of morphemes in verbal prefix clusters, deriving shapes that will be referred to here as *quasi-portmanteaux*. These rules derive new morphemes by combining pairs of forms found in the lexicon. For example the verbal prefixes *ba-* and *kuN-* occur independently in the lexicon, but combine in different ways in different grammatical environments. In the presence of a non-participant subject they combine to produce the derived shape *bungka-*, while in the presence of a participant subject they produce the shape *bu-*. These postlexical rules thus derive new morphemes from pairs of underived forms. The derived shapes are then subject in turn to other more general phonological rules such as vowel harmony.

To avoid confusion, the morphophonemic rules described here are listed with their rule numbers as presented in the *Grammar of Worrorra* (GW) (Clendon 2000) in brackets, where they are different.

3.1 Morpheme-specific rules

These lexicon-internal rules account for the allomorphic shapes of 13 morphemes in Worrorra.

<u>Rule 1: nasal assimilation</u>
Assimilatory nasal phonemes (/N/) are found in the 3f prefix *nyiN-* and in the 3w prefix, in its three allomorphs *kuN-*, *ØN-* and *ᵏwuN-*. Assimilatory nasals represent underlying nasal consonants that are unspecified as to place of articulation, such that their surface form copies the place of articulation of the consonant that comes after it:[29]

$$/N/ \longrightarrow [\alpha \text{ place}] / \_\_\_ C [\alpha \text{ place}]$$

Eg: |nyi**N**-| —> ny**im**- / ____ b
      —> ny**ing**- / ____ k
      —> ny**in**- / ____ d
      —> ny**irn**- / ____ rd
      —> ny**iny**- / ____ j

The 3f index *nyaN-* ~ *nyiN-* ~ *nyuN-* loses its underlying nasal phoneme in at least three situations:

(i) In front of a root morpheme that starts with /ee/, such as *=ee* 'put, place' and *=eenda* 'cook:'

|N| —> Ø / nyV__ =ee.....

Eg: /nyeerla/   <— |nyi-Ø=ee-rla| s/he set her down
                    3f-3=place-PAST[30]

It appears from this that when an assimilatory nasal occurs in front of a verb root that begins with a vowel, /N/ takes on phonetic features of that vowel, so that eg |nyi**N**-Ø=**ee**-rla| ([3f-3=place-PAST]) becomes *nyeerla* 's/he set her down' by the following process:

|nyi**N**-Ø=**ee**-rla| —>
nyi**ny**-Ø=**ee**-rla —>
nyi**y**-Ø=**ee**-rla —> (cf rule 24)
nyi-Ø=**ee**-rla —> (rule 18)
/nyeerla/   s/he set her down

In this example /N/ absorbs the features [+high, –back] from the following vowel /ee/ to become (/ny/). /ny/ is then lenited to /y/ and eventually to /Ø/. The selection of which process an

---

[29] Cf the Sanskrit *anusvāra* (ṃ).
[30] See §1.7 for explanation of glossing conventions.

assimilatory nasal undergoes is probably governed by the features of the vowel that comes in front of it, such that |kuN-Ø=ee-rla| ([3w-3=place-PAST]) becomes *kunyeerla* 's/he set it (celestial-class) down'. In this instance the [+back] vowel /u/ coming before /N/ prevents /ny/ from being lenited and deleted in similar circumstances:

|ku**N**-Ø=ee-rla| —>
ku**ny**-Ø=ee-rla —>
/kunyeerla/   *s/he set it (celestial-class) down*

(ii) Before the root of the irregular verb =*ya* 'go:'

    Eg.:   /nyenga/   <— |nya=ya-nga| *she went*
                                        3f=go-TNS

(iii) before the root *Grarl/Grarlya* 'CLAN COUNTRY NAME:'

    /nyeegrarlya/   <— |nyi=grarlya| *woman from* Grarl

Morphemes containing assimilatory nasals are probably more accurately characterized at some level as containing underlying nasalized vowels, such that eg the 3f morpheme is |nyṼ|, and 3w is |ᵏwũ|. These two morphemes are treated as if they ended in a vowel by *nya*-epenthesis rule 26 and V-metathesis rule 8. However it is useful to posit a dummy archiphone /N/ here for the sake of pattern congruity in hardening rules.

<u>Rule 2: velar glide hardening</u> (GW P-5)
Nasals and glides regularly alternate with stops at the same places of articulation in the morphology. For this reason glides will be said to harden, rather than requiring distinct suites of lenition and fortition rules to account for processes undergone by glides and nasals respectively. In a couple of morpheme-specific contexts, the underlying glide |ᵏw| hardens to /ngk/ after unrounded vowels:

    |ᵏw| —>   ngk / V[–round] _____

The morpheme -*ᵏwurri* 'NUM' becomes -*ngkurri* after the sound /rri/ that occurs in the continuous aspect marker -*eerri* and in plural participant pronouns:

    /kunjeerri**ngk**urri/   <— |kunjeerri-**ᵏw**urri| *they say*
    /ngarri**ngk**urri   <— |ngarri-**ᵏw**urri| *we few (inc)*

The morpheme -*aal* 'hither, CENTRIPETAL' has underlying shape |-ᵏwaal|, and becomes -*ngkaal* after the verb roots =*ya* 'go' and =*yoolee* 'move, travel:'

    /be**ngk**aal/   <— |ba=ya-**ᵏw**aal| *come here*
                                CFT=go-hither

    /nyijoolee**ngk**aal/   <— |nyirr=yoolee-**ᵏw**aal| *come over here, you lot*
                                   2p=move-hither

<u>Rule 3: deretroflexion</u> (GW P-8)
The locative morpheme -*rnanya* hardens to -*danya* after an apico-alveolar consonant:

    -rnanya   —>   -danya / d, l, rr _____

    Eg.:   /manga**d**anya/   <— |manga**rr-rn**anya| *in the pouch*
             /aambu**ld**anya/   <— |aambu**l-rn**anya| *in his eye(s)*

Here the first phoneme /rn/ of *-rnanya* hardens to a stop (/rd/) (rule 11), then assimilates to the place of articulation of the preceding consonant. Another instance of deretroflexion is described in rule 17.

Rule 4: relict consonant deletion (GW P-11)
Some morphemes show evidence of relict or ghost consonants in their underlying forms, which leave traces of their presence in the morphemes' surface shapes, by effecting consonants that come after them:

$$|C| \longrightarrow \emptyset \,/\, \underline{} \,\#$$

For instance *-ᵏwunya* 'PURPOSIVE' hardens to *-kunya* after a consonant (rules 10 & 11), but also appears as *-kunya* after a final vowel in words like *mamangkunu* 'morning' and *anguja* 'what?:'

mamangkunu**k**unya	*until the morning*
anguja**k**unya	*what for?*

One explanation for this is that the underlying shapes of *mamangkunu* and *anguja* end in relict consonants (|C|): |mamangkunuC|, |angujaC|.

The 3w-indexing morpheme has a series-2 allomorph /ØN-/ (see §8.1.1). This zero morph has an effect on following consonants, in that glides that come after it are hardened to stops; the examples offered here use the glide-initial roots =*raarreya* 'big' and =*yakarri* 'other:'

/**rd**aarreya/ <—	|ØN=**r**aarreya|	*big (celestial-class)*
/**j**akarri/ <—	|ØN=**y**akarri|	*another (celestial-class) one*

The best explanation for this phenomenon is that in its underlying structure the zero morph /ØN-/ ends in a relict assimilatory nasal, which triggers glide-hardening rule 10 in following morphemes.

Rule 5: strange hardening (GW P-13)
Ungarinyin has a morphophoneme $|y_2|$, which hardens to /d/ (Rumsey 1982:17).[31] This type of hardening, to a non-homorganic stop, does not occur in Worrorra, except in the case of just two morphemes that I know of that start with $|y_2|$: *-y₂aka* 'EMPHATIC' and *-y₂irdaka* 'from:'

/kajirn berrwun**d**aka/ <—	|berrwun-**y₂**aka|	*we mustn't hit him*
/anjol**d**irdaka/ <—	|anjol-**y₂**irdaka|	*out of the sky*

3.1.1 Quasi-portmanteaux

A subset of morpheme-specific rules deals with five morphemes in Worrorra that are synchronically analysable as fusions of other, constituent shapes. Their status as quasi-portmanteau forms will be discussed after the rules themselves have been presented.

Rule 6: velar sequence lenition (GW P-21)
This rule applies specifically to transitive verbs with first person plural inclusive subjects *(-ngarr-)* acting on third person singular celestial objects *(kuN-)*. The underlying sequence |kuN-ngarr-| is replaced by *warr-*:[32]

---

[31] McGregor & Rumsey (2009) argue plausibly that $|y_2|$ is derived diachronically from a dental glide /yh/ in an earlier historical period (their putative proto-Worrorran), where there was a conditioned alternation between /yh/ and /th/ in morpheme-initial position.

[32] Ie, kuN-ng —> kungng —> kung —> w.

kuN-ngarr —> warr / ____ ....

|kuN-ngarr=ᵇwu| —>
3w-1pin=hit
kung-ngarr=ᵇwu   (rule 1) —>
w-arr=ᵇwu   (rule 6) —>
/warrwu/   *we can hit it*

|kuN-ngarr=yi| —>
3w-1pin=do
kuN-ngarr=y**u**   (vowel harmony)
kung-ngarr=yu   (rule 1) —>
w-arr=yu   (rule 6) —>
w-arr=ju   (rule 11)—>
w-a=ju   (rule 15)—>
/waju/   *let's do it*

In this example, vowel harmony changes the vowel /i/ in the root =*yi* 'do' to /u/ in surface form, under influence from the vowel in |kuN|.

<u>Rule 7: velar nasalization</u> (GW P-23)
This rule applies specifically to intransitive counterfactual verbs with third person singular masculine subjects (*ka-*), and to transitive counterfactual verbs with third person singular subjects *(-Ø-)* and third person singular masculine objects (*ka-*); ie to any prefixial string of the shape |ba-ka (-Ø)|. In this environment the masculine singular morpheme |-ka-| turns into -*ngka-*.

k —> ngk / ba ____ a ...

/ba**ng**k**a**nin/   <— |ba-**ka**=ni-n| *he should be*
                             CFT-3a=be-NON.P

/ba**ng**k**o**nya/   <— |ba-**ka**-Ø=ᵇwu-nya| *s/he should hit him*
                             CFT-3a-3=hit-PAST

This leads naturally to an alternative interpretation of the counterfactual morpheme *ba-* as underlying *baN-*, as discussed in §8.3.

<u>Rule 8: vowel metathesis</u> (GW P-24)
This rule applies specifically to intransitive counterfactual verbs with third person singular celestial subjects (*ᵏwuN-*), and to transitive counterfactual verbs with third person subjects and third person singular celestial objects (*ᵏwuN-*); ie to any prefixial string of the shape |ba-kuN-(3(p))|. In this sequence the vowel /a/ and the underlyingly nasalized vowel /uN/ change places. /N/ then becomes /ng/ before /k/ by rule 1:

ba-kuN —> buN-ka / ____ [–I, –II] ...

The end result is surface forms like *bungkanin* 'it should be' and *bungkonya* 's/he should have hit it:'

|ba-kuN=ni-n| —>
CFT-3w=be-NON.P
 bu**N**-ka=ni-n   —>
/bu**ng**kanin/   (rule 1)   *it should be*

|ba-kuN-Ø=ᵇwu-nya| —>
CFT-3w-3=hit-PAST
bu**N**-ka-Ø=ᵇwu-nya   —>
bu**ng**-ka-Ø=ᵇwu-nya   (rule 1) —>
/bungkonya/   (rule 18)   *s/he should have hit it*

|ba-kuN-ᵇwarr=yi-n| —>
CFT-3w-3p=say-NON.P
bu**N**-ka-ᵇwarr=yi-n   —>
bu**ng**-ka-ᵇwarr=yi-n   (rule 1) —>
bung-kaarr=yi-n   (rule 23)—>
bung-kaarr=ji-n   (rule 11)—>
/bungkaajin/   (rule 15)   *they should say*

Vowel metathesis is also apparent in some intransitive counterfactual verbs with 'you singular' (*ngun-*) subjects. Here the vowels of the morphemes in the string |ba-ngun -| change places: |ba-ngun-| —> /bu-ngan-/

|ba-ng**u**n=ni-n| —>
CFT-2=be-NON.P
b**u**-ng**a**n=ni-n —>
/bunganin/   *you should be*

<u>Rule 9: counterfactual—3w assimilation</u> (GW P-25)
This rule applies specifically to counterfactual transitive verbs with first or second person subjects acting on third person singular celestial *(kuN-)* objects; ie to any prefixial string of the shape |ba-kuN-(1(p), 2(p))|. In these verbs the morphemes |ba-| and |-kuN-| merge or blend together to make *bu-,* or *bi-* under vowel harmony:

  ba-kuN —> {bu, bi} / ____ {[+I], [+II]} ....

|ba-kuN-nga=ᵇwu-n|—>
CFT-3w-1=hit-NON.P
b**u**-ng**a**=ᵇwu-n —>
/bungon/   (rule 18)   *I should hit it*

|ba-kuN-rra=yi-n| —>
CFT-3w-2p=say-NON.P
b**u**-rra=yi-n   —>
b**i**-rri=yi-n   (regressive vowel harmony from =*yi*)
/birreen/   (rule 18)   *you should all say*

Here *bu- ~ bi-* really is a portmanteau morpheme, covering two meanings; *ba-* 'Counterfactual' and *kuN-* '3rd person singular celestial.'

While there is indeed at least one genuine portmanteau index in Worrorra, *jan-* '2(p)>1' 'a second person subject acting upon a first person singular object,' the set of quasi-portmanteau forms discussed here is less unequivocal. Vowel metathesis rule 8, for example, is clearly an elaborate form of vowel harmony, which is a regular prosodic process in Worrorra (§2.6.1). No-one would want to argue that the shape *bungan-* (underlying |ba-ngun-| [CFT-2-]) is anything more than a metathesized sequence. This being the case, it is hard to escape the conclusion that the shape *bungka-* (|ba-kuN-| [CFT-3w-]) is likewise a metathesized string. Yet *bungka-* is in complementary distribution with *bu-* (rule 9) in terms of its syntactic environment, and *bu-* is a much better candidate for portmanteau status. But to list *bu-* and *bungka-* as members of separate morpholexical categories is to miss the syntactic motivation underlying their different constructions. Likewise the shape *bangka-* 'CFT-3a-'

(rule 7) is clearly a nasalized version of underlying |ba-ka-|, explicable by reference to an alternative shape for the counterfactual morpheme in morphophonology, as |baN-|. Like *bu-*, the 1pin>3w shape *warr-* (rule 6) is a good candidate for portmanteau status. Yet the string /arr/ in its construction is reminiscent of that string as it occurs in *-ngarr-* '1pin.' This leads naturally to a consideration of the phoneme /w/ in this morpheme as a lenition of |kuN-ng| (—> |kung|): a sequence of [+back] phonemes (velar consonants + /u/) melted down to the labio-velar glide /w/.

3.2 General rules

There are a number of very prominent 'hardening' rules in Worrorra that turn glides and nasals into stop consonants at the same place of articulation. Importantly, there are two labio-velar glide morphophonemes, designated |^{b}w| and |^{k}w|, that harden to /b/ and /k/ respectively after certain types of consonant. The full set of homorganic glide, vowel and nasal–stop pairs is as follows:

Table 3.1: homorganic hardening correspondences

^{b}w, m	—>	b
n	—>	d
r, rn	—>	rd
y, ny	—>	j
^{k}w, ng	—>	k, ngk
aa / ^{k}wa	—>	ka, ngka

Rules 2, 5, 10, 11, 12 and 13 are all hardening rules in Worrorra.

<u>Rule 10: glide hardening</u> (GW P-2)
Glides turn into the stop consonant at the same place of articulation when they come after a nasal consonant.

$$G \longrightarrow T\ /\ N\ \underline{\hspace{1cm}}$$

Eg: yoolee —> joolee / n ____

/ngunjoolee/ <— |ngun=yoolee| *you travel*
                    2=travel

Exception: the root morpheme of the irregular verb *=ya* 'go' does not harden after a nasal:

/ngunyanga/ <— |ngun=ya-nga| *you went*
                    2=go-TNS
/kunyanga/ <— |kuN=ya-nga| *it went*
                    3w=go-TNS

The irregular paradigm of the verb *=ya* 'go' noted here and in rule 1 may be accounted for by a diachronic process of homorganic NT cluster reduction (cf rule 28), which also accounts for the 3p>3w prefix *kubarr-* from underlying |kuN-^{b}warr-|:

$$C^N[\alpha\ \text{place}],\ C^T[\alpha\ \text{place}] \longrightarrow C^{\{N,T\}}$$

That is:

	|ngun-ya-nga|,	|kuN-ᵇwarr-| —>
(glide hardening)	ngun-**j**a-nga,	kuN-**b**arr —>
(N assimilation to following T)	ngu[**ny**-j]a-nga,	ku[**m**-b]arr —>
(CC reduction)	ngu[ny-]a-nga,	ku[-b]arr —>
	ngunyanga,	*kubarr-*

<u>Rule 11: hardening (general)</u> (GW P-3)
Nasal consonants and glides become stops after lateral consonants or /rr/.

   N, G —> T / L, rr ____

Eg: /nyirringkaal**k**urri/   <— |nyirringkaal-**ᵏw**urri| *come here, you lot*
      /nyamaal**d**u/   <— |nyamaal-**n**u| *s/he will get it for you*
      /Arr**b**alandiya/   <— |arr=**m**alandiya| *the Prince Regent River clan*
      /kaa**j**oolinerri/   <— |kaarr=**y**oolinerri| *they were travelling*

This last example involves the deletion of /rr/ before /j/ (see rule 15).
Exception: there is one exception to this rule: the glide /ᵇw/ does *not* harden at the start of a verbal root morpheme, although it does harden in other environments:

/ngarr**b**arr**w**una/   <— |ngarr-ᵇwarr=ᵇwu-na| *they hit us*
                                1pin-3p=hit-PAST

The following two rules, as well as velar elision rule 22, describe the relationship between the [+back] phonemes /a/, /aa/ and /ᵏw/. These three rules in effect describe three phonological outcomes of essentially the same morphophonemic phenomenon.

<u>Rule 12: open vowel — open glide equivalence</u> (GW P-4)
When it comes at the start of a morpheme, the long vowel /aa/ has the underlying allophonic shape |ᵏwa-|. This means that the same things happen to /aa/ as would happen to the glide-vowel pair /ᵏwa-/.

   aa —> |ᵏwa| / + ____

The morpheme *-aarndu* 'Dual' hardens to *-karndu* after a consonant, as if it began with |ᵏw|; and *-aara* '1DAT' becomes *-kara* after a consonant:

/nyirringkaal**k**arndu/   <— |nyirringkaal-**ᵏw**arndu| *come here you two*
/maal**k**ara/   <— |maal-**ᵏw**ara| *get it for me*

The verb root =*aangurru* 'take, carry' may be underlyingly represented as |=ᵏwangurru|, as it becomes =*kangurru* after a nasal. Accordingly, *nyiN-* '3f' becomes *nying-* in front of /=aa/:

|nyiN=ᵏwangurru| —>
 nyiN=**k**angurru   —>
 nyi**ng**=kangurru   —>
 /nyi**ngk**angurru/   *take/carry her*

And =*aangurru* manifests as =ᵏ*wangurru* in future tense forms:

|a-Ø-nya=ᵏwangurru| —>
3a-3-OPT=carry
e=ᵏwangurru   —>
/ewangurru/   *s/he will take/carry him*

Note also the shape *ngaangurru* 'I will take it (celestial),' underlyingly |ØN-ng**a**=ᵏ**wa**ngurru|, with elision of |ᵏw| between /a/ and /a/ by velar elision rule 22. Because /aa/ has phonemic status elsewhere in the phonology, it is sufficient to posit /ᵏwa/ as a morphologically-conditioned allophone of /aa/.

Rule 13: distance hardening (GW P-12)

This rule applies specifically to morphemes of the shape /#C₁VN₍ₐ₎T₍ₐ₎ .../, where C₁ is a glide or nasal, and [α] indexes a specific place of articulation. Examples of such morphemes are =*ningka* 'bite,' -*nangka* 'DAT,' =*ninja* 'look' and =*rambima* 'extended family/patriclan.' The rule states that when C₁ is in a position to be hardened, then N₍ₐ₎ will also be hardened:

$$N_{[\alpha]} \longrightarrow T_{[\alpha]} \;/\; C_2 \# C_1V \underline{\quad} T_{[\alpha]} .....$$

Here C₂ is a nasal, a lateral or /rr/, whichever type of consonant causes C₁ to harden under hardening rules 10 or 11. The application of this rule results in a geminate stop (T₍ₐ₎T₍ₐ₎):

$$C_1VN_{[\alpha]}T_{[\alpha]} ..... \longrightarrow TVT_{[\alpha]}T_{[\alpha]} .....$$

which is now shortened under degemination rule 27.

Eg: |maal-**n**a**ng**ka| —>
      maal-**d**a**ng**ka   (rule 11) —>
      maal-**d**a**kk**a   (distance hardening) —>
      /maal**d**a**k**a/   (rule 27)   *bring it to him/her*

      |ngarr-Ø=**n**inja| —>
      1pin-3=look
      ngarr-Ø=**d**inja   (rule 11) —>
      nga-Ø=**d**inja   (rule 15) —>
      nga-Ø=**d**i**jj**a   (distance hardening) —>
      /nga**d**i**j**a/   (rule 27)   *s/he can see us*

The next two rules are more or less complementary; rule 14 describes how nasals are deleted before trills and laterals, and rule 15 describes how trills are deleted before nasals and laterals.

Rule 14: nasal deletion (GW P-6)
Nasals are deleted in front of laterals and /rr/.

$$N \longrightarrow \emptyset \;/\; \underline{\quad} L, rr$$

Eg: /ngulardu/   <— |ngu**n**=lardu| *your back*
      /kurloonangka/   <— |ku**N**=rloonangka| *s/he'll talk to him/her*

Nasals are deleted very specifically before the 2p subject morpheme /-rra/ in transitive verbs:

/nyirrona/   <— |nyi**N**-rrona| *you all hit her*
/jarrona/   <— |ja**n**-rrona| *you all hit me*

Rule 15: trill deletion (GW P-7)
The trill /rr/ is deleted before the stops /d, rd/ and /j/:

$$rr \longrightarrow \emptyset \ / \ \_\_\_\_ \ T \ [+coronal]$$

Before being deleted, though, it frequently hardens a glide or nasal in accordance with hardening rule 11, as in these examples:

|arr=nu-na|	—>	
1px=be-PAST		
arr=du-na	(rule 11)—>	
a=du-na	(trill deletion)—>	
/aduna/	*we were*	
|arr=yakarri|	—>	
3p=other		
arr=jakarri	(rule 11) —>	
a-jakarri	(trill deletion) —>	
/ajakarri/	*the others*	

And /rr/ may or may not be deleted before laterals; here /rr/ and /Ø/ are in free variation:

mana kaaladingeerri *or* mana kaarrladingeerri	*they live here*
korru kubarloonya *or* korru kubarrloonya	*let them speak*

An elaboration on this aspect of trill deletion is dealt with in rule 17.
 Also, /rr/ may be deleted before nasals in verbal prefix clusters, and in prefixes used to construct pronouns:

/angkenga/	<—	|arr-ngkenga|	*when they went*
/anbuna/	<—	|arr-nbuna|	*s/he hit us*
/kaangona/	<—	|kaarr-ngona|	*I hit them*
/anja/	<—	|arr=nja|	*these*
/arno/	<—	|arr=rno|	*those*

But in other situations /rr/ is *not* deleted before nasals: eg note the /rr+ng/ cluster in *Arnngarrngoyu* 'CLAN COUNTRY NAME' and *mamurrnguma* 'separate (adj).'
 Rules 3 and 16 deal with apical consonants and are also complementary; rule 3 describes how retroflex consonants lose their retroflexion, and rule 16 describes how alveolar consonants become retroflexed.

Rule 16: retroflexion (GW P-9)
Apical consonants become retroflexed before a retroflex consonant at the beginning of a root morpheme:

$$C \ [+coronal, -distrib] \longrightarrow [-anterior] \ / \ \_\_\_\_ =C \ [+coronal, -distrib, -anterior]$$

Eg: |ngun=rno| —>
    ngurn=rno   (retroflexion) —>
    /ngurno/   (degemination)   *I'll give it to you*

|kaan=ṟema| —>
kaan=ṟdema (rule 10) —>
kaaṟn=ṟdema (retroflexion) —>
/kaaṟndema/ *s/he'll cry for them*

Rule 17: disambiguation before laterals (GW P-10)
When any plural NP index (1pin *ngarr-*, px *arr-* or 2p *nyirr-*) occurs before a derived noun root that begins with a lateral, then the /rr/ phoneme is not deleted, as rule 15 would otherwise predict:

Eg: /ngaṟṟlardu/ <— |ngaṟṟ=lardu| *our backs*
/aṟṟlungkum/ <— |aṟṟ=rlungkuma| *their knees*

This happens in order to distinguish between *nyiN-* '3f' and *nyirr-* '2p', and between *nga-* '1' and *ngarr-* '1pin' in this position:

ngaladu *my back*   ngaṟṟlardu *our backs*
nyiladu *her back*   nyiṟṟlardu *your backs*

When any of the morphemes *ngarr-*, *arr-* or *nyirr-* occur before intransitive verb roots that begin with laterals, then the same thing happens:

/ngaṟṟlelwana/ <— |ngaṟṟ=rlelwana| *we were born*
/nyiṟṟlelwana/ <— |nyiṟṟ=rlelwana| *you were all born*

Again, this enables pairs such as the following to be distinguished:

ngarlelwana *I was born*   ngaṟṟlelwana *we were born*
nyirlelwana *she was born*   nyiṟṟlelwana *you were all born*

This may not happen with transitive verb roots like *kuN[ ]=rloo* 'talk, speak' because there is no danger of confusion. Note also that /rl/ becomes /l/ after these prefixes; this is another case of deretroflexion (cf rule 3).

Rule 18: V-expansion (GW P-15)
The long vowels (/aa/, /ee/, /oo/, /e/ and /o/) may be |V-(G)-V| sequences in morphophonology. The V-expansion rule is concerned with /ee/, /oo/, /e/ and /o/: the underlying representation of the vowel /aa/ is dealt with by rule 23. Rule 18 states that certain underlying V-(G)-V sequences are converted to specific long vowels in surface phonology.

That is: |a + (y)i|
          |a + (y)a| —>   /e/

          |a + (w)u| —>   /o/

          |i + (y)i|
          |u + (y)i| —>   /ee/

          |u + wu| —>   /oo/

Examples of these cluster assimilations follow:

/e/	/nge/		<—		ØN-nga=**yi**		*I will do it*
	/ngenga/		<—		ng**a**=ya-nga		*I went*
	/ke/	<—	ØN=kaya <—		ØN=ᵏw**a**ya		*that one*

| /o/ | /ngo/ | | <— | |ØN-ng**a**=ᵇwu| | *I will hit it* |

| /ee/ | /kunjee/ | <— | kuN-nji=yi <— | |kuN-nj**a** =yi| | *you do it* |
| | /barrweenya/ | | <— | |ba-ka-ngarr=ᵇw**u**-**yi**nya| | *we should've hit him* |

| /oo/ | /nyidoorri/ | | <— | |nyirr=n**u**-ᵏwurri| | *2p 'be' NUM* |

Rule 19: V+V contraction (GW P-16)
When two short vowels, or a long vowel and a short vowel, are separated by only a morpheme boundary, one of the vowels (usually but not always the short one) may disappear.

V + V —> V

In the following examples the bold-type vowels are deleted:

/maalkara/	<—		m**a**-aalkara		*get it for me*
/kunjeerri/	<—		kunj**i**-eerri		*he's doing it*
/ngengurreerri/	<—		ngengurr**u**-eerri		*I'm going away*
/minyiyaara/	<—		minyiy**i**-ᵏwara		*tell me*
/ngarrwaarndeerri/	<—		ngarrw**u**-aarnd**u**-eerri		*he's hitting us two*
/irrayaalkara/	<—		irra=**ee**yaalkara		*you all put it here for me*

Rule 20: *y*-epenthesis (GW P-17)
When two long vowels are separated by only a morpheme boundary, the glide /y/ may be inserted between them, although this does not always happen.

Ø —> y / V ___ # V

/irnoyaarndum/	<—		irno-aarndum		*there they both are*
/kangoyeerri/	<—		kango-eerri		*I'm hitting him*
/kubajeyeerri/	<—		kubaje-eerri		*they're doing it*

Rule 21: *a*-fronting and raising (GW P-18)
When /a/ comes in between two lamino-palatal consonants, and in front of a root morpheme, it turns into /i/.

a —> i / C [+high, –back] ___=C [+high, –back]

In the following examples the effected vowel is in bold type:

| /miny**i**yaara/ | <— | |miny**a**=yi-ᵏwara| 2>3w=say-1DAT | *tell me* |

| /nyimny**i**yawana/ | <— | |nyiN-mny**a**=yawa-na| 3f-DD=rub-PAST | *she rubbed it on herself* |

| /kunj**i**yeerri/ | <— | |kuN-nj**a**=yi-eerri| 3w-2=do-PROG | *you're doing it* |

/anbajiyaariwuna/   <— |arr-n-ᵇwarr-ny**a**=yaariwu-na| *they gave it to us*
                         1px-INV-3p-EP-give-PAST

Rule 22: velar elision (GW P-19)
In some circumstances velar consonants may disappear when they come between two /a/ phonemes or between /a/ and /aa/.

C [+back] —> Ø / V [+back, –round] ____ V [+back, –round]

When this happens, two short /a/ sounds originally found on either side of a velar consonant blend together under V+V contraction rule 19. In the following examples the consonants in bold are deleted:

|ba-**k**aarr=[i-nga]-n| —>
CFT-3p=[go-TNS]-NON.P
ba-aarr=i-nga-n   —>
/baarringan/   (rule 19)   *they should go*

|ka-**ng**arr=ᵇwu| —>
CFT-1pin=hit
ka-arr=ᵇwu   —>
karr=ᵇwu   (rule 19)   —>
/karrwu/   *we can hit him*

|a-**ng**arr-a=ᵇwu| —>
3a-1pin-OPT=hit
a-arr-a=ᵇwu   —>
arr-a=ᵇwu   (rule 19)   —>
/arro/   (rule 18)   *we will hit him*

|ba-**k**aarr-nga=ᵇwu-nya| —>
CFT-3p-1=hit-PAST
ba-aarr-nga=ᵇwu-nya   —>
baarr-nga=ᵇwu-nya   (rule 19)   —>
baa-nga=ᵇwu-nya   (rule 15)   —>
/baangonya/   (rule 18)   *I should have hit them*

|ba-**k**a-**ng**arr=ᵇwu-yinya| —>
CFT-3a-1pin=hit-PAST
ba-**k**a-arr=ᵇwu-yinya   —>
ba-a-arr=ᵇwu-yinya   —>
barr=ᵇwu-yinya   (rule 19)   —>
/barrweenya/   (rule 18)   *we should have hit him*

Rule 23: peripheral glide lenition (GW P-20)
This rule is a reflex of open vowel–open glide equivalence rule 12, and at the same time an extension of V expansion rule 18. It states that the underlying string |awa| may find surface expression as /aa/.

/aanangka/   <— |**awa**-nangka| *his*
                  he-DAT

/maarrwu/	<—	|ma-ᵇwarr=ᵇwu| 3m-3p=hit	*they can hit it*
/ingkaarrwu/	<—	|i-ngka-ᵇwarr=ᵇwu| 3a-SJTV-3p=hit	*when they hit him*

Rule 24: *ny*-lenition (GW P-26)

The results of this rule never appear in surface forms. It applies quite specifically to the optative morpheme -*nya*- and to the transitive first person plural exclusive subject morpheme *nyarr*-. The /ny/ sound in these morphemes turns into /y/ when it comes after /a/.

ny —> y / a _____ a

This results in the sequence |aya| which then turns into /e/ by the application of rule 18.

|**a-nya**=nu| 3a-OPT=be	—>		
a-ya=nu	—>		
/enu/	(rule 18)		*he will be*

|**a-Ø-nya**=ᵇwu| 3a-3-OPT=hit	—>		
a-Ø-ya=ᵇwu	—>		
/ewu/	(rule 18)		*s/he will hit him*

|nyaN-nyarr=ᵇwu| 3f-1px=hit	—>		
ny**any-nya**rr=ᵇwu	(rule 1)	—>	
nya-**nya**rr=ᵇwu	(rule 27)	—>	
ny**a-ya**rr=ᵇwu	—>		
/nyerrwu/	(rule 18)		*we hit her*

|**a-nya**rr-ngun=ᵇwu| 3a-1px-SJTV=hit	—>		
a-nyarr-kum=bu	(rules 10 & 11)	—>	
a-yarr-kum=bu	—>		
/errkumbu/	(rule 18)		*when we hit him*

Rule 25: *ba*-epenthesis (GW P-27)

There is a rather weak tendency or preference for Worrorra words not to end in consonants. If a word does end in a consonant, an epenthetic morpheme /-ba/ may be added to the end.

Ø —> ba / C # ___

For example the underlying shape |bundurl| 'the bush' adds the morpheme -*rnanya* 'LOC' to make *bundurldanya* (rule 11) 'in the bush,' but on its own it usually appears as *bundurlba*. Other examples are: *dalorr* and *dalorrba* 'well, sink hole,' *kajirn* and *kajirnba* 'unable,' *marneen* and *marneenba* 'hang up,' *baraan* and *baraanba* 'shaved (head),' and =*reen* and =*reenba* 'real.' When the SPECIFIC morpheme -*maan*- appears as a separate phonological word, it has the shape *maanba*. The clan country name *Grarl* may also appear as *Meegrarlba*. Verbs may also very occasionally appear with *ba*-epenthesis: *banjamnyeenba* (|ba-ka-nja-mnya=ee-n-ba| [CFT-3a-2-DD=place-NON.P-EP]) 'you should put him down.'

Rule 26: *nya-* and *a*-epenthesis (GW P-28)

A meaningless shape /a/ is always inserted after the third person plural subject–third person singular masculine object prefix cluster /ka-^{b}warr-/ in verbs in present and past tenses:

/kawarro/   <— |ka-^{b}warr-**a**=^{b}wu| *they hit him*
                       3a-3p-EP=hit

/kawarrarema/   <— |ka-^{b}warr-**a**=rema| *they cry for him*
                       3a-3p-EP=cry.for

Epenthetic /a/ occurs sporadically throughout Worrorra morphology.

A meaningless shape |nya| may be inserted between a prefix cluster and a verb root, on any verb marked for present or past tense, provided that the prefix cluster ends in a consonant:

$\emptyset \longrightarrow$ nya / .... C ___ =[+tense]

Compare these pairs of verb forms with and without epenthetic |nya|:

arr=nu-na   >   aduna
1px=be-PAST   *we were*
arr-**nya**=nu-na   >   ajanuna
1px-**EP**=be-PAST

kaarr=i-nga   >   kaarringa
3p=go-PAST   *they went*
kaarr-**nya**=ya-nga   >   kaajenga
3p-**EP**=go-past

ngan-ngun=nu-na   >   nganngununa
1-SJTV=be-PAST   *when I was*
ngan-ngun-**nya**=nu-na >   nganngunyanuna
1-SJTV-**EP**=be-past

ngun-Ø=^{b}wu-na   >   ngunbuna
2-3=hit-PAST   *s/he hit you*
ngun-Ø-**nya**=^{b}wu-na >   ngunyona
2-3-**EP**=hit-PAST

ngun-Ø-ngun=^{b}wu-na   >   ngunngumbuna
2-3-SJTV=hit-PAST   *when s/he hit you*
ngun-Ø-ngun-**nya**=^{b}wu-na > ngunngunyona
2-3-SJTV-**EP**=hit-PAST

kaarr-n-Ø=^{b}wu-na   >   kaanbuna
3p-INV-3=hit-PAST   *s/he hit them*
kaarr-n-Ø-**nya**=^{b}wu-na > kaanyona
3p-INV-3-**EP**=hit-PAST

ba-ka-nyarr=^{k}wulkuna-yinya   >   berrkulkunenya
CFT-3a-1px=fear-PAST   *we should've been*
                                                 frightened of him
ba-ka-nyarr-**nya**=^{k}wulkuna-yinya > bejolkunenya
CFT-3a-1px-**EP**=fear-PAST

The appearance of the shape |nya| is phonologically conditioned; that is, it does not appear on a verb form that has a vowel or an assimilatory nasal (/N/) before the verb root, and it does not occur on a verb marked with the phonologically competing morpheme *-mnya-* 'Discourse Deictic.' After /rr/, |nya| turns into /ja/ (rule 11). Its use is entirely optional.

3.2.1 Redundancy rules

There are also at least a couple of redundancy rules that ensure that words produced by the morphology conform to the language's more basic phonological and phonotactic requirements. These rules may be stated as:

Rule 27: degemination (GW P-14)
This rule simply states that any long consonants that arise in the course of deriving a surface word from an underlying form are shortened: that is, there are no long consonants in Worrorra:

$$CC\ [\alpha\ \text{place},\ \alpha\ \text{manner}] \longrightarrow C$$

See the examples given under rule 13 for instances of degemination rule 27.

Rule 28: initial CC reduction
Where zero morphs occur word-initially at a morphophonemic level, nasal-stop consonant clusters are sometimes left stranded at the start of words. Such CCs are illegal in the phonology in this position (§2.4.1), and when this happens the nasal member of such a CC is deleted:

$$N \longrightarrow \emptyset\ /\ \#\underline{\quad}T \quad \text{or} \quad NT \longrightarrow T\ /\ \#\underline{\quad}$$

|ØN-**nj**a=ᵇwu|	—>	
3w-2=hit		
ØN-**j**a=ᵇwu	—>	
/jo/	(rule 18)	*you will hit it (celestial)*
|ØN-Ø-**ngk**a=rloo|	—>	
VCOMP-3-SJTV=speak		
ØN-Ø-**k**a + rloo	—>	
/karloo/		*when s/he talks/speaks*

There are actually a few more morphophonemic rules than the 28 listed here, but most of the other rules follow naturally from the rules of allophony and vowel harmony outlined in Chapter Two, and affect only one or two morphemes in quite restricted places. These rules will be further exemplified, and some of them will be repeated in Chapters Five, Eight and Fifteen, where verb morphologies are described in greater detail.

3.2.2 Rule Ordering

Morphophonemic processes often involve a number of rules acting in unison, or one rule coming into force before or after another is applied. Some underlying shapes need several rules to be applied in order to derive surface forms. Some instances of processes of this sort have already been offered in the examples listed under Velar elision rule 22, Vowel metathesis rule 8, and *ny*-lenition rule 24. Two more examples of complex ordering of rules are shown here as well:

input	|nyaN-ngarr=rno|	—>
	3f-1pin=give	
(i) rule 11	nyaN-ngarr=**rd**o	—>
(ii) rule 15	nyaN-nga=rdo	—>
(iii) rule 1	nya**ng-ng**a=rdo	—>
(iv) rule 27	nya-**ng**-a=rdo	—>
(v) rule 22	nya-a=rdo	—>
(vi) rule 19	nya=rdo	—>
output	/nyardo/	*let's give it to her*

Here Hardening rule 11 must apply before Trill deletion rule 15: if it were otherwise, the hardening rule could not be applied. Rules 22 and 19 must also apply in that order if they are to cooperate to produce the correct outcome. Nasal assimilation rule 1 and degemination rule 27 are examples of 'background' rules that come into operation indiscriminately, that is, whenever derivational processes throw up strings to which they apply.

input	ba-ka-nyarr-nya=^kwulkuna-yinya	—>
	CFT-3a-1px-EP=fear-PAST	
(i) rule 22	b**a-a**-nyarr-nya=^kwulkuna-yinya	—>
(ii) rule 19	b-**a**-nyarr-nya=^kwulkuna-yinya	—>
(iii) rule 11	ba-nya**rr-j**a=^kwulkuna-yinya	—>
(iv) rule 15	ba-nya-ja=^kwulkuna-yinya	—>
(v) rule 24	ba-ya-ja=^kwulkuna-yinya	
	b**a-ya**-ja=^k**wu**lkuna-**yi**nya	
(vi) rule 18	b-**e**-j-**o**-lkun-**e**-nya	
output	bejolkunenya	*we should have been frightened of him*

In this example we can see that V expansion rule 18 is the last rule to apply, and can only apply after rules 22, 19, and 24 have produced the vowel—glide strings upon which rule 18 feeds.

In many cases where there is a possibility of two rules applying to one cluster, one of the rules will have precedence, to the exclusion of the other. For example V-expansion rule 18 normally applies to |awu| strings at morpheme boundaries:

/ing**o**/   <— |i-ng**a**=^b**wu**| *I will hit him*
                    3a-1=hit

When the morpheme -^k*warndu* 'DUAL' is suffixed to this form, however, V+V Contraction rule 19 is applied to the sequence *before* rule 18 has a chance to apply:

/inga**waa**rndu/   <— |i-ng**a**=^bw**u-aa**rndu| *I will hit them both*
                              3a-1=hit-DU

In this example V+V contraction rule 19 applies to the string /u-aa/ and deletes the /u/ sound in =^b*wu* before V-expansion rule 18 can be applied to the string /a-wu/ to produce /o/. In this case note that it is clear that the grammar deals with the sequence |i-nga=^bwu-aarndu| as if it were an autonomous unit, and not merely an inflected form of the singular shape *ingo*. Thus each of the surface shapes *ingo* and *ingawaarndu* is derived from their underlying morphemes independently, without reference to the other as a paradigmatically prior or more basic form. The implication of this situation is that the language's morphology, even in the typically inflexional context of verb paradigms, is not inflexional at all but derivational, with each word-form assembled out of the lexicon independently.

In summary, it can be said that only general morphophonemic rules are ordered: morpheme-specific and redundancy rules are 'background' rules as described above. Of the 17 or so general morphophonemic rules, 7 of them (rules 14, 16, 17, 20, 21, 25 and 26) are independent. Rule 17 is simply an exception to trill deletion rule 15, and rules 20, 25 and 26 involve different kinds of epenthesis. The remaining three (14, 16 and 21) likewise do not feed other processes. Rules 10, 11 and 13 are hardening rules, feeding trill deletion rule 15. Rules 18, 19, 22 and 24 all effect vowels, and rules 12 and 23 deal with the /aa/—/^{k}wa/ allomorphy in Worrorra.

```
22 —> 19 —> 18 <— 24

10 ⎫
11 ⎬ —> 15
13 ⎭

23 <——> 12
```

Figure 3.1: summary of general rule ordering

Four: nouns and noun classes

This chapter is concerned with nouns as word-forms that refer to *types* of things, while Chapter Six deals with nominal expressions as denoting *instances* of those types (cf Langacker 1991:51). Worrorra referring expressions may be described by reference to at least three independent parameters with formal consequences:

>   Classificatory: by way of a five-way gender partition
>   Lexical: by way of a four-way morpholexical division
>   Animacy: by way of a two-way split, pluralizable vs non-pluralizable

<u>Classificatory</u>
Worrorra nouns occur as members of one of five classes or genders. These are a *masculine* class, a *feminine* class, a *celestial* class, a *terrestrial* class, and a minor class of *collective* nouns containing probably about a dozen members. Although some genders may be neutralized in some situations (see especially Chapter Nine), genders and noun classes do not constitute separate categories in Worrorra, as they do in some languages such as Mayali (Evans 2003), so that the terms 'gender' and 'noun class' may be used here synonymously. The two non-human genders referred to here and in Clendon (1999) as *celestial* and *terrestrial*, are referred to by Love (1934) as the *wuna* and *mana* classes respectively. Love named these genders after the definite articles used with their members *(wunu* and *mana* in my experience) (see Chapter Seven). Gender-marking is exhaustive and unique; the gender of the head of a noun phrase controls agreement on adjectives, inalienable nouns, pronouns and verbs and is essentially invariable with respect to each noun. Gender in Worrorra is described in §4.1.

<u>Lexical</u>
Simple nouns are fully lexicalized, meaning that they do not require additional bound morphemes in order to become utterable words. They may or may not display gender-signalling morphemes as part of their formal construction. The second and third nominal categories (below) constitute examples of external possession, as described in the volume edited by Payne & Barshi (1999).

The second lexical category comprises nouns that refer to parts of some whole which, when viewed from the perspective of traditional Worrorra culture, are deemed to be inalienable, or, as Chappell & McGregor (1996) put it, fall within the 'personal sphere' of some 'owner' or some whole of which the denotatum is a part. The 'whole' entity is indexed on nouns of this category by way of a set of inflexional person, number and gender-marking prefixes, with the result that inalienable nouns exhibit double agreement-class marking. Most inalienable nouns refer to parts of the body, but some refer to parts of the person such as =*ngumbu wunu* 'name,' =*yula inja* 'anger' and =*ngaanja inja* 'shadow; soul, spirit.'

The third category contains nouns that refer to kinfolk, or kinship nouns. These are derived from underlying root (vocative) morphemes by way of a set of derivational suffixes that index the agreement-class of the propositus (the 'possessor') on the head noun.

The fourth subcategory is derived from underlying root morphemes by way of a set of person, number and gender-marking affixes. These forms refer underlyingly to states rather than to entities, and are here termed adjectives.

Lexical subcategories may be summarized as follows:
(i) *simple nouns:* have inherent gender,
(ii) *inalienable nouns:* composite, inflexional, display double agreement-class marking,
(iii) *kinship nouns:* composite, derivational, have natural gender,
(iv) *adjectives:* composite, derivational, gender agreement with head.

Simple nouns are discussed in this chapter. Inalienable nouns and adjectives are described in Chapter Six. Kinship nouns are discussed in Chapter 13, and an inventory of kinship nouns is provided in Chapter 18.

Animacy

Human nouns and nouns that refer to important animals and to foods may be pluralized. Nearly all pluralizable nouns are either masculine or feminine; I know of only two that are not; *wunu marruku* 'flower' is promoted to the set of pluralizable nouns when flowers are being considered as food for some animals such as possums or echidnas, and *mana rambarr* 'avoidance-category kin.' This last appears to be a *Wanderwort* in the Kimberley, denoting in Worrorra a superordinate or category term covering a number of kinship designations whose referents stand in restricted or prohibited relationships to the speaker. There is, therefore, an abstract dimension to its meaning, which is something like 'polar opposite' or 'antithesis.' The same word in Ungarinyin means 'barrier' or 'screen',[33] and so it is probably safe to assume that in Worrorra this word's primary or underlying meaning has to do with the semantics of separation rather than with the denotation of human beings. Not all masculine and feminine nouns by any means are able to be pluralized; rather the subset of masculine and feminine nouns that can be pluralized may be characterized as being highly placed on a scale of animacy (or notional topicality, or cultural importance). As it happens, highly animate nouns are just the sort that make good candidates for inclusion in either masculine or feminine genders. Plurality in Worrorra is described in §4.2.

4.1 Agreement classes

Most of this chapter is concerned with the systematics of the five agreement classes that encode gender in the language. Gender represents one kind of nominal classification system found in Australia, the other being represented by systems of noun classification. Both types of system operate by partitioning the nouns of a language into distinct categories or partition classes (Silverstein 1986). Noun classifiers are lexicalizations of the intensional properties of their partition classes, that also function as heads of the phrases in which they occur. Gender systems are able to be described in similar terms, but without the requirements of lexicalization and headedness. Gender in Worrorra is a lexical property of the noun which bears it, and the articles listed in (4.4) below, that overtly signal gender, are frequently absent from noun phrases.

Referring expressions in Worrorra are partitioned into ten agreement classes, signalled morphologically on adjectives, pronouns, inalienable nouns, kinship nouns and possessive phrases, and on verbs in intransitive subject, transitive object, agent and non-subcategorized object positions. The parameters that define agreement class are of two types: person and number are higher-level parameters employed in the definition of all classes, while participation (that is, whether or not an addressee is included in the reference) and gender are lower-level parameters operating on only a subset of classes defined by the higher-level parameters. There are analytical disparities in agreement-class membership: five of the agreement classes contain only one high-frequency member each (first and second persons) while the other five contain thousands of members (third persons). Emically, however, there are no significant grounds for distinguishing between agreement classes on the basis of

---

[33] Alan Rumsey, pers comm.

person; all agreement classes have equal (and equally obligatory) access to each agreement locus. Although gender is not signalled on morphemes marking agents and non-subcategorized objects on verbs, there are no other morphological cues to indicate that the category 'third person singular' constitutes a subset of agreement classes defined by gender.

Table 4.1: nominal agreement-classes

CLASS LABEL	ABBREV	DERIVATIONAL PREFIX
first person singular	1	nga-
second person singular	2	ngun-
third person singular masculine	3a	i-, a-
third person singular feminine	3f	nyi(N)-
third person singular celestial	3w	ØN-, ᵏwuN-
third person singular terrestrial	3m	ma-
first person plural inclusive	1pin	ngarr-
first person plural exclusive	1px	arr-
second person plural	2p	nyirr-
third person plural	3p	arr-

Grammatical person does not operate independently of other agreement-class parameters as it does in other gendered languages such as French or Arabic. To illustrate the way in which inflected person, number, participation and gender categories constitute a single morphosyntactic parameter in Worrorra, it may be helpful to consider the noun *nyinjorinya* 'widow.' Although semantically a prototypical human noun, it is nevertheless morphologically derived, and is underlyingly adjectival in terms of the analysis offered here. Its meaning is in part derived by morphemes signalling agreement class; the morphological processes that it undergoes are the same as those undergone by all other agreement targets. *Nyinjorinya* is marked for feminine gender; a widower is *iyoru*, and is marked for masculine gender. If you were to keep two red-winged parrots (*wunu marrirri*) in a cage, and one of them were to die, the remaining parrot could be referred to as *wunjoru* 'it (who has) lost its mate.' If two red-tailed black cockatoos (*mana darraanma*) were kept in a cage and if one were to die, the survivor could be referred to as *mayorama* 'it (who has) lost its mate.' If I were to lose my spouse, I would refer to myself as *ngayoru* 'I (who am) a widow(er);' and similarly with other agreement-class categories: *ngunjoru* 'you singular (who are) a widow(er),' *ngajoyoru* 'we inclusive (who are) widow(er)s,' *ajoyoru* 'we exclusive (who are) widow(er)s,' *nyijoyoru* 'you plural (who are) widow(er)s' and *ajorayoru* 'widow(er)s.' In this paradigm, grammatical person is not manifested in a separate form-class from that of gender; the first person singular shape, for instance, cannot bear gender-marking affixes as adjectives do in French: *je suis content* 'I am happy (male referent)' vs *je suis contente* 'I am happy (female referent).'

There are, then, no *formal* grounds for separating the category 'gender' from other agreement-class meanings in Worrorra; in all agreement paradigms, person, gender, number and participation together constitute a single morphological parameter. Syntactic and semantic criteria are required to define the category 'gender' in Worrorra.

Gender partitions the third person singular category only. However there is a small class of collective nouns (about a dozen) whose agreement forms are homophonous with those of the third person plural agreement class. Collective nouns constitute an ambiguous category; they are formally identical to the third person plural agreement class, but morphosyntactically analogous to members of the set of third person singular agreement classes defined by gender. It should be borne in mind that there are at least two competing ways to account for collective nouns in Worrorra: one is to constitute collective nouns as an eleventh (homophonous) agreement class, and the other is to describe the third person plural agreement class as containing both plural and collective nouns. Neither approach seems to offer any clear analytical advantage over the other.

Worrorra nouns frequently co-occur with members of a set of determiners that serve as definite articles. These are *inja* (masculine), *nyina* (feminine), *wunu* (celestial) and *mana* (terrestrial); and they will be used to identify the gender of nouns occurring in this text. The following sentence exemplifies their use as definite articles:

(4.1)
Wankaleeninjaa,	jurlwun	injaa,	warinyinaa,
wankaleena-inja-aa	jurlwun	inja-aa,	warinya-nyina-aa
k'roo.sp-3aDEF-and	k'roo.sp	3aDEF-and	k'roo.sp-3fDEF-and

karroninyinaa	buju	kubarrwunanangka.
karroninya-nyina-aa	buju	kuN-ᵇwarr=wu-na-nangka
k'roo.sp-3fDEF-and	finish	VCOMP-3p=hit-PAST-DAT

They killed the male plains kangaroos, the male grey kangaroos, the female grey kangaroos and the female plains kangaroos.

The haplological contraction of noun and article seen here is discussed in §4.1.2. In (4.1) the types of kangaroo listed (*wankaleena, jurlwun, warinya, karroninya*) are followed by articles of appropriate gender, with the final vowel lengthened by the encliticized conjunction *aa* 'and.' These determiners may function deictically, and may also be used anaphorically to refer to members of the classes they signal, with quite precise meanings: in prototypical usage the human class markers *inja* and *nyina* refer to 'he, him' and 'she, her' respectively, and *mana* is used to mean 'here:'

(4.2)   Mana aja banu
        Sit here

Wunu is used as a determiner with subjunctive verbs (*nganngunjineerri* in 4.3a) and to mark the definite status of whole clauses, as in (4.3b):

(4.3a) Waawa nguru banyankangurrun, [wunu nganngunjineerri]?
        How come you don't listen to me, [when I speak to you]?

(b)   Baanjamurlomurlonyeerri [wunu]!
        ([You know that]) you should have been looking after them!

In (4.3a) the definite (backgrounded) status of the subordinate clause is marked by the use of the article of the appropriate class (*wunu*). In (4.3b) the propositional content of the utterance is rhetorically marked as being already known to the listener, and so receives definite marking by way of the celestial article.

Nouns typically denote concrete things in space, while the events depicted by verbs occur typically in time. Hence the meanings of the deictic functions of Worrorra determiners in prototypical usage are as follows:

(4.4)
ARTICLE	CORE DENOTATUM	'MEANING'
inja	male	he
nyina	female	she
wunu	time	when
mana	place	here

The following overview is based on a survey of some 600 nouns. While the sample is too small to convey meaningful statistics, the following tendencies may be noted. Where percentages are stated they are usually rounded, and should be recognized as being intended to convey tendencies and relative proportions only.

The class with the most membership is the masculine class. Over one third of all nouns belong to this class. Masculine is the most unmarked class, and typically genderless anaphors like *anguja* 'what?,' *angujakana* 'something' and *angujakane* 'all kinds of things' take masculine agreement markers, so in this sense the masculine class is semantically also the most neutral or residual class:

(4.5)
Awa	inja	angujakana	baa	kamurrkarla
awa	inja	angujakana	baa	ka-Ø=murrka-rla
3aNAR	3aDEF	something	rise/appear	3a-3=go.to-PAST

Something came up towards him

The feminine, celestial and terrestrial classes each contain about one fifth of all nouns in the sample. This rather even spread of nouns among the three non-masculine classes may suggest that allocation to gender may to some extent be arbitrary. However in real terms the feminine class is certainly the smallest of the genders (the collective gender excluded) when nouns that refer to females are discounted.

Inalienable nouns display significant differences from other nouns in the way they are distributed among genders. Of the seventy or so inalienable nouns recorded, three quarters of them are shared equally between the celestial and terrestrial classes. The remaining quarter is shared between the masculine and feminine classes; less than one fifth of the total sample being masculine and only five being feminine (see §4.1.3 (ii) and §4.1.6 (i)).

This discussion excludes from consideration derived nouns such as *nyinjorinya* (|nyiN=yoru-nya| [3f=widowed-3f]) 'widow,' referred to above. These word-forms are derived productively from underlying root morphemes by way of derivational affixes that code for all ten agreement classes, and are isomorphic with semantic adjectives such as *nyiniyanya* (|nyiN=niya-nya| [3f=good-3f]) 'good (feminine).' The root morphemes in question constitute a lexical category devoid of inherent gender.

4.1.1 Gender and culture

Worrorra genders constitute bounded sets whose core references are, as we shall see, complex, covert and opaque to analysis.[34]

Since Dixon (1982:178 ff) first described the semantic basis of the allocation of nouns to noun classes in Dyirbal, it has become apparent that some kind of organizational principles with respect to gender allocation may apply to other languages where nouns appear at first sight to be distributed among genders in a more or less random or arbitrary manner. As Lakoff & Johnson (1980) and Silverstein (1986) have pointed out, languages map classification onto experience by reference to a culturally specific set of symbolic structures. This is to say that language plays an integral part in the way that cultures structure the symbols by which societies create their own realities, and in the way that they manipulate those symbolic structures. This being the case, it would be a conceit to imagine that we could fully understand the organizational principles behind gender allocation in Worrorra without being in a position to comprehend much better than we do, the symbolic structures upon which such allocation is based. The result of this situation is that there must inevitably be a degree of analytic opacity or arbitrariness entering into an account of gender in Worrorra without our being in a position to determine to what extent such perceived randomness is real or merely apparent.

To illustrate this point it may be useful to look at some instances where culture determines gender independently of linguistic considerations. In these instances we are in a position to appreciate the cultural factors involved, but as our understanding of traditional Worrorra society is partial at best, a great deal of this sort of information is unavailable. In instances of this sort the question must inevitably arise as to whether gender is determined by some extra-linguistic cultural (usually narrative) mandate, or whether gender previously allocated thereby makes some entity felicitously available for a cultural role that requires a participant of that gender. In each of these examples it will be seen that the former is the case; in these examples at least, culture determines gender.

The moon has a recognizable physiognomy, and despite (or perhaps because of) periodic changes is recognizable as a single entity. The sun however has no physiognomy and was seen in traditional Worrorra culture as a multiplicity of entities. The operation of the sun was envisaged as follows: there

---

[34] As is the case with most gender, as opposed to classifier, systems, Worrorra gender semantics are generally beyond the 'limits of awareness' (Silverstein 1981) of native speakers.

is a mother sun who stays behind the world giving birth to daughter suns, each of whom in turn travels through the sky and dies at the end of each day. This story, *Iwarnbarnngarri nyangkaningkarla marangunya* ('The snake that bit the sun') is recounted in Utemorrah 2000:31-36. Because the parent sun, *nyina marangunya*, must in this cosmology be a mother in order to reproduce, it is female and allocated with other female things to the feminine gender.

Over much of the world and including North-Western Australia, snakes are phallic symbols and we could expect them to be allocated to masculine genders. However in Worrorra the black-headed python, *mawunkunya* is feminine. It has another name, *nyimrimaaingarrinya*, also feminine. *Nyimrimaaingarrinya* is a compound noun derived from the root =*mri* 'head' and the preverb *maai* '(a woman) shaves and blackens her head in mourning.' Its morphology is as follows: |nyiN=mri-maai-ngarri-nya| [fem=head-{shave-&-blacken-in-mourning}-relativizer-fem] 'her-head-is-shaved-and-blackened-in-mourning.' This name refers to the funerary requirement of a woman to shave her head and blacken it with soot as a sign of mourning for a specified period after the death of some relatives, most importantly her husband. In Worrorra culture the black-headed python is taken to be the aetiological prototype of this custom. Because only women perform this funerary duty the black-headed python is considered to be a woman and is allocated to the feminine gender.

In traditional Worrorra society the manufacture of stone spear-heads was an important and time-consuming activity and the best of the results were highly prized. There are a number of nouns referring to stone spear-heads and I am not sure of the connotations of all of them. However two types of spear-head are of interest here. The normal, all-purpose, functional spear-point is referred to by the noun *jimara*. *Jimara* is a masculine noun for reasons that will be discussed below. Another type of spear-head was essentially non-functional, at least in the way that spear-heads typically function. This type was made of shiny or semi-translucent stone such as jasper or agate, and of bottle-glass after European contact. They were beautifully crafted and often so thin as to be impractical for use in hunting. Their closest comparison is with the Solutrean leaf-shaped points of the European Upper Palæolithic, and they are often referred to as 'Kimberley points.' These points were not made for hunting but for their æsthetic value and for the magic and curative powers they derived from that value. They were prized trade items and were traded as far away as the Western Desert where they were referred to as *jinala* (from Worrorra *jinalya* 'spear'). The commonest general term for this type of spear-head is *jimbeerlanya*, and is feminine. The special properties of *jimbeerlanya* and the role they played in Worrorra society meant that they were not only culturally highly significant items but were also shiny and dangerous by virtue of their magical properties. As such they were allocated to the semantically marked gender which in Worrorra is feminine. The construction of markedness in Worrorra and its manifestation in gender-marking is discussed in §4.1.6 (i). If this piece of cultural information were not available, it might be assumed that *jimara* and *jimbeerlanya* were allocated to different genders more or less capriciously, and that gender allocation was at least in this instance arbitrary.

A comparable situation is seen in the two nouns that mean 'buttocks.' *Wumbarranu* is a celestial noun and =*malab* is terrestrial. I know of no reason why these two apparent synonyms should be allocated to different genders, but that ignorance does not mean that such allocations are necessarily arbitrary. Again, *wunu ngubunu, mana ngujalama* and *nyina wiyarrinya* (feminine) are all species of stingray. Examination of the animals themselves and of information about them may reveal some kind of pattern to their distribution among genders but as things stand, no such pattern is apparent.

Associations made by one culture are not necessarily those made by another. To put it another way, any given thing in the world will empirically exhibit a number of attributes, from among which different cultures will select those which are for them significant from those which are not, with respect to the ways in which such things are categorized. For example in Worrorra *manjuma* 'wind' is terrestrial, and we would expect that *jalawuna* 'whirlwind, willy-willy' would be in the same category as 'wind,' whereas in fact it is masculine. The reason for this is that Worrorra culture personifies the whirlwind as something like a large, sulky and bad-mannered adolescent, and when one is immanent older Worrorra people will loudly exhort it to go around them or away from them and leave them alone. And so *jalawuna* is masculine, along with other human figures. Likewise most bright, reflective things are celestial, and we would expect *nyungumanja* 'reflection' to be in that gender too; the semantic core of the word 'reflection' has to do with light. However the semantic core of *nyungumanja* is the image of a human being (seen in still water), and so the word is masculine, again with other human figures. The surface of the sea may appear bright on still, hot days, but the semantics of *wondum* 'sea, salt water' has to do with the opacity and palatability of the water itself; *wondum* is applied to salty, unpalatable water generally, and is terrestrial.

4.1.2 Gender and phonology

With reference to the sample of Worrorra nouns mentioned above, nearly three quarters (73%) display a phonological segment that pertains to their class membership. Gender is lexically inherent in Worrorra nouns, that is to say that gender is part of a noun's lexical construction, whether or not it is overtly signalled on the noun itself. Phonological segments do not signal class membership uniquely, and, with one case exception, members of a given class do not display one segment exclusively. However the above figure gives evidence that there are strong tendencies for certain phonological segments to be associated with particular genders. Phonology may serve to indicate or signal class membership, but it does not determine it. Once class membership has been assigned (and I will argue that this is accomplished by reference to criteria that are primarily semantic), then membership may (or may not) be signalled phonologically. A rather nice illustration of this sequence is provided by Love (1934:20):

> The Worrorra word for vegetable-fibre string is irkalja, a masculine noun, represented by the pronoun indja. Sisal hemp was grown and used for string making. When asked the gender of hemp the men replied "indja"; but one man asked the English name of the leaf. He was told "Hemp". The men repeated " 'emp, 'emp, mana". At first they designated the hemp plant indja, probably thinking "Irkalja"; but, on hearing the sound of the English word, ending in p, they declared that the word is mana.

In this account we can see that sisal was at first assigned gender by reference to semantic criteria until its phonological shape as an English word was ascertained, which was then taken to signal a predetermined or pre-existing gender.

The forms in question are suffixes or rarely prefixes, essentially the same as those used to derive adjectives and pronouns, and are displayed in Table 4.2.

Table 4.2: gender morphemes

	word-initial	word-final
masculine	i-	-ya *or* -i
feminine	ny-	-nya
celestial	wu- /u- /oo-	-u
terrestrial	ma-	-m(a) *or* -b(a)
collective		-ya or -i

Collective gender-signalling suffixes have the same shape as suffixes used on plural nouns (§4.2.2).

Gender-signalling morphemes are, as a general rule, not productive on nouns; they are for the most part lexicalized components of their hosts. The exceptions to this are nouns of the feminine and terrestrial classes. In these classes, the gender suffixes *-nya* and *-m(a)* may be detached from their host lexemes under certain (mainly phonological) conditions. For instance when a feminine noun is followed by a determiner or appropriate postposition, the noun's gender-signalling suffix is usually deleted under haplology (4.6a & b) or distant haplology (4.6c) in normal fast speech:

(4.6a)   Balangkarra**nya** nyangke   —>   balangkarra nyangke   *A storm-wave*

(b)   Wangayi**nya** nyina   —>   wangayi nyina   *The woman*

(c)   Karranangka**nya** - ᵏwunya —> karranangkawunya   *For his mother*

Note as well the haplologically reduced forms *warinyinaa* 'the female grey kangaroo' and *karroninyinaa* 'the female plains kangaroo' already seen in (4.1). The feminine noun *ngeenya* 'honey' exchanges its feminine marker (*-nya*) for a plural one (*-ya*) in a form *ngeeya* that refers to a mass of honey or lots of honey.

Adverbial suffixes are usually interposed between the root lexeme and the gender-marking suffix of a terrestrial noun, as in (4.7a); otherwise the gender morpheme may be lost altogether, as in (4.7b):

(4.7a)   dambee-ma-nyini   —>   dambee-nyini-ma   —>   dambeenyinim
         place-3m-ENDPOINT   place-ENDPOINT-3m
         To/at home, homeward

(b)   dambee-ma-ᵏwunya   —>   dambeewunya
         place-3m-PURP
         Homeward

Another example of this phenomenon is to be seen in (4.18). Nouns such as *kulum mana* 'hot (baking) sand' lose gender-marking suffixes when used as preverbal elements in complex predicates, eg *kulu =ma* 'burn, scorch with hot sand.'

It will be helpful now to look at each gender in turn to see the ways in which, and the extent to which gender is signalled phonologically.

The feminine gender is the one exception referred to above, in which all the nouns in this class (in my sample) display one underlying segment (|-nya|) exclusively. This makes feminine the most phonologically marked gender in the language. Feminine nouns end in *-nya*, *-(r)lja*, *-j* or *-Vja*. In these words, however, *-ja* is underlying |-nya|. |ny| hardens to /j/ after laterals and /rr/ (rule 11), such that the sequence |rr-ny| always finds surface expression as /j/ (rule 15). Take, for example, the masculine words *kanangkurri* 'dog,' *kalakalaarri* 'sea-turtles on-shore to mate or lay eggs' and *karnamarri* 'large shark.' These have feminine equivalents *kanangkuja* 'bitch,' *kalakalaaja* 'female sea-turtles on-shore to lay eggs' and *karnamaja* 'large female shark,' and are underlyingly |kanangkurr+nya, kalakalaarr+nya| and |karnamarr+nya|. So it may be assumed that feminine words such as *balkuja* 'dugong,' *banaja* 'bustard' and *kuyoja* 'great-billed heron' end in underlying |... rr-nya| sequences as well. The feminine words *mamangkalja* 'woman friend, female relation,' *ngorlja* 'large green frog sp.' and *yarnkalja* 'spear thrower' show the segment |-nya| hardening after lateral consonants. Three feminine nouns in my sample end in *-j*: *jimbirrij* 'giant groper,' *jalaj* 'axe handle' and *karruj* 'silver gull.' As no noun of any other gender ends in this segment, it may be assumed that *-j* in this situation is a reduced form of *-ja* and is therefore underlyingly |-nya| as well.

Of the four feminine endings listed above, *-nya*, *-(r)lja*, *-j* and *-Vja*, only the ending *-Vja* does not signal feminine gender exclusively on common nouns. This is because the phonological hardening process referred to above applies as well to glides, such that the masculine segment |-ya| also hardens after the trill /rr/, and it may be that the underlying sequence |... rr-ya| finds surface expression as *-ja* in such masculine words as *rnamaja* 'bigamist.' Regardless of the difficulty of sorting out words that just happen to end in *-ja* from those whose endings are derived from underlying |rr-(n)ya| sequences, the ending *-Vja* is found on both masculine and feminine nouns, as well as on one celestial noun; *ngaja* 'custom, precedent.' Over nine tenths (91%) of the feminine nouns in my sample end in one of the three endings that signal feminine gender on common nouns exclusively.

While all feminine nouns may thus be seen to end in |-nya|, not every noun that ends in *-nya* is feminine. There are a number of place names that end in *-nya* that belong to other classes: *Karnmanya* 'Kunmunya Mission' (terrestrial), *Mangadanya* 'place name' (terrestrial), *Mingkunya* 'Port George IV' (terrestrial) and *Ngayangkarnanya* 'Mount Trafalgar' (celestial). Some of these are diachronic compounds containing the relational morpheme *-rnanya* 'LOCATIVE,' eg |mangarr-rnanya| [pouch-LOC] —> *Mangadanya* 'In the pouch,' and another may be compounded with the morpheme *-ᵏwunya* 'GOAL.' These grammatical morphemes impart a superficially feminine appearance to these names.

The one masculine word in the sample that ends in -*nya*, *aalkunya* 'young man, initiate,' is almost certainly such a compound.

Four fifths of all terrestrial nouns in the sample end in /-B(a)/, where B stands for a bilabial nasal or stop. In this score I have included a few nouns on which -*ma* or -*ba* appear to be epenthetic:

karnmern *or* karnmernma	*cave*
rambarr *or* rambarrba	*avoidance relation*
dalorr *or* dalorrba	*well, sink-hole*
kulnmerr *or* kulnmerrba	*tail*
bundurl *or* bundurlba	*countryside; 'the bush'*
Yarloon *or* Yarloonma	*Cone Bay*
jerr *or* jerrba	*shade*

The longer epenthesized forms are citation forms, while the occurrence of the truncated forms is environmentally conditioned. In the last example, the monosyllabic form *jerr* is very restricted in terms of the phonological environments within which it may occur. In the following example, the epenthetic morpheme is deleted under haplology with the first syllable of the following adjective:

(4.8)   Jerr maniyam mana
        The deep shadow

Despite the high proportion of terrestrial words ending in /-B(a)/, this ending is not exclusive to that class, as the following masculine nouns demonstrate: *karimba* 'golden bandicoot,' *burlkumba* 'Northern brush-tailed possum,' *joomba* 'bone in forearm,' *joonba* 'ceremony,' *wundukuwundukum* 'nocturnal gecko sp,' *maaba* 'old man' and *kurruma* 'wife's mother's brother or father.' The celestial noun =*ngumba*/=*ngumbu* 'name' is also of interest in this respect.

Over one half of all celestial nouns in the sample end in the segment -*u*. Included in this score are a few nouns for which that segment appears to be epenthetic, insofar as alternative forms exist without it, or it is elided in the presence of grammatical suffixes:

angkuban *or* angkubanu	*cloud*
jeerr *or* jeerru	*eyebrows*
braarr *or* braarru	*first light at dawn*
wungkurr *or* wungkurru	*sacred pool*
kayuk *or* kayuku	*rock*
mangarr *or* mangarru	*(kangaroo's) pouch*

anjolu	*sky*	anjoldanya	*in heaven*
nguwanu	*tree*	nguwarnanya	*in the tree*
wiyanu	*fire*	wiyarnanya	*in/by the fire*
aambulu	*his eyes*	aambuldanya	*in his eyes*
mangarru	*pouch*	mangadanya	*in the pouch*

As word-final -*u* does not behave in this manner when it is found on nouns of other classes, it appears that this ending serves a double function as well, namely that of epenthesis and of signalling class membership. A number of nouns ending in -*u* are not celestial; the following are all masculine: *karnmangku* 'yam (generic),' *korru* 'jaw,' *murlku* 'boil, sore,' *rangku* 'heart,' *waraku* 'father's sister's son,' *broolku* 'cicatrice,' *irnarruku* 'blanket' and *jeembu* 'kangaroo-bone pressure-flaking tool.' And three belong to the terrestrial class: =*reenu* 'body,' *dungundu* 'side, of eg a building or a hill, and *kanaalu* '(spatially) opposite side or place.'

A little over one third of the masculine nouns in the sample end in the segment |-ya| and a little over one fifth end in the segment -*i*. Altogether, over one half of all masculine nouns in the sample end in a segment that may be said to signal gender. As indicated above, |-ya| may find realization in a fairly wide range of surface-level phonemes, hence the segments -*Vja, (r)nja, -ya* and -*lya* may all signal masculine gender. There are two pieces of evidence that suggest that |-ya| is a gender-signalling segment. The first is that -*ya* occurs in complementary distribution to the feminine segment -*nya* as a suffix to some nouns that refer to male things and have masculine gender. Masculine kinship nouns in their first person singular propositus or citation shapes contrast with feminine kinship nouns in this respect (see below). The suffixes -*waaya* (masculine) and -*waanya* (feminine) derive nouns with human reference from the names of some patriclan countries, and nouns that refer to introduced things and roles, such as goats and nurses, may also display alternations between the -*nya* and -*ya* suffixes to represent female and male roles and animals respectively. At least one non-introduced role, that of 'friend, countryman, relation' also shows this alternation. The pro-form *burn*- takes class and number suffixes in agreement with its denotatum in any given context. And finally at least one preverb can be seen transparently to employ -*ya* to derive a masculine human noun (the usual way of doing this is by the use of the relativizing suffix -*ngarri* 'associated with, characterized by or pertaining to (something)'). In three of the pairs in the following list, the segment -*ya* is hardened to -*ja* after a nasal consonant:

FEMININE		MASCULINE	
babaanya	*Mo Fa sister*	babaaya	*mother's father*
barnmarnya	*nurse*	barnmarnja	*doctor*
naningkunya	*nanny goat*	naningkunja	*billy goat*
mamangkalja	*woman friend*	mamangkalya	*friend*
burnya	*pro-noun*	burnja	*pro-noun*
jikarl (preverb)	*lie*	jikarlya	*liar*
Wurnbangkuwaanya	*CLAN NAME*	Wurnbangkuwaaya	*CLAN NAME*

The second line of evidence referred to above is that this suffix is almost entirely restricted to the masculine class. The segment |-ya| occurs on the end of only three non-masculine nouns, once the occurrence of -*ja* on feminine nouns (where it is a reflex of |-nya|) is discounted. Two of these are celestial: *barndaya* 'mainland' and *murndaaleya* 'plateau, platform,' and one is terrestrial: *Grarlya* 'clan country name,' which has alternate forms *Grarl* and *Meegrarlba*. Two other celestial nouns, *ngaja* 'custom, precedent' and *oomanja* 'round bone at the base of the big toe' end in a segment that may be a hardened reflex of |-ya|, but these are the only two that do so, and no terrestrial noun ends in this segment. This amounts to a possible total of five (or three) non-masculine nouns, as opposed to over 70 masculine nouns displaying the ending |-ya|.

A significant number of masculine nouns that display phonological signalling of their class membership end in the segment /-lya/, and this ending is almost exclusive to masculine nouns. Rather than propose /-lya/ as a gender-signalling suffix in addition to -*ya* and its hardened form -*ja*, I take it to represent an underlying |-L-ya| sequence. The occurrence of such a sequence in the morphophonology is supported by comparing the nouns *mamangkalya* and *jikarlya* in the above list with the words with which they are paired.

The ending -*(r)nja* is almost exclusive to masculine nouns because |-ya| hardens to -*ja* after a nasal consonant (rule 10), whereas nasals do not harden after other nasal consonants, so that underlying |... N+nya| sequences find surface expression as -*(r)nya*. The only non-masculine noun ending in -*(r)nja* is *wunu oomanja*, referred to above.

The proportion of masculine nouns ending in -*i* is so small (one fifth) that it is tempting not to recognize this segment as one signalling gender. Nevertheless, on adjectives and pronouns -*i* (like |-ya|) does function as a morpheme deriving masculine gender, and it does occur on more masculine nouns than on those of any other gender. In pairs of words like *kanangkurri* 'dog' and *kanangkuja* 'bitch,' referred to above, -*i* appears to alternate with |-nya| to produce masculine and feminine pairs (|kanangkurr-i, kanangkurr-nya|). A number of celestial nouns also end in -*i*: *wijali* 'burnt grass,' *jalaani* 'deep water,' *marlinji* 'oyster,' *marrirri* 'red-winged parrot,' =*mri* 'head,' *namandi* 'canoe,' *ngarli* 'paperbark,' =*rnorri* 'hand, fingers,' *wanawi* 'egg' and *warnangkali* 'cliff.' One terrestrial noun ends in -*i*: *aajaajirri* 'rainy season.'

The endings that signal masculine gender are homophonous with those that signal plural number (§4.2.1). The shapes of plural masculine nouns may be homophonous with their singular counterparts, or they may employ stem reduplication as well as suffixation to mark plural number. Be that as it may, the endings that signal masculine gender in Worrorra do not signal gender uniquely; the suffixes concerned are systematically shared with plural number. There is thus no unique gender-marking for masculine, not even if statistical criteria are used. So in this sense the masculine gender is essentially unmarked phonologically in Worrorra.

Of the nine collective nouns in the sample, eight end in *-i* or |-ya|. This sample is too small to be useful for purposes of comparison with other noun classes, and moreover the segments in question are primarily plural number-marking morphemes (§4.2.2).

Table 4.3: distribution of gender-signalling suffixes

SEGMENT	SIGNAL	FEMININE	TERRESTRIAL	CELESTIAL	MASCULINE
-Vja	masc, fem	10		1	11
-nya	fem	93			1
-(r)lja	fem	3			
-j	fem	3			
-ya	masc			3	21
-(r)lya	masc				21
-(r)nja	masc			1	18
-i	masc		1	10	45
-B(a)	terrestrial		119	1	7
-u	celestial		3	70	8
	N / %	109 / 100	119 / 79	70 / 57	116 / 57

Gender in Worrorra is signalled phonologically, but not in any straightforward way. The distribution of gender-signalling suffixes is summarized in Table 4.3. Proper nouns (including anomalous place names) are not included in this summary. Place names present some difficulties with respect to gender and will be discussed in §4.1.4 (i). In the table the number of nouns from the sample displaying each gender-signalling segment is listed for each agreement class. Below this are listed the number of gender-marked nouns in each class (N), and then that number expressed as a percentage of the total number of nouns in each class.

Less than 12% of nouns in the sample display initial segments that could be said to correspond to their gender. In Table 4.4 the numbers of nouns displaying initial segments corresponding to (some) gender are listed for each agreement-class.

Table 4.4: Distribution of gender-signalling prefixes

SEGMENT	MASCULINE	FEMININE	CELESTIAL	TERRESTRIAL
i-	**19**	2	3	2
ny-	1	**8**		
wu- /u- /oo	4	2	**18**	5
ma-	11	10	8	**23**

Among those 20% or so of nouns that display one or another of the initial segments in question, it is clear that there is a tendency for the shape of segments to correlate with the gender of the nouns on which they appear. That is to say that while the correlation between initial segment and gender is very far from being absolute, neither is it entirely random. The existence of a pair of nouns minimally distinguished by gender-marking segments demonstrates that initial segments can be involved in signalling gender, at least in a minor way: *rlarlangkarram mana* 'the sea' and *irlarlangkarra inja* 'salt-water crocodile.' Only 13 such nouns (2%) bear 'correct' initial segments without also bearing gender-signalling segments word-finally. The proportions of initial and final gender-signalling segments are as follows:

gender signalling by final segment only	62%
gender signalling by both initial and final segments	9%
gender signalling by initial segment only	2%

Although almost three quarters of Worrorra nouns in the sample display phonological signalling of class membership, this figure is not uniform for all classes. The number of nouns that signal gender phonologically falls away from the feminine class, in which all nouns can be seen to display gender-signalling, to the terrestrial (four fifths), and to the celestial and masculine classes (with roughly three fifths each). This trend is interesting in that it defines a scale of phonological markedness which is at least partly correlated with semantic markedness, and which will be discussed further in §4.1.6 (i) below.

4.1.3 Semantic assignment

While it is possible that the large and phonologically largely unmarked masculine gender contains a subset of residually classified nouns, that is to say of nouns whose allocation to gender is by default rather than by reference to semantic criteria, the systematics underlying the gender partition are nevertheless so pervasive as to afford us some insight into the interplay between Worrorra culture and language. Nouns are partitioned by reference to a semantic structure that acts as an organizing principle with respect to the denotata to which they refer. This structure is outlined in Figure 4.1 in §4.1.5, in terms of what I will refer to as a system of *meta-intensions*. In order to understand the basis of such a meta-intensional structure, it is necessary to investigate the lower-level semantic domains and the integrational principles of which the system as a whole is comprised.

In attempting to describe the operation of the semantic structure responsible for setting up partition-classes in Worrorra, it may be helpful to engage the geometric analogy of a multi-dimensional semantic space. A number of dimensions or parameters may be imagined within such a space, each describable, as in geometry, by reference to a set of coordinates. As far as I am aware, such a semantic space in Worrorra is defined in at least four parameters (dimensions), but there could be more of which I am unaware. The coordinates describing these four parameters are in the form of polar oppositions, to one or other of which any given noun is attracted with respect to each parameter. A more precise geometry might describe two semantic spaces, or two regions within semantic space: one region defined by parameters the coordinates of which are drawn from observations of human shape and experience, and the other drawing from experience of the world external to the human body. These two regions are mutually exclusive, that is to say there is no overlap between them, and they constitute two superordinate partitioning structures that will be referred to as macrogenders (§4.1.6). The parameters of this semantic space and their coordinates are shown in Table 4.5:

Table 4.5: gender intensions

Parameter	Coordinates	
human macrogender	MASCULINE	FEMININE
sex	male	female
shape	extended	rounded
non-human macrogender	CELESTIAL	TERRESTRIAL
dimension	time	place
luminosity	bright, translucent	dark, opaque

The term 'human' as a macrogender label applied to the formal marking of the partition is used here to capture those characteristics of denotata that acquire meaning and significance for gender allocation by analogy with meaningful and significant properties and characteristics of human beings. Semantic markedness constitutes another pervasive coordinate-set defined by the dynamics of bipolarity; markedness however is a macrogender parameter and is discussed in §4.1.6 (i).

Some of the parameters of semantic space exhibit more clearly than others core–fadeout properties as category properties in natural language. Prototypical members of a luminous category, for example, such as fire and water, become associated by analogy with things that exhibit luminous properties less unambiguously, along a core–fadeout continuum. For example the most culturally important or 'visible' stones were those capable of producing a sharp cutting edge, such as quartz or agate, and these happen to be shiny, especially after being flaked. Further along the continuum other reflective or pale-coloured stones are included, then dark reflective stones, then any stones, rocks and rocky hills. The point is that core–fadeout properties in categorization do not make the categories in which they appear less significant for nominal partition than categories with relatively straightforward distinctions. Core–fadeout categories may indeed produce secondary semantic parameters, such as that labelled 'topography' in §4.1.3 (v). In reality many if not most nouns must 'appear' in more than one parameter, but only the result or outcome of competing polarities can be evident lexically, in terms of the gender ultimately assigned to nouns. When a number of denotational attributes make a noun eligible for membership of more than one formal class, then the selection of criteria that determine allocation proceeds in ways that are not etically predictable. Although the structural parameters discussed below are clearly observable, they constitute a far from complete account of gender semantics in Worrorra, as the many exceptions to these parameters, which represent generalizations or tendencies only, demonstrate.

The outline displayed in Table 4.5 represents a kind of superstructure, around and within which cluster other semantic fields that may be related to the superstructure to a greater or lesser extent, or which may not be related to it at all. Categories are defined by core–fadeout properties, added to which are historical considerations: gender semantics are liable to change over time (Corbett 1991:248), although gender itself, as a lexically inherent property of a given noun, may be retained to become an exception to synchronic trends, ie an archaism. The result of this kind of process would be to have preserved islands of residual or archaic gender assignment in a sea of more general semantic tendencies, and this is more or less what we find in Worrorra.

4.1.3 (i) sex differentiation

All humans and a good many higher animals are allocated gender on the basis of biological sex, that is to say that they are sex-differentiable. Terms referring to lower-order animals are not sex-differentiated. The gender to which males are allocated is here termed masculine and that to which females are allocated is termed feminine. Male–female pairs usually show phonological correspondence or equivalence, but such correspondence is not necessary, as the following list of male and female pairs indicates. Kinship pairs of this sort are usually related affinally.

	MALES		FEMALES	
person	eeja	*man*	wangayinya	*woman*
child	awanja	*boy*	nyangkanya	*girl*
adolescent	weerla		mrnangkanya	
demon	akurla		jilinya	
spirit-bird	kaakaaja		meemeenya	
parent	irraaya	*father*	karraanya	*mother*
spouse	kulaaya	*husband*	mangkaanya	*wife*
in-laws	ibaaya	*husband's father*	jalinjaanya	*husband's mother*
	waaya	*wife's father*	kurrumaanya	*wife's mother*
father's parents	ngawaaya	*father's father*	mangkaanya	*father's mother*
mother's parents	jamaaya	*mother's father*	kajaanya	*mother's mother*

Some kinship pairs of this sort, however, are consanguineal; most notably those that are closest to you – your parents and their opposite-sex siblings, and your children, reckoned patrilineally:

patrilateral	irraaya	*father*	bamaraanya	*father's sister*
matrilateral	kakaaya	*mother's brother*	karraanya	*mother*
children	irraaya	*son*	bamaraanya	*daughter*
wife's family	waaya	*wife's brother*	mangkaanya	*wife*

Usually however the male and female forms of words show phonological correspondence. Most kinship nouns are of this sort: pairs of kinship nouns exhibiting phonological correspondence are always consanguineal, not affinal kin.

offspring	kawurla 'son'	kawurlanya 'daughter'
husband's family	kulaaya 'husband'	kulaanya 'husband's sister'
wife's family	kurruma 'wife's uncle'	kurrumaanya 'wife's mother'
matrilateral cross-cousin	jamaaya	jamaanya
patrilateral cross-cousin	waraku	warakunya
matrilineal descendants	ibaaya 'son'	ibaanya 'daughter'
elder sibling	ngawaaya (abiya)	ngawaanya (abeenya)
younger sibling	ngawmaleya	ngawmalenya
old person	maaba	maabanya
child	warrala 'boy'	warralinya 'girl'
	wangalang 'child'	wangalangunya 'girl child'
European	aalmara	aalmarinya
friend, relation	mamangkalya	mamangkalja

That the correspondences exemplified in the above list represent the most productive way of deriving male and female forms of any type, is shown by recent innovations:

medical practitioner	barnmarnja 'doctor'	barnmarnya 'nurse'
goat	naningkunja	naningkunya

In its traditional sense the noun *barnmarnja inja* meant 'sorceror' and that role was the exclusive domain of men: as Patsy Lulpunda told me, *'eejamaanja barnmarnja* – only men are sorcerors.' Recently however this noun has extended its reference to include Western-style doctors and has productively acquired a feminine ending to refer to nurses and women doctors.

Important animals are sex-differentiated. When the sex of some animal is unknown or is not contextually pertinent, the masculine term is always used to refer to a member of that species:

	MALES	FEMALES
grey kangaroo	arr'ra ~ jurlwun	warinya
plains kangaroo	wankaleena	karroninya ~ balngkoninya
salt-water crocodile	koyoya ~ irlarlangkarra	meerrinya
perentie (goanna)	kariyali	irroninya
green sea-turtle	juluwarra	rlanonya
dog	kanangkurri	kanangkuja
dingo	arroli	arrolinya
large shark	karnamarri	karnamaja

<u>4.1.3 (ii) shape</u>
Most animals are allocated to the masculine and feminine genders, with the majority being masculine. Squat or rounded animals, however, are almost all feminine: *balkuja* or *warlinya* 'dugong' is a ponderous and bulky animal, and is contrasted with sea turtles, which are masculine: *warli* 'sea-turtle (generic),' *mawurnkareenja* 'large sea turtle,' *mungurdi/mungurldi* 'loggerhead turtle,' and *nawarralya* 'hawksbill turtle.'

Other large and ponderous sea animals are *murnumbanya* 'whale,' *jimbirrij* 'giant groper/rock cod' and *nyalikanya* 'baler shell (*Melo amphora*)' which are also feminine. Animals may become rounded by curling themselves into balls; *mirimiringarrinya* 'echidna,' *joonya* 'mouse, antechinus' and *rlangkumanya* 'sugar glider' are feminine. Pigeons are plump and bulbous birds and are mostly feminine: *kunbalawaja* 'crested pigeon,' *wawarranya* 'rock pigeon' and *barnbarrngunya* 'bronzewing pigeon.' The rounded or bulbous shape of ankles may be the reason that the words =*rlawarndinya* 'ankle' and =*yalngkanya* 'ankle' are feminine.

Extended and/or rigid things are masculine, especially in the field of made goods and chattels or artefacts. These include *jinalya* 'spear' and associated *jimara* 'spear blade,' *jandoorri* 'staff,' *karli* 'boomerang' (an introduced term for an introduced item) and *kalambarna* 'wooden paddle for raft.' Extended flexible things are also masculine: *irrkalya* and *mamurlanja* 'spun vegetable-fibre string or rope,' *banjaya* 'string spun from eucalypt bark' and *kulijarri* 'steel wire.' Bones and bony or bone-like body parts are masculine: =*rnaarri* 'bones, skeleton,' *dingkalya* 'bone in lower leg,' *joomba* 'bone in forearm,' =*yoowa* 'elbow' (although words for the corresponding body part 'knee,' =*rlungkum* and =*yoorrkum*, are terrestrial), =*rnangalya* 'wrist' (although words for 'ankle,' =*rlawarndinya* and =*yalngkanya*, are feminine), *korru* 'jaw,' *kurleerla* 'shoulder blades' and *keyingka* 'finger nails.' Bone tools are masculine; *jeembu* 'kangaroo-bone pressure-flaking tool' contrasts with *mana karrinjalba* 'wooden pressure-flaking tool' and *wunu keembu* 'stone pressure-flaking tool.' Stone things are typically celestial, as is *durrku* 'mortuary cairn.' However the large erect stone monuments called *yarndulya* are masculine, as are termite mounds of comparable shape, *irrulya*.

4.1.3 (iii) dimension

Just as the masculine and feminine genders have 'maleness' and 'femaleness' as their core denotational prototypes, so 'place' is the corresponding denotatum for the terrrestrial class. Any adjective or pronoun marked for terrrestrial agreement without a stated head noun is taken to refer to 'place' by default. In the following sentence examples the adjective =*yakarri* 'other' is marked for terrestrial agreement as *mayakarrima*, and is not co-referential with any noun in the preceding discourses. In this situation the reference is always to 'place:'

(4.9a) Ke **mayakarrima** bariy maarrburrkarla
Then they got up and went on to another place

(b) Waa **mayakarrima** berringenya
We didn't go to other places

(c) Mangkanangkanya marno nyimnyenga **mayakarrima**rnanya, nyinjorinya nyingke
His wife, the widow, would move away to another place

The terrrestrial class is in some respects a locative gender as nominals marked for terrrestrial need not (and very often do not) take locative or allative suffixes when used in these functions. Example (4.9b) shows this use of terrrestrial marking with the verb =*ya* 'go.' Example (4.9c) shows =*ya* 'go' used with an adjective marked for terrrestrial class and inflected with the locative suffix -*rnanya*. The following sentences are further examples of noun phrases with terrestrial heads used in locative and allative senses without local postpositional ('case') inflection. This usage is rather more common than that *with* local case inflection, and in §4.1.4 (i) we will see that locative inflection may actually induce derivational terrrestrial class marking.

(4.10a) Aja   nganunerri   ngayanangkama   mayaram.
         aja   nga=nu-na-eerri   ngayu-nangka-ma   mayaram
         sit   1=be-PAST-PROG   I-DAT-3m   house
I stayed home at my place.

(b) Kaarringoorri molnganem mana.
     kaarr=i-nga-oorri molnganem mana
     3p=go-TNS-U/AUG river 3mDEF
     She went with them to the river.

The superordinate lexeme for the terrestrial class is *dambeem* 'place.' Nearly all nouns that refer to locations or to topography are terrestrial, with the exception of a subset of nouns that refer to high, rocky or steep places. Nevertheless the generic term for hills, *werrim*, is terrestrial, as are:

(a) Low, flat places: *marayuma* 'plain,' *waawima* 'flat, open ground,' *wondum* 'the sea' and *rlarlangkarram* 'the sea'
(b) Grasses that grow in flat areas: *majalba* 'grass,' *ngalarrama* 'long grass' and *wurrkalama* 'grass'
(c) Ground effected by fire: *bimbinalba* 'ashes,' *kulum* 'hot sand' (used for baking vegetables) and *maalkarram* 'grass fire'
(d) Soil types: *mangubam* 'mud,' *jirrkalima* 'sand,' *mirijim* 'river sand,' *anmolba* 'white clay,' *kumbarruma* 'yellow ochre,' *joornim* 'dust' and the generic type *kabalba* 'ground, earth'
(e) Some edible root species: *inkalba*, 'edible root sp,' *wangkarlum* 'edible root sp' and *wungunimbim* 'edible root sp;' although the generic term *karnmangku* 'yam' is masculine
(f) Rivers, which for most of the year are dry sandy beds dotted with pools: *marolalem* 'river' and *molnganem* 'river'
(g) Dark, concave places: *karnmern* 'cave,' *barnjam* 'cave,' *dalorr* 'sink hole, well,' *rdakulama* 'pit, deep hole,' *rlaard* 'fissure, gap, crack,' *maarnduwalba* 'tunnel,' *maarndabrlam* 'gap, gorge' and *balaayuma* 'rock shelter'
(h) Places created by people for their use: *yandalba* 'bark shelter,' *mayaram* 'house,' *yarram* 'hut,' *karlumba* 'path' and *karndirrim* 'mortuary platform'
(i) Unoccupied places: *bundurlba* 'the bush'
(j) Spatial abstracts: *dungundu* 'side (of eg. a hill),' *kanaalu* 'opposite side' and *kangurram* 'non-visible or hidden side'
(k) Some trees: *jungurim* 'boab' (but see §4.7.1), *bunjuma* 'fig,' *jinkarnma* 'tree sp.' and *krooma* 'white cypress pine.'

Other things acquire terrestrial marking by analogy with these imageries of place. Large concave artefacts are terrestrial: *namarrkama* 'large wooden bowl' and *angkam* 'wooden bowl,' although the more general term *karraki* 'container' is masculine and is applied to modern hand-bags and briefcases.

Reference to events involves the indexation of temporal, as opposed to spatial coordinates. As Alan Rumsey has noted with respect to Ungarinyin (1982:40): 'If -m- is the gender of 'place,' w_2 is the gender of time.' If an adjective in Worrorra is marked for celestial agreement without being co-referential with any noun in the surrounding discourse, its reference is interpreted as one of time:

(4.11) Jakarri wunu
        ØN=yakarri wunu
        3w=other 3wDEF
        The next day

(b) Jarrungu wunu ...
     ØN=yarrungu wunu
     3w=QUANT 3wDEF
     One day ......

(c) Wungunenali
ᵏwuN=ngu<ne>nali
3w=new<AUG>
These days/nowadays

This interpretation is as guaranteed for celestial forms as the interpretation of the corresponding terrestrial forms is with respect to place: compare with the forms in (4.11) *mayakarrima* 'another place,' *mayarrunguma* 'one place' and *mangunalima* 'a new place.'

Verba dicendi in Worrorra constitute a formal/functional subcategory of transitive verbs which obligatorily index complement clauses in object position. The celestial class-marking morpheme *kuN-* and its allomorphs *ᵏwuN-* and *ØN-* are used to index complement clauses on these verbs. In effect, *verba dicendi* index sentential objects just as other transitive verbs index noun objects, and the class marker used in this function is that of the celestial class. Furthermore, complex predicates may consist of a preverb placed under the scope of an inflecting verb. Such arrangements constitute examples of nuclear-core subordinate nexus in clause linkage typology (Foley & Van Valin 1984:249). In these types of predicates the preverb is indexed on the inflecting verb (the verb classifier) in object position as a celestial morpheme (glossed 'VCOMP' – see sentence example (4.1), where *buju* 'finish' is a preverb). Nor does this phenomenon result merely from the use of an empty, default or residual neuter category: as has been seen, the default category in Worrorra is masculine. There is, moreover, a small set of preverbs that control *terrestrial* VCOMP marking on verb classifiers: *murn* 'look, gaze' is one such:

(4.12) Murn maarrwuna.
murn ma-ᵇwarr=ᵇwu-na
gaze VCOMP-3p=hit-PAST
They gazed all around.

But verbal nouns or preverbs and abstract nouns that refer to actions or events normally belong to the celestial class: *budurrwu* 'snoring,' *buju* 'finish,' *mungurr* 'argument,' *wurrkunu* 'trouble,' *ngarlangarla* 'speech,' *ngarlungarlu* 'the sound of people talking,' *yarrorl* 'the sound of voices,' *kuyoya* 'whisper,' *ngaja* 'custom, precedent,' *wurnarn* '(ritual) sharing,' *wurloo* 'purification,' *wurdoo* 'blessing,' *lalai* 'the dreamtime,' *wunurr* 'begging,' *kulunu* 'sleep' *kurdu* 'chase, follow' and many other preverbs employed as verbal nouns. In (4.13) the verbal noun *kulunu* 'sleep' is qualified by the adjective =*n-ngal* 'these several' (ie several 'sleeps'). Note that gender agreement is with the celestial class (glossed as '3w'):

(4.13) Ke kulunu wunngengalu bariy kanunaal
ke kulunu ᵏwuN=n-nge-ngal-u bariy ka=nu-na-aal
and sleep 3w=DEF-AUG-several-3w rise 3a=be=PAST-hither
And after sleeping for a few days he got up

However, rough or violent events are terrestrial: *barurruma* 'feud,' *malanim* 'battle,' *manjuma* 'wind' and *warrambam* 'flood waters.' Verbal nouns that refer to places or country are usually terrestrial as well: *rdarlurn* 'looming' (with reference to eg a bluff or cliff that 'looks like it's looking down on you'), and *murn* 'gazing' (typically out over an expanse of country, see example 4.12).

Subjunctive verbs are employed in subordinate and some other clause types. In relativizing constructions, subjunctive predicates may occur with markers signalling agreement with the gender of the nominal head of the phrase in which they occur (§15.6.3). However in adverbial subordinate function the only gender-markers they may occur with are celestial, such as the determiner *wunu*, as seen in §15.6.1, and as illustrated in (4.3a) and (4.14):

(4.14)
Kaarringoorri molnganem mana, ke **[woo nyangkawanangurru] wunu**, aakumarnanya mana, jarnda ngenu kenga aaku ke, mara nyimbeena; nyungumanja aaya mara kona.
*She went with them to the river, and [**when she bent down**] over the water intending to scoop some up, she saw herself; she saw her reflection.*

In (4.14) the subjunctive predicate (in square brackets) falls within the scope of the following determiner *wunu*. That this determiner is part of the verb phrase and not the following noun phrase (*aakumarnanya mana* '(over) the water'), is indicated by a pause, marked in transcription by the comma after *wunu*.

When any verb-form accepts gender agreement, that agreement is always with the celestial class, with exceptions as exemplified in (4.12). And as has been seen in (4.3b), there are a variety of sentence types that may be topicalized, or made definite by the use of the definite article *wunu*, which in these constructions has scope over the entire sentence. Example (4.15a) shows another definite sentence construction, and (4.15b & c) show how events of all sorts may receive celestial marking:

(4.15a)   Ngani   bungenjeerri   wunu!
          ngani   ba-kuN-nga=yi-n-yeerri   wunu
          what   CFT-VCOMP-1=do-NON.P-PROG   3wDEF
          I'm not doing anything! (as I've already told you)

(b)   Ke   binjiyeerri.
          ke   ba-kuN-nja=yi-eerri
          3wREF   CFT-VCOMP-2=do-PROG
          Don't do that.

(c)   Aaya   anguja,   burnu   kunjeeng?
          aaya   anguja   burn-u   kuN-nja=yi-ng
          3aREF   what   PRO-3w   VCOMP-2=do-PAST
          What was that, did you fart?

Example (4.15a) is another rhetorical form, used when the speaker believes that the listener already knows the propositional content of an utterance. The determiner here refers to the entire utterance. Example (4.15b) shows an extra-linguistic event referred to by the contextual/topicalizing deictic pronoun =^{k}*waya* marked for celestial agreement as *ke*. Example (4.15c) shows the same pronoun inflected for masculine agreement (as *aaya*) with the interrogative anaphor *anguja* 'what?' The event itself, however, is referred to euphemistically by way of the pro-form *burn-* inflected for celestial agreement.

4.1.3 (iv) luminosity
The celestial–terrestrial dichotomy encompasses what might be referred to as an abstract–concrete distinction. The prototypically most concrete thing is the earth, and the notion of place is derived directly from it. Just as solid, heavy, dark things tend to be terrestrial, so abstract and bright things are celestial. Bright, translucent things or things with reflective surfaces belong to the celestial class:

(a) Atmospheric/celestial/meteorological phenomena: *anjolu* 'the sky,' *angkubanu* 'clouds,' *braarr* 'illumination,' *lewarra* 'daylight,' *mamangkunu* 'dawn,' and *wungoru* 'air'
(b) Liquids are typically bright and reflective: *aaku* 'fresh water,' *wunjuku* 'continuous or sheet rain,' *wungkurr* 'sacred pool,' *bijurlu* 'shallow water' and *jalaani* 'deep water,' although atmospheric or 'dispersed' water is masculine; *aaja* 'rain' and *wilmi* 'mist'
(c) Bodily fluids: *kurloo* 'blood,' *bongkul* 'urine,' *ngamuku* 'milk' and *jelu* 'saliva'
(d) Soft, bright, liquid things: =^{k}*wambulu* 'eyes' and *marlinji* 'oyster'
(e) Hard bright things: *wanawi* 'egg,' =*mlarru* 'forehead,' *kayuku* 'rock, stone,' *karrku* 'rock, stone' and =^{b}*wiyaku* 'teeth'

(f) Fire and associated things: *wiyanu* 'fire, firewood,' *welkunke* 'torch,' *yorlu* 'torch,' *wulurrku* 'coals, charcoal,' *bijaku* 'smoke,' *br'nalu* 'ashes,' *wijali* 'burnt grass,' *bululuku* 'tinder, kindling' and *leerruku* 'fire spindle'

(g) Brightly coloured living things: *marrirri* 'red-winged parrot' (associated with fire in myth) and *marruku* 'flower'

(h) Bright or shiny parts of living things: *ilulu* 'feather,' *marnda* 'tree gum' and *idmangkanu* 'leaf'

(i) Grease: *wunjawarra* 'grease off meat' and *wrrngeewa* 'bone marrow.'

The field of bodily fluids is extended to include bodily extracts such as *ngoku* 'fæces.'

Just as the celestial class can be seen to be composed of luminous things along some kind of core–fadeout continuum, so the terrestrial class is composed of dark, opaque things. We have already noted some dark, concave places in the list of topographies in the preceding section, and the sea, also in that section. Fresh water *(aaku wunu)* and sea water *(wondum mana)* are opposed in Worrorra symbolism; fresh water is essential to humans while sea water is unpalatable. Water may be specified as being fresh as opposed to salty by being referred to as *aaku rdeenu* 'real water;' sea water is, by implication, not 'real' water, in the sense that one of the defining characteristics of water is that it is something people drink. The sea around the Kimberley coast is characteristically dark, cloudy and opaque when compared to fresh water. Other dark or opaque things in the terrestrial class are:

(a) Atmospheric/celestial phenomena: *karlumarlum* 'evening, dusk,' *karlakarlem* 'evening, dusk,' *wundukum* 'night,' *warlorluma* 'night,' and *jerrba* 'shade,' although interestingly *marram* 'light' and *yankarndama* 'star' are also terrestrial.

(b) Dark-coloured or nocturnal birds: *darraanma* 'red-tailed black cockatoo,' *barrom* 'tawny frogmouth' and *booboom* 'coucal pheasant;' crows, however, *(wangkuranya)* are feminine.

<u>4.1.3 (v) topography</u>

The parameters of dimension and luminosity produce another and secondary opposition, that of relative topographic position or height. We have already seen that low, flat places are terrestrial, and that rocks and firewood are celestial. This gender distinction comes about naturally as a result of the terrestrial class's coordinate position on the dimension parameter as 'place,' and the celestial class's coordinate position on the luminosity parameter as 'luminous.' This dynamic now produces a topographic contrast between low, flat areas on the one hand, and high or raised things on the other, and is expressed by way of an opposition between the earth/place and low, flat areas as terrestrial, and tree/hill/height as celestial.

The sea is low and flat as well as being dark and opaque, and things associated with it are terrestrial: *wondum* 'the sea, salt water,' *rlarlangkarram* 'the sea,' *kalaarrba* 'sandy beach,' *kalam* 'double raft' and *jindim* 'mangrove.' However landforms defined in terms of their contradistinction to the sea, that is in terms of their raised position above the sea, are celestial: *ungujonu* 'island,' *murdu* 'island,' *barlurlu* 'coastline, sea-shore' and *barndaya* 'the mainland.'

Trees as well are characteristically raised above the land upon which they grow. The generic term *nguwanu* 'tree' is celestial and most trees belong to this class. Possible primary reasons for this are that firstly the trees most characteristic of Worrorra country (apart from boabs) are eucalypts with shiny white bark; and secondly the most common use of these and indeed of most trees is as firewood *(wiyanu wunu)*. Things obviously cut out of trees are also celestial: *namandi* 'canoe' (an introduced item), *barrawara* 'canoe' and *jinyinu* 'shield.'

Rocks present hard reflective surfaces and rocks and stony things are celestial:

(a) Rocks: *karrku* 'rock, stone,' *kayuku* 'rock, stone,' *murndaaleya* 'plateau, platform, flat rock' and *durrku* 'mortuary cairn.'

(b) Steep, high and/or rocky hills: *kurrandu* 'hill,' *rdarlambanu* 'high and/or steep hill,' *kenjanu* 'high and/or steep hill,' *kurraarrandu* 'line of hills' and *warnangkali* 'cliff, mountain.'

The two most prominent peaks in Worrorra country are *Ngayangkarnanya* 'Mount Trafalgar' and *Nubungarri* 'Mount Waterloo,' two large and spectacular mesas on the Northern shore of

Ngarlangkarnanya (The St. George's Basin) at the mouth of the Prince Regent River. They have high quartzite or sandstone cliffs that glow red and gold at sunrise and sunset.

The distinction between low, flat things and superior rocky or wooden things discussed here in terms of a semantics of 'topography' is represented iconically in the genders assigned to *barlarlonma* 'mortar/grinding stone' (terrestrial) and its complementary artefact *rnoku* 'pestle' (celestial).

4.1.4 Functional properties

The clearest manifestation of a category's intension is the derivational function of that category's tokens within a system of reference. The intensions of Worrorra gender categories are made explicit by virtue of the derivational functions of gender marking.

It has been suggested to me that gender systems in northern Australia may be of two types.[35] In one type of system, gender is correlated with 'semantic field' or 'lexical domain,' and all members of a particular semantic field are allocated to the same gender. In this system it would appear that the oppositional dynamic that characteristically structures gender systematics is relaxed or absent with respect to the way in which relations between particular semantic fields are conceived emically (eg Gaagudju (Harvey 1992), Ngalakan (Merlan 1983), Ngandi (Heath 1978), Ngan'gityemerri (Reid 1991) etc). In the other type, gender is used to make distinctions between denotata within semantic fields, and the oppositional dynamic appears to function systematically at every level of gender reference. We may characterize this difference as one between gender systems that function to create lexical domain categories, and others that function to signal lexical differentiation between similar or comparable denotata. Worrorra for the most part exhibits the second type of system: but the first type is also found, as described below in §4.1.4 (ii).

<u>4.1.4 (i) lexical differentiation</u>
We have already observed the derivation of male–female pairs of nouns in §4.1.3 (i), and locational derivation in §4.1.3 (iii), showing that 'male,' 'female' and 'place' at least are intensional properties of the masculine, feminine and terrestrial classes.

A change of gender may signal a change in sense (eg such as recorded by Heath 1984:188). The masculine noun *jungura* means 'boab tree,' while the terrestrial noun *jungurim* means 'shade of the boab tree.' Indeed large old boab trees have status as places rather than as trees only, and their wide trunks do provide shade in a rather open and unshaded landscape. Kangaroos are precisely named. The term used specifically for the female grey kangaroo, *warinya*, has masculine shape *wara* 'kangaroo (generic)' used not for the male animal (*jurlwun* and *arr'ra* are used for that), but as a superordinate noun covering all kangaroos regardless of species or sex. The inflexional inalienable noun $=^k$*wambulu* 'eye' is celestial. When this noun exhibits terrestrial marking it undergoes a change in sense: *maambulba mana* '(tidal) whirlpool.' The gender-marking in this case is coreferential with *rlarlangkarram mana* 'the sea.' Literally this word means 'its eye.' When *aaku* 'water' is thought of as a substance, ie as that which people drink, it is celestial. When water is referred to as a body of water (that is as a place) and marked with a locative postposition, it takes derivational terrestrial class-marking:

(4.16a)   Juward   kanuna   mana   aakumarnanya
           juward   ka=nu=na   mana   aaku-ma-rnanya
           jump   3a=be-PAST   3mDEF   water-3m-LOC
           He jumped into the water

The terrestrial class functions as a locative gender in what probably amounts to a large proportion of its occurrences. When used in this locational sense, *aaku* usually acquires locative (terrestrial) gender derivation (marked by the morpheme -*ma*) as well as locative case inflection. Note that this gender derivation is not simply a matter of a lexeme-specific case allomorph -*marnanya*. In this usage, as in

---

[35] I am grateful to Jeffrey Heath for pointing this out to me.

example (4.16a), *aaku* exhibits a derived or outer gender that controls anaphor agreement on the article *mana*. The locative-marked phrase in this sentence is derived as indicated:

(4.16b) [TERR mana [CEL aaku CEL] ma + rnanya TERR]

This phrase is composed of an inner inherent gender (celestial) overlain by an outer derived gender (terrestrial). In this instance the language employs derivational gender affixation to make a sense distinction between water as substance, and a body of water as place or location. Other nouns may also occur in derived terrestrial form, with or without the gender affix *-ma*. When *-ma* is not attached, the derived status of such a noun is indicated by the shape of the article (*mana*). For example the masculine noun *jardi inja* 'spinifex' may occur as *jardirnanya mana* 'in (a wad of) spinifex,' and *karrku wunu* 'rock, hill' may occur as *mana karrkurnanya* 'on the rocks.'

Conversely, some terrestrial nouns may take derived celestial marking when their aspectual or *aktionsart* properties are brought to the fore; *wundukum mana* 'night' is one such:

(4.17)
Ke **wundukumarnanya wunu** anja wangalaalunguyu kubajunganangkorri, 'Yarrorl birriyeerri, meemeenya binyinmaa, yoowa ke kaakaaja kurde.'
And **at night** *they told their children, 'Don't make too much noise, or the meemeenya bird might get you, or the boobook owl, or the kaakaaja bird.'*

In this derivation *wundukum* 'night' is denoted as an interval of time with internal structure, and acquires celestial marking to signal this typically verbal (aspectual) characteristic. Here gender-marking is used to signal aspectual properties of nouns. This phenomenon is not uncommon in languages; in French, *jour* (masculine) 'day' and *soir* (masculine) 'evening' become *journée* and *soirée* (both feminine) under the same circumstances. The same also occurs in Arabic, eg. *lail* (masculine) 'night' and *laila* (feminine) 'night (aspectual),' although in Arabic the distinction may also be lexicalized: *nahaar* 'day' and *yaum* 'day (aspectual).' Another Worrorra noun that behaves in this way is *karlumarlum mana* 'evening.' Derivational process may be signalled by apparent dis-agreement, or 'wrong' gender-marking morphemes appearing elsewhere in the clause in which the derived noun occurs, as in (4.18). The suffix *-nyini* 'until, then' usually comes between the root morpheme of a terrestrial noun to which it is suffixed and the gender-marking morpheme *-ma* or *-m* (see example 4.7a):

(4.18)
Yarriba	nyimnyawanangurreerri,	karlumarlunyinim
yarriy-ᵇwa	nyiN-mnya=ᵇwa-na-ngurru-eerri	karlumarlu-nyini-m
descend-PROG	3f-DD=fall-TNS-away-PROG	evening-until-3m

kumnyanuna	karle	imaya.
kuN-mnya=nu-na	karle	imaya
3w-DD=be-PAST	then	cool

[The sun] went down and then evening came on and it got cool.

Even though occurring in a construction which picks out, as it were, the gender-marking suffix *-m*, the noun *karlumarlum* here receives celestial subject indexation on the following verb (*kumnyanuna* 'it (celestial) was (inchoative)'), as indicated by the intransitive subject prefix morpheme *kuN-*. The semantic properties of nouns such as *wundukum* and *karlumarlum*, which acquire gender from one part of their denotation (darkness), but which also denote intervals of time, render them inherently liable to this type of derivation.

A few other instances of a change in sense resulting from a change in gender arise when singular or plural noun-forms are homophonous with collective nouns: *wari* 'kangaroos' (plural) vs 'kangaroo meat' (collective); *burnarri* 'animals' or 'birds' (plural) vs 'meat' (collective) and *barnmarnja* 'sorceror' (singular) vs 'sorcery' (collective).

There are only a few instances that I am aware of in which gender changes induce changes in meaning. One of these is *rlarlangkarram mana* 'the sea' and *irlarlangkarra inja* 'estuarine crocodile' (ie 'the salt-water one' or 'salty'). The other example is *warli inja* 'sea-turtle (generic)' and *warlinya nyina* 'dugong.' This pair shows an interesting and unusual phonological correspondence that treats members of two zoological classes of large, highly-prized marine vertebrates anthropomorphically, ie as if the distinction were a sex-differentiable one. The plural shape *warli* refers to turtles and dugongs collectively, just as for example the plural shape *arroli* refers to both dingo dogs and bitches. This special treatment is almost certainly related to the highly prized status of turtle and dugong meat in Worrorra culture. And a third example is seen in the pair *wungkurru wunu* 'sacred pool,' and *wungkuja nyina* 'rock python' (underlyingly |wungkurr-nya| with feminine suffix *-nya*). This pair consists of nominalizations of the adjective *wungkurr* 'sacred,' with celestial derivation to produce 'sacred water,' and feminine to produce 'sacred python.'

Other instances of gender change do not result in changes of meaning. Love (1934:19-20) describes how the noun *karlumba* 'path' which is terrestrial, changed gender to become masculine when it referred to the road built under missionary supervision between Port George IV (Mingkunya) and Kunmunya. At present *karlumba* is terrestrial, but a synonym *juwalya* 'path' is masculine.

Animals may change gender when they are personified as humans. Most animals are members of the masculine or feminine genders, and when they appear in myths they are personified as men or women depending upon their gender. However there is one example of a mythically important bird in the non-human macrogender, *marrirri wunu* 'red-winged parrot,' which is personified as a woman and which may take feminine gender agreement in mythic contexts:

(4.19)
Marrirri **wunu** murn mona: 'inja wiyanu ngarraangkowa kumalangaayeerri?' kunjunganangka; wululu **nyim**banaalnyale **nyangka**.
*The red-winged parrot looked around: 'Why is he taking the fire away?' it/she asked; then **she** flew down towards him.*

In this sentence *marrirri* at first controls celestial agreement on the article *(wunu)* but subsequently triggers feminine agreement shapes at the opposite end of the sentence in the NP index *nyim-* and by the pronoun *nyangka* 'she.'

A final area of gender fluidity in Worrorra appears to involve place names. I have had some difficulty in ascertaining gender for many place names as nearly all place names appear to be able to control terrestrial agreement, especially in citation contexts. In some instances however terrestrial marking may be taken to be an outer gender assignment. In these circumstances place names are able to control agreement for other genders as well, and such 'inner' genders appear to be allocated according to the topographic type of the referent, as described in §4.1.3 (v). For instance *Ngayangkarnanya* 'Mount Trafalgar' may be referred to as *Ngayangkarnanya mana* '(the place) Ngayangkarnanya' or as *Ngayangkarnanya wunu* '(the mountain) Ngayangkarnanya.' Mountains *(warnangkali wunu, rdarlambanu wunu)* appear to have an inner celestial class: *Ngayangkarnanya wunu* 'Mount Trafalgar,' *Nubungarri wunu* 'Mount Waterloo,' *Majerrin wunu* 'Mount Hann' and *Wundamarro wunu* 'MOUNTAIN NAME.' Some islands *(ungujonu wunu, murdu wunu)* appear to be of the same class: *Wurrurlku wunu* 'Augustus Island,' *Karlinji wunu* 'ISLAND NAME' and *Jinbeenu wunu* 'ISLAND NAME,' while others are terrestrial: *Numen mana* 'ISLAND NAME,' and *Yawijaba mana* 'The Montgomery Islands.' Other place names are also celestial: *Dulooku wunu* 'land of the dead,' located out over the Western Ocean, probably acquires gender by analogy with *barndaya wunu* 'mainland,' as may also be the case for *Wurnbangku wunu* 'patriclan country name,' located on the coast around the St. George's Basin, although it is possible that this term may acquire gender by virtue of its initial and final segments as well. An example of the way in which this kind of dual gender allocation functions in practice is seen in a description of the activities of a dreamtime crocodile who left his liver behind in the form of a large liver-shaped rock:

(4.20) Warndi kumnyona wunu Yuwulam mana.
warndi kuN-Ø-mnya=ᵇwu-na wunu yuwulam mana
make 3w-3-DD=hit-PAST 3wDEF 'Liver' 3mDEF
He made (the rock called) 'The Liver.'

The place name *Yuwulama* 'The Liver' is derived from the terrestrial noun =ᵏ*wulama* 'liver,' and occurs here with the articles of both the celestial and terrestrial classes. We may thus infer outer terrrestrial and inner celestial assignments for *Yuwulam*. At the same time a celestial undergoer is indexed on the verb *warndi* =ᵇ*wu* 'make.' From context, and from the undergoer-gender indexed on the verb, *karrku wunu* 'rock' or *kayuku wunu* 'rock' is automatically inferred as the verb's object. This is an example of the way in which gender-marking morphology functions indexically by restricting the range of possible referents. Another rather lovely example of the dual nature of gender allocation with respect to place names is found in a story told by the late Daisy Utemorrah (Utemorrah 2000:13-20); in this story two boys are gazing out to sea at the island called *Karlinji*. As they look at it they sing:

(4.21) Karlinji bawarra, mawe wurno, mawe wurno.
Karlinji Island so far away, there it is away over there.

In this song the island is referred to by two anaphors: =ᵏ*we* 'presentational' and =*rno* 'that (distal).' The first is inflected for terrestrial agreement *(mawe)* while the second bears celestial inflection *(wurno)*. *Ngarlangkarnanya* 'The St George's Basin' appears to have an inner gender which is feminine, probably because of the shape of its final segment -*nya*, although of course it may also accept terrestrial agreement. And some place names are clauses, such as *Imalala Jujurr Ingkaarrbanga* 'Where they carried the handsome man,' and *Jilinya Jaarr Nyangkawana* 'Where the spirit-woman travelled upstream.'[36]

<u>4.1.4 (ii) lexical domains</u>
Despite what is described above, and in order to set it in perspective, it will be useful to observe how semantic fields are dealt with in the Worrorra gender system. Correlations between gender and semantic field are scanty and not particularly consistent. Most minor semantic fields are unipolar; ie they do not display the coordinate polarities exhibited by the semantics of the gender superstructure displayed in Table 4.5.

Sexuality provides powerful metaphors by which nouns may be classified according to the imagery of masculinity and femininity. Snakes are usually phallic and tend to be masculine, but several are feminine; Heath (1984:181) plausibly suggests that the imagery of swallowing may be sexual, and associated with femaleness. In Worrorra pythons are feminine (*mawunkunya/ nyimrimaaingarrinya* 'black-headed python' and *wungkuja* 'rock python') as well as some other snakes: *kawaanya* 'black snake' and *rlongkungkunya* 'sea snake *sp*' Spears *(jinalya)* are masculine, and spear-throwers *(yamarlbanya* and *yarnkalja)* are feminine. Gender is assigned to spear-throwers by reference to the iconic imagery of how a spear fits into the slightly concave spear-thrower when it is about to be released.

As noted above, body parts are mostly celestial or terrestrial. Body parts are only semantically 'visible' when distinguished apart from the whole beings to which they are attached. Body parts are prototypically parts of human beings, and human beings belong to the human or highly animate genders masculine and feminine. Gender semantics again employs an oppositional dynamic in order clearly to distinguish body parts from their human 'owners' by classifying them in the non-human macrogender. Another way of putting this is to say that body parts only come into existence when reified apart from their human 'owners;' and their categorization in the non-human macrogender serves the function of grammaticizing the reification. Body parts belonging to the human macrogender are of fairly clear types. Bones and bony or bone-like parts are masculine, as noted. The 'heart,' *rangku* is masculine, as are two words for 'thigh,' *wanjarra* and =ᵏ*wuda*. Non-material emanations from the body are masculine as well; =*ngaanja* 'shadow, spirit' and =*yula* 'anger.' Feminine body parts are *mangajanya* 'sweat,' *jurlwaanya* 'sinew,' *nyaarnkanya* 'Achilles tendon' and =*rlawarndinya*

---
[36] See §15.6.6.

and =*yalngkanya*, both meaning 'ankle.' The significance of the relationship between the shape of ankles and their gender has already been suggested, and the gender of sinews and tendons is discussed in §4.1.6 (i).

Bodily ornaments are masculine; these include women's pubic aprons (woven from hair-string or kangaroo fur) *warlbirri*, *yawurna* and *kuduwaanja*, as well as *jangkunja* 'hair-string belt,' *broolku* and *bankulaja* 'cicatrices,' *boordi* 'mans long hair bun, wrapped in paperbark' and the introduced ornament *dress*. Interestingly however, *wanala* and *wudbeenu* 'woven hair string' (ie before being made up into some artefact or ornament) are celestial.

Major food classes (vegetables, meat, etc.) are all in the collective gender. Such items include 'vegetable food,' *mangarri* and *maya*; 'meat,' *burnarri*; and 'kangaroo meat,' *wari* (see §4.2.2).

The following tendencies may be briefly noted about the way that other semantic fields cluster with respect to gender.

(a) Animals (including insects and birds) are mostly either masculine or feminine, with the majority being masculine. Larger birds and some insects tend to be feminine, as discussed in §4.1.6 (i).
(b) Topography is mostly terrestrial or celestial, with the majority of terms being terrestrial.
(c) Plants are mostly terrestrial or celestial.
(d) Collocation is a pervasive factor in gender allocation, for instance *kambananya* 'shovel, scoop, poker' is used mainly by women to manipulate food in a fire, and is feminine.
(e) Most semantic fields are not correlated with gender categories. Artefacts are an example, and marine invertebrates also appear to disport themselves heedlessly across genders.

4.1.5 Meta-intensional references of gender categories

In order to capture the underlying denotational properties of gender as the system operates in Worrorra, it is necessary to distinguish between levels of intensional reference. The semantic coordinates of a gender system (see Table 4.5) represent discrete clusters of intensions of the sort to which such systems make reference. Meta-intensions, as the term is used here, are essentially image schemata that, by referring to the embodied nature of our experience, motivate the coherence of such intension-clusters. Image schemata are

> structures that organize our mental representations at a level more general and abstract than that at which we form particular mental images (Johnson 1987:23-24) ... recurring dynamic pattern[s] of our perceptual interactions and motor programs that give coherence and structure to our experience (idem: xiv).

An embodied schema is one that refers to the body's physical location in, and operation as a part of the world. Meta-intensions are essentially the symbols to which partition-classes make differential reference at an underlying level.

The male-female opposition encoded by the human macrogender is clear enough to speakers of a language such as English that employs this dichotomy as a gender distinction. What is perhaps less immediately clear is the incorporation of the parameter of shape within this semantics, with its phallic imagery with respect to males and with its imagery of pregnancy with respect to females. Nevertheless it should be clear that the underlying or meta-intensional references of these categories of sex and shape are to the embodied image schemata of human beings, ie to *man* and *woman* respectively.

What is less clear, perhaps, is the opposition between notions of [place/dark/concrete] on the one hand and [time/luminous/abstract] on the other. I will argue that like the opposition in the human macrogender, the non-human macrogender opposition involves embodied image schemata, in Johnson's (1987) terms.

The dynamic of polar opposition constitutes the main structural principle involved in the partitioning of lexical categories generally, and this is particularly evident in the structure of the Worrorra partition. As has been suggested, the prototypically most concrete thing is the earth, and it should be apparent that reference to the earth is an important part of the intension of the terrestrial class. We should also expect that whatever the underlying intension, or meta-intension of that class may be, it will exhibit an oppositional dynamic with respect to that of the celestial class. So far we have observed a series of systematic oppositions in the non-human macrogender between time and place, luminous and non-luminous, and between abstract and concrete. We have also noted an opposition between the sea and low places on the one hand, and hills and high places on the other. Now it appears that all the intensional properties of the two categories constituting the non-human macrogender may be captured by reference to an oppositional dynamic between *earth* and *sky*. The earth is the intension of the notion of place. The earth also provides dark, concave places (caves, burrows etc) away from the light. Time is the creation of celestial phenomena: the passage of the sun, moon and stars across the sky, and the variations in colour and luminosity exhibited by the sky create our understanding of time. Furthermore, the sky is luminous; even at night the moon and stars define the sky as the abode of brightness. The sky is also an essentially abstract phenomenon: it can be apprehended only visually; no other sensory mode is able to detect it. Central to an understanding of the semantics of this dynamic is the notion of relative height. The celestial class refers to things that are in general high, while the terrestrial class refers to things that are in general low. The structure of the Worrorra gender system is displayed in Figure 4.1, together with the forms of the definite article required by each lexical category:

MAN *inja*	SKY *wunu*
WOMAN *nyina*	EARTH *mana*

Figure 4.1: Worrorra gender categories

The oppositional dynamic between earth and sky is quite consistent with our understanding of embodied image schemata: it is an all-pervasive feature of our existence as physical beings in the world. Earth and sky are the objective or externalized manifestations of our embodied experience of UP–DOWN. The UP–DOWN schema, in external manifestation, is available and suitable for grammaticization because it is *bounded*, by the sky above and the earth below. Other (eg horizontal) dimensions are unbounded. Furthermore, the bounded, external manifestation of the UP–DOWN schema is all-pervasive in the lives of people who live entirely out-of-doors. It is entirely natural that a gender system should make use of such a schema as an underlying structural principle in the oppositional dynamic of which such systems are constituted. Earth and sky, then, are meta-intensional principles that underly other denotational functions of gender in Worrorra. Worrorra society is structured at a very basic and important level according to the parameters described here. Apart from the biological gender distinction, the two patrimoieties, *Adbalarriya* and *Arrwunarriya*, refer underlyingly to the UP–DOWN schema – see §6.2.4 for discussion.

The system outlined here is inherently covert: its core denotata are overlain by other intensional references whose relationship to their category's meta-intension is not immediately apparent. The extent of the system's opacity implies that the system itself is an ancient one. Its survival is due to its status as an embodied image schema; that is to say, as a primary semantic structure in memory and cognition; ie, in the apparatus of mental representation.

4.1.6 Macrogender

The four overt genders described above may be grouped together along orthogonal axes to produce two covert macrogender pairs. The masculine and feminine genders together constitute a human macrogender, and the terrestrial or celestial classes together constitute a non-human macrogender. Similarly, the feminine and terrestrial classes constitute a macrogender whose members are characterized by phonological markedness, and which typically display features characteristic of some kind of semantic markedness. The masculine and celestial classes constitute a macrogender of typically unmarked nouns.

Table 4.6: macrogenders as defined by the semantics of animacy and markedness

	+MARKED	−MARKED
+HUMAN	feminine	masculine
−HUMAN	terrestrial	celestial

These four macrogenders are covert, that is to say that they lack consistent overt morphosyntactic marking. However the morphology of one set of referring expressions, that of the independent interrogative substitutes meaning 'who?' or 'what?,' clearly displays the operation of parameters that define macrogender. The paradigm of the anaphor |ang(k)uYa| 'who/what?' does not pattern like that of other derived nominals that refer to third persons. This anaphor accepts gender-marking affixes, but only with reference to members of the marked macrogender, that is to say, it accepts gender-marking in agreement with feminine and terrestrial nouns only. The morphologically unmarked forms constitute default categories that trigger either masculine or celestial agreement on verbs:

(4.22a) Anguja **ka**njamurrkerri? *What are you looking for?*
(b) Anguja worr **ka**nungu ngeenya kajirn? *What's that that smells like honey?*
(c) Angkuyu **ka**rdangoo? *Whom can we ask to go and get it?*
(d) Anguja nee **ka**njaangurreerri? *What are you thinking about?*

In each of these examples the prefix *ka-* on the verb signals masculine agreement with *anguja* 'what?' or *angkuyu* 'who?' In other situations, however, *anguja* controls celestial agreement. The verb *kuN[ ]=yi* 'do' only accepts objects marked for celestial class: for an example of this phenomenon see example (4.15b) in §4.1.3 (iii). In that example the textual deictic object *ke* 'that referred to previously, or already known to the addressee' is the celestial form required by the verb. This verb may also employ *anguja* in object role (although the VP anaphor *nguni* 'what?' is more common in this situation):

(4.23) Anguja kunjiyeerri?
anguja kuN-nja=yi-eerri
what VCOMP-2=do-PROG
What are you doing?

A functional paradigm of this anaphor gives a clearer indication of its semantics:

(4.24) |ang(k)uYa|
    HUMAN: *who?* angkuyu
        specifically plural angkuyangkuya
        specifically feminine angkunya
    NON-HUMAN: *what?* anguja
        specifically terrestrial angujama

The parameters operating here produce a human—non-human split, and give evidence of another split corresponding to phonological markedness:

(4.25)

	+MARKED	−MARKED
+HUMAN	angkunya	angkuyu
−HUMAN	angujama	anguja

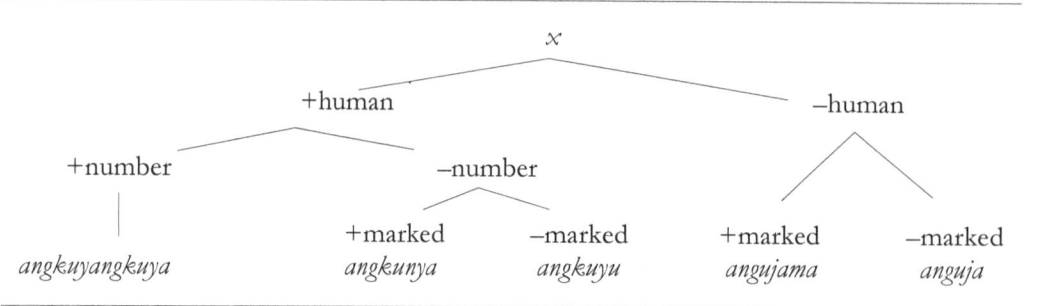

Figure 4.2: features of interrogative anaphors

Independent interrogative substitutes refer by definition to things the identities of which are unknown. In order to operate the anaphor system, a speaker must make decisions about the identity status of any given denotatum, and such decisions draw the denotatum from an unknown to a (partially) known state in a systematic and graded way (Figure 4.2). At each decision-node a choice of 'unknown (decision failed)/not pertinent (decision refused)' automatically yields a default category. Below the feature [human] decisions to register 'known' information yield marked categories. In each case, a feature bearing a negative value means that with respect to that feature, information has either failed or been refused registration, ie information is either not available or is not contextually pertinent. So for instance for the anaphor *angkuyu*, the specification [+human, –number, –marked] indicates that the denotatum is human, but that its number and gender properties are either unknown or not pertinent to the context of the utterance in which it occurs. The properties of each output-category may be more clearly stated as follows:

(a) *anguja* is used when any of the following apply: (1) the referent's animacy-status is unknown, (2) a non-human referent's gender is unknown or is not contextually pertinent, (3) a non-human referent's gender is known to be masculine, feminine or celestial.
(b) *angujama* is used when: (1) a non-human referent's gender is known to be terrestrial and (2) its gender is contextually pertinent.
(c) *angkuyu* is used when either of the following apply: (1) a human referent's sex is unknown or is not contextually pertinent, (2) a human referent is known to be male.
(d) *ankuyangkuya* is used when: (1) a human referent's number is plural and (2) its number is contextually pertinent.
(e) *angkunya* is used when: (1) a human referent is known to be female and (2) her sex is contextually pertinent.

From this account it is clear that relations between the members of the set of independent interrogative substitutes are structured with respect to each other, that is to say that some operate as superordinate lexemes with respect to others:

(4.26)   anguja: ——— angujama
         angkuyu: ——— angkuyangkuya
                       angkunya

Those that are not superordinate are either marked for number or marked in terms of the semantics of gender.

The features that conjointly define covert macrogender categories operate in parallel to the four overt genders. Moreover, there seems to be no requirement that the semantics of macrogender should be mapped precisely onto the morphosyntax of overt gender. The marked macrogender is partitioned by the feature [human] and the resulting covert categories [+marked, +human] and [+marked, -human] correspond closely to the overt feminine and terrestrial classes respectively, although *rambarr mana* 'avoidance category kin' is a member of the [+human, +marked] category that is not feminine. However the partitioning of the unmarked macrogender does not correspond closely to that of the overt masculine and celestial classes: note that both *angkuyu* and *anguja* require masculine agreement. The gender specifications of *anguja* are not stated in terms of an overt category; its primary gender specifications are acquired from its macrogender membership only, as [-marked, -human]. Nevertheless, overt gender concord is obligatory in Worrorra and *anguja* selects promiscuously and pragmatically from the two overt genders encompassed by the unmarked macrogender. When *anguja* substitutes for some noun it selects the least marked or default overt gender category, which is masculine; and when it substitutes for a VP it selects the gender appropriate to VP, which is celestial. *Anguja* is able to behave in this way because it is unspecified for overt gender membership.

4.1.6 (i) markedness

Possessive phrases in Worrorra show agreement with both head and dependent nouns. Head noun agreement is accomplished by suffixation upon a possessive pronoun, *-Ø* for agreement with masculine and celestial heads, *-nya* for feminine and *-ma* for terrestrial heads; that is to say that head agreement is covert for members of the unmarked macrogender, but overt for members of the marked macrogender. The following examples employ the possessive pronoun *ngayanangka* 'my:'

(4.27a)	inja karraki ngayanangka	*my bag*
(b)	wunu kayuku ngayanangka	*my money (stones)*
(c)	nyina yamarlbanya ngayanangka**nya**	*my spear-thrower*
(d)	mana angkam ngayanangka**ma**	*my bowl*

While both overt gender members of the marked macrogender show phonological markedness, it would appear that only the feminine gender is used systematically to signal semantic markedness. Only one semantic domain displaying characteristically 'marked' criteria occurs in the celestial class (see below). Semantic markedness is therefore not a major feature of this class. It is possible to further differentiate the celestial and masculine genders on the basis that the celestial class is associated with a set of gender-signalling inflections that are unique to itself, whereas the masculine gender shares some of its gender inflections with the plural/collective/mass agreement class (see Table 4.2); that is to say that its gender-marking phonology is not unique. The masculine gender is therefore the least marked category of the unmarked macrogender. This situation gives evidence of a hierarchy of markedness types, as shown in Table 4.7.

Table 4.7: markedness types

GENDER	MARKEDNESS TYPE
feminine	+phonological, +semantic
terrestrial	+phonological, ~semantic
celestial	~phonological, −semantic
masculine	−phonological, −semantic

Semantically marked categories are those whose denotata exhibit a culturally perceived assymetry when compared to other things of the same or similar general type (Lakoff 1987:59). Such a semantic assymetry usually involves some kind of desirability or conversely repulsion (ie 'anti-desirability'), although it may involve other things as well. Within the food domain there is a marked subcategory easily characterized as 'delicacies:' *ngeenya* 'honey' and *jubakunya* 'tobacco,' both feminine. Also feminine are a number of dangerous things that need to be treated with respect or avoided altogether. The semantics of one of these, *jimbeerlanya* 'spear blade,' has been discussed in §4.1.1. Other members of this category are *balangkarranya* 'storm wave' and *malngeerrinya* 'lightning.' The vulnerability felt during a tropical lightning storm by people living out in the open can be well imagined. The Worrorra double-raft *(kalam)* is reputed to have been unsinkable and was used for quite long-range sea journeys around the coast and to offshore islands. Riders on *kalam* were apparently vulnerable to only one natural phenomenon, and that was storms at sea; storm waves could sweep people off their rafts and leave them in the water to drown. Biting arthropods cause pain or irritation, and are feminine: *maanya* 'centipede,' *bijileenya* 'mosquito,' *nyinyinya* 'sandfly,' *kungkunya* 'march fly' and *kubadeenya* 'meat ant.'

Also feminine is *rdarrkenya* 'grasshopper,' although this large and fearsome-looking insect is quite harmless.

A specific type of danger is allocated to the terrestrial class. Violent things and things associated with interpersonal violence belong here: *malanim* 'battle, fight,' *barurruma* 'feud,' and the only specifically offensive weapon, *rdiyama* 'fighting club' (compare this implement with the masculine *rdiya inja* 'club used to deliver the *coup de grace* to wounded kangaroos'). Also naturally-occurring violent phenomena belong in this class: *manjuma* 'wind' and *warrambam* 'flood waters.'

Most raptors are masculine: *baardmarra* 'white-breasted sea eagle,' *dindiwalya* 'black kite,' *jarroo* 'brahminy kite' and *jindiwal* 'peregrine falcon.' The largest and most spectacular raptor, however, is feminine: *warraananya* and *arndangarrinya* 'wedge-tailed eagle.' Birds that are special by being large and terrestrial or largely terrestrial, and esteemed sources of meat are also feminine: *jebarranya* 'emu,' *kurrongkalinya* 'brolga,' *kuyoja* 'great-billed heron' and *banaja* 'bustard.' Fresh-water turtles were highly-esteemed sources of meat and two of the three terms in the sample for fresh-water turtles are feminine: *kanjorrinya* 'fresh-water turtle sp' and *wurlumaranya* 'northern snake-necked turtle,' while *dijakurri* 'northern snapping turtle' is masculine.

While woven vegetable-fibre string is masculine (*irrkalya, banjaya* and *mamurlanja*) and hair-string is celestial *(wanala* and *wudbeenu)*, string taken from animals (and therefore present in, if not taken from humans) is feminine: *jurlwaanya* 'sinew' and *nyaarnkanya* 'Achilles tendon.'

4.2 Plurality

Worrorra exhibits two kinds of grammatical number-marking category: a class of overt forms, described in Chapter Nine, and a covert category. The covert category consists of two numbers, singular and plural. Singular nouns occur as unmarked citation forms, such as are discussed in §4.1. Formally plural nouns may be distributed among three functionally-motivated types: those exhibiting non-singular (plural) number, mass plural nouns and collective nouns.

4.2.1 Plural nouns

A subset of nouns in the human macrogender may exhibit plural forms (two pluralizable nouns in the non-human macrogender are mentioned at the beginning of this chapter). Nouns that have plural forms are typically human nouns or nouns that refer to important animals, foods or artefacts. An exception to this is *jalwaya* 'skinks.' Pluralizable artefacts are *jimareya* 'spearheads' and *ardarruku* 'blankets.' Love (1934:25) records a plural form for 'spears' but modern Worrorra people reject this.

All genders collapse into a single plural-agreement form-class, ie gender is not realized in plural number. The plural definite article is *anja* 'the, these.' Plural number is signalled on the noun morphologically and by agreement patterns registered on all possible agreement targets. Plural-marking morphology is not straightforward and varies in accordance with both phonological and semantic considerations. The simplest plural shapes are homonymous with their singular forms. Nouns of this sort are bisyllabic, with the first vowel long, and the second back, low and short:

	SINGULAR	PLURAL
man	eeja	eeja
fish	jaaya	jaaya
adolescent boy	weerla	weerla

The next most simple shapes involve only the addition of the plural suffix *-ya*; social roles (orator, initiate, sorceror, demon) take this type of plural marking, as well as lower-order animates such as skinks and plants:

orator	jorlbarda	jorlbardaya
initiate	mamaa	mamaaya
sorcerer	barnmarnja	barnmarnjiya
demon	akurla	akurlaya
bandicoot	karimba	karimbaya
brush-tailed possum	burlkumba	burlkumbaya
skink	jalwa	jalwaya
yam (generic)	karnmangku	karnmangkuya
flower	marruku	marrukuya

A variant of this type of plural-marking puts /e/ in front of the plural suffix:

spear-head	jimara	jimareya
bullock	buluman	bulumaneya

Feminine nouns lose their final segment *-nya* and replace it with *-ya*:

woman	wangayinya	wangaya
emu	jebarranya	jebarreya
snake-knecked turtle	wurlumaranya	wurlumareya
female plains kangaroo	karroninya	karroniya

After a stem ending in a nasal consonant, the suffix *-ji* may occur:

grey kangaroo	jurlwun	jurlwunji

After /rr/ the pural ending /-i/ occurs:

animal	burnarra	burnarri
sheep	kukunja	kukunjarri

The plural NP index prefix *arr-* (§6.1) may occasionally be used, sometimes with epenthetic *-nya-* (rule 26):

blanket	irnarruku	ardarruku
young adolescent boy	angkanabija	arrangkanabiji
person	aarrinja	arrkarrinjiya

When masculine and feminine forms share a common plural shape, the plural form may resemble, or be homonymous with the masculine shape:

	MASCULINE	FEMININE	PLURAL
friend	mamangkalya	mamangkalja	mamangkalya
white person	aalmara	aalmarinya	aalmareya
dingo	arroli	arrolinya	arroli
large shark	karnamarri	karnamaja	karnamarri
goat	naningkunja	naningkunya	naningkunjiya
kangaroo (generic)	wara	warinya	wari
turtle/dugong	warli	warlinya	warli

Stem extension or reduplication is used with humans and dogs only; nearly all kinship nouns are of this type. Reduplicated plurals usually employ the suffix *-ya* as well. The phonological process concerned is a Type 3 extension as described in §6.2.6 (ii), and further discussed in §13.1.1; it is exemplified below:

| ka-**n**angkurri | dog | \|ka-**n**aa-**n**angkurri\| | kanaanangkurri | dogs |
| wanga-langu | child | \|wanga-laa-langu-ya\| | wangalaalunguyu | children |

	SINGULAR	PLURAL
girl	nyangkanya	nyangkaangkaya
adolescent girl	mrnangkanya	mrnaarnangkaya
young man	aalkunya	aalkalkunyeya
sibling	ankurnda	ankaankurndeya
boy	awanja	awaawanja
father	irraaya	irraarreya
mother	karraanya	karraarreya
mother's brother	kakaaya	kakaakaya
father's sister	bamaraanya	bamaamareya
elder brother	abiya	abaabiya
elder sister	abeenya	abaabiyeya
mother of many	karrernbarrinya	karraarrernbarriya

	MASCULINE	FEMININE	PLURAL
old person	maaba	maabanya	maabaabaya
boy, girl	warrala	warralinya	warraarraleya
child	wangalang	wangalangunya	wangalaalunguyu
dog	kanangkurri	kanangkuja	kanaanangkurri

One noun at least inflects as if it were an adjective, with both prefixing and stem-reduplication:

| young woman | nyimbarijinya | arrwaawarija |

There are two nouns in the sample that have plural shapes with plural reference, but which may control only singular agreement:

| cake, ball | imarulya inja | imarumarulya inja |
| hill | kurrandu wunu | kurraarrandu wunu |

The reduplicated shapes of these nouns refer to 'a pile (collectivity) of cakes' and 'a line of hills' respectively.

Worrorra nouns may overtly signal dual, unit augmented and collective number, but these morphologies also appear on adjectives, pronouns and verbs, and so are treated separately in Chapter Nine. Number- (eg dual-) marking morphemes attach to the *plural* shapes of nouns:

	SINGULAR	PLURAL	DUAL
girl	nyangkanya	nyangkaangkaya	nyangkaangkaarndinya
dog	kanangkurri	kanaanangkurri	kanaanangkurrkarndu
child	wangalang	wangalaalunguyu	wangalangaarndu *or* wangalaalangaarndu

Most non-human, non-edible nouns do not have plural forms, and do not trigger plural agreement. Paucal adjectives meaning 'several *x*' or 'a number of *x*' may be used with these nouns if clarification or emphasis call for their use (§6.2.6 (i), §7.3.4), otherwise number may be signalled contextually. More often however the language does not require an overt number choice to be made.

4.2.2 Collective and mass plural nouns

Some nouns can only control plural agreement, that is to say that they have no singular agreement forms. These are collective nouns which constitute a fifth noun-class in Worrorra. There are three types of collective noun:

(a) Classes of food/consumables: *mangarri* 'vegetable food,' *maya* 'vegetable food,' *burnarri* 'meat,' *jubakuya* 'tobacco,' *wari* 'kangaroo meat' and *aarlngarra* 'food cooked in an earth oven'
(b) Dangerous things: *barnmarnja* 'magic, sorcery, medicine'
(c) Collective items: *wurlarnbirri* 'personal effects or belongings,' *iwaawurleya* 'teenage boys'

The first type refers to classes of food such as meat or vegetables, not to particular items of food. Another type refers to things that are too dangerous to be spoken about directly, but which prefer indirect reference, such as things to do with death or magic. And the third type refers to collective groups of things.

Although there are a wealth of words denoting age grades and stages of growth *(angkanabija* 'young teenage boy' and *weerla* 'teenage boy' are two examples); and although the singular nouns *kawurla* 'son' and *kawurlanya* 'daughter' have a shared plural shape *kawaawurleya*, the collective noun *iwaawurleya* 'teenage boys' has no singular shape that I know of.

The collective nouns *burnarri* 'meat' and *wari* 'kangaroo meat' have homophonous (plural) shapes meaning 'animals' and 'kangaroos' respectively; that is to say that the homonyms display differences in denotational sense. In these meanings these words do have semantically corresponding singular shapes (ie 'animal' and 'kangaroo'), but there are no singular shapes for these forms when used with collective meaning; that is to say that there are lexically-motivated paradigmatic gaps:

	SINGULAR	PLURAL/COLLECTIVE
animal	burnarra	burnarri
meat	—	burnarri
kangaroo	wara	wari
kangaroo meat	—	wari

A similar gap, though of a different type, occurs with *barnmarnja* 'sorcerer' and *barnmarnja* 'sorcery:'

sorcerer	barnmarnja	barnmarnjiya
sorcery	—	barnmarnja

Some plural shapes signal not multiple instantiations of some item, but rather a relatively large amount of that item. This type marks amount rather than number, and is homophonous with plural morphology. Most mass plural nouns refer to valuable commodities:

	SINGULAR	MASS
honey	ngeenya	ngeeya
tobacco	jubakunya	jubakuya
grease	wunjawarra	ajawarre
piece of meat	iwileerri	arrwileerri
brideprice	embarri	arrembarri, ajembarri
group of people	belangkarra	belangkarraya

Although the feminine form *jubakunya* is known to modern Worrorra speakers, *jubakuya* is now used exclusively, and this lexeme has become in effect a collective noun.

Five: indicative mood, and basic verbal morphology

This chapter is concerned with a description of the morphology and semantics of minimally-extended, fully-finite, active verb forms in canonical or characteristic usage; that is, with the inflexion of morphemes signalling core argument structure, tense and aspect. To achieve this, the formally and functionally unmarked indicative category will be taken as an exemplar. Indicative verb forms denote positive, factual assertions and questions in typical reference-and-predication discourse styles.

Worrorra finite verbs occur in four inflexional categories or form-classes, as follows:
(i) Indicative mood, described in this chapter,
(ii) Optative mood (§8.1 & §8.2),
(iii) Counterfactual mood (§8.3 & §8.4),
(iv) Subjunctive mood (§15).

As well, a lexical category consisting of non-finite verb forms (preverbs) is described in §11.2.

Classes of verb-forms are defined by the shapes of their prefix clusters and by the shapes of their tense-marking morphemes, both of which are specific to each form-class. These formal distinctions encode a separate and specific semantics in each case, and in each case the entire formal and functional package will be referred to as a mood. Different modalities within each mood are brought into being by constraints on the occurrence of tense and aspect morphemes in order classes [9] and [13].

Indicatives are unmarked forms, while the other three moods are marked. Indicative forms are therefore simpler than the shapes of the other moods, and so indicative prefix clusters are employed in §5.3 to illustrate the way grammatical relations are indexed. The prefix clusters that uniquely characterize indicative forms are set out in Tables 5.1 and 5.2 in §5.3.2. The other forms signalling this mood are its tense markers, which appear in order-class [9] and are displayed in Tables 5.4 and 5.5 in §5.4.

5.1 The verb phrase

A number of phrasal constituents are discernable below the level of the sentence, and in this section I will discuss some evidence supporting the notion of a verb phrase in Worrorra. The verb phrase is the projection of an inflecting verb, and constitutes a distinct predicative phrase type.

Verb phrases consist optionally of a negative operator (*waa* 'not' or *kajirn(ba)* 'unable') plus a preverb followed by an inflecting or classifying verb. In the phrase-types under consideration here, the only obligatory element is the phrasal syntactic head, the inflected form. A phrase-type involving preverbs only is discussed in §11.2.1, but is not pertinent here. The optionally extended phrase is exemplified in (5.1):

(5.1a) Kajirnba   joli   banganin
       kajirnba   joli   ba-nga=ni-n
       can't   return   CFT-1=be-NON.P
       I can't go back

(b)   Waa   minjarl   bungkenya
       waa   minjarl   ba-kuN-Ø=yi-nya
       not   eat   CFT-VCOMP-3=do-PAST
       S/he didn't eat (it)

In (5.1a) the semantic load is carried by the preverb *joli* 'return;' and the classifier *banganin*, a form of =*nu* 'be,' carries inflexion for subject, tense and reality-status. In (5.1b) the preverb *minjarl* 'eat' carries the clause's semantic load while the classifier *bungkenya*, a form of *kuN[ ]=yi* 'do,' carries inflexion for subject, object, tense and reality-status. (Root morphemes are indicated by the use of an equals sign (=) to mark the left-hand morpheme boundary). That the negative operators are part of the verb phrase is signalled by their control over the shape of the verb: all verbs governed by these operators must have counterfactual form (they must contain the counterfactual morpheme *ba-* 'CFT,' see §8.3), and thus fall within the scope of the operators in question. Other material may intercede between these elements; either (i) between the negative operator and the rest of the phrase as in (5.2), where the adjective *ngamurlooku* 'I-well, healthy' comes between the operator *kajirnba* and the verb *banganin*;

(5.2) Kajirnba   ngamurlooku   banganin
       kajirnba   nga=murlooku   ba-nga=ni-n
       NEG   1=healthy   CFT-1=be-NON.P
       I'm not well

Or (ii) between the two elements of a complex predication, as in (5.3):

(5.3a) Kurdey   maa   kawarronerri.
       kurdey   maa   ka-ᵇwarr-a=ᵇwu-na-eerri
       ask   PROG   3a-3p-EP=hit-PAST-PROG
       They kept on asking him.

(b)   Nanjan   mana   waay   ngarraa   kanuna.
       nanjan   mana   waay   ngarraa   ka=nu-na
       ladder   3mDEF   throw   wrongly   3a=be-PAST
       He maliciously threw the ladder away.

In (5.3a) the adverb *maa* has aspectual (continuous/iterative) force with respect to a preceding preverb, in this case *kurdey* 'ask'. In (5.3b) the adverb *ngarraa* 'wrongly, maliciously' occurs between the preverb *waay* 'throw' and the classifier *kanuna*, another inflected form of =*nu* 'be.'

Adverbs may also occur *before* preverbs, as in (5.4):

(5.4) Wajulu   ruluk   kengkunaal.
       wajulu   ruluk   ka=ya-ngku-na-ᵏwaal
       close   move   3a=go-EP-PAST-hither
       He moved in closer.

Here the adverb *wajulu* 'close' precedes the preverb *ruluk* 'move' and the classifier, an inflected form of =*ya-ᵏwaal* 'come.' Otherwise, two preverbs may occur serially, as in (5.5):

(5.5a) Kaarri maa   waa   wala   durr   bungkonya.
        kaarri maa   waa   wala   durr   ba-kuN-Ø=ᵇwu-nya
        in.vain   not   cry   stop   CFT-VCOMP-3=hit-PAST
        S/he wouldn't stop crying

(b)   Mana   we   ngarrwaarndu   kulunu.
      mana   we   ngarr=ᵇwa-ᵏwarndu   kulunu
      3mDEF   lie   1pin=fall-DU   sleep
      Let's lie down here and go to sleep

In (5.5a) the operator *waa* 'not' is followed by the preverbs *wala* 'cry' and *durr* 'cease, stop'. The classifier is an inflected form of =ᵇwu 'hit.' In (5.5b) the preverb *we* 'lie down' occurs before the classifier, and another preverb, *kulunu* 'sleep,' occurs *after* the classifier, which is an inflected form of =ᵇwa 'fall.' In this sentence the usually consecutive forms *we kulunu* 'lie down and go to sleep' are separated for discourse-pragmatic purposes: the postposition of *kulunu* indicates a purposive meaning in this case.

Adverbs are not the only kind of material that can intervene between a negative operator and the rest of its phrase; various kinds of objects may also occur there. This is exemplified in (5.6):

(5.6a)
Waa   barndaya   binyengenyeerri   kaarri.
waa   barndaya   ba-nya=[ya-nga]-yinya-eerri kaarri
not   mainland   CFT-3f=[go-TNS]-PAST-PROG   3pNEG
She didn't go up onto the land at all

(b)
Waa   aambulkarndu   wunu,   waa   kuman
waa   a=ᵏwambul-ᵏwarndu   wunu   waa   kuman
not   3a=eye-DU   3wDEF   not   close

bungkamenyaarndu.
ba-kuN-Ø=ma-yinya-ᵏwarndu
CFT-VCOMP-3=get-PAST-DU
Neither of them closed their eyes

In (5.6a) the object noun *barndaya* 'mainland' occurs between the negative operator and the verb *binyengenyeerri*. In (5.6b) *waa* 'not' is followed by the object noun *aambulkarndu_wunu* 'their (dual) eyes,' and also by the preverb *kuman* 'close, shut (eyes).' The classifying verb *bungkamenyaarndu* is an inflected form of =*ma* 'get.'

Instrumental arguments may also occur between the negative operator and the head verb. In (5.7) the noun *kulum mana* 'hot (cooking) sand,' functionally an oblique (instrumental) argument, has been granted derived preverb status and incorporated into a complex predicate meaning 'to burn with hot sand.' Here in predicate position it loses its nominal gender-marking morphology (-*m*) (cf. (5.9a) below):

(5.7)   Mana   dambeem   kulu   ingkamangaarndu
        mana   dambeem   kulu   i-Ø-ngka=ma-nga-ᵏwarndu
        3mDEF   place   burn   3a-3-SJTV=get-PAST-DU
        The place where they (dual) burned him with hot sand

The classifying verb *ingkamangaarndu* is another inflected form of =*ma* 'get.'

Complement clauses or their predicates may also occur in this position, after a negative operator and before the matrix verb itself, as in (5.8):

(5.8a) Waa kubajeerri bungkaajeenyanangkorri arrka wangalaalunguyu.
They didn't know that their children were doing it /
They didn't know what their children were doing.

In this complex sentence, both clauses are discontinuous. We will look at the matrix clause first:

(5.8b) Waa   bungkaajeenyanangkorri
       waa   ba-kuN-ᵇwarr=yi-yinya-nangkorri
       not   CFT-VCOMP-3p=do-PAST-3pDAT
       They didn't know about them

The verb is an inflected form of *kuN[ ]=yi* 'do.' In the sense employed here it is a *verbum dicendi* operating as a verb of cognition, hence 'know.' The verb indexes two objects: the prefixed object *kuN-* 'sentential complement (VCOMP)' refers to the entire complement clause. The suffixed object *-nangkorri* '3pDAT' refers to the subject of the complement clause. The complement clause itself is as follows:

(5.8c) Kubajeerri   arrka   wangalaalunguyu
       kuN-ᵇwarr=yi-eerri   arrka   wangalaalunguyu
       VCOMP-3p=do-PROG 3pNAR children
       The children are doing it

Here the verb *kubajeerri* is another inflected form of *kuN[ ]=yi* 'do,' with *arrka wangalaalunguyu* 'the children' as its subject. The matrix's suffixed object index *-nangkorri* '3pDAT' is coreferential with the complement's subject. This sentence is discussed in more detail in §14.1 and §14.3.4.

Returning now to the three forms first proposed as constituting the verb phrase, that is, negative operator plus preverb and inflecting verb, it appears that all material intervening between any of these constituents must also be considered as part of the phrase. In summary, this material consists of (i) predicate adjectives, (ii) adverbs, (iii) object nouns and (iv) sentential complements.

Complement clauses in Worrorra constitute core object arguments of their matrix verb, as is intimated in the gloss and subsequent discussion of sentence example (5.8b) (see Chapter 14 for extended discussion). And as will be seen in §11.5.2, many preverbs are core object arguments of their inflecting verbs, and it will be argued there that there is a class of complex predicate in Worrorra that constitutes an example of subordinate nexus in predicate linkage typology (Foley & Van Valin 1984:249). So it should not be surprising to find that objects generally form part of the verb phrase in Worrorra. Nor should it be surprising that adverbs form part of verb phrases; as modifiers of verbs, adverbs are dependent upon verbs in Nichol's (1986) terms. Predicate adjectives themselves function as part of the predicate. Cross-linguistically, adjectives in predicate positions often take reduced nominal inflection in accordance with their more verbal function:

(5.9a)   German: eine schöne Frau   *a beautiful woman*
                                die Frau ist schön   *the woman is beautiful*
(b)   Arabic: albint aljamiila   *the beautiful girl*
                                albint jamiila   *the girl is beautiful*

In these examples the German adjective *schön* 'beautiful' loses feminine gender-inflection *(-e)* in predicate position, and the Arabic adjective *jamiila* 'beautiful (fem)' loses definiteness marking *(al-)* under the same circumstances.

The structure of the Worrorra verb phrase is summarized in Figure 5.1. In this figure the constituent OBJ includes sentential complement clauses, and PV is 'preverb:'

VP   →   V´, (ADV), (ADJ), (OBJ)
V´   →   (NEG), (PV), V

Figure 5.1: verb phrase structure

The preverb and the inflecting verb (V) taken together will be referred to as a 'complex predicate.' The inflecting verb functions normally to classify the predicate, as will be shown in Chapter 11. When an inflecting verb occurs on its own, that is in a simplex construction, it will be referred to simply as a 'verb.' Thus any form functioning as a classifier in complex constructions may also serve as a fully lexical verb in simplex constructions. As a lexical simplex verb, such a form will be endowed with its full semantic import. As a classifying verb that may bear properties of an auxiliary, however, the same form will be lexically 'bleached.' Compare the functions of the form =^{b}wu 'hit' in (5.10a) and (b):

(5.10a)   Wunu   nguwanu   kungona
           wunu   nguwanu   kuN-nga=^{b}wu-na
           3wDEF   tree   3w-1=hit-PAST
           I hit the tree

(b)   Wunu   nguwanu   mara   kungona
           wunu   nguwanu   mara   kuN-nga=^{b}wu-na
           3wDEF   tree   see   3w-1=hit-PAST
           I saw the tree

In (5.10a) the verb =^{b}wu 'hit' bears its full lexical-semantic load. In (5.10b) the lexical load is borne by the preverb *mara* 'see, find,' while the classifying form =^{b}wu 'hit' contributes only the grammar of transitivity to the predicate's semantics. The present chapter is concerned with simplex verbs.

5.2 Properties of verb roots

Simplex verbs contain a lexical core or root morpheme that may not occur without inflexion, although some constructions may appear to involve something very like an uninflected root morpheme:

(5.11)   Aaku   maal.
            aaku   ØN=ma-^{k}waal
            water   3w=get-hither
            Get some water.

The celestial object *aaku* 'water' is indexed on the verb =*ma* 'take, get' by a prefixed zero morpheme in this instance, giving the appearance of a more or less uninflected root. However the amount of inflexion that a verb root may undergo is one of the typologically defining features of the language. The schematic layout of the Worrorra verb is shown below in Table 5.1. The schema illustrated here represents a string of grammatical signs the ordering of which is invariant. When a token of a clause constituent is indexed on its syntactic head, the verb or verb classifier, that constituent's marking is strictly ordered with respect to the marking of any other co-occurring constituent of the verb. All of the order classes shown here are filled by inflexional morphemes except for those hard on either side of the root morpheme, order classes [6] and [8], which are filled by derivational morphemes.

Table 5.1: verbal form-order classes
> [1] Counterfactual
> [2] Undergoer
> [3] Subject
> [4] Optative/Subjunctive
> [5] Discourse deixis
> [6] Augmenting
> [7] ROOT
> [8] Middle voice
> [9] Tense
> [10] Direction
> [11] Non-subcategorized object
> [12] Dual/unit augmented
> [13] Aspect
> [14] Collective
> ([15] Adverbial)

This chapter is concerned with basic finite verbal morphology only, as revealed by morphemes occurring in order-classes [2], [3], [6], [7], [9] and [13]. Subject- and object-indexing morphemes (classes [2] and [3]) are discussed in §5.3. A derivational morphology occurring in order-class [6] is described in §5.2.2. Morphemes signalling tense in order class ([9]) are described in §5.4, and aspect-marking in order class ([13]) is described in §5.2.1.

Certain grammatical properties of verbs may be characterized as being properties inherent or localized in their root morphemes. The most compelling of these are their distributional and lexical properties. In distributional terms, as noted above, a subset of verbs (15 out of a total of about 100 in the database) have the ability to take part in complex constructions as verb classifiers. And by text count, as opposed to dictionary count, simplex verbs are relatively infrequent, the majority of verbal instantiations being in the form of complex predicates.

In lexical terms, simplex verbs may be intransitive or transitive. Transitive verbs may be further divided into those that select their objects freely, and a small subset that obligatorily take sentential complement clauses as objects, referred to here as *verba dicendi*. There are only four *verba dicendi* in the database, but they are frequent and important in the grammar. There are only 15 intransitive verbs in the database, including nine deponents but not including derived middle forms. The vast majority of verbs are transitive and the majority of intransitive verbal expressions are formed from preverbs combined with one or another of a set of four intransitive verb classifiers.

There are only three irregular verbs in Worrorra: =*ya* 'go,' =*ya-ᵏwaal* 'come' and *kuN[ ]*=*yi* 'do' (see Appendix 2). The root =*ya* has a surface-level word-final allomorph =*yu*. The verb roots =*ya* and =*ya-ᵏwaal* have suppletive plural-subject allomorphs =*i* and =*i-ᵏwaal* respectively.

5.2.1 Aspect

As a nuclear-level operation, aspect, or the kind of internal structure an event has, is a property with scope over the verb root. Verbs in all form-classes may be inflected for continuous aspect in order-class [13] by the morpheme *-(y)eerri* 'continuous/progressive.' This morpheme is opposed to Ø-marking for punctual or non-continuous (unmarked) aspect. The ordering contradicts Foley & Van Valin's prediction (1984:210, 392) that aspect marking, as a nuclear-level operation, will always occur closer to the verb root than a peripheral-level tense marker. In Worrorra the verbal aspect marker in order-class [13] is outside the tense marker in order-class [9]. Again phonology is responsible for this situation. Primary stress is preferentially placed on a penultimate syllable and upon a long vowel. The continuous aspect morpheme is thus custom-made, as it were, to appear at the end of a word, where it nearly always takes primary stress on its long vowel, which in this position is also penultimate. Morphemes appear only quite rarely to the right of order-class [13] (see examples 8.31c in §8.4.3 and examples in §9.2 & §9.6.2), so that the continuous aspect morpheme is at the end of its verb in most instances.

As described in Chapter Ten, aspect may also be marked by enclitics attached to preverbs and to verbs in order-class [15]: *-je/-ji* 'again' and *-biji* repeatedly' (§10.1.1 (iii)). A number of important adverbs also signal aspect, and these are discussed in §10.1 as well.

Verb forms are recognizable both by the general characteristics of the morphological classes to which they belong, as well as by specific tense- and aspect-marking morphologies. These morphemes typically encode more than tense and aspect only; in different combinations they usually conspire to signal other meanings as well (cf Lyons 1977:682). So the occurrence of the progressive marker *-(y)eerri* on Worrorra verbs controls other functions apart from aspect: in indicative mood its absence signals aorist forms (§5.4.5), and in counterfactual mood its presence or absence decides whether certain speech acts are monitive or prohibitive (§8.5.2).

5.2.2 Semantic augmentation

Verbs roots with extended meanings are derived from normal roots by a phonological process manifested in order-class [6], and glossed AUG. This process is underlyingly a stylized kind of reduplication in which the first consonant of the root morpheme is copied and preposed, and then followed by /e/. It is essentially the same, but not quite as involved, as the kinds of reduplication undergone by adjectives and derived nouns, as described in §6.2.6 (ii), and may be formalized as:

$$\emptyset \longrightarrow C_i e \: / \: \underline{} \: = C_i \ldots$$

So, for example, the root morpheme *=ninja* 'look at' has its first consonant *(n)* copied and preposed: |-n=ninja|, and then followed by *e*: /-ne=ninja/. In this way new root morphemes are derived which may be used, for example, as in the negative imperative forms shown in (5.12) (see §8.5.2):

(5.12a) Barraneninjerri   kunyila   aaya
         ba-ka-rra-ne=ninja-eerri   kunyila   aaya
         CFT-3a-2p-AUG=look.at-PROG moon   3aREF
         Don't stare at the moon

(b)   Bardernoyeerri   ngeeya
         ba-ka-ngarr-rne=rno-yeerri   ngee-ya
         CFT-3a-1pin-AUG=give-PROG   honey-3p
         Let's not give him any honey

(c)   Baarrangenguyoyeerri   ajakarri
         ba-kaarr-rra-nge=nguyo-yeerri   arr=yakarri
         CFT-3p-2p-AUG=abuse-PROG   px=other
         Don't go round swearing at other people

Although it is clear in these forms that phonological extensions of their root morphemes signal extensions of their meanings, it is difficult to be precise about the kinds of semantic extensions involved. As derived forms, the extended or augmented roots probably have lexically specific and possibly quite idiosyncratic meanings. In the database, forms of the two roots *=ninja* 'look at' and *=murrka* 'SUBJ go to OBJ; go (telic)' make up over half of the instances of semantic augmentation. The form *-ne=ninja* seems to mean something like 'SUBJ looks intently at, stares at OBJ,' and *-me=murrka* seems to mean 'SUBJ goes to OBJ with some particular purpose in mind.' Note the examples of this form in (5.13):

(5.13a) Kamemurrkarlaal
ka-Ø-me=murrka-rla-ᵏwaal
3a-3-AUG=go.to-PAST-hither
He came up to him

(b) Nyimbarrbemurrkarla
nyiN-ᵇwarr-me=murrka-rla
3f-3p-AUG=go.to-PAST
They all ran out to see her

(c)
Yarriyarriy	kawanaal	nyimnyamemurrkarlangurru
yarriy-yarriy	ka=ᵇwa-na-ᵏwaal	nyiN-Ø-mnya-me=murrka-rla-ngurru
descend-REDUP	3a=fall-TNS-hither	3f-3-DD-AUG=go.to-PAST-away

He scrambled down (the hill) and ran over to her

In (5.13a) one man is going to confront another with an accusation, and in (5.13b) the people involved have been told that the object is a spirit, and are certainly curious to see her. Example (5.13c) describes a reunion between a husband and wife. It would seem, then, that semantic augmentation involves actor intensity or concentration with respect to an event's motivation, ie that an actor performs an action for a particular purpose, and with particular intensity. This is borne out by other examples; reconsider (5.12b), for instance, where the action (refusal to supply honey) is motivated by feelings of rage, as part-punishment for a man's crime. And in (5.12c) the verb =*nguyo* 'abuse verbally, tell off' becomes -*nge=nguyo* 'swear at, revile' under augmentation. Some other examples are shown in (5.14):

(5.14a)
Abiyarnanya	ajaaja	nganunerri,	waa
abiya-rnanya	ajaaja	nga=nu-na-eerri	waa
el.br-LOC	dwell	1=be-PAST-PROG	not

bangayeyangenyeerri	kaarri
ba-nga-ye-[ya-nga]-yinya-eerri	kaarri
CFT-1-AUG-[go-TNS]-PAST-PROG	3pNEG

I stayed at my brother's place, I didn't use to go out walking around

(b)
Marndum	mamnyawewuna,	nyingulum	blaablaai
marndum	ma-Ø-mnya-ᵇwe=ᵇwu-na	nyiN=ngulum	blaai-blaai
stomach	3m-3-DD-AUG=hit-PAST	3f=stomach	pound-pound

mamnyona.
ma-Ø-mnya=ᵇwu-na
3m-3-DD=hit-PAST
She pounded her stomach, she kept on pounding her stomach.

(c)
Mangarri	anja	kaanyarrbemrangerri,	*garden*-ngarri	anja.
mangarri	anja	kaarr-nyarr-me=mra-nga-eerri	garden-ngarri	anja
food	3pDEF	3p-1px-AUG=gather-PAST-PROG	garden-REL	3pDEF

We could always get food out of the garden.

In (5.14a) the speaker is emphasizing her chastity, in not engaging in an act that is regarded in Worrorra culture as one in which women supposedly promenade to attract men's attention. In using an augmented form, the speaker is drawing attention to the commonly assumed motivation behind a woman's act of walking around or promenading. Example (5.14b) is somewhat mysterious, as it occurs in a story in which a female crocodile pounds her stomach in an act of mourning for the loss of someone dear to her. The point of the example is the event's motivation, and the apparent synonymity of the augmented form, -^{b}we=^{b}wu, with another verb, the reduplicated preverb *blaablaai* 'pound,' more specific than the unaugmented shape =^{b}wu 'hit.' Example (5.14c) is more idiosyncratic; the augmented shape -*me=mra* 'gather' appears to mean 'gather (food) diligently, conscientiously.' Note also the idiomatic expression in (5.15), where the inalienable noun =*ngulum mana* 'stomach' has a secondary sense meaning, 'feelings:'[37]

(5.15)   Awa   ingulum   maadedija
             awa   i=ngulum   ma-^{b}warr-ne=ninja
             3aNAR   3a=stomach   3m-3p-AUG=look.at
They occupied his thoughts ('they stare at his stomach (feelings),' ie, he was unhappy on account of them).

A second type of semantic augmentation in Worrorra involves a more transparent kind of stem-reduplication, in which the first two syllables of a verb root are copied and preposed. This type is quite rare in the database, and I am unable to say very much about its semantics (but see example 17.23b in §17.3.1 and discussion there); three instances are offered in (5.16):

(5.16a =17.23b)
Kamarlamarlaarndorna   wunu.
ka-Ø-marla=marlaarndo-rna   wunu
3a-3-REDUP=follow-PAST   3wDEF
She followed along after him.

(b)
Mara   kubajonya   wunu   karrku
mara   kuN-^{b}warr-nya=^{b}wu-nya   wunu   karrku
see   3w-3p-EP=hit-HORT   3wDEF   rock

ingkaarrkarnaarnamalunerri.
i-ngka-^{b}warr-^{k}warna=^{k}warnamalu-na-eerri
3a-SJTV-3p-REDUP=shoot-PAST-PROG
Let them see all the stones that they threw at him.

(c)
Angujakunya   karrolkolkunerri   aalmara   aaya?
anguja-^{k}wunya   ka-rra-^{k}wulku=^{k}wulkuna-eerri   aalmara   aaya
what-PURP   3a-2p-redup=fear-PROG   European   3aREF
Why are you all so afraid of that white man?

And occasionally an entire verb root with prefixes may be repeated in this manner, as in (5.17):

---

[37] In Worrorra the stomach *(=nguluma mana, marnduma mana)* is the main metaphor of emotion, just as the heart is in English. However note that in English the stomach is used as a metaphor for one particular emotion, namely courage; as in 'he has no stomach for it,' and 'guts' used as a euphemism for 'courage,' and 'shit oneself' (evacuation of stomach) as a euphemism for the failure of courage. This metaphor is firmly grounded in physiology (cf Grossman 1995:70). Note also its use in Shakespeare's Richard II, Act I, Sc 1: 'High-stomach'd are they both, and full of ire.'

(5.17a)

Mee maa	jajarrwa	nyinunyinuna	nyangka	wala
mee maa	jajarrwa	nyiN=nu-nyiN=nu-na	nyangka	wala
just	shiver	3f=be-3f=be-PAST	3fNAR	cry

She just began to tremble and cry

(b)

Arnawurnkarnawurnka,	warawunya	ankangurru
arr-n-Ø=rnawurnka-arr-n-Ø=rnawurnka	wara-ᵏwunya	arr-n-Ø=ᵏwangurru
px-INV-3/2=lead-px-INV-3/2=lead	k'roo-PURP	px-INV-3/2=carry

Take them away with you, take them out hunting for kangaroos

In (5.17a) the classifier =*nu* 'be' has scope over both the preverbs *jajarrwa* 'shiver' and *wala* 'cry,' although the latter is postposed to the inflecting verb upon which it depends (§11.2.2). In (5.17b) the verbs are imperative forms (§8.5.3), the verb =*rnawurnka* meaning 'take, lead, look after,' depending upon context. Again, I am unable to say much about the semantic motivation for these forms, as they are rare in the database.

5.3 Argument indexation

One or two predicate arguments are indexed by appositional verbal prefixes occurring in order-classes [2] and [3]. One of these always codes subject grammatical function and the second when it occurs codes object grammatical function. Verbs are lexically subcategorized into those that index one and only one predicate argument (intransitive verbs), and those that are required to index two arguments (transitive verbs). The indexation of subjects and objects in prefix position is obligatory on all verbs, whether or not the NPs to which they refer are overtly present in the discourse environment. All ten agreement classes (§4.1) are coded by subject- and object-marking prefixes; that is to say that NP-indexing prefixes on verbs are portmanteau forms that code both grammatical function and agreement class in all situations where they occur.

As transitive verbal prefix-clusters represent 53 different argument combinations, a shorthand system will be used to refer to their components, without which discussion of these kinds of phenomena in a language such as Worrorra is awkward, to say the least. The system employed here is as follows:

1	first person	a	masculine	in	inclusive
2	second person	f	feminine	x	exclusive
3	third person	w	celestial		
p	plural	m	terrestrial		

Where number is not marked by p 'plural', reference is to singular by default. In transitive combinations the actor is listed first, followed by an arrow (>) to indicate direction of transitivity, then an undergoer listing. So for instance 2>3a means 'a second person singular actor acting upon a third person singular masculine undergoer', ie 'you did it to him,' and 1pin>3p means 'a first person plural inclusive actor acting upon a third person plural undergoer,' ie 'we did it to them,' and so on.

5.3.1 Grammatical relations

Relations between predicate arguments in Australian languages are frequently less than straightforward (see, eg, Nordlinger 2011 on Murrinh-Patha, another Arafuran language; and *to appear*). I will take as a starting point the notion of grammatical subject, defined in the first instance pragmatically as the term upon which some other expression is predicated.

In order to gain an appreciation of the way in which predicate arguments are coded in Worrorra, we will need to look at the formal marking of grammatical relations in more detail, starting with the sentences presented below in (5.18). Following Dixon (1979) and Foley & Van Valin (1984), grammatical functions will be referred to by the mnemonics S (intransitive subject), A (agent/actor/transitive subject), U (undergoer/transitive object) and DAT (non-subcategorized object):

(5.18a) Wangayinya nyimbana
wangayinya nyiN=^{b}wa-na
woman 3f=fall-TNS
A woman fell

(b) Anja eeja kaarrwana
anja eeja kaarr=^{b}wa-na
3pDEF men 3p=fall-TNS
The men fell

(c) Anja eeja nyimbarrburrkarla wangayinya
anja eeja nyiN-^{b}warr=murrka-rla wangayinya
3pDEF men 3f-3p=go.to-PAST woman
The men went to a woman

(d) Anja eeja wangayinya kaanmurrkarla
anja eeja wangayinya kaarr-n-Ø=murrka-rla
3pDEF men woman 3p-INV-3=go.to-PAST
A woman went to the men

In these sentences, word order does not reflect grammatical relations (subject or object) of NPs. Note also that the noun phrases themselves do not bear any indications of case marking. Instead, the coding of grammatical relations is accomplished by morphological markers on the verbs.

In (5.18a) the noun *wangayinya* 'woman' is indexed (cross-referenced) on the verb =^{b}wa 'fall' by the morpheme |nyiN-| (glossed '3f' or 'third person singular feminine'), and in (5.18b) the noun phrase *anja eeja* 'the men' is indexed by the morpheme |kaarr-| (glossed '3p' or 'third person plural') on the same verb. In these intransitive sentences the NPs are in S grammatical function.

In (5.18c & d) the verb is transitive *(=murrka* 'SUBJ go to OBJ'). In (5.18c) the shape |nyiN-| occurs again, and again it indexes *wangayinya* 'woman.' And in (5.18d) the shape |kaarr| occurs again, indexing *anja eeja* 'the men.' Notice however that in these sentences, the noun phrases indexed by |nyiN-| and |kaarr-| are in U grammatical function. In verb morphology so far, then, we can note that the indices of NPs in S and U grammatical functions receive the same formal marking, ie that the morphemes that index transitive objects have the same shape as those that index intransitive subjects, or put briefly, that S=U.

Turning again to (5.18c), we can note that the subject of this sentence, *anja eeja* 'the men,' is also indexed upon the verb, this time by the morpheme |-^{b}warr-|. In (5.18d), the subject *wangayinya* 'woman,' receives zero-marking by way of indexation, and a morpheme /-n-/ is also present, between the morphemes that index object and subject grammatical functions. Now it is clear that the indices of NPs in A grammatical function receive different formal markers from those in S and U functions, and that Worrorra has an ergative-absolutive system of verbal agreement-marking.

This is not, of course, the whole story. What happens, for instance, when actor and undergoer are of the same agreement class, for instance a man *(eeja inja)* and a dog *(kanangkurri inja)*? How does the language distinguish subjects from objects in these circumstances? The answer is, that in signalling grammatical relations, an extensive system of pragmatic reference is employed, which operates in conjunction with the morphological coding of argument structures on verbs. This pragmatic system of argument coding is examined in Chapter 17. Note as well that in elicitation Worrorra speakers use

SVO word order to distinguish the grammatical functions of denotata of the same agreement class, as in (5.19):

(5.19a) | Inja | eeja | mara | kona | inja | kanangkurri
| inja | eeja | mara | ka-Ø=ᵇwu-na | inja | kanangkurri
| 3aDEF | man | see | 3a-3=hit-PAST | 3aDEF | dog

The man saw the dog

(b) | inja | kanangkurri | mara | kona | inja | eeja
| inja | kanangkurri | mara | ka-Ø=ᵇwu-na | inja | eeja
| 3aDEF | dog | see | 3a-3=hit-PAST | 3aDEF | man

The dog saw the man

Although displaying ergative-absolutive alignment in verbal prefixes, a subject grammatical relation in Worrorra, subsuming S and A functions, is warranted on a number of grounds. In typical acts of predication, subjects correspond to terms in predicate logic (see Chapter 17): that is to say that the subject relation signals a particular and indispensable pragmatic status with which some predicate argument is associated. Subject arguments prototypically occupy the semantic roles of 'actor' or 'agent,' that is, as the volitional initiators, animate experiencers, performers and/or controllers of events and actions. These observations are as pertinent to Worrorra as they are cross-linguistically.[38]

The clearest syntactic evidence for subjecthood is found in the grammatical relations that hold between complement clauses and their matrices (see Chapter 14). Complement clauses may be classified as having S or A arguments with references that are either (i) the same as, or (ii) different from, that of the A argument of their matrix. While different-subject complement clauses are not constrained with respect to the indexation of their arguments, same-subject complement clauses obligatorily encode their S or A arguments as first person singular. This is the case whether the complement-clause verb is intransitive, with a single S argument, or transitive, with an A argument. The grammar treats S and A arguments alike in this context, encoding both types as first person singular.[39] Without the notion of a subject grammatical relation in Worrorra, important syntactic generalizations having to do with the way in which complement clauses are embedded within their matrices would be lost.

As well, a subject relation uniting S and A functions is signalled by anaphor configuration, as is described in §17.4.

The object relation is, however, more complicated. Object arguments fulfil a variety of semantic roles such as 'patient', 'theme,' 'goal', 'utterance', 'recipient', 'deprivee,' 'event,' 'source' etc. As well as by way of prefixes in order-class [2], objects may also be indexed on verbs as suffixes in order-class [11]. In all verbs, material appears in order-class [11] by semantic warrant, that is to say that no assignment rules seem to operate with respect to this position, which is available for the indexation of non-subject arguments as required by the pragmatics of particular predications. In other words, this order class is filled only 'optionally.' In a transitive verb, the prefixed object position is filled obligatorily, even in object-demoting constructions (§11.5.2). For this reason, the prefixed object position is a privileged one: in transitive verbs only one argument may be indexed there, and one argument *must* be indexed there. What we have, then, is an unequivocal subject relation, and a formal indication of a privileged object relation, for which all non-subject arguments of a verb compete.

It is likely, then, firstly that there is some criterion or criteria operating to regulate competition for prefixed-object indexation, and secondly, that such a criterion has a semantic basis (cf Fillmore 1968). In considering this issue more widely, other authors have proposed a hierarchy of semantic roles with general application (see eg Allen 1995:122 and references there). The assumption underlying this position is that, of all the arguments a predicate may have, one and only one will be selected to enter into a subject grammatical relation with it, and one and only one will be selected for entry into direct

---

[38] Some experiencer constructions are exceptions to this generalization; see §12.3.

[39] Except when the matrix subject is first person plural, in which case same-subject complements also encode their subject arguments as first person plural.

object relation. In selecting among arguments as candidates for occupancy of these privileged grammatical relations, language appeals to the semantic roles that candidate-arguments fill. Semantic roles in turn are cross-linguistically ordered as to whether they are more naturally suited to occurring as subjects or as objects. When all the arguments of a particular predicate are considered, the one with the most subject-like semantic role, ie the argument whose referent typically initiates and controls an event, achieves what Foley & Van Valin (1984) describe as semantic macrorole status as *actor*, and enters into subject grammatical relation with its predicate. And the one with the most object-like semantic role is awarded a macrorole status that, following Bloomfield (1933:165), Foley & Van Valin refer to as *undergoer*, and enters into 'direct' object grammatical relation with its predicate. In effect, verbal arguments compete for access to macrorole status according to the semantic roles that they fill in any particular utterance.

This framework has obvious potential to account for the distinction in Worrorra between those non-subject arguments indexed by verbal prefixes and those indexed by verbal suffixes. Prefixed arguments are privileged in being obligatory, and we can guess at this stage that in general, their privileged morphological status probably signals a privileged semantic status as macroroles. Henceforth, then, the NP in subject grammatical relation to a verb will be referred to by its relational label as subject, by its semantic-role label, or by its semantic macrorole label as actor. Prefixed objects will be referred to by their macrorole label as undergoers (mnemonically abbreviated to U) to distinguish them from other object arguments which receive indexation as suffixes, or which receive no indexation at all.

One other point may be noted. Not only do S and U indices (marking absolutive agreement) have the same shape, but they also occur at the front of the verb, that is to say that the order of NP-indexing morphemes prefixed to transitive verbs is U–A. In order to keep the glosses in sentence examples as uncluttered as possible, the grammatical functions of prefixed NP indices will *not* be indicated, and the reader should be aware that where only one index occurs (as in (5.18a & b)) it will be in S function, and where two occur (as in (5.18c & d)) they will be ordered in U–A configuration. This convention may seem a little confusing at first, but its purpose is to make sentence glosses more legible in the long run.

In the rest of this section I will attempt to clarify the Worrorra system of verbal NP indexation and agreement, as it is evidenced in the sentences in (5.18) and in other sentences like them. Here we will be concerned with the formal apparatus of argument indexation, and more or less exclusively with prefixed NP indices, as these feed the morphophonemic processes which define form classes, and which in turn code semantic properties on predicates.

5.3.2 Alignment

Argument indices display two quite separate and independent systems of alignment, one ergative and the other inverse/accusative. Morphemes referring to the language's ten agreement classes thus occur in four order-classes, as in Table 5.2:

Table 5.2: Series-1 NP indices

	S [2/3]	U [2]	A [3]	DAT [11]
1	nga-	nga-n-	nga-	-^{k}wara
2	ngun-	ngun-	-nja-	-nu
3a	ka-	ka-	-Ø-	-nangka
3f	nyiN-	nyiN-	-Ø-	-nangka
3w	kuN-	kuN-	-Ø-	-nangka
3m	ma-	ma-	-Ø-	-nangka
1pin	ngarr-	ngarr-	ngarr-	-ngarri
1px	arr-	a-n-	-nyarr-	-nyarri
2p	nyirr-	nyi-n-	-rra-	-noorri
3p	kaarr-	kaa-(n)-	-^{b}warr-	-nangkorri

Worrorra employs two sets of NP indices, one fully inflexional (above) and another doubling as a set of derivational prefixes (see Chapter 6). I will refer to these sets as series-1 and series-2 respectively. Series-2 forms will be described in Chapter 8.

The S order-class indexes the subjects of intransitive verbs, and occurs as prefixed morphemes in position [2/3]. The U class indexes the undergoers of transitive verbs and occurs as prefixed morphemes in position [2]. The A class indexes the subjects of transitive verbs and occurs as prefixed morphemes in position [3]. The class of non-subcategorized object indices (glossed DAT) may occur on both transitive and intransitive verbs as suffixed morphemes in position [11] (see Chapter 13). This 'indirect object' marking appears on both heads and dependents in possessive phrases, as well as marking predicate objects of all kinds, outranked for undergoer status.

The form *nyiN-* has a variant *nyaN-* that may appear when the assimilatory nasal finds expression as /ng/. Vowel harmony may upon occasion produce the shape *nyuN-*. The underlying form of this morpheme is probably |nyVN-|, where |V| represents some short vowel. Also note that the second person prefix indices are different syllables of the second person free pronouns: *ngun-, -nja-* cf *ngunju* 'you singular' and *nyirr-, -rra-* cf *nyirri* 'you plural.'

Worrorra distinguishes five different number categories. Singular and plural are the only two number categories signalled by prefixed argument indexation, and denote grammatical number in a conventional sense. The dual number category and two morphemes signalling trial and paucal number are indexed upon verbs as suffixes in positions [12] and [14], and are described in Chapter Nine.

Two vertical syncretisms involve the third person singular actor indices (all represented by zero morphs), and the third person singular non-subcategorized object indices, which are all *-nangka*.[40] These constitute the only morphological cues defining the category 'third person singular' as a subset of agreement classes also definable by gender partitioning (§4.1). Gender is only registered by indices in third person singular absolute agreement (S and U functions); it is not registered by plural or agent indices.

It should be pointed out that with reference to the prefixed S, U and A forms only, patterns of syncretism produce several 'splits' in the agreement paradigm (Silverstein 1976a), as displayed in Figure 5.2:

1	accusative alignment
1pin	complete syncretism — no alignment
1px, 2p, 3p	no syncretism — accusative-ergative overlap
2, 3	ergative alignment

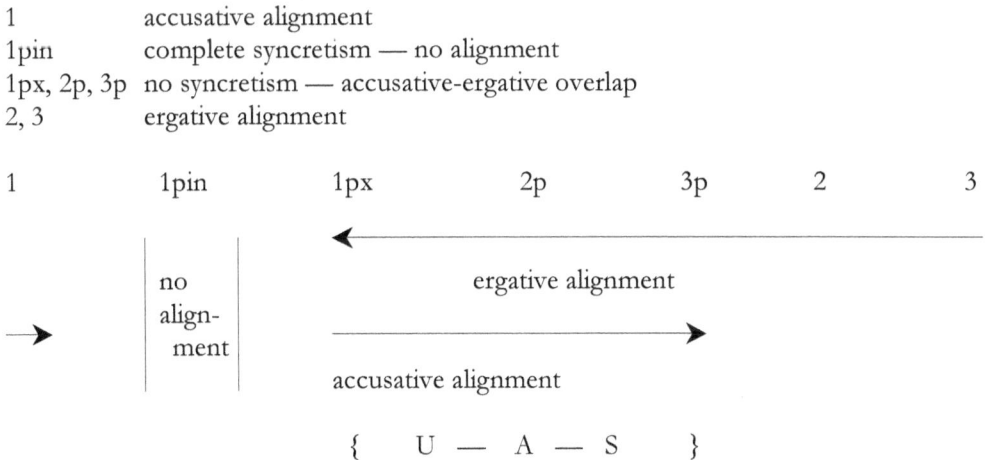

Figure 5.2: split alignment system

The type of splits observed are brought about through the operation of two independent verbal agreement systems. NP indices signal grammatical relations by way of no less than three independent coding systems, resulting in a double redundancy:

---

[40] 3sg A arguments are not claimed to have null-anaphoric coding: rather, I will use the symbol Ø as a place-holder in glosses, again to make them easier to read.

ORDER: U–A configuration
FORM 1: ergative alignment
FORM 2: inverse/accusative alignment

Any one of these would suffice on its own to code grammatical relations.

This system gives evidence of a hierarchy of grammatical feature-clusters as displayed in Figure 5.3:

[+I, –NUM] > [+NUM] > [–I, –NUM]

Figure 5.3: NP feature hierarchy

This hierarchy is one of natural agency, with natural actors or agents on the left receiving accusative marking when in an 'unnatural' grammatical relation (undergoer-hood); and natural patients on the right receiving ergative marking when in an 'unnatural' grammatical relation (agency). Note that this hierarchy describes the system of verbal agreement generally, and is quite different from the specifically inverse/accusative hierarchy displayed in Figure 5.4 below, particularly in the way it treats second person indices.

In order to examine these two alignment systems as they apply in Worrorra it is necessary to observe the underlying shapes of prefix clusters before the operation of morphophonemic rules.

In indicative intransitive verbs the S indices displayed in Table 5.2 are prefixed to the verb root in a straightforward manner, subject only to phonological constraints at morpheme boundaries as described in §3.2. The morpheme boundary to the left of a verb root is a phonologically complex one, but not opaque to analysis. Prefix clusters in front of transitive verb roots involve a number of morphosyntactic processes as well as some phonological complexity. These clusters are displayed in Table 5.3, along with the morphemes involved underlyingly in their construction and with notes on the morphological processes involved in their derivation (numbers refer to the pertinent phonological rules (§3)).

Table 5.3: transitive prefix-clusters: indicative mood

1>2	ngun-	|ngun-(n)-Ø|	INV, neutralization
1>3a	kanga-	|ka-nga|	
1>3f	nyanga-	|nyaN-nga|	
1>3w	kunga-	|kuN-nga|	
1>3m	manga	|ma-nga|	
1>2p	nyin-	|nyirr-n-Ø|	15, INV, neutralization
1>3p	kaanga-	|kaarr-nga|	15
2>1	jan-	|jan|	portmanteau
2>3a	kanja-	|ka-nja|	
2>3f	nyinja-	|nyiN-nja|	
2>3w	kunja-	|kuN-nja|	
2>3m	manja-	|ma-nja|	
2>1px	kaanja-	|kaarr-nja|	15, neutralization
2>3p	kaanja-	|kaarr-nja|	15
3>1	ngan-	|nga-n-Ø|	INV
3>2	ngun-	|ngun-(n)-Ø|	INV
3>3a	ka	|ka-Ø|	
3>3f	nyiN-	|nyiN-Ø|	
3>3w	kuN-	|kuN-Ø|	
3>3m	ma-	|ma-Ø|	
3>1pin	ngarr-	|ngarr-Ø|	

3>1px	an-	|arr-n-Ø|	15, INV
3>2p	nyin-	|nyirr-n-Ø|	15, INV
3>3p	kaan-	|kaarr-n-Ø|	15, INV
1pin>3a	karr-	|ka-ngarr|	22
1pin>3f	nyarr-	|nyaN-ngarr|	22
1pin>3w	warr-	|ᵏwuN-ngarr|	6
1pin>3m	marr-	|ma-ngarr|	22
1pin>3p	kaangarr-	|kaarr-ngarr|	15
1px>2	ngunbarr-	|ngun-(n)-ᵇwarr|	INV, neutralization
1px>3a	kerr-	|ka-nyarr|	24
1px>3f	nyerr-	|nyaN-nyarr|	24
1px>3w	kunyarr-	|kuN-nyarr|	
1px>3m	merr-	|ma-nyarr|	24
1px>2p	nyinbarr-	|nyirr-n-ᵇwarr|	15, INV, neutralization
1px>3p	kaanyarr-	|kaarr-nyarr|	15
2p>1	jarra-	|jan-rra|	14, portmanteau
2p>3a	karra-	|ka-rra|	
2p>3f	nyirra-	|nyiN-rra|	14
2p>3w	kurra-	|kuN-rra|	14
2p>3m	marra-	|ma-rra|	
2p>1px	kaarra-	|kaarr-rra|	neutralization
2p>3p	kaarra-	|kaarr-rra|	
3p>1	nganbarr-	|nga-n-ᵇwarr|	INV
3p>2	ngunbarr-	|ngun-(n)-ᵇwarr|	INV
3p>3a	kawarra-	|ka-ᵇwarr-a|	26
3p>3f	nyimbarr-	|nyiN-ᵇwarr|	
3p>3w	kubarr-	|kuN-ᵇwarr|	NT hardening
3p>3m	maarr-	|ma-ᵇwarr|	23
3p>1pin	ngarrbarr-	|ngarr-ᵇwarr|	
3p>1px	anbarr-	|arr-n-ᵇwarr|	15, INV
3p>2p	nyinbarr-	|nyirr-n-ᵇwarr|	15, INV
3p>3p	kaanbarr-	|kaarr-n-ᵇwarr|	15, INV

5.3.3 Morphophonological processes

A number of phonological processes occur in these clusters that are not found elsewhere. Discussion of the inverse-hierarchy morpheme -*n*- is kept for the following section.

<u>5.3.3 (i) trill deletion</u>
The most obvious process is the deletion of the trill /rr/ before nasals (rule 15). This occurs in every cluster involving the 1px, 2p and 3p morphemes in undergoer function, such that these morphemes could be argued to have underlying U-function forms |a-|, |nyi-| and |kaa-| respectively, instead of |arr-|, |nyirr-| and |kaarr-| as proposed here. A more efficient description relies on a phonological explanation of the surface shapes of these morphemes for the following reasons: a surface series-2 3p shape /a-/ occurs in S function in intransitive verbs before the subjunctive morpheme -*ngka*- in shapes such as *angkenga* 'when they went' |arr-ngka=ya-nga| [3p-SJTV=go-TNS]. This shape involves the series-2 3p absolutive prefix *arr*-, which also indexes the 1px function in series-2, so that it appears on the 1px intransitive subject verb form in the same shape: *arrkunyenga* 'when we (exc) went' |arr-

ngun=ya-nga| [1px-SJTV=go-TNS]. Here the different shape of the subjunctive morpheme (-*ngun*- as opposed to -*ngka*-) could be said to reveal the subject-indexing morpheme in its full form. It could nevertheless be argued that series-2 really has a separate shape for each function, /arr-/ for 1px and /a-/ for 3p, but this would not be borne out by the prefixes of the optative form-class, which also employs series-2 indices; for example *arreyu* means both 'they will go' and 'we (exc) will go' |arr-a=ya| [1px/3p-OPT=go]. The only other explanation is that the 3p morpheme takes on a different form (/a-/) in series-2 prefixes when used upon intransitive verbs marked with the subjunctive morpheme, but then we have to ask for the reason why this should be so. A phonological explanation involving the incompatibility of the shapes /arr/ and /ngka/ is the most natural, since such incompatibility is elsewhere attested by hardening rule 11, which if applied here would produce |arr + ngka| > */adkka/ > */aka/. If phonology can in this manner explain the shape of *angkenga* and similar verb forms by a rule that deletes /rr/ before nasals in series-2 prefix clusters, then the rule is available for, and could be expected to apply to series-1 prefix clusters where the same phonological conditions pertain. The shapes /a-/, /nyi-/ and /kaa-/ all occur before nasals except when followed by the 2p transitive subject morpheme -*rra*-, in which instance the shapes of the undergoer morphemes in question are as likely to end in /rr/ as not.

It is now possible to observe the underlying shapes of the 1px, 2p and 3p morphemes in U function:

1px |arr-n| > /a-n-/
2p |nyirr-n| > /nyi-n-/
3p |kaarr-n| > /kaa-(n)-/

It is apparent that the underlying shapes of these morphemes match those of the equivalent S-function forms shown in Table 5.1. When we exclude -*n*- from the first person singular U prefix as well, we are left with a paradigm of the U order-class that exactly matches that of the S class. Now the 1 index exhibits complete syncretism in all prefixed order-classes, and in this it is comparable to the 1pin index. And the rest of the paradigm now shows a thoroughly ergative prefix morphology, with S=U shapes opposed to A.

5.3.3 (ii) nasal deletion

The opposite situation to trill deletion rule 15 also occurs; that is, nasal deletion rule 14 deletes nasal consonants when they occur before the trill /rr/ in the 2p A index -*rra*-. This process is likewise confined to verbal prefix clusters and can be observed in 2p>1, 2p>3f and 2p>3w:

(5.20)   2p>3f   Nyirramurrkarla
                   nyiN-rra=murrka-rla
                   3f-2p=go.to-PAST
                   You lot went to her

5.3.3 (iii) velar elision

Rule 22 velar elision applies when there is a 1pin agent, and can be observed in 1pin>3a, 1pin>3f and 1pin>3m. This rule derives /a/ from underlying |anga| sequences:

(5.21)   1pin>3f   Nyarrburrkarla
                    nyaN-ngarr=murrka-rla
                    3f-1pin=go.to-PAST
                    We (inc) went to her

5.3.3 (iv) velar cluster lenition
The very specific velar cluster lenition rule 6 applies to 1pin>3w, and derives /w/ from underlying |ᵏwuN-ng|:

(5.22) 1pin>3w   Nguwanu   warrburrkarla
                   nguwanu   ᵏwuN-ngarr=murrka-rla
                   tree   3w-1pin=go.to-PAST
                   We (inc) went to the tree

5.3.3 (v) palatal nasal lenition
Rule 24 /ny/-lenition applies to clusters with a 1px agent and is seen in 1px>3a, 1px>3f and 1px>3m. This rule operates in tandem with vowel expansion rule 18, first to derive |aya| from underlying |anya| sequences, and then to derive /e/ from |aya|:

(5.23) 1px>3f   Nyerrburrkarla
                  nyaN-nyarr=murrka-rla
                  3f-1px=go.to-PAST
                  We (exc) went to her

5.3.3 (vi) peripheral glide lenition
Peripheral glide lenition rule 23 applies to the cluster 3p>3m. This rule derives /aa/ from underlying |awa| sequences:

(5.24) 3p>3m   Werrim   maarrburrkarla
                 werrim   ma-ᵇwarr=murrka-rla
                 hill   3m-3p=go.to-PAST
                 They went to the hill

The cluster 3p>3w displays a homorganic cluster-hardening rule that derives *kubarr-* from underlying |kuN-ᵇwarr| via the sequence |Nᵇw > Nb > mb > bb| > /b/:

(5.25) 3p>3w   Nguwanu   kubarrburrkarla
                 nguwanu   kuN-ᵇwarr=murrka-rla
                 tree   3w-3p=go.to-PAST
                 They went to the tree

Finally the cluster 3p>3a includes an epenthetic /a/ before a following morpheme.

(5.26) 3p>3a   kawarramurrkarla
                 ka-ᵇwarr-a=murrka-rla
                 3a-3p-EP=go.to-PAST
                 They went to him

5.3.3 (vii) first and third person neutralization
Indices separately bearing the features [+I] and [+II] cannot co-occur in the same prefix cluster. The grammar deals with this constraint in two ways. The first is by a process of first and third person neutralization, whereby first person functions in prefix clusters whose other member consists of a second person function, are reassigned to a third person index form. When the subject in such a cluster is first person singular, the expected form *-nga-* is replaced by the third person singular shape /-Ø-/ (1>2, 1>2p). When the subject is first person plural exclusive, the expected form *-nyarr-* is replaced by the third person plural shape *-ᵇwarr-* (1px>2, 1px>2p). And when the undergoer in such a cluster is first person plural exclusive, the expected form *arr-* is replaced by the third person plural shape *kaarr-* (2>1px, 2p>1px):

(5.27a) 1>2   Ngunmurrkarlaal
                   ngun-(n)-Ø=murrka-rla-^kwaal
                   2-(INV)-3/1=go.to-PAST-hither
                   He/I came to you

(b)   1px>2p   Nyinbarrburrkarlaal
                   nyirr-n-^bwarr=murrka-rla-^kwaal
                   2p-INV-3p/1px=go.to-PAST-hither
                   We/they came to you lot

(c)   2>1px   Kaanjamurrkarlaal
                   kaarr-nja=murrka-rla-^kwaal
                   3p/1px-2=go.to-PAST-hither
                   You came to us/them

<u>5.3.3 (viii) 2>1 portmanteau</u>
The second way in which the grammar conforms to this constraint is by way of a portmanteau morpheme *jan-* which denotes 2>1, and occurs in clusters where a second person subject is opposed to a first person singular undergoer, ie 2>1 and 2p>1. In the latter cluster the 2p morpheme is placed after the portmanteau; |jan-rra| > *jarra-*, such that this cluster analyses functionally as [2 [2p] >1], the embedded function securing the feature [+NUM] to the second person function:

(5.28)   2p>1   Jarramurrkarlaal
                   jan-rra=murrka-rla-^kwaal
                   2>1-2p=go.to-PAST-hither
                   You lot came to me

5.3.4 Inverse marking

It now remains to discuss the role of the morpheme *-n-* (see examples (5.18d), (5.27a,b)). Transitive prefix clusters give evidence of another hierarchy of grammatical person and number features with respect to their naturalness or likelihood of agency:

   2 > 1 > 3p > 3

   Figure 5.4: inverse hierarchy

When an A index bears grammatical features below (or further to the right of) those of the undergoer, then an inverse hierarchy marker *-n-* appears after the undergoer morpheme.

Note that this is quite a different hierarchy from that described in Figure 5.3. The hierarchy in Figure 5.4 refers specifically to the way in which inverse-hierarchy marking is encoded, and not to the verbal agreement system as a whole. The most dramatic difference between the two hierarchies is in the treatment of second person indices: the second person singular index, for example, is at the opposite end of each hierarchy.

The inverse hierarchy marker (glossed INV) appears when a first person agent acts upon a second person undergoer (1>2, 1>2p, 1px>2, 1px>2p), when a third person agent acts upon a second person undergoer (3>2, 3>2p, 3p>2, 3p>2p), when a third person agent acts upon a first person undergoer (3>1, 3>1px, 3p>1, 3p>1px) and when a third person singular agent acts upon a third person plural undergoer (3>3p). The second person singular index /ngun-/ appears to have INV built into its form, making a separate marker /-n-/ redundant when it occurs in the clusters 1>2, 1px>2, 3>2 and 3p>2. Examples of inverse clusters are shown in (5.29):

(5.29a) 3p> 2p   Nyinbarrburrkarlaal
                 nyirr-n-ᵇwarr=murrka-rla-ᵏwaal
                 2p-INV-3p=go.to-PAST-hither
                 They came to you lot

(b)   3>1px   Anmurrkarlaal
                 arr-n-Ø=murrka-rla-ᵏwaal
                 1px-INV-3=go.to-PAST-hither
                 He came to us (exc)

(c)   3p>1   Nganbarrburrkarlaal
                 nga-n-ᵇwarr=murrka-rla-ᵏwaal
                 1-INV-3p=go.to-PAST-hither
                 They came to me

With one exception, the morpheme -*n*- in this position consistently signals an inverse of hierarchical ordering with respect to direction of transitivity. And with one exception the inverse marker occurs wherever the hierarchy displayed in Figure 5.4 predicts that it should. This morpheme is an obligatory morphological ('semantic') inverse in Givón's (1994:23) terms. More particularly it is a 'purely pronominal-morphological' inverse, type C-ix in his typology of inverse clauses *(ibid:*29). Far from representing an incipient ergative construction as he claims *(ibid:*32), inverse-hierarchy marking in Worrorra is in effect a form of accusative marking, sensitive only to certain grammatical (person and number) features. A similar morphology occurs in Ungarinyin (Heath 1976:181 ff), where Heath refers to -*n*- as a form 'which can be taken as Accusative.'

The INV marker also appears in the equipollent 3p>3p cluster *kaanbarr-*, where it marks accusative relationship exclusively:

(5.30) 3p>3p   Kaanbarrburrkarlangurru
                 kaarr-n-ᵇwarr=murrka-rla-ngurru
                 3p-INV-3p–go.to-PAST-away
                 They went over to them

The marker appears in an accusative role as well in an imperative verb prefix where the underlying second person subject has null (zero) representation, which is understood or misread by the grammar as encoding the third person singular agent index-function (which is also /-Ø-/). This phenomenon is discussed further in §8.5.3.

As may by now be expected, phonological processes may intervene in morphosyntactic ones and take precedence over them. The 1pin index does not accept INV when it occurs in undergoer position in the clusters 3>1pin and 3p>1pin, respectively: |ngarr-Ø| > *ngarr-* and |ngarr-ᵇwarr| > *ngarrbarr-*:

(5.31) 3>1pin   Ngarrburrkarlaal
                 ngarr-Ø=murrka-rla-ᵏwaal
                 1pin-3=go.to-PAST-hither
                 S/he came to us (inc)

The reason for this omission is phonological; in prefix clusters trill deletion rule 15 appears to override hardening rule 11, such that the unattested sequence *|ngarr-n-| would produce the surface shape *ngan-*. This surface form does occur, but as an index of 1 in the equivalent clusters 3>1 and 3p>1. The grammar therefore uses INV to disambiguate the forms of the 1 and 1pin indices, and INV does not appear in clusters with 1pin in object function, as would otherwise be expected.

This kind of disambiguation is possible in Worrorra because inverse-hierarchy marking is redundant there. Morphological inverse-hierarchy marking typically occurs in languages in order to assign grammatical function when pronominal affixes are ordered according to some person and/or number hierarchy (see eg Heath 1984:362 on Wubuy). In Worrorra indexing affixes are unexceptionally ordered syntactically in U–A configuration, so there is no possibility of confusion over grammatical function. Historically, it is likely that the morpheme *-n-* has cycled between accusative and inverse marking patterns (cf. Heath 1976:182 *et seq*). The point of diachronic interest is not that *-n-* occurs in an equipollent position (3p>3p) or that it is missing from 3(p)>1pin clusters, but rather its overall redundancy. The shapes *ngan-* '1', *an-* '1px', *ngun-* '2', *nyin-* '2p' and *kaan-* '3p' are as it were ready-made accusative forms if an accusative system were to develop. And the present inverse system may well have developed out of just such an accusative system. Syntactic index-configuration in Worrorra may have arisen if gender-marking suffixes had been copied from a preceding undergoer NP onto a following verb, and had come to be treated as prefixes to that verb. Subsequently participant NPs could have been generalized to this paradigm.

5.4 Tense-marking

In indicative mood each Worrorra verb employs a set of one or two tense allomorphs to signal time reference. Reference may be to present, past or future time, but each verbal lexeme selects only one set of suffixes for tense-marking; that is, selection of tense-marking allomorphs forms part of a verb's lexical specification. The tense-marking morphology described in this section applies to indicative verbs, and also to verbs in the hypotactic and avertive functions of the subjunctive mood (Chapter 15).

5.4.1 Tense-marking on intransitive verbs

With respect to tense-marking there are two types of intransitive verbs. The first type has separate tense morphemes for present and past tenses. The second type has only one morpheme that serves to mark both present and past tenses. Intransitive tense-marking morphology is summarized in Table 5.4.

Table 5.4: intransitive tense morphemes: indicative mood

		PRESENT	PAST
(a)	=nu *'be'*	-ngu	-na
	=ya-^{k}waal *'come,'* =ninjawa *'burn'*	-Ø	-na
	middle voice	-ng	-na
	subset of middle voice	-ng	-nya
(b)	=^{b}wa *'fall'*		-na
	=ya *'go'*		-nga

For the first type (a), the usual present tense allomorph is *-ng*. The phonology of this form is discussed below, but at this point it should be noted that the present tense marker on =*nu* 'be' (*-ngu*) is almost certainly /-ng/ underlyingly. And the most common past tense allomorph is *-na*. This combination of tense forms is an index of intransitivity, and middle (derived intransitive) verbs nearly all show these forms.

The verbs =*ya* 'go' and =*ya-^{k}waal* 'come (go-hither)' are irregular. The past tense marker of =*ya-^{k}waal* is a little problematic; compare *ngengkaal* 'I come' with *ngengkunaal* 'I came,' where the difference seems to be in the insertion of a form *-un-* into the directional morpheme *-(ngk)aal*. However I suspect that the tense morpheme is better described as *-na*, with an epenthetic vowel /u/ appearing after the cluster /ngk/ (which is a reflex of the morphophoneme |^{k}w| in the directional morpheme), and the vowel of the tense allomorph blended with the following directional morpheme: |^{k}w-u-na-^{k}waal > ngk-u-na-aal|. The tense morphology of =*ya-^{k}waal* 'come' and =*ninjawa* 'burn' (*-Ø* for present and *-na* for past) is more typical of transitive verbs (see Table 5.5).

At least four middle verbs take the past tense allomorph *-nya*; they are are =*ᵇwalke* 'stand', =*ᵇwarnke* 'grow,' =*ᵏwulkune* 'be afraid' and =*ngarnde* 'rain.' The continuous aspect morpheme does not blend with this tense shape, that is to say that V expansion rule 18 does not apply here, and the past continuous suffix shape is *-nyeerri* on these deponent verbs.

The second type of intransitive verb exhibits a future/non-future tense system, with non-future forms marked by a suffix and with optative (future) forms unmarked by suffixes. The high-frequency irregular verb =*ya* 'go' employs the suffix *-nga* to mark both present and past tenses. When the directional morpheme *-ngurru* 'away' is suffixed to =*ya* 'go,' the tense marker normally undergoes haplological reduction in fast speech:

(5.32)　　Kengurru
　　　　　ka=ya-nga-ngurru
　　　　　3a=go-TNS-away
　　　　　He went away

The verb =*rlelwa* 'be born,' appears to be composed of an incorporated element diachronically fused to the front of =*ᵇwa* 'fall,' and is conjugated like =*ᵇwa*.

5.4.2 Time-reference on transitive verbs

The continuous aspect morpheme *-(y)eerri* has an auxiliary function coding tense on transitive verbs. Present time is signalled by the absence of a tense-marking suffix in order class [9] and the presence of the continuous aspect morpheme in order class [13]: /-Ø-(y)eerri/. In the following exchange, note the way in which the continuous aspect morpheme *-eerri* signals present time in the absence of a tense morpheme:

(5.33)
(a)　Ngayu kaangamarlaarndoyeerri marru.　　　*I'm going off with them.*
(b)　Joli banaal!　　　　　　　　　　　　　　　　*Come back!*
(c)　Kaarriyaka, jaa maa kaangamarlaarndoyeerri.　*No I won't, I'm going with them.*
(d)　Arri angujakunya?　　　　　　　　　　　　　*What for?*
(e)　Marru dambeewunya.　　　　　　　　　　　　*To have a look at the country.*
(f)　Wangalaalunguyu kurde kaanjaangurreerri?　　*Are you taking the children too?*

Sentence (5.33b) has a verb in imperative form, sentences (5.33d,e) are verbless constructions and sentences (5.33a,c,f) have verbs in present continuous form, constructed as follows:

(g=(a,c))　　Kaangamarlaarndoyeerri
　　　　　　kaarr-nga=marlaarndo-yeerri
　　　　　　3p-1=follow-PROG
　　　　　　I'm following them

(h=(f))　　　Kaanjaangurreerri
　　　　　　kaarr-nja=ᵏwangurru-eerri
　　　　　　3p-2=carry-PROG
　　　　　　You're taking them

The absence of both tense and aspect suffixes from a transitive indicative verb normally signals an aorist form, the semantics of which are discussed in §5.4.5.

There are two types of transitive past-tense suffix. The most common type includes all but a handful of verbs, and has past tense forms marked by *-na*, *-nga* or *-rla*. The suffix *-rla* is confined to transitive verbs, but apart from that, these suffixes do not signal verbal conjugation, as tense-marking allomorphs frequently do in other Australian languages. The selection of tense-marking forms is not correlated to any other property of verbs. The other two suffixes *-na* and *-nga* occur on both transitive and intransitive verbs.

A second type has past tense forms marked by *-rna* and *-ng*. The allomorph *-rna* appears to be a variant of *-na* used only with transitive verbs. It may be that *-na* and *-rna* are in free variation in transitive verbs; at any rate they are not always easy to distinguish. I have only discerned the form *-rna* with certainty on four verbs: =*rno* 'give', =*marlaarndo* 'follow', =*ᵇwalkenju* 'erect' and =*rnaajo* 'copy, imitate'. It is possible that in three of these verbs the retroflex form of the tense allomorph harmonizes with retroflex consonants in the verb root morphemes, but the sample is too small to make any realistic generalizations. At any rate it is the case that the retroflex allomorphs *-rla* and *-rna* are confined to transitive verbs, and this is the only correlation able to be drawn between allomorphic shape and the semantics of verbal root morphemes.

The past tense marker *-ng* I have found on only two verbs, the high-frequency irregular verb *kuN[ ]=yi* 'do' and =*ᵏwalkara* 'discard, throw out'. Transitive tense-marking morphology is summarized in Table 5.5.

Table 5.5: transitive tense morphemes: indicative mood

	PRESENT	PAST
Subsets of transitive only	-Ø	-rna, -rla
kuN[ ]=yi 'do'	-Ø	-ng
Elsewhere	-Ø	-na, -nga

The shape of the morpheme *-ng* is not unambiguous. It occurs as a present tense marker on intransitive verbs as well as a past tense marker on a couple of transitive verbs. Occurrences of this shape are exemplified in (5.34):

(5.34a) Nganungu   *I am*
nga=nu-ng
1=be-PRES

(b) Kunjungu   *S/he did it*
kuN-Ø=yi-ng
VCOMP-3=do-PAST

(c) Kunjunganangka   *S/he said to him/her*
kuN-Ø=yi-ng-a-nangka
VCOMP-3=do-PAST-EP-DAT

(d) Kunjingeerri   *S/he was doing it*
kuN-Ø=yi-ng-eerri
VCOMP-3=do-PAST-PROG

(e) Kumnyeng   *S/he did it*
kuN-Ø-mnya=yi-ng
VCOMP-3-DD=do-PAST

(f) Kenga   *When s/he did it*
ØN-Ø-ngka=yi-ng
VCOMP-3-SJTV=do-PAST

The tense allomorph exhibits the surface shapes *-ngu* (5.34a,b), *-nga* (5.34c,f) and *-ng* (5.34d,e) in these examples, and it is likely that only one of them is underlying.

V-expansion rule 18 allows us to rule out the shape *-nga* as underlying; if it were so, the past continuous shape in (5.34d) would be |-nga + eerri| > *-ngerri*, which is not what is found there. The shape *kumnyeng* in (5.34e) may appear with an epenthetic final /a/ at the end of an intonation group or in slow speech, and correspondingly the unepenthesized forms are found in rapid speech. This phenomenon is a result of an apparent preference for ending words in a vowel, a tendency which is far from being a rule. The most likely explanation for the shape of the tense morpheme is that underlying |-ng| naturally attracts word-final vowel epenthesis, which is nevertheless not obligatory. This is seen in (5.34f), in which vowel epenthesis is employed to avoid a monosyllabic form. Although there are a number of monosyllabic words in Worrorra, the language prefers to avoid monosyllabic forms in those cases where this can be achieved by some kind of epenthesis.

The shape *-ngu* only occurs when the surface shape of the preceding verb root morpheme contains the vowel /u/. Furthermore, *-ngu* changes to *-nga* when followed by material immediately containing the vowel /a/, as in (5.34c), and when it occurs in a position of primary stress, as in *kùnjungánu* 's/he told you (sg).' The occurrence of *-ngu* is therefore phonologically conditioned and represents an instance of vowel epenthesis and progressive vowel harmony, in this case moving forward from the vowel in the root lexeme, and in the case of (5.34b), ultimately from the shape of the undergoer morpheme *kuN-*. The presence of the discourse-deictic morpheme *-mnya-*, or of *nya-*epenthesis blocks the forward movement of vowel harmony, as in (5.34e).

5.4.3 Tense and time reference

Present tense-marking forms are not tightly correlated to their overt or characteristic time-referential function. Present tense forms may also refer to past time, or more frequently to future time. The following sentence examples illustrate the use of present tense morphemes to refer to *future time*. In situations that involve some kind of modal semantics, an optative or hortative shape is preferred to code future time reference (§8.1, §8.5.1).

(5.35a) Angujaaw   jaraai   kanungu?
         anguja-aaw   jaraai   ka=nu-ngu
         what-TIME   laugh   3a=be-PRES
         When is he going to laugh?

(b)   Mamangkunu   ke   ngarringurraarndu
         mamangkunu   ke   ngarr=i-nga-ngurru-^{k}warndu
         morning   3wREF   1pin=go-TNS-away-DU
         We'll go in the morning

(c)
Wardi   ngarringa   marru,   warnangkali   ke   warranganyarro.
wardi   ngarr=i-nga   ma=rru   warnangkali   ke ^{k}wuN-ngarr-a=nganyarro
hope   1pin=go-TNS   3m=LAT   mountain   3wREF   3w-1pin-OPT=look for
We'd like you to go with us to look for that mountain.

In (5.35b) the irregular verb root *=ya* 'go' has a plural-subject allomorph *=i*. The tense morpheme and the directional morpheme undergo haplological reduction (|nga-ngurru| > *-ngurru*). In (5.35c) the form *warranganyarro* is optative, as is usual in purposive clauses (see §8.2.1). However the form *ngarringa* is a non-future form, and this is unusual after the modal adverb *wardi* 'hopefully' in this context.

The following sentence examples illustrate the use of present tense morphemes to refer to *past time*.

(5.36)
Marno	Maangkayarnanya	aja	adungaarndeerri,	mamaa
ma=rno	Maangkaya-rnanya	aja	arr=nu-ng-aarndu-eerri	mamaa
3m=DIST	NAME-LOC	sit	1px=be-PRES-DU-PROG	secluded

warnda-warnda	nganuna
warnda-warnda	nga=nu-na
dwell-REDUP	1=be-PAST

I stayed with Maangkaya, I lived there by myself

In (5.36) the complex predicate *aja adungaarndeerri* 'we (du exc) sat/stayed, I sat/stayed with him/her' is inflected for present tense, although it refers to events that took place several decades ago, and is coordinated with a verb in past tense *(nganuna)*.

(5.37a)
Nyengurreerri	abeerla	maa,	ke	manja	kaweengaarndu
nya=ya-nga-ngurru-eerri	abeerla	maa	ke	manja	ka=ᵇwee-ng-aarndu
3f=go-TNS-away-PROG	slow	PROG	and	meet	3a=hit.MID-PRES-DU

inja	iwarnbarnngarri
3aDEF	snake.sp

She went along slowly until she met up with the king brown snake

(b)
Jijaaya	nguru	kerrkangurreerri	karloorlerri
jijaaya	nguru	ka-nyarr=ᵏwangurru-eerri	ØN-Ø-ngka=rloo-rla-eerri
Mr Love	hear	3a-1px=carry-PROG	VCOMP-3-SJTV=speak-PAST-PROG

ke,	karrangarri,	Karnmanya
ke	karrangu-ngarri	Karnmanya
3wREF	high-REL	Kunmunya

We used to listen to Mr. Love at Kunmunya when he talked about heaven

In (5.37a) the complex predicate *manja kaweengaarndu* 'they two meet each other' is in present tense form in a text that refers to past events. And in (5.37b) the complex predicate *nguru kerrkangurreerri* 'we (exc) are listening to him' includes a classifying verb with present time-marking, dominating a subordinate verb in past tense (*karloorlerri* 'when s/he was speaking'). This is from a text referring to events that happened half a century previously: *jijaaya* 'dad' is the Revd J R B Love, referred to here by the name by which he was affectionately known to Worrorra people.

Although this kind of thing is not all that common, neither is it particularly uncommon, and it is a good indication of the generally less-than-tight relationship between tense form and time-referential function in Worrorra.

5.4.4 Verbs unmarked for time reference

Some indicative forms that are unmarked for both tense and aspect may nonetheless have patterns of occurrence quite distinct from formally identical aorist verbs. The reason for their occurrence is phonological: the verb =*nu* 'be' often sheds its past tense morpheme -*na* under haplology in fast speech: /=nuna/ > =*nu*, as in (5.38):

(5.38) Wali ajaaja ajanoorri
 wali ajaaja arr-nya=nu-ᵏwurri
 PERF live 1px-EP=be-NUM
 We lived with them

Furthermore, and quite importantly, past tense morphemes on all verbs may be optionally deleted in fast speech when time reference is unambiguous. Note the absence of tense markers from the complex predicates *mara ko* 'see, find' in (5.39a) and *rok kee* 'bury' in (5.39b):

(5.39a)
Jarroo mara ko marno, jeyi kanunerri jaayawunya.
jarroo mara ka-Ø=ᵇwu ma=rno jeyi ka=nu-na-eerri jaaya-ᵏwunya
kite.sp see 3a-3=hit 3m=DIST spear 3a=be-PAST-PROG fish-PURP
There he found the brahminy kite spearing fish

(b) Rok kee
 rok ka-Ø=ee
 bury 3a-3=place
 S/he buried him

This phonological process is iconic of fast, dramatic or emotional utterances and is grammaticized to depict events of that nature in aorist verbs.

5.4.5 Aorist

The indicative mood contains two functional subcategories. Declarative functions are used to make positive assertions, statements and questions that refer to events in past or present time. Aorist is a subcategory of indicative functions that makes no specific temporal reference, either deictically by tense-marking or in terms of internal structure (aspect). Aorist is used in those discourse situations where a speaker wishes to demote time as a salient category in the depiction of events. The term 'aorist' is used here to refer to the functions of indicative verbs lacking tense and aspect marking. These forms denote vividness, habitual action, universal statements ('gnomic aorist'), imminence ('future aorist') and enablement. The Worrorra aorist bears some semantic similarities to the aspect of that name found in Classical Greek and English (Foley & Van Valin 1984:226-228). Aorist aspect in those languages (i) ignores a predicate's internal temporal structure (aspect), and (ii) expresses timeless, universal statements, vivid descriptions of actions, habitual actions, events that are vague or generalized with respect to time reference, present time reference, and a specific kind of future time reference. Because of these similarities the name of the aspect will be used here opportunistically to refer to a subcategory of the indicative mood; that is, to a set of verb functions signalled by the absence of both aspect and tense marking.

5.4.5 (i) vividness

Aorist verbs are used to depict events vividly. Note the shapes of the verb classifiers *kubaju* in (5.40a), *kama* and *kayabu* in (5.40b), and *kumnyama* in (5.40c):

(5.40a) Arrkeka   yarrorl   kubaju   belangkarraya!
         arrka-y₂aka   yarrorl   kuN-ᵇwarr=yi   belangkarraya
         3pNAR-EMPH   voices   VCOMP-3p=do   everyone
         There's all their voices!

(b)   Jarrangurlak   kama,   wurluk   kayabu   aworle
         jarrangurlak   ka-Ø=ma   wurluk   ka-Ø=yabu   awa-ᵏwurle
         lift.up   3a-3=get swallow   3a-3=throw 3aNAR-first
         He picked up the first one and swallowed him

(c)   Mamaamangkunu   wunu   ingak   kumnyama.
         ma-maa-mangkunu   wunu   ingak   kuN-Ø-mnya=ma
         ↳-AUG-morning   3wDEF   dead   VCOMP-3-DD=get
         By the morning he was dead.

5.4.5 (ii) habitual action

Aorist signals the demotion of time as a salient category in the depiction of an event. In these circumstances the resulting form denotes action not related to a specific temporal framework, and which is usually to be understood as habitual or characteristic action. Aorist verbs may refer to habitual, customary or prescribed *actions* as in (5.41):

(5.41a)
Kulaaya   debarr   ingkenganyarri,   arrbri   baraanba
kulaaya   debarr   i-ngka=ya-nga-nyarri   arr=mri   baraan-ba
husband   die   3a-SJTV=go-TNS-1pxDAT px=head   shaved-EP

kerrburrka
ka-nyarr=murrka
3a-1px=go.to
When our husbands die we shave our heads for them

(b)
Waa   ngawurriy   bungajin   wunu   mrnangkanya
waa   ngawurriy   ba-kuN-ngarr=yi-n   wunu   marnangkanya
not   drink.gravy CFT-VCOMP-1pin=do-NON.P   3wDEF   adolescent.girl

ngarrkunungu,   ke   arrka   maa   ngarrbardo
ngarr-ngun=nu-ng   ke   arrka   maa   ngarr-ᵇwarr=rno
1pin-SJTV=be-PRES   and   3pNAR   SPEC   1pin-3p=give
We don't drink the cooked blood in the body-cavity of a kangaroo when we are adolescent girls, until they give it to us

(c)
Kunyajunangkorri   anja   wangalaalunguyu   wenngarri   maa.
kuN-nyarr=yi-nangkorri   anja   wangalaalanguya   weni-ngarri maa
VCOMP-1px=do-3pDAT   3pDEF   children   now-REL   PROG
We still tell it to our children these days

5.4.5 (iii) universal statements

Sometimes aorist mood may be used to make universal statements that refer to situations established in the dreamtime, as in (5.42), although again, subjunctive verbs are more usual in conveying this kind of meaning:

(5.42)
Arrigrarlya	arrke	gee	kaanbarrwu	anja	burnarri
arr=igrarl-ya	arrke	gee	kaarr-n-^{b}warr=^{b}wu	anja	burnarri
px=Grarl-3p	3pREF	represent	3p-INV-3p=hit	3pDEF	animals

These animals are the totemic emblems of the people of Grarl

In (5.42) the complex predicate *gee =^{b}wu* 'SUBJ be represented totemically by OBJ' has a similar semantics but an opposite predicate perspective to English verbs such as 'represent,' 'symbolize' or 'stand for.'

5.4.5 (iv) imminence

Aorist is used to refer to events that are imminent. Imminence is a privileged type of projection, and denotes future events that are not irrealis in so far as their occurrence is impending, necessary and more or less obvious. Projection is discussed in §8.2.2, but for the time being it should be noted that future time reference in these utterances is an essentially epistemic category, that is to say that certain facts about the present are treated as constituting premises for making judgements about conditions in the immediate future, as may be seen in (5.43):

(5.43a)
Manmaa	kerdaarnaarndu
ma-n-maa	ka-nyarr=rnaarna-^{k}warndu
3m-DEF-3mREF	3a-1px=await-DU

We'll wait here for him

(b)
Kawarro	wali	aaya	ngamba	ke
ka-^{b}warr-a=^{b}wu	wali	aaya	ngamba	kee
3a-3p-EP=hit	PERF	3aREF	now	3wREF

They're going to kill him soon

(c)
Marreya	nganngunungu,	ngurru	maa	barnmarnja	kangarnaarna
marreya	ngan-ngun=nu-ng	ngurru	maa	barnmarnja	ka-nga-rnaarna
sick	1-SJTV=be-PRES	here	3mREF	doctor	3a-1=await

If I get sick I'll wait right here for the doctor

(d)
Wunu	kaarri	ngarrkunyanungu,	ngani	nyini	kubaje?
wunu	kaarri	ngarr-ngun-nya=nu-ng	ngani	nyini	kuN-^{b}warr-nya=yi
3wDEF	3pNEG	1pin-SJTV-EP=be-PRES	what	until	VCOMP-3p-EP=do

When we're all gone, what are they going to do then?

In (5.43c & d) the time reference of the main clause is relative to that of the subordinate clause, such that the subordinate clauses constitute premises sufficient for the occurrence of the main clause events.

5.4.5 (v) enablement

Aorist verbs may also denote the semantics of a schema of enablement (Johnson 1987:47, 53). Enablement is a type of root modality, that is, a force originating in the physical, rather than the logical world. In discussing the lexicalization of enablement in the English modal verb *can*, Johnson (*ibid*:52) says,

> *Can* thus involves a sense of internal power or capacity to act. The actor is a source of energy sufficient to perform some action. Although *can* tends to assume an absence of restricting barriers, its primary focus is on potentiality or capacity to act.

This description also applies well to Worrorra tense-less and aspect-less indicative verb forms used in a root modal sense. This meaning is closely related to the epistemic sense in which these forms denote imminent future reference; indeed the distinction between the two senses is often less than sure. Nevertheless an opposition may be discerned in paradigmatic cases, between imminent reference and enablement. Aorist forms denoting enablement are shown in (5.44):

(5.44a) Majerrin kunganinja wurno-wurno
majerrin kuN-nga=ninja wurno-wurno
Mt.Hann 3w-1=look.at 3wDIST-3wDIST
I can see Mount Hann over there

(b) Dambeem mana marramnyaana nyirrkanangka mana
dambeem mana ma-rra-mnya=^{k}wana nyirr=^{k}wa-nangka mana
place 3mDEF 3m-2p-DD=keep 2p=NAR-DAT 3mDEF
You can keep this land to be your own

(c) Ngani kungenu wunu?
ngani kuN-nga=yi-nu wunu
what VCOMP-1=do-2DAT 3wDEF
What can I do for you?

(d) Inja kajarimu?
inja ka-ngarr-nya=rima
3aDEF 3a-1pin-EP=name
Can we say his name?

As the phonologically and semantically unmarked morphological category, the indicative mood has been employed in this chapter in order to illustrate some of the basic formal properties of Worrorra verbs, and the kinds of meanings (declarative and aorist) that are signalled by these forms. The semantics of other kinds of verbal modality in the language are explored in Chapter Eight.

Because argument indexation is so exhaustive in Worrorra, it functions frequently to refer elliptically to NPs that are not overtly stated, but which are recoverable either from previous discourse or from context. Indexation by inflexional or derivational morphology is the main reference-monitoring mechanism employed by the language; because inflexion is obligatory on all verbs, other referential systems such as switch reference are not required. The rigorousness of NP indexation on verbs marks Worrorra as a language of a particular type (or a particular 'linguistic system' in Foley & Van Valin's (1984:374) view). In this view languages are seen as gestalt systems, that is, as constellations of forms that collectively constitute semiotic apparati that are themselves of greater significance than the sum of their component parts. Systems of voice opposition, gender, pivoting, switch-reference and switch-function determine the nature of such apparati, and hence their type. In Foley & Van Valin's terms *(ibid:*361) Worrorra is an example of a language employing an elaborate gender system (§4.1). Such systems are said characteristically to imply the absence of switch reference, the absence of voice oppositions and the absence of pivots from a language. Nevertheless Worrorra does have a voicing opposition, as well as a reference-monitoring morpheme in order class [5]. More importantly, it is the case that although the linguistic type to which Worrorra conforms is characterized as one of elaborate gender, gender marking is only a part of the system of agreement-class indexation. And it is this system of agreement-class indexation, rather than gender only, that constitutes the elaboration and delicacy by means of which the language achieves its semiotic function.

Six: adjectives and inalienable nouns

In undertaking an act of reference, a speaker must fulfil at least two conditions (Searle 1969, Silverstein 1986); the first consists of denoting a type of referent, and the second of identifying a particular instance of such a type. A nominal expression therefore includes a simple noun as well as some referential extension of it, in order to pick out, among all the instances of a particular denotatum that may exist in the world, just which instance or set of instances may be uniquely intended. Extensions of this sort are typically created by way of co-reference, which consists of a relationship between a word used to denote a type of thing in the world, and other words or morphemes that are dependent upon it for their referential value.

In this chapter and elsewhere the term 'noun phrase' or 'NP' will be used fairly informally to refer to any nominal expression, the tokens of which depend for their reference on a noun (lexical or derived) acting as the syntactic head of that expression. The literature on non-configurationality, discontinuous NPs and constituency generally in Australian languages is considerable (see, eg, Austin & Bresnan 1996 and references therein), and no more than a rather loose and informal characterization of this phrase type will be attempted here.

In Worrorra, agreement morphology is used to signal coreference. In this chapter we will look at adjectives and other more or less adjective-like or nominal expressions, and particularly at the ways in which agreement occurs between head nouns and their referential extensions. As Nichols (1986:57-58) puts it, 'the function of the morphology of government, agreement, cross-reference etc, is to identify syntactic relations by appropriately marking either the head ... or the dependent.' Dependent adjectives in Worrorra are marked in agreement with their heads (§6.2.1), while inalienable nouns are phrasal heads which are marked in agreement with their dependents (§6.3). Members of a third lexical category of derived nouns obligatorily include agreement-class affixes in their construction, without being dependent on any head, and without themselves needing to have any dependent (§6.2.3). The function of those affixes in this case is not to signal agreement, but to index meanings constitutive of a particular denotation. And in this case no syntactic relations are identified by these now derivational affixes, in a category that is formally indistinguishable from that of adjectives.

6.1 Agreement-class indices

In Worrorra coreferentiality is signalled by the indexation of the agreement class of one constituent upon another (§4.1). Nominal types defined by this morphological pattern include adjectives, derived nouns and inalienable nouns (this chapter), and pronouns and demonstratives (Chapter Seven).

The combination of root lexemes with agreement-class indices in Worrorra represents arguably one of the most productive morphologies observable anywhere. If any one feature of Worrorra were to be selected to characterize the language in general typological terms, it would be the productive capacity of its derivational morphology. This amounts to an acknowledgement of the role of what are sometimes referred to as elaborate gender systems (eg Foley & Van Valin 1984:373), but which in the case of Worrorra is really an elaborate system of agreement-class marking. Such productivity allowed the Revd J R B Love to coin words for 'apostle,' 'disciple,' 'elect' (ie 'chosen ones'), 'tempter,' 'vision' and so on from Worrorra lexemes without needing to resort to English words. It is a process complicated by phonological cluster assimilations that occur at both the left- and right-hand boundaries of the root morpheme involved, and by occasional irregularities in the combination specifications of root morphemes. Root lexemes and agreement-class indices are combined analogically, producing an exhaustive referential system with reflexes in most lexical categories. The sheer productivity of the resulting system gives evidence of the efficacy of analogy or pattern-association as a cognitive process in morphology.

Worrorra derivational agreement-class affixes are displayed in Table 6.1 below:

Table 6.1: derivational agreement-class indices

	PREFIXES	SUFFIXES
1	nga-	-Ø, -u
2	ngun-	-Ø, -u
3a	i-, a-	-ya, -i, -iya, -Ø
3f	nyi(N)-	-nya
3w	ØN-, ᵏwuN-	-u
3m	ma-	-ma
1pin	ngarr-	-Ø, -u
1px	arr-	-Ø, -u
2p	nyirr-	-Ø, -u
3p	arr-	-ya, -i, -iya

The affixes in Table 6.1 function derivationally by enabling root morphemes to move between agreement categories, and thus to create new lexical forms. Observe the outcomes of this process in the examples in (6.1):

(6.1a) Jakarri wunu Mayakarrima mana
ØN=yakarri wunu ma=yakarri-ma mana
3w=other 3wDEF 3m=other-3m 3mDEF
The next day *Another place*

(b) Larlangkarrama Irlarlangkarra
rlarlangkarra-ma i-rlarlangkarra
sea-3m 3a-sea
The sea *Salt-water crocodile*

(c) Aarrinja Nyingkarrinjinya
a=ᵏwarrinja nyiN=ᵏwarrinja-nya
3a=human 3f=human-3f
Aboriginal man *Aboriginal woman*

(d) Nyungujaja Ingujarri
nyiN=ngujarr-nya i=ngujarr-i
3f=new.born-3f 3a=new.born-3a
Baby girl *Baby boy*

(e) Loolim Nyiloolinya
looli-ma nyi=looli-nya
PATRICLAN.NAME-3m 3f=PATRICLAN.NAME-3f
Loolim (clan country) *Woman of Loolim*

(f)   Maai   Maayinya   Maaya
      (preverbal infinitive)   maai-nya   maai-ya
                                  mourn-3f   mourn-3a
      Undergo ritual mourning   *Bereaved woman*   *Bereaved man*

(g)   Ngunmeembu   Wumeembiya
      ngun-Ø=meembu   ᵏwuN=meembu-ye
      2-3/1=show   3w=show-MID
      I show you   *Sign*

(h)   Ke   Maa
      ØN=ᵏwaya   ma=ᵏwa(ya)
      3w=REF   3m=REF
      That (event)   *There (that place)*

(i)   Wungkurru   Wungkurri   Wungkuja
      wungkurr-u   wungkurr-i   wungkurr-nya
      sacred-3w   sacred-3a   sacred-3f
      Sacred pool   *Mythical Ancestor*   *Rock Python*

(j)   Ngawaaya   Ngawaanya   Ngawaama
      ngawaa-ya   ngawaa-nya   ngawaa-ma
      el.sib/fa.fa-3a   el.sib/fa.fa.si-3f   el.sib/fa.fa-3m
      Elder brother   *Elder sister*   *Clan estate*

The prefixes are largely homophonous with the series-2 optative NP indices shown in Table 8.4 in §8.1.1. Discussion of the morphophonology of these shapes is to be found in that section.

For the most part, agreement class indexation is the only way in which lexical root morphemes can acquire utterable form. In doing so, a root morpheme also acquires membership of one or other of the ten Worrorra agreement classes,[41] and it is in this sense that agreement-class indexation is obligatory on derived lexemes. Their derivational function, therefore, makes of this set of indices a productive referential tool, with the power to project all kinds of underlying forms into all ten agreement classes, with lexical consequences as evidenced by (6.1a,b,e,i & j) above in particular. This system ensures that agreement class is indexed on the vast majority of dependent lexemes, and that the co-references of nominal expressions can be stated precisely in terms of ten denotational categories. An important corollary of such an exhaustive indexing system is that most dependent forms may be used anaphorically to substitute for the heads of their phrases (eg example 6.1a).

6.1.1 Prefixes

Worrorra has nine agreement class prefixes that attach to lexical root morphemes. With one case of syncretism, these prefixes refer to the ten agreement classes described in §4.1. The prefixes are formally and functionally analogous to the inflexional NP indices displayed in Table 5.1 in §5.3.1, and the two sets of forms are clearly reflexes of each other. As well as signalling agreement class upon adjectives, derived nouns, inalienable nouns, pronouns and demonstratives, their series-2 inflexional counterparts are found on subjunctive verbs and on finite verbs in optative mood (§8.1.1).

Derivational/inflexional series-2 prefixes differ formally from their inflexional series-1 counterparts with respect to three agreement classes only: those of the unmarked macrogender

---

[41] Actually this is not strictly true: adjectives may lose agreement-class indexation when functioning as preverbal infinitives (ie with an adverbial function) in complex predicates. See sentence examples (11.26) and (11.27) in §11.3.3 and discussion.

(masculine and celestial) and third person plural. Note that the 1px and 3p indices are syncretized, producing a morpheme that bears only the grammatical features [+NUM, –II]. Where the morphology does not distinguish between 1px and 3p functions, the morphemes at issue are glossed *px* 'plural exclusive.' The only grammatical features distinguishing plural agreement classes here are [I] and [II], with [II] the higher-ranking feature, as shown in Figure 6.1:

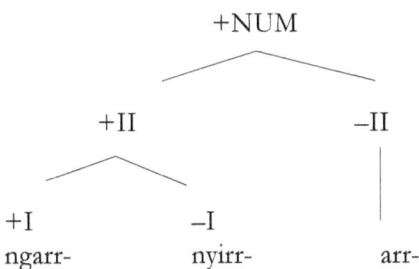

Figure 6.1: feature specifications of plural derivational prefixes

6.1.2 Suffixes

As well as the derivational agreement-class prefixes shown in Table 6.1, there is a further set of suffixes which are found only on members of certain lexical categories. For any given agreement class, the affixes shown in Table 6.1 commonly occur together on the same root morpheme, although a number of derived forms are found with only the prefixes. A small subset of adjectives are found with suffixes only; that is to say that they do not occur with prefixes. The morphophonolgy of derived forms is not straightforward, and the following points may be noted about the suffixes in Table 6.1 above:

(i) The 3a and 3p suffixes are commonly *-i* or *-iya* after /rr/, these two forms being in free variation. One common root lexeme, =*yakarri* 'other, different' has a 3a suffix *-a: iyakarra* 'other (masc).'

(ii) Suffixes on participant forms are all /-Ø/ or epenthetic *-u*. The epenthetic nature of this vowel becomes clear when we compare two derived forms, one with a phonemic final *-u*, =^{b}*wulku* 'first-born child,' and another with an epenthetic final vowel, =*warr(u)* 'wrong, bad; sick.' The form =*warr* is slightly irregular in that the initial /w/ does not harden. Also the initial /^{b}w/ in =^{b}*wulku* does not harden after /rr/ (rule 11). These shapes are shown in Table 6.2. In these paradigms the participant suffix may be said to be /-Ø/ on =^{b}*wulku*. The epenthetic *-u* on =*warr* disappears in the presence of suffixes on third person forms (eg *nyiwaja*), whereas this does not happen with =^{b}*wulku* (eg *nyimbulkunya*).

Table 6.2: derivational paradigms
(1) =^{b}*wulku* 'first-born child'

1	ngawulku	|nga=^{b}wulku-Ø|	*I'm the eldest*
2	ngunbulku	|ngun=^{b}wulku-Ø|	*you're the eldest*
3a	iwulku	|i=^{b}wulku-Ø|	*eldest son*
3f	nyimbulkunya	|nyiN=^{b}wulku-nya|	*eldest daughter*
3w	wumbulku	|^{k}wuN=^{b}wulku-u|	*it's the eldest*
3m	mawulkuma	|ma=^{b}wulku-ma|	*it's the eldest*
1pin	ngarrwulku	|ngarr=^{b}wulku-Ø|	*we're the eldest*
1px	arrwulku	|arr=^{b}wulku-Ø|	*we're the eldest*
2p	nyirrwulku	|nyirr=^{b}wulku-Ø|	*you're the eldest*
3p	arrwulkuya	|arr=^{b}wulku-ya|	*the eldest ones*

(2) =*warr* 'bad, sick'

1	ngawarru	|nga=warr-u|	*I'm bad/unwell*
2	nguwarru	|ngu(n)=warr-u|	*you're bad/unwell*
3a	iwarriya	|i=warr-iya|	*he's bad/unwell*
3f	nyiwaja	|nyi=warr-nya|	*she's bad/unwell*
3w	warru	|ØN=warr-u|	*it's bad/unwell*
3m	mawarrba	|ma=warr-ma|	*it's bad/unwell*
1pin	ngarrwarru	|ngarr=warr-u|	*we're bad/unwell*
1px	arrwarru	|arr=warr-u|	*we're bad/unwell*
2p	nyirrwarru	|nyirr=warr-u|	*you're bad/unwell*
3p	arrwarriya	|arr=warr-iya|	*they're bad/unwell*

Finally, note how the near homonymity of the 3a and 3p suffixes unites these two classes as essentially unmarked, default categories, and which are, as it turns out, both 'melting pot' categories in terms of markedness and gender resolution (see §4.1.6 (i) and §9.4.2).

In order to illustrate how this referential system works, it will be useful to consider a lexical category referred to briefly at the beginning of Chapter Four, as that of adjectives.

6.2 Adjectives and derived nouns

Adjectives and derived nouns constitute a single formal category in Worrorra, but the two types are distinguishable on semantic grounds. Formally, both classes consist of root lexemes affixed by the derivational morphemes shown in Table 6.1. This means that the same root lexeme may appear in different agreement categories, with different referential meanings.

6.2.1 Adjectives

Adjectives in Worrorra may be characterized by means of two orthogonal sets of parameters, formal and functional. The formal parameter reflects the amount of morphology displayed by any given form:
  (i) simplex underived forms (*simplex* forms)
  (ii) forms with derivational suffixes only (*suffixial* forms)
  (iii) forms with full derivational affixation (*affixial* forms)
The functional parameters reflect the notional lexical categories involved:
  (i) adjectives
  (ii) passive participles
  (iii) derived nouns
Love (1934:29) notes that 'uninflected [ie simplex] adjectives are rare.' It would appear that the great majority of adjectives in Worrorra are derived; there is however a smallish class of underived, simplex forms.

The semantic domains into which adjectives may be divided (eg Dixon 1982:16) do not appear to be correlated with their morphological type. For instance the domain 'colour' is spread across all morphological types:

SIMPLEX	SUFFIXIAL	AFFIXIAL
jarlewa 'red'	dubudubulya 'red (masc)'	=roro 'white'
wakumaada 'black'		
rowa 'white'		

Other semantic domains show similar morphological diversity:

(i) Words for relative location or position include *bale* 'behind, last' (simplex) and *bulaka* 'middle' (simplex), but the suffix -*ᵏwurle* or the affixial form =*ᵏwurle* is used for 'first.' The simplex adverb *marnngale* 'in front' is a reflex of the inalienable noun =*marnngalema mana* 'chest.'

(ii) Words for 'strong, powerful' are in different morphological categories: *darranku* (suffixial), =*yulwarra* (affixial) and =*yurrul(ba)* (affixial).

(iii) The domain of dimension includes *birdeen* 'small' (suffixial) and =*raarreya* 'big' (affixial), as well as *karranken* 'extended' (simplex) and =*yawu* 'short' (affixial).

(iv) The domain of speed is denoted by forms that are essentially adverbial; *abeerla* 'slow, quiet' (simplex) may be used as an adjective but is more usually an adverb, and its adverbial function may be indexed syntactically by its co-occurrence with *maa* 'CONTINUOUS' as *abeerla maa* 'slowly.' Words for 'fast' or 'quick' are all adverbial: *mayakirrkam* 'quickly,' *bulumba* (preverb) '(move) fast, (be) quick' and the preverbal suffix -*mirri* 'quickly.' The adverb *mana-manangarri* 'quickly' is composed of *mana-mana* (3mDEF-3mDEF) 'right here' (§7.3.1) + -*ngarri* 'RELATIVIZING.'

(v) Human propensity adjectives are morphologically diverse, and include the affixial forms =*malala* 'handsome, personable,' =*manngulaaya* 'inoffensive, meek, quiet,' =*ᵏwawiya* 'pleasant (of food or people),' and =*mara* 'murderous, hostile.' Words for 'strong, powerful' also fall into this category (see above). Also the simplex forms *karlikarli* 'sulky,' *yulu* 'stubborn,' *wirriwirriny* 'busy, preoccupied' and *rlulwa* 'generous,' and the suffixial form *wangala* 'senseless, silly.' Other human propensities are denoted by preverbs: *jukurl* '(be) happy,' *kadaada* '(be) tired, aching' *mungurr* 'argue, (be) jealous' and *ngarlingka* 'torment, (be) cruel.' And at least one form is an inalienable noun: =*yula inja* 'anger.'

(vi) A number of adjectives denoting human physical properties such as afflictions, ailments and oddities are also morphologically diverse, such as the simplex forms *aarra* 'sick,' *marreya* 'sick,' *ngarla* 'sick,' *wirrkeman* 'unburied' and the adjectives describing the head listed below. Affixial forms include =*albakurr* 'having a withered arm,' =*marreya* 'sick,' =*mawu* 'left-handed,' =*moy* 'left-handed,' =*murlooku* 'healthy, safe,' =*ᵏwurrinjal*[42] 'lame,' =*ᵇwarndaaja* 'lame' and =*man* 'dead.' Some adjectives of this type are derived from inalienable body-part nouns (§6.3) with an added suffix -*ja*. These include =*ᵏwambilija* 'blind' from =*ᵏwambul(u) wunu* 'eye' and =*ᵏwarlija* 'having a crippled arm' from =*ᵏwarluma mana* 'arm.'

A few semantic domains however are correlated with morphological form:

(vii) The two adjectives describing taste are simplex: *wulaba* 'sweet (=good-tasting)' and *kurlakurla* 'sour (=bad-tasting).'

(viii) Adjectives describing hair or its absence also appear to be simplex: *balaababa* 'bald,' *baraan* 'shaved (head)' and *marrurlu* 'grey (hair).

(ix) The semantic domain of age appears to contain only affixial forms: =*ngunali* 'new,' =*rnirndeerr* 'old' and =*rnungkule* 'ancient.'

(x) The domain of value contains affixial forms; =*niya* 'good' and =*warr* 'bad, wrong, sick.'

(xi) Physical-property adjectives appear to be mostly simplex: *maramara* 'hot,' *rnima* 'heavy,' *yangkarliba* 'limp' and *mirimiri* 'prickly, spiky.' *Aalingarri* 'soft' is a suffixial form derived by the suffix -*ngarri* 'RELATIVIZING.' Also in this category are the sensation preverbs *imaya* 'cold' and *yali* 'cold.' However at least one physical property adjective is based on the inalienable body-part noun =*ᵏwarluma mana* 'arm:' =*ᵏwarlinjarri* 'branching, spreading' (typically used to refer to the way in which tuber-bearing roots spread out underground).

(xii) Some important abstract concepts are realized as affixial adjectives, including: (a) =*rnora* 'be without (something), have none (of something),' as in *ngarnora* (|nga=rnora| [1=have.not]) 'I haven't got any;' (b) =*yilem* 'with (someone) present, in (someone's) presence,' as in *iyilem* (|i=yilem| [3a=present]) 'in his presence, while he's here' (although the antonym *wurdun* '(be) absent, silent' is a preverbal infinitive); and (c) =*rnamaanya* 'private (of property), reserved, set aside,' which has third person reference only and does not accept agreement-class suffixes, as seen in (6.2a):

---

[42] =*ᵏwurrinjal* 'lame' is an irregular adjective. The initial consonant /ᵏw/ hardens to a nasal stop under progressive consonant harmony: *ngangurrinjal* (|nga=ᵏwurrinjal| [1=lame]) 'I am lame.'

(6.2a)   Wunu   motor-car   wurnamaanya   wali ke.
         wunu   motor-car   ᵏwuN=rnamaanya   wali ke
         3wDEF   car   3w=reserved   PM
         This car is reserved (for someone else's use).

(b)   Ngarnaarruba   marno   kamnyengkunaal.
         nga=rnaarruba   ma=rno   ka-mnya=ya-ngku-na-ᵏwaal
         1=AT.HOME.OF   3m=DIST   3a-DD=go-EP-PAST-hither
         He came around to my place.

There is however a plural form *ardamaaya* (|arr=rnamaa-ya| [3p=reserved-PL]). While morphologically an inalienable noun (§6.3) the form *=rnaarruba mana* 'at the home of X, at X's place'[43] belongs here as well; its terrestrial gender marks it as a locational adverb, used in expressions such as *ngarnaarruba* 'at/to my place,' seen above in (6.2b).

From the foregoing it can be seen that the set of simplex adjectives shows a random scatter across a wide range of semantic domains. Some simplex adjectives are derived from reduplicated simplex noun stems, for example *manjumanju* 'windy' from *manjuma mana* 'wind' and *maramara* 'hot' from *marangunya nyina* 'the sun.'

Some simplex forms may also function as nouns by zero derivation, for example *mamaa* 'secluded' (adjective)/'initiate' (masculine noun), *barnmarn* 'medicinal' (adjective)/'sorceror' (masculine noun) and *wungkurr* 'sacred' (adjective)/'sacred pool' (celestial noun). Other simplex adjectives may also function as preverbal infinitives (§11.2): *joy* 'famous,' *rdarlurn* 'looming,' *jukurl* 'happy,' *jilibeerd* 'closed' and quite a number of others. Although affixial adjectives may lose agreement morphology when functioning as preverbal infinitives (§11.3.3), this loss appears to be restricted to that specific context. There is however at least one lexeme which can occur as a member of two morphological categories as an adjective: *marreya* (simplex)/*=marreya* (affixial) 'sick.'

Suffixial forms are an even smaller category than simplex forms, and include *wangala* 'senseless, silly, confused; lost,' *dubudubulu* 'red' and *birdeen* 'small.' Also in this category are forms derived by -*ngarri* or -*ngarra* 'REL' (§10.6.2 (i)) such as *raarrkarri* 'clean' (from preverb *braarr* 'clean, clear'), *aawangarri* 'open' (from *aawa* 'open') and *maramarangarri* 'hot' (from *maramara* 'hot'). Forms derived by -*ngarri* are underlyingly nominal: -*ngarri* is essentially a derivational morpheme that derives surface adjectives and sometimes adverbs; so *bulakangarri* (|bulaka-ngarri| [middle-REL]) 'the one(s) in the middle,' *wijingarra* (|wiji-ngarra| [boil-REL]) 'the one with boils, ie the spotted quoll,' *mirimiringarrinya* (|mirimiri-ngarri-nya| [thorny-REL-3f]) 'the thorny one, ie the echidna' and *yalingarri* (adverb) (|yali-ngarri| [cold-REL]) 'early in the morning.'

Two adjectives exhibit suppletive plural forms; these are *birdeen* 'small' (suffixial) and *=ᵏwujal* 'raw, unripe' (affixial). Their morphology is displayed below:

Table 6.3: adjective paradigms: suppletion

	birdeen 'small'		*=ᵏwujal* 'raw, unripe'	
1	birdeen(u)	|birdeen(-u)|		
2	birdeen(u)	|birdeen(-u)|		
3a	birdeenja	|birdeen-ya|	iwujalya	|i=ᵏwujal-ya|
3f	birdeenya	|birdeen-nya|	nyingkujalja	|nyiN=ᵏwujal-nya|
3w	birdeenu	|birdeen-u|	wungkujalu	|ᵏwuN=ᵏwujal-u|
3m	birdeenma	|birdeen-ma|	mawujalama	|ma=ᵏwujal-a-ma|
PL	beewurdu		arrangkaya	

Some root morphemes may be suffixed with -*waa*- 'PERSONIFYING' when referring to human and personified human denotata. This shape is another derivational morpheme which may itself take

---
[43] Cf the meaning of French *chez*, Latin *apud*.

derivational suffixes, 3a and 3p *-ya*, 3f *-nya* and 3m *-ma*, producing the forms *-waaya* for masculine singular and all plural human references, *-waanya* for feminine singular reference and *-waama* for terrestrial (cf 6.1j and Table 6.7). Examples are *bulmarrwaaya* 'squashed, flattened' and *marnduwaanya* (|marndu-waa-nya| [stomach-PERS-3f]) 'pregnant.'

6.2.2 Passive participles

Passive participles in Worrorra appear to be forms derived from verb roots with the middle-voice suffix *-ye* added in form-order class [8]. Love made extensive use of these forms in translating Christian terms into Worrorra, but no examples of them occur in unelicited contexts in all of the 150-odd pages of the Worrorra database. And so we are faced with a problem: were these forms merely coined by Love out of a highly productive morphology to create words that would be comprehensible if not natural to his flock? Or are they forms that are simply unlikely to occur in the narrative, predicating-and-referring style of speech of which the database is mainly composed? There is some evidence to suppose that the latter might be the case, and that these forms really do represent an original feature of the morphology, although one whose resulting meanings were rather more 'fixed' or lexically frozen than is implied by Love's account:

> Worrorra speech does not include many abstract ideas. Abstract nouns, however do occur. On examination these are found to be, ... The neuter-wuna form of a verb in the future passive ... In this manner, abstract nouns may be coined from the corresponding verb, or less often adjective. Thus, if the language has a verb, or an adjective, containing the thought required to be expressed by a noun, this can be intelligibly given. (Love 1934:27)

As examples, Love cites *wun'djo:rie* 'hatred' from *=yora* 'hate' (underlying |^{k}wuN=yora-ye| [3w=hate-MID]), and *umi'imbai'e (wumeembiya)* 'sign' from *=meembu* 'show' (underlying |^{k}wuN=meembu-ye| [3w=show-MID]). This quotation from Love illustrates very well the missionary concern with linguistics as essentially a science of translation, from English into some target vernacular. This is the opposite of modern linguistic endeavour, which is concerned to account for what is there, rather than to create what is not there. Specifically, Love was interested in coining abstract nouns by morphological derivation from verb roots, and so he lists among others *ardjalgai'eja* 'hidden things' (Love 1939b:53) and *wundjai'elgai'e* 'secret' (1939b:95), both from the transitive verb root *=yalke* 'hide;' *adbi'imbai'eja* 'signs' (1941a:3) and *imi'imbai'e* 'teacher' (1939b:113) from *=meembu* 'show;' *adburi'eja* 'elect, chosen ones' (1939b:35) from *=mra* 'gather,' and *ar'didji'eja* 'vision' (1939b:124, 1941a:4) from *=ninja* 'look at.' The question remains as to the extent to which he was simply making use of a derivational process already available, or forcing the grammar into forms and meanings which it had not previously taken.

A number of these forms are recoverable today by elicitation, although with meanings somewhat different from those given by Love. As an example, note the following partial paradigm of the root *=meembiya* '(still) recognizable,' in Table 6.4:

Table 6.4: participial paradigm

1	ngameembiya	|nga=meembu-ye|	[1=show-MID]
2	ngunmeembiya	|ngun=meembu-ye|	[2=show-MID]
3a	imeembiyeya	|i=meembu-ye-ya|	[3a=show-MID-3a]
3f	nyimeembiyanya	|nyiN=meembu-ye-nya|	[3f=show-MID-3f]
3w	wumeembiya	|^{k}wuN=meembu-ye|	[3w=show-MID]
3m	mameembiya	|ma=meembu-ye|	[3m=show-MID]
3p	arrbeembiyeya	|arr=meembu-ye-ya|	[3p=show-MID-3p]

These forms have meanings such as: *nyimeembiyanya* 'she's still the same' and *arrbeembiyeya* 'they haven't changed much,' etc, and are also used in expressions such as that shown in (6.3):

(6.3)   Ngunminguma   mameembiya
        ngun=minguma   ma=meembu-ye
        2=face   3m=recognizable-MID
        You haven't changed (Lit: 'your face is still recognizable')

In (6.3) the participle *mameembiya* modifies the inalienable noun =*minguma mana* 'face, nose,' and so shows terrestrial agreement. Love recorded these forms as (3w) *umi'imbai'e* 'sign,' (3p) *adbi'imbai'eja* 'signs' and (3a) *imi'imbai'e* 'teacher,' showing both phonological and semantic discrepancies with modern forms. The meanings that Love lists for these words are based directly on the meaning of the root verb =*meembu* 'show;' that is to say that Love's meanings are predictable from the meaning of the root verb. So a sign is 'that which is shown,' and a teacher is 'he who shows.' The modern meaning, however ('recognizable' or something like it), while clearly related semantically to the root verb, is certainly not predictable from it; that is to say that the derived forms represent new lexical entries.

The phonological discrepancies are more involved, and relate to the tension in phonology between allophonic and morphophonemic rules. It is clear from Love's notes that he was well aware of the underlying morphophonemic processes that drive Worrorra grammar (cf, eg, Love 1934:102). The shapes of the unsuffixed (participant and non-human macrogender) forms shown in Table 6.4 allow us to posit a root morpheme =*meembiya* 'recognizable.' It is also clear that the verbs that underlie the participial forms are transitive, but have lost an argument in the process of their derivation, suggesting that some kind of valency-reducing process is occurring. As far as Love would have been concerned this would have involved the loss of either a subject argument (*umi'imbai'e* 'sign') or an object argument (*imi'imbai'e* 'teacher'). Added directly to the underlying verb root is the segment |-ya|, formally and apparently functionally reminiscent of the middle morpheme -*ye*. It is likely that Love recognized the syllable -*ya* as a reflex of the middle (his passive) morpheme, and treated it as an allophonic variant of -*ye* rather than as a phonological reflex of the morpheme |-ye|. This approach would have been supported by the shape of the morpheme when further suffixed by -*ya* (masculine and plural), which is -*ye*. This phenomenon however is not related to the syllable's morphophonemic shape, being simply an instance of open vowel fronting and raising between palatal glides:

$$|a| \longrightarrow e \ / \ y \_ y \quad \text{eg imeembi}\mathbf{yey}\text{a}$$

Hence Love represents the middle reflex consistently as [-*i'e*] in his transcriptions, probably because having correctly recognized this segment as a variant of the middle morpheme, he collapsed the levels of description involved.

Another middle form is *adijiyeya* (|arr=ninja-ye-ya| [3p=look.at-MID-3p]), which essentially refers to a recollection, dream or some other non-mundane experience (a 'calling up') of deceased people, or of people you haven't seen for a long time and whom you want to see. This is a more specific modern translation than Love's 'vision,' and again reflects a more lexically idiosyncratic derivation, and one less predictable than simply 'vision.' And so there is more than one possible interpretation of the sentence offered by Love in 1941a:4:

(6.4)   Adijiyeya   mara   kaangona.
        arr=ninja-ye-ya   mara   kaarr-nga=^{b}wu-na
        3p=look-MID-3p   see   3p-1=hit-PAST
I saw a vision /
I saw/remembered/thought about that/those old (deceased) person/people.

6.2.3 Derived nouns

Most adjectival lexemes are derived forms which, in terms of the range of semantic types they display, grade imperceptibly into a notional category of derived nouns. Morphologically, derived forms constitute a single, unitary category with denotata ranging from prototypically adjectival states such as =*nija* 'good' and =*warr* 'bad' through to prototypical nouns such as *iyarnda* 'little boy,' *ngawmalenya* 'my little sister' and *nyinjorinya* 'widow.' At first glance, this provisional distinction among derived forms in semantics would seem to be an entirely etic one, not able to be justified in the morphology. The last three examples given above have underlying forms =*yarnda* 'infant,' =*w(a)male* 'younger sibling' and =*yoru* 'widowed,' so that other forms may be produced as well; eg. *nyinjarndanya* |nyiN=yarnda-nya| [3f=infant-3f] 'little girl,' *ngarrwmalenya* |ngarr=wmale-nya| [1pin=jnr.sibling-3f] 'our little sister' and *iyoru* |i=yoru| [3a=widowed] 'widower,' and so on for all of the ten agreement classes in the language. Nevertheless, while derived adjectives and derived nouns are morphologically indistinguishable, there do appear to be emic (language internal) grounds for making lexical-semantic distinctions among derived forms.

Derived forms may occur in apposition to each other, as seen in (6.5):

(6.5) Iyarnda iniya
 i=yarnda i=niya
 3a=infant 3a=good
 A good little boy

The term *iniya* 'good (masc)' typically denotes a value state, in which state may be found people, artefacts, food and other substantive things. On the other hand *iyarnda* 'little boy' has as its core meaning, the denotation of a human being of a specific age. Although the root morphophoneme =*yarnda* 'young, infant' may also be applied to the young of animals, all surface shapes indexed for human macrogender agreement refer to humans by default, unless some specific animal reference is prominent in the context of a discourse. Semantically, then, we may say that the core denotation of *iyarnda* is essentially substantive, while that of *iniya* is not.

Syntactic headedness in the context of phrases like that shown in (6.5) is important in determining which of the forms, if either, is functioning typically, cross-linguistically, as a noun; that is as the non-anaphoric head of an NP in phrase structure. Phrases of the sort shown in (6.5) have at least two structural possibilities. One is that neither word is the phrasal head, both being dependent upon some other implied head noun, while the other possibility is that one of these words does function as a phrasal head, with the other serving as its modifier. Note how in (6.6a), the phrase in (6.5) may function as a predicate argument:

(6.6a) Iyarnda iniya kaarn kaningeerri.
 i=yarnda i=niya kaarn ka=ni-ng-eerri
 3a=infant 3a=good sing 3a=be-PRES-PROG
 A good little boy is singing.

(b) Angkuyu kaarn kaningeerri? Iyarnda.
 angkuyu kaarn ka=ni-ng-eerri i=yarnda
 who sing 3a=be-PRES-PROG 3a=infant
 Who is singing? A little boy.

In (6.6b) the proposition in (6.6a) is questioned and answered. In some constrained context the answer could be *awa iniya inja* 'the good one,' set about with foregrounding ('nominalizing') pronouns (see §17.2.2, §17.4); but without fairly detailed circumstantial constraints, *iyarnda* serves as the normal, unmarked denotation of a substantive entity, not *iniya*.

Considerations of this sort enable us to make a distinction among derived forms, between terms denoting physical entities that may also serve as syntactic heads of NPs, and words denoting attributes, states and qualities that modify NP heads. Our ability to draw such a distinction is consequent upon the semantic properties of the root lexemes concerned. Nevertheless the boundary between the lexical-semantic categories of derived adjectives and derived nouns is nothing if not fuzzy. What we end up with is an opposition between typically nominal forms on the one hand and typically adjectival forms on the other, with a good deal of material intervening.

Derivational morphology may sometimes be used simply as a tool for making lexical-semantic distinctions, without regard to the denotational properties of the agreement categories themselves. As an example, note the abstract root form =*yawarra* 'shiny, edible fluid; juice, grease.' This lexeme has a masculine shape *iyawarra inja* 'juice from fruit,' a celestial shape *wunjawarra wunu* 'grease off meat,' and a mass plural shape *ajawarre anja* 'lots of grease off meat' (see §4.2.2).

6.2.4 Social categories

Most, but not all, of the material at the nominal end of the scale denotes social categories of human beings. These include the bereavement categories =*yoru* 'widowed' and =*ye* 'orphaned,' the referents of which are clearly nominal (eg *nyinjorinya* 'widow'). Age-grade terms also constitute a set of social categories: =*ngujarr* 'new born,' =*yarnda* 'infant,' =*marurr* 'young adolescent' and =*rnayurr* 'adult.' This latter root has as well a metaphoric or extended meaning, as 'elder, leader, boss.' Other social categories denoted by these forms are =*rnawurrkunja* 'enemy' and =*ᵏwarrinja* 'human.'

A number of important kinship nouns are derived: =*ᵇwarnkarra* 'grown-up child of some parent,' =*ᵇwulku* 'first-born child of some parent,' =*w(a)male* 'younger sibling' and =*ᵏwurlu*/=*ᵏwurla* 'man's son, woman's brother's son, conceived of as a member of her patriline.' This last is an irregular, verb-like form, which Love (1941b:108, 1939b:27, 103) describes as a verb meaning 'beget' (see also comments in §7.7, §13.1.1, §18). It contains a subjunctive morpheme and indexes both propositus in agent position, and referent in undergoer position, as shown in the examples in (6.7):

(6.7a) Ingkorlu
        i-Ø-ngka=ᵏwurlu
        3a-3-SJTV='beget'
        His son

(b)   Inganngunyorlu
        i-ngan-ngun-nya=ᵏwurlu
        3a-1-SJTV-EP='beget'
        My son

(c)   Ingkaarrkurlu
        i-ngka-ᵇwarr=ᵏwurlu
        3a-SJTV-3p='beget'
        Their son

These terms locate a boy in his father's (ie his father's father's) clan or patriline (among his *abaabiya* 'elder brothers,' see Chapter 18). Love offers an example of a form meaning 'my daughter' in 1939b:27, but no mention of this is made in Love 1941b:108, the words based on =*ᵏwurlu* being given as 'man's son.'[44] An important part of the meaning of =*ᵏwurlu*, however, is that it may also be used by women, when referring to their brothers' sons as members of their own patriline. For example the dual exclusive term *errkunyorlaarndu* in (6.8a) may be used by a woman talking to (vocative), or about her brother's son, in which case it indexes a tripartite relationship between a brother and sister and the brother's son. The trial inclusive form (6.8b), in turn, may be used by a woman talking to two of her brothers or sisters while referring to their brother's son:

(6.8a) Errkunyorlaarndu
        a-nyarr-ngun-nya =ᵏwurlu-ᵏwarndu
        3a-1px-SJTV-EP='beget'-DU
        Our (dual exclusive) 'son'

---

[44] While claiming that these are subjunctive forms (relativized forms, see §15.6.3), and offering the example *ingkorlu*, Love also gives non-relativized examples *kangorlu* (|ka-nga=ᵏwurlu| [3a-1='beget']) 'my son' and *nyingorlu* (|nyiN-nga=ᵏwurlu| [3f-1='beget']) 'my daughter' (1939b:27), as well as a number of other forms (1939b:103).

(b) Arrkunyorloorri
     a-ngarr-ngun-nya=ᵏwurlu-oorri
     3a-1pin-SJTV-EP='beget'-TRI
     Our (trial inclusive) nephew

As these terms may refer to the relationship between a woman and her brothers' sons, as well as to that between her brothers and their sons, the translations 'beget' and 'son' are not quite accurate. Nevertheless the forms of these Worrorra words clearly involve the root morpheme in some verbal or quasi-verbal function: some kind of semantically extended type of 'begetting.'

In terms of the set of necessary-and-sufficient conditions for external possession proposed by Payne & Barshi (1999), this construction is arguably not an instance of that syntactic type. Although the possessor is coded as a core argument (here subject) of a verb, the verb =ᵏ*wurlu* 'beget' requires a possessor subject in its argument frame.[45] This root is discussed further in §7.7 below.

Other quasi-verbal or gerund-like forms are derived from the intransitive root =ᵏ*wangkarre* 'SUBJECT'S image exists.' This root occurs only in present tense forms such as *ngaangkarrenga* (|nga=ᵏwangkarre-ng| [1=IMAGE.EXIST-PRES]) 'my picture is there.' The shape /nga/ at the end of the root is apparently a frozen present tense suffix. This verb appears as well in subjunctive shape, producing in effect an adjectival form, as in (6.9), with reference to a Wandjina painting:

(6.9)
Mana	barnjama	ingkaangkarrengama,	irnurnu	warndi
mana	barnjama	i-ngka=ᵏwangkarre-ng-a-ma	i=rnurnu	warndi
3mDEF	cave	3a-SJTV=image.exist-PRES-EP-3m	3a=hand	create

konama.
ØN-Ø-ngka=ᵇwu-na-ma
3w-3-SJTV=hit-PAST-3m
The cave where his picture is, where he painted his hands.

The second clause contains the inalienable noun =*rnurnu wunu* 'hand,' with indexation for a masculine singular dependent NP (see §6.3).

Worrorra society was traditionally in extended social contact with a number of other linguistically-defined groups, the largest of which appear to have been Ngarinyin and Wunambal (§1.3). The word Worrorra is invariant, and is used as an adjective and a noun, to denote the people, the society, the culture and the language of the region concerned. The term *Ngarinyin wunu* refers to the group of people who speak Ungarinyin as their first language, but other references are derived from the root form =*ngarinyin*. So, the Ungarinyin language is *Wungarinyinu wunu*, and Ngarinyin people are *Arrkarinyinja anja*. Likewise, *Wunambal wunu* is the group name for the people who live north of Worrorra country, but other terms are derived from the root =ᵏ*wunambal*. The Wunambal language, therefore, is *Wunambalu wunu*, and Wunambal-speaking people are *Arrkunambalya anja*. The allocation of the group names of these people to the celestial class indicates that the underlying principle by which these groups are defined is linguistic.

The names of the two Worrorra patrimoieties, *Arrbalarriya* (phonetic *Adbalarriya*) and *Arrwunarriya*, are derived from the roots =*malarr* and =ᵇ*wunarr* respectively (Table 6.5). These roots may contain an archaic plural marker in the phoneme /rr/, which is iconic of plurality in its trilled allophone (a series of repeated, audible beats of the tongue apex against the alveolum).[46] Note that this phoneme occurs at the end of all the language's plural NP indices and in none of the singular forms (§6.1). Factoring out this sound, and ignoring their status as root forms, we are left with *mala and *wuna. Love (1934)

---

[45] And is in this respect like verbs such as 'have' and 'own' which require a possessor in subject grammatical function.

[46] Capell & Coate (1984:105 et seq) discuss the widespread occurrence of /rr/ as a plural morpheme in the North Kimberley and Arnhem Land.

recorded the shape of the celestial definite article quite consistently as *wuna*, although I, just as consistently, heard it as *wunu*. Be that as it may, what we clearly have here are archaic cognates of the markers of the non-human macrogender, *mana* and *wunu* (§4.1.6). Love (1950:280) clearly states, 'I do not know any meaning for the moiety names; they are just the names of moieties.' Nevertheless Blundell (1976) records reference to the moiety names as *arbulari (Arrbalarri)* 'plains people' and *arungari (Arrwunarri)* 'rocky people,' terms that are congruent with the semantic analysis offered in §4.1.5. Blundell offers no discussion of these designations, however, and it could be, for instance, that they simply refer to the relative locations of certain patriclans on their traditional land. We need only note that in reckoning kinship, the Worrorra patrimoieties classify the world into two dynamically opposed (exogamous) groups. Such a cultural partition runs orthogonally to the biological male-female division, and the appropriate orthogonal classificatory apparatus (the non-human macrogender) is enlisted to label its members.

Table 6.5: patrimoiety terms

	=*malarr*	=*bwunarr*
1	ngamalarru	ngawunarru
2	ngunmalarru	ngunbunarru
3a	imalarri	iwunarri
3f	nyimalaja	nyimbunaja
3w	wumalarru	wumbunarru
3m	mamalarrba	mawunarrba
1pin	ngarrbalarru	ngarrwunarru
1px	arrbalarru	arrwunarru
2p	nyirrbalarru	nyirrwunarru
3p	arrbalarriya	arrwunarriya

Animals, places and plants, as well as people, are allocated to one or other of the two patrimoieties. This projects the root forms of the patrimoiety terms into all agreement classes, as shown in Table 6.5. In sentence example (6.10), Patsy is describing the patrimoiety affiliation of the sulphur-crested cockatoo *(kuyaarriya inja)*. With reference to its totemic status, the cockatoo, like other totemic beings, may be denoted in terms of its geographic affiliation, as *mamalarrba* '(belonging to) the land of (the people of) the Adbalarriya moiety,' as well as in terms of its own inherent masculine gender, as *imalarri*:

(6.10) Kuyaarriya   mamalarrba;   imalarri   kuyaarriya.
        kuyaarriya   ma=malarr-ma   i=malarr-i   kuyaarriya
        cockatoo.sp   3m=PATRIMOIETY-3m   3a=PATRIMOIETY-3a   cockatoo.sp
        The sulphur-crested cockatoo belongs to the Adbalarriya moiety.

People who spoke Worrorra as their first language were traditionally grouped in around about a dozen patrilineally-reckoned extended families or patriclans (Love 1935:230-231, Blundell & Layton 1978, Blundell 1980). These were exogamous, virilocal, patrilineal groups sociocentrically named for the country or territory in which they were located. Being exogamous, each clan belonged to one or other of the two patrimoieties. By Love's account, five clans belonged to the Arrbalarriya moiety, and five to the Arrwunarriya moiety. Consanguineal clan members all bore the same clan and moiety titles, as opposed to women who married into the clan, and who retained their own clan and moiety affiliations. Love's population estimate of 300 for Worrorra society as a whole at contact allows each patriclan c 25 members on average: this figure at least gives us an indication of the order of magnitude of the groups under discussion.

The patriclan appears to have been essentially an extended patrilineal family defined by descent, and by religious and emotional allegiance to a particular location. The underlyingly locational definition of clans is reflected in both the shape and gender of the word for 'patriclan:' =*rambim mana* (an inalienable noun, see §6.3). This word is clearly cognate with *dambeem mana* 'place.' Although in theory a clan could have been composed of a number of unrelated patrilines, in practice all members of a clan were probably descended from a common ancestor. Members referred to themselves collectively as *abáabiya* 'brothers,' or *abàabiyéya* 'sisters.' All members bore their clan as well as their patrimoiety titles, and upon marriage women retained both. Marriage appears to have been generally uxorilocal at first, then virilocal, that is, in the husband's clan territory, after a wife (and presumably her family) had gained confidence in her husband. Although on occasion men appear to have travelled fairly widely outside their clan territory, women and children were probably tied more closely to it. As Patsy says, speaking of her childhood before contact with Europeans:

(6.11)
Kaarri	waa	mayakarrima	bejengenya	kaarri,
kaarri	waa	ma=yakarri-ma	ba-nyarr-nya=[ya-nga]-yinya	kaarri
3pNEG	not	3m=other-3m	CFT-1px-EP=[go-TNS]-PAST	3pNEG

dambeema mawi.
place 3mNEG
We never used to go to other places.

In one case at least, that of *Arnngarrngoyu* (not listed in Love 1935), the name of a clan is phonologically unrelated to the name of the country it occupied: *Malamalorn mana* 'the Glenelg River.' However most clan titles *were* derived from the name of the country they occupied. The Prince Regent River, for example, *Malanduma mana*, was the home of a clan of the same name, whose titles were derived as shown below in Table 6.6.

The names and partial derivations of a few other clan countries are displayed in Table 6.7 for comparison. Note the variety of morphological patterns in this Table. The personifying suffix *-(ʷw)aaya* (feminine *-(ʷw)aanya*) is used typically do denote a person as coming from the place marked by the suffix.[47] Three of the terms in Table 6.7 use this suffix instead of derivational prefixes; Love (1934:30) also gives *Karnmanyawaaya* 'person from Kunmunya,' and the root *=mangurraama* takes this suffix as well as derivational prefixes. The gender of most clan countries is terrestrial, except for *Wurnbangku* which is celestial (see §4.1.4 (i)). The name *Meegrarlba* also appears as both *Grarl* and *Grarlya*. The people of *Yawijaba mana* 'the Montgomery Islands,' probably had patriclan status in Worrorra society – the islands are so small, they probably could not have supported more than a clan-sized group at most.

Table 6.6: Adbalandiya – the Prince Regent River clan

1	ngamalandu	1pin	ngarrbalandu
2	ngunmalandu	1px	arrbalandu
3a	imalandu	2p	nyirrbalandu
3f	nyimalandinya	3p	arrbalandiya
3w	wumalandu		
3m	mamalanduma		

Table 6.7: some patriclan terms

PLACE	FEMININE	MASCULINE	PLURAL
Meegrarlba mana	Nyeegrarlja	Igrarlya	Arrigrarlya
Loolim mana	Nyiloolinya	Iloola	Arrlooliya
Wurnbangku wunu	Wurnbangkuwaanya	Wurnbangkuwaaya	
Larrinyima mana	Larrinyuwaanya	Larrinyuwaaya	
Mamangurraama mana	Nyimangurraanya	Imangurraaya	
Yawijaba mana	Yawijibaanya	Yawijibaaya	

---

[47] Note also the related adjectives *bulmarr* 'prostrate' and *bulmarrwaaya* 'crushed, flattened;' and the noun *marnduma* 'stomach' and the adjective *marnduwaanya* 'pregnant.'

Animals and other significant things can be totemic emblems for particular clans, and such animals and things are said to 'represent' that clan, and may thereby have membership of it:

(6.12)
Ngurlandangarri	nyina	malyaawam	Wurnbangkuwaanya
ngurlandangarri	nyina	malyaawam	Wurnbangku-waa-nya
little.corella	3fDEF	REASON	CLAN.NAME-PERS-3f

bungajinangkerri;	nyangka	Wurnbangkuwaamaanya.
ba-kuN-ngarr=yi-nangka-eerri	nyangka	Wurnbangku-waa-maa-nya
CFT-VCOMP-1pin=do-DAT-PROG	3fNAR	CLAN.NAME-PERS-SPEC-3f

That's the reason why we call the little corella 'the Wurnbangku woman,' she belongs only to the land of Wurnbangku.

6.2.5 Pro-form burn-

The base form *burn-* (glossed PRO) serves as the all-purpose pro-form in the language, and takes agreement-class suffixes as shown in Table 6.8:[48]

Table 6.8: pro-form *burn-*

3a	burnja
3f	burnnya
3w	burnu
3m	burnma
3p	burnji

The pro-form is used in Worrorra as a substitute for nouns that a speaker is unable for the time being to remember, as in English, 'whatsit' or 'that thing.' It is also used to refer to amorphous or anonymous materials, such as are referred to by the nouns 'thing' or 'stuff' in English. Such materials may be dangerous, in which case the plural shape will be used with collective meaning, as seen in (6.13a) below.

The fact that the agreement class of the denotatum substituted for is obligatorily encoded on the pro-form, supports Silverstein's (1986:509) contention that in undertaking an act of reference, there are certain base-level, language-specific, denotational structures (eg in this case gender and number) that constitute preconditions for the successful accomplishment of such an act. Examples of the use of *burn-* are shown below:

(6.13a)
Burnji	anja	kaankarndenganangka	nyineemarnanya.
burnji	anja	kaarr-n-Ø=ᵏwarnde-nga-nangka	nyiN=neema-rnanya
3pPRO	3pDEF	3p-INV-3=place-PAST-DAT	3f=ear-LOC

He put a spell on her (lit: he put magic in her ears).

(b)
	Waa	burnu	bungkaajin,	kaarri.
	waa	burnu	ba-kuN-ᵇwarr=yi-n	kaarri
	not	3wPRO	CFT-VCOMP-3p=do-NON.P	3pNEG

They don't do that (listen properly) at all.

---

[48] The morphophonolgy of the pro-form burn- is as follows: |burn-ya| > *burnja,* |burn-nya| > *burnnya,* |burn-u| > *burnu,* |burn-ma| > *burnma,* |burn-yi| > *burnji.*

(c)
Aambulkarndu	wunu	karle	wayarl	kumiyena	wunu
a=ᵏwambul-ᵏwarndu	wunu	karle	wayarl	kuN=ma-ye-na	wunu
3a=eye-DU	3wDEF	then	clean	3w=get-MID-PAST	3wDEF

burnma,	kuma	mana.
3mPRO	gum	3mDEF

Their eyes were cleansed of that stuff, that gum.

In (6.13c) the speaker refers to *kuma mana* 'gum' by the terrestrial pro-form, *burnma*, but determines it with the celestial definite article, *wunu*. In the database the noun *kuma* 'gum, glue' behaves as if it could belong to both genders: Daisy makes switches of this sort more than once. In (6.13a) the 'stuff' referred to is sorcery, and gets plural/collective marking, on the proform and on the verb in undergoer position (cf. §4.2.2). The 'owner' ('her') of the locative adjunct (*nyineemarnanya* 'in her ears') is indexed on the verb as a non-subcategorized object (glossed DAT) (see §13.2.2 (iii)).

The celestial shape *burnu* substitutes for verbal or sentential constituents, as shown in (6.13b) above. In this case, reference is made to events by nominal forms; that is to say that events are reified as things (cf. §11.2.3 and §17.1.1). The form *burnu* is also used in complex predicates euphemistically to refer to dangerous, unpleasant, rude or embarrassing events or acts, the denotation of which the speaker would prefer not to have to utter (cf diffuse reference in §7.1). Some examples of this phenomenon are seen below in (6.14). Another example of this use of *burnu* is seen in (7.43b).

(6.14a)
Iwarndu	wunu	burnu	bungkenya.
i=ᵇwarndu	wunu	burnu	ba-kuN-Ø=yi-nya
3a=lower.arm	3wDEF	3wPRO	CFT-VCOMP-3=do-PAST

He broke his arm.

(b)
Larlangkarranyinim	burnu	ko
rlarlangkarra-nyini-ma	burnu	ka-Ø=ᵇwu
sea-until-3m	3wPRO	3a-3=hit

He perished at sea.

(c)
Ngani	kunjeeng?	Angkuyu	burnu	ngunbunerri?
ngani	kuN-nja=yi-ng	angkuyu	burnu	ngun-n-Ø=ᵇwu-na-eerri
what	VCOMP-2=do-PAST	who	3wPRO	2-INV-3=hit-PAST-PROG

What happened to you? Who did this to you?

(d)
Aaya	anguja,	burnu	kunjeeng?
aaya	anguja	burnu	kuN-nja=yi-ng
3aREF	what	3wPRO	VCOMP-2=do-PAST

What was that, did you fart?

6.2.6 Number and reduplication

This section deals with two separate but related phenomena. The first part looks at the way in which plural entities are encoded in singular agreement-class forms, and the second at the way in which singular agreement forms may signal plurality by way of phonological extensions to their root shapes.

<u>6.2.6 (i) number</u>
In §4.2.1 it was observed that plural marking is only available to human nouns and nouns referring to important animals, foods or artefacts; that is, to denotata that are highly animate. For other, less animate beings, singular forms are used to refer to just one instance, and also to a number of instances of such things. So:

inja manjawarra	*the* manjawarra *berry or the* manjawarra *berries*
wunu kayuku	*the stone or the stones*
mana angkam	*the bowl or the bowls*
nyina meerrinya	*the female crocodile or the female crocodiles*
mana mayarama	*the house, the houses, station or settlement*

It is as if the language treats all low-animate nouns the way English treats mass/food nouns such as *rice, honey, sugar, wine*. These forms may not take plural marking, as they do not refer to the kinds of things that are conceived of as being able to be counted. Similarly in Worrorra, it is as if low-animate nouns refer to entities that are not conceived of as being the kinds of things that warrant individuation beyond the identification of a single instance of such a thing.[49] It follows therefore that adjectives behave in the same manner: that is to say that for some less animate entity, singular adjectival agreement shapes are used to refer to both singular and plural occurrences of that entity. The phrases below use the adjective =*yakarri* 'other:'

inja karraki iyakarra	*the other bag or bags*
motor-car jakarri wunu	*the other car or cars*
mana mayaram mayakarrima	*the other house or houses*
nyina kambananya nyinjakarrinya	*the other shovel or shovels*

The third person plural shape of adjectives, then, is applied only to people and other things highly placed on a scale of animacy (which varies according to context). And in this case, of course, gender is neutralized in plural marking. The phrases below use the adjective =*raarreya* 'big:'

nyina nyangkanya nyirndaarreyinya	*the big girl*
anja nyangkaangkaya ardaarreya	*the big girls*
inja eeja iraarreya	*the big man*
anja eeja ardaarreya	*the big men*

Even an inherently plural adjective like =*raarrawa* 'many' requires singular forms with reference to low-animate denotata:

(6.15a) Anja   ardaarrawaaya
         anja   arr=raarrawa-waa-ya
         3pDEF   px=many-PERS-3p
         Many people

---

[49] On one recorded occasion when being bitten by ants, Patsy says in English, 'ants I got it.' Besides a typically Worrorra word order (noun+[verb+arg indices]), this expression shows a plural noun cross-referenced by a singular pronoun ('it').

(b)   Mamangkunu   rdaarrawa   wunu
        mamangkunu   ØN=raarrawa   wunu
        morning   3w=many   3wDEF
        Every morning/each morning

The demonstrative adjective =*n-ngal* 'these few, several, some' also requires singular forms with reference to low-animate (non-human) denotata:

koyoya inngalya	*several crocodiles*
marrirri wunngalu	*several red-winged parrots*
rdarrkenya nyinngalja	*several grasshoppers*
mayaram manngalba *or* manngalima	*several houses*
wangaya anngalya	*several women*
eeja anngalya	*several men*

Here the plural agreement form of the adjective, *anngalya*, is reserved for reference to highly animate denotata; all other nouns induce singular agreement-class prefixes on adjectives, even when a number of such things are specifically referred to.

Highly animate (human) denotata trigger plural agreement on adjectives, but they appear not to be *restricted* to occurring with plural agreement forms. Such denotata may on occasion induce *singular* (masculine or feminine) agreement prefixes when a number of them are being referred to. I do not fully understand the grammar of this phenomenon, as there are few occurrences of it in the database, and elicitation of these forms out of context is inherently unreliable. Under dual number marking (§9.3), adjectives prefer singular prefix shapes when referring to human denotata, although duality is a special case. Nevertheless, note the occurrence of singular agreement marking on a form referring to a number of humans in (6.16):

(6.16)
Ngayu	nyinjorinya	nyinngalja,	yorr
ngayu	nyiN=yoru-nya	nyiN=n-ngal-nya	yorr
I	3f=widowed-3f	3f=DEF-several-3f	sit.together

nyangkawanjeerri	nyirno-nyirno;	nyirno	ninjarrungunya.
nyaN-ngka=ᵇwa-ny-yeerri	nyiN=rno	nyiN=rno	nyiN=yarrungu-nya
3f-SJTV=fall-MIR-PROG	3f=DIST	3f=DIST	3f=QUANT-3f

I am one of these widows that live all around here, all on their own.

My best guess is that in this example, and possibly in some others like it, the singular reference of the first word (*ngayu* 'I') triggers singular agreement marking throughout the rest of the sentence, on co-referential derived nouns, demonstratives, verbs and adjectives (*ninjarrungunya* 'one (fem):' see Table 9.2 in §9.1). Love (1934:28) notes precisely this phenomenon with respect to =*raarrawa* 'many:' reference to women and girls is usually by way of the 3p shape *ardaarrawaaya* (cf. 6.15a), but occasionally by way of the feminine shape *nyirndaarrawaanya* (|nyiN=raarra-waa-nya| [3f=many-PERS-3f]). Plural agreement-marking on adjectives and pronouns is summarized below in Table 6.9. This phenomenon is discussed again in §7.3 and §9.5.

Table 6.9: plural agreement prefixes found on adjectives and pronouns

	HUMAN	NON-HUMAN
3a	i-	i-
3f	nyiN-	nyiN-
3w		ᵏwuN-, ØN-
3m		ma-
3p	arr-	

<u>6.2.6 (ii) reduplication</u>

In §4.2.1 we saw that many highly animate nouns, that is those denoting humans and dogs, and including nearly all kinship nouns, form plurals by phonological extensions of their stems. Some inanimate nouns as well, are able to encode different kinds of semantic extension by means of reduplication:

imarulya inja	*ball (of food), cake*	imarumarulya inja	*a pile of cakes*
kurrandu wunu	*hill*	kurraarrandu wunu	*a line of hills*
mamangkunu wunu	*morning*	mamaamangkunu wunu	*dawn*
wundukum mana	*darkness, night*		
wunduwundukum mana	*the darkest part of the night; the dark before dawn*		

Derived nouns and adjectives also commonly signal some kind of semantic augmentation by phonological extension of their stems, in a manner quite similar to that described for verbs in §5.2.2. Such extensions take a number of different forms, but all derive underlyingly (diachronically) from reduplications of different kinds. The usual, but by no means the only motivation for this process is to mark plurality. There are two interesting things to note about the forms listed above and others like them:

(i) The first is that these examples represent an instance of iconicity in language: phonological extensions of root morphemes signal semantic extensions of their denotations.
(ii) The second has to do with the animacy status of words such as *imarulya* and *kurrandu*. As these words refer to low-animate denotata, all their agreement forms must be singular (cf Table 6.9). Phonological extension, therefore, is the only way open to the grammar to signal plural or mass quantities of low animate denotata:

(6.17a)   Kulunu   wunngengalu
           kulunu   ᵏwuN=n-nge-ngal-u   (=*n-ngal* 'these several')
           sleep   3w=DEF-AUG-several-3w
           (After) a number of/ quite a few days ('sleeps')

(b)   Wungunenali
           ᵏwuN=ngu-ne-nali   (=*ngunali* 'new')
           3w=↳-AUG-new
           These days

At least three types of phonological extension may be identified. In the illustrations that follow (6.18–6.21), the first line lists the relevant root morpheme, the second picks out the extensional material in square brackets, the third shows the output root shape and the fourth illustrates the output shape affixed for 3p agreement:

<u>Type 1</u>

In the first type, the first morpheme or segment of the root lexeme is reduplicated, as shown in (6.18). Here the roots illustrated are =*yadangurru* 'long and straight,' derived from *jada* 'straight, direct' and -*ngurru* 'away;' =ᵏ*warlinjarrija* 'branching, spreading,' derived from =ᵏ*warluma mana* 'arm, wing;' and =*yakarri* 'other, different.'

(6.18)

=yadangurru	=ᵏwarlinjarrija	=yakarri
=yada + [yada] + ngurru	=ᵏwarl + [aarl] + injarrija	=yaka + [yaka] + rri
=yadayadangurru	=ᵏwarlaarlinjarrija	=yakekarri
ajadayadangurriya	aarlaarlinjarrija	ajakekarri

The 3p derived forms are *ajadayadangurriya* 'arranged in parallel lines,' *aarlaarlinjarrija* 'a mass of branching things/spreading out in all directions' (both these 3p forms coding agreement with the collective noun *mangarri anja* 'vegetable food,' and here referring to the way in which edible tubers grow underground), and *ajakekarri* 'all the others.' By this interpretation, V-expansion rule 18 turns the sequence |aya| in |=yak**aya**karri| into /e/ in the output shape =*yakekarri*. The first syllable of the irregular lexeme =ᵏ*wawiya* 'nice, pleasant (of food or people)' is reduplicated to signal plural reference, but the initial glide /ᵏw/ becomes a velar nasal in the reduplicated segment:

(6.19)   =ᵏwawiya
         =ᵏwa + [nga] + wiya
         =ᵏwangawiya
           arrkangawiya

Type 2

In the second type of phonological extension, the first consonant of the root morpheme is copied and preposed, and followed by a long unrounded vowel, either /aa/ or /e/, or rarely, /ee/:

$$\emptyset \longrightarrow \{C_iaa, C_ie\} \: / \: \_\_\_ =C_i \ldots$$

This process is illustrated in (6.20) with the root lexemes =*warr* 'bad,' =*niya* 'good' and =*rnayurr* 'adult, grown.'

(6.20)

=warr	=niya	=rnayurr
=[w + aa] + warr	=[n + ee] + niya	=[rn + e] + rnayurr
=waawarr	=neeniya	=rnernayurr
arrwaawarriya	adeeniya	ardernayurriya

The shape *wunngengalu* in (6.17a) is of this sort. Note also the dual derived form *iwaawunarrkarndu* (|i + [ᵇw + aa]=ᵇwunarr + ᵏwarndu| [3a + [AUG]=MOIETY + DU]) 'two people of the *Arrwunarriya* moiety,' with a type 2 extension.

Type 3

In a third pattern, it is the first consonant of the second syllable of the root morpheme that is selected for augmentation. This process is illustrated in (6.21) with the roots =*ngunali* 'new' (cf 6.17b), =*yakarri* 'other, different' and =ᵏ*warrinja* 'human/Aboriginal.' The augmented shape of the root =*yakarri* may be explained by this interpretation as well, giving evidence of a link between reduplication as shown in (6.18) and other forms of extension:

(6.21)

=ngunali	=yakarri	=ᵏwarrinja
=ngu + [n + e] + nali	=ya + [k + e] + karri	=ᵏwa + [rr + aa] + rrinja
=ngunenali	=yakekarri	=ᵏwarraarrinja
arrkunenali	ajakekarri	arrkarraarrinjiya

This last output shape, *arrkarraarrinjiya*, is one of the usual words used to refer to Aboriginal people as opposed to non-Aboriginal people, although before European contact it would have referred to human beings as opposed to other forms of life and spirits.

Many forms referring to highly animate things appear to have two options for pluralization: either plural agreement-class indexation alone, or plural agreement-class indexation *and* reduplication, as exemplified by the following alternatives, indexed for 3p agreement:

=ᵏwarrinja	*human*	arrkarrinjiya	arrkarraarrinjiya
=man	*dead*	arrbanjiya	arrbaamanjiya
=mara	*dangerous*	arrbareya	arrbaamareya
=marreya	*sick*	arrbarreya	arrbaamarreya
=warr	*bad*	arrwarriya	arrwaawarriya
=niya	*good*	adiya	adeeniya
=yakarri	*other*	ajakarri	ajakekarri

It is not clear to me whether such alternatives are synonymous, or if the reduplicated forms signal a somewhat larger number of items. There is a third plural shape of the root =*man* 'dead,' *arrbanja*, used to make oblique or 'diffuse' (euphemistic) reference to a single deceased person (§7.1).

Derived nouns referring to categories of humans do not have this option, they *require* both plural agreement-class indexation *and* reduplication:

=rnayurr	*adult*	ardernayurriya	
=yoru	*widow(er)*	ajoyoriya, ajorayoriya	
=yarnda	*little child*	ajaayarndeya	
=ᵇwarnkarra	*adult offspring*	arrwaawarnkarreya	
ngawmaleya	*my little brother*	ngawmaamaleya	*my little brothers*

Reduplication does not always signal plurality. The adjective =*yarrungu* 'QUANTIFIER' (§9.1) has a 3p shape *ajarrunguya* 'all of them.' The reduplicated form *ajarrinjarrunguya*, however, means 'only a few;' in this case, semantic intensification reduces the scope of reference. The adjective =*raarreya* 'big' undergoes type 3 reduplication to produce a form =*raarraarreya* 'huge,' without any reference to number: *kanangkurri iràarráarreya* 'a huge dog.'

Reduplicated morphologies are available to all plural agreement classes, but are most commonly found on 3p forms. They are less frequent on participant (1pin, 1px, 2p) forms, as evidenced in (6.22), with the adjective =*warr* 'bad:'

(6.22)
Arri	waa	benbeenyeerri	arrwarr	arrkununa.
arri	waa	ba-nyarr-n-Ø=ᵇwu-yinya-eerrri	arr=warr	arr-ngun=nu-na
we/us	not	CFT-1px-INV-3=hit-PAST-PROG	px=bad	1px-SJTV-be-PAST

He never used to hit us when we were naughty.

6.3 Inalienable nouns

A lexical category quite distinct from the nominals we have considered so far is that of inalienable nouns. These are nouns that denote things occurring in what Chappell & McGregor (1996) refer to as someone's 'personal sphere;' that is, within the range of interactions that are conceptually very close to a person. Inalienable nouns denote things that are regarded emically as forming essential or inseparable parts of a person's being; that is, they refer to inalienable parts of some other (typically human) whole. These may be abstract things that are culturally definitive of personhood, such as

=*ngumbu wunu* 'name,' =*ngaanja inja* 'shadow; soul' =*rambim mana* 'patriclan' and =*yula inja* 'anger.' Most nouns of this sort however, refer to parts of the body.

Chappell & McGregor (1996) characterize inalienability in a way that is entirely congruent with this phenomenon as it is found in Worrorra. They describe inalienable relationships in terms of a set of inextricable, essential and unchangeable relations holding between someone (a 'possessor') and an aspect of their being (that which is 'possessed'), over which the possessor has little or no control. The conceptual proximity that holds within such a relationship is rendered iconically in Worrorra and other languages by the affixation of a token of the possessor (in this case an NP-indexing prefix) to the noun denoting of the possessed. This results in an externally possessed construction in Payne & Barshi's (1999) exposition, in terms of which a possessor may be expressed as a pronominal affix within the NP headed by the possessed noun.

Both the grammar of inalienability, and the grammar of external possession are discussed and exemplified at length by McGregor (1996b & 1999), with respect to the Nyulnyulan languages of the West Kimberley. These languages are located to the south-west of Worrorra country, and many of the phenomena canvassed in those articles are applicable to these syntactic strategies as they are found in Worrorra.

While some body-part nouns such as *keyingka inja* 'fingernails', *kurleerla inja* 'shoulder-blades' and *ngamuku wunu* 'breast(s)' are simplex, most body-part nouns are inalienable, that is, they obligatorily take agreement-class indices that refer to the whole of which they are a part. English denotes such part-whole relationships by way of possessive phrases such as 'his hand,' with the whole (the 'possessor' of the part) marked by a possessive morphology, while the head noun (the part) is left unmarked. Worrorra refers to the whole by way of an agreement-class index that is prefixed to the head noun, which again denotes the part. This system is comparable to affixial pronominal possessive-marking in Afro-Asiatic languages such as Arabic: *kitaab* 'book,' *kitaabiy* 'my book,' *kitaabik* 'your (fem) book,' *kitaabuhu* 'his book' etc. The noun stem is the head of its phrase and the coreference of the inflexional index represents an NP dependent upon the head in phrase structure:

(6.23a) Irnurnu wunu (b) Nyimri wunu
i=rnurnu wunu   nyiN=mri wunu
3a=hand 3wDEF   3f=head 3wDEF
His hand(s)   *Her head*

(c) Ngunkubulu wunu (d) Ardaarriya anja
ngun=ᵏwambul wunu   arr=rnaarri-ya anja
2=eye 3wDEF   3p=bones-PL 3pDEF
Your eyes   *Their bones*

(e) Nyingarnima mana (f) Ngardabim mana
nyiN=ngarnima mana   ngarr=rambim mana
3f=odour 3mDEF   1pin=clan 3mDEF
Her smell   *Our family (patriclan)*

While hosting prefixes that refer to some other NP, such nouns also bear gender in the usual lexically specified manner. Inalienable nouns, therefore, are often doubly-marked for gender, as in (6.23a, b & e); showing the gender of the dependent NP in prefix position, as well as their own inherent gender marked on other agreement loci, such as the determiners in (6.23).

Although the prefixes found on inalienable nouns are homophonous with the derivational indices shown in Table 6.1, their function here is primarily inflexional. They do not usually alter the agreement category or gender of the head noun, which retains its inherent gender. Moreover, the gender of the head noun determines the gender of its phrase, a process illustrated in (6.24):

(6.24)

		Nyina	wangayinya	nyungkubulu		wunu	
[WUNU	[FEM	nyina	wangayinya	|nyiN FEM\]=^kwambul|		wunu	WUNU]
		3fDEF	woman	|3f	=eye|	3wDEF	

The woman's eyes

The body-part noun in this example is =*^kwambul(u) wunu* 'eyes', and the dependent NP within the phrase is *wangayinya nyina* 'the woman'. The phrase itself compels celestial agreement, that is to say that the phrase's outer gender category is celestial.

As shown in (6.24), whole-part phrases of this type consist of an inner dependent NP and an outer head noun that controls agreement-marking for the discourse section in which it occurs (cf example 4.16 in §4.1.4 (i) where outer gender controls agreement in derived-gender phrases). In (6.25) the inalienable noun =*mri wunu* 'head' receives 2p indexation (*nyirrbri* 'your heads') and feminine indexation (*nyimri* 'her head'). Regardless of which dependent NPs are indexed, anaphor and verb agreement is nearly always controlled by the gender of the head noun (which is in this case celestial):

(6.25a)
Wunu	nyirrbriaarndu	wakumaadamaade	kaninjeerri	wunu.
wunu	nyirr=mri-^kwarndu	wakumaada-maade	ØN-ngka=ni-ny-yeerri	wunu
3wDEF	2p=head-DU	black-RESULT	3w-SJTV-be-MIR-PROG	3wDEF

So now both your heads are black.

(b)
	Wunu	nyimri	wakumaada	kumnyanungu.
	wunu	nyiN=mri	wakumaada	kuN-mnya=nu-ng
	3wDEF	3f=head	black	3w-DD=be-PRES

Her head is black.

Note here that the verbs involved (forms of =*nu* 'be') index agreement for celestial subjects.[50] This rule, however, is not without exception. In some situations a highly topical dependent (owner) appears to be able to outrank a head noun for head-of-phrase status, as in the verbless sentence shown in (6.26):

6.26
	[TERM	]	[PRED	]
	Nyingumbu	Kankanarlonya	wali nyina.	
	nyiN=ngumbu	kankanarlonya	wali nyina	
	3f=name	NAME	PM	

Her name is Kankanarlonya.

Predicate markers (here *wali nyina*) agree in gender with their terms (here *nyingumbu* 'her name') (see §17.8). However in (6.26) the predicate marker agrees not with the gender of the term's head (=*ngumbu wunu*), but with that of the term's *dependant* (feminine) NP.

Unlike in some north Australian languages, terms for human body-parts do not appear to be extended metaphorically to non-animate denotata. In Wubuy, for example, parts of plants and artefacts (the belly [= berry] of a tree, the tongue [= blade] of a spear) are referred to by derived forms with the whole entity indexed on the part by derivational noun-class prefixes (Heath 1984:173-177).

---

[50] Love (1934:30) claims that adjectives qualifying inalienable nouns may be marked for agreement not only with the head noun itself, as described here, but with dependent nouns as well, offering as an example the adjective =*niya* 'good' combined in a phrase with the terrestrial noun =*ngarnima* 'scent, odour,' as *nyingarnima maniyanya* (|nyiN=ngarnima ma=niya-nya| [3f=smell 3m=good-3f]) 'her good smell,' a claim cited by Capell & Coate (1984:69). However my instructors rejected this and constructions like it, producing adjectives marked only for agreement with their head nouns. Note however that there is indeed an important class of forms that does exhibit double gender-marking, that of subjunctive verbs, as eg. the shape *ingkaangkarrengama* 'where his picture is' in (6.9), with 3a prefix *i-* and 3m suffix *-ma*.

In this language derived adjectives, derived nouns (Heath's 'defective' roots) and inalienable nouns appear to form the same kind of continuum or 'squish' as derived adjectives and derived nouns do in Worrorra. In Worrorra syntactic criteria clearly distinguish inalienable nouns from the other categories, and the references of inalienable nouns appear to be confined pretty much to body parts and to human and animal wholes.

In verbal argument structure, an inalienable part-whole compound may function directly as an undergoer, as in (6.27a), or in apposition to some other noun in undergoer position, as in the possessor-ascension construction shown in (6.27b). This is to say that either the whole or the part may be indexed as undergoer. These sentence examples employ the complex predicate *burr =^{b}wu* 'SUBJ fall on OBJ:'

(6.27a)   Ngamri   burr   kumbuna.
          nga=mri   burr   kuN-Ø=^{b}wu-na
          1=head   fall.on   3w-3=hit-PAST
          It hit my head (lit: it fell on my-head)

(b)   Burr   nganbuna   ngamri.
          burr   nga-n-Ø=^{b}wu-na   nga=mri
          fall.on   1-INV-3=hit-PAST   1=head
          It hit me on the head (lit: it fell on me my-head)

In (6.27a) the verb's 3w undergoer is *=mri wunu* 'head,' while in (6.27b) the undergoer is indexed as first person singular.

Inalienable nouns change gender to agree with that of their dependents when those dependents are celestial or terrestrial, so that in this case the agreement-class indices really do function derivationally. Hence *maambulba mana* (|ma=^{k}wambul-ma| [3m=eye-3m]) 'tidal whirlpool' derived from *=^{k}wambul wunu* 'eye,' where the whole indexed on the inalienable noun is *rlarlangkarrama mana* 'the sea' – so this word means literally 'its eye.' The change of gender involved (from celestial to terrestrial) is evidenced by terrestrial agreement on the determiner and on the adjective *=raarreya* 'big' in (6.28a):

(6.28a)
Maraarreyim   kungurr   kumnyeng,   maambulb   mana
ma=raarreya-m   kungurr   kuN-Ø-mnya=yi-ng   ma=^{k}wambul-ma mana
3m=big-3m   stab   VCOMP-3-DD=do-PAST   3m=eye-3m   3mDEF
She stabbed the big one, the eye-of-the-sea.

(b)   Mangumbam   nganama?
          ma=ngumba-ma   ngani-ma
          3m=name-3m   where-3m
          What's the place called?

In (6.28b) the interrogative *nga-(ni)* 'where?/what?' (§7.4.1) is predicated upon the inalienable celestial noun *=ngumbu wunu* 'name.' This noun has changed its gender to agree with that of its implied dependent NP, *dambeem mana* 'place,' and this change is reflected in the gender marked on both the noun itself and on the interrogative.

This phenomenon of gender derivation to agree with a dependent of the non-human macrogender is illustrated by the noun *=rnaarri inja* 'bones, skeleton:'

        Wurnaarru wunu   *Its (celestial) bones*
        Marnaarrba mana   *Its (terrestrial) bones*
        Ardaarriya anja   *Their bones*

This noun also shows derived gender agreement with a 3p dependent, as seen here and in (6.23d); this probably occurs because of the collective nature of the noun's denotation. Note as well the idomatic expression in (6.29):

(6.29)   Wunu   wiyanu   wurnaarru.
         wunu   wiyanu   ᵏwuN=rnaarr-u
         3wDEF   fire   3w=bones-3w
         The bones of the fire (ie charcoal and ash).

The experiencer constructions in (6.30) show the syntax of the inalienable noun =*yula inja* 'anger'. The experiencer of the emotion denoted by this noun is indexed on it in prefix position, as the 'whole' of whom anger is an inalienable 'part,' to yield a form that translates literally as 'my anger, his anger' etc. In predications the experiencer is the grammatical agent of the verb =*ma* 'get,' while the inalienable noun itself is the undergoer. This syntax produces a construction of the type 'AGENT/EXPERIENCER seizes his/her anger.' The inalienable noun is indexed on the verb (verb classifier) in undergoer position as *ka-* '3a:'

(6.30a) Ngayu   ngayula   kangamerri.
         ngayu   nga=yula   ka-nga=ma-eerri
         I   1=anger   3a-1=get-PROG
         I'm getting angry.

(b)   Bamaraanya   nyinjula   kamerri.
         bamaraanya   nyiN=yula   ka-Ø=ma-eerri
         fa.si   3f=anger   3a-3=get-PROG
         My aunt is getting angry.

Note however, that when an experiencer of the non-human macrogender is indexed in dependent (prefix) position, the gender of =*yula* 'anger' changes to agree with that of its dependent, and this change is manifested in the shape of the verb's undergoer index, *kuN-* '3w' and *ma-* '3m' respectively in (6.31), rather than by *ka-* '3a' as expected. This morphology indicates that =*yula* may indeed have changed gender in agreement with its dependent noun:

(6.31a) Wunu   marrirri   wunjula   kumerri.
         wunu   marirri   ᵏwuN=yula   kuN-Ø=ma-eerri
         3wDEF   parrot.sp   3w=anger   3w-3=get-PROG
         The red-winged parrot is getting angry.

(b)   Mana   darraanma   mayula   mamerri.
         mana   darraanma   ma=yula   ma-Ø=ma-eerri
         3mDEF   cockatoo.sp 3m=anger   3m-3=get-PROG
         The red-tailed black cockatoo is getting angry.

An alternative explanation for this phenomenon is advanced in §12.4.

'Parts-of-parts' type constructions are represented by only one example in the database, =*yardu umalab mana* 'heel' (literally 'the buttock of the foot'). This nominal is a more nested (or more embedded) form of the construction shown in (6.24), involving the nouns =*yardu wunu* 'foot' and =*malab mana* 'buttocks':

(6.32)

	Nyinjardu		umalab		mana
[MANA [WUNU [FEM	nyiN FEM]	=yardu	ᵏwuN WUNU]	=malab	mana MANA]
	3f	=foot	3w	=buttock	3mDEF

Her heel

A synonym is the simplex noun *umalaku wunu* 'heel', diachronically derived from =*malab mana* 'buttocks' with celestial affixation *(-(ᵏw)u-)*.

Seven: pronouns, demonstratives, anaphors, deictics

7.1 Substitution

This chapter is concerned primarily with anaphora and deixis in Worrorra, involving the substitution of a set of replacement forms for other expressions. The expressions usually substituted for in Worrorra are noun phrases and sentences, the replacement forms comprising a lexical category of pronouns, including demonstrative pronouns.

Worrorra pronouns and demonstratives make primary reference to the substantive person, number and gender categories or agreement classes whose tokens, as inflexional (§5.3.1) and derivational (§6.1) NP indices, have already been encountered. The grammar treats sentences and sentential complements of all sorts as if they were celestial, or occasionally terrestrial nouns (§4.1.3 (iii)). While these person-and-number categories are evidenced widely in the morphology, this chapter is concerned primarily with their manifestation as lexical words.

Because of the small number of Worrorra speakers, I have not been able to observe much of the indexical use of person-and-number categories, that may have pertained between different classes of kin, between different age groups, between men and women, or in various social circumstances and ritual contexts. The material presented in this chapter, therefore, suffers from that deficiency. One observation, however, may be noted here, and that has to do with a function that I will refer to as *diffuse* reference.

Diffuse reference is found in euphemistic constructions used in referring to socially or physically dangerous things. Such reference is signalled by the use of the third person plural category, especially in situations where other categories could be expected. The use of the non-participant third person category precludes dangerous things from being represented in the speech event itself, that is to say, third person reference enables people to undertake a speech act while yet excluding unwanted things from participating in the act. The use of the plural number category has the effect of *dispersing* such reference, so that its connotational weight is not concentrated at any one metaphorical point. The dispersal or deflection of illocutionary force may be observed in the use of the counterfactual mood prefix *ba-* in intransitive imperative singular verb forms (eg *bayu!* |ba=ya| [CFT=go] 'go!'), where the counterfactual morpheme is employed to deflect the inherent illocutionary forcefulness of commands (§8.5.3).

Within the person-indexical system, 3p marking achieves a similar effect. For example reference to the dangerous practice of sorcery is oblique, by means of the collective noun *barnmarnja anja*. This noun accepts only 3p agreement and has no singular shape (§4.2.2). References to death are typically accomplished by 3p forms: the adjective *=man* 'dead' has singular shapes (eg *imanja*, masculine and *nyimanya*, feminine), but an alternative shape *arrbanja* (|arr=man-ya| [3p=dead-3p]) is also used in diffuse reference, typically outside of mourning and funerary contexts where the awfulness of death is not only allowed, but required to enter. Note that this form is distinct from the genuinely plural shapes *arrbanjiya* and *arrbaamanjiya* seen in §6.2.6 (ii). And as seen in §6.2.2, the recollection of a deceased person or people is accomplished by the plural passive participle *adijiyeya* 'vision.'

Dangerous things may be referred to obliquely, especially in the context of their dangerous behaviour (cf Bloomfield 1933:400-1). This kind of oblique reference is always situated in the 3p category, as is the case in sentence example (7.1) below:

(7.1)   Inja   eeja   burnarri   arrke   kawarraningkarla.
        inja   eeja   burnarri   arrke   ka-ᵇwarr-a=ningka-rla
        3aDEF   man   animals   3pREF   3a-3p-EP=bite-PAST
        A snake bit the man ('those animals' bit the man).

The snake in question was the black snake *kawaanya nyina*, a very dangerous species, and in this context the speaker employed diffuse reference (*burnarri arrke* 'those animals') rather than actually name the animal itself. This type of consideration probably underlies Silverstein's (1976b:39) passing mention of 'deference' in Worrorra, presumably in relation to the socially dangerous avoidance category kin *(rambarr mana)*.

Pronouns and demonstratives bear number-marking morphemes; number is marked not only as part of the package of references of agreement class indices, but also overtly by way of a set of suffixes described in Chapter Nine. These suffixes are -ᵏ*warndu* 'dual,' -*oorri* 'trial' and -ᵏ*wurri* 'paucal,' and their allomorphy is described in §9.1 and §9.6.1. The trial morpheme appears to occur only on the pronoun =ᵏ*wa* 'Anaphoric/Narrative.' The trial and paucal morphemes never occur on the same root form, that is, they are in complementary distribution (cf. §9.6.2). The paucal morpheme is less restricted in its occurrence, and the dual morpheme is ubiquitous. Overt number marking in Worrorra is not straightforward, and is discussed in more detail specifically in relation to pronouns in §9.4.3, §9.6.1 and §9.6.3.

There is an important distinction made in pronouns between speech-act participants (first and second persons) and non-participants (third persons). This distinction has significance for number marking, as discussed below and in §9.5.

7.2 Personal pronouns

The criteria for making a distinction between personal and non-personal pronouns in Worrorra are less than clear. Although a distinction between personal and demonstrative third person pronouns is unmotivated on purely formal grounds, by combining morphological and semantic criteria it is possible to set up such a distinction to include participant forms, and in a way that has significance for other parts of the grammar. Morphologically, it may be claimed that personal pronouns are those that take possessive marking. Semantically, it may be claimed that participant pronoun forms are inherently personal, and that anaphoric third person forms, that is, those without a demonstrative function, may also qualify as personal pronouns. These criteria do not wholly cover the personal – non-personal distinction in Worrorra, as there are participant forms that are clearly demonstrative, and Love (1934:12) lists demonstrative forms that appear to take possessive marking. Nonetheless, among these considerations may be discerned some grounds at least for discovering a class of personal pronouns, opposed to one of non-personal or demonstrative forms.

Table 7.1: participant personal pronouns

PERSON	SINGULAR	PLURAL	DUAL	PAUCAL
1 inc		ngarri *we*	ngarrerndu *you & I*	ngarringkurri *you two & I*
1 exc	ngayu *I*	arri *we*	arrerndu *s/he & I*	arringkurri *them two & I*
2	ngunju *you*	nyirri *you all*	nyirrerndu *you two*	nyirringkurri *you & them two*

There are three types of personal pronoun. The first kind consists of forms that denote only participant persons, as shown in Table 7.1. This is a semantically unmarked set based on the root shapes =*ya* in the singular and =*i* in the non-singular.[51] Interestingly, these allomorphs are homophonous with the root allomorphs of the verb 'go,' although it is not clear why this should be so. In their non-singular possessive shapes, these pronouns appear to be based on a root form =*ᵏwa*. Notice in Table 7.1 that the first person singular exclusive shape begins with a velar nasal, making it similar in this respect to the first person *inclusive* series: the other first exclusive forms begin with /a/.

The morphophonology of the dual and paucal shapes involves V-expansion rule 18 and velar glide hardening rule 2 respectively, exemplified as follows:

    ngarri-ᵏwarndu —> ngarrerndu
    ngarri-ᵏwurri —> ngarri**ngk**urri

Note also the split between singular and non-singular: the dual and paucal number markers -*ᵏwarndu* and -*ᵏwurri* are attached to the plural shape of the pronouns, not to the singular.

The second kind of personal pronoun consists of third person anaphors with the root shape =*ᵏwa* 'Anaphoric/Narrative' (glossed NAR). This is again a denotationally empty form, functioning as a determiner when inside the same NP as the noun to which it refers, and anaphorically when appearing outside of that NP. It is one of the most widely-used anaphoric pronouns and is common in narrative discourse styles. Its morphology is displayed in Table 7.2.

Table 7.2: =*ᵏwa* 'Anaphoric/Narrative'

	SINGULAR		DUAL	TRIAL	PLURAL	
3a	awa	'he'	awaarndu	awoorri	arrka	'they'
3f	nyangka	'she'	awaarndu	awoorri	arrka	
3w	kawa	'it'	kawaarndu	kawoorri		
3m	mawa	'it'	mawaarnduma	mawoorrima		

The non-singular possessive shapes of the forms in Table 7.1, as well as the shapes in Table 7.2, are all based on the same root (=*ᵏwa*) (cf example 7.7c). This fact is suggestive of an underlying identity between the two sets, as participant and non-participant forms of the same root lexeme, and justifies their inclusion together in a category of personal pronouns. Possessive pronouns are described below in §7.7.

The trial series is discussed in §9.4.3. Note also the following points in Table 7.2:
(i) The classes of the human macrogender are neutralized in the non-singular number series.
(ii) Note also and in particular that here, in contrast to Table 7.1, there is a split between plural and non-plural forms. The dual and trial number markers are attached to the *singular* shape of the pronouns, not to the plural.
(iii) Only highly animate entities in the human macrogender can be represented by plural forms. There are therefore no plural shapes for the non-human classes.

Free personal pronouns are employed in equational sentences, as seen in (7.2) and (7.3). Note the highly elliptical, quasi-idiomatic expression in (7.2e):

---

[51] The morphophonolgy of the pronouns in tables 7.1 and 7.2 is as follows:

    |nga=ya| —> /ngayu/ |a=ᵏwa| —> /awa/
    |ngun=ya| —> /ngunju |nyaN=ᵏwa| —> /nyangka/
    |ngarr=i| —> /ngarri/ |ØN=ᵏwa| —> /ka(wa)/
    |arr=i| —> /arri/ |ma=ᵏwa| —> /mawa/
    |nyirr=i| —> /nyirri/ |arr=ᵏwa| —> /arrka/

(7.2a) Ngayu ngawarrekuwali.
   ngayu nga=warr-a-y₂akuwali
   I   1=bad-EP-EMPH
   I'm feeling really sick.

(b) Ngunju angkunya?
  you who (fem)
  Who are you (fem)?

(c) Ngayu ke   wali!
  I   3wREF RESUM
  It's me!

(d) Ngayu wali wunu.
  I   PM
  It's me.

(e) Anguja ngarri wunu?
  what/how we(inc) 3wDEF
  How will we do this?

(7.3)
Arrerndu ninjarrungunya karrernbarrinya, karraanyarrerndinya
arri-ᵏwarndu nyiN=yarrungu-nya karrernbarrinya karraa-[nyarri-ᵏwarndu]-nya
we(exc)-DU 3f=QUANT-3f mother.of.many mother-[1pxDAT-DU]-3f

ninjarrungunya, awa iwulku, ngayu wangalang nganunangurru.
nyiN=yarrungu-nya awa i=ᵇwulku ngayu wangalang nga=nu-na-ngurru
3f=QUANT-3f 3aNAR 3a=1st.born I child 1=be-PAST-away
He and I had the same mother, he was the eldest and I was just a child.

In (7.3) note the pronouns *arrerndu* 'we two (exc)' and *awa* 'he' used in verbless clauses. Note also that the pronoun *ngayu* 'I' is used to point up a contrast between the referent of *awa* and the speaker. This contrastive use is another important function of free pronouns, as shown again in (7.4), and in (7.5), which records an exchange between two people:

(7.4) Ngayu marru, awa ngurru.
   ngayu ma=rru awa ngurru
   I   3m=LAT he here
   I'm over there, and he's right here. (reference to points on a map)

(7.5) 'Maa maa ngadunerringkurri.'
   maa maa ngarr=nu-na-eerri-ᵏwurri
   PROG PROG 1pin=be-PAST-PROG-NUM
   'We were living with you.'

   'Ngayu karle eejakurde nganngunu.
   ngayu karle eeja-kurde ngan-ngun=nu
   I   then man-ASSOC 1-SJTV=be
   'I was married by that time.'

Second person pronouns are frequent in focus position in imperative clauses:

(7.6a) Ngunju   maa   bayungurru.
       ngunju   maa   ba=ya-ngurru
       you   PROG   CFT=go-away
       You go on ahead.

       Ngunjunyale   minyamaara.
       ngunju-nyale   minya=ma-ᵏwara
       you-too   2>3w=get-1DAT
       You get me some, too.

(c)   Bariy   bamnyanu   ngunju!
       bariy   ba-mnya=nu   ngunju
       rise   CFT-DD=be   you
       You get up!

Free personal pronouns are also used more widely to signal focus and topicalization. They occur typically in situations where a speaker wishes to pick out the pronoun's referent for particular attention, as in the sentence examples in (7.7):

(7.7a)
Ngayu   kungenganyale;   ngayu,   ngayu.
ngayu   kuN-nga=yi-ng-a-nyale   ngayu   ngayu
I   VCOMP-1=do-PAST-EP-too   I   I
I've done that myself, too.

(b)
Ngayu   ingo   ngana   kubajungaara.
ngayu   i-nga=ᵇwu   ngana   kuN-ᵇwarr-yi-ng-ᵏwara
I   3a-1=hit   PROB   VCOMP-3p=do-PAST-1DAT
They must have wanted to kill me.

(c)
Ngarri   wali   ngarrkanaanangkaya   anja   wangalaalunguyu!
ngarri   wali   ngarr=ᵏwa-naa-nangka-ya   anja   wangalaalanguya
we (inc) still   1pin=NAR-AUG-DAT-3p   3pDEF   children
They are our children!

Sentence (7.7b) contains the sentential complement of the *verbum dicendi kuN[ ]=yi* 'do, want,' a situation described in Chapter 14.

The third kind of personal pronouns are negative pronouns, as displayed in Table 7.3. These consist of forms based on the root =ᵏwi 'Negative' (glossed NEG), with the meaning 'not (someone)'.

Table 7.3: negative pronouns: =ᵏwi 'Negative'

1	ngawi	*not me*
2	ngunki	*not you*
3a	kawi	*not him*
3f	nyungki	*not her*
3w	kuwi	*not it*
3m	mawi	*not it*
3p	kaarri	*not them*

The plural shape *kaarri* is used for all plural references, as well as being a very widely-used negative interjection: *kaarri!* 'No!/No way!/Not at all!/Certainly not!/Nothing!' (see eg example 7.12). The expression *kaarri maa* 'in vain' is also commonly used (§6.4.2 (xi)). Sentence example (7.12) also contains an example of the use of *mawi* '3mNEG,' and further examples of the use of these forms can be seen in sentence (7.8):

(7.8)
Irranangkorri	kawi,	karranangkorrinya	nyungki,	kaarri.
irra-nangkorri	kawi	karra-nangkorri-nya	nyungki	kaarri
father-3pDAT	3aNEG	mother-3pDAT-3f	3fNEG	3pNEG

Their father's never there, their mother's not around, there's no-one.

7.3 Demonstrative pronouns

Unlike in most languages, demonstrative pronouns in Worrorra constitute an open, or at least a semi-open, class.[52] Pronominal forms combine with adverbial and adjectival deictic morphemes to create a highly productive referential system, rather than a finite list of pronominal words only. The meanings of many of the forms created in this system are not completely clear to me, as I have not been able to observe their use in a variety of contexts and situations. I will not be able, therefore, to provide a precise semantic description of each form, but will rather try, here and in Chapter 17, to outline the operation of the system as a whole.

7.3.1 Definiteness and deixis

Among its determiners Worrorra has a set of three demonstratives, used to bring entities onstage in the speech events in which they occur. These are =*n* 'the, this, DEFINITE/PROXIMAL' (glossed DEF), =*rno* 'that, DISTAL' and =*rru* 'LATERAL' (glossed LAT). The proximal forms serve as definite articles, and their functions have been touched on already in §4.1. The paradigm of =*n* 'the, this' is shown in Table 7.4:

Table 7.4: definite article: =*n* 'this, DEFINITE'

	SING	DUAL	PAUCAL	HUM PAUC	PLURAL
3a	inja	inkarndu	inkoorri	ankoorri	anja
3f	nyina	inkarndu	inkoorri	ankoorri	anja
3w	wunu	wunkarndu	wunkoorri		
3m	mana	mankarnduma	mankoorrima		

The paucal suffix is heard as either -*kurri* or -*koorri*, but usually as the latter. There is no reason from its use to believe that this is a trial form, rather the lengthening of the back vowel seems to be phonologically motivated: being stressed, it attracts length. There is a split between on the one hand the dual and non-human paucal forms which are based on the singular shape, and on the other, the human or highly-animate paucal form, based on the plural shape.[53] Highly animate (human) denotata may be referred to by either human or non-human paucal forms in line with the usual constraints on number-agreement marking on nominals – see Table 6.8 in §6.2.6 (i). Also note again how the human genders are neutralized in the non-singular number series, and that plural shapes are unavailable to non-human denotata.

---

[52] Inupiaq has a similar kind of demonstrative system (with thanks to an anonymous reviewer).
[53] The morphophonolgy of the proximal demonstratives is as follows: |i=n-ya| > *inja*, |ᵏwuN=n-u| > *wunu*, |arr=n-ya| > *anja*. The marked macrogender forms are slightly irregular, the predicted forms /ˣnyinya/ *(nyina)* and /ˣmanma/ *(mana)* not occurring.

This pronoun has three distinguishable functions or senses; its main function is almost certainly that of a definite article: it is frequently pleonastic, and serves to indicate that the speaker believes that the referent is identifiable by the hearer. That is, the main and most frequent function of =*n* in Worrorra appears to be to grammaticize identifiability (cf Lyons 1999:278); in Lyons' terms, =*n* occupies a structural position activating definiteness in the NP in which it occurs. When a denotatum first appears in a narrative text, it may occur with the contextual deictic =*kwaya* (Table 7.8), which both introduces and topicalizes it. Subsequently, the denotatum typically appears with =*n*, in situations where a token of its definite status is required. As an article =*n* signals what Bloomfield (1933:203) calls the 'identificational character' of a denotatum, or what Silverstein (1986:509) refers to as its preconditions of reference. The article signals number (singular, dual, paucal or plural, within the constraints imposed by animacy status), gender and definiteness: that is, a referential framework upon which denotation may be hung. The use of =*n* as an article signalling general-knowledge definiteness has been seen in sentence example (4.1), where the existence and nature of the animals listed are all part of Worrorra speakers' encyclopaedic knowledge. The construction of definiteness in Worrorra and the uses of =*n* 'DEFINITE' are discussed more fully, and in relation to discourse pragmatics generally, in §17.1.

The anaphoric use of =*n*, as listed in (4.4) above, is widespread, and may be seen in (5.44d) *(inja)*, in (6.34) *(nyina)*, in the second occurrence of *anja* in (9.7), and elsewhere. As a subcategory of definiteness (Lyons 1999:159), we might expect anaphora to be represented by a definite article-*cum*-proximal demonstrative.

There is, cross-linguistically, a broad overlap between definite articles and proximal demonstratives (Lyons 1999:332), and this is true of Worrorra. The article =*n* has a proximal deictic sense ('this') in many of its occurrences, as if physical location near the addressee were a metaphor for an item's presence in the addressee's attention. Here people's general knowledge of the world, and the contents of their immediate discourse and physical environments are squished and represented by a single set of forms. In fact, Worrorra is able to disentangle this set of meanings by reduplicating the definite article to produce forms that are purely proximal demonstratives. Note that in many instances the *unreduplicated* article also occurs in the same NP pleonastically, serving solely to activate definiteness. Reduplicated demonstratives recoverable from the database are masculine *injinja*, celestial *wunu-wunu* or *wununu*, and plural *anjanja*. The terrestrial form *mana-mana* is frequent, but appears to serve as an adverb meaning 'right here, just here,' as is also often the case with *wununu* when referring to celestial denotata. A possible feminine shape *nyimnyininya* has only one occurrence, and there is as well a dual form *inkarnd-inkarndu*. Examples are offered below, and others may be seen in (9.24, 10.74) and (17.11).

(7.9a)
Injinja	inja	irnurnu	warndi	kona	lalai.
inja-inja	inja	i=rnurnu	warndi	ØN-Ø-ngka=^{b}wu-na	lalai
3aDEF-REDUP	3aDEF	3a=hand	make	3w-3-SJTV=hit-PAST	dreamtime

This one [Wandjina] painted his hands in the dreamtime.

(b)
Injinja	inja	we	ingkawanjeerri.
inja-inja	inja	we	i-ngka=^{b}wa-ny-yeerri
3aDEF- REDUP	3aDEF	lie.down	3a-SJTV=fall-MIR-PROG

This is him lying down here.

(c)
Wunu-wunu	ngenangka	kungenganu.
wunu-wunu	ØN-nga=yi-nangka	kuN-nga=yi-ng-a-nu
3wDEF- REDUP	VCOMP-1=do-DAT	VCOMP-1=do-PAST-EP-2DAT

This is what I wanted to say to you.

(d)

Ngayu	kajaajeya	anjanja.
ngayu	kajaajeya	anja-anja
I	mother's mothers	3pDEF- REDUP

These are my mother's mother's family.

(e)

Nguru	kanuna	inkarnd-inkarndu	aja	ingkaninykarndeerri.
nguru	ka=nu-na	i=n-^{k}warndu-i=n-^{k}warndu	aja	i-ngka=ni-ny-^{k}warndu-eerri
hear	3a=be-PAST	3a=DEF-DU-3a=DEF-DU	sit	3a-SJTV=be-MIR-DU-PROG

He heard these two where they were sitting.

The distal demonstrative =*rno* 'that' refers to things situated away from the centre of some point of reference, or beyond the immediate vicinity of the speech event, that is, at all distances beyond =*n*. The lateral demonstrative =*rru* refers to things that are both beyond the immediate vicinity of the speech event, and at the side of, or behind its participants. The complementary ranges of these two pronouns are shown in Figure 7.1, where the small circle at the centre indicates a speaker or participant in the speech situation, and the arrow shows the direction in which that participant is facing:

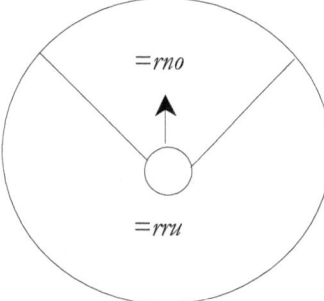

Figure 7.1: ranges of =*rno* 'distal' & =*rru* 'lateral'

Love (1934:8) describes the difference between these forms as indicating something 'at-a-distance-but-within-sight' *(=rno)*, versus something out of sight *(=rru)*. Although these meanings are almost certainly involved in the coding specifications of these two forms, my instructors indicated a primary distinction along the lines shown in Figure 7.1. Note that being a long way out of sight is frequently referred to as being in a lateral direction by analogy, such that 'way over that way' becomes a metaphor for 'out of sight,' because in most cases something is referred to as being in a lateral position if you cannot turn and face it directly. That the visual parameter of the distinction is not primary, however, is suggested by expressions such as that shown in (7.10):

(7.10)

Grarlya	marno	yakuwalima	bawarra.
Grarlya	ma=rno	yakuwali-ma	bawarra
COUNTRY	3m=DIST	EMPH-3m	far

The land of Grarl is a very long way away.

When this sentence was uttered, the land in question was several hundred miles distant, but was not conceived of as being located laterally with respect to the speaker's attitude. Again, note the expression in (7.11), where the speaker refers to her own position as 'lateral' ('behind'). This sentence comes from a text about the travels of an ancestral giant groper *(nyina jimbirrij)* and the baler shell *(nyina nyalikanya)*. In this story the groper races on ahead, leaving the baler shell behind, to crawl through the mud of the St. George's Basin *(Ngarlangkarnanya)*:

(7.11)
Nyangka	Nyalikanya,	'Marru	ngayu,	marru-marru	nganungu.'
nyangka	nyalikanya	ma=rru	ngayu	ma=rru-ma=rru	nga=nu-ng
3fNAR	baler.shell	3m=LAT	I	3m=LAT-REDUP	1=be-PRES

The baler-shell (said), 'I'll be behind, I'm staying behind.'

The paradigm of =*rno* 'Distal' is shown in Table 7.5, and that of =*rru* 'Lateral' in Table 7.6. The same constraints apply here as in Table 7.4: number morphemes are based on the singular pronoun shape, the human genders are neutralized, and plural forms are not available to non-human denotata.

Table 7.5: distal demonstrative: =*rno* 'that'

	SINGULAR	DUAL	PAUCAL	PLURAL
3a	irno	irnoyaarndu	irnowurri	arno
3f	nyirno	irnoyaarndu	irnowurri	arno
3w	wurno	wurnoyaarndu	wurnowurri	
3m	marno	marnoyaarnduma	marnowurrima	

Table 7.6: lateral demonstrative: =*rru*

	SINGULAR	DUAL	PLURAL
3a	irru	irraarndu	arru
3f	nyirru	irraarndu	arru
3w	wurru	wurraarndu	
3m	marru	marraarnduma	

Love (1934:10) appears to list a trial series for these forms: *i'no:juri* (*irnoyoorri* ?) but my instructors rejected these. Further, he does not list the paucal series provided here (forms ending in -*wurri*). He also gives a trial/paucal series for the lateral demonstrative, *i'ruri* (*irroorri* ?), but my instructors rejected this even more firmly. This does not mean that Love was necessarily mistaken, or that Worrorra never had trial or paucal series in these categories; I am simply recording here the language as I found it in the 1990s. I would however note two important factors influencing paradigms of this nature: (i) they are the output of a highly productive morphology, from which nothing ought to be discounted out-of-hand, and (ii) speakers' intuitions about indexical forms like these are very vulnerable. My instructors at first rejected *irru* and *nyirru* until I contextualized them: these forms even occur in unelicited narrative texts in the database. For further discussion see §9.6.1 and §9.6.3.

On this note, observe that the number of series-distinctions occurring in the demonstrative paradigms given above declines with distance from the speech act, from 5 in Table 7.4, to 4 in 7.5 and 3 in 7.6 – probably a quite natural progression.

Love also gives number-marked feminine forms for most demonstrative pronouns; that is, he does not record a neutralization in the human macrogender under number marking. My instructors also provided such forms in elicited paradigms: my reasons for rejecting them here are given in §9.4.3.

7.3.2 Presentational =^{k}*we*

A second set of demonstratives are presentational forms based on the root =^{k}*we* 'Presentational' (glossed PRSNTL), used to point out something that is highly topical in terms of the speech act in which it occurs. This paradigm involves singular participant agreement classes, and is shown in Table 7.7. Other forms are available for plural participant reference (cf eg sentence example 7.2c).

Table 7.7: presentational pronouns: =^{k}we 'PRESENTATIONAL'

1	ngawe	*here I am!*
2	ngunke	*there you are!*
3a	awe	*there he is!*
3f	nyangke	*there she is!*
3w	kawe	*there it is!*
3m	mawe	*there it is!*
3p	arrke	*there they are!*

Examples of their use are shown in (7.12). The suffix *-wurrurru* 'by oneself' may be attached to these pronouns, as shown in (7.12c & d). In (7.12a) the subject is *mana mayarama* 'house(s),' and the verb is in hortative mood:

(7.12a) Mawe   mamnyaninyeerri.
         ma=^{k}we   ma-mnya=ni-nya-eerri
         3m=PRSNTIL   3m-DD=be-HORT-PROG
         They (terrestrial things) can stay the way they are.

(b)   Ngawe   ngemnyanu.
         nga=^{k}we   nga-nya-mnya=nu
         1=PRSNTIL   1-OPT-DD=be
         I'll stay here.

(c)   Ngawewurrurru   ngenga.
         nga=^{k}we-wurrurru   nga=ya-nga
         1= PRSNTIL-by.oneself   1=go-TNS
         I went by myself.

(d)   Awewurrurru   baay   kanuna.
         a=^{k}we-wurrurru   baay   ka=nu-na
         3a= PRSNTIL-by.oneself   climb   3a=be=PAST
         He climbed up there all by himself.

(e)   Irnurnu   werr   kumnyona,   awewe   maa.
         i=rnurnu   werr   kuN-Ø-mnya=^{b}wu-na   awe-we   maa
         3a=hand   sing   3w-3-DD=hit-PAST   3aPRSNTIL-REDUP   3mREF
         There he was, and he sang about his hands.

7.3.3 Contextual =^{k}waya

Finally there is an important set of topicalizing or contextual deictics, that are used to bring something that is already onstage in the speech event into focus. The difference between these forms and the demonstratives is quite subtle. If, for example, you were pointing out a black cockatoo in a tree to someone, you would probably say, '*darraanma wali marno* – there's a black cockatoo.' If, however, you heard one screeching in the branches above you, you might still look up and point to it, but say, '*darraanma wali maa* – that's a black cockatoo.' The difference is that in the first expression you are drawing the denotatum on stage, by establishing ('creating') it as a feature of the arena in which the speech act takes place; while in the second you are only highlighting one that is already on stage – in this case one that has already brought itself to your attention by its own actions. Contextual deictics are based on the root shape =^{k}waya 'Contextual' (glossed REF), and are shown in Table 7.8:[54]

Table 7.8: contextual deictics: =^{k}waya 'CONTEXTUAL'

	SINGULAR	DUAL	HUMAN DUAL	PLURAL
3a	aaya	aayaarndu	arrkeyaarndu	arrke
3f	nyingke	aayaarndu	arrkeyaarndu	arrke
3w	ke			
3m	maa			

The first vowel in the feminine form here is quite variable. It may be heard as either *nyingke* or *nyangke*, and occasionally as *nyungke*.

There is a split here in the dual number-marked forms: human dual is based on the plural shape, while non-human dual is based on the singular shape. In this paradigm my instructors unhesitatingly rejected feminine dual-marked forms. No number-marked forms at all are available to non-human denotata.

The pronoun =^{k}waya functions as a contextual deictic, a distal demonstrative and as a topic marker in Worrorra. Although these uses are quite varied, it seems that the pronoun's contextual deictic function, as exemplified in (7.13), is primary:

(7.13a)
Ngarru	inja	kanangkurri,	iraarreya	aaya?
ngarru	inja	kanangkurri	i=raarreya	aaya
whither	3aDEF	dog	3a=big	3aREF

Where's the dog (gone), that big one?

(b)
Nyirramurrkangurru	bamaranoorrinya	nyangke.
nyiN-rra=murrka-ngurru	bamara-noorri-nya	nyangke
3f-2p=go.to-away	FaSi-2pDAT-3f	3fREF

You lot go over to that aunty of yours.

(c)
Aaya	anguja	rdu-rdu-rdu-rdu	mamerri?
aaya	anguja	rdu-rdu-rdu-rdu	ma-Ø=ma-eerri
3aREF	what	du-du-du-du	3m-3=get-PROG

What's that that's going du-du-du-du?

(d)
Mr Love	aaya	irnayurri,	aawali	minister
Mr Love	aaya	i=rnayurr-i	aaya-^{b}wali	minister
Mr Love	3aREF	3a-adult-3a	3aREF-RESUM	minister

That Mr. Love was an elder, he was the minister

(e)
Angujakunya	karrolkolkunerri	aalmara	aaya?
angujakunya	ka-rra-^{k}wulka=^{k}wulkuna-eerri	aalmara	aaya
why	3a-2p-AUG=fear-PROG	European	3aREF

---

[54] The morphophonolgy of the contextual deictics is as follows: |a=^{k}waya| > *aaya*, |nyiN=^{k}waya| > *nyingke*, |ØN=^{k}waya| > *ke*, |ma=^{k}wa(ya)| > *maa*, |arr=^{k}waya| > *arrke*. Note the operation of V-expansion rule 15 here: |aya|>/e/, and peripheral glide lenition rule 20: |awa|>/aa/. The 3m shape is slightly irregular.

Irnayurri wali aaya.
i=rnayurr-i wali aaya
3a-adult-3a PM
Why are you so afraid of that white man? He's an elder.

(f)
Wenngarri aaya eeja, waa ngarrkunjaangarri
weni-ngarri aaya eeja waa ngarrkunjaa-ngarri
now-REL 3aREF man not long.ago-REL

bangkaninyangarri aaya.
ba-ka=ni-nya-ngarri aaya
CFT-3a=be-PAST-REL 3aREF
That man lived quite recently, he was not from a very long time ago.

(g)
Ke binjiyeerri.
ke ba-kuN-nja=yi-eerri
3wREF CFT-VCOMP-2=do-PROG
Don't do that.

In all these examples, the referents marked by =*ᵏwaya* are already present in the immediate linguistic and attentive context in which the utterances occur. That is to say that this pronoun is used deictically, to point to things present in the context of speech-and-memory shared by the participants in a speech act, just as the spatial deictics are used to point to things in the visual environment.

Just as in English, and as would be expected, the boundary between the mnemonic and visual deictic functions becomes blurry at times. The contextual deictic pronoun may from time to time enter service as a distal demonstrative, but in such cases its spatial references are related to and derived from its contextual ones, as already discussed, and as may be seen again in (7.14):

(7.14a)
Darraanma wali maa.   Marrirri wali ke.
cockatoo PM   parrot PM
There's a red-tailed black cockatoo.   *There's a red-winged parrot.*

(b)
Marno binyineerri nyangke.
ma=rno ba-nyiN=nu-eerri nyangke
3m=DIST CFT-3f=be-PROG 3fREF
Don't let her stay over there.

(c)
Arno ajarrungoorri arrke wali.
arr=rno arr=yarrungu-oorri arrke wali
3p=DIST 3p=QUANT-TRI 3pREF RESUM
There's three of them out there.

(d)
Arrke baarramurrkerri awaawanja.
arrke ba-kaarr-rra=murrka-eerri awaawanja
3pREF CFT-3p-2p=go.to-PROG boys
Don't you lot go over to those boys.

(e)
Yarrorl	nguru	kanungunyale		mana	dambeemarnanya.	'Arrke
yarrorl	nguru	ka=nu-ng-u-nyale		mana	dambeema-rnanya	arrke
voices	hear	3a=be-PRES-EP-then		3mDEF	place-LOC	3pREF

ngani	kubajeerri?'		kunjungu		ineemarnanya.
ngani	kuN-ᵇwarr=yi-eerri		kuN-Ø=yi-ng		i=neema-rnanya
what	VCOMP-3p-do-PROG		VCOMP-3=do-PAST		3=ear-LOC

Then he heard shouting coming from back at the camp. 'What are they doing?' he wondered.

In these examples the contextual deictics are open to either spatial-visual or contextual interpretations. In practice, what is contextually salient is also very often visually prominent. The repetition of contextual deictics is commonly used to mark *linear extent* or *lines of progress* through space. In this use they are repeated, usually about three times, in an iconic representation (a 'frame-by-frame' representation) of an entity's motion, as shown in (7.15):

(7.15a)
'Nyangke!	Nyangke!	Nyangke!'	kubajeng.
nyangke	nyangke	nyangke	kuN-ᵇwarr-nya =yi-ng
3fREF/3fPRSNTIL	nyangke	nyangke	VCOMP-3p-EP=do-PAST

'There she goes! There she goes!' There she goes!' they cried.

(b)
Wara	inja	juwardba	kengkunaal	aaya,	aaya,	aaya.
wara	inja	juward-ᵇwa	ka=ya-ngku-na-aal	aaya	aaya	aaya
kangaroo	3aDEF	jump-PROG	3a=go-EP-PAST-hither	3aREF		

The kangaroo came jumping along towards them.

(c)
Jujurrwa	kubarrkangurrurlaaleerri,	ke,	ke,	ke.
jujurr-ᵇwa	kuN-ᵇwarr=ᵏwangurru-rla-aal-eerri	ke	ke	ke
haul-PROG	3w-3p=carry-PAST-hither-PROG	3wREF		

They were hauling it (celestial) along this way.

(d)
Jamaramaram	mana	mengkunaal	maa,	maa,	maa.
jamaramaram	mana	ma=ya-ngku-na-aal	maa	maa	maa
lizard.sp	3mDEF	3m=go-EP-PAST-hither	3mREF		

The dragon lizard came walking along.

(e)
Kamnyengkunaalkarndu	wajulu	aayaarndu,	aayaarndu,	aayaarndu.
ka-mnya=ya-ngku-na-aal-ᵏwarndu	wajulu	aayaarndu	aayaarndu	aayaarndu
3a-DD=go-EP-PAST-hither-DU	close	3aREF.DU		

They (dual) came closer and closer and closer.

A third important function of =ᵏ*waya*, that of topic marking, is discussed in §17.2.1. There is a preference for the determiners =ᵏ*waya* 'Contextual' and =*n* 'Definite' to occur after the noun over which they have scope. This is a preference only, occurring in pragmatically unmarked situations, as shown in (7.16a); in pragmatically marked arrangements ordering can be quite fluid. There is a corresponding preference for =ᵏ*wa* 'Anaphoric' to occur in front of its head noun, as shown in (7.16b). All three determiners may occur in the same noun phrase as the head noun, or outside the phrase. And in some pragmatically marked contexts all three determiners are found together in the same NP, as shown in (7.16c):

(7.16a)
Inbali	manjawarra	inja,	manjawarra	aaya	blaai	kaadingeerri.
i=nbali	manjawarra	inja	manjawarra	aaya	blaai	kaarr=ni-ng-eerri
3a=RESUM	berry.sp	3aDEF	berry.sp	3aREF	pound	3p=be-PRES-PROG

They're pounding up those manjawarra *berries.*

(b)
Awa	imalalamaanja	inja.
awa	i=malala-maan-ya	inja
3aNAR	3a=handsome-SPEC-3a	3aDEF

He is particularly handsome.

(c)
Awanyale	inja	koyoya	aaya	moorr	kunjunganangkorreerri.
awa-nyale	inja	koyoya	aaya	moorr	kuN-Ø=yi-ng-a-nangkorri-eerri
3aNAR-too	3aDEF	crocodile	3aREF	hate	VCOMP-3=do-PAST-EP-3pDAT-PROG

There was this crocodile that hated them.

The semantics and configurational ordering of these three pronouns define an elaborate system of pragmatic reference, described in more detail in §17.2.2 and §17.4.

7.3.4 Paucal DEF-ngal-

The morpheme *-ngal-* 'several x, a number of x' is suffixed to =n 'Definite' and =rno 'Distal.' This paucal number morpheme is quite distinct from the paucal number-marking morpheme *-ᵏwurri* described in §9.6.1. Whereas the semantics of *-ᵏwurri* is augmentational at bottom, and has to do with the construction of sets, that of *-ngal-* is comparatively straightforward, denoting simply a number of items (between about five and a dozen) under consideration. The unmarked and distal paradigms of these forms are shown in Table 7.9. Examples of their use in sentences are seen in (7.17):

Table 7.9: *-ngal-* 'SEVERAL'

	=n-ngal-'several'	=rno-ngal- 'those several'
3a	inngalya	irnongalya
3f	nyinngalja	nyirnongalja
3w	wunngalu	wurnongalu
3m	manngalima ~ manngalba	marnongalba
3p	anngalya	arnongalya

(7.17a)
	Wangaya	anngalya	kaarringkaaleerri
	wangaya	arr=n-ngal-ya	kaarr=i-ᵏwaal-eerri
	women	px=DEF-several-3p	3p=go-hither-PROG

Several women are coming

(b)
	Wunngalu	marrirri	kunyangkaaleerri
	ᵏwuN=n-ngal-u	marirri	kuN=ya-ᵏwaal-eerri
	3w=DEF-several-3w	parrot.sp	3w=go-hither-PROG

A number of red-winged parrots are coming

(c)   Ngayu   nyinjorinya   nyinngalja
ngayu   nyiN=yoru-nya   nyiN=n-ngal-nya
I   3f=widow-3f   3f=DEF-several-3f
I am one of a number of widows/I am one of these widows

7.4 Interrogative pronouns

There are three important sets of interrogative pronouns.

7.4.1 *nga-(ni)- 'where?'*

In adverbial locative functions, these forms require suffixial agreement-class coding in agreement with their referents. In adverbial vector functions they take the suffixes =*rru* 'Lateral' (also possibly a contraction of -*ngurru* 'Allative') and -*aalba* 'Ablative,' as seen in Table 7.10. The second syllable of this root form is deleted in adverbial vector functions. This adverbial pronoun may also take the discourse-deictic infix -*mnya*- after the first syllable, as well as number suffixes and non-subcategorized object (DAT) marking, as seen in the examples in (7.18).

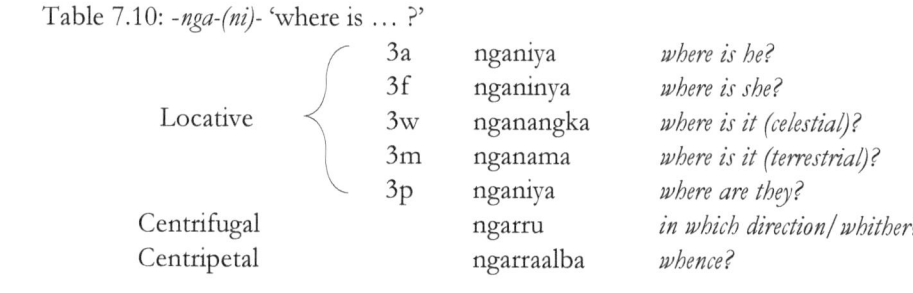

Table 7.10: -*nga-(ni)*- 'where is … ?'

Locative	3a	nganiya	*where is he?*
	3f	nganinya	*where is she?*
	3w	nganangka	*where is it (celestial)?*
	3m	nganama	*where is it (terrestrial)?*
	3p	nganiya	*where are they?*
Centrifugal		ngarru	*in which direction/whither?*
Centripetal		ngarraalba	*whence?*

(7.18a)   Nyinjarndanya   nganinya?
nyiN=yarnda-nya   ngani-nya
3f=infant-3f   where-3f
Where's the litte girl?

(b)   Nyinjarndanya   ngamnyaninya?
nyiN=yarnda-nya   nga-mnya-ni-nya
3f=infant-3f   ↳-DD-where-3f
Where's that little girl?

(c)   Inkarndu   ngamnyaniyaarndu?
i=n-ᵏwarndu   nga-mnya-ni-ya-ᵏwarndu
3a=DEF-DU   ↳-DD-where-3a-DU
Where have those two got to?

(d)   Wurlarnbirri   nganiyaareya?
wurlarnbirri   ngani-ᵏwara-ya
belongings   where-1DAT-3p
Where's all my things?

The terrestrial shape *nganama* is used as a general locative interrogative for participant persons, and when location is in focus:

(7.19a) Nganama   kaanjaarndengaara?
         ngani-ma   kaarr-nja=^kwarnde-nga-^kwara
         where-3m   3p-2=place-PAST-1DAT
         Where did you put all my (things)?
         Lit: *'Where's (the place) that/ at what (place) did you put all my (things)?'*

(b)   Nganama   ngadunerri   karle maa?
         ngani-ma   ngarr=nu-na-eerri   karle maa
         where-3m   1pin=be-PAST-PROG   REM.P
         Where did we use to live?

The anaphor *nga-(ni)-* is idiomatically predicated upon the inalienable noun *=ngumbu wunu* 'name,' as seen in (6.27b) in §6.3 and in (7.20):

(7.20a) Nyingumbu   nganangka?
         nyiN=ngumbu   nganangka
         3f=name   where.3w
         What's her name?

(b)   Ngunngumbu   nganangka?
         ngun=ngumbu   nganangka
         2=name   where.3w
         What's your name?

7.4.2 /ang(k)uYa/ 'who? what?'

These interrogative pronouns are described in §4.1.6. Note as well however the forms *angujakunya* (|angujaC-^kwunya| [what-PURP]) 'What for? Why?' and *angujaaw* (|anguja-aaw| [what-TIME]) 'When?' A relict consonant |C| appears in the underlying shape of *angujakunya*, to harden the following purposive morpheme *-^kwunya* 'Purposive.'[55] There is also a rhetorical form *angujabirri* 'Why the hell ... ? Why on earth ... ?' as seen in (7.21):

(7.21)   Angujabirri   jandu-jandu   bungunindaka?
         angujabirri   jandu-jandu   ba-ngun=ni-n-y₂aka
         why   mock-mock   CFT-2=be-NON.P-EMPH
         Why on earth do you have to make fun of it?

Anguja as a masculine noun may also mean 'something' or 'thing,' as in (7.22):

---

[55] The relict consonant is probably *ng* by reduplication: |angujang|. This in turn suggests the development of the modern form from a reduplicated ancestral form **yangu*:

	yangu-yangu
Medial glide hardening	yangu-jangu
Initial glide deletion	angu-jangu
Final vowel deletion	angu-jang—> |angujang|

Note that in this scenario the ancestral shape **yangu* is almost identical to the modern Wubuy word *yangi* (Heath 1984:455), the functional equivalent of Worora *anguja*. Note also Nyulnyulan **yangki* 'what.'

(7.22a)
Inja   anguja   wori   ngarrwaarndeerri?
inja   anguja   wori   ngarr-Ø=ᵇwu-ᵏwarndu-eerri
3aDEF   something surround   1pin-3=hit-DU-PROG
What's that creeping around us?

(b)
Angujakunya   anguja   inja   kurdu   kunjeenga   wunu?
angujaC-ᵏwunya   anguja   inja   kurdu   kuN-nja=yi-ng   wunu
what-PURP   thing   3aDEF   follow   VCOMP-2=do-PAST   3wDEF
What did you have to go chasing after that thing for?

The masculine noun *angujakana inja* 'something' is also used with this meaning:

(7.23)   Awa   inja   angujakana   baa   kamurrkarla.
         awa   inja   angujakana   baa   ka-Ø=murrka-rla
         3aNAR   3aDEF   something   appear   3a-3=go.to-PAST
         Something came up towards him.

Another form *angujakane inja* 'all kinds of things' is used in this function with plural reference. Finally there is an infrequent variant of *anguja, angujanu*, with which it appears to be synonymous.

7.4.3 Existential =aani

The existential interrogative *=aani* asks, 'Is there any *x*?/Does some *x* exist?/Do you have *x*?' This word takes agreement-class prefixes as shown in Table 7.11. Note that no distinction is made in the unmarked macrogender:

Table 7.11: existential *=aani* 'is there (any)?'
3a/3w	kaani
3f	nyaani
3m	maani
3p	kaarrani

The use of these forms is exemplified by such expressions as *Ngeenya nyaani?* 'Is there any honey?' *Burnarri kaarrani?* 'Is there any meat?' and *Ngeeya kaarrani?* 'Is there a lot of/much honey?' These forms accept the discourse-deictic infix *-mnya-*, eg 3f *nyimnyaani* and 3a *kamnyaani*, as shown in example (7.24):

(7.24)   Kulanoorri   kamnyaani?
         kula-[nu-ᵏwurri]   ka-mnya=aani
         husband-[2DAT-NUM]   3a-DD=EXIST
         Is your (pl) husband still alive?

The plural shape may be used with *-nya-* epenthesis, as in *burnarri kaajaani?* (|kaarr-nya=aani| [3p-EP=EXIST]) 'is there still some meat left?'

7.5 Directional =*rru-nangkowa*

The root shape =*rru-nangkowa* 'Directional' (glossed DIR) comes about by way of a small set of lateral demonstrative adverbs with the suffix -*nangkowa* attached. The demonstratives in question are *marru* 'over that way' and *ngarru* 'whither?' with a pair of collateral forms, *maangurru* 'over there' and *wurru* 'that (celestial) one.' The resulting forms yield a number of sense meanings centred around the notion of 'general or unspecified, usually lateral, direction or extent.' The word *marrunangkowa* 'this/that side, this/that way' is used without regard to distance: what is denoted is the general nature of the direction referred to, rather than the distance from the speaker. Such expressions are often accompanied by manual gestures:

(7.25a) Marrunangkowa bengkaal.
　　　　ma=rrunangkowa ba=ya-ᵏwaal
　　　　3m=DIR CFT=go-hither
　　　　Come over to this side.

(b) Marrunangkowa dambeem mawarrakuwalima.
　　ma=rrunangkowa dambeem ma=warr-(y₂)akuwali-ma
　　3m=DIR place 3m=wrong-EMPH-3m
　　That's the wrong place over that way.

(c) Marrunangkowa keey nyinuna.
　　ma=rrunangkowa keey nyiN=nu-na
　　3m=DIR peep 3f=be-PAST
　　She peeped over the side.

The interrogative *ngarrunangkowa* 'on which side?/in which direction?/which way?' may be used in a locative-lateral sense as in (7.26a), or in a directional sense, as in (7.26b & c):

(7.26a)
Ngarrunangkowa kaningkarla?
ngarrunangkowa ka-Ø=ningka-rla
which.way 3a-3=bite-PAST
Where (=on which side) did it bite him?

(b)
Ngarrunangkowa nyenga? Marrunangkowa nyimnyenga.
ngarrunangkowa nya=ya-nga marrunangkowa nyiN-mnya=ya-nga
which.way 3f=go-TNS that way 3f-DD=go-TNS
Which way did she go? She went that way.

(c)
Mee ngarrunangkowa kamnyengaarndu.
mee ngarrunangkowa ka-mnya=ya-nga-ᵏwarndu
I.don't.know which.way 3a-DD=go-TNS-DU
I don't know which way they went.

The function of the English manner interrogative 'how?' may be assumed by *anguja* 'what/(how)' as in (7.2e), or by *ngarrunangkowa*, as in (7.27). That is to say that 'which way?' in Worrorra may have both directional or manner-adverbial senses, as in English:

(7.27a) Ngarrunangkowa   ngama   wali   welkunke?
         ngarrunangkowa   ØN-nga=ma   wali   welkunke
         which way/how   3w-1=get   still   torch
         How can I get a torch?

(b)   Ngarrunangkowa   wayarl   karrba?
         ngarrunangkowa   wayarl   ka-ngarr=ma
         which way/how   remove   3a-1pin=get
         How can we get rid of it (masc)?

The paired terms *marrunangkowa, marrunangkowa* and *maangurrunangkowa, marrunangkowa* 'this way and that way/on either side/every which-way' denote items or actions extending centrifugally all around the speaker, as in (7.28):

(7.28a)
Daya   kubajingeerri   marrunangkowa, marrunangkowa.
rdaya   kuN-ᵇwarr=yi-ng-eerri   marrunangkowa, marrunangkowa
ignite   3w-3p=do-PAST-PROG   this.way.and.that.way
They were lighting fires all over the place.

(b)
Walambarr-walambarr   nyimbuna   marrunangkowa, marrunangkowa.
Walambarr-walambarr   nyiN-Ø=ᵇwu-na   marrunangkowa, marrunangkowa
throw.out-throw.out   3f-3=hit-PAST   this.way.and.that.way
He threw it (fem) all out, left, right and centre.

(c)
Malka   kanunerringkurri   maangurrunangkowa marrunangkowa.
malka   ka=nu-na-eerri-ᵏwurri   maangurrunangkowa marrunangkowa
play   3a=be-PAST-PROG-NUM   this.way.and.that.way
They were playing about all over the place, every which-way.

Finally, the celestial-terrestrial opposition in the non-human macrogender may be enlisted to denote bilateral symmetry, as in (7.29a), which is part of a description of the way in which crocodiles are butchered for food. Extended bilateral symmetry may be marked by a directional form paired with an ablative form, as in (7.29b).

(7.29a)
Jarlewa   kanungu   mana   inganabarnanya,
jarlewa   ka=nu-ng   mana   i=nganaba-rnanya
red   3a=be-PRES   3mDEF   3a=body-LOC

marrunangkowaa   wurrunangkowa.
ma=rrunangkowa-aa   ᵏwuN=rrunangkowa
3m=DIR-and   3w=DIR
There are red markings in its body, all up and down each side.

(b)
Marrunangkowa   warnangkali,   marraalba   warnangkali.
ma=rrunangkowa   warnangkali   ma=rru-aalba   warnangkali
3m=DIR   cliff   3m=LAT-from   cliff
Cliffs rearing up on either side.

7.6 Highly presentational forms

Highly presentational pronoun forms direct the listener's attention to their referents by extracting them from their conversational or narrative background, and endowing them with a special emotive significance. In Worrorra such forms are marked by suffixes containing the adverbial shape -^{b}wali (§10.1.1 (i)).

7.6.1 Emphatic -y$_2$akuwali

The emphatic suffix -y$_2$akuwali has been seen in examples (7.2a) and (7.10). This shape is composed of -y$_2$aka 'EMPHATIC' (see §10.2.1 (ix)), and -^{b}wali 'RESUMPTIVE' (§17.5), although I am unable to ascertain the difference in meaning between -y$_2$aka and -y$_2$akuwali. -y$_2$akuwali is also found suffixed to personal participant pronouns and to the definite article =n, as shown in Table 7.12. The word-forms in this table have meanings something like '*x* is the one!' Note that the morpheme is a postposition in plural participant expressions. In this table the following phonological processes apply:

$y_2 \longrightarrow d\ /\ n\ \_\_\_$
$a \longrightarrow u\ /\ k\ \_\_\_\ w$:

Table 7.12: -y$_2$akuwali EMPHATIC, '*x* is the one!'

	PERSONAL FORMS		DETERMINER FORMS
1	ngayekuwali	3a	indakuwali
2	ngunjekuwali	3f	nyindakuwalinya
1pin	ngarri yakuwali	3w	wundakuwali
1px	arri yakuwali	3m	mandakuwalima
2p	nyirri yakuwali	3p	andakuwali

The shape -y$_2$akuwali is also found suffixed to SPECIFIC pronoun forms, in a sequence -maandakuwali, as occurs in *iyarrungumaandakuwali* (|i=yarrungu-maan-y$_2$aka-^{b}wali| [3a-QUANT-SPEC-EMPH-RESUM]) 'he's the very one!' For further discussion of these forms see §17.7.1.[56] Further examples of the use of -y$_2$akuwali are shown in (7.30):

(7.30a)
Nyindakuwalinya	kungurr	kunjunganangka!
nyiN=n-y$_2$aka-^{b}wali-nya	kungurr	kuN-Ø=yi-ng-a-nangka
3f=DEF-EMPH-RESUM-3f	stab	VCOMP-3=do-PAST-EP-DAT

She's the one who stabbed him!

(b)
Arrke	kaarri	yakuwali.
3pREF	3pNEG	EMPH

There's no-one there/They've all gone.

---

[56] The morphophonology of emphatic pronouns is as follows: |ngaya-y$_2$aka-^{b}wali| > *ngayekuwali*, |ngunja-y$_2$aka-^{b}wali| > *ngunjekuwali*, |i=n-y$_2$aka-^{b}wali| > *indakuwali*, |nyiN=n-y$_2$aka-^{b}wali-nya| > *nyindakuwalinya*, |^{k}wuN=n-y$_2$aka-^{b}wali| > *wundakuwali*, |ma=n-y$_2$aka-^{b}wali-ma| > *mandakuwalima*, |arr=n-y$_2$aka-^{b}wali| > *andakuwali*.

7.6.2 Presentational/empathic

The demonstrative/ indexical postposition *(-)yirdabali* is quite difficult to understand, appearing to have at least two distinct sense meanings. Most commonly, it is found marking presentational speech acts, in which the speaker is presenting or offering something to the listener, either in a literal sense, as in (7.31a & c) below, or in a metaphorical, demonstrative sense, as in (7.31b). In this function it appears as either a separate word with the shape *irdabali*, or as a suffix to nouns and pronouns. As a pronoun suffix, it takes agreement-class marking as shown in Table 7.13:

Table 7.13: examples of *-yirdabali* 'Presentational'

1	ngayirdabali		1pin	ngarrirdabali
2	ngunjirdabali		1px	arrirdabali
3a	irdabali		2p	nyirrirdabali
3f	nyinjirdabalinya		3p	arrkerdabali
3w	wunjirdabali			
3m	manjirdabalima			

This table represents not so much a paradigm, as one example only of the way in which the suffix may be attached to pronouns. For instance the 3f, 3w and 3m shapes here are based on the pronoun =*n* 'Definite,' while the 3p shape is based on =^{k}*waya* 'Contextual.' The 3a shape appears to have only the masculine agreement-class index *i-* as its prefix – cf also example (7.31b) below. The presentational function of this form is illustrated in (7.31):

(7.31a)
Karle   irdabali   rnaaya   kungmanga.
karle   irdabali   rnaaya   kuN-nga=ma-nga
now   PRSNTIL   gather   3w-1=get-PAST
There they are now, I've gathered them (celestial) all together.

(b)
Nyingkeyirdabalinya   nyirno   ilardurnanya!
nyiN=^{k}waya-yirdabali-nya nyiN=rno   i=lardu-rnanya
3f=REF-PRSNTIL-3f   3f=there   3a=back-LOC
There she is, there, she's on his back!

(c)
Yaw,   nyijengurraarndu,   nyimnyaangurrungurru
yaw   nyirr-nya=ya-ngurru-^{k}warndu   nyiN-mnya=^{k}wangurru-ngurru
yes   2p-EP=go-away-DU   3f-DD=carry-away

mangkanyirdabalinya   nyina.
mangkanya-yirdabali-nya   nyina
wife-PRSNTIL-3f   3fDEF
Yes, she can go with you, take her away, she's your wife now.

In (7.31c) a father is presenting his daughter to his son-in-law, after the pair have been living with her family for a while, and as they set out to move to her husband's home.

The second sense-function of *-yirdabali* appears to be to show sympathy or empathy with someone, especially for someone suffering some kind of trouble. Expressions of this sort are quite common in northern Australia, for example *japurtu* in Nyangumarta and *wiyarrpa* in Warlpiri both convey this meaning. The core meaning of these forms is not to denote the referent as an object of pity, but rather to register the speaker's projection of his or her self into some other person's situation;

that is, to register empathy with someone in a particular situation. Examples of this are given in (7.32):

(7.32a) Anguja   kaningkarla   irdabali   inja?
         anguja   ka-Ø=ningka-rla   irdabali   inja
         what   3a-3=bite-PAST   PRSNTIL   3aDEF
         What's bitten the poor little thing?

(b) Ngani   wajunangkerdabali   nyinmurruma?
     ngani   ᵏwuN-ngarr=yi-nangka-yirdabali   nyiN=n-murru-ma
     what   VCOMP-1pin=do-DAT-PRSNTIL   3f=DEF-SEQ.FIN-?
     Now what are we going to tell that poor old thing back there?

It may be that the presentational and empathic-projectional meanings of *-yirdabali* are related as centrifugal gestures towards some goal, typically an addressee in both cases. So also in English, presentational expressions are used to comfort distressed children ('there we are,' 'here we go'); presentation being used in these instances metaphorically, as a vehicle for the projection of the speaker's sympathy toward an addressee/goal.

7.7 Possessive pronouns

Possessive pronouns are produced by suffixing the indirect or non-subcategorized object morpheme *-nangka* (glossed DAT, discussed in Chapter 13) to pronouns in the following ways:
(i) The first and second person singular pronouns |ngaya| and |ngunja|, have *-nangka* attached directly.
(ii) All other possessive pronouns, including non-singular participant forms, are based on the anaphoric/narrative pronoun =ᵏwa, described above in §7.2 and seen in Table 7.2; along with agreement-class prefixes.

Table 7.14: possessive pronouns

FUNCTION		FORM	MORPHOLOGY	TRANS
Singular:	first	ngayanangka	|nga=ya-nangka|	'my'
	second	ngunjanangka	|ngun=ya-nangka|	'your'
	third masc	aanangka	|a=ᵏwa-nangka|	'his'
	third fem	nyangkanangka	|nyaN=ᵏwa-nangka|	'her'
Plural:	first inc	ngarrkanangka	|ngarr=ᵏwa-nangka|	'our'
	first exc	arrkanangka	|arr=ᵏwa-nangka|	'our'
	second	nyirrkanangka	|nyirr=ᵏwa-nangka|	'your'
	third	arrkanangka	|arr=ᵏwa-nangka|	'their'
Dual:	first inc	ngarrkanangkaarndu	|ngarr=ᵏwa-nangka-ᵏwarndu|	'our'
	first exc	arrkanangkaarndu	|arr=ᵏwa-nangka-ᵏwarndu|	'our'
	second	nyirrkanangkaarndu	|nyirr=ᵏwa-nangka-ᵏwarndu|	'your'
	third	aanangkaarndu	|a=ᵏwa-nangka-ᵏwarndu|	'their'
Paucal:	first inc	ngarrkanangkorri	|ngarr=ᵏwa-nangka-ᵏwurri|	'our'
	first exc	arrkanangkorri	|arr=ᵏwa-nangka-ᵏwurri|	'our'
	second	nyirrkanangkorri	|nyirr=ᵏwa-nangka-ᵏwurri|	'your'
	third	arrkanangkorri	|arr=ᵏwa-nangka-ᵏwurri|	'their'

This paradigm is not without problems. The paucal number series is represented in the database only in elicited paradigms, it is not found in spontaneous texts. (See §9.6.1 below on the difference between plural and paucal pronouns.) Love (1934:13) lists a trial possessive pronoun series ending in *-uri*, which may represent the trial morpheme *-oorri* discussed in §9.6.3. Love (1934:12) also lists possessive pronouns *not* based on =*ᵏwa*: he gives examples of demonstrative pronouns with possessive inflection. While such forms may have been produced within the context of a full linguistic community, (or perhaps in an elicitation context), my instructors would not agree to them. Both Love's and my elicited paradigms include a feminine dual shape **nyangkanangkaarndinya*, but as predicted, this is absent from the spontaneous database, and I do not consider it to be a genuine form (for discussion see §9.4.3).

There are only two spontaneous occurrences of dual possessive pronouns in the database, and they are both third person. There are no examples of celestial or terrestrial possessive pronouns; that is, of possessive pronouns with celestial or terrestrial antecedents. It appears, then, that the possessor in a possessive construction must be human.

Possessive constructions using pronouns are discussed in §13.1.2, but a few comments here are necessary in order to account for the forms of possessive pronouns. Cross-linguistically nominal possessive constructions are naturally complex, composed of at least two parts: a head nominal, that is the thing possessed; and a dependent, that is the possessor or owner of the thing possessed. I will refer to these categories as 'heads' and 'possessors' respectively. In Worrorra, possessive pronouns are syntactically dependent upon their heads: like English possessive determiners they refer to whatever their heads refer to. They display morphological agreement with their heads when those head nouns are plural, collective, or of the marked macrogender.[57] Such agreement-marking is by means of suffixes: *-nya* feminine, *-ma* terrestrial and *-ya* collective and plural. Some examples follow:

(7.33a) (3a head) Ngayanangka   abiya
                    ngaya-nangka   abi-ya
                    I-DAT   El.Sib-3a
                    My elder brother/father's father

(b)   (3f head)   Abeenya   ngunjanangka**nya**
                    abi-nya   ngunja-nangka-nya
                    El.Sib-3f   you-DAT-3f
                    Your elder sister/father's mother

(c)   (3w head)   Ngarlangarla   ngarrkanangka
                    ngarlangarla   ngarr=ᵏwa-nangka
                    language   1pin=NAR-DAT
                    Our language

(d)   (3m head)   Rambarrba   nyangkanangka**ma**
                    rambarrba   nyaN=ᵏwa-nangka-ma
                    avoidance.kin   3f=NAR-DAT-3m
                    Her avoidance-category kinsman

(e)   (3p head)   Ngunjanangkaya   nyangkaangka**ya**
                    ngunja-nangka-ya   nya-ngkaa-ngka-ya
                    you-DAT-3p   ↳AUG-girl-3p
                    Your girls

---

[57] And so can be said to display negative or default agreement with the masculine and celestial genders.

(f)	(collective head)	Arrkanangka**ya** arr=ᵏwa-nangka-ya px=NAR-DAT-3p *Their/ our food*	mangarri mangarri food

From these examples it can be seen that a pronoun's morphological stem, *=ya-nangka* or *=ᵏwa-nangka* in Table 7.14, is doubly inflected; agreement with the phrasal head is marked by suffixes, and coding of the agreement-class of the phrasal dependent (the possessor) is marked by prefixes.

Possessive pronouns often co-occur with their base (uninflected) form in apposition. The following sequences, sometimes metathesized, are found in the database:

ngayu ngayanangka	*my*
ngarri ngarrkanangka	*our (inc)*
arri arrkanangka	*our (exc)*
arrka arrkanangka	*their*

This is part of a wider phenomenon discussed in §13.1.2, in which possessor nouns occur in apposition with, and in the same phrase as possessive pronouns. A by-product of this syntax is that the 1px and 3p possessive forms may be disambiguated, as seen above.

Curiously, in pronouns and only in pronouns, the possessive (DAT) morpheme *-nangka* behaves as if it were a root morpheme, in so far as it may undergo Type 2 phonological extension (§6.2.6 (ii)):

Ø —> naa / ___ nangka

In the database this phenomenon is quite restricted in its occurrence. It is found in possessive pronouns modifying nouns that (i) denote humans or dogs, and (ii) are marked for plural number, and (iii) have their own root shapes reduplicated or extended. In the following examples the extension material is glossed AUG:

(7.34a)	Abaabiya abi-abi-ya El.Sib-El.Sib-3p *Our/ their elder brothers*	arrkanaanangkaya arr=ᵏwa-naa-nangka-ya px=NAR-AUG-DAT-3P	
(b)	Ngayanaanangkaya ngaya-naa-nangka-ya I-AUG-DAT-3p *My big boys*	iwaawurleya i-ᵏwaa=ᵏwurla-ya ↳-AUG-man's.child-3p	
(c)	Ngunjanaanangkaya ngunja-naa-nangka-ya you-AUG-DAT-3p *All your dogs*	kanaanangkurri ka-naa-nangkurri ↳-AUG-dog	
(d)	Kawaawurlanangkaya ka-ᵏwaa=ᵏwurla-nangka-ya ↳-AUG=man's.child-DAT-3p *Her nephews and nieces*	nyangkanaanangkaya nyaN=ᵏwa-naa-nangka-ya 3f=NAR-AUG-DAT-3P	

Head nouns denoting humans in the above examples are doubly marked for plural number: by stem-augmentation and by suffixation (*-ya* '3p'), and their possessive pronoun dependents are doubly marked in the same way. Although this process is common, it is not obligatory: example (7.33e) above shows a reduplicated head noun modified by a possessive pronoun that is *not* itself augmented.

Examples (7.34b & d) involve the somewhat problematic root =ᵏwurla/=ᵏwurlu 'man's child; woman's brother's child,' already seen in §6.2.4. The appearance of the DAT morpheme on the kinship noun in (7.34d) is addressed in §13.1.1 below. The Type 2 phonological extension -ᵏwaa- preposed to the roots of the kinship nouns in the (b) and (d) examples (*iwaawurleya* and *kawaawurlanangkaya* respectively) indicates fairly clearly that these forms are derived from an underlying root, probably =ᵏwurla. There are two ostensibly underived nouns, *kawurla* 'man's son, woman's brother's son,' and *kawurlanya* 'man's daughter, woman's brother's daughter' that also appear to incorporate this morpheme, although the initial segment /ka-/ is clearly not a masculine marker in this case. The apparently collective noun *iwaawurleya* 'big boys, adolescents' noted in §4.2.2 also appears to incorporate this root, or possibly the root =ᵏwurle 'first' (§10.6.4 (ii)); and again the ostensibly masculine singular initial segment *i-* is not singular here. In the morphology of possessive pronouns, it is the DAT morpheme that undergoes phonological extension in agreement or harmony with a plural, high-animacy head whose root is also phonologically extended.

7.8 Intimations of other forms

A number of other pronoun forms occur in the database that are neither well represented nor well understood. For some of these, paradigms have been obtained, and a few are sketched here.

(i) The proximal pronouns (=*n*) are able to take the first person singular non-subcategorized object suffix -ᵏ*wara* (1DAT), in the sequence |=n-ᵏwara| ([=DEF-1DAT]), producing forms with a meaning something like 'here/there *x* is, my *y*!'

Table 7.15: =n-ᵏwara 'Here's my x!'

3a	inkarawa
3f	nyinkarawanya
3w	wunkara
3m	mankarawama
3p	ankarawaya

An example of the use of this form is shown in (7.35):

(7.35) Mangkaanya   nyinkarawanya   nyina!
       mangka-aa-nya   nyiN=n-ᵏwara-wa-nya   nyina
       wife-1DAT-3f   3f=DEF-1DAT-?-3f   3fDEF
       Here she is, my own wife!

Non-subcategorized object morphemes occur in all sorts of unexpected places, cf the shape *nganiyaareya* 'where are my (things)?' in (7.18d).

(ii) The shape -*murru* 'at last, SEQUENCE FINAL' appears to mark something as being one found at last, after a series of events. In the database this morpheme occurs suffixed to the spatial deictics =*n* 'Definite, this' and =*rno* 'Distal' as shown in Table 7.16, as well as to the 3m contextual deictic *maa*.

Table 7.16: -*murru* 'SEQUENCE FINAL'

	PROXIMAL	DISTAL
3a	inmurru	irnomurru
3f	nyinmurru	nyirnomurru
3w	wunmurru	wurnomurru
3m	manmurru	marnomurru
3p	anmurru	arnomurru

Under elicitation, pronouns with -*murru* occur as in Table 7.16, but in the database nearly all forms occur with an additional suffix -*m(a)* (see (iv) below). This shape has already been seen in (7.32b), and further examples are shown in (7.36).

(7.36a) Irnomurrum!
i=rno-murru-ma
3a-DIST-SEQ.FIN-?
There he is at last!

(b)
Ke	wunmaanmurru	nyerrkunyo	wunu ...
ke	ᵏwuN=n-maan-murru	nyaN-nyarr-ngun-nya=ᵇwu	wunu
and	3w=DEF-SPEC-SEQ.FIN	3f-1px-SJTV-EP=hit	3wDEF

And so now, when we kill them (fem) ...

(c)
Nyinmurrum	wunu	kamnyaninjeerri	maade
nyiN=n-murru-ma	wunu	ØN-ngka-mnya=ni-ny-yeerri	maade
3f=DEF-SEQ.FIN-?	3wDEF	3w-SJTV-DD=be-MIR-PROG	RESULT

And so that's the way it is for her now ...

In (7.36b & c) the celestial forms refer to time: so *wunmaanmurru* 'this particular time now,' and the 3w subject of the verb *kamnyaninjeerri* is also to be taken as time, ie '(now) it is (thus).'

(iii) The determiner =*n* may appear with the relativizing suffix -*ngarri*. In this form it refers to 'things associated with this or these (things).' Two examples are shown in (7.37):

(7.37a)
Wunngarrima	bardi	arrkunyaninykarndeerri
ᵏwuN=n-ngarri-ma	bardi	arr-ngun-nya=ni-ny-ᵏwarndu-eerri
3w=DEF-REL-?	go.home	1px-SJTV-EP⁻be-MIR-DU-PROG

mana	dambeem.
3mDEF	place

From now on we're staying at home.

(b)
Nyangkanyini	nyina	kawurlanya,	nyinngarriwa
nyangka-nyini	nyina	kawurlanya	nyiN=n-ngarri-wa
3fNAR-ENDPOINT	3fDEF	daughter	3f=DEF-REL-?

ngarrkunyameembinjeerri	marram	mana.
ngarr-Ø-ngun-nya=meembu-ny-yeerri	marram	mana
1pin-3-SJTV-EP=show-MIR-PROG	light	3mDEF

So now it's the daughter, and her (sisters and daughters) who show us the light.

In (7.37a) the celestial reference of the word *wunngarrima* is to time, hence 'intervals of time associated with this time/from now on.' The feminine shape *nyinngarriwa* in (7.37b), 'things associated with her/her ones,' refers to other female relations of the daughter, in this case either her sisters or daughters, or both.

(iv) A segment *-m* or *-ma*, homophonous with the terrestrial suffix, occurs quite rarely word-finally on some pronouns in the database, where 3m marking would not be expected. In this chapter we have seen this segment occur in *nyinmurrum(a)* in (7.32b) and (7.36c), *irnomurrum* in (7.36a) and *wunngarrima* in (7.37a). As well as this, almost all instances of the morpheme *-murru* 'SEQ.FIN' in the database occur as *-murrum(a)* (7.36b contains an exception). The pronouns showing this phenomenon are =*n* 'DEF,' =*rno* 'DIST' and *nyangke* '3fREF' which occurs as *nyangkem* (see example 11.31b in §11.4.2). Some more examples are shown in (7.38):

(7.38a)
Nyinma	kanangkuja	ngarru	nyimnyenga?
nyiN=n-ma	kanangkuja	ngarru	nyiN-mnya=ya-nga
3f=DEF-?	bitch	whither	3f-DD=go-TNS

Where's that dog gone?

(b)
Aalmara	iniya,	irnayurr	wali	inma.
aalmara	i=niya	i=rnayurr	wali	i=n-ma
European	3a=good	3a=adult	PM	3a=DEF-?

The European is a good man, he's a leader.

(c)
Nyangkem	aja	nyangkaninjeerri.
NyaN=ᵏwaya-m	aja	nyaN-ngka=ni-ny-yeerri
3f=REF-?	sit	3f-SJTV=be-MIR-PROG

There she is, sitting down.

In these examples the forms with *-m(a)* all appear to function just as do their more conventional counterparts; *nyina* '3fDEF,' *inja* '3aDEF' and *nyangke* '3fREF,' even to the point of *inma* substituting for the more usual *inja* in predicate-marking syntax in (7.38b) (see §17.8). Although at first glance it appears that these forms have acquired terrestrial marking, this is probably not the case, as such extra class-marking appears to be unmotivated in the instances in which it occurs. Example (7.38c), for instance, contains an evidential mirative verb form as well as a presentational or contextual pronoun; in this situation terrestrial marking, indexical of place, would seem to be quite superfluous. And the semantics of place do not enter into (7.38b) at all. Rather, my guess is that these forms are simply stylistic variants, perhaps influenced by borrowing from another language, rare in the database but optionally available none the less.

The uses of the three important pronouns =*n*, 'Definite,' =ᵏ*wa* 'Anaphoric/ Narrative,' and =ᵏ*waya* 'Contextual' have been sketched in this chapter. The form =ᵏ*wa* 'Anaphoric' is the language's most common NP anaphor, and it appears most often and most characteristically in this function. It is also discussed in §9.4.3 in relation to its role in marking number. However =*n*, 'Definite' and =ᵏ*waya* 'Contextual' have important pragmatic functions, in marking definiteness and topicality over stretches of discourse, as well as combining with a variety of adverbial morphemes and other morphemes whose meanings are primarily or exclusively pragmatic. Consideration of these important functions of Worrorra pronouns involves the analysis of discourse-level phenomena such as rhetoric and 'global' predication, and is reserved for Chapter 17.

The class of pronouns in Worrorra may be characterized quite fairly as a semi-open one. I am far from being sure that I have encountered all of the pronominal morphemes available in the language, and while the number of pronominal words is probably not infinite, when all possible combinations of morphemes are taken into account, it must be large indeed, especially when identity-maintaining and specific pronouns are included in the total (§17.5, §17.7).

Eight: optative, counterfactual and exercitive moods

Worrorra verbs display four formal-functional categories that correspond well to categories called 'mood' in other languages. Verbs display distinctions that may be termed indicative, optative, counterfactual and subjunctive moods. The term 'mood' is applied here to sets of forms that signal functional categories of the same name. Each verbal utterance must be in one and only one of these classes, which is to say that they are in complementary distribution. Constraints on the co-occurrence of morphemes in any one verb form define the shapes of Worrorra moods:

Table 8.1: mood-signalling

MOOD	NP INDEX TYPE	SLOT [1]	SLOT [4]	FUNCTION
Indicative	series-1	Ø	Ø	actualized events
Counterfactual	series-1	ba	Ø	unactualized events
Optative	series-2	Ø	a, nya, Ø	projected events
Subjunctive	series-2	Ø	ngun, ngka	averted events

In this chapter Worrorra's optative (§8.1, §8.2) and counterfactual (§8.3, §8.4) moods will be described, as well as a set of exercitive forms also appropriately called 'moods:' hortative, monitive, prohibitive and imperative (§8.5). Indicative mood is described in Chapter Five, and a fourth, irrealis, category of subjunctive forms is described in Chapter 15. The labels 'indicative,' 'optative' and 'subjunctive' are borrowed from Indo-European linguistics without, of course, any suggestion that more than typological or convergent similarity is involved: it just happens that the semantics of Worrorra verbal categories correspond generally with those of some Indo-European languages.[58]

Reality status is signalled overtly by mood categories, with indicative signalling actualized events, and counterfactual signalling unreal or unactualized possibilities. All Worrorra verb forms apart from declarative signal some kind of irrealis meaning; the term 'irrealis' will therefore be reserved as a general descriptor of semantic properties common to a number of verbal functions. An irrealis category of projected events is signalled by optative mood forms.

As in many other languages (see eg Sweetser 1990:49), a given Worrorra verb form may signal both epistemic and root modality. In Sweetser's account, epistemic modality is derived from root modality by metaphorical process, and the two are in complementary distribution. Forms may therefore be ambiguous between these two senses, and this is what is found in Worrorra. Modality in Worrorra is signalled both by verbal inflexion and by the set of modal adverbs described in §10.2.1.

---

[58] A more circumspect approach might label the four Worrorra verbal form-classes as something like the A-, B-, C- and D-series respectively.

8.1 Optative prefix-clusters

The optative mood is used to depict events in future time. Such events are either projected to occur on the basis of present circumstances, or intended as future states. In Worrorra future time reference is not marked by a tense morpheme in order class [9], but by a number of other means, including a morpheme in order class [4]. In this way the language distinguishes real (past, present) from non-real (future) time reference.

The sets of prefix clusters that uniquely characterize optative forms are set out in Tables 8.2 and 8.3 below. The absence of tense-marking morphemes from order-class [9] also signals optative form, although this absence does not preclude aspect marking in order class [13]. This mood is not signalled in a straightforward way. It is marked by a number of formal devices, none of which signal optative function exclusively or uniquely: rather each of them acts in cooperation with other forms to signal the required meaning. The clearest signals of optative form are the occurrence of the allomorphs -*nya*- or -*a*- in order class [4], and the use of a special set of NP indices in order classes [2] and [3]. In the underlying representations in the following tables the optative allomorphs are in bold:

Table 8.2: intransitive prefix-clusters: optative mood

	SINGULAR			PLURAL	
1	nge-	|nga-**nya**|	1pin	ngarra-	|ngarr-**a**|
2	ngunya	|ngun-**nya**|	1px	arra-	|arr-**a**|
3a	e-	|a-**nya**|	2p	nyirra-	|nyirr-**a**|
3f	nye-	|nyaN-**nya**|	3p	arra-	|arr-**a**|
3w	nya-	|ØN-**nya**|			
3m	me-	|ma-**nya**|			

Table 8.3: transitive prefix-clusters: optative mood

1>2	ngunya-	|ngun-(n)-Ø-**nya**|
1>3a	inga-	|i-nga|
1>3f	nyinga-	|nyiN-nga|
1>3w	nga-	|ØN-nga|
1>3m	manga-	|ma-nga|
1>2p	nyinya-	|nyirr-n-Ø-**nya**|
1>3p	anga-	|arr-nga|
2>1	janya-	|jan-**nya**|
2>3a	inja-	|i-nja|
2>3f	nyinja-	|nyiN-nja|
2>3w	ja-	|ØN-nja|
2>3m	manja-	|ma-nja|
2>1px	anja-	|arr-nja|
2>3p	anja-	|arr-nja|
3>1	nganya-	|nga-n-Ø-**nya**|
3>2	ngunya-	|ngun-(n)-Ø-**nya**|
3>3a	e-	|a-Ø-**nya**|
3>3f	nye-	|nyaN-Ø-**nya**|
3>3w	nya-	|ØN-Ø-**nya**|
3>3m	me-	|ma-Ø-**nya**|
3>1pin	ngaja-	|ngarr-Ø-**nya**|
3>1px	anya-	|arr-n-Ø-**nya**|
3>2p	nyinya-	|nyirr-n-Ø-**nya**|
3>3p	anya-	|arr-n-Ø-**nya**|

1pin>3a	arra-	|a-ngarr-**a**|
1pin>3f	nyarra-	|nyaN-ngarr-**a**|
1pin>3w	warra-	|ᵏwuN-ngarr-**a**|
1pin>3m	marra-	|ma-ngarr-**a**|
1pin>3p	angarra-	|arr-ngarr-**a**|
1px>2	ngunbarra-	|ngun-(n)-ᵇwarr-**a**|
1px>3a	erra-	|a-nyarr-**a**|
1px>3f	nyerra-	|nyaN-nyarr-**a**|
1px>3w	nyarra-	|ØN-nyarr-**a**|
1px>3m	merra-	|ma-nyarr-**a**|
1px>2p	nyinbarra-	|nyirr-n-ᵇwarr-**a**|
1px>3p	anyarra-	|arr-nyarr-**a**|
2p>1	jarre-	|jan-rra-**nya**|
2p>3a	irre-	|i-rra-**nya**|
2p>3f	nyirre-	|nyiN-rra-**nya**|
2p>3w	wurre-	|ᵏwuN-rra-**nya**|
2p>3m	marre-	|ma-rra-**nya**|
2p>1px	arre-	|arr-rra-**nya**|
2p>3p	arre-	|arr-rra-**nya**|
3p>1	nganbarra-	|nga-n-ᵇwarr-**a**|
3p>2	ngunbarra-	|ngun-(n)-ᵇwarr-**a**|
3p>3a	ewarra-	|a-**nya**-ᵇwarr-**a**|
3p>3f	nyewarra-	|nyaN-**nya**-ᵇwarr-**a**|
3p>3w	barra-	|ØN-ᵇwarr-**a**|
3p>3m	mewarra-	|ma-**nya**-ᵇwarr-**a**|
3p>1pin	ngarrbarra-	|ngarr-ᵇwarr-**a**|
3p>1px	anbarra-	|arr-n-ᵇwarr-**a**|
3p>2p	nyinbarra-	|nyirr-n-ᵇwarr-**a**|
3p>3p	anbarra-	|arr-n-ᵇwarr-**a**|

8.1.1 Optative NP indices

The special NP indices used in optative mood forms occur only in S and U positions, and are homophonous with the derivational agreement-class indices described in §6.1 in Table 6.1.

Table 8.4: series-2 NP indices

	S	S/O	O
1	nga-		nga-n-
2		ngun-	
3a		i-	
3f		nyiN-	
3w	ØN-		ᵏwuN-
3m		ma-	
1pin		ngarr-	
1px	arr-		a-n-
2p	nyirr-		nyi-n-
3p	arr-		a-n-

This is the set of series-2 inflexions mentioned in §5.3.2. In optative verb-forms their function is not derivational, rather their presence here contributes to the formal marking of optative mood. These forms differ from their indicative counterparts (Table 5.2) only in the unmarked macrogender (masculine and celestial) and third person plural.

(i) The 3a shape *i-* occurs as |a-| in front of velar and palatal nasals, in the 3>3a, 1pin>3a, 1px>3a and 3p>3a clusters in Tables 8.2 and 8.3. Also note that *i-* disappears before a stem beginning with /aa/. In this situation there are three descriptive options; either *i-* becomes Ø- before /aa/, *i-* is assimilated into /aa/ by vowel contraction rule 22, or *i-* has an allomorph *a-* before /aa/ and is assimilated by rule 22. I prefer the latter option because it is congruent with the variant forms of the 3f index (ie the open vowel form *nyaN-* before velar consonants, see §5.3.1: *aa-* is underlying |ᵏwa-|):

(8.1)   ... i ... —> ... a ... / __ |C [+velar]|

(ii) The 3w allomorph ØN- is reconstructed with a final nasal consonant because it has the effect of hardening following glides but not nasals. It therefore induces glide-hardening rule 10 and behaves as if it ended in a nasal consonant (see §3.1, rule 4).

(iii) The 2>3w prefix cluster |ØN-nja| leaves the 2 agent morpheme *-nja-* stranded at the start of words, presenting an illegal word-initial nasal-stop consonant cluster. In this situation the first member of the CC is deleted under Initial CC reduction rule 28:

|ØN-nja=ᵇwu|	[3w-2=hit]	—>	
ØN-ja=ᵇwu	(rule 28)	—>	
jo	(rule 18)		*you will hit it*

(iv) The allomorph ᵏwuN- is only employed in the transitive 1pin>3w and 2p>3w clusters *warra-* and *wurra-*, and in imperative and subjunctive verb forms.

(v) The series-2 3p shape is syncretized with the 1px shape, (both *arr-*), resulting in a form that signals plural exclusive reference only (glossed 'px,' see §6.1.1).

8.1.2 The morpheme nya ~ a

This section further discusses features of the prefix-clusters illustrated in Tables 8.2 and 8.3 above. The allomorphs *-nya-* and *-a-* may be seen in bold in those tables.

The morpheme *-nya-* appears in order class [4] in the following circumstances:

(a) On intransitive verbs with singular subjects,
(b) On transitive verbs with third person singular subjects,
(c) On transitive verbs with second person plural subjects,
(d) On verbs with 1>2, 1>2p and 2>1 argument structures,
(e) On verbs with 3p>3a, 3p>3f and 3p>3m argument structures.

The allomorph *-a-* occurs in order class [4] after subject indices ending in the trill /rr/. That is, it occurs after all plural subjects except second person plural agents.

There is as well a set of forms that lack any kind of optative marking in order-class [4]. These are transitive verbs with first and second person singular subjects, except as listed in (d) above. Added to this situation are the facts that the absence of tense-marking suffixes from order class [9] does not uniquely signal optative form, and that some optative/series-2 indices are homophonous with their indicative counterparts. The result of this is that there are a few verb forms that do not distinguish optative from aorist shapes. These are forms with first or second person singular agents acting upon undergoers of the marked macrogender, ie 1>3f, 1>3m, 2>3f and 2>3m.

It is also clear that -*nya*- and -*a*- are phonologically conditioned variants. These shapes are elsewhere epenthetic in this position (rule 26). When they co-occur with optative NP indices and in the absence of tense-marking morphemes in order class [9], they function to signal optative mood. Outside of this formal context they retain their epenthetic role.

Note the underlying shapes of the 3p>3a, 3p>3f and 3p>3m indices. In these shapes the optative morpheme occurs twice; first as -*nya*- after the undergoer-indexing morpheme, and a second time in its post-trill shape -*a*-. This configuration, schematized in (8.2), represents a violation of the general ordering of constituents described in Table 5.1:

(8.2)   OBJ + OPT + SUBJ + OPT + ... ROOT

Another idiosyncratic violation of constituent order of this nature is found in subjunctive verb forms (§15.2).

In most situations where the optative morpheme -*nya*- occurs, it is found after the morphophoneme |a| and is subject to extensive alteration that results in the surface-level phoneme /e/:

(8.3) (i) |a-nya| —> aya   (/ny/-lenition rule 24)
       (ii) aya —> /e/   (V-expansion rule 18)

The 3a morpheme *i*- also has morphophonemic shape *a*- before optative -*nya*-, resulting in the surface outcome /e/. This shape reveals the underlying form of verb roots starting in /aa-/ (|ᵏwa-|):

(8.4)   Ewangurraal
         a-Ø-**nya**=ᵏwangurru-aal
         3a-3-**OPT**-carry-hither
         S/he will bring him

Note the shape of the 3>1pin index *ngaja*- (|ngarr-Ø-nya|). In this shape the morphophoneme |ny| hardens to /j/ after |rr|, and constitutes the only instance of hardening rule 11 operating in a verbal prefix cluster at the expense of the expected trill deletion rule 15. Again the reason for this is phonological and has to do with disambiguation; if rule 15 operated upon this cluster initially, the resulting surface shape **nganya*- would not be distinguishable from the attested 3>1 shape, also *nganya*-.

8.2 Optative constructions

The typical denotation of optative is volition. By text count some form of volition is by far the most common meaning of optative forms.

A second denotation is that of projection. Projected functions are epistemic predictions used to make positive assertions, statements and questions that refer to events in future time. Although future events may also be signalled by declarative (§5.4.3) or by aorist forms (§5.4.5), the optative mood is the typical, most unequivocal and commonest form used in this function.

8.2.1 Morphological volition

In many languages the distinction between futurity and intention is not clear-cut. For example the English sentence 'I'm staying here' may denote the speaker's intention (='I intend to stay here') or his prediction about a future state of the world (='I conclude that I will stay here') or both (or neither). So in Worrorra the distinction may also be a hazy one. Compare the two senses of that English sentence, with the senses of the following Worrorra sentences:

(8.5a) Arri ngayu manmaa aja ngenu
arri ngayu ma=n-maa aja nga-**nya**=nu
but I 3m-this-3mREF sit 1-**OPT**=be
But I'll stay right here/But I want to stay right here

(b) Yaw, bija wali ngemnyeyungurru
yaw bija wali nga-**nya**-mnya=ya-ngurru
yes FUT PERF 1-**OPT**-DD=go-away
Yes, I'll go/Yes, I'd like to go

(c) Maangurrinyini ngayanangkamarnanya ngunyaangurru
maa-ngurru-nyini ngayu-nangka-ma-rnanya ngun-Ø-**nya**=ᵏwangurru
3mREF-away-until I-DAT-3m-LOC 2-3/1-**OPT**=take
I'll take you away to my own country/I'd like to take you away to my own country

In (8.5c), terrestrial marking on the possessive pronoun refers to 'place' by default (§4.1.3 (iii)); and in (8.5c) and (8.6a) below, first person singular agent reference on the verb is neutralized with third person singular marking *(-Ø-)* in the presence of a second person (undergoer) index (see §5.3.3 (vii)). The adverb *bija* 'Future' in (8.5b) appears to convey pretty much the same semantics as the does optative mood itself, and is quite common in optative sentences.

But optative morphology is also employed to denote a clearer sense of volition, as the following sentence examples show:

(8.6a)
Ruluk bamnyayu, wook ngunyamnyongurru!
ruluk ba-mnya=ya wook ngun-Ø-**nya**-mnya=ᵇwu-ngurru
move CFT-DD=go pass 2-3/1-**OPT**-DD=hit-away
Move over, I want to get past you!

(b)
Nanjan maa angujakunya waay ngununa? Yarribaa
nanjan maa anguja-ᵏwunya waay ngun=nu-na yarribaa
ladder 3mREF what-PURP throw 2=be-PAST descend.PL

nyarramnyengurru!
ØN-nyarr-**a**-mnya=yi-ngurru
VCOMP-1px-**OPT**-DD=do-away
What did you take the ladder away for? We want to get down!

(c)
Ngayu geenyale barramnyiyaara anja Arrbalandi.
ngayu gee-nyale ØN-ᵇwarr-**a**-mnya=yi-aara anja arr=maland-i
I represent-next VCOMP-3p-**OPT**-DD=do-1DAT 3pDEF px-PLACE.NAME-3p
Now the Prince Regent River people want me to be their totemic emblem.

Example (8.6c) is spoken by a dreamtime ancestor about to be killed and 'deified' as a totem. The preverb *gee* 'totemic representation' occurs here with the verb classifier *kuN[ ]=yi* 'do,' with the meaning 'SUBJ be represented totemically by OBJ.' Here there are two objects; the first is the verb classifier's subordinated complement (*gee*), indexed in prefixed undergoer position as the sentential object index 'VCOMP.' The second is the animate object indexed as a suffix in order class [11] as 1DAT.

8.2.2 Periphrastic volition

A third type of volition is represented by a periphrastic construction. Here the verb *kuN[ ]=yi* 'do' acts as a matrix predicate to an optative complement clause. In most of its occurrences the verb *kuN[ ]=yi* is the most semantically bleached of all the Worrorra verb classifiers, being used in both transitive and intransitive predicates (§11.4.1). As the language's universal pro-verb, it is almost devoid of lexical content in complex predicates. *KuN[ ]=yi* 'do' has, however, a second, distinct meaning as an all-purpose verb of cognition, as seen in cognitional constructions such as that shown in example (5.8) in §5.1, where it has a meaning something like 'know/think about.' Related to this meaning, *kuN[ ]=yi* has a third sense as a *verbum dicendi*, in which case it means 'say/tell,' and a fourth sense as a verb of volition, with a meaning roughly equivalent to 'think/want.'

Periphrastic volitional constructions employ *kuN[ ]=yi* in this fourth, volitional, sense as a matrix predicate whose object argument is a complement clause expressing propositional content. This syntax denotes volition unambiguously in Worrorra. It appears to involve the semantics of volition projected from OPT morphology in the complement clause, up to the matrix verb *kuN[ ]=yi*, which then functions as if it were a volitional lexeme meaning 'want' (for a more complete discussion see §14.2). Consider example (8.7), with the complement clause in square brackets:

(8.7) [Dambeewunya ngeyu] kungayeerri.
dambeem-ᵏwunya nga-**nya**=ya kuN-nga=yi-eerri
place-PURP 1-**OPT**=go VCOMP-1=do-PROG
I want [to go home]

While the expression *dambeewunya ngeyu* by itself is ambiguous between volitional or future-time sense meanings (as 'I want to go home' or 'I will go home') the construction in (8.7) can only mean 'I want to go home'. Another example of this kind of construction is shown in (8.8).

(8.8) [Derluk ngewangurru] kenga, ...
derluk nga-**nya**=ᵇwa-ngurru ØN-Ø-ngka=yi-ng
between 1-**OPT**=fall-away VCOMP-3-SJTV=do-PAST
When she tried [to pass between them], ...

In these constructions the matrix subject is indexed on the matrix clause verb (as -Ø- '3' in this instance), and is co-indexed obligatorily by the first person singular morpheme (*nga-* '1') in the complement clause. This produces what appears to be at first sight a direct-speech kind of syntax of the sort: 'when she thought *(kenga)*: ['I will pass between *(derluk ngewangurru)*'] ...' Again, for explanation see §14.2.

8.2.3 Purposive clauses

In Role-and-Reference terms, purposive clauses in Worrorra contain optative verb forms linked in peripheral coordination to a logical protasis. The purposive clause is then structurally although not logically independent of its predecessor. The nature of the linkage is therefore of the loosest sort, and produces essentially *de facto* purposive constructions. Some examples of purposive clauses are shown below, in square brackets. Note the absence of an OPT morpheme from the purposive clause in (8.9a), with its 1>3w prefix (see §8.1.2 above).

(8.9a)
Karle ngengerri molnganem [aaku ngama].
karle nga=ya-nga-eerri molnganem aaku ØN-nga=ma
now 1=go-TNS-PROG river water 3w-1=get
I'm going to the river [to get some water].

(b)
Nyirringkaal!	Nyirringkaal!	[Bunjuma	minjarl-minjarl	nyirranu!]
nyirr=i-^kwaal	nyirr=i-^kwaal	bunjuma	minjarl-minjarl	nyirr-**a**=nu
2p=go-hither	2p=go-hither	fig	eat-eat	2p-**OPT**=be

Come on! Come on! (Come) [and eat the figs]!

(c)
Erramnyaangurru		marno	[warli	arrke	iyilem
a-nyarr-**a**-mnya=^kwangurru		ma=rno	warli	arrke	i=yilem
3a-1px-**OPT**-DD=take		3m=there	turtle	3pREF	3a=present

jeyi-jeyi	nyarre].
jeyi-jeyi	ØN-nyarr-a=yi
spear-spear	VCOMP-1px-OPT=do

We want to take him out [so we can spear turtles in his presence] =
We want to take him out [to show him how to spear turtles].

The first part of the utterance in (8.9b) is an imperative form of =*ya-^kwaal* 'come,' and the second part is the purposive clause, of the form 'in order to eat figs.'

8.2.4 Projection

In Worrorra the optative mood signals projected reality as well as volition. Optative forms may denote epistemic necessity. In the following examples the speakers are claiming that available evidence and processes of reasoning compel them to the conclusions they come to. In (8.10) a man has just fallen down a deep hole. When all attempts to get him out have failed, he says,

(8.10)
	Ngurru	maanbali	ngenu,	korru.
	ngurru	maanbali	nga-**nya**=nu	korru
	here	FOCUS	1-**OPT**=be	alright

Alright, I'll stay here/Alright, I'll really have to stay here.

The epistemic adverb *maaji* 'DELIBERATIVE, I-had-better' denotes conclusions reached by processes of reasoning based on the speaker's knowledge of the circumstances of his or her situation. In (8.11) the second clauses contain the premises for the conclusions reached in the clauses controlled by *maaji*.

(8.11a)
Maaji-maaji	burnma	mangaarndenangkorri,	ke
maaji-maaji	burn-ma	ma-nga=^kwarnde-[nangka-^kwurri]	ke
had.better-REDUP	PRO-3m	3m-1=place-[3pDAT]	and

murndey	maade	barrayeerri	anja	belangkarraya.
murndey	maade	ØN-^bwarr-**a**=yi-eerri	anja	belangkarrya-ya
cross	RESULT	VCOMP-3p-**OPT**=do-PROG	3pDEF	many.people-3p

I think I'd better put something there for them, and then everyone will [be able to] get across.

(b)
Barnmarnngarrirnanya	maaji	angaangurru,	wardi	ngana
barnmarn-ngarri-rnanya	maaji	arr-nga=^kwangurru	wardi	ngana
medicine-REL-LOC	had.better	3p-1=carry	I.hope	PROB

wurlingkarr	nyenangkorri.
wurlingkarr	ØN-Ø-**nya**=yi-[nangka-ᵏwurri]
rub.clean	VCOMP-3-**OPT**=do-[3pDAT]

I'd better take them to a doctor, maybe he'll be able to cure them.

Another epistemic category referred to by optative forms is that of prediction. In (8.12) a dreamtime ancestor foresees her own death:

(8.12)

Ngayu	maa	ngemnyeyu	marru,	Daraarlu	marru,
ngayu	maa	nga-**nya**-mnya=ya	ma=rru	rdaraarlu	ma=rru
I	3mREF	1-**OPT**-DD=go	3m=LAT	PLACE.NAME	3m=LAT

maangurru	bija	nganbarro,	wirrkeman	nganbarree.
maa-ngurru	bija	nga-n-ᵇwarr-**a**=ᵇwu	wirrkeman	nga-n-ᵇwarr-**a**=ee
3mREF-away	FUT	1-INV-3p-**OPT**=hit	unburied	1-INV-3p-**OPT**=place

I will go away over there to Daraarlu, and there they will kill me and leave my body unburied.

(8.13)

Nyijoolee	marno	Wadoyrnanya;	yorr	nyirrwa,	ke
nyirr=yoolee	ma=rno	Wadoy-rnanya	yorr	nyirr=ᵇwa	ke
2p=go	3m=DIST	spotted.nightjar-LOC	sit.together	2p=fall	and

arrka	Wadoyngarri	mana	Jrr'nkurnanya	yorr
arrka	wadoy-ngarri	mana	jrr'nkurn-rnanya	yorr
3pNAR	spotted.nightjar-REL	3mDEF	owlet.nightjar-LOC	sit.together

arrawa.
arr-**a**=ᵇwa
3p-**OPT**=fall

You lot go over to Wadoy's place and live there, and Wadoy's (daughters) will (come and) live at Jinkun's place.

Example (8.13) is from a story describing how the two culture heroes Jinkurn and Wadoy agreed to exchange daughters, and thereby institute the patrimoiety system common to Worrorra-, Ungarinyin- and Wunambal-speaking people. The optative form *yorr arrawa* 'they will abide' is predictive in this instance.

Promises are performative acts of prediction, in which a speaker's guarantee constitutes the epistemic warrant for his or her claims about the future, as seen in (8.14):

(8.14)

Kaarriyaka	wunu,	bija	murlard	erramnyoyeerri.
kaarri-y₂aka	wunu	bija	murlard	a-nyarr-**a**-mnya=ᵇwu-yeerri
3pNEG-EMPH	3wDEF	FUT	look.after	3a-1px-**OPT**-DD=hit-PROG

There's no way that'll happen, we're going to be looking after him.

An important epistemic category identified by Brisard (1997:276) is referred to by him as that of evaluatives. The two types of evaluative functions recognizable in the Worrorra database are hopes and resultatives (expectations and outcomes), both of which are signalled by specific epistemic adverbs. *Resultative* expressions are usually signalled by the enclitic adverb *maade* 'so, RESULT,' which occurs as either a postposition or a suffix to a verb or preverb. The second clause in (8.11a) is a resultative clause of this type. The examples in (8.15) come from the same story as example (8.13):

(8.15a)
Warrarloowaarndu ngarlangarla ke ngenangka,
ᵏwuN-ngarr-**a**=rloo-ᵏwarndu ngarlangarla ke ØN-nga=yi-nangka
VCOMP-1pin-**OPT**=speak-DU speech 3wREF VCOMP-1=do-DAT

ke ngurumaade janyaangurru.
ke nguru-maade jan-**nya**=ᵏwangurru
and hear-RESULT 2>1-**OPT**=take

I want to discuss something with you that I will tell you about, and then you will understand me.

(b)
Wunu ngunjanangkaya nyangkaangkaya anja
wunu ngunju-nangka-ya nya-ngkaa-ngka-ya anja
3wDEF you-DAT-3p ↳-AUG-girl-3p 3pDEF

angkengkaal ngayurnanya, ke wurlarl baade nyanu.
arr-ngka=ya-ᵏwaal ngayu-rnanya ke wurlarl baade ØN-**nya**=nu
3p-SJTV=go-hither I-LOC 3wREF suitable RESULT 3w-**OPT**=be

If your daughters were to come over to my place, then that would be fitting.

Hopes are signalled by the epistemic adverb *wardi* 'I hope,' which occurs most frequently with potential (counterfactual) verb forms. However it may also control optative verb forms, as may be seen in examples (8.11b) and (8.16). Clauses of this type denote hope with a sense of expectation; that is, the speaker both hopes and expects that the event depicted will happen.

(8.16)
Adijaarndeerri ngani-ngani nye, wardi
a-ngarr=ninja-ᵏwarndu-eerri ngani-ngani ØN-Ø-**nya**=yi wardi
3a-1pin=look.at-DU-PROG what-what VCOMP-3-**OPT**=do I.hope

ngana yarriy ewaal.
ngana yarriy a-**nya**=ᵇwa-ᵏwaal
PROB descend 3a-**OPT**=fall-hither

Let's watch him and see what he's going to do, I hope he does come down.

8.3 Counterfactual forms

The counterfactual mood is used to depict non-factual (irrealis) and counterfactual events. It is the only form able to appear in negative constructions, which constitute its typical and most frequent occurrence.

Counterfactual mood is marked by a morpheme *ba(N)*- in order class [1], and by a distinct set of tense suffixes in order class [9]. The prefix clusters that uniquely characterize these forms are set out in Tables 8.5 and 8.6 below. Counterfactual verbs have the following formal properties:

(i) A prefix whose underlying shape can be reconstructed as either *ba*- or *baN*- appears in order-class [1].
(ii) Counterfactual verbs encode a past/non-past tense system in order class [9], with the morpheme -*n* signalling non-past and -*(yi)nya* signalling past on all verbs.
(iii) When order class [9] is empty, potential verb forms are indicated (§8.4.3).

The shape of the counterfactual morpheme will be taken as *ba*- for practical purposes, although the morphophonology could be made to work nearly as easily with a shape *baN*-, and in all probability the synchronic morpheme results from an archiphoneme *baN-. Wubuy in south-eastern Arnhem Land has a morpheme -w₂an- (-ᵇwan-) in similar position and function (Heath 1984:360). Velar nasalization rule 7 specifically inserts a nasal phoneme after ba- in some situations, and would be redundant if a form baN- were postulated. Vowel metathesis rule 8 and the alternating shapes of the 2(p)>1 portmanteau jan- ~ -nyan- would also be better explained if the morphophoneme were nasalized (see §8.3.1 below). Against this, another rule would be needed to remove nasal-stop clusters where 3a and 3p morphemes occur in absolutive (S/U) function if a shape baN- were postulated. It seems that an overall simpler synchronic description is achieved by adopting the shape ba-, although the evidence points to an historical shape *baN- for the counterfactual prefix. Prefix clusters are listed below, along with phonological rules for the derivation of surface shapes from underlying abstract formulations.

Table 8.5: intransitive prefix-clusters: counterfactual mood

	SINGULAR			PLURAL	
1	banga-	|ba-nga|	1pin	barr-	|ba-ngarr|
2	bungun-	|ba-ngun|	1px	berr-	|ba-nyarr|
3a	bangka-	|ba-ka|	2p	binyirr-	|ba-nyirr|
3f	binyiN-	|ba-nyiN|	3p	baarr-	|ba-kaarr|
3w	bungka-	|ba-kuN|			
3m	bama-	|ba-ma|			

Table 8.6: transitive prefix-clusters: counterfactual mood

1>2	bungun-	|ba-ngun-(n)-Ø|	V harmony
1>3a	banga-	|ba-ka-nga|	22
1>3f	binyinga-	|ba-nyaN-nga|	21
1>3w	bunga-	|ba-kuN-nga|	9
1>3m	bamanga-	|ba-ma-nga|	
1>2p	binyin-	|ba-nyirr-n-Ø|	21
1>3p	baanga-	|ba-kaarr-nga|	22
2>1	banyan-	|ba-jan|	
2>3a	banja-	|ba-ka-nja|	22
2>3f	binja-	|ba-nyiN-nja|	21
2>3w	binja-	|ba-kuN-nja|	9
2>3m	bamanja-	|ba-ma-nja|	
2>1px	baanja-	|ba-kaarr-nja|	22
2>3p	baanja-	|ba-kaarr-nja|	22
3>1	bangan-	|ba-nga-n-Ø|	
3>2	bungun-	|ba-ngun-(n)-Ø|	V harmony
3>3a	bangka-	|ba-ka-Ø|	7
3>3f	binyiN-	|ba-nyiN-Ø|	21
3>3w	bungka-	|ba-kuN-Ø|	8
3>3m	bama-	|ba-ma-Ø|	
3>1pin	barr-	|ba-ngarr-Ø|	(22)
3>1px	ben-	|ba-nyarr-n-Ø|	24
3>2p	binyin-	|ba-nyirr-n-Ø|	21
3>3p	baan-	|ba-kaarr-n-Ø|	22
1pin>3a	barr-	|ba-ka-ngarr|	22
1pin>3f	binyarr-	|ba-nyaN-ngarr|	21, (22)
1pin>3w	bungarr-	|ba-kuN-ngarr|	9
1pin>3m	bamangarr-	|ba-ma-ngarr|	
1pin>3p	baangarr-	|ba-kaarr-ngarr|	22

1px>2	bungunbarr-	|ba-ngun-(n)-ᵇwarr|	V harmony
1px>3a	berr-	|ba-ka-nyarr|	22, 24
1px>3f	binyerr-	|ba-nyaN-nyarr|	21, 24
1px>3w	binyarr-	|ba-kuN-nyarr|	9
1px>3m	bamerr-	|ba-ma-nyarr|	24
1px>2p	binyinbarr-	|ba-nyirr-n-ᵇwarr|	21
1px>3p	baanyarr-	|ba-kaarr-nyarr|	22
2p>1	banyarra-	|ba-jan-rra|	
2p>3a	barra-	|ba-ka-rra|	22
2p>3f	binyarra-	|ba-nyaN-rra|	21
2p>3w	burra-	|ba-kuN-rra|	9
2p>3m	bamarra-	|ba-ma-rra|	
2p>1px	baarra-	|ba-kaarr-rra|	22
2p>3p	baarra-	|ba-kaarr-rra|	22
3p>1	banganbarr-	|ba-nga-n-ᵇwarr|	
3p>2	bungunbarr-	|ba-ngun-(n)-ᵇwarr|	V harmony
3p>3a	bawarra-	|ba-ka-ᵇwarr-a|	22
3p>3f	binyimbarr-	|ba-nyiN-ᵇwarr|	21
3p>3w	bungkaarr-	|ba-kuN-ᵇwarr|	8, 23
3p>3m	bamaarr-	|ba-ma-ᵇwarr|	23
3p>1pin	bangarrbarr-	|ba-ngarr-ᵇwarr|	
3p>1px	benbarr-	|ba-nyarr-n-ᵇwarr|	24
3p>2p	binyinbarr-	|ba-nyirr-n-ᵇwarr|	21
3p>3p	baanbarr-	|ba-kaarr-n-ᵇwarr|	22

8.3.1 Morphophonological processes

The morpheme *ba-* is prefixed to the inflexional NP indices listed in Table 5.2 in a relatively straightforward manner. However there are four important phonological rules operating in counterfactual prefix clusters, three of which apply exclusively to counterfactual verbs: they are velar elision rule 22, velar nasalization rule 7, vowel metathesis rule 8 and CFT-3w assimilation rule 9.

(i) Velar elision rule 22 applies to the S/U indices \|ka\| '3a', \|ngarr\| '1pin' and \|kaarr\| '3p'. When these morphemes occur in a cluster with *ba-*, their initial velar consonants are usually elided.
(ii) Velar nasalization rule 7 applies to the S/U index \|ka\| '3a,' and turns the initial velar consonant into a prenasalized stop (/ngk/) after *ba-* if no other phonetic indexing material follows.
(iii) Vowel metathesis rule 8 and CFT-3w assimilation rule 9 induce transformations upon the S/U 3w index *kuN-* after *ba-*. Vowel harmony is prominent in counterfactual prefix clusters, and rule 8 is after all an elaborate vowel harmony rule. Rule 8 metathesizes the underlying sequence \|ba-kuN\| to \|buN-ka\|, which is then subject to the operation of other phonological rules to derive surface forms. Rule 9 blends *ba-* with the 3w U index *kuN-* to produce the surface shapes *bu-* and *bi-* in the presence of a participant agent index.

Other phonological operations evidenced in these clusters are as follows:

(iv) The shape *ba-* becomes *bi-* before /ny/, that is before *nyiN-* '3f' and *nyirr-* '2p'. This is a variation upon /a/-fronting and raising rule 21.
(v) *ba-* becomes *bu-* before *ngun-* '2'.

(vi) The 2(p)>1 portmanteau morpheme *jan-* has the shape *-nyan-* after *ba-*. The underlying shape of this morpheme could be construed as either of these two forms.

(vii) The shape *barr-* occurs in three situations; as intransitive |ba-ngarr| 'CFT-1pin', as transitive |ba-ngarr-Ø| 'CFT-3>1pin' and transitive |ba-ka-ngarr| 'CFT-1pin>3a'. In all these situations *barr-* is in free varation with *bangarr-*.

(viii) The CFT 1pin>3f shape occurs as either *binyarr-* or *binyangarr-*; underlyingly |ba-nyaN-ngarr|, either with or without velar elision rule 22.

(ix) The intransitive 1px morpheme copies the transitive shape *-nyarr-* in counterfactual verbs. In this way the intransitive CFT 1px shape *berr-* (|ba-nyarr|) is distinguishable from the 1pin shape *barr-* (|ba-ngarr|). Here /ny/-lenition rule 24 and V-expansion rule 18 derive /e/ from underlying |a+nya|.

(x) The 2>3f shape *binja-* shows haplological reduction as follows (the 2 agent morpheme *-nja-* is phonetic [-nyja]):

    (i) |ba-nyiN-nja| —>

    (ii)   bi-nyiny-nyja   —>

    (iii) b-[iny-iny]-ja   —>

    (iv) b-iny-ja   —>   *binja-*

This makes this shape homophonous with the 2>3w shape, which in turn derives its form from CFT-3w asimilation rule 9 (see (iii) above).

8.3.2 Tense-marking

Tense and aspect morphemes in order classes [9] and [13] combine in different ways to signal a variety of counterfactual functions. This system is summarized in Table 8.7:

Table 8.7: counterfactual tense and aspect marking

Nonpast:	*-n*
Nonpast continuous	|-n+yeerri| —> *-njeerri*
Past	*-(yi)nya*
Past continuous	|-(yi)nya+eerri| —> *nyeerri*
Potential	*-Ø*
Potential continuous	|-Ø+eerri| —> *-eerri*

The continuous aspect morpheme is *-jeerri* after *-n*, and it combines with pat tense *-(yi)nya* to produce *-nyeerri*. The shape |-yi-| in this allomorph is essentially a dummy segment, being discernable only by the effect it has upon vowels preceding it:

(8.17)   Waa   bangkawenya

           waa   **ba**-ka=^{b}wa-yinya

           not   **CFT**-3a=fall-PAST

           He didn't fall

The only way to account for the surface shape of the vowel /e/ in the root morpheme in (8.17) is to posit some influence by the following tense morpheme along the lines of V-expansion rule 18. Essentially the past tense shape *-nya* can be said to have a raising and fronting effect on vowels occurring on both sides of it.

In counterfactual forms of the irregular verb *=ya* 'go,' the indicative tense morpheme *-nga* remains bonded to the root, producing a shape |-yanga-|. This shape is then re-inflected with counterfactual tense suffixes, as exemplified in (8.18):

(8.18)   Waa   bangengenya
         waa   **ba**-nga=[ya-nga]-yinya
         not   **CFT**-1=[go-TNS]-PAST
         I didn't go

Likewise, the irregular verb =*ya-ᵏwaal* 'come' retains its indicative past tense morphology *-ngku-na-* ([EP-PAST]) as described in §5.4.1, but redundantly, and only in present-tense shapes: so, *bangengkunaal* (|ba-nga=ya-ngku-na-ᵏwaal| [CFT-1=go-EP-PAST/EP-hither]) 'I should come.' Here the meaningless shape *-na* is effectively epenthetic. In genuine past-tense forms of this verb, the morph *-na* is replaced by the counterfactual past-tense morpheme *-(yi)nya*: so, *bangengkunyaal* (|ba-nga=ya-ngku-nya-ᵏwaal| [CFT-1=go-EP-PAST-hither]) 'I should have come.' The verb =*ya-ᵏwaal* also uses a variant *-jeerri* of the continuous morpheme in counterfactual present continuous shapes after the directional morpheme *-ᵏwaal* (see Appendix 2.2 for examples). So: *bangengkunaaljeerri* (|ba-nga=ya-ngku-na-ᵏwaal-yeerri| [CFT-1=go-EP-EP-hither-PROG]) 'I should be coming.'

When followed by a tense-marking morpheme, the verb =*nu* 'be' has the shape =*ni* in counterfactual forms.

8.4 Counterfactual meanings

Negative utterances involve a typically irrealis semantics, and the use of the counterfactual mood in these constructions marks it as the inflexional category dedicated to non-factual and counterfactual meanings. The counterfactual mood is used outside of negative contexts in two important functions: (i) forms marked for tense denote obligations, conceived of in both deontic and epistemic senses, and (ii) forms unmarked for tense denote statements of potential reality, typically depicting a speaker's hopes and fears.

8.4.1 Negation

Clauses can only be negated by using either of the two negative adverbs *waa* 'not' or *kajirn(ba)* 'unable' (see §5.1). These adverbs denote non-modal and root modal senses of negation respectively, and control verbs in counterfactual mood. The use of *waa* has already been seen in examples (8.17) and (8.18). The use of *kajirn(ba)* is seen in example (8.19):

(8.19)
Anja	kajirnba	baadinkurri	anja	ngawaawanangkorri!
anja	kajirnba	**ba**-kaarr=ni-n-ᵏwurri	anja	nga-waa-wa-[nangka-ᵏwurri]
3pDEF	can't	**CFT**-3p=be-NON.P-NUM	3pDEF	↳-AUG-El.Sib-[3pDAT]

Kajirn	baangarnonangkorri	ngawaawanangkorri!
kajirn	**ba**-kaarr-nga-rno-n-[nangka-ᵏwurri]	nga-waa-wa-[nangka-ᵏwurri]
can't	**CFT**-3p-1=give-NON.P-[3pDAT]	↳-AUG-El.Sib-[3pDAT]

They can't live with their brothers! I can't give them to their own brothers!

Negative verbs are marked for tense. Non-past tense-marking refers to events in present or future (projected) time. Present time reference may be conveyed by the marker *-n* 'NON.P', as in the examples in (8.20):

(8.20a)
Nyangke	ngeenya	waa	wali	binyangarreendandaka
nyangke	ngeenya	waa	wali	**ba**-nyaN-ngarr=eenda-n-y₂aka
3fREF	honey	not	PERF	**CFT**-3f-1pin=cook-NON.P-EMPH

Of course we don't cook honey

(b)   Waa   jukurljukurl   banganineerri
         waa   jukurl-jukurl   **ba**-nga=ni-n-nu-eerri
         not   happy-happy   **CFT**-1=be-**NON.P**-2DAT-PROG
         I'm not happy to see you

In (8.20b), and in the verb *baangarnonangkorri* in (8.19) the tense marker *-n* is obscured by the first phoneme of the following object morphemes, |-nu| and |-nangka| respectively. Support for the claim that the tense marker is underlyingly present in these situations is to be found by reference to a paradigm such as that shown in (8.21):

(8.21a)   Ngunju   waa   binjee**n**karerri
            ngunnju   waa   **ba**-kuN-nja=yi-**n**-ᵏwara-eerri
            you   not   **CFT**-VCOMP-2=do-**NON.P**-1DAT-PROG
            You're not telling me

(b)   Awa   waa   bungke**n**ngarreerri
         awa   waa   **ba**-kuN-Ø=yi-**n**-ngarri-eerri
         3aNAR   not   **CFT**-VCOMP-3=do-**NON.P**-1pinDAT-PROG
         He's not telling us

(c)   Ngunju   waa   binjee**n**angkerri
         ngunju   waa   **ba**-kuN-nja=yi-**n**-nangka-eerri
         you   not   **CFT**-VCOMP-2=do-**NON.P**-DAT-PROG
         You're not telling him/her

The marker *-n* is clearly present in (8.21a) and (b), and its presence may be inferred in situations such as that shown in (c) by analogy with the other two examples. It is therefore possible to claim that all verbs employed in negative constructions are tensed. Negative future projected time reference may also be conveyed by the marker *-n*, as seen in example (8.19) and in the following examples:

(8.22a)   Waa   jakarl   bangawan.
            waa   jakarl   **ba**-nga=ᵇwa-n
            not   swim   **CFT**-1=fall-NON.P
            I won't go swimming.

(b)   Waa   minjarl   bungen,   karle   ngawarru.
         waa   minjarl   **ba**-kuN-nga=yi-n   karle   nga-warr
         not   eat   **CFT**-VCOMP-1=do-NON.P   now   1-sick
         I won't eat anything, I feel sick.

(c)   Mara   errkumbu,   kajirn   berrwundaka.
         mara   a-nyarr-ngun=ᵇwu   kajirn   **ba**-ka-nyarr=ᵇwu-n-y₂aka
         see   3a-1px-SJTV=hit   can't   **CFT**-3a-1px=hit-NON.P-EMPH
         When we find him, we won't hurt him

8.4.2 Anaphors and adverbs used with counterfactual verbs

In sentences containing indefinite anaphors, either the anaphor or the verb may be marked negatively, as in English: (i) We have nothing to eat (ii) We haven't eaten anything (iii) No one's eaten it (iv) Somebody hasn't eaten theirs. In (i) and (iii) negative anaphors are used with positive verb forms, while in (ii) and (iv) positive anaphors are used with negative verb forms. When sentences with indefinite anaphors are negated in Worrorra, it is usual for an interrogative anaphor to occur with a counterfactual verb. The following sentence examples demonstrate constructions of this sort with the interrogatives *angkuyu* 'who?/some one,' *anguja* 'what?/something,' *ngani* 'what?/anything' and *angujabirri* 'why on earth … ?'

(8.23a)
Karraarrangarri	aa	irraarrangarri	kaarriyaka
ka-rraa-rra-ngarri	aa	i-rraa-rra-ngarri	kaarri-y₂aka
↳-AUG-mother-1pinDAT	and	↳-AUG-father-1pinDAT	3pNEG-EMPH

wali,	angkuyu	mara	barrwunjeerri.
wali	angkuyu	mara	**ba**-ngarr-Ø=ᵇwu-n-yeerri
PERF	who	see	**CFT**-1pin-3=hit-NON.P-PROG

Our mothers and fathers aren't here, no one will see us.

(b)
Mee	anguja	minjarl	bungajindaka
mee	anguja	minjarl	**ba**-kuN-ngarr=yi-n-y₂aka
I.don't.know	what	eat	**CFT**-VCOMP-1pin=do-NON.P-EMPH

There's nothing for us to eat/I don't know what we're going to eat

(c)
Ngani	bungenjeerri	wunu!
ngani	**ba**-kuN-nga=yi-n-yeerri	wunu
what	**CFT**-VCOMP-1=do-NON.P-PROG	3wDEF

I'm not doing anything!

(d)
Angujabirri	jandujandu	bungunindaka?
angujabirri	jandu-jandu	**ba**-ngun=ni-n-y₂aka
why	mock-mock	**CFT**-2=be-NON.P-EMPH

Why do you have to make fun of it? (=You shouldn't make fun of it)

The interrogative *angujabirri* 'why?' is used in rhetorical questions with deontic force, to suggest that in the opinion of the speaker an event ought not to happen, and is more or less equivalent to an English expression like 'Why on earth … ?'

Other rhetorical phrases are used when people are deliberating what to do. These are *Ngani nge?* 'What shall I do?' and *Ngani waju?* or *Ngani waje?* 'What shall we do?' and are equivalent to English deliberative expressions such as 'I know what I'll do …' and 'I know what we can do …' An idiomatic variant of this type of expression is seen in (8.24):

(8.24)
	Anguja	bangamemurrkanjeerri?
	anguja	**ba**-ka-nga-me=murrka-n-yeerri
	what	**CFT**-3a-1-AUG=go.to-NON.P-PROG

Where shall I go now?

Two sentence-level adverbs govern counterfactual mood in verbs with which they are associated. These are the negative interrogative adverb *waawa* 'why not …/is it not so (that) … ?' and *malyaawam* 'that's the reason that …/it's not for no reason that …' Their use is illustrated below:

(8.25a)
Waawa	joy	baadinyeerri?
waawa	joy	**ba**-kaarr=ni-nya-eerri
NEG.INTER	famous	CFT-3p=be-PAST-PROG

Didn't they use to be famous?

(b)
Waawa	nguru	banyankangurrun?
waawa	nguru	**ba**-jan=^kwangurru-n
NEG.INTER	hear	CFT-2>1=carry-NON.P

How come you don't listen to me?

(c)
Wunu	malyaawam	'Dilangarri'	bungkaajeenyanangkorri
wunu	malyaawam	dila-ngarri	**ba**-kuN-^bwarr=yi-yinya-[nangka-^kwurri]
3wDEF	REASON	dog-REL	CFT-VCOMP-3p=do-PAST-[3pDAT]

That's the reason why they called them 'Dog-People'

(d)
Ngurlarndangarri	nyina	malyaawam	'Wurnbangkuwaanya'
ngurlarndangarri	nyina	malyaawam	Wurnbangku-waa-nya
little.corella	3fDEF	REASON	CLAN.COUNTRY-PERS-3f

bungajinankerri
ba-kuN-ngarr=yi-n-nangka-eerri
CFT-VCOMP-1pin=do-NON.P-DAT-PROG

That's the reason why we call the little corella 'the woman of Wurnbangku'

8.4.3 Obligation

Obligations in Worrorra are unactualized events expressed in terms of deontic modality. Deontic obligation denotes physical and social forces acting upon humans, and is metaphorically extended to epistemic obligation (Johnson 1987, Sweetser 1990). In Worrorra the counterfactual mood is used for both types of obligation, and verbs used in these functions are tensed. Sentence examples illustrating deontic obligation are presented below; in (8.26a) & (b) the obligations are expressed in the second clauses:

(8.26a)
Nyangke	ngeenya	waa	wali	binyangarreendandaka	nyangke,
nyangke	ngeenya	waa	wali	**ba**-nyaN-ngarr=eenda-n-y₂aka	nyangke
3fREF	honey	not	PERF	CFT-3f-1pin=cook-NON.P-EMPH	3fREF

wunu	mee maa	minjarl	binjeen.
wunu	mee maa	minjarl	**ba**-kuN-nja=yi-n
3wDEF	just	eat	CFT-VCOMP-2=do-NON.P

We certainly don't cook that honey, you should eat it just as it is.

(b)
Nyinma	kanangkuja	ngarru	nyimnyenga?	Jolimirri
nyinma	kanangkuja	ngarru	nyiN-mnya=ya-nga	joli-mirri
3fDEF	bitch	whither	3f-DD=go-TNS	return-quickly

binyimnyaninba!
ba-nyiN-mnya=ni-n-ba
CFT-3f-DD=be-NON.P-EP
Where's that dog gone? She'd better get back here quickly!

(c)
Baanjamurlomurlonyeerri	wunu!
ba-kaarr-nja=murlomurlo-nya-eerri	wunu
CFT-3p-2=look.after-PAST-PROG	3wDEF

You should have been looking after them!

Sentence examples illustrating epistemic obligation are shown below:

(8.27a)
Anja	ngarlungarlu	yarrorl	bungkaajin;	ngarru
anja	ngarlungarlu	yarrorl	**ba**-kuN-ᵇwarr=yi-n	ngarru
3pDEF	talking	voices	**CFT**-VCOMP-3p=do-NON.P	whither

kaajooleena	anja?
kaarr=yoolee-na	anja
3p=go-PAST	3pDEF

There should be voices (coming from) their (camp); where have they gone?

(b)
Manjamanja	bangarrbajonkarndu.
manja-manja	**ba**-ngarr-ᵇwarr-nya=ᵇwu-n-ᵏwarndu
meet-meet	**CFT**-1pin-3p-EP=hit-NON.P-DU

They should be coming out to meet us.

(c)
Kanaanangkurri	arrke	beewurdungarri	birdeen	bangkaninya,	burnja
kanaanangkurri	arrke	beewurdu-ngarri	birdeen	**ba**-ka=ni-nya	burn-ya
dogs	3pREF	small.PL-REL	small	**CFT**-3a=be-PAST	PRO-3a

kajirnja	iraarraarreya	yolow	kenga	inja	kanaanangkurri.
kajirnja	i=raa-rraa-rra-ya	yolow	ka=ya-nga	inja	kanaanangkurri
like	3a=↳-AUG-big-3p	stand.PL	3a=go-TNS	3aDEF	dogs

[You'd think that] those puppies would have been small, but these dogs were as huge as anything.

In (8.27a, b) the actors are not physically or morally obliged to be at home or to come out to meet the speakers, respectively. But the speakers are claiming that on the basis of their knowledge of past circumstances and events, they would expect the protagonists to be at home, or to come out to meet them, because that is how they have characteristically behaved in the past. And the evidence of past events constitutes premises on the basis of which they expect that on this occasion too, they will behave characteristically.

Example (8.27c) is a complex sentence and requires some commentary. Firstly it illustrates very well how dogs fall in between humans, whose referents may be pluralized, and animals, whose referents usually may not. Dogs in this sentence display both singular and plural agreement morphologies. *Birdeen* and *beewurdu* are the suppletive singular and plural agreement forms respectively of the adjective meaning 'small' (§6.2.1) Here *birdeen* takes no agreement-class marking because it is used predicatively, falling under the scope of the following counterfactual verb, *bangkaninya*. The phrase *kanaanangkurri beewurdungarri* 'small dogs' refers here to 'puppies.' The speaker is claiming that these particular puppies, as puppies, should by analytic logic be small. That is to say that logic compels us to conclude that puppies, as 'small dogs,' are thereby small. However that this is not the case is shown by the counterfactual form of the verb *bangkaninya*, and the following clause, which states that contrary to expectation, the puppies are huge.

8.4.4 Potential reality

Potential reality is an epistemic category that denotes the possibility of event actualization on the basis of given premises. In placing an event within the domain of potential reality, a speaker asserts no more than that the event is located on one of the 'paths that reality's momentum is not precluded from following,' to paraphrase Langacker (1991:277). Potential reality is a type of futurity with less likelihood of actualization than projection, but greater likelihood than non-reality (Langacker 1991:243). In Worrorra potential reality is indicated by the use of counterfactual verb forms without tense marking (§8.3.2). Examples of this type of clause follow; in (8.28b) the first, and in (830c) the second clauses express potential reality:

(8.28a)
Korru	wooy	bangayu	mana.
korru	wooy	**ba**-nga=ya	mana
alright	swim	**CFT**-1=go	3mDEF

It might be alright for me to swim here.

(b)
Karle	joliyolimirri	bungkaajaal,	jukurley
karle	joli-joli-mirri	**ba**-kuN-ᵇwarr=yi-aal	jukurley
now	return-return-quickly	**CFT**-VCOMP-3p-do-hither	tickle

ajama	ke	jaraai	baade	enu	inja	kanangkurri.
a-ngarr-nya=ma	ke	jaraai	baade	a-nya=nu	inja	kanangkurri
3a-1pin-EP=get	and	laugh	RESULT	3a-OPT=be	3aDEF	dog

They could get back any time now; lets tickle the dog and make it laugh.

(c)
Wununu	wunu	abeerlawa,	ngurr	bungenangkeka
wunu-wunu	wunu	abeerla-ᵇwa	ngurr	**ba**-kuN-nga=yi-nangka-y₂aka
3wDEF-3wDEF	3wDEF	slow-PROG	strike	**CFT**-VCOMP-1=do-DAT-EMPH

wunu	joli	nyangkanungaal!
wunu	joli	nyaN-ngka=nu-ng-aal
3wDEF	return	3f-SJTV=be-PRES-hither

This is taking so long; I'll really belt her when she gets back!

In (8.28c) the speaker is under no obligation to hit his dog, nor does he state that he intends to do so, although this is not obvious from the English translation. He is asserting only that such an action has become a possibility, where no such possibility existed before. A possibly more accurate although less comfortable translation might read 'I might really belt her …' or 'I could really belt her …' The context of the verb *bungenangkeka* makes it clear that it is a potential form, and that therefore there is no tense marker in its construction, in contrast to (8.21).

In the great majority of instances, however, potential verb forms are used to express people's *hopes* and *fears*. In denoting fears, potential verbs carry out a function variously referred to as *aversive*, *apprehensive* or *evitative*. These functions are exemplified below and again in §8.5.2. Potential forms occur in this context in negative-purposive ('lest') clauses, seen below as the second clauses in each sentence. In (8.29a) the first clause is imperative (§8.5.3) and in (8.29b) & (c) the first clauses are prohibitions (§8.5.2):

(8.29a)
Ininjerri   yangarnay   bangkawaarndu.
i=ninja-eerri   yangarnay   **ba**-ka=ᵇwa-ᵏwarndu
3a-watch-PROG   escape   **CFT**-3a=fall-DU
Watch them (dual) so they don't escape.

(b)
Ke   bungajeerri,   yawarrarra   bungaju.
ke   **ba**-kuN-ngarr=yi-eerri   yawarrarra   **ba**-kuN-ngarr=yi
3wREF   **CFT**-VCOMP-1pin=do-PROG   sink.PL   **CFT**-VCOMP-1pin=do
Let's not do that, or we might get drowned.

(c)
Yarrorl   birriyeerri,   meemeenya
yarrorl   **ba**-kuN-rra=yi-eerri   meemeenya
voices   **CFT**-VCOMP-2p=do-PROG   spirit.bird

binyinmaa,   yoowa   ke   kaakaaja   kurde.
ba-nyirr-n-Ø=ma-aa   yoowa   ke   kaakaaja   kurde
CFT-2p-INV-3=get-and   boobook.owl   and   spirit.bird   ASSOC
Don't make too much noise, or the meemeenya *bird might get you, or the boobook owl, or the* kaakaaja *bird.*

Potential forms are also commonly employed in the apodoses of *if ... then ...* conditional constructions (hypothetical constructions):

(8.30a)
Wunu   marnowa   nganngunyaangurru,   jaa   wurlingkarr
wunu   marnowa   ØN-ngan-ngun-nya=ᵏwangurru   jaa   wurlingkarr
3wDEF   carry   VCOMP-1-SJTV-EP=carry   PERF   rub.off

bungkayaara.
ba-kuN-Ø=yi-ᵏwara
CFT-VCOMP-3=do-1DAT
If I were to carry it, I'm sure it would rub off all my (paint).

(b)
Arri   ingujulum   inganngunyamaalima,   ke   bangamaalimaarndu.
arri   i=ngujulum   i-ngan-ngun-nya=maalima   ke   **ba**-ka-nga=maalima-ᵏwarndu
but   3a=ribcage   3a-1-SJTV-EP=spear   3wREF   **CFT**-3a-1=spear-DU
But if I spear him in the ribs, I might get those two (boys).

(c)
Aai   kaaju   ke,   ngarrkanangka
aai   ØN-ngka-ᵇwarr=yi   ke   ngarr=ᵏwa-nangka
reply   VCOMP-SJTV-3p=do   3wREF   1pin=NAR-DAT

ngarlangarlanyine   aai   kaajaal,   ke
ngarlangarla-nyine   aai   ØN-ngka-ᵇwarr=yi-aal   ke
language-INST   reply   VCOMP-SJTV-3p=do-hither   3wREF

yawarrarra	bungaju	wali	ke.
yawarrarra	**ba**-kuN-ngarr=yi	wali	ke
sink.PL	**CFT**-VCOMP-1pin=do	PERF	3wREF

If they answer, if they answer back in our own language, then we might all get drowned.

Potential verbs are also the commonest forms occurring with *wardi* 'hope.' These constructions are the semantic opposites of the aversive forms seen above. Optative verb forms may also occur with *wardi*, (see §8.2.4), in which case they denote some degree of expectation as well as hope. In potential constructions, hope is referred to without necessarily any sense of expectation. Following are some examples: in (8.31c) the first clause expresses a hope, while the second contains a complement clause expressing a fear.

(8.31a)
Wardi	ke	ngambal	bangkawa.
wardi	ke	ngambal	**ba**-ka=ᵇwa
I hope	3wREF	satisfied	**CFT**-3a=fall

I hope he'll be happy about that.

(b)
Ke	wardi	wurlarl	bungkanunu?
ke	wardi	wurlarl	**ba**-kuN=nu-nu
3wREF	I.hope	suitable	**CFT**-3w=be-2DAT

Would this be suitable for you?

(c)
Wardi	murlard	barroyeerringkurri,	balangkarra	nyangke
wardi	murlard	**ba**-ka-rra=ᵇwu-yeerri-ᵏwurri	balangkarra	nyangke
I.hope	look.after	CFT-3a-2p=hit-PROG-NUM	storm.wave	3fREF

bangkawaara	kungayeerri.
ba-ka=ᵇwa-ᵏwara	KuN-nga=yi-eerri
CFT-3a=fall-1DAT	VCOMP-1=do-PROG

I just hope you look after him [properly], I'm worried that he might fall off [when] a big wave [comes along].

The complement-clause construction in the second clause of (8.31c) is described in §14.3.4. The 1DAT morpheme *-ᵏwara* occurring here is in affective dative function (see §13.2.2 (ii)).

8.5 Exercitive structures

A class of exercitive speech acts was proposed by Austin (1955 [1976:155]) to unite those acts by means of which a speaker exercises or seeks to exercise power over events and other people. The prototypical exercitive speech act is imperative, characterized by Searle (1969:124, footnote) as follows: 'the aim of imperatives is to get the world to conform to words, whereas [the aim of other illocutionary acts is] in getting words to conform to the world.' However there is no guaranteed correlation between form and function in the construction of speech acts (see eg Levinson 1983:263-276): interrogative forms may be used with imperative illocutionary force, as in 'have you quite finished?' or with requesting force, as in 'can you pass the salt?' or with hortative force ('shall we go?'). Examples of indirect speech acts in Worrorra follow:

(8.32a)
Marno	malkalka	ngarranaarndu	jindimarnanya
ma=rno	malka-malka	ngarr-a-nu-ᵏwarndu	jindima-rnanya
3m=there	play-play	1pin-OPT=be-DU	mangrove-LOC

marno,	baay-baay	ngarranaarndu.
ma=rno	baay-baay	ngarr-a-nu-ᵏwarndu
3m=DIST	climb-climb	1pin-OPT=be-DU

Let's go over there and play in the mangroves and climb around in them.

(b)
Dumbi	inbali!	Arrowurri!
dumbi	i=nbali	a-ngarr-a-ᵇwu-ᵏwurri
barn-owl	3a=RESUM	3a-1pin-OPT=hit-NUM

There's that owl! Let's kill it!

The verbs in (8.32) have optative form, but function with hortative illocutionary force. The verb in (8.33) below has hortative form (see below, §8.5.1) but in the context in which it was spoken, that is in the referent's clear hearing, it had imperative illocutionary force.

(8.33)   Karle   nyengenya.
         karle   nya=[ya-nga]-yinya
         now   3f=[go-TNS]-HORT
         She can go now/Let her go now.

Without close observation of the daily use of language in a largish community of speakers, it would be difficult to exhaustively correlate linguistic form and speech-act function in any systematic way. In this section I will attempt to describe the forms that typically and frequently signal exercitive speech acts, and which seem to be dedicated specifically to those speech acts. In this way I will be describing a set of structures with characteristic functions. In Worrorra they include imperative, hortative, monitive and prohibitive forms.

8.5.1 *Hortative*

Hortative speech acts are attempts 'to get the world to conform to words' in the same way that imperatives are, but without the addressee being involved as a predicate subject. In making such an attempt, a speaker may use a variety of modal schemata to achieve his or her ends. So hortatives in Worrorra grant a licence or a warrant for such-and-such an event to occur. The granting of such a licence may involve various modal semantics, such as permission or enablement, epistemic warrants such as futurity, or imperative illocutionary force. Regardless of which modal sense an hortative utterance may be framed in, the function of such speech acts is in essence to licence some part of the world to conform to the speaker's wishes.

Hortative verbs are indicative forms usually marked by the suffix *-(yi)nya* in order-class [9]. This shape combines with the continuous aspect morpheme without the application of V-expansion rule 18, producing the shape *-nyeerri*. A segment |yi| is hypothesized to occur in front of the shape /nya/ because of the effect that this morpheme has on preceding vowels (see §8.3.2):

(8.34)   We   kawenya!
         we   ka=ᵇwa-yinya
         lie   3a=fall-HORT
         Let it fall! (=drop it!)

Just as in counterfactual forms (see (8.18) in §8.3.2), the non-future tense morpheme *-nga* of the irregular verb *=ya* 'go' remains bonded to the verb root. This phenomenon can be seen in (8.33) above. Other examples of intransitive hortative forms are as follows:

(8.35a)   Korru   kaajaninyeerri.
             korru   kaarr-nya=ni-nya-eerri
             alright   3p-EP=be-HORT-PROG
             Let them have it their way. (=Let them be.)

(b)   Ajakarri   mana   bija   aja   kaadinyaal.
          arr=yakarri   mana   bija   aja   kaarr=ni-nya-^{k}waal
          3p=other   3mDEF   FUT   sit   3p=be-HORT-hither
          Make a space for someone else to sit down (=Let others come and sit here).

(c)   Ngurru   nyimnyengkunyaal   arrirnanya!
          ngurru   nyiN-mnya=ya-ngku-nya-^{k}waal   arri-rnanya
          here   3f-DD=go-EP-HORT-hither   we(exc)-LOC
          Let her come over here to us!

Example (8.35c) was uttered in the course of a dispute between patriclan members over the allocation of wives. Example (8.33) above is another instance of this type of hortative predicate. The suffix *-(yi)nya* is absent from intransitive forms with plural participant subjects (1pin, 1px, 2p). The only exception to this rule is the irregular verb *=ya-^{k}waal* 'come.' In these situations the hortative shape is homophonous with indicative declarative or aorist forms. An example of such a form has already been seen in (5.5b), repeated here as (8.36), with other examples in (8.37).

(8.36)   Mana   we   ngarrwaarndu   kulunu.
           mana   we   ngarr=^{b}wa-^{k}warndu   kulunu
           3mDEF   lie.down   1pin=fall-DU   sleep
           Let's lie down here and go to sleep.

(8.37a)   Aaku   maa   joyo   ngadaarndeerri.
             aaku   maa   jo-jo   ngarr=nu-^{k}warndu-eerri
             water   3mREF   drink-drink   1pin=be-DU-PROG
             Let's get a drink from that pool.

(b)   Injinja   kurrkujaal   ngadunangkaarndu.
          inja-inja   kurrkujaal   ngarr=nu-nangka-^{k}warndu
          3aDEF-3aDEF   climb.up.on   1pin=be-DAT-DU
          Let's climb up onto this one.

Plural participant hortative forms of the irregular verb *=ya* 'go' may be homophonous with optative forms, but note (8.38b):

(8.38a)   Karle   ngarreyu
             karle   ngarr-a=ya
             now   1pin-OPT/EP=go
             Let's go/We'll go

(b)   Karle   ngajeyu
          karle   ngarr-nya=ya
          now   1pin-EP=ya
          Let's go

The verb forms in (8.38a) and (b) are synonymous in hortative contexts, indicating that the second morpheme of the verb in (a) may function epenthetically (by *a*-epentheseis rule 26) in those contexts. However the verb form in (8.38b), with *nya*-epenthesis, is only open to an hortative interpretation. Compare this example with the hortative expression in (8.39):

(8.39)   Korru   nyijengurroorri.
            korru   nyirr-nya=ya-ngurru-^kwurri
            alright   2p-EP=go-away-NUM
            Alright, he can go with you/you can go with him.

Examples of (formally) transitive hortative forms are as follows:

(8.40a)
Wali   wulaa   kubajeenyeerri.
wali   wulaa   kuN-^bwarr=yi-yinya-eerri
PERF   rest   VCOMP-3p=do-HORT-PROG
Let them sleep on.

(b)
Korru   anmarlaarndonya   warliwunya   ke.
korru   arr-n-Ø=marlaarndo-nya   warli-^kwunya   ke
alright   1px-INV-3=follow-HORT   turtles-PURP   3wREF
Let him come with us after turtles.

(c)
Wali maa   awarl   kamnyamenya   wara,   ke   ngarramnyeyu
wali maa   awarl   ka-Ø-mnya=ma-yinya   wara   ke   ngarr-a-mnya=ya
CONT   cook   3a-3-DD=get-HORT   kangaroo   and   1pin-OPT-DD=go

dambeem.
place
Let the kangaroo cook first, and then we'll go home.

Transitive hortative forms with first person plural agents are arranged in a fairly chaotic formal paradigm, summarized in Table 8.8:

Table 8.8: transitive hortative (indicative) prefix clusters, first person plural subjects

         1pin>3a   arr- |a-ngarr|
         1pin>3f   nyarr- |nyaN-ngarr|
         1pin>3w   warr- |^kwuN-ngarr|
         1pin>3m   marr- |ma-ngarr|
         1pin>3p   angarr- |arr-ngarr|

         1px>2   ngunbarr- |ngun-^bwarr|
         1px>3a   erra- |a-nyarr-a|
         1px>3f   nyerr- |nyaN-nyarr|
         1px>3w   nyarra- |ØN-nyarr-a|
         1px>3m   merr- |ma-nyarr|
         1px>2p   nyinbarr- |nyirr-n-^bwarr|
         1px>3p   anyarra- |arr-nyarr-a|

The features of this paradigm are as follows:

(i) The suffix *-(yi)nya* is absent,
(ii) Series-2 undergoer NP indices are employed (Table 8.4).

First person plural *exclusive* agent forms have the above features, as well as:

(iii) An epenthetic /a/ is inserted in front of the verb root when the undergoer is a member of the unmarked macrogender (masculine or celestial) or plural,
(iv) The agent index has the shape -*ᵇwarr*- in the presence of a second person undergoer (§5.3.4 (vi)).

Examples of verbs of this sort have already been seen in the first verb in (8.16) and the second verb in (8.28b). Two other examples are as follows:

(8.41a) Karle   nyardo,   karle   arrbanangka   wara.
        karle   nyaN-ngarr=rno   karle   a-ngarr=ma-nangka wara
        now   3f-1pin=give   now   3a-1pin=get-DAT   kangaroo
        Let's give it to her, let's get her a kangaroo.

(b)   Manmaa   korru   arrkarnde   karndirrimarnanya.
        ma-n-maa   korru   a-ngarr=ᵏwarnde   karndirrima-rnanya
        3m-this-3mREF   alright   3a-1pin=place   burial.platform-LOC
        Let's put him up there on the burial platform.

8.5.2 Warnings, prohibitions & negative commands

As seen in §8.4.4, people's fears are usually encoded in potential verb forms. Utterances of this sort may in some contexts constitute warnings. This is apparent in the first verb in example (8.28b), the second verbs in examples (8.29b) and (c), and the third verb in example (8.30c). Examples of two other warnings of this sort are contained in the final clauses of the sentences in (8.42):

(8.42a)
Maangurru   bungunyeyeerri,   maa-maa   dalorr   wali   maa,
maa-ngurru   ba-ngun=ya-yeerri   maa-maa   dalorr   wali   maa
3mREF-away   CFT-2=go-PROG   3mDEF-3mDEF   sink-hole   PERF   3mREF

yawak   barrwa   marru   ke
yawak   ba-ngarr=ᵇwa   ma=rru   ke
sink   CFT-1pin=fall   3m=LAT   3wREF
Don't go over there, there's sink-holes there and we might fall down one

(b)
Irrangunyaninjanykarndu   ke,   yarriy   bangkawaal
i-rra-ngun-nya=ninja-ny-ᵏwarndu   ke   yarriy   ba-ka=ᵇwa-ᵏwaal
3a-2p-SJTV-EP=look.at-MIR-DU   3wREF   descend   CFT-3a=fall-hither
If you stare at it, it might come down

The predicates of prohibitive utterances consist of potential verb forms marked for continuous aspect. When such verbs have second person subjects, they function as negative imperative forms; a couple may be seen in sentence examples (5.12a,c), and a couple more given in this chapter are collected here for convenience:

(8.43a) Yarrorl birriyeerri,
 yarrorl ba-kuN-rra=yi-eerri
 voices CFT-VCOMP-2p=do-PROG
 Don't make any noise

(b) Maangurru bungunyeyeerri,
 maa-ngurru ba-ngun=ya-yeerri
 3mREF-away CFT-2=go-PROG
 Don't go over there

(c) Ke binjiyeerri
 ke ba-kuN-nja=yi-eerri
 3wREF CFT-VCOMP-2=do-PROG
 Don't do that

When potential verb forms marked for continuous aspect have first- or third-person subjects, they function as negative hortative forms:

(8.44a) Anja wangalaalunguyu baay baadeerri wunu nguwanu
 anja wangalaalanguya baay ba-kaarr=ni-eerri wunu nguwanu
 3pDEF children climb CFT-3p=be-PROG 3wDEF tree
 Don't let those children climb the tree

(b) Bardoyeerri ngeeya.
 ba-ka-ngarr=rno-yeerri ngee-ya
 CFT-3a-1pin=give-PROG honey-3p
 Let's not give him any honey.

Another negative hortative form is shown in (5.12b) in §5.2.2. Of course not all potential verbs marked for continuous aspect denote prohibition: the first verb in example (8.31c) is an instance of one that does not. In this case context defines which continuous potential forms are prohibitive and which are not.

A common syntax in which prohibitive forms occur is in constructions of the sort X-PROHIB, Y-POT, meaning 'Let X not happen, or/lest Y might happen.' These may be termed *counterfactual hypothetical* constructions. In these constructions the first clause is prohibitive and the second is monitive (aversive). Sentence examples (8.29b & c) are examples of constructions of this sort. Another example is given below:

(8.45)
Birriyaarndeerrije, akurlanyini wanji
ba-kuN-rra=yi-ᵏwarndu-eerri-je akurla-nyini wanji
CFT-VCOMP-2p=do-DU-PROG-again devil-until find

bangkaweenurrerrndu wuneerda
ba-ka=ᵇwee-[nu-ᵏwurri]-ᵏwarndu wunu-yirda
CFT-3a=hit.MID-[2pDAT]-DU 3wDEF-try
Don't do it again or a devil might come looking for you another time

8.5.3 Imperative

Imperative illocutionary force in Worrorra is signalled by a variety of formal types, both indicative and counterfactual. Imperative forms may or may not be marked for continuous aspect: the first verb in sentence example (8.29a) is a continuous imperative form.

Intransitive singular imperative forms are constructed simply by attaching the counterfactual prefix *ba-* to an intransitive verb root, without NP indexation. The first verb in sentence example (8.6a) is an imperative of this type, as are the verbs in (8.46):

(8.46a) Nguru   banu!
        nguru   ba=nu
        hear   CFT=be
        Listen!

(b) Baya!
    ba=ya
    CFT=go
    Get out of it! (usually spoken to dogs)

(c) Aja   bawa.
    aja   ba=ᵇwa
    sit   CFT=fall
    Take a seat.

(d) Bengkaal!
    ba=ya-ᵏwaal
    CFT=go-hither
    Come here!

Note also the unanalysable expression *kakaaw!* 'Come here!' used as an alternative to *bengkaal*, called out over long distances. Intransitive plural imperative forms are constructed by attaching the 2p S index (*nyirr-*, see Table 5.2) to the front of a verb root. The first and second verbs in example (8.13) are imperatives of this type, as are the verbs in (8.47):

(8.47a) Aja   nyideerri.
        aja   nyirr=nu-eerri
        sit   2p=be-PROG
        Don't anyone get up!/(keep sitting)

(b) Aja   nyirrwa.
    aja   nyirr=ᵇwa
    sit   2p=fall
    Be seated.

(c) Nyirringkaaleerri!
    nyirr=i-ᵏwaal-eerri
    2p=go-hither-PROG
    Keep coming!

Transitive imperative forms are constructed by placing series-2 undergoer NP indices (Tables 8.4 & 6.1) before a verb root. Plural-subject forms occur with the 2p A index *-rra-* next to the root morpheme. The transitive imperative prefix paradigm is set out in Table 8.9 below.

Transitive imperative prefix clusters exhibit the following features:

(i) The addressee (agent) is indexed as -Ø- in singular and -*rra*- in plural forms.
(ii) There are two portmanteau morphs, 2(p)>1 *jan*- and 2>3w *minya*-.
(iii) In 2>3w clusters ØN- and *minya*- are in free variation.
(iv) 1px and 3p undergoers (px) require inverse-hierarchy marking (-*n*-) when they occur with a singular agent (§5.3.3). In this situation the grammar treats the zero morpheme as if it indexed a third person singular agent argument (also -Ø-), and is accordingly allocated to the bottom of the inverse hierarchy (see Figure 5.5). Here, then, the role of the inverse marker is strictly accusative.

Table 8.9: transitive imperative prefix clusters

OBJ	SINGULAR AGENT	
1	jan-	|jan|
3a	i-	|i-Ø|
3f	nyiN-	|nyiN-Ø|
3w	ØN-, minya-	|ØN-Ø|, |minya-|
3m	ma-	|ma-Ø|
px	an-	|arr-n-Ø|

OBJ	PLURAL AGENT	
1	jarra-	|jan-rra|
3a	irra-	|i-rra|
3f	nyirra-	|nyiN-rra|
3w	wurra-	|ᵏwuN-rra|
3m	marra-	|ma-rra|
px	arra-	|arr-rra|

The first verb in (8.29a) is an imperative of this type. Other examples follow. Note the idiomatic expression in (8.48c):

(8.48a) Yarribaa wurriyaal!
yarribaa ᵏwuN-rra=yi-aal
descend.PL VCOMP-2p=do-hither
Come down!

(b) Ngunju maa jaarr mongurru.
ngunju maa jaarr ma=ᵇwu-ngurru
you 3mREF go.upstream 3m=hit-away
You go upstream.

(c) Kekaka ju.
kekaka ØN=yi
thus VCOMP=do
It serves you right.

8.6 Semantic summary

The following semantic functions of verb forms are identified in this chapter and in Chapters Five and Fifteen:

Indicative	*Declarative reference to past, present and future time* §5.4.1-5.4.4
Aorist	*Vividness* §5.4.5 (i) *Habitual/characteristic action* §5.4.5 (ii) *Universal statements* §5.4.5 (iii) *Imminence* §5.4.5 (iv) *Enablement* §5.4.5 (v)
Optative	*Volition* §8.2.1-8.2.2 *Purposive clauses* §8.2.3 *Epistemic necessity* §8.2.4 *Predictions* §8.2.4 *Resultatives* §8.2.4 *Hopes, expectations* §8.2.4
Counterfactual	*Epistemic negation* §8.4.1 *Root modal negation* §8.4.1 *Anaphoric negation* §8.4.2 *Deontic obligation* §8.4.3 *Epistemic obligation* §8.4.3 *Potential reality* §8.4.4 *Aversives* §8.4.4 *Hopes* §8.4.4
Exercitives	*Hortatives* §8.5.1 *Warnings* §8.5.2 *Prohibitions* §8.5.2 *Imperatives* §8.5.3, 8.5.2
Subjunctive	*Averted/unconsummated events* §15.4.1 *Frustrative mood* §15.4.2 *Inference* §15.5.4 *Immediacy* §15.5.2 *Mirative* §15.5.3

Nine: number

9.1 Introduction

Worrorra has five inflexional categories that may be described under the rubric of 'quantity' or 'number,' although the semantics of these categories are different in many ways from Western number concepts.

Number morphemes may occur as suffixes to nominals, namely simplex nouns, inalienable nouns, derived nouns, kinship nouns, adjectives and pronouns. Where they occur on verbs, number-marking morphemes may index or refer to arguments in all core grammatical functions: S, A, U and D (DAT; ie non-subcategorized or indirect objects).[59] They have somewhat different sense meanings when they appear on verbs and on nominals respectively.

The singular and plural number categories are signalled inherently, as it were, as part of the meanings of sets of inflexional NP prefixes on verbs, already encountered in Table 5.2 in §5.3.1, and of derivational agreement-class prefixes on nominals, shown in Table 6.1 in §6.1. Our present concern, however, is with three overt number-marking morphemes that occur as suffixes on verbs and nominals, and which are displayed in Table 9.1 below:

Table 9.1: number-marking suffixes

MORPHEME	ORDER CLASS	NOMINAL	NOMINAL & VERBAL	VERBAL
-ᵏwarndu	[12]		dual	
-oorri	[12]	trial		unit augmented
-ᵏwurri	[14]		collective plural	

Note that the 'collective plural' and 'trial/unit augmented' categories are only distinct in certain highly-constrained contexts; elsewhere they fall together as a single form. The allomorphy of these forms is as follows:

(i) The dual morpheme *-ᵏwarndu* hardens to *-karndu* (rule 12).
(ii) The collective morpheme *-ᵏwurri* hardens to *-kurri* after consonants (rules 10 & 11).
(iii) The same morpheme hardens to *-ngkurri* after /-rri-/ (rule 2), to make the combined shape *-rringkurri*.
(iv) The shape *-ᵏwurri* becomes *-orri* after /a/ by V-expansion rule 18:
　　|a-ᵏwurri| —> -orri
(v) As well, *-ᵏwurri* becomes *-oorri* after /u/ by the operation of the same rule:
　　|u-ᵏwurri| —> /-oorri/

The outcome of this process is a shape homophonous with the trial/unit augmented morpheme, with the result that the distinction between trial/unit augmented and collective number is neutralized after

---

[59] Non-subcategorized objects are treated in Chapter 13.

/u/. Historically, the trial/unit augmented morpheme is probably derived from the collective one by reduplication and the application of V-expansion rule 18:

*/-ᵏwu-ᵏwurri/ —> /-oorri/

On verbs, the dual morpheme occurs in order-class [12], and the collective morpheme in order-class [14]. The unit augmented morpheme never occurs in the database in the same verb form as the continuous aspect morpheme (order-class [13]), and so it is impossible to be precise about its location. It is here conservatively allocated to order-class [12], along with the dual morpheme.

An important point to note is that the three morphemes in question signal marked categories, that is to say that they only appear when issues of number and participation are contextually foregrounded. Compare, by way of example, the two expressions in (9.1):

(9.1a) Ngarreyu!
ngarr-a=ya
1pin-OPT=go
Let's go!

(b) Ngarriyaarndu!
ngarr-a=ya-ᵏwarndu
1pin-OPT=go-DU
Let's go!/ I'll go with you (sg)!/ You (sg) come with me!

The form in (9.1a) may be spoken to a group of people or to just one person, with the clear understanding that the speaker is referring to himself or herself and the addressee(s). The form in (9.1b), however, with the dual morpheme -ᵏ*warndu*, is employed when the speaker intends to distinguish a single addressee from someone else or from a group of other people, and to include only that addressee in his or her predication. Both forms in (9.1) may be used to refer to two people (the speaker and one addressee): the second expression however is a marked form used when the speaker wants to make it clear to the addressee that only he or she is intended, or that he or she in particular is intended.

Worrorra has an adjectival root morpheme =*yarrungu* 'QUANTIFIER' which is denotationally empty, but which serves as a base for the attachment of agreement-class indices (§6.1) and number suffixes. Forms derived from =*yarrungu* are numbers in the strict sense: despite an elaboration of agreement-class affixation, these forms denote absolute numerical quantities of the class depicted. They are displayed in Table 9.2 below.

With respect to this table, note that:
(i) A fourth set of plural forms ('many,' 'all of __') is declined:

1pin	ngajarrungu
1px	ajarrungu
2p	nyijarrungu
3p	ajarrunguya

(ii) Prefixed morphemes index agreement-classes, as listed down the left-hand side of the table. The suffixes -*nya* on 3f forms, -*ma* on 3m forms and -*ya* on 3p forms code those agreement classes as well (see §6.1).
(iii) The feminine suffix -*nya* is optional on 3f forms: common alternatives are SG *ninjarrungu*, DU *ninjarrungaarndu*, TRI *ninjarrungoorri*.
(iv) The initial phoneme of the 3f forms is /n/ rather than the expected /ny/, under dissimilation with the following [nyj] cluster

Table 9.2: numbers

	One	Two	Three
1	ngayarrungu nga=yarrungu		
2	ngunjarrungu ngun=yarrungu		
3a	iyarrungu i=yarrungu	iyarrungaarndu i=yarrungu-^{k}warndu	iyarrungoorri i=yarrungu-oorri
3f	ninjarrungunya nyiN=yarrungu-nya	ninjarrungaarndinya nyiN=yarrungu-^{k}warndu-nya	ninjarrungoorrinya nyiN=yarrungu-oorri-nya
3w	jarrungu ØN=yarrungu	jarrungaarndu ØN=yarrungu-^{k}warndu	jarrungoorri ØN=yarrungu-oorri
3m	mayarrunguma ma=yarrungu-ma	mayarrungaarnduma ma=yarrungu-^{k}warndu-ma	mayarrungoorrima ma=yarrungu-oorri-ma
1pin		ngajarrungaarndu ngarr=yarrungu-^{k}warndu	ngajarrungoorri ngarr=yarrungu-oorri
1px		ajarrungaarndu arr=yarrungu-^{k}warndu	ajarrungoorri arr=yarrungu-oorri
2p		nyijarrungaarndu nyirr=yarrungu-^{k}warndu	nyijarrungoorri nyirr=yarrungu-oorri
3p		ajarrungaarndiya arr=yarrungu-^{k}warndu-ya	ajarrungoorriya arr=yarrungu-oorri-ya

9.2 Outranked actors

On the face of it, the number system signalled by these suffixes is, typologically, a system of *augmentation*, comparable in some ways to that found in other Australian Arafuran languages such as Rembarrnga and Ndjebbana (McKay 1978). A more detailed study of aspects of augmenting pronoun systems may be found in Greenberg (1988), and referral to this phenomenon in neighbouring Nyulnyulan languages may be found in McGregor (1989). The formal marking of the system in Worrorra, however, does not appear to be cognate with that of any other language, and the system itself is reasonably distinct from other systems of numerical augmentation.

In Worrorra, an augmented quantity is characterized as a set, the members of which may then be manipulated conceptually as an entire unit. Consider example (9.1b) above, in which the use of the dual morpheme indexes the speaker and the addressee as being included in a set distinct from other people around them. The most important function of number marking, therefore, is to index an act of *inclusion*, by means of which referents are characterized as being co-members of a set. Sets are encoded in the language by virtue of the fact that in any given instance, the co-referents of forms indexed by a number morpheme constitute a set. All verbal arguments co-indexed by a number morpheme must appear in the same grammatical function; that is to say that while a set may occur in S, A, U or D function, all members of the set must appear in the same function as each other. Pronouns marked for number characteristically occur with included referents in apposition to the pronoun, as in (9.2):

(9.2a)
Doreen	arrerndu	kajaanya	nyiman	nyimnyanu.
Doreen	arri-ᵏwarndu	kajaanya	nyiN=man	nyiN-mnya=nu
Doreen	we(exc)-DU	MoMo	3f=dead	3f-DD=be

Doreen's and my grandmother died.

(b)
Arrerndu	Aalkaalja	marru	jarriy	kunyarrbaarndu.
arri-ᵏwarndu	Aalkaalja	ma=rru	jarriy	kuN-nyarr=ma-ᵏwarndu
we (exc)-DU	Aalkaalja	3m=LAT	run	VCOMP-1px=get-DU

Aalkaalja and I ran away.

Forms overtly marked for number can be described with a collective or expanded plural interpretation, as 'all these items together/we all did something.' This interpretation comes out of the *set-inclusive* function of number marking, in picking out or indexing all the items that go to make up a set. Inclusiveness is a feature of the person-indexical system as well, and the two occurrences of this meaning are not unrelated.

A somewhat different sense meaning comes out of the *set-restrictive* function of number marking, picking out just those items that a speaker intends to include in the set, and no others. So forms marked for overt number may also be described with a restrictive/paucal interpretation, as 'these few items/we few did something'. The actual denotation of number in Worrorra may be summed up by a formula such as 'all of those items and just those particular items,' with either one or the other of these senses brought into focus by pragmatic considerations that come out of the context in which they are uttered.

The interpretation of number marking is contextually bound: not only in terms of which sense meaning is in focus in any utterance, but also in terms of which argument (S, A, U or D) is intended. It is not at all uncommon for different instances of number marking occurring in the same short stretch of discourse to index different predicate arguments (§9.5). The construal of sets in Worrorra appears to be pragmatically motivated, and number marking serves an essentially pragmatic function.

Set-formation is accomplished by way of a particular type of enumeration, one in which some quantity is augmented by another quantity. This process of augmentation is depicted abstractly in (9.3): in this notation the augmenting quantity precedes the augmented quantity:

(9.3a) dual: $1 + 1$
collective plural: $x + (n>1)$

From this it is clear that what is here termed 'dual' is really a 'unit–unit augmented' morpheme, although the term dual will be retained. The collective plural notation simply states that in this type of set, some number greater than one is augmented by another quantity. Unit augmentation is a special, marked type of collective number marking, in which $x = 1$:

(9.3b) unit augmented: $1 + (n>1)$

This notation states that some number greater than one is augmented by one. Attached to some nominals, the unit augmented morpheme has a distinct sense, 'trial.' This comes about apparently as the result of a special type of unit augmentation, in which the augmented number (n>1) is understood to be dual:

(9.3c) trial: $1 + (1 + 1)$

This situation gives evidence of a hierarchy of markedness, with the most general function giving way to increasingly more specific ones, as shown in (9.4):

(9.4)   Trial > Unit Augmented > Collective > Plural

What this means in effect is that collective is a marked type of plurality, unit augmentation is a marked type of collectivity, and that trial in turn is a marked type of unit augmentation.

An important outcome of the inclusive function and augmentative construction of number marking is that the language is able to encode a type of predicate argument that I will refer to as *outranked actor*, following Foley & Van Valin (1984:87). Outranked actors are 'potential actors ... which do not occur as actor[s]' (*ibid*). That is to say that they are outranked for actor (subject) status by some other argument with a stronger claim. It should be stressed that this is an almost entirely *de facto* category in Worrorra, as number morphemes may index objects as well as actors. Nevertheless the very common use of number to encode this type of argument is manifest. Consider the examples in the paradigm in (9.5):

(9.5a) Waa   malka   bedeenya.
        waa   malka   ba-nyarr=ni-yinya
        not   play   CFT-1px=be-PAST
        We (exc) never used to play.

(b)   Waa   malka   bedinyaarndu.
        waa   malka   ba-nyarr=ni-nya-ᵏwarndu
        not   play   CFT-1px=be-PAST-DU
        I never used to play with him/her.

(c)   Waa   malka   bedinyoorri.
        waa   malka   ba-nyarr=ni-nya-oorri
        not   play   CFT-1px=be-PAST-U/AUG
        I never used to play with them.

(d)   Waa   malka   bedinyorri.
        waa   malka   ba-nyarr=ni-nya-ᵏwurri
        not   play   CFT-1px=be-PAST-NUM
        We never used to play with them.

Note that (9.5b) is also translatable as 'he (or she) never used to play with me, we (dual exc) never used to play together,' (9.5c) as 'they never used to play with me,' and (9.5d) as 'they never used to play with us, we (exc) never all used to play together.'

The outranked actor interpretation comes out of the augmentative construction of number in the language, encoding the augmentation of one actor/participant by another. Note that augmentation is a function of the entire predicate itself, not just of its arguments: the marked shape of the predicate signals that its argument, or one of its arguments, is augmented. The interpretation of which argument that is, comes about by implicature from context. (For examples of context-determined interpretations of augmenting and augmented actors, see §9.6.2, esp examples (9.39, 9.41) and (9.42)). In signalling that their arguments are indexed by 'number' morphemes, the sentences in (9.5) encode the augmentation of that argument by some other actor, the outranked co-indexee of the number morpheme. In such sentences the discourse topic is generally interpreted as occupying subject grammatical function. Number marking, however, signals another participant or potential argument, dependent upon the same lexical predicate, and fulfilling the same semantic role as the topic-subject. But this other argument is outranked for subject status by the topic – in a pragmatic process the pragmatically most salient argument wins out. Although outranked, the other argument may still be included in the predicate's argument structure by being co-indexed with the 'real' subject. The outranked-actor function of number marking is pervasive, and represents the single most common discourse function of this morphology.

Outranked actors may occur as free-standing NPs, in which case their core-argument status is confirmed by the fact that they do not usually accept postpositions, nor are they marked by conjunctions (cf example 9.2). Most importantly, the referents of outranked actors are not co-referential with the subject of their verb; they may often contradict the person and/or gender specifications of the subject, making it impossible to construe them as included in the reference of the subject. This is particularly clear when the subject is second person. The injunction in (9.6a), for example, is addressed to a group of girls: the outranked actor noun, *iwaawurleya* 'adolescent boys,' cannot be construed as denoting addressees in this instance. Nor can *bamaranoorrinya* 'your (pl) father's sister' possibly be construed as an addressee in (9.6b):

(9.6a)
Nyirri	iwaawurleya	malka	binyideerringkurri.
nyirri	iwaawurleya	malka	ba-nyirr=nu-eerri-ᵏwurri
you.PL	adolescent.boys	play	CFT-2p=be-PROG-NUM

Don't you lot play with the big boys.

(b)
Nyirramurrkangurru	bamaranoorrinya	nyangke	ajaaja
nyiN-rra=murrka-ngurru	bamara-[nu-ᵏwurri]-nya	nyangke	aja-aja
3f-2p=go.to-away	FaSi-[2pDAT]-3f	3fREF	sit-sit

nyidoorri.
nyirr=nu-ᵏwurri
2p=be-NUM

You lot go to your aunty and live with her.

In other situations, while subject and outranked actor specifications may be reconcilable, context makes it impossible that they should be co-referential:

(9.7)
Ngayu	karle	irri	kaangamrerri	anja	ngayu
ngayu	karle	irri	kaarr-nga=mra-eerri	anja	ngayu
I	now	not.want	3p-1=gather-PROG	3pDEF	I

ngayanaanangkaya	nyangkaangkaya	arrke:	anja	kajirnba
ngaya-naa-nangka-ya	nya-ngkaa-ngka-ya	arrke	anja	kajirnba
I-AUG-DAT-3p	↳-AUG-girl-3p	3pREF	3pDEF	NEG

baadinkurri	anja	ngawaawanangkorri.
ba-kaarr=ni-n-ᵏwurri	anja	nga-waa-wa-[nangka-ᵏwurri]
CFT-3p=be-NON.P-NUM	3pDEF	↳-AUG-El.Sib-[3pDAT]

I don't want to keep these daughters of mine any longer: they can't live with their own brothers.

In the second clause of (9.7) the first occurrence of *anja* '3pDEF' refers to the girls, while the second refers to their brothers: the two are not co-referential.

(9.8)
Awaawanja	kaarri,	waa	berringenyeerringkurri	kaarri.
awaawanja	kaarri	waa	ba-nyarr=[i-nga]-yinya-eerri-ᵏwurri	kaarri
boys	3pNEG	not	CFT-1px=[go-TNS]-PAST-PROG-NUM	3pNEG

Not the boys, they didn't come with us/we didn't go with them at all.

In (9.8) the speaker is stating that while she and some other girls *did* go, the boys did not. The two groups cannot be co-referential, since under semantic decomposition the polarity of the predicate refers to only one of the groups, not both.

There are of course other strategies for denoting comitative relationships. The postpositions *-rnanya* 'LOCATIVE,' *(-)kurde* 'too, as well, ASSOCIATIVE' and *-nyina* 'HUMAN COMITATIVE' are also available, especially when the locative sense of such a relationship is in focus; but these are not nearly as frequent as instances of outranked actor marking:

(9.9a)
Irraayaa	karraanyarnanya	nganunerri.
irraaya-aa	karraanya-rnanya	nga=nu-na-eerri
my.father-and	my.mother-LOC	1=be-PAST-PROG

I lived with my father and mother.

(b)
Nyimnyininya	aja	ajanunerringkurri
nyi(na)-mnya-(nyi)na-nya	aja	arr-nya=nu-na-eerri-ᵏwurri
3fDEF-DD-HCOM-3f	sit	1px-EP=be-PAST-PROG-NUM

dambeem,	nyangkanangkamarnanya	nyina.
dambeem	nyangka-nangka-ma-rnanya	nyina
place	3fNAR-DAT-3m-LOC	HCOM

We all lived with her, at her place.

9.3 Dual

Sections §9.4 and §9.5 will explore how Worrorra resolves competition for the formal marking of various gender and number categories on lexical words. These processes mostly involve, and are best observed in, dual number morphemes, although they also effect other number categories. In order better to understand gender and number resolution in Worrorra, it will be useful first to undertake a general overview of the dual number category.

Dual number marking denotes a set of two people or things, usually one thing of a type and another of a similar type. With well over 700 occurrences, dual morphemes make up three quarters of all attested instances of number marking in the database. Duality is a grammatical category of the same order as 'singularity' and 'plurality;' it is a cultural category grammaticized in morphological marking throughout most of Australia. Where it occurs, dual number marking usually appears on all sentence constituents able to host it: note its marking on both the pronoun and the verb in (9.2b); determiners, nouns and verbs in (9.10a) and the sentences in (9.22) in §9.4.3, and even on the interrogative anaphor in (9.10b). Dual marking is also regularly indexed across clauses with co-referential arguments, as in (9.10c). In the following transitive sentence examples, number morphemes are bracketed with the argument indices to which they refer, and are subscripted for U, A or D grammatical function.

(9.10a)
Awaarndu	wangalaalangaarndu	malkalka	kanunaarndeerri
awa-ᵏwarndu	wangalaalangu-ᵏwarndu	malka-malka	ka=nu-na-ᵏwarndu-eerri
3aNAR-DU	children-DU	play-REDUP	3a=be-PAST-DU-PROG

inkarndu	awaawankarndu.
i=n-ᵏwarndu	awaawan-ᵏwarndu
3a=DEF-DU	boys-DU

The two boys were playing.

(b)
Angkuyaarndu inkarndu?
angkuyu-ᵏwarndu i=n-ᵏwarndu
who-DU 3a=DEF-DU
Who're these two?

(c)
Nyirringkaalkarnndu jarrernawajaarndu.
nyirr=i-ᵏwaal-ᵏwarndu jan-[rra]-nya=rnawaja-[ᵏwarndu_A]
2p=go-hither-DU 2>1-[2p]-OPT-help-[DU_A]
Come here, you two, and help me.

Attested simplex nouns marked for dual are humans, body parts and dogs (highly animate), and some other entities personified in myth. However it seems likely that dual marking could probably be applied to any noun, if its dual status were important enough. The dual morpheme is normally attached to the plural shape of human nouns, if that shape is different from the singular (§4.2.1):

SINGULAR		PLURAL	DUAL
eeja	*man*	eeja	eekarndu
wangayinya	*woman*	wangaya	wangayaarndinya
awanja	*boy*	awaawanja	awaawankarndu
nyangkanya	*girl*	nyangkaangkaya	nyangkaangkaarndinya
wangalang	*child*	wangalaalunguyu	wangalangaarndu, wangalaalangaarndu
kanangkurri	*dog*	kanaanangkurri	kanaanangkurrkarndu
jebarranya	*emu*	jebarreya	jebarranyaarndinya
marangunya	*sun*	—	marangunyaarndinya

Note that although the plural stem forms of nouns are used in dual marking, the feminine singular suffix -*nya* is used on those same forms. The dual morpheme is consistently inconsistent with respect to its selection of host (singular or plural) morphologies (§9.5). Note also that the feminine agreement-class suffix -*nya* usually comes after the dual affix; that is, that the dual morpheme is inserted between the noun stem and its gender suffix: cf eg *nyangkanya* (|nyangka-nya| [girl-3f]) 'girl,' and *nyangkaangkaarndinya* (|nya-ngkaa-ngka-ᵏwarndu-nya| [↳-AUG-girl-DU-3f]) 'two girls.' Feminine forms optionally end in -ᵏ*warndu* instead of -ᵏ*warndinya*; there is no statistical preference for one form over the other: *wangayaarndu* 'two women,' *nyangkaangkaarndu* 'two girls,' *jebarranyaarndu* 'two emus' and *marangunyaarndu* 'two suns.'

Derived nouns may also take dual marking:

(9.11a) Imalarrkarndu
i=malarr-ᵏwarndu
3a=MOIETY.NAME-DU
Two people of the Adbalarriya moiety

(b) Nyimalajaarndinya
nyiN=malarr-nya-ᵏwarndu-nya
3f=MOIETY.NAME-3f-DU-3f
Two women of the Adbalarriya moiety

(c) Iwunarrkarndu or iwaawunarrkarndu
i=ᵇwunarr-ᵏwarndu i-ᵇwaa=ᵇwunarr-ᵏwarndu
3a=MOIETY.NAME=DU 3a-AUG=moiety.name=DU
Two people of the Arrwunarriya moiety (cf. §6.2.6 (ii))

(d)	Nyimbunajaarndinya
	nyiN=ᵇwunarr-nya-ᵏwarndu-nya
	3f=MOIETY.NAME-3f-DU-3f
	Two women of the Arrwunarriya moiety

Adjectives may also take dual marking. The quantifier =*yarrungu* shown in Table 9.2 in §9.1 is formally adjectival.

(9.12a)	Iniyaarndu
	i=niya-ᵏwarndu
	3a=good-DU
	Two good (people)

(b)	Iyakarraarndu
	i=yakarri-ᵏwarndu
	3a=other-DU
	Two others/another two

Kinship nouns contain possessive suffixes (glossed DAT; see §13.1.1), which may be marked for dual number:

(9.13a)	Karraangarrerndinya
	karraa-[ngarri-ᵏwarndu]-nya
	mother-[1pinDAT-DU]-3f
	Our (dual inc) mother

(b)	Mangkaangkanangkaarndiya
	ma-ngkaa-ngka-[nangka-ᵏwarndu]-ya
	↳-AUG-wife-[DAT-DU]-3p
	Their (dual) wives

Note again in these examples how the feminine and plural agreement-class suffixes come after the dual number affix. Inalienable body-part nouns may also take dual marking, in which case two people are being referred to, not two organs:

(9.14a)	Iyardaarndu
	i=yardu-ᵏwarndu
	3a=foot-DU
	(Two people's) feet or sets of tracks

(b)	Aarlaarnduma
	a=ᵏwarlu-ᵏwarndu-ma
	3a=arm-DU-3m
	(Two people's) arms

(c)	Aambulkarndu
	a=ᵏwambul-ᵏwarndu
	3a=eye-DU
	(Two people's) eyes

(d) Ingulumaarnduma
 i=ngulu-ma-ᵏwarndu-ma
 3a=stomach-3m-DU-3m
 (Two people's) stomachs or feelings

Note in (9.14b) and (d) how the mana-class suffix -*ma* comes after the dual morpheme.

Some nouns of the marked macrogender lose their gender suffixes in front of the dual marker, as does =ᵏ*warluma mana* 'arm' in (9.14b) (underlyingly |=ᵏwarlu| in this construction), and some do not, making instead a form doubly-marked for gender, as does =*nguluma mana* 'stomach' in (9.14d) (cf also *nyimalajaarndinya* and *nyimbunajaarndinya* in (9.11b & d). Word forms of this sort, with two gender morphemes, constitute clear examples of the sequential application of morphology. While the left-hand gender morpheme occurs as part of the noun's lexical construction, the presence of the right-hand gender morpheme appears to be due to a post-lexical process.

9.4 Gender resolution

As is the case in many gendered languages, it sometimes happens in Worrorra that denotata of different genders are included in the same set, that is, are co-indexed by the same number morpheme. When this occurs the genders concerned may, as it were, compete for access to some agreement locus, for instance for registration in prefix position on verbs or pronouns. In this section we will look at the strategies Worrorra uses to resolve potential conflicts of this sort, brought about by number marking on verbs, inalienable body-part nouns and pronouns.

Gender resolution in Worrorra appears to involve the combined application of three principles:
(i) only highly animate denotata are eligible for number marking,
(ii) for highly animate denotata, gender anomalies are resolved by re-allocation to masculine, and
(iii) in some lexical categories, feminine gender markers and number markers do not appear on the same word concurrently.

On verbs, number morphemes may refer to arguments in any core grammatical function. The gender of third person singular core arguments is indexed on verbs in S and U functions (absolutive agreement), but not in A and D functions (see Table 5.2 in §5.3.1). Therefore verbal arguments marked for both number and gender occur in absolutive function only.

9.4.1 Animacy

In §4.2.1 it was seen that plural marking is only available to human nouns and nouns referring to important animals, foods or artefacts, that is to denotata highly placed on a scale of animacy and/or salience. Overt (dual, trial/unit augmented and collective) number marking is also the privilege of mainly highly animate denotata. Normally, non-human denotata, including nearly all members of the non-human macrogender, are ineligible for number marking, so that a number of entities of this sort are referred to by singular agreement forms:

(9.15a)
Angujakunya	kubarrbrerri	wunu	karrku?
anguja-ᵏwunya	kuN-ᵇwarr=mra-eerri	wunu	karrku
what-PURP	3w-3p=gather-PROG	3wDEF	stone

What are they picking up all those stones for?

(b)
Arrka	karnmangku	wok	kawarrona
arrka	karnmangku	wok	ka-ᵇwarr-a=ᵇwu-na
3pNAR	yam	cook	3a - 3p-EP=hit-PAST

They cooked the yams

(c)

Manjawarrawunya	buluba	kaarringa,	kawarramrangerri
manjawarra-ᵏwunya	buluk-ᵇwa	kaarr=i-nga	ka-ᵇwarr-a=mra-nga-eerri
berry.sp-PURP	seek-PROG	3p=go-TNS	3a-3p-EP=gather-PAST-PROG

angkam   mana
bowl   3mDEF

They went out looking for manjawarra *berries, and gathered them up into bowls*

(d)

Ngani	kubaje	nyini	mana	mayaram?
ngani	kuN-ᵇwarr-nya=yi	nyini	mana	mayaram
what	VCOMP-3p-EP=do	then	3mDEF	house

What are they going to do with the houses?

In (9.15a) and (c) the verb =*mra* 'gather' refers to a number of object entities by definition (rocks and berries respectively), which are marked however by a singular determiner *(wunu)* in (9.15a), and by singular object indices (*kuN*- '3w' and *ka*- '3a'). In (9.15b) the object *karnmangku inja* 'yam' is clearly used in a plural sense in the passage in which it occurs, but is indexed on the verb by the masculine singular U form. In (9.15c) as well, *angkam mana* 'bowl,' while used with a singular determiner, refers to a number of bowls, and in (9.15d) *mana mayaram* 'house' here refers to a number of houses under discussion.

When nouns from different classes are potentially conjoint arguments of some predicate, then the grammar needs somehow to address the issue of gender resolution. One way of doing this is to list such nouns in separate clauses, as shown in (9.16), thus avoiding the issue altogether:[60]

(9.16)

Kulju	inja	kamangaa,	marlinji	wunu	rderdeba
kulju	inja	ka-Ø=ma-nga-aa	marlinji	wunu	rdeyi-rdey-ᵇwa
snail.sp	3aDEF	3a-3=get-PAST-and	oyster	3wDEF	crack-crack-PROG

kumbuna
kuN-Ø=ᵇwu-na
3w-3=hit-PAST

She gathered sea-snails and broke open oysters

Otherwise, a number of entities highly placed on a scale of animacy/salience/topicality (in this case food) may be indexed by plural agreement marking, as in (9.17), where the objects (honey and yams) are co-indexed on the verb by the plural agreement morpheme *kaarr*- '3p:'

(9.17)

Ngeeyaa	karnmangku	wanji	kaanbunaal
ngeeya-aa	karnmangku	wanji	kaarr-n-Ø=ᵇwu-na-aal
honey-and	yam	find	3p-INV-3=hit-PAST-hither

She came back with honey and yams

Although most inalienable body-part nouns belong to the non-human macrogender, owing to their core denotations as parts of the human body, they are potentially highly animate. The sentence examples in (9.18) and (9.19) below show dual number marking on celestial and terrestrial inalienable nouns. In these sentences number marking is found on both the body-part nouns themselves and on the verbs of which they are arguments:

---

[60] Exactly the same device is used in Ungarinyin — see Rumsey 1982:137.

(9.18)
Imriyaarndu	wakumaada	kumnyanungaarndu	wunu
i=mri-y-ᵏwarndu	wakumaada	kuN-mnya=nu-ng-ᵏwarndu	wunu
3a=head-EP-DU	black	3w-DD=be-PRES-DU	3wDEF

Both their heads are black

The intransitive verb in (9.18), *kumnyanungaarndu*, is marked for dual number and for the gender of its subject, *=mri wunu* 'head.' The sentence in (9.19) shows dual marking on a terrestrial inalienable noun in undergoer function:

(9.19)
Aarlaarndum	mana	kurriybiji	mamangaarndu
a=ᵏwarlu-ᵏwarndu-ma	mana	kurriy-biji	[ma]-Ø=ma-nga-[ᵏwarndu_U]
3a=wing/arm-DU-3m	3mDEF	cut.off-REPEAT	[3m]-3=get-PAST-[DU_U]

karlinyine
karli-nyine
boomerang-INST

He cut off their wings with his boomerang

The verb's terrestrial undergoer is the inalienable noun *=ᵏwarlum mana* 'arm, wing,' with dual number marking on itself and on the verb. On both *imriaarndu* and *aarlaarndum* in (9.18) and (9.19), note the masculine indexation (prefixed) of the possessors of these inalienable nouns (§6.3), which in both these instances actually refer to two emus *(jebarranyaarndinya)*, which are feminine (see also 9.24 in §9.4.3).

9.4.2 Re-allocation to masculine

Usually, when a number of highly animate entities are denoted, plural agreement forms are used to refer to them. However when only two or three highly animate entities of different genders are included in the same number-set, gender marking collapses into the largest and most unmarked gender, which is masculine (§4.1.2 & §4.1.6 (i)), as in (9.20):

(9.20a)
Wangalangaarndu	marno	**ka**walkenyaarndeerri	karrkurnanya,
wangalangu-ᵏwarndu	ma=rno	ka=ᵇwalke-nya-ᵏwarndu-eerri	karrku-rnanya
child-DU	3m=there	**3a**=stand-PAST-DU-PROG	rock-LOC

awanjaa   nyangkanya
awanja-aa nyangkanya
boy-and   girl

Two children were standing on a hill, a boy and a girl

(b)
Minjarlminjarl	**ka**nunaarndeerri.	Ke	awa	minjarl
minjarl-minjarl	ka=nu-na-ᵏwarndu-eerri	ke	awa	minjarl
eat-eat	**3a**=be-PAST-DU-PROG	and	3aNAR	eat

kanunerri	karrangu	maa	marno	nguwarnanya,	ke
ka=nu-na-eerri	karrangu	maa	ma=rno	nguwanu-rnanya	ke
3a=be-PAST-PROG	high	3mREF	3m=there	tree-LOC	and

nyangka	kabalbarnanya	kaanmrangerri	minjarlminjarl
nyangka	kabalba-rnanya	kaarr-n-Ø=mra-nga-eerri	minjarl-minjarl
3fREF	ground-LOC	3p-INV-3=gather-PAST-PROG	eat-eat

nyinunerri
nyiN=nu-na-eerri
3f=be-PAST-PROG

They were both eating. He was eating (fruit) high up in the tree, and she was gathering them up off the ground and eating them.

(c)

Marrkaayaarndu	kamnyaweenaarndu		iyarrungaarndu.
marrka-y-ᵏwarndu	ka-mnya=ᵇwee-na-ᵏwarndu		i=yarrungu-ᵏwarndu
sibling-EP-DU	3a-DD=hit.MID-PAST-DU		3a=QUANT-DU

Lose'm	kamnyaweenaarndu.	Nyina	ngawanangkorrinya
lose'm	ka-mnya=ᵇwee-na-ᵏwarndu	nyina	ngawa-[nangkorri]-nya
die	3a-DD=hit.MID-PAST-DU	3fDEF	El.Sib-[3pDAT]-3f

laburru	**ka**mnyamiyengoorri,	ajarrungaarndiya.
laburru	ka-mnya=ma-ye-ng-oorri	arr=yarrungu-ᵏwarndu-ya
follow	**3a**-DD=get-MID-PRES-U/AUG	px=QUANT-DU-3p

The two brothers used to fight. They both died. They went at about the same time as their elder sister, both of them.

In (9.20a) the dual subject (a boy and a girl) is indexed on the verb *kawalkenyaarndeerri* by the masculine form *ka-* '3a.' Similarly, the first verb in (9.20b), *kanunaarndeerri*, has the man and the woman together as its subject, and is marked for dual number, with the subject index showing masculine gender agreement. Example (9.20c) involves all middle-voice verbs, that is to say transitive verbs with an argument removed. That the siblings concerned are brothers (and not sisters) is shown by the masculine gender marking on the quantifier *iyarrungaarndu* 'two (masc).' Note that they are later referred to by the quantifier *ajarrungaarndiya* 'two (human),' showing that with reference to humans, these two forms are synonymous (cf Table 6.9 in §6.2.6 (i)). The English verb *lose'm* is here used to mean 'die,' and the verb's classifier =ᵇ*wee* 'hit(middle)' is used as a general middle-voice pro-verb. The sentence in which it occurs could more accurately be translated euphemistically as 'they were lost.' As an argument has been removed from the middle-voice predicate *laburru kamnyamiyengoorri*, a reciprocal meaning may have been produced in this instance, 'they followed each other,' so it is impossible to state which actor (the two brothers or their sister) is referred to by the prefixed NP index *ka-* '3a' (but see discussion in §16.2). The point is that under number marking mixed masculine-feminine subjects of this sort are indexed by masculine forms. Note that the unit augmented morpheme marks three actors in this instance: if sets of this make-up (1+2) were particularly salient or reasonably frequent in the past, it may explain how the unit augmented morpheme came to be treated as a trial form on nominals.

The database contains no instances of masculine or feminine denotata being co-indexed for number with denotata of the celestial or terrestrial classes; that is to say that denotata of the human macrogender are not co-indexed with those of the non-human macrogender. This makes sense in the light of the semantic properties of human and non-human denotata respectively: humans are prototypically natural agents, while non-human things are natural patients (Silverstein 1976a). These two semantic types are therefore functionally opposed to each other: in a world of argument types, they are in a kind of functional complementary distribution. Recall from §9.2 that all members of a set must appear in the same grammatical function: it now becomes clear that with respect to a given predicate, typical agents and typical patients are unlikely to be found together in the same set. Indeed in Worrorra there seems to be a prohibition against nouns of opposing semantic types appearing together in the same set. And if two such arguments were ever required to appear together, some strategy other than number indexation could be readily found to accommodate them; listing in separate clauses, as in (9.16) would appear to be most likely. This is not an uncommon stylistic device, as seen below in (9.21) with masculine and feminine denotata:

(9.21a)   Rorrij   kamangaa   nyangka   rorrij   kamanga
           rorrij   ka-Ø=ma-nga-aa   nyangka   rorrij   ka-Ø=ma-nga
           snatch   3a-3=get-PAST-and   3fDEF   snatch   3a-3=get-PAST
           *He snatched some (masc) and then **she** snatched some*

(b)   Marnuk   nyimaa,   marnuk   kama
      marnuk   nyiN-Ø=ma-aa   marnuk   ka-Ø=ma
      lift   3f-3=get-and   lift   3a-3=get
      *He picked **her** up, then he picked **him** up*

Example (9.21a) shows masculine undergoers, with a switch from masculine to feminine agent marked by the feminine anaphor *nyangka*, while (9.21b) shows feminine and masculine undergoers indexed on the verbs.

9.4.3 Feminine gender and number-marking

Certain lexical categories (verbs, pronouns and inalienable nouns) appear to be unable to host both number morphemes *and* feminine gender-marking morphemes at the same time. The result of this situation is that in these categories the masculine and feminine genders are neutralized to masculine under number marking. In the examples in (9.22) below, notice how feminine denotata in S function are indexed on the verb and on pronouns by masculine agreement forms:

(9.22a)
Inkarndu   wangayaarndu   ngarru   kengaarndeerri?
i=n-ᵏwarndu   wangaya-ᵏwarndu   ngarru   ka=ya-nga-ᵏwarndu-eerri
3a=DEF-DU   women-DU   whither   **3a**=go-TNS-DU-PROG
Where are those two women off to?

(b)
Awaarndu   nyangkaangkaarndinya   aja   **ka**ningaarndeerri
awa-ᵏwarndu   nyangkaangka-ᵏwarndu-nya   aja   ka=ni-ng-ᵏwarndu-eerri
3aNAR-DU   girls-DU-3f   sit   **3a**=be-PRES-DU-PROG

wiyarnanya
wiyanu-rnanya
fire-LOC
The two girls are sitting by the fire

The feminine nouns in (9.22) occur with the dual-marked masculine determiners *awaarndu* and *inkarndu*, as well as being indexed by masculine forms on the verbs. With respect to verbs and pronouns, this reflects the situation found in all examples from naturally occurring, unelicited texts: wherever women or other feminine denotata are marked for number, they are indexed by masculine forms. Note in particular the sentence in (9.23); here the discourse topic is a woman, who has been the subject of discussion and a good deal of interest, and of whom it is said:

(9.23)   Ke   **ka**mnyanunaarndeerri   inja   eeja
          ke   ka-mnya=nu-na-ᵏwarndu-eerri   inja   eeja
          and   **3a**-DD=be-PAST-DU-PROG   3aDEF   man

And she lived with that man

The verb =*nu* 'be' in this sentence is used in its sense meaning 'dwell, abide.' The woman, as discourse topic, is understood to be the subject, with *inja eeja* 'the man' an outranked actor. Number marking, however, induces a masculine NP prefix. The marking of the human macrogender is also collapsed into masculine for undergoer arguments. Example (9.24) is taken from a text about two emus, which although feminine, here appear indexed by masculine forms:

(9.24)
Wali maa	injinja	karlinyine	ingaarnamalaarndu
wali maa	inja-inja	karli-nyine	[i]-nga=aarnamalu-[ᵏwarndu_U]
CONT	3aDEF-REDUP	boomerang-INST	[3a]-1=shoot-[DU_U]

I'll get them (dual) with this boomerang

The reduplicated determiner *injinja* refers to *karli* 'boomerang.'

Inalienable nouns are another lexical category in which feminine gender morphemes and number morphemes are prohibited from co-occurring. In sentence examples (9.18) and (9.19) in §9.4.1 we have already seen inalienable body-part nouns with the gender of feminine possessors neutralized to masculine. There is however a way in which both the feminine gender of a possessor and the number of items denoted by the inalienable noun itself may be referred to separately. This construction involves the adjective =*yarrungu* 'QUANTIFIER,' as seen in example (9.25) below:

(9.25)
Nyingumbu	wunu	jarrungaarndu	wali wunu;
nyiN=ngumbu	wunu	ØN=yarrungu-ᵏwarndu	wali wunu
3f=name	3wDEF	3w=QUANT-DU	PM

nyimrimaaingarrinyaa	mawunkunya.
nyiN=mri-maai-ngarri-nya-aa	mawunkunya
3f=head-blackened-REL-3f-and	python.sp

She has two names; they are, her-head-is-shaved-and-blackened-in-mourning and mawunkunya.

In this sentence the number *jarrungaarndu* 'two (celestial)' agrees with its head, =*ngumbu_wunu* 'name.' The number of denotata referred to by the inalienable noun is marked periphrastically, rather than morphologically by some disallowed form such as **nyingumbaarndu*.

Another important class of gender-restricted nominals is that of pronouns, number-marked instances of which have already been observed in (9.22). Although pronouns are described in more detail in Chapter Seven, the paradigm of the pronoun =ᵏ*wa* 'Anaphoric/Narrative' (glossed NAR) is shown here for illustrative purposes. This is one of the very few forms that displays trial number marking. Its morphology is displayed in Table 7.2 in §7.2, reproduced here in part as Table 9.3. The collapsing of the human macrogender in the non-singular categories is apparent in these forms.

Table 9.3: =ᵏ*wa* 'Anaphoric/Narrative'

	SINGULAR		DUAL	TRIAL
3a	awa	*he*	awaarndu	awoorri
3f	nyangka	*she*	awaarndu	awoorri
3w	kawa	*it*	kawaarndu	kawoorri
3m	mawa	*it*	mawaarnduma	mawoorrima

However there does appear to be a discrepancy in the data. Love (1934:36-64, 85-89) presents paradigms of intransitive verb forms with feminine shapes marked for number. He lists as well separate number-marked feminine pronouns (*ibid.*: 9-10), although he does show masculine and feminine genders collapsed in dual possessive pronouns (*ibid.*:13). Furthermore, I have also found that such forms, both verbal and pronominal, are readily elicited, especially in paradigms. The form *nyangkaarndinya (=^{k}wa 'anaphoric/narrative' feminine dual) appears in Love's paradigm (Love 1934:9) and in my own elicited paradigms, but is unattested in numerous textual instances where it could appear, but where *awaarndu* appears instead. Love (1934:10) also lists *njiŋ'gurinja* (?*nyingkoorrinya*) as a feminine trial form of =^{k}wa, but this was consistently rejected by my instructors. A feminine dual definite article *nyinkarndinya is also readily elicited, but again, in all textual situations where it could occur, the masculine shape *inkarndu* appears instead (cf 9.22a). The point is that unattested forms like *nyinkarndinya, *nyangkaarndinya and *nyingkoorrinya are completely predictable by analogy with the rest of the morphology, which may be what prompts people to recite paradigms of this sort, that show forms not actually in use. Given the verb forms *kenga* 'he went,' *kengaarndu* 'they (dual) went' and *nyenga* 'she went,' an unattested form *nyengaarndu 'they (fem dual) went' is completely predictable.

With some 950 instances of number marking attested in the database, I am reasonably confident about its general reliability in this respect. A number of reasons could be put forward to account for the discrepancy between elicited and attested forms, eg: (i) the discrepancy is a peculiarity of just those few Worrorra speakers remaining in the 1990s, or (ii) is a result of the late stage of the language in terms of its social use. Other explanations that I think are rather more likely, are that (iii) a highly productive morphology is liable to throw up bogus forms in elicited paradigms, (iv) the highly marked feminine-number forms may be available for particular types of focus or emphasis only, not represented in the database, or (v) there may be a stylistic prohibition against including two highly-marked kinds of morpheme (number and feminine gender) in the same word form; such a prohibition not being manifested in the decontextualized style of paradigm-recitation.

On this point I should make reference to an obscure passage in Love (1934:75-76) having to do with number-marking on feminine objects (undergoers):

> N.B. For feminine object in all numbers the dual, trial and plural subjects are same as singular subject. ... Note 4. With feminine object in the dual, trial, or plural, the subject uses (1) the same forms as for a masculine object; or (2) if necessary to distinguish the feminine gender in the object, the same forms are used, in all numbers of the subject, as given in the above table for singular subject.

It seems possible that the reason Love included this passage, and why these comments are obscure, is that his attempts to elicit number-marking on feminine objects foundered. Because the interpretation of number morphemes is so context-dependent, confusion between subjects and objects in these paradigms is to be expected, and was certainly the case in my experience. The situation is reminiscent of Rumsey's (1982:106) warning about the unreliability of elicited responses in relation to number marking. The discrepancy as it stands represents a good example of the difference between what people say, and what they say they say.

9.5 Number resolution

In this section we will look at interactions between the two types of number marking that I will refer to as 'overt' and 'inherent.' As suffixes, overt number morphemes are normally attached to a word form already bearing some indication of number by means of either inflectional or derivational NP prefixes. As these prefixes include coding for either singular or plural number, then overt number shapes will be attached to word forms already inflected for these inherent number categories. Overt number morphemes are not consistent with respect to which inherent number categories they select to host them. In this section we will look only at how dual morphemes are hosted; consideration of this phenomenon in collective and unit augmented forms is reserved for §9.6.

I have already mentioned in §9.3 that the dual morpheme is consistently inconsistent with respect to its selection of host morphology, and already it may be apparent that there is an important split in the system by which the dual morpheme selects its host. Grammatical person in Worrorra shows a split between speech act participants (first and second persons) and non-participants (third persons). When the dual morpheme co-indexes or refers to some *participant* person, then the relevant NP index must be a *plural* form. Examples of this phenomenon are shown in (9.1b, 9.2, 9.5b, 9.10b) and (9.13a). But when the dual morpheme refers to some *non-participant* person, then the NP index must be a *singular* form. Examples of this phenomenon are shown in (9.11, 9.12, 9.14, 9.18, 9.19, 9.20, 9.22, 9.23, 9.24) and (9.25).

Adjectives agreeing with non-participant heads normally take singular prefix shapes when marked for dual number (see examples in 9.12). However the word *ajarrungaarndiya* 'two (human)' in (9.20c), contains a dual morpheme suffixed to a form with the third person *plural* (non-participant) prefix *arr-*. Given the constraints on plural marking on adjectives discussed in §6.2.6 (i), this shape is quite regular. The form *=yarrungu* 'QUANTIFIER' is an adjective, and as such would normally take plural indexation (*arr-* '3p') when referring to a number of highly animate entities, such as humans. But adjectives may also appear in singular agreement forms when referring to a number of humans (see Table 6.9 in §6.2.6 (i)), and so the singular-prefix forms *iyarrungaarndu* 'two (masc)' and *ninjarrungaarndinya* 'two (fem)' are just as acceptable as, and are in fact statistically preferred to, the plural-prefix shape *ajarrungaarndiya*. And of course low-animate denotata may only be referred to by the singular third person prefix forms in Table 9.2. It would appear that for human denotata, the choice between *iyarrungaarndu* or *ninjarrungaarndinya* and *ajarrungaarndiya* is stylistic, and indeed both forms appear together in example (9.20c).

It is claimed above that words with number morphemes, including dual morphemes, are marked forms, and this being so, it ought to be possible to refer to two entities together in an unmarked way. This is indeed the case, of course, and such reference is achieved by way of plural NP indexation:

(9.26a)
Awa	irranangkaa	karranangkorrinya	aja	kaadunerri
awa	irra-nangka-aa	karra-nangkorri-nya	aja	kaarr=nu-na-eerri
3aNAR	father-DAT-and	mother-3pDAT-3f	sit	3p=be-PAST-PROG

Their mother and father were sitting down

(b)
Irranangkorri	aa	karranangkorrinya	jandoorri	kawarramanga
irra-nangkorri	aa	karra-nangkorri-nya	jandoorri	ka-^{b}warr-a=ma-nga
father-3pDAT	and	mother-3pDAT-3f	staff	3a-3p-EP-get-PAST

Their father and mother got staves

(c)
Ngarru	kamnyengaarndu?	Angkuyu	kaanmranga?
ngarru	ka-mnya=ya-nga-^{k}warndu	angkuyu	kaarr-n-Ø=mra-nga
whither	3a-DD=go-TNS-DU	who	3p-INV-3=gather-PAST

Where've they (dual) gone? Who took them?

(d)
Kaangurrurlaarndeerri,	maangurru	ingkenga	jaa maa
[ka]-Ø=^{k}wangurru-rla-[^{k}warndu$_U$]-eerri	maa-ngurru	i-ngka=ya-nga	jaa maa
[3a]-3=carry-PAST-[DU$_U$]-PROG	3mREF-away	3a-SJTV=go-TNS	always

kamarlaarndornaarndeerri.	Ke	kengorri
ka-[Ø]=marlaarndo-rna-[^{k}warndu$_A$]-eerri	ke	ka=ya-nga-^{k}wurri
3a-[3]=follow-PAST-[DU$_A$]-PROG	and	3a=go-TNS-NUM

maangurrunangkowa,	marrunangkowa	kengorri
maa-ngurru-nangkowa	ma=rru-nangkowa	ka=ya-nga-^{k}wurri
3mREF-away-DIR	3m=LAT-DIR	3a=go-TNS-NUM

kaankangurrurlerri
kaarr-n-Ø=ᵏwangurru-rla-eerri
3p-INV-3=carry-PAST-PROG

He would take them (dual) with him; when he went away they (dual) would always go with (follow) him. He went with them way over this way and over that way; he took them with him.

In (9.26a) the two parents are referred to by the plural S index on the verb; in (9.26b) by the plural A index; and in (9.26c) two people are referred to by the plural U index in the second sentence. In (9.26d) two boys are referred to as dual undergoers in *kaangurrurlaarndeerri*, and as dual agents in *kamarlaarndornaarndeerri*. In the final verb, *kaankangurrurlerri*, however, they are referred to as plural undergoers by way of the 3p index *kaarr-*.

Sometimes two agents are indexed by a singular NP prefix when in the presence of a plural undergoer prefix. In the second clause in (9.27a) the two actors referred to in the first clause receive singular indexation *(-Ø-)* as agents, in the presence of a 3p undergoer *(kaarr-)*:

(9.27a)
Kengkunaalkarndeerri	aja	kaanyeerla	jed	mana
ka=ya-ngku-na-aal-ᵏwarndu-eerri	aja	kaarr-n-Ø-nya=ee-rla	jed	mana
3a=go-EP-PAST-hither-DU-PROG	sit	3p-INV-3-EP=place-PAST	shade	3mDEF

They (dual) came along and set them down in the shade

(b)
Kaarringkunaal	nyangka	jebarranya	nyina,
kaarr=i-ngku-na-aal	nyangka	jebarranya	nyina
3p=go-EP-PAST-hither	3fNAR	emu	3fDEF

kaaninjangaaleerri
kaarr-n-Ø=ninja-nga-aal-eerri
3p-INV-3=look-PAST-hither-PROG

(Two) emus had come up, and were watching them

Example (9.27b) contains the first appearance of two emus in a narrative text. Consistently indexed by the dual morpheme subsequently, here they are referred to in the first clause by the singular topicalizing NP *nyangka jebarranya nyina*, and also by the plural S prefix *kaarr-* '3p' on *kaarringkunaal*, a result of their ambiguous status as personified animals. In the second clause, note, they are indexed by a singular A prefix *(-Ø-)*, again in the presence of a plural U prefix.

In summary, then: two participants are always referred to by plural NP indices, whether marked as a dual set or not. Two non-participants, on the other hand, are usually referred to by plural indices if unmarked for duality, but by singular indices if marked for duality. This situation is set out in Table 9.4:

Table 9.4: shapes of prefixes indexing two entities

	PARTICIPANT	NON-PARTICIPANT
Marked for Dual	PL	SG
Unmarked for Dual	PL	PL/(SG A)

In Worrorra then, the underlying reference of plurality is to some number greater than one; that is, to some non-singular number.

As can be seen from sentence example (9.1b) and all subsequent examples with intransitive verbs, number morphemes are available to mark arguments in S grammatical function. As well, example (9.26d) shows the dual morpheme indexing co-referential A and U arguments in the same sentence. Another number-marked argument in A function is seen in (9.10b), and other number-marked arguments in U function are seen in (9.19) and (9.24). Example (9.19) shows the verb *mamangaarndu* with a dual undergoer argument. Sentence (9.28) shows the same verb form, but this time with a dual *agent* argument:

(9.28) (cf 9.19)
Kambananyine   maa   jaluk   mamangaarndu   mana   kulum
kambana(nya)-nyine maa   jaluk   ma-[Ø]=ma-nga-[ᵏwarndu_A]   mana   kulum
shovel-INST   3mREF   scoop   3m-[3]=get-PAST-[DU_A]   3mDEF   oven-sand
They both scooped up shovelfuls of hot cooking-sand

Comparing (9.19) and (9.28), it is clear that the interpretation of the number morpheme must be made from context: there are no morphosyntactic clues available.

Number morphemes may also index non-subcategorized object arguments (abbreviated to D and glossed DAT), as in (9.29):

(9.29)
'Angujakunya   irriwa   nyidunaarndaara,
anguja-ᵏwunya   irri-ᵇwa   [nyirr]=nu-na-[ᵏwarndu]-ᵏwara
what-PURP   not.want-PROG   [2p]=be-PAST-[DU]-1DAT

mangkaangkaya   aai?'   kunjunganangkaarndu
ma-ngkaa-ngka-ya   aai   kuN-Ø=yi-ng-a-[nangka-ᵏwarndu_D]
↳-AUG-wife-3p   hey   VCOMP-3=do-PAST-EP-[DAT-DU_D]
'Why have you (dual) turned against me, my wives?' he asked them (dual)

In this sentence it is the non-subcategorized object of the verb *kunjunganangkaarndu* 'he said to them (dual)' that is marked for dual number, as is clear from the preceding material. But compare this example with the sentence in (9.30); the homonymous verb form there indexes dual actors instead:

(9.30)   Jarrungu   wunu   kunjunganangkaarndu ...
         ØN=yarrungu   wunu   kuN-[Ø]=yi-ng-a-nangka-[ᵏwarndu_A]
         3w=QUANT   3wDEF   VCOMP-[3]=do-PAST-EP-DAT-[DU_A]
         One day they (dual) said to him ...

And just as we saw in (9.26d), switcheroos of this kind can quite readily appear in the same or adjacent sentences, as is seen in (9.31):

(9.31)
'Marno   malkalka   nyidaarndu,'   kunjunganangkaarndu.
ma=rno   malka-malka   nyirr=nu-ᵏwarndu   kuN-Ø=yi-ng-a-[nangka-ᵏwarndu_D]
3m=DIST   play-REDUP   2p=be-DU   VCOMP-3=do-PAST-EP-[DAT-DU_D]

'Kaarriyaka,   manmaa   ajaaja   arramnyanaarndu,'
kaarri-y₂aka   ma=n-maa   aja-aja   arr-a-mnya=nu-ᵏwarndu
3pNEG-EMPH   3m=DEF-3mREF   sit-sit   1px-OPT-DD=be-DU

kunjunganangkaarndu,   kubajunganangka   inja
kuN-[Ø]=yi-ng-a-nangka [ᵏwarndu_A]   kuN-ᵇwarr=yi-ng-a-nangka
VCOMP-[3]=do-PAST-EP-DAT-[DU_A]   VCOMP-3p=do-PAST-EP-DAT   3aDEF

irranangkorri
irra-nangkorri
father-3pDAT

'Go and play over there,' he said to them (dual). 'No way, we're (dual) going to stay right here,' they (dual) told their father.

In this text the father starts off speaking to his two sons, and the first occurrence of the verb *kunjunganangkaarndu* 'he said to them (dual)' indexes the boys as dual addressee objects. But when the boys reply to their father in the next sentence, the same verb form is used, only this time indexing them as dual agents; 'they (dual) said to him.' In this situation, with homonymous forms occurring adjacent to each other, a speaker may feel that some kind of clarification is in order. Clarification is effected in this instance by the juxtaposition of the unambiguous form *kubajunganangka* 'they said to him,' immediately after the second dual form, substituting a plural agent shape for the by now ambiguous dual agent form. Clarification of this sort is available because unmarked dual reference makes use of plural NP indices, rather than singular ones.

The full references of Worrorra number morphemes can only be discovered in the context of an unfolding speech event in which their pragmatic values are set up or established over a stretch of discourse. In such circumstances clarification is always available, either by extra-linguistic means such as pointing, or by substituting unmarked expressions for the forms in which they occur, as in (9.31). The set-inclusive function of number marking is foregrounded when number morphemes occur on verbs, at the expense of enumeration: enumeration above two is certainly possible, but often fuzzy, as we will see in the next section.

9.6 Collective plural

While the dual morpheme has a clear enumerative function, by and large the collective morpheme lacks such a function. Being concerned with denoting sets of entities greater than two, the collective morpheme's functional load is almost exclusively concerned with set-construal. Indeed, set-construal is really all that the dual and collective morphemes have in common, and all that motivates their inclusion together in the same general 'number' category.

The collective morpheme signals a set of entities defined in ways dictated by Worrorra culture. So social groups are typically referred to, such as nuclear families, extended families and, rarely, patriclans. Also referred to are orthogonally constructed social groups, such as all the women, all the men or all the children of an extended family group, conceived of as a distinct social unit (set) for the purposes of some activity. In fact any group of more than two acting together may be marked for collective number (glossed NUM): so, 'all of us (did something), they all (did something),' etc. Typically, however, collective number marking seems to be applied to a group of more than two, but one which is not too big, either. It appears to define a set of a size that is socially functional, in terms of the typical day-to-day economic and social activities of a Worrorra family or extended family.

The only two simplex nouns marked for collective number that I have encountered are *eekurri* [man-NUM] 'all the men' and *wangayoorri* [women-NUM] 'all the women.' The only collectively-marked modifiers in the database are the quantifier *ajarrungoorri* 'three' and the adverb *bulakorri* (|bulaka-ᵏwurri| [middle-NUM]) 'in the middle of them all, amongst all the others.' It is likely, however, that collective number was more productive in a traditional linguistic context.

On verbs, the collective number morpheme may index arguments in S, A or rarely, U grammatical function. Non-subcategorized objects appear not to be indexed by collective morphemes in the same way that other arguments are: second and third person non-singular non-subcategorized object-indexing morphemes have the collective morpheme frozen unproductively into their shapes, where they simply mark non-singular number (see Table 5.2 in §5.3.2; Table 13.1 in Chapter 13). Take, for instance, the declension of the second person non-subcategorized object suffix:

(9.32) SINGULAR   PLURAL   DUAL
        -nu   -noorri   -nurrerndu
        |-nu| |-nu-ᵏwurri| |-[nu-ᵏwurri]-ᵏwarndu|
        -2DAT   -2DAT-NUM   -[2DAT-NUM]-DU

Here it is clear that the collective (NUM) morpheme merely forms a non-singular base that may be further inflected for dual number. Love (1934:14) lists a collective or trial series based on the plural shapes, as well as a dual series, but these forms do not occur in the database. It is therefore possible or maybe probable that non-subcategorized objects were on some occasions marked for collective reference, but as no instances of this occur in the database, this possibility will not be explored further. The upshot of this situation is that as far as the material in the database goes, collective number is not marked on non-subcategorized objects.

Collective number morphemes also violate ordering constraints when frozen into a plural non-subcategorized object index. Reference to Table 5.1 in §5.2 shows that in other circumstances the collective morpheme occurs in order-class [14], that is, after the continuous aspect morpheme in order-class [13], as may be seen in examples (9.6a, 9.8 & 9.9b) above, and (9.34) below. Non-subcategorized object indices, however, occur in order-class [11], before the continuous morpheme, whether in singular or non-singular shape, as may be seen in (9.33):

(9.33) Kurloonurreerri
        kuN-Ø=rloo-[nu-^{k}wurri$_D$]-eerri
        VCOMP-3=speak-[2DAT-NUM$_D$]-PROG
        He's talking to you lot

Although undergoers may be set up to receive collective number marking in elicited contexts, of the 75 examples of the collective number morpheme indexing verbal arguments in the database that do not occur in elicited paradigms, only three instances index undergoers; and of those only one occurs spontaneously, presented here as (9.34):

(9.34) Jandu-jandu   ngardaarnarlerringkurreka   inja.
        jandu-jandu   [ngarr]-Ø=rnaarna-rla-eerri-[^{k}wurri$_U$]-y$_2$aka   inja
        mock-REDUP   [1pin]-3=await-PAST-PROG-[NUM$_U$]-EMPH   3aDEF
        He really made fools out of us all.

The overwhelming majority of collectively indexed predicate arguments from naturally-occurring contexts, therefore, are in S and A functions; that is, they function as typical actors. While it is possible to index U arguments, as (9.34) shows, and while it may well have been possible to index non-subcategorized object arguments, there seems to be a strong preference for restricting collective number marking to actors. This tendency is, of course, completely in accordance with the outranked actor function of number marking: most occurrences of the collective morpheme seem to be motivated at least in part by an outranked actor interpretation.

Collectively marked verb forms take plural NP indexation, thus solving at once all issues having to do with gender and number resolution. The only exception to this is with unit augmented forms, where singular NP indexation is a possibility for third person arguments.

9.6.1 *Paucal pronouns*

Collectively marked (paucal) pronouns are discussed more fully in Chapter Seven. Love (1934:10, 13-15) describes a paucal pronoun category; he uses the term 'trial,' however, which serves in this exposition to label a slightly different category (see §9.6.3). In this section, reference will be made to the semantics of paucity in the particular context of collective pronouns.

A referential-indexical category such as 'inclusive' may have a number of sense meanings operating concurrently. In this case we have noted (i) the set-inclusive sense ('the set of all contextually pertinent instances of this particular denotation'), which leads to a plural interpretation; (ii) the outranked actor interpretation, and (iii) the set-restrictive sense ('just these particular ones and no others'), which may lead to a paucal interpretation. Different senses may be foregrounded in different lexical categories: in pronouns, it is the set-restrictive sense of collective meaning that is in focus, giving collectively marked pronouns a strong paucal interpretation.

The pronouns involved in paucal number marking are: (i) possessive pronouns, (ii) personal participant (first and second person) pronouns (Table 7.1) and (iii) some demonstrative pronouns: =n 'DEFINITE, PROXIMAL' and =rno 'that, DISTAL.' Love (1934:10) lists a collective series for =rru 'LATERAL' but my instructors rejected this (for further discussion, see §7.3.1). All examples of collectively marked pronouns, however, occur in Love's (1934) and my own recorded paradigms; none appear in spontaneous texts. The following examples also come from elicitation:

eeja arnowurri	*those few (3-5) men/all those men together*
eeja inkoorri	*these few men/all these men together*
wangayoorri irnowurri	*those few women/all those women together*
wangayoorri inkoorri	*these few women/all these women together*
kenjanu wurnowurri	*those few hills/all those hills*

The collective morpheme -^{k}*wurri* has an allomorph -*koorri* very specifically after the pronoun =n 'DEF,' and apparently nowhere else. The numerical denotation of paucity is three, four or five; that is, greater than dual, and with the number of fingers on one hand apparently as the upper limit.

9.6.2 Unit augmentation

Unit augmentation is a type of collective number marking that focuses or foregrounds the outranked-actor sense-meaning of that category. Evidence for its status as a separate (sub-)category is found in minimal pairs of the sort shown in (9.5c & d) and in (9.35):

(9.35a) Kaarringoorri
kaarr=i-nga-oorri
3p=go-PAST-U/AUG
S/he went with them/they went with her

Kaarringorri
kaarr=i-nga-^{k}wurri
3p=go-PAST-NUM
They all went together

(b) Arringoorri
arr=i-nga-oorri
1px=go-PAST-U/AUG
S/he went with us/we went with him/her

Arringorri
arr=i-nga-^{k}wurri
1px=go-PAST-NUM
We (exc) all went together

(c) Nyirringoorri
nyirr=i-nga-oorri
2p=go-PAST-U/AUG
You went with them/they went with you

Nyirringorri
nyirr=i-nga-^{k}wurri
2p=go-PAST-NUM
You all went together

The verb *kamnyamiyengoorri* in (9.20c) is also clearly marked for unit augmentation, contrasting as it does with an alternative collective form *kamnyamiyengorri*.

The foregrounded outranked-actor function of the category appears to arise from the relative ease with which one entity (as opposed to a number of entities) may be picked out for mental attention. Consequently, it would seem that a set can more easily be conceived of as being augmented by just one entity, than by a larger number of entities. In this aspect of its function, unit augmentation has more in common with dual marking than with the collective category generally, as the following pair of expressions suggests:

(9.36a) Bija   warrarluwarndu
         bija ^{k}wuN-ngarr-a=rloo-^{k}warndu
         FUT   VCOMP-1pin-OPT=talk-DU
         I want to talk to you

(b)   Bija   warrarluwoorri
         bija ^{k}wuN-ngarr-a=rloo-oorri
         FUT   VCOMP-1pin-OPT=talk-U/AUG
         We want to talk to you (sg)/I want to talk to you lot

Unit augmentation is a form that appears to be dedicated to encoding the outranked actor status of predicate arguments. The unit augmented morpheme only occurs in S/A grammatical function, and it may occasionally be used to encode outranked actor-hood in situations where the augmentation involved is not strictly unitary. The sentence in example (9.37) comes from a mythical text about the discovery of fire. With reference to a group of people not involved in the discovery, the narrator says:

(9.37)   Burnarrinyale   angarreendoorri   kubajungu.
         burnarri-nyale   arr-ngarr=eenda-oorri   kuN-^{b}warr=yi-ng
         meat-too   3p-1pin=cook-U/AUG   VCOMP-3p=do-PAST
         They wanted to cook their meat, too.

The verb *angarreendoorri* is the head of a complement clause of the sort in which the complement subject must be indexed by a first person shape (here *-ngarr-* '1pin') if co-referential with the matrix subject (*-^{b}warr-* '3p' in *kubajungu*). The complement object (*burnarri* 'meat') is indexed on its verb by the collective shape *arr-* '3p.' Suffice to say for now that the complement clause here is a form of direct speech, such that the whole may be paraphrased: 'they thought: we will cook (our) meat too.' The use of the unit augmented form in this instance focuses the outranked actor status of the group who discovered fire, and who are here dependent upon the same lexical predicate, and fulfil the same semantic role.

It is often unclear where unit augmentation is and where it isn't. Because |u+wu| > /oo/ (V expansion rule 18), then any verb form ending in /u/ suffixed by the collective morpheme *-^{k}wurri* is liable to result in a surface shape *-oorri*. It would seem, therefore, that collective/unit-augmented homophony could be quite common. As examples, note the sentences in (9.38), where the final morphemes are conservatively glossed as *-^{k}wurri*, but could just as easily be analysed as *-oorri*, as a unit augmented meaning is involved in both cases. In (9.38a) one person is being addressed:

(9.38a) Aja   nyidoorri   wangalaalangaarndu   inkarndu.
         aja   nyirr=nu-^{k}wurri wangalaalangu-^{k}warndu i=n-^{k}warndu
         sit   2p=be-NUM   children-DU   3a=DEF-DU
         You stay here with the two children.

(b)   Korru   nyijengurroorri
         korru   nyirr-nya=ya-ngurru-^{k}wurri
         alright   2p-EP=go-away-NUM

Alright, he can go with you

The surface shapes of some words may end in /u/, even though their underlying shapes do not. In this situation it is difficult to know at what level the collective/unit-augmented morpheme is applied: at an underlying level (|a+oorri| > /oorri/) or at a surface level (|u+ᵏwurri| > /oorri/). This situation is again suggestive of a distinction between lexical and postlexical phonological processes. In the examples in (9.39), the unaugmented surface shapes of the verbs in question are *ngarreyu, arreyu* and *kubajungu* respectively, that is, they are all shapes that end in /u/. However none of the underlying shapes of these forms do so. In these glosses, the more conservative option is again adopted:

(9.39a)
Nyinyameembu!   Nyinyameembu!   Ngarriyoorri!
nyirr-n-Ø-nya=meembu nyirr-n-Ø-nya=meembu ngarr-a=ya-ᵏwurri
2p-INV-3/1-OPT=show   2p-INV-3/1-OPT=show   1pin-OPT/EP=go-NUM
I'll show you! I'll show you! Come with me!

(b)
Ngunju   jeewa   arriyoorri   kunjiyeerri?
ngunju   jeewa   arr-a=ya-ᵏwurri   kuN-nja=yi-eerri
you   ENQ   1px-OPT/EP=go-NUM   VCOMP-2=do-PROG
Do you want to go with them?

(c)
Kaarringerringkurri,   warli   jeyi   kubajungoorri.
kaarr=i-nga-eerri-ᵏwurri   warli   jeyi   kuN-ᵇwarr=yi-ng(u)-ᵏwurri
3p=go-PAST-PROG-NUM   turtles spear   VCOMP-3p=do-PAST-NUM
They went off together and he speared turtles with them.

Sentence (9.39b) is another complement clause of the form, 'Are you thinking: I will go with them?' In all the examples in (9.38) and (9.39), a unit augmented analysis would make perfect sense, both phonologically and semantically. However it should be pointed out that we cannot know whether such an analysis would be quite accurate, especially as in this case we cannot be sure that the collective morpheme is not attached to the surface, rather than to the underlying shapes of verbs. Sentence example (9.40) shows a verb form that is clearly not marked for unit augmentation; no individual is intended and no outranked actor sense-meaning is involved. The verb form here, however, exhibits a surface shape homophonous with the unit augmented morpheme:

(9.40)   Mana   aja   ngadoorri
         mana   aja   ngarr=nu-ᵏwurri
         3mDEF   sit   1pin=be-NUM
         Let's all sit down here/let's sit down here together

As well as this, the collective morpheme frequently appears in a unit augmented sense, as the following examples show:

(9.41a)
Malka   ngamnyanunerri,   malka   adunerringkurri
malka   nga-mnya=nu-na-eerri   malka   arr=nu-na-eerri-ᵏwurri
play   1-DD=be-PAST-PROG   play   1px=be-PAST-PROG-NUM

anja   wangalaalunguyu   ajakekarri
anja   wangalaalnguya   arr-ya-ke-karri
3pDEF   children   px-↳-AUG-other

I used to play, I played with all the other children

(b)
Awaawanja	arrke	korru,	karle	bedinkurri
awaawanja	arrke	korru	karle	ba-nyarr=ni-n-ᵏwurri
boys	3pREF	alright	now	CFT-1px=be-NON.P-NUM

The boys are alright, they can stay with me

(c)
Jeengurru	awa	jeyi-jeyi	arraneerringkurri
jeengurru	awa	jeyi-jeyi	arr-a=nu-eerri-ᵏwurri
by.oneself	3aNAR	spear-spear	1px-OPT=be-PROG-NUM

We want him to come out spear-fishing with us on his own

Two observations are worth making here; the first is that the unit augmented morpheme never occurs in the presence of the continuous aspect morpheme: in this environment the unit augmented and collective categories appear to be neutralized (cf examples 9.6a, 9.8, 9.9b, 9.39c, 9.41a, c & 9.42). The second follows on from this, and is simply to repeat that the unit augmented category is essentially a marked type of collective morphology. The collective morpheme appears to be able to stand in for the unit augmented one in any situation where extra semantic markedness is not called for.

As with the collective category, unit-augmented verb forms normally take plural NP indexation. However when the single (augmenting) entity is in focus as the discourse topic or for some other reason, the language has the option of using singular masculine indices to refer to third person arguments. This is the case whether the unit augmenting or the collective morpheme is used to signal this function. We have already seen this phenomenon in the collectively-marked form *kengorri* 'he went with them' in (9.26d). Other examples are shown in (9.42):

(9.42a)
Warnda	kanunerringkurri	mangkanangkanyaa
warnda	ka=nu-na-eerri-ᵏwurri	mangka-nangka-nya-aa
camp	3a=be-PAST-PROG-NUM	wife-DAT-3f-and

wangalaalangaarndu	awaawankarndu
wangalaalangu-ᵏwarndu	awaawan-ᵏwarndu
two.children	two.boys

He lived with his wife and their two boys

(b)
Wrrorra	ngarlangarla	ke	barrabarra	kunjeerringkurri
wrrorra	ngarlangarla	ke	barrabarra	kuN-Ø=yi-eerri-ᵏwurri
Worrorra	stories	3wREF	narrate	VCOMP-3=do-PROG-NUM

awaa	awoorri	Kowan	aa	Angaburra,	Rurrngawala,	Ambagai
awa-aa	awoorri	kowan	aa	angaburra	rurrngawala	ambagai
3aNAR-and	3NAR.TRI	Daisy	and	Patsy	Amy	Sam

Worrorra stories as told by Daisy, Patsy, Amy and Sam Umbagai

In (9.42b) the unit augmented construction of the sentence is made clear by the use of pronouns. The masculine singular shape *awa* '3aNAR' is conjoined to the trial form of the pronoun, *awoorri*. The set is clearly made up of three women augmented by one man, who is also the singular subject of the augmented verb.

In (9.20c) the complex predicate *laburru kamnyamiyengoorri* |laburru ka-mnya=ma-ye-ng-oorri| [follow 3a-DD=get-MID-PRES-U/AUG] 'they followed after each other' constitutes a special case. The set here is made up of a woman and two men, but the verb is passivized, that is, it has an argument removed, and the language does not specify which one (the men or the woman – see discussion in §9.4.2). If the woman is interpreted as the underlying subject, then the singular indexation on the verb follows for the reasons under discussion. If the two men are interpreted as the subject, however, then singular indexation is still to be expected for the reasons discussed in §9.5; that is, that two third person entities marked for number require masculine singular indexation on their predicate (Table 9.4).

9.6.3 Trial

The Worrorra trial morpheme appears to occur on a few nominal forms only: being highly marked, it is infrequently used. Love (1934) did not recognize separate trial and paucal categories in Worrorra; the entire morphology here termed 'collective,' he seems to have understood as more or less strictly numerical forms denoting three or four, which he termed 'trial.' Not usually recording a phonemic contrast in vowel length, he did not distinguish the forms -^{k}*wurri* and -*oorri*. With respect to his trial category, Love says:

> The trial number denotes three, or several; as many as may be gestured by the fingers of one hand. A Worora man, when questioned about several, will show three, or four, rarely five fingers. The trial number is really thus a limited plural, rather than denoting precisely three; but, in speaking English, the Worrorra man will usually say 'three' for several. (Love 1934:10)

Love may have conflated the paucal sense of collectively-marked pronouns with those forms that do genuinely mark trial number. In my data genuinely trial forms are based on the quantifying adjective =*yarrungu* displayed in Table 9.2 and on the pronoun =^{k}*wa* displayed in Tables 7.2 and 9.3, and on these forms only. The contrast between collectively-marked pronouns and trial forms is seen in the following pairs, offered for illustrative purposes:

kenjanu wurnowurri	*those few hills/ all those hills*
kenjanu kawoorri	*the three hills*
eeja arnowurri	*those few men/ all those men together*
eeja awoorri	*the three men*

Love (1934:10, 13) lists pronouns that are possibly trial forms (as that term is used here). For example, where my instructors offered the collective form *irnowurri* 'just those (distal) together/those few,' Love lists *i'no:juri (irnoyoorri?)*, an apparently trial form. And where my instructors offered the collective *arrkanangkorri* 'of them all together,' Love lists *'arkanaŋ'guri (arrkanangkurri? arrkanangkoorri?)*, one of which may be a trial form. For further discussion of pronoun forms generally, see §7.2 & §7.3. Love (1934:30) offers trial adjectives, one at least of which (*'wora'luri i'wor'kuri* 'three bad boys') is clearly paucal-collective, and which my instructors rephrased as *warraarraleya iwaawarrkurriya* 'some bad boys/all the bad boys together,' using the reduplicated forms of the base lexemes. Of the other trial adjective offered, *i:'guri 'iniuri* 'three good men,' my instructors seemed unsure, although *eekurri iniyoorri* (trial) is a possibility.

Native speakers' intuitions about pragmatic meanings are vulnerable in elicitation, and it is uncertain, of course, if and to what extent Love regularized his data. But I would certainly not want to discount Love's observations on these points out of hand: obviously he had access to a full and viable speech community, and was able to record the full, productive capacity of this very productive morphology. It seems quite likely that there originally were more than the two genuinely trial forms that I have recorded, or that the trial morphology was much more productive than appears to be the case in my data.

Unequivocally trial forms occurring in spontaneous texts are quite few: example (9.42b) is one such, and (9.43) contains another:

(9.43)
Arno	ajarrungoorri	arrke	wali;	inja	iyakarra
arr=rno	arr=yarrungu-oorri	arrke	wali	inja	i=yakarra
3p=dist	px=QUANT-TRI	3pREF	PERF	3aDEF	3a=other

ngarru	kenga?
ngarru	ka=ya-nga
whither	3a=go-TNS

There's only three of them out there; where's the other one gone?

In conclusion, I should emphasize that number marking, as a pragmatic as well as a referential operation, has a dimension that may well extend beyond the scope of the limited amount of recorded material, and the limited types of context in which I experienced the language. As an essentially pragmatic way of encoding argument structure, the outranked actor function of number marking in Worrorra has parallels in the way in which pronouns are used, as described in Chapter 17. Nor am I, in commenting on Love's data, intending to imply that the system of number marking in Worrorra has never been other than what I found and recorded at Mowanjum in the 1990s.

Ten: adverbs and postpositional phrases

Adverbs in Worrorra modify predicates at nuclear, core and peripheral levels.[61] Nuclear- and peripheral-level adverbs are discussed in §10.1, while core-level or modal adverbs are discussed in §10.2. In addition, §10.3 looks at some demonstrative adverbs used to locate events in space, §10.4 at some adverbs used to locate events at specific times, and §10.5 at a couple of interrogative adverbs. §10.6 will survey a number of very frequently encountered suffixes and postpositions attached to nouns, that form phrases or phrasal words functioning as de-nominal adverbs.

A number of important adverbs are enclitic on preceding material. A small number of aspectual morphemes are encliticized to preverbs, with scope over a complex predicate: these are *-mirri* 'quickly,' *-je, -ji* 'again,' and *-biji* 'repeatedly' (§10.1.1 (iii)). Of these, *-mirri* attaches only to preverbs, and *-je* and *-biji* attach to both preverbs and finite verbs. Sentence examples showing the use of *-je/-ji* may be seen at (10.15a, 10.61c) and (15.10f), and those showing the use of *-mirri* may be seen at (8.26b) and (8.28b). The clause-linking morpheme *-maade* 'so, RESULT' (§8.2.4) is found after preverbs and also after nouns, deictics, adjectives in preverbal position, and most frequently after finite verbs. The enclitics *-nyini* 'ENDPOINT, until' (§10.1.2 (v)), and *-nyale* 'next in sequence' (§10.6.4 (i)) appear to be unrestricted in their distribution, attaching to members of nearly every lexical category.

10.1 Aspectual adverbs

It is useful in Worrorra to try to distinguish between temporal structure as it is found applying to verbal root morphemes as denotative types, and as it is found applying to clauses, as the depictions of fully instantiated events. The first situation we may refer to as nuclear-level aspectual modification, and the second as peripheral-level aspect.

10.1.1 Nuclear-level aspect marking

These adverbs and adverbial affixes depict a predicate's internal temporal structure.

10.1.1 (i) ᵇ*wali* 'PERFECT'

The adverb ᵇ*wali* signifies a continuing state, that is, that no change of state has occurred or is occurring. In effect, this adverb signals perfect aspect independently of tense-marking, and frequently in verbless sentences. Spoken on its own, '*wali!*' means 'wait!'

---

[61] The nucleus represents a predicate's non-finite denotation: usually a verb root in Worrorra. The core contains the nucleus as well as its core arguments, a subject and up to two objects. The periphery contains everything outside the core. A fuller explanation of these terms is provided in Appendix 4.

(10.1)   Wali   nyinjarndanya   nyinunerri   nyina.
         wali   nyiN=yarnda-nya   nyiN=nu-na-eerri   nyina
         PERF   3f=infant-3f   3f=be-PAST-PROG   3fDEF
         She was still a little girl

Used in combination with verbs, *ᵇwali* signals perfect aspect unambiguously: although an action may be completed, its effects are still felt in, or are still important to the present:

(10.2a) Irrolija   wali   nguyul   kubajenganangka.
         irra-wulija   wali   nguyul   kuN-ᵇwarr-nya=yi-ng-a-nangka
         father-2KIN   PERF   strike   VCOMP-3p-EP=do-PAST-EP-DAT
         They have killed your father

(b)   Jardi   aaya   karlaa   mona   wali   mana   dalorrba.
         jardi   aaya   karlaa   ma-Ø=ᵇwu-na   wali   mana   dalorr-ba
         spinifex 3aREF   cover   3m-3=hit-PAST   PERF   3mDEF   sink.hole-EP
         Spinifex had covered over the sink-hole.

(c)   Ngarru   inja   kanangkurri   wali   burnu   angkona?
         ngarru   inja   kanangkurri   wali   burnu   arr-Ø-ngka=ᵇwu-na
         whither   3aDEF   dog   PERF   3wPRO   3p-3-SJTV=hit-PAST
         Where's the dog who has done this thing to them?

<u>10.1.1 (ii) *ᵇwali maa* 'EXTENDED PROGRESSIVE'</u>
ᵇwali maa signals extended progressive aspect:

(10.3)
Wali maa   walaawirri   kaadunerri,   jeejeerr   kubajungu.
wali maa   walaawirri   kaarr-nu-na-eerri jeejeerr   kuN-ᵇwarr=yi-ng
PROG   keen   3p=be-PAST-PROG   scream   VCOMP-3p=do-PAST
They kept on wailing and screaming

<u>10.1.1 (iii) *biju / -biji* 'REPEAT'</u>
Biju signals repetitive, ongoing action; it has a suffixial form *-biji*.

(10.4a)
Wangalaya   biju   kaajoolinerri   ngunjanaanangkaya   kanaanangkurri.
wangala-ya   biju   kaarr=yoolee-na-eerri ngunja-naa-nangka-ya   ka-naa-nangkurri
lost-3p   RPTV   3p=travel-PAST-PROG you-AUG-DAT-3p   ↳-AUG-dog
All your dogs keep wandering around all over the place.

(b)
Waaybiji   nganbajabunerri
waay-biji   nga-n-ᵇwarr=yabu-na-eerri
throw-RPTV   1-INV-3p=throw-PAST-PROG
They threw me (up in the air) again and again

10.1.1 (iv) *jaa* 'PERFECTIVE'

Jaa 'PERFECTIVE' signals not only that an action is complete, but that the results of that action are irreversible:

(10.5a)   Jaa   warrabarl   kerrwuna.
           jaa   warrabarl   ka-nyarr=^{b}wu-na
           PERFV   throw.away   3a-1px=hit-PAST
           We just threw it all away.

(b)   Jaa   bangkawaara   rlarlangkarram   mana.
       jaa   ba-ka=^{b}wa-^{k}wara   rlarlangkarram   mana
       PERFV   CFT-3a=fall-1DAT   sea   3mDEF
       He might fall into the sea, and that would be it.

(c)   Jaa   wurlingkarr   bungkayaara.
       jaa   wurlingkarr   ba-kuN-Ø=yi-^{k}wara
       PERFV   rub.off   CFT-VCOMP-3=do-1DAT
       It might all rub off me.

In these examples the presence of *jaa* signals that (a) what was thrown away was in this case irretrievable; (b) if (a boy) were to fall into the sea, he would perish, and that (c) once (the paint) is rubbed off, it can't be put back on again.

10.1.1 (v) *jaa maa* 'all the way, always'

This important adverb combines perfective and continuous aspects (*maa* 'Progressive') to signal that an action is accomplished after a reasonably lengthy process. It has two main sense meanings, one referring to space ('all the way'), and another that refers metaphorically to time ('always').

(10.6a)   Jaa maa   kurdu   konerri.
           jaa maa   kurdu   ka-Ø=^{b}wu-na-eerri
           all.way   follow   3a-3=hit-PAST-PROG
           He chased all the way after him.

(b)   Jaa maa   rlerlewa   nyengerri.
       jaa maa   rlerlewa   nya=ya-nga-eerri
       all.way   crawl   3f=go-PAST-PROG
       She crawled all the way.

(c)   Jaa maa   kamarlaarndornaarndeerri.
       jaa maa   ka-[Ø]=marlaarndo-rna-[^{k}warndu$_A$]-eerri
       all.way   3a-[3]=follow-PAST-[DU$_A$]-PROG
       They (dual) always went with him.

(d)   Jaa maa   ngaja   nyejamanga.
       jaa maa   ngaja   nyaN-nyarr-nya=ma-nga
       all.way   emulate   3f-1px-EP=get-PAST
       We always followed the custom that she established.

(e)
Nyinke   maanbali   balorru   wunu   jaa maa   ngaja   nyejamanga.
nyingke   maanbali   balorru   wunu   jaa maa   ngaja   nyaN-nyarr-nya=ma-nga
3fREF   FOCUS   everyone   3wDEF   all.way   emulate   3f-1px-EP=get-PAST
She is the one whose precedent we all follow scrupulously.

Other meanings of *jaa maa* are derived metaphorically from this pair of sense meanings. One important sense refers to an action as being completed with difficulty, against forces that tend to impede or prevent its completion; that is, that the process involved in its accomplishment is not only lengthy but difficult. This sense allows a translation something like 'determinedly:'

(10.7a)　　Jaa　　　kurdey　　maa　　nyimbarrwunerri
　　　　　　jaa　　　kurdey　　maa　　nyiN-ᵇwarr=ᵇwu-na-eerri
　　　　　　PERFV　ask　　　　PROG　3f-3p=hit-PAST-PROG
　　　　　　They kept on asking her

(b)　　　　Jaa maa　minyamiyangkanaara
　　　　　　jaa maa　minya=miyangkana-ᵏwara
　　　　　　all.way　　2>VCOMP=understand-1DAT
　　　　　　You must try to understand me

10.1.2 Peripheral-level aspect marking

These adverbs depict the temporal structure of entire clauses, often in relation to events immediately preceeding or immediately following.

10.1.2 (i) *karle* 'change of state'
The adverb and conjunction *karle* signifies a change of state from one situation to another, and so has the opposite meaning to *ᵇwali*. It corresponds to the English words 'now' and 'then' when these words are used to introduce a different set of circumstances or a new situation from that which has previously obtained. It is commonly heard at the beginning or the end of utterances, signalling essentially a change or impending change in speech act participant, in which case it corresponds to 'that's all.'

(10.8)　　　Nyirringkaalkarndu,　　karle　　wundukum!
　　　　　　nyirr=i-ᵏwaal-ᵏwarndu　　karle　　wundukum
　　　　　　2p=go-hither-DU　　　　now　　　night
　　　　　　Come here you two, it's night-time now!

10.1.2 (ii) *ᵇwali waa* 'not yet'
(iv) *ᵇwali waa*, with a verb in counterfactual mood, means 'not yet:'

(10.9)　　　Wali waa　　laiburru　　binyideenya　　　wunu　　aalmarangarri.
　　　　　　wali waa　　laiburru　　ba-nyirr=ni-yinya　wunu　　aalmara-ngarri
　　　　　　not yet　　　know　　　CFT-2p=be-PAST　3wDEF　European-REL
　　　　　　You still didn't know the Europeans' (language) yet.

10.1.2 (iii) *karle wali* 'CHANGE'
The term *karle wali* signifies that that a situation has changed, and that the change is permanent or at least reasonably long-lasting:

(10.10)　　Yarribaa　　waje,　　　　　　　karle wali　　kaarri.
　　　　　　yarribaa　　ᵏwuN-ngarr-nya=yi　karle wali　　kaarri
　　　　　　descend.PL　VCOMP-1pin-EP=do　CHANGE　　　3pNEG
　　　　　　We can go down now, it's all over.

10.1.2 (iv) *jadbengurru* 'for good'

The adverb *Jadbengurru* 'permanently, for good' marks something as permanent:

(10.11)   Ngurrinyini   ngajaningeerri,   jadbengurru.
          ngurru-nyini   ngarr-nya=ni-ng-eerri   jadbengurru
          here-ENDPOINT   1pin-EP=be-PRES-PROG   for.good
          We're here now, for good.

10.1.2 (v) *-nyini* 'until, ENDPOINT'

The enclitic suffix *-nyini* 'until, ENDPOINT' is a very common adverbial form with a number of sense meanings, as well as being frequently homophonous with the human comitative/locative morpheme *-nyina* (§10.6.2 (iii) below). There is probably nothing that *-nyini* cannot occur with, as suffix or postposition. It is found with adverbs (10.11, 10.12, 10.27b, 10.31b, 10.47a), preverbs (10.16b), adjectives (10.17b), pronouns (10.13, 10.18b), nouns (10.13), as a suffix on postpositions (10.31a), and as a postposition to finite verbs (10.49b). Love (1934:31, 34) translates *-nyini* as 'until, yet,' and this is probably as good a translation as any for its most frequently encountered meaning. English *until* and Worrorra *-nyini* denote in different ways the endpoint of a line of events, or of an extended event leading up to a particular point in time:

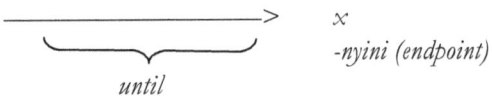

English *until* refers to the time leading up to the endpoint (*x* in the diagram above): so, *this did not happen until 1958* depicts 1958 as the endpoint of a stretch of time during which 'this did not happen.' Worrorra *-nyini*, in contrast, tags the endpoint, as an endpoint. So 'OUTCOME' is often denoted by *-nyini*, in situations where a translation *until* is not optimal.

The word *dambeewunyinim*, translatable as something like 'homeward at last,' or 'until (they) got home,' occurs twice in the database, both times at the end of stories in which characters have a number of adventures and then go home:

(10.12)   Keyaaw,   ke   kamnyengaarndu   dambeewunyinim.
          ke-aaw   ke   ka-mnya=ya-nga-ᵏwarndu   dambee-ᵏwunya-nyini-m
          and-TIME   3wREF   3a-DD=go-TNS-DU   place-PURP-ENDPOINT-3m
          And now they both went home together.

Not uncommonly, *-nyini* marks the endpoint or outcome of a series of events in a story. In (10.13) the outcome of an event in the Dreamtime was that a ceremony was created to commemorate it:

(10.13)
Nyinbalinya   jilinya   jandu   nyimbajamanga   joonbanyiniya.
nyiN-nbali-nya   jilinya   jandu   nyiN-ᵇwarr-nya=ma-nga joonba-nyini-ya
3f-RESUM-3F   spirit.woman   perform   3f-3p-EP=get-PAST   ceremony-ENDPOINT-3p
So then they used to perform ceremonies about that spirit-woman.

The suffix *-nyini* frequently marks the endpoint of a journey, as in (10.76) below and (10.14):

(10.14)   Mingkunyarnanya   ajengkunaal   Karnmanyanyini.
          Mingkunya-rnanya   arr-nya=ya-ngku-na-ᵏwaal Karnmanya-nyini
          PLACE.NAME-LOC   1px-EP=go-EP-PAST-hither PLACE.NAME-ENDPOINT
          We came from Mingkunya to Kunmunya.

In (10.15a) the outcome of two boys wandering off through the bush on their own is predicted, and in (10.15b) a disaster is described in terms of the events that led up to it:

(10.15a)
Birriyaarndeerrije,	akurlanyini	wanji
ba-kuN-rra=yi-ᵏwarndu-eerri-je	akurla-nyini	wanji
CFT-VCOMP-2p=do-DU-PROG-again	devil-ENDPOINT	find

bangkaweenurrerndu	wuneerda.
ba-ka=ᵇwee-[[nu-ᵏwurri]-ᵏwarndu]	wunu-yirda
CFT-3a=hit.MID-[[2pDAT]-DU]	3wDEF-try

Don't do it again; another time a demon might find you both.

(b)
Larlangkarram	mana	kaarri maa	keekeey	kanunerri	wunu
rlarlangkarram	mana	kaarri maa	keekeey	ka=nu-na-eerri	wunu
sea	3mDEF	in vain	peer	3a=be-PAST-PROG	3wDEF

kalam	mana,	ke	bloy	kumanga	ke
kalam	mana	ke	bloy	kuN-Ø=ma-nga	ke
raft	3mDEF	and	slip	VCOMP-3=get-PAST	and

rlarlangkarranyinim	burnu	ko.
rlarlangkarra-nyini-ma	burnu	ka-Ø=ᵇwu
sea-ENDPOINT-3m	3wPRO	3a-3=hit

He was trying to peer over the side of the raft into the water, but he slipped and perished in the sea.

The semantics of change-of-state may arise naturally from those of 'endpoint,' in that the endpoint of one state or situation may be taken as the beginning of another:

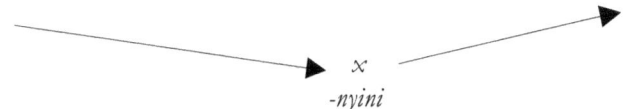

This meaning is exemplified in (10.16); (10.16a) is an exchange between two people:

(10.16a)
'Ke	arrinyini	baawaa	kunyajaal.'
ke	arri-nyini	baawaa	kuN-nyarr=yi-(ᵏw)aal
and	we(exc)-ENDPOINT	appear.PL	VCOMP-1px=do-hither

'Nyirrinyini	Daisy,	maa-maa	nyimnyarlelwana.'
nyirri-nyini	Daisy	maa-maa	nyiN-mnya=rlelwa-na
you(pl)-ENDPOINT	NAME	3mREF-3mREF	3f-DD=born-PAST

'And then we came along (=were born)'
'Then you lot and Daisy, she was born there.'

(b)
Nyambalaknyini	kamnyimiyenaarndu
nyambalak-nyini	ka-mnya=ma-ye-na-ᵏwarndu
stick.together-ENDPOINT	3a-DD=get-MID-PAST-DU

And so now they were stuck together

Sometimes it is not clear whether *-nyini*'s primary reference is to 'endpoint' or to 'change-of-state.' Example (10.17a) occurs at the end of an adventure in a story, and so is able to denote 'endpoint.' It also depicts a changed state, in that it is now the daughter sun, rather than the mother, who goes up into the sky. Similarly in (10.17b); the new moon is both the endpoint of a sequence, and a change of state from what there was before. In situations like this *-nyini* denotes both meanings at once:

(10.17a)
Nyangkanyini	nyina	kawurlanya,	nyinngarriwa
nyangka-nyini	nyina	kawurlanya	nyiN=n-ngarri-wa
3fNAR-ENDPOINT	3fDEF	daughter	3f=DEF-REL-?

ngarrkunyameembinjeerri		marram	mana.
ngarr-Ø-ngun-nya=meembu-ny-yeerri		marram	mana
1pin-3-SJTV-EP=show-MIR-PROG		light	3mDEF

So now it's her, the daughter, and her sisters who show us the light.

(b)
Ke	kenga	awa	yarriy	ingkawana	inja	kunyila,
ke	ka=ya-nga	awa	yarriy	i-ngka=^bwa-na	inja	kunyila
and	3a=go-PAST	3aNAR	descend	3a-SJTV=fall-TNS	3aDEF	moon

ke	ingunalinyini	baa	kamnyengkaal.
ke	i=ngunali-nyini	baa	ka-mnya=ya-^kwaal
and	3a=new-ENDPOINT	appear	3a-DD=go-hither

The moon goes along, and when it goes down, then a new one appears.

In sentences where *-nyini* occurs with a change-of-state meaning, the apparently synonymous adverb *karle* (§10.1.2 (i) above) often occurs close by. This co-occurrence may be seen in (4.18) in Chapter Four, and in the following examples:

(10.18a)
Karle	maalkarram	kaarri	wijalinyini	ke	wirndiba
karle	maalkarram	kaarri	wijali-nyini	ke	wirndiy-^bwa
then	grass.fire	3pNEG	burnt.grass-ENDPOINT	and	spear-PROG

kawarraangurrurlu	inja	wara.
ka-^bwarr=^kwangurru-rla	inja	wara
3a-3p=carry=PAST	3aDEF	kangaroo

Then the grass burned down to black stubble, and they would go out hunting kangaroos.

(b)
Kenyini	malka	ajanaarndeerri,	karle	kayalkayal
ke-nyini	malka	arr-nya=nu-aarndu-eerri	karle	kayal-kayal
and-ENDPOINT	play	1px-EP=be-DU-PROG	then	hold.hand-hold.hand

ngankangurrurlu.
nga-n-Ø=^kwangurru-rla
1-INV-3-carry-PAST

After that I always used to play with her, and she would hold my hand wherever we went.

Two other aspectual morphemes used mainly with preverbal infinitives, *-^bwa* 'PROGRESSIVE' and *maa* 'PROGRESSIVE,' are discussed in §11.3.2.

10.2 Modal adverbs, adverbs of manner

The distinction between modal and manner adverbial functions is blurry in Worrorra, and both kinds are presented here for convenience.

10.2.1 Modal adverbs

The epistemic modal adverb *maaji* 'Deliberative' and the enclitic/postpositional adverb *maade* 'so, RESULT' are described and exemplified in §8.2.2. The adverb *wardi* 'I hope' is described in §8.2.2 and §8.4.3, and *bija* 'Future' is described in §8.2.1. The counterfactual adverbs *waawa* 'Negative Interogative' and *malyaawam* 'REASON' are described in §8.4.1. The emphatic adverb *(-)y₂akuwali* is discussed in §7.6.1.

There are other modal adverbs that also have scope over the entire clause in which they occur. Some are listed below, with examples of their use:

<u>10.2.1 (i) *jee, jeewa* 'Question/Enquiry'</u>
This word (glossed ENQ) signals that the speech act in which it occurs is a question or a reported question, in which case it translates as 'I wonder (if) ...' The adverb *jee/jeewa* usually occupies second position in a sentence:

(10.19a)
Mangarri	jeewa	minjarl	kunjee?
mangarri	jeewa	minjarl	kuN-nja=yi
food	ENQ	eat	VCOMP-2=do

Do you want something to eat?

(b)
Ngayu	jeewa	marno	dambeem	kabalbarnanya	dalulu
ngayu	jeewa	ma=rno	dambeem	kabalba-rnanya	dalulu
I	ENQ	3m=DIST	place	ground-LOC	shed

kaadungu	anja	marrukuya.
kaarr=nu-ng	anja	marrukuya
3p=be-PRES	3pDEF	flowers

I wonder if any flowers have fallen down onto the ground over there.

<u>10.2.1 (ii) *mee* 'I don't know'</u>
This sentence in English is lexicalized as an adverb in Worrorra:

(10.20)
Mee	angkuyu	kaanyamranga.
mee	angkuyu	kaarr-n-Ø-nya=mra-nga
unknowing	who	3p-INV-3-EP=gather-PAST

I don't know who took them.

<u>10.2.1 (iii) *ngana* 'probably'</u>
The adverb *ngana* 'probably, possibly, perhaps' (glossed PROB) gives an irrealis meaning to a sentence in which it occurs. It may be seen in sentence example (10.29) below.

The three modal adverbs shown so far may be used together in a more or less idiomatic expression: *mee jee ngana* 'I'm not so sure (about that)/I don't really want to.'

10.2.1 (iv) *yakurnu* 'try'

This adverb is nearly always found in future time-reference contexts, that is with imperative, hortative or optative verb forms:

(10.21) Ngunju bayungurru yakurnu.
ngunju ba=ya-ngurru yakurnu
you CFT=go-away try
You try and go on ahead.

10.2.1 (v) *-yirda* 'try'

This suffix is found attached to verbs and pronouns, and may occur in the same clause as *yakurnu*, with an apparently similar meaning. Its use is shown in (10.22):

(10.22a)
Ngunju yakurnu baay baneerda.
ngunju yakurnu baay ba=nu-yirda
you try climb CFT=be-try
You try and climb up there.

(b)
Wunmaanbali, wunmaanjirda kurdu
ᵏwuN-n-maanbali ᵏwuN-n-maan-yirda kurdu
3w-DEF-FOCUS 3w-DEF-SPEC-try follow

warrkunyonjeerri.
ᵏwuN-ngarr-ngun-nya=ᵇwu-ny-yeerri
VCOMP-1pin-SJTV-EP=hit-MIR-PROG
We still follow, we are still trying to follow this (custom) now.

Example (10.22b) occurs at the end of a description of Worrorra marriage laws, at a point where the narrator amends her explanation to take into account recent social changes that have resulted in marriages that may be socially incomprehensible by traditional standards.

10.2.1 (vi) *niji, nijiwa* 'truely, really'

This adverb is seen in (10.23):

(10.23)
Nijiwa nganbardongkurlanangka irraayaa karraanya?
nijiwa nga-n-ᵇwarr=rnongku-rla-nangka irraaya-aa karraanya
truely 1-INV-3p=take.away-PAST-DAT father-and mother
Would they really have taken me away from my father and mother?

10.2.1 (vii) *korru* 'alright'

This adverb may be used as an interjection meaning 'that's alright,' or with scope over an entire proposition, as may be seen in example (10.24):

(10.24) Ngurru maanbali ngenu korru.
ngurru maanbali nga-nya=nu korru
here FOCUS 1-OPT-be alright
It's alright, I'll stay right here.

10.2.1 (viii) *ngaali* 'WRONG SUPPOSITION'

This adverb declares that some supposition is wrong, as in 'I wrongly thought that … :'

(10.25a)   Maniyama   ngaali   kungenga.
              ma=niya-ma   ngaali   kuN-nga=yi-ng
              3m=good-3m   WRONG   VCOMP-1=do-PAST
              I (wrongly) thought this was a good place.

(b)   Karle   kenga   ngaali   kunyajunganu.
              karle   ka=ya-nga   ngaali   kuN-nyarr=yi-ng-a-nu
              now   3a=go-TNS   WRONG   VCOMP-1px=do-PAST-EP-2DAT
              We thought you'd gone.

10.2.1 (ix) *-y₂aka* 'Emphatic'

This suffix, glossed EMPH, contains the phoneme /y₂/ which hardens to /d/ under Strange Hardening rule 5. See also *(-)y₂akuwali* in §7.6.1. The suffix *-y₂aka* is seen in the examples in (10.26) and (10.30), and again in (10.39a) where the very common negative word *kaarriyaka* 'no way, not at all' is seen.

(10.26a)   Kajirn   berrwundaka.
              kajirn   ba-ka-ngarr=ᵇwu-n-y₂aka
              can't   CFT-3a-1pin=hit-NON.P-EMPH
              We mustn't hurt him.

(b)   Awa   iyarrungaareka   wali   kurleen   kangona.
              awa   i=yarrungu-ᵏwara-y₂aka   wali   kurleen   ka-nga=ᵇwu-na
              3aNAR   3a=QUANT-1DAT-EMPH   PERF   born   3a-1=hit-PAST
              He is the only child ever born to me.

10.2.2 Manner adverbs

These adverbs are used to describe, in fairly abstract ways, the manner in which events takes place.

10.2.2 (i) *mee, mee maa* 'just, only'

This adverb is used to narrow the focus of attention onto just one action of possibly several being performed or considered at any one time:

(10.27a)   Ajengerri   bundurlba,   kaarri,   arri   mee maa.
              arr-nya=ya-nga-eerri   bundurlba   kaarri   arri   mee maa
              1px-EP-go-PAST-PROG   'the bush'   3pNEG   we(exc)   only
              We just travelled around through the bush, that's all we used to do.

(b)   peanut   inja   minjarlminjarl   ajanuna   meenyini
              peanut   inja   minjarl-minjarl   arr-nya=nu-na   mee-nyini
              peanut   3aDEF   eat-eat   1px-EP=be-PAST   just-ENDPOINT
              until we just ate the peanuts

When one action only is being performed, then it may be implied that that action is being performed with concentration and intensity. *Mee* often signals intense or determined activity:

(10.28a)
Nyungkubulu wunu mee kaaninjangurreerri.
nyiN=ᵏwambulu wunu mee kaarr-n-Ø=ninja-nga-ngurru-eerri
3f=eyes 3wDEF just 3p-INV-3=look.at-PAST-away-PROG
She was straining her eyes to catch sight of them.

(b)
Kaarri maa mee maa kurdey nyimbunerri.
kaarri maa mee maa kurdy nyiN-Ø=ᵇwu-na-eerri
in vain just ask 3f-3=hit-PAST-PROG
He kept on asking and asking her, but it was no use.

Both meanings of *mee* (shown in §10.2.1 (ii) and §10.2.2 (i)) may occur together:

(10.29)
Mee ngarru ngana kenga, mee
mee ngarru ngana ka=ya-nga mee
I.don't.know whither PROB 3a=go-TNS just

kejanduwerlaarndu.
ka-[nyarr_A]=yanduwe-rla-[ᵏwarndu_A]
3a-[1px_A]=leave-PAST-[DU_A]
I've no idea where he could have gone, we (dual) just left him.

<u>10.2.2 (ii) *kaarri maa* 'in vain'</u>
This expression is used typically to denote frustration or failure, as when something does not happen despite your efforts. An example is seen in (10.30):

(10.30) Kaarri maa kaarri, kajirnba wayarl bangamandaka.
kaarri maa kaarri kajirnba wayarl ba-ka-nga=ma-n-y₂aka
in vain 3pNEG can't remove CFT-3a-1=get-NON.P-EMPH
It's no good, I just can't get it off.

Negative pronouns such as *kaarri* '3pNEG' are treated in §7.2.

<u>10.2.2 (iii) *malyaa, malyaama* 'purposelessly'</u>
This adverb has a meaning something like 'purposelessly, idly, uselessly, for no reason.' In the first sentence example Patsy describes how her family felt when Europeans became established in their land:

(10.31a) Malyaama kajirnnyini karle laiburru aduna.
malyaama kajirn-nyini karle laiburru arr=nu-na
NO.REASON like-ENDPOINT now know 1px=be-PAST
Now it was as if we didn't know anything at all.

(b) Wurno malyaanyinim ajaaja nganingeerri
wurno malyaa-nyini-m ajaaja nga=ni-ng-eerri
3wDIST NO.REASON-ENDPOINT-3m dwell 1=be-PRES-PROG
Now I'm just living idly over there.

The adverb *malyaawam* 'not for no reason, NO.REASON' (§8.4.1) is diachronically produced from *malyaama* 'for no reason' and *waa* 'not.'

<u>10.2.2 (iv) *ke maa* 'thus'</u>
This is the celestial shape of the specific-topic pronoun =*ᵏwaya-maan*, described in more detail in §17.7.1. It has a semi-idiomatic use as an adverb corresponding to some degree to the English adverb 'thus,' or 'in this manner.' Further examples of the use of this form are given in (17.54) and (17.55).

(10.32a)
Ke maa   kumnyengaara.
kee maa   kuN-Ø-mnya=yi-ng-aara
thus   VCOMP-3-DD=do-1DAT
That's what he said to me.

(b)
Ke maa	kubajunganyarri	mamangkunu	rdaarrawa	wunu.
ke maa	kuN-ᵇwarr=yi-ng-a-nyarri	mamangkunu	ØN=raarrawa	wunu
thus	VCOMP-3p=do-PAST-EP-1pxDAT	morning	3w=many	3wDEF

This is what they did for us every morning.

(c)
Ke maa	kaningaayenaarndeerri,	ke maa.
kee maa	ka=ningaaye-na-ᵏwarndu-eerri	kee maa
thus	3a=do.MID-PAST-DU-PROG	thus

They did this to each other time and again.

10.3 Demonstrative adverbs

Demonstrative pronouns (§7.3) enter into morphological and syntactic arrangements with a number of adverbial forms, which will be described here. The grammar of the arrangements themselves will be commented on further in Chapter 17. Adverbs meaning 'here,' 'there,' 'hither,' 'thence' etc are mostly terrestrial forms of demonstrative pronouns: so *mana* 'here,' *marno* 'there' and *marru* 'over that way/behind.' The form *maa* 'there/that (place)' is used to refer to a place already known from context. The phrase *marno maa* '(that place) over there' is used to indicate a place that is both some distance away, and already known from context:

(10.33a)
Marno maa   nganingeerri.
marno maa   nga=ni-ng-eerri
over.there   1=be-PRES-PROG
I live over there.

(b)
Nyangka	aja	kaarnaarnarlerri	marno maa	werrim.
nyangka	aja	kaarr-n-Ø=rnaarna-rla-eerri	marno maa	werrim
3fNAR	sit	3p-INV-3=await-PAST-PROG	over.there	hill

She was sitting waiting for them over there on the hill.

(c)
Arrka	awaawanja	kaarringenya	maangurru,	marno maa	mamaa.
arrka	awaawanja	kaarr=[i-nga]-yinya	maa-ngurru	marno maa	mamaa
3pNAR	boys	3p=[go-TNS]-HORT	3mREF-ALL	over.there	secluded

The boys can go off that way over there by themselves.

Allative forms are *maangurru* 'over there/that way/thither' and *marrungurru* 'away over that way/away back there/thither.' Although these forms refer primarily to movement, as seen in (10.33c) and (10.34a), they may also denote linear extent, as in (10.34b) and in the hyperbolic expression in (10.34c):

(10.34a)
Marrungurru   bungunyeyeerri.
ma=rru-ngurru   ba-ngun=ya-yeerri
3m=LAT-ALL   CFT-2=go-PROG
Don't go over that way.

(b)
Nyangka   marrungurru   aja   nyiningeerri.
nyangka   ma=rru-ngurru   aja   nyiN=ni-ng-eerri
3fNAR   3m=LAT-ALL   sit   3f=be-PRES-PROG
She's living over that way.

(c)
We   kamnyawana   marndum   maa   maangurru,   maangurru.
we   ka-mnya=ᵇwa-na   marndum   maa   maa-ngurru   maa-ngurru
lie   3a-DD=fall-TNS   stomach   3mREF   3mREF-ALL   3mREF-ALL
He lay down with his bloated stomach extended way out in front of him.

Ablative forms are *marnoyaalba* 'thence' and *marraalba* 'from away over there/thence.' The metaphor of motion as linear extent is common with these forms as well:

(10.35)
Marraalba   kumanga   ngarlangarla   marru,   awa
ma=rru-aalba   kuN-Ø=ma-nga   ngarlangarla   ma=rru   awa
3m=LAT-from   3w-3=get-PAST   word   3m=LAT   3aNAR

ingumbu   kubarrkarndenga,   mayakarrima   dambeem   aalb.
i=ngumbu   kuN-ᵇwarr=ᵏwarnde-nga   ma=yakarri-ma   dambeem   aalb
3a=name   3w-3p=place-PAST   3m=other-3m   place   from
He got (that) word from over that way, they gave him his name over there, in another country.

Another common locative adverb is *ngurru* 'hither/here.' Although formally identical to the centrifugal morpheme (§10.6.1), its meaning as a separate word is quite distinct. It has two senses, one locative, as seen in (10.36) below; and another centripetal, as seen in (10.37).

(10.36a)   Ngurru   kaangaarndenu.
           ngurru   kaarr-nga=ᵏwarnde-nu
           here   3p-1=place-2DAT
           I'll put them here for you.

(b)   Korru   jarrorawe   ngurru.
           korru   jan-rra=ᵏwurawe   ngurru
           alright   2>1-2p=leave   here
           Alright, leave me here.

(10.37a)   Kangurraal   ngurru.
           ØN=ᵏwangurru-aal   ngurru
           3w=carry-hither   hither

Bring it (celestial) here.

(b) Mamurlanjaaya yarrkorli irriyaara ngurru.
mamurlanja-aaya yarrkorli i-rra=ee-ᵏwara ngurru
rope-3aREF hang.down 3a-2p=put-1DAT hither
Hang that rope down here for me.

(c) Ngurru nyimnyengkunyaal arrirnanya!
ngurru nyiN-mnya=ya-ngku-nya-aal arri-rnanya
hither 3f-DD=go-EP-HORT-hither we(exc)-LOC
Let her come over here to us!

The adverb *ngurru maa* means 'right here' or 'right there.' Its use is exemplified in (10.38):

(10.38a) Ngayu ngurru maa aja nganungu.
ngayu ngurru maa aja nga=nu-ng
I right here sit 1=be-PRES
I live right here.

(b) Ngurru maa rok kejeerla kabalbarnanya.
ngurru maa rok ka-nyarr-nya=ee-rla kabalba-rnanya
right there bury 3a-1px-EP=place-PAST gound-LOC
We buried it right there in the ground.

(c) Jarrorawe ngurru, ngurru maa ngenu.
jan-rra=ᵏwurawe ngurru ngurru maa nga-nya=nu
2>1-2p=leave here right here 1-OPT=be
Leave me here, I'll stay right here.

An adverb with a similar meaning is *manmaa* (|ma=n-maa| [3m=DEF-3mREF]) 'right here.' This is a contrastive form, used to focus on one place as opposed to, or in contrast to, another (cf *wunmaa* in §10.4.1 (i) below):

(10.39a)
Kaarriyaka, manmaa ajaaja arramnyanaarndu.
kaarri-y₂aka manmaa ajaaja arr-a-mnya=nu-ᵏwarndu
3pNEG-EMPH right here stay 1px-OPT-DD=be-DU
No way, we're going to stay right here.

(b)
Ngunju maa bayungurru jaarr mongurru dambeem
ngunju maa ba=ya-ngurru jaarr ma=ᵇwu-ngurru dambeem
you 3mREF CFT=go-away upstream 3m=hit-away place

maa, arri ngayu manmaa aja ngenu.
maa arri ngayu manmaa aja nga-nya=nu
3mREF but I right here sit 1-OPT=be
You go on upstream to that place, but I'll stay right here.

(c)
Malka binyidaarndeerri ngalarramarnanya marno,
malka ba-nyirr=nu-ᵏwarndu-eerri ngalarrama-rnanya ma=rno
play CFT-2p=be-DU-PROG long.grass-LOC 3m=DIST

manmaa	aja	nyidaarndu.
manmaa	aja	nyirr=nu-^kwarndu
right here	sit	2p=be-DU

Don't play over there in the long grass, you two stay right here.

A suffix *-yirdaka* with a likely meaning 'from' was elicited in reference to some of Love's notes. It was offered suffixed to *maa* '3mREF' to produce a form *maayirdakama* 'thence;' and also to *ngurru* 'hither/here' to produce *ngurreerdaka* 'hence,' as seen below:

(10.40a) Kengkunaal maayirdakama.
         ka=ya-ngku-na-^kwaal maa-yirdaka-ma
         3a=go-EP-PAST-hither 3mREF-?from-3m
         He came from there.

(b) Dambeem maayirdakama.
     dambeem maa-yirdaka-ma
     place   3mREF-?from-3m
     There's your home.

(c) Kengangurru ngurreerdaka.
     ka=ya-nga-ngurru ngurru-yirdaka
     3a=go-PAST-ALL   here-?from
     He went away from here.

The sentence in (10.40b) is anomalous with a meaning 'from,' but was spontaneously produced. It is just possible that the shape *-yirdaka* may incorporate *-y2aka* 'EMPHATIC' as seen above in §10.2.1 (ix). I am uncertain about the precise meaning of this form.

10.4 Temporal adverbs

Time is marked by nouns denoting times of the day: *braarru wunu* 'first light before sunrise' *yalingarri* (|yali-ngarri| [cold-REL]) (adverb) 'dawn,' *mamangkunu wunu* 'morning,' *nyinaarringeenya nyina* 'midday; early afternoon, hottest part of the day,' *karlumarlum mana* and *karlakarlem mana* 'late afternoon; evening, dusk' (a brief event in the north Kimberley) *warlorlum mana* 'night,' *wundukum mana* 'darkness' and *wunduwundukum mana* 'the darkest part of the night, the dark before dawn.' Seasons are also named: *mawingki inja* 'winter, the cool season,' c June-July; *mirringunu wunu* 'the hot season,' c October-mid-December, and *aajaajirri* 'the wet season,' c mid-December-April. Note also the adverb *weni* 'now, today;' and that in my data seasons are defined by core periods, in a system not designed to be exhaustive.[62]

10.4.1 Time-referential adverbs

Apart from the verbal tense system described in §5.4, §8.1.2 and §8.3.2, there are a number of deictic expressions in the language that refer or point to time in relation to the speech event or its reported equivalent.

---

[62] Elsewhere in the Kimberley it appears that exhaustive five- or six-term naming-systems for seasons are found, which leads me to wonder whether there may be gaps in the information I collected.

10.4.1 (i) *Wenmaa, wunmaa* 'now/right now'

These are contrastive forms comparable to *manmaa* 'right here' seen in §10.3 above. The adverb *weni* 'now, today' is incorporated into the first form: see (10.50) for an example of its use. These words are used to focus on the present as opposed to some other, past or future time.

(10.41a)   Wenmaa   joli   banu.
           wenmaa   joli   ba=nu
           right now   return   CFT=be
           Go back right now.

(b)   Wunmaa   maade   wunu   nyarrkunyaninjanjeerri.
           wunmaa   maade   wunu   ØN-nyarr-ngun-nya=ninja-ny-yeerri
           now   RESULT   3wDEF   3w-1px-SJTV-EP=look.at-MIR-PROG
           So that's how we see them (celestial) now.

In (10.41a) the implication is that the addressee wants to procrastinate, and (10.41b) is a resultative clause, contrasting a present situation with a past one.

10.4.1 (ii) *karle maa* 'REMOTE PAST'

The expression *karle maa* marks time reference to a distant past, as seen in (10.42):

(10.42)
Karle maa   ke   kaadunerri   belangkarraya   inja
karle maa   ke   kaarr=nu-na-eerri   belangkarraya   inja
REM.P   3wREF   3p=be-PAST-PROG   everyone   3aDEF

ingkayoolinerri.
i-ngka=yoolee-na-eerri
3a-SJTV=travel-PAST-PROG
Back at that time everyone used to go travelling around from place to place.

10.4.1 (iii) *-aaw* 'TIME'

This suffix has already been seen in §7.4.2, attached to *anguja* 'what?' to produce *angujaaw* 'at what time?/when?'

(10.43a)   Angujaaw   ngunyangkunaal?
           anguja-aaw   ngun=ya-ngku-na-aal
           what-TIME   2=go-EP-PAST-hither
           What time did you get here?

(b)   Angujaaw   joli   ngunungaal?
           anguja-aaw   joli   ngun=nu-ng-aal
           what-TIME   return   2=be-PRES-hither
           When are you coming back?

This is a deictic suffix, and its default reference is to present time where the more abstract concept of 'time' itself is not appropriate or relevant. It is used to refer to present time where no tense-marking morphology is available, as in (10.44):

(10.44)   Karle   kaarriyaaw,   karle   kawi   imanjaaw.
           karle   kaarri-aaw   karle   kawi   i=man-ya-aaw
           now   3pNEG-TIME   now   3aNEG   3a=dead-3a-TIME
           Now its over, now he's dead.

It may also be used either to bring time reference into the plane of the present, as in (10.45a), or where verbal present tense morphology is vague, as in (10.45b):

(10.45a)
Keyaaw,   ke   kamnyengaarndu   dambeewunyinim.
ke-aaw   ke   ka-mnya=ya-nga-ᵏwarndu   dambee-ᵏwunya-nyini-m
and-TIME   3wREF   3a-DD=go-TNS-DU   place-PURP-ENDPOINT-3m
And now they both went home.

(b)
Karleyaaw   ngunyangerri?
karle-aaw   ngun=ya-nga-eerri
Change.of.State-TIME   2=go-TNS-PROG
Are you going now?

It is also used where some other tense or mood morphology excludes present tense marking, as in (10.46):

(10.46a)   Marno   maaji   ngeewunya   ngeyaaw.
           ma=rno   maaji   ngee-ᵏwunya   nga-nya=ya-aaw
           3m=DIST   had.better   honey-PURP   1-OPT=go-TIME
           I think I'll go off now and find some honey.

(b)   Bengkaalaaw!
           ba=ya-ᵏwaal-aaw
           CFT=go-hither-TIME
           Come here now!

(c)   Ajaaja   banaaw.
           ajaaja   ba=nu-aaw
           stay   CFT=be-TIME
           Stay here, meanwhile.

In this connection note the unanalysable form *kakaaw!* 'Come here!' mentioned in §8.5.3.

10.4.2 *Time-relative ngamba*

This important time adverb appears to have three distinct sense meanings, corresponding to 'later,' 'now/soon' and 'when' (relative-adverbial). These meanings seem to share some general common semantic, in marking the time of a particular event as being relative to the time of some other event. The functions of *ngamba* are illustrated below:

10.4.2 (i) now, soon, later
The adverb and conjunction *ngamba* may mean 'later' as in the examples in (10.47), or 'now' as in (10.48a) or 'soon' as in (10.48b):

(10.47a)   Ngambanyini   ke   wala   kaanyajona.
           ngamba-nyini   ke   wala   kaarr-nyarr-nya=ᵇwu-na
           later-ENDPOINT   3wREF   like   3p-1px-EP=hit-PAST
           At last we got to like them.

(b) Mamangkunu ke ngamba ngarriyaarndu.
    mamangkunu ke ngamba ngarr-a=ya-ᵏwarndu
    morning 3wREF later 1pin-OPT=go-DU
    Later on we'll go, in the morning.

(c) Yaw, bija bija ngenangka wali ngamba.
    yaw bija bija ØN-nga=yi-nangka wali ngamba
    yes FUT FUT VCOMP-1=do-DAT PERF later
    Yes, I'll be sure to tell him later.

(10.48a) Ngamba jolimirri nyidaalkarndu!
    ngamba joli-mirri nyirr=nu-aal-ᵏwarndu
    now return-quickly 2p=be-hither-DU
    Come back here at once!

(b) Kawarro wali aaya ngamba ke.
    ka-ᵇwarr-a=ᵇwu wali aaya ngamba ke
    3a-3p-EP=hit PERF 3aREF now 3wREF
    They're going to kill him now.

10.4.2 (ii) subordinate relative function

In this function, *ngamba* usually marks subordinate clauses that describe the time at which the event depicted in the main clause occurs. Typically, subjunctive verbal morphology signals the subordinate status of clauses controlled by *ngamba*, as may be seen in the examples shown in (10.49):

(10.49a)
Minyiyaara ngamba ngeyu jungunju dambeemangurru.
minya=yi-ᵏwara ngamba nga-nya=ya ØN-nja-ngun=yi dambeema-ngurru
2>3w=do-1DAT when 1-OPT=go VCOMP-2-SJTV=do place-ALL
Tell me when you want to go home.

(b)
Anja ngamba maabaabaya burnu kaaju, ngani
anja ngamba maabaabaya burnu ØN-ngka-ᵇwarr=yi ngani
3pDEF when old.people 3wPRO VCOMP-SJTV-3p=do what

kubaje nyini?
kuN-ᵇwarr-nya=yi nyini
VCOMP-3p-EP=do ENDPOINT
When these old people pass away, what will they do then?

(c)
Ngamba wurnarnngarri ingkenga wunu, kolkol
ngamba wurnarn-ngarri i-ngka=ya-nga wunu kol-kol
when exchange-REL 3a-SJTV=go-TNS 3wDEF share-trade

ngarrkunungaayenga
ngarr-ngun=ningaaye-ng
1pin-SJTV=do.MID-PRES
We'll share it out when it goes into the wurnarn *exchange cycle.*⁶³

---

⁶³ The ritual exchange cycle called *wurnarn wunu* was an important part of the culture of Worrorra-, Ungarinyin- and Wunambal-speaking people. Participants in the cycle were said to perform (='do,' *wurnarn kuN[ ]=yi*) the

However subordinate clauses controlled by *ngamba* are not obligatorily subjunctive. In (10.50), *ngamba* controls a relative clause dependent upon *ngarlangarla wunu* 'word, speech, story' as its head noun.

(10.50)
Weni	wali maa	kunyarrkangurreerri	ngarlangarla	ke,
weni	wali maa	kuN-nyarr=ᵏwangurru-eerri	ngarlangarla	ke
today	PROG	3w-1px=carry-PROG	story	3wREF

ngamba	ke	barraneninjerri	kunyila	aaya.
ngamba	ke	ba-ka-rra-ne=ninja-eerri	kunyila	aaya
when	3wREF	CFT-3a-2p-AUG=look.at-PROG	moon	3aREF

Today we still tell that story, about how you shouldn't stare at the moon.

10.5 Interrogative *ngani*, confirmatory *yama*

While *anguja* 'what?' substitutes for nouns (§7.4.2), *ngani* 'what?' substitutes for denotations of events – typically, for clauses or their verbal heads. The use of *ngani* in negative-counterfactual constructions has been discussed in §8.4.2. *Ngani* 'what?' is used *only* with *kuN[ ]=yi* 'do,' the verb with the most general semantics, where it is indexed in undergoer position as this verb's celestial-class direct object. Its use in interrogative function may be seen in (10.49b) & (10.51). This word is quite distinct from *nga-(ni)-* 'where?' seen in §7.4.1.

(10.51a) Ngani kunjiyeerri?
ngani kuN-nja=yi-eerri
what VCOMP-2=do-PROG
What are you doing?

(b) Ngani wajiyaarndu?
ngani ᵏwuN-ngarr-nya=yi-ᵏwarndu
what VCOMP-1pin-EP=do-DU
What shall we (du inc) do?

There is also a reduplicated form *ngani-ngani* 'what on earth? what in the world?' shown in (10.52):

(10.52a) Ngani-ngani kunjeerri?
ngani-ngani kuN-Ø=yi-eerri
what-what VCOMP-3=do-PROG
What on earth's s/he doing?/What on earth's going on?

(b)
Wali	ngani-ngani	ngenangkorri	anja	wali?
wali	ngani-ngani	ØN-nga=yi-nangkorri	anja	wali
PERF	what-what	VCOMP-1=do-3pDAT	3pDEF	PERF

Well now, what can I do to them?

Both of these forms may function non-interrogatively as general (ie as non-temporal) relative adverbs, as shown in (10.53):

---

exchange, while goods put into the cycle were said to 'walk' (*marduk =ya* [walk =go]) around the exchange routes or pathways between groups.

(10.53a)   Mee   ngani   nge.
     mee   ngani   ØN-nga=yi
     I.don't.know   what   VCOMP-1=do
     I don't know what I'll do.

(b)   Ngani   kunjungu   wardi   bungkaajaara.
    ngani   kuN-Ø=yi-ng   wardi   ba-kuN-^{b}warr=yi-^{k}wara
    what   VCOMP-3=do-PAST   hope   CFT-VCOMP-3p=do-1DAT
    I hope they know what's happened to me.[64]

(c)   Adijaarndeerri   ngani-ngani   nye.
    a-ngarr=ninja-^{k}warndu-eerri   ngani-ngani   ØN-Ø-nya=yi
    3a-1pin=look.at-DU-PROG   what-what   VCOMP-3-OPT=do
    Let's watch him (and see) what he's going to do.

The confirmatory interjection *yama?* seeks to confirm a statement or line of reasoning. It is used in the same way as the German *nicht wahr?* and the French *n'est-ce pas?*

(10.54)   Wurnbangku   kurdu   bungonya,   yama?
     wurnbangku   kurdu   ba-kuN-nga=^{b}wu-nya   yama
     CLAN.COUNTRY   follow   CFT-VCOMP-1=hit-PAST   CONFIRM
     I should have talked about the Wurnbangku-clan part of the story, shouldn't I?

10.6 Postpositional phrases

Like other Australian languages, Worrorra has a set of forms that attach to nouns to signal a number of 'non-core' case-like relations. That is, relations that are neither subject nor object, but instead convey locative, allative, ablative, instrumental, comitative, associative and other meanings. This morphology is derivational, producing de-nominal adverbs modifying, delimiting or expanding the reference of the verb in the clause in which they occur. The morphemes occur as suffixes or postpositions, or they may be both on different occasions.

10.6.1 Spatial structure and vector deixis

Attached to nouns the locative suffix *-rnanya* and its hardened allomorph *-danya* (Deretroflexion rule 3 in §3.1) are ubiquitous, and may be seen above in (10.12b, 10.37c, 10.38b, 10.39c), and throughout this grammar. Some place names appear to have this morpheme frozen into their shapes: ones that I know of are *Mangadanya* (|mangarr-rnanya| [pouch-LOC]) 'PLACE NAME,' *Ngayangkarnanya* 'Mount Trafalgar' and *Ngarlangkarnanya* 'the St. George's Basin.'

   Functionally related to locative are the allative and ablative forms. These need to be discussed in relation to each other and to a pair of verbal suffixes with corresponding meanings. Taken in combination these nominal and verbal affixes constitute a system of vector deixis that has overarching application to the denotation of events in Worrorra, and which are frequently depicted in terms of real or metaphorical direction or extent. In Worrorra an event's spatial structure, that is the directional movement, orientation or extent of one or more actors in relation to some other entity, is highly salient and frequently coded. Spatial structure in Worora is semantically isomorphic with the coding of temporal structure as verbal aspect. In this sense, Worrorra's depiction of spatial structure may be thought of by analogy as a kind of 'nominal aspect.'

---

[64] Literally, 'I hope they think/say/know of me: 'what's happened/what's he done?'' See Ch 14.

One or other of a pair of morphemes occurs in verbal form-order class [10]; these are *-aal* (underlyingly |-*kwaal*|) 'hither' and *-ngurru* 'away.' They formally coincide with a pair of directional postpositions that occur with nouns, *(-)aalb(a)* 'Ablative' and *-ngurru* 'Allative.'

The attachment of the verbal forms to the verb *=ya* 'go,' is lexicalized as *=ya-kwaal* 'come' and *=ya-ngurru* 'leave, depart.' Their denotation is of movement towards *(-aal)* or away from *(-ngurru)* a speaker or some other referent, from whose point of view some event is seen as unfolding. These meanings are diagrammed in Figure 10.1a, where S indicates a speaker or some other focal referent.

The nominal forms denote some referent as either a *source* (ablative, *aalba*) or as a *goal* (allative, *-ngurru*). These meanings are diagrammed in Figure 10.1b, where R is a referent, to which the postposition is attached.

(a) VERBAL *-kwaal*   *-ngurru*
S <— 'towards S'   S —> 'away from S'
eg *bengkaal* 'come here'   eg *bayungurru* 'go away'

(b) NOMINAL *(-)aalba*   *-ngurru*
R —> 'from R (ablative)'   R <— 'towards R (allative)'
eg *molnganem aalb* 'from the river'   eg. *molnganemangurru* 'to the river'

Figure 10.1: directional semantics

Note that the English translations of these forms are contradictory: 'towards' may be applied to both forms, as may 'from.' The semantics of vector deixis in Worrorra may be captured, however, by the notions of centripetal and centrifugal grounding. Grounding refers in this case to linear extent or motion with respect to some real world (speech event) participant or some narrative actor. The ground is represented by the actor from whose viewpoint the action is regarded; the empathic, subjective projection of speaker-and-hearer into the event depicted. This kind of projection is obligatorily marked in Worrorra in all kinds of situations where it would not be in English, eg as in (10.55):

(10.55a) Kaarn   kanunaal.
         kaarn   ka=nu-na-kwaal
         sing   3a=be-PAST-hither
         He came/was facing this way/towards (some actor), singing.

(b)   Aja   kanungurreerri.
         aja   ka=nu-ng-ngurru-eerri
         sit   3a=be-PRES-away-PROG
         He's sitting away over there.

The equivalence of linear extent and motion in this context is discussed in Heath (1984:287) for Wubuy, and the same considerations apply here.

The morpheme *(-)aal(ba)* 'hither, ABLATIVE' denotes centripetal motion, away from some referent (R in Figure 10.2) and towards the ground (S in Figure 10.2), as shown in Figure 10.2a. And conversely, the morpheme *-ngurru* 'away, ALLATIVE' denotes centrifugal motion, away from the ground, and towards some other referent, as shown in Figure 10.2b. The formal and functional coincidence of centripetal motion and ablative case is also apparent in Wubuy (Heath 1984:283).

(-)aal(ba)   *-ngurru*
R —> S   R <— S
(a) Centripetal grounding   (b) Centrifugal grounding

Figure 10.2: vector deixis

The use of these forms in their different senses in the same sentence is common, as is seen in (10.56):

(10.56a) Kengkunaal   molnganem   aalb.
          ka=ya-ngku-na-aal   molnganem   aalb
          3a=go-EP-PAST-hither river   from
          He came from the river.

(b)   Kengangurru   molnganemangurru.
          ka=ya-nga-ngurru   molnganema-ngurru
          3a=go-TNS-away   river-ALL
          He went to the river.

While *-ngurru* is always a suffix, *(-)aalb(a)* occurs as either a suffix (*marraalba* in (10.35)) or a postposition (10.56a, & *dambeem aalb* in (10.35)).

10.6.2 *Associative postpositions*

Worrorra has a number of suffixes coding relationships of physical proximity, either actual or metaphorical. These morphologies derive adverbial words from nouns, except in the case of *-ngarri* 'REL,' which sources a broader range of phrase types.

10.6.2 (i) relativizing *-ngarri, -ngarra*

The two forms of the relativizing morpheme, *-ngarri* and *-ngarra*, appear to be interchangeable, but *-ngarri* is more frequent in the database:

iwarnbarnngarri ~ iwarnbarnngarra   *king brown snake*
Ngarinyinngarri ~ Ngarinyinngarra   *of or associated with Ungarinyin-speaking people*

The initial nasal hardens to a stop in the right environment: *Wunambalkarra* (|wunambal-ngarra| [LANGUAGE.NAME-REL]) 'of or associated with Wunambal-speaking people.'

This very common predicative morpheme depicts an abstract relationship between its term and the object to which it is suffixed. It is a two-place stative predicate, and is available to denote a wide and very general range of relationships:

   -ngarri (x, y)
   be-associated-with (x, y)

The form *-ngarri* is suffixed to its object *(y)*, and predicated upon its term, *x*. Typically the object is a noun, but it can be a noun phrase, and adjective, an adverb, or a whole sentence. A brief introduction to this morpheme is to be found in §6.2.1. The suffix *-ngarri* functions to make its object syntactically dependent upon its term. In the course of doing so it derives a new word from its object; frequently the derived outcome is an adjective or an adverbial phrase, in line with its relativizing function. Whatever the outcome, the term becomes the head of a phrase within which the derived relativized constituent is embedded. The most transparent manifestation of this process is observed in modifiers ('adjectives') derived from nouns; such modifiers display gender agreement with their heads, if those heads are of the marked macrogender:

(10.57a)   mangarringarrim   dambeem
           mangarri-ngarri-m   dambeem
           vegetable.food-REL-3m   place
           place associated-with-vegetable food = garden

(b)   mangarri   *garden*-ngarri
            vegetable.food   garden-REL
            food associated-with-(a/ the) garden = food from the garden

(c)   aalmarangarrim   kajirn   dambeem
            aalmara-ngarri-m   kajirn   dambeem
            European-REL-3m   like   place
            places like those-associated-with-Europeans = European-style houses

(d)   mana   kuma   kunyilangarrima
            mana   kuma   kunyila-ngarri-ma
            3mDEF   gum   moon-REL-3m
            gum associated-with-the moon[65] = 'moon-glue'

More often, however, the term is deleted and the derived form, the erstwhile dependent constituent, stands for the whole, as in (10.58):

(10.58a)   wurnarnngarri
                wurnarn-ngarri
                ceremonial.exchange-REL
                (goods that are) part of the wurnarn *ceremonial exchange cycle*

(b)   Bulakangarri   (c)   karrangarri
        bulaka-ngarri   karrangu-ngarri
        middle-REL   high-REL
        '(people)-in-the-middle'[66]   *heavenly (things) (Christian context)*

(d)   wurnirndeerrngarri   (e)   bijakungarri
        ᵏwuN=rnirndeerr-ngarri   bijaku-ngarri
        3w=old-REL   smoke-REL
        in the old (days)/ long ago   *smoking (ceremony)*

(f)   wungunalingarri   (g)   yalingarri
        ᵏwuN=ngunali-ngarri   yali-ngarri
        3w=new-REL   cold-REL
        these (days), recent (events)   *cold (time) = early in the morning*

In the following examples the derived forms refer to (a) a person or persons (from or associated with Kalumburu), and (b) a language (associated with Europeans), respectively. In both cases the erstwhile heads of these relativized phrases (persons and language) are unstated:

(10.59a)
Kalamburrungarri   nganmurrkarlaalkarndu.
Kalamburru-ngarri   nga-n-[Ø]=murrka-rla-ᵏwaal-[ᵏwarndu]
PLACE.NAME-REL   1-INV-[3$_A$]=go.to-PAST-hither-[DU$_A$]
Two (men) from Kulumburu came to see me.

---

[65] The traditional explanation for bacterial conjunctivitis.
[66] Real people who lived in an historical, as opposed to the mythical period.

(b)
'Wrrorra	maa	kunyarloorlerri		wangalang	arrkununa.'
wrrorra	maa	kuN-nyarr=rloo-rla-eerri		wangalang	arr-ngun=nu-na
Worrorra	only	VCOMP-1px=speak-PAST-PROG		child	1px-SJTV=be-PAST

'Wali waa	laiburru	binyideenya	wunu	aalmarangarri.'
wali waa	laiburru	ba-nyirr=ni-yinya	wunu	aalmara-ngarri
not.yet	know	CFT-2p=be-PAST	3wDEF	European-REL

'We only spoke Worrorra when we were children.'
'You didn't know the Europeans' (language) yet.'

As seen at the head of this section, an entity may be linked to a social group by this derivational process. In (10.60) the term is *Wanjurna*, and the relativized dependent is *Ngarinyinngarri*. Note here how the frequently deleted phrasal head may be recalled if required:

(10.60)
Awa	irno	bariy	kanunaal	Ngarinyinngarri,	inja
awa	i=rno	bariy	ka=nu-na-^{k}waal	Ngarinyin-ngarri	inja
3aNAR	3a=DIST	rise	3a=be-PAST-hither	Ngarinyin-REL	3aDEF

iyakarra	Wanjurna.
i=yakarra	wanjurna
3a=other	DEITY

That Ngarinyin one over there rose up, the other Wandjina.

Some names (particularly of animals) have *-ngarri / -ngarra* frozen into their forms:

BASE	MEANING	DERIVED FORM	MEANING
wiji	*boil, sore*	wijingarra	*quoll*
mirimiri	*thorny*	mirimiringarrinya	*echidna*
iwarnbarn	?	iwarnbarnngarri	*king brown snake*
nyimri maai	*her head blackened*	nyimrimaaingarrinya	*black-headed python*
barnmarn	*magic, sorcery*	barnmarnngarri	*sorcerer*
nubu	?	Nubungarri	*Mount Waterloo*
ngurlarnda	?	ngurlarndangarrinya	*little corella*

Used with reference to people, the suffix *-ngarri* usually denotes a person's generational peers, as seen in (10.61) below. In (10.61c) the phrases *wunu-walingarri* and *wungunalingarri* are probably more or less synonymous, as 'current/younger generation.' The expression *wunu wali* is rare in the database, but may mean something like 'meanwhile, at the same time.'

(10.61a)
Anja	kulaayangarri
anja	kula-aa-ya-ngarr
3pDEF	husband-1POSS-3a-REL

my husband's friends and relations

(b)
Daraarlu	Bajawalakurdengarri	arrkanangka.
daraarlu	Bajawala-kurde-ngarri	arr=^{k}wa-nangka
PLACE.NAME	NAME-ASSOC-REL	3p=NAR-DAT

(The place called) Daraarlu belongs to Bajawala's family.

(c)
Wunu-walingarri	bujuje	kaajaningeerri	weni,
wunu-wali-ngarri	buju-je	kaarr-nya=ni-ng-eerri	weni
3wDEF-PERF-REL	finish-again	3p-EP=be-PRES-PROG	now

wungunalingarri	ke,	ngurru	aja	arrkunyawanjeerri.
ᵏwuN=ngunali-ngarri	ke	ngurru	aja	arr-ngun-nya=ᵇwa-ny-yeerri
3w=new-REL	3wREF	here	sit	px-SJTV-EP=fall-MIR-PROG

Modern people are still dying now, this new generation who live here.

As well as creating nominal modifiers or adjectives, *-ngarri* may also create absolutive adverbial phrases, with the suffix having scope over an entire phrase, as bracketed and italicized in the following examples. In (10.62a) the celestial reference in the absolutive phrase is to time, while in (10.62b) it is to *namandi wunu* 'canoe.' In (10.62c) the adverb *dande* 'travelling' is relativized to produce a meaning '(those) associated with travel; travelling/nomadic (people).'

(10.62a)
Yakurnu	jakarl	nyirrwaarndeerri	*[wunu*	*maramarangarri].*
yakurnu	jakarl	nyirr=ᵇwa-ᵏwarndu-eerri	wunu	maramara-ngarri
try	swim	2p=fall-DU-PROG	3wDEF	hot-REL

You two try and go for a swim [in the heat of the day].

(b)
Anja	bundurlba	angkengerri	*[namandi*	*kaarringarri*	*wunu].*
anja	bundurlba	arr-ngka=ya-nga-eerri	namandi	kaarri-ngarri	wunu
3pDEF	the.bush	3p-SJTV=go-PAST-PROG	canoe	3pNEG-REL	3wDEF

Those who were travelling through the bush [with no canoes].

(c)
Anbajiyaariwuna	nyina	*lolly,*	*[karle-karle*	*dandengarri*
arr-n-ᵇwarr-nya=yaariwu na	nyina	lolly	karle-karle	dande-ngarri
1px-INV-3p-EP=give-PAST	3fDEF	lollies	CHANGE.OF.STATE	travel-REL

ke],	kaarri maa,	waa	minjarl	binyajeenya.
ke	kaarri maa	waa	minjarl	ba-kuN-nyarr=yi-yinya
3wREF	in.vain	not	eat	CFT-VCOMP-1px=do-PAST

They gave us lollies [but at that time (we were) nomadic, so] it was pointless, we didn't eat them.

There are at least two idiomatic adverbial relativizations using *-ngarri*: *mana-manangarri* 'immediately, then-and-there,' and *ngarrkunjaangarri* 'long before our time/before we were born,' seen in (10.63a) below. This latter word is a variant of *ngarrkunjaa* with the same meaning. These frozen forms look like they could be lexicalizations of perhaps previously more productive forms, something like *|ngarr-ngun=yaa-(ngarri)| [1pin-SJTV=?be.born-(REL)] 'when we (are/were) born.' There is a modern uninflectable preverbal infinitive *nyaa* 'be born.'

Whole sentences may be subordinated using *-ngarri*, with either a relative interpretation, as in (10.63a) where *eeja* 'man' is modified; or an adverbial subordinate interpretation as in (10.63b):

(10.63a) = (7.13f)
Wenngarri	aaya	eeja,	*[waa*	*ngarrkunjaangarri*	*bangkaninya]ngarri*	aaya
weni-ngarri	aaya	eeja	waa	ngarrkunjaa-ngarri	ba-ka=ni-nya-ngarri	aaya
now-REL	3aREF	man	not	long.ago-REL	CFT-3a=be-PAST-REL	3aREF

That man lived quite recently, he was not from a long time ago.

(b)
[*Wali waa   nyaa   bangawenya*]ngarri,   karraanya
wali waa   nyaa   ba-nga=ᵇwa-yinya-ngarri   karraanya
not.yet   born   CFT-1=fall-PAST-REL   my.mother

ngankangurrurlerri   marndumarnanya.
nga-n-Ø=ᵏwangurru-rla-eerri   marnduma-rnanya
1-INV-3=carry-PAST-PROG   stomach-LOC
Before I was born my mother carried me in her stomach.

Adjectives may also be relativized, but it is not at all clear to me what difference, if any, this makes to their meaning. Relatived–unrelativized pairs of adjectives, used as adjectives, taken from the database are as follows (see §6.2.1).

wuniya	wuniyangarri	*good (celestial)*
maramara	maramarangarri	*hot*
beewurdu	beewurdungarri	*small (plural)*
manjumanju	manjumanjungarri	*windy*

In one example, *manjumanjungarri* 'windy' modifies *rlarlangkarram* 'the sea' to denote wild, stormy water:

(10.64)
Manjumanjungarrim   maa   bariy   kaanmurrkarla   rlarlangkarram.
manju-manju-ngarri-m   maa   bariy   kaarr-n-Ø=murrka-rla rlarlangkarram
wind-wind-REL-3m   3mREF   rise   3p-INV-3=go.to-PAST   sea
The storm-tossed sea rose up around them.

<u>10.6.2 (ii) associative *(-)kurde*</u>
Etically, there appear to be three degrees of closeness of association denoted by this suffix or postposition. The closest association is when something is physically a part of, or embedded in, something else. In the database thorns and spears sticking into people, and fruit on trees, are marked by *(-)kurde*:

(10.65a)   Awa   jinalyakurde   we   kawanerri.
           awa   jinalya-kurde   we   ka=ᵇwa-na-eerri
           3aNAR   spear-ASSOC   lie.down   3a=fall-TNS-PROG
           He's lying down with a spear sticking into him.

(b)   Wunu   nguwanu   mangarrikurde.
           wunu   nguwanu   mangarri-kurde
           3wDEF   tree   vegetable.food-ASSOC
           The tree with fruit.

A second, comitative use with humans typically denotes marriage:

(10.66a)   Karle   eejakurde   nganuna.
           karle   eeja-kurde   nga=nu-na
           change.of.state   man-ASSOC   1=be-PAST
           Then I got married.

(b)   Inkarndu   mangkaangkanangkaarndiya   kurde.
           i=n-ᵏwarndu   ma-ngkaa-ngka-[nangka-ᵏwarndu]-ya   kurde
           3a=DEF-DU   ↳-AUG-wife-[DAT-DU]-3p   ASSOC

The two (men) with their wives.

When used with humans and suffixed by *-ngarri* 'REL,' the resulting shape *-kurdengarri* refers to a person's immediate or extended family (see (10.61b) above).

The third, loosest association is one of addition, fairly translatable as 'as well, also:'

(10.67a) Jilinya   kurde   aja   nyinunanangkaarndeerri.
          jilinya   kurde   aja   nyiN=nu-na-[nangka-^{k}warndu]-eerri
          demon   ASSOC   sit   3f=be-PAST-[DAT-DU]-PROG
          A female demon was sitting with them (dual) as well.

(b)   Arrka   kurde   kaarringkunyaal.
          arrka   kurde   kaarr=i-ngku-nya-^{k}waal
          3pNAR   ASSOC   3p=go-EP-HORT-hither
          They can come too.

An idiomatic expression *=neem kurdekurde* [ear ASSOC-ASSOC] 'with (your) ears' means to listen out for, or watch out for something while doing something else, such as a woman being aware of her children playing nearby while she is otherwise engaged.

10.6.2 (iii) human comitative/locative *(-)nyina*

This suffix and postposition is heard as *(-)nyini* as often as *(-)nyina*, and is to that extent homophonous with the aspectual suffix described in (10.1.2 (v)) above. In elicitation and as a postposition it is heard as *(-)nyina*. The following partial paradigm of pronoun and determiner forms was elicited:

Table 10.1: human comitative/locative *-nyina* 'with (someone)' (partial paradigm)

PERSONAL PRONOUNS

	SINGULAR	DUAL	COLLECTIVE	DEFINITE ARTICLES
1	ngayunyina			
2	ngunjunyina			
3a	awanyina	awaarndunyina		injanyina
3f	nyangkanyina			nyinyaninya ~ nyinyini
1pin	ngarrinyina		ngarringkoorrinyina	
2p		nyirrerndunyina		
3p	arrkanyina			

The feminine definite article form (at least) may be infixed with the discourse-deictic morpheme to produce the shape *nyimnyininya*, probably composed as follows: |nyi(na)-mnya-(nyi)na-nya| [3fDEF-DD-HCOM-3f].

It's use as a comitative form appears to be restricted to human beings, and is illustrated in the following examples:

(10.68a)
Ke	marru	ruluk	kungenga	nyinyini
ke	ma=rru	ruluk	kuN-nga=yi-ng	nyina-nyina
and	3m=LAT	move	VCOMP-1=do-PAST	3fDEF-HCOM

nyangojirdarla,	adunaarndeerri	marno	mayakarrim
nyaN-nga=^{k}wujirda-rla	arr=nu-na-^{k}warndu-eerri	ma=rno	ma=yakarri-ma
3f-1=keep.company-PAST	1px=be-PAST-DU-PROG	3m=DIST	3m=other-3m

mayaram	nyina.
house	HCOM

And I moved over there with her to keep her company, I lived with her there at the other house.

(b)
Kerrkulkunarla	ke	nyimnyininya	aja
ka-nyarr=ᵏwulkuna-rla	ke	nyiN=(n-a)-mnya-(nyi)na-nya	aja
3a-1px=fear-PAST	and	3f-(DEF)-DD-HCOM-3f	sit

ajanunerringkurri	dambeem,	nyangkanangkamarnanya	nyina.
arr-nya=nu-na-eerri-ᵏwurri	dambeem	nyaN=ᵏwa-nangka-ma-rnanya	nyina
1px-EP=be-PAST-PROG-NUM	place	3f=NAR-DAT-3m-LOC	HCOM

We were afraid of him so we lived with her at her place.

(c)
'Marno	ngarreyu	kulurrkunya	jurujuru	ngarranaarndu,
ma=rno	ngarr-a=ya	kulurr-ᵏwunya	juru-juru	ngarr-a=nu-ᵏwarndu
3m=DIST	1pin-EP=go	water.lily-PURP	dive-dive	1pin-OPT=be-DU

ngarranoorri' –	yankarndamaa	kunyilaa	awaarndunyina
ngarr-a=nu-oorri	yankarndama-aa	kunyila-aa	awa-ᵏwarndu-nyina
1pin-OPT=be-NUM	star-and	moon-and	3aNAR-DU-HCOM

marangunyaarndinya.
marangunya-ᵏwarndu-nya
sun-DU-3f

'Let's go and dive for water-lily roots, let's all go' - the stars and the moon along with the two suns.

At the end of the sentences in (10.68a & b) the postposition *nyina* functions as a locative, in both cases marking places where someone lived, if not quite the people themselves.

A distinct but related sense meaning 'too, as well' is found when *(-)nyina* is attached to a nominal denoting an extra item, as shown below:

(10.69a)
Ke	ngeenyiniya	minjarlminjarl	kaaduna.	Wari	anjaa,
ke	ngee-nyina-ya	minjarl-minjarl	kaarr=nu-na	wari	anja-aa
and	honey-too-3p	eat-eat	3p=be-PAST	kangaroos	3pDEF-and

karimbinjaa,	burlkumba,	mirimiringarrinya	arrkenyini	minjarlminjarl
karimba-inja-aa	burlkumba	mirimiringarrinya	arrke-nyina	minjarl-minjarl
bandicoot-3aDEF-and	possum	echidna	3pREF-too	eat-eat

kaaduna.
kaarr=nu-na
3p=be-PAST

And they used to eat honey as well. Kangaroos, bandicoots, possums, echidnas; they ate those, too.

(b)
Wurrkunu	angujakunya	mara	kumbunaara	malyaama?
wurrkunu	angkujakunya	mara	kuN-Ø-ᵇwu-na-ᵏwara	malyaama
trouble	what.for	see	3w-3=hit-PAST-1DAT	needlessly

Kubarrwunaara			ngayunyinóo.
kuN-ᵇwarr=ᵇwu-na-ᵏwara		ngayu-nyina-óo
3w-3p=hit-PAST-1DAT		I-too-EMPH
What did he have to go and make trouble for me for? They made (trouble) for me too.

In (10.69b) the final vowel of *(-)nyina* is extended, stressed and rounded for emphasis.

<u>10.6.2 (iv) privative *-yeye*</u>
There is only one example of this suffix in the database: *wiyanuyeye* |wiyanu-yeye| [fire-PRIV] 'without fire.' The more usual denotation of privative meaning is by way of the adjective *=rnora* 'be without, lack (something):'

(10.70a)   Kayuku   ngarnora.
           kayuku   nga=rnora
           rock   1= be.lacking
           I haven't got any money.

(b)   Awanyale   kulnmerrbarnanya   iwajam   irnora.
      awa-nyale   kulnmerrba-rnanya   i=ᵇwajam   i=rnora
      3aNAR-next   tail-LOC   3a=fur   3a=be.lacking
      After that he had no fur on his tail.

10.6.3 Other derivational suffixes

Worrorra has two other important case-like suffixes, in addition to the locative, allative and ablative forms seen in §10.6.1. These mark purposive and instrumental relations, as seen below. Again these de-nominal forms serve derived adverbial functions.

<u>10.6.3 (i) purposive *-ᵏwunya*</u>
Like the locative suffix *-rnanya*, purposive *-ᵏwunya* (glossed PURP) ends in the segment *-nya*, homophonous with the feminine gender marker. The shape *-ᵏwunya* hardens to *-kunya* after laterals, nasals and /rr/ under hardening rules 10 and 11, and after the words *anguja* 'what?' and *mamangkunu* 'morning' under Relict Consonant Deletion rule 4. Nouns of the marked macrogender commonly have their gender suffixes *(-m(a)* and *-nya)* deleted before *-ᵏwunya*:

         dambeem   'place'   —>   dambeewunya   'homeward'
         ngeenya   'honey'   —>   ngeewunya   'for honey'

The purposive suffix marks goals; that is, entities or states that are desired but not yet attained. Most frequently in the database *-ᵏwunya* marks the goals of hunting and gathering: so people go out *kulurrkunya, ngeewunya, wariwunya, karnmangkuwunya, jaayawunya,* and *aakuwunya;* that is, looking for lily roots, honey, kangaroos, yams, fish and water, respectively, among many other things. *Dambeema* 'place,' when suffixed by *-ᵏwunya* to form *dambeewunya*, can only mean 'homeward;' it may not refer to any other kind of place. The word *mamangkunukunya* (|mamangkunuC-ᵏwunya| [morning-PURP]) 'until morning' uses the purposive suffix somewhat idiomatically, perhaps because people look forward to the morning, in Worrorra culture at least. Preparations for ritual occasions may be referred to by the purposive suffix. So we find *wurloowunya* 'for ritual purification by smoking,' *bijakuwunya* 'for smoke' (with the same reference) and *wurnarnkunya* 'for the ritual exchange cycle.' Activities denoted by preverbal infinitives may also be goals, as *minjarlkunya* 'for eating/edible.'

The suffix *-ᵏwunya* appears in many situations where there is a strong allative component to its semantics:

(10.71a)
Imnyaangurrunangka   karranangkanyawunya.
i-mnya=ᵏwangurru-nangka   karra-nangka-nya-ᵏwunya
3a-DD=carry-DAT   mother-DAT-3f-PURP
Take him to his mother.

(b)
Dalja   kungengeerri   ke   ajengerri   bundurlkunya.
dalja   kuN-nga=yi-ng-eerri   ke   arr-nya=ya-nga-eerri   bundurl-ᵏwunya
grow   VCOMP-1=do-PAST-PROG   3wREF   1px-EP=go-TNS-PROG   bush-PURP
As I was growing up we used to travel through the bush ('go bush').

Nevertheless GOAL, as the term is used here, is not synonymous with ALLATIVE; people may go to a place without that location being desired for its own sake. So allative and purposive suffixes may appear in the same sentence, as in (10.72):

(10.72)   Marru   ngengerri   *lolly*-wunya   *shop*-ngurru.
          ma=rru   nga=ya-nga-eerri lolly-ᵏwunya   shop-ngurru
          3m=LAT   1=go-TNS-PROG   lolly-PURP   shop-ALL
          I'm going over to the shop for some lollies.

In (10.71a) the referent is a small, crying child, for whom location with his mother was desired but not yet attained. The sentence in (10.71b) refers to families living on a mission who used to 'go bush' at regular intervals to find food, visit their country and escape from mission controls. On these occasions the bush was a goal, a place of enjoyment for its resources and for its own sake.

Causes may also be marked by the purposive suffix, if a cause is a cause by virtue of its desired status. The commonest example, however, *angujakunya* (|angujaC-ᵏwunya| [what-PURP]) 'for what purpose/reason?/what for?,' has a more general meaning, 'why?' Other examples may be seen in Chapter 17 in sentences (17.13a, 16, 18d, 19a, & 20a), and below:

(10.73a)
Bardawaai   nyimbeenerri   wangalanguwunya   wunu.
bardawaai   nyiN=ᵇwee-na-eerri   wangalangu-ᵏwunya   wunu
writhe   3f=hit.MID-PAST-PROG   child-PURP   3wDEF
She writhed about in an agony of grief for her child.

(b)
Anja   iyaaw   kawarraangurrurlu   irraaya,
anja   iyaaw   ka-ᵇwarr-a=ᵏwangurru-rla   irra-aa-ya
3pDEF   abuse   3a-3p-EP=carry-PAST   father-1DAT-3a

ngayu   irraaya   ngayuwunya.
ngayu   irra-aa-ya   ngayu-ᵏwunya
I   father-1DAT-3m   I-PURP
They abused my father, my own father, because of me.

At the time of (10.73b), the speaker was a young woman and the object of a dispute over who should marry her; she was therefore the cause of a dispute because she was desired. In (10.73a) the preverb *bardawaai* denotes a cultural expression of emotional agony. The object of the woman's grief, being desired, is the cause of her pain.

In a few examples the semantics of 'goal' disappear entirely, and *-ᵏwunya* is used to mark a noun's semantic role as beneficiary (10.74a) or theme (10.74b) (cf §13.2.2 (i, iv)):

(10.74a) Jaaya   jeyi-jeyi   kanunanangkerri   nyina   karranangkawunya.
          jaaya   jeyi-jeyi   ka=nu-na-nangka-eerri   nyina   karra-nangka-ᵏwunya
          fish   spear-spear⁶⁷   3a=be-PAST-DAT-PROG   3fDEF   mother-DAT-PURP

He was spearing fish for his mother.

(b)   Nyangkawunya   ngenangka   wali   kungenganu.
          nyangka-ᵏwunya   ØN-nga=yi-nangka   wali   kuN-nga=yi-ng-a-nu
          3fNAR-PURP   VCOMP-1=do-DATᵢ   PERF   VCOMP-1=do-PAST-EP-2DATᵢ

I've been wanting to tell you about her.

If anything could be said to be desired in (10.74a) it is the fish, but the beneficiary role (*karranangkanya* 'his mother') is marked by *-ᵏwunya*, not the noun in patient role (*jaaya* 'fish'). In (10.74b) the theme argument appears in a complement-clause construction.⁶⁸ Sentences of this kind are described in §14.3.2, but for now it may be noted that the main clause pronominal object (*-nu* '2DAT - of/about you) is co-referential with the complement clause's pronominal object (*-nangka* 'DAT - him/her / to him/her'). As this is the only purposive expression of this sort in the database, little more can be said about it.

<u>10.6.3 (ii) instrumental *-nyine, -ningke, -nyiningke*</u>
The form found in the database is almost universally *-nyine*, but I was also given synonymous alternatives *-ningke* and *-nyiningke*. Love (1934:32) gives only *-nyiningke* as the instrumental suffix. Instrumental suffixes may agree with their host nouns of the marked macrogender, taking *-m(a)* and *-nya* inflection, optionally. So *kalam(a)* 'double-raft' may be inflected with *-nyine* in the following ways: *kalanyinema, kalamanyinem* or *kalamanyine*. Definite articles referring to instruments anaphorically are marked with *-nyine;* masculine and celestial *injanyine* and *wunyine* 'with it/this' are found in the database, as exemplified in (10.75):

(10.75)   Wununu   kungurr   mango   wunyine.
          wunu-wunu   kungurr   ma-nga=ᵇwu   wunu-nyine
          3wDEF-3wDEF   stab   3m-1=hit   3wDEF-INST

I'll stab it with this.

Instrumental suffixes most commonly mark tools used to effect or achieve some desired outcome. So people are stabbed with spinifex, *jardinyine,* or with spears, *jinalnyine* or *jinalyanyine;* they are hit with sticks, *nguwanunyine,* or with boomerangs, *karlinyine;* food is pounded up, and grieving women gash themselves, with stones, *karrkunyine;* people get splashed with water, *aakunyine;* things are covered over with paperbark, *ngarlinyine;* hot sand is scooped out of fires with shovels, *kambananyine;* and children are blessed or purified in smoking ceremonies with their (parents') hands, *ardurnunyine.* The instrumental suffix also marks vehicles: babies are carried round in coolamons, *angkamanyine;* and people travel in cars, *motor-car-nyine,* on rafts, *kalamanyinem,* and in canoes:

(10.76)
Kengkunaal   Warruwarlaalb   barrawarranyine   Ngokonyini.
ka=ya-ngku-na-ᵏwaal   Warruwarlu-aalb   barrawarra-nyine   Ngoko-nyini
3a=go-EP-PAST-hither   PLACE-from   canoe-INST   PLACE-ENDPOINT

He came from Warruwarlu to Ngoko in a canoe.

Locations may also be marked as instrumental in bringing about desired outcomes: things may be swung through the air in (people's) arms, *arrwarndunyine* (|arr=ᵇwarndu-nyine| [px=arm-INST]); and food may be pounded up in mortars, *rnokunyine.*

---

⁶⁷ Preverb *jeyi* 'spear (something) at close range.'
⁶⁸ Literally, 'Of you I wanted/thought: 'I will tell him/her about her." See §14.3.2 for the syntax of this construction.

Instrumental suffixes also mark media, that is, intervening substances through which things are achieved. So people are anointed with arm-pit sweat, *marlambardbanyine;* and smeared with charcoal, *wulurrkunyine.* Language is a medium also marked by instrumental suffixes:

(10.77a)   Ngarrkanangka   ngarlangarlanyine   aai   kaajaal.
           ngarr=^{k}wa-nangka   ngarlangarla-nyine   aai   ØN-ngka-^{b}warr=yi-(^{k}w)aal
           1pin=NAR-DAT   language-INST   call   VCOMP-SJTV-3p=do-hither
           If they call out in our language.

(b)   Kurloonangkorreerri   Wrrorranyine.
     kuN-Ø=rloo-[nangka-^{k}wurri]-eerri   Wrrorra-nyine
     VCOMP-3=speak-[DAT-NUM]-PROG   Worrorra-INST
     He's talking to them in Worrorra.

Temporal adverbs may also host instrumental suffixes. In the database *weni* 'now, today' appears with instrumental marking:

(10.78)   Kunyajenangkerri   weninyine.
           kuN-nyarr-nya=yi-nangka-eerri   weni-nyine
           VCOMP-1px-EP=do-DAT-PROG   now-INST
           We still call it that today.

The expression *ngarrkunjaa* 'before our time/before we were born' has been discussed above in §10.6.2 (i) and illustrated in (10.63a). As well as being suffixed by *-ngarri* 'REL,' this time adverb may also be suffixed by *-ningke* 'INST,' illustrated below in (10.79). The variants *ngarrkunjaa, ngarrkunjaangarri* and *ngarrkunjaaningke* appear to be synonymous, frozen forms.

(10.79)   Nyinunerri   nyirnungkurlenya   nyangke   ngarrkunjaaningke.
           nyiN=nu-na-eerri   nyiN=rnungkurle-nya   nyangke   ngarrkunjaa-ningke
           3f=be-PAST-PROG   3f=ancient-3f   3fREF   long.ago-INST
           She lived a long time ago, long before we were born.

<u>10.6.3 (iii) customary *-barda*</u>

This suffix may be related to the form *-da* that Love (1934:108) describes as 'customary.' Love (1934:3) also notes *tjo:lbada* 'orator' (see below). Preverbal infinitives may be suffixed by the form *-barda* to derive a noun meaning '(person) habitually performing the action of the preverb.' Examples follow:

PREVERB		DERIVED NOUN	
jaraai	*laugh*	jaraaibarda	*someone who's always laughing*
yarrorl	*sound of voices*	jorlbarda	*orator*
ajaajin	*lie, pretend*	ajaajinbarda	*liar*

There is also a word *maambulbarda,* literally 'it's (terrestrial) eye,' which refers to either a particular tidal whirlpool off the north Kimberley coast, or to tidal whirlpools generally. The terrestrial reference in this word is to *rlarlangkarram mana* 'the sea,' so *maambulbarda* is translated as 'eye-of-the-sea.' Its derivation is either |ma=^{k}wambul-ma-rda| [3m=eye-3m-CUST], or |ma=^{k}wambul-barda| [3m=eye-CUST]. Either way, the customary morpheme here is surely idiomatic.

<u>10.6.3 (iv) essive *-aanjanu*</u>

The suffix *-aanjanu* attached to nouns derives adverbs indicating that some event occurred while the noun so marked existed. This suffix is unusual in that an essentially verbal meaning may be marked only by nominal affixation. Examples from the database are *wangalangaanjanu* |wangalang-aanjanu|

[child-ESS] 'while (someone) was a child,' *wangalaalangaanjanu* |wangalaalangu-aanjanu| [children-ESS] 'while (some people) were children,' and *lewarraanjanu* |lewarra-aanjanu| [daylight-ESS] 'while there's still daylight.' The use of such derived adverbs is illustrated in (10.80a) below. When attached to a clause, the clause must be subjunctive, as seen in (10.80b):

(10.80a) Arrke   kaangamnyaangurrurlungurru   wangalaalangaanjanu.
        arrke   kaarr-nga-mnya=ᵏwangurru-rla-ngurru   wangalaalangu-aanjanu
        3pREF   3p-1-DD=carry-PAST-away   children-ESS
        I looked after them for a time while they were children.

(b)   Kunyila   baa   ingkengaanjanu.
        kunyila   baa   i-ngka=ya-nga-aanjanu
        moon   appear   3a-SJTV=go-TNS-ESS
        While the moon is out.

10.6.4 Sequential suffixes

This section deals with two morphologies that, unlike the other forms in §10.6, are not derivational.

<u>10.6.4 (i) sequential *-nyale*</u>
This ubiquitous suffix has a wide-ranging meaning, marking something as coming after something else in a sequence of items or events, as 'next in sequence.' This general meaning can be somewhat artificially broken down as follows: (i) repeated action - an action performed again or in sequence; (ii) joining - comparable items listed together; (iii) next - coming immediately after something else.

The sense meaning 'repeated action; again' is illustrated below:

(10.81a)
Wali maa   kengaarndeerrinyale   karle   wundukum   manunerri.
wali maa   ka=ya-nga-ᵏwarndu-eerri-nyale karle   wundukum   ma=nu-na-eerri
PROG   3a=go-PAST-DU-PROG-again   then   night   3m=be-PAST-PROG
They went on again until night fell.

(b)
Joli   kamnyanuna   mana   jawenyale   nyangka   ingkaarndengama.
joli   ka-mnya=nu-na   mana   jawe-nyale   nyangka   i-ngka-Ø=ᵏwarnde-nga-ma
return 3a-DD=be-PAST   3mDEF   same-again   3fNAR   3a-SJTV-3=place-PAST-3m
He went back again to the same place where she had left him.

(c)
Wali   mamangkununyale   kununa,   kaanmurrkarlanyale.
wali   mamangkunu-nyale   ku=nu-na   kaarr-n-Ø=murrka-rla-nyale
PERF   morning-again/then   3w=be-PAST   3p-INV-3=go.to-PAST-again
The next morning he went to them again / 'Again it was morning, again he went to them.'

A distinct sense, 'comparable items listed together,' translatable as 'too, also, as well' is illustrated in (7.7a) in Chapter Seven, and below:

(10.82a)   Bajawala   nyinjorinyalenya   nyangka.
           Bajawala   nyiN=yoru-nyale-nya   nyangka
           NAME   3f=widow-too-3f   3fNAR
           Bajawala is a widow too.

(b)   Awa   iman   kanuna,   awanyale   aalkunya.
    awa   i=man   ka=nu-na   awa-nyale   aalkunya
    3aNAR   3a=dead   3a=be-PAST   3aNAR-too   young.man
    He died too, as a young man.

(c)   Iyaaw   kaanbajaangurrurlu   ajakekarrinyale.
    iyaaw   kaarr-n-ᵇwarr-nya=ᵏwangurru-rla   arr=ya-ke-karri-nyale
    scold   3p-INV-3p-EP=carry-PAST   px=↳-AUG-other-too
    They scolded all the others as well.

A third sense meaning appears to denote an event as coming after, or immediately after, some other event; here a translation of 'next, then, after that' seems to fit, as seen in (10.70b) above and in the following:

(10.83a)   Wululu   nyimbanaalnyale   nyangka.
     wululu   nyiN=ᵇwa-na-ᵏwaal-nyale   nyangka
     fly,flutter.down   3f=fall-TNS-hither-next   3fNAR
     Then she flew down.

(b)   Ke   jakarrinyale   mamangkunu   bariy   nyinuna.
    ke   ØN=yakarri-nyale   mamangkunu   bariy   nyiN=nu-na
    and   3w=other-next   morning   rise   3f=be-PAST
    Then one morning she got up.

It is often unnecessary to invoke these etic distinctions in situations where an overarching semantics of something like 'next in sequence' is clearly intended, as can be seen in these examples:

(10.84a)
Nyangka   kambananya   nyimangaa,   nyangkanyale   nyimanga
nyangka   kambananya   nyiN-Ø=ma-nga-aa   nyangka-nyale   nyiN-Ø=ma-nga
3fNAR   shovel   3f-3=get-PAST-and   3fNAR-too   3f-3=get-PAST

kambananya.
shovel
She₁ took up her shovel, and she₂ also took up her shovel.
She₁ took up her shovel, and then/next she₂ took up her shovel.

(b)
Inja   birdeenja   kamanganyale,   jarrangurlak   kamanga   ke
inja   birdeen-ya   ka-Ø=ma-nga-nyale   jarrangurlak   ka-Ø=ma-nga   ke
3aDEF   small-3a   3a-3=get-PAST-too   lift.up   3a-3=get-PAST   and

we   keerlanyale   marno   kubadeernanya.
we   ka-Ø=ee-rla-nyale   ma=rno   kubadeenya-rnanya
lie.down   3a-3=place-PAST-too   3m=DIST   meat.ant-LOC
He got the little one next, lifted him out and laid him on a nest of meat-ants too.

<u>10.6.4 (ii) -ᵏwurle 'first'</u>
This suffix hardens to *-kurle* after nasals, laterals and /rr/, and undergoes cluster assimilations as follows: |a-ᵏwu| > /o/, as in |awa-ᵏwurle| > *aworle* 'he first,' and |u-ᵏwu| > /oo/, as in |i=ᵇwulku-ᵏwurle| > *iwulkoorle* 'elder brother first.' Note however that 'me first' and 'you (sg) first' are *ngayorle* and *ngunjorle* respectively, indicating that the underlying shapes of the first and second person singular free pronouns end in |a|, not /u/: |ngaya-ᵏwurle| > *ngayorle*, |ngunja-ᵏwurle| > *ngunjorle*.

The suffix *-ᵏwurle* is hosted by far the most commonly by pronouns; but nouns, derived nouns, adjectives, verbs and preverbal infinitives may all host this suffix. An entity may be denoted as the first in a series, as in (10.85a), or an event may be denoted as occurring first in relation to some other event, as in (10.85b):

(10.85a)
Aworle	wali,	nyangkorle,	aworlewurle	kulnmerrba
awa-ᵏwurle	wali	nyangka-ᵏwurle	awa-ᵏwurle-ᵏwurle	kulnmerrba
3aNAR-first	PERF	3fNAR-first	3aNAR-first-first	tail

rireey	nyinunanangka	mana.
reey-reey	nyiN=nu-na-nangka	mana
pluck-pluck	3f=be-PAST-DAT	3mDEF

It was him, no it was her, it was him who first got all the fur on his tail pulled out.

(b)
Mangarriwurle	minjarl	ju,	bija	joli	ngenaal.
mangarri-ᵏwurle	minjarl	ØN=yi	bija	joli	nga-nya=nu-(ᵏw)aal
food-first	eat	VCOMP=do	FUT	return	1-OPT=be-hither

I'll come back after you've had lunch. (Lit, 'eat lunch first, I'll come back here.')

Even though in (10.85a) the speaker is momentarily confused about who did what first, with the final pronoun doubly-marked with *-ᵏwurle*, one of the actors is indicated as having been the first to undergo an event. In (10.85b) two events are juxtaposed, their sequence being marked again by *-ᵏwurle*. The suffix in this sentence is attached to the initial noun, but has scope over the entire clause in which it occurs. It is often unclear whether *-ᵏwurle* has scope over its whole clause, or over just its host nominal. In (10.86) the pronouns at the start of each clause are marked for *-ᵏwurle*, with ambivalent scope:

(10.86a)
Ankurle	kaarringerri.
arr=n-ᵏwurle	kaarr=i-nga-eerri
3p=DEF-first	3p=go-TNS-PROG

These people are going first.

(b)
Abiorle	maanja	karlelwana,	aworle	karlelwana
abiya-ᵏwurle	maan-ya	ka=rlelwa-na	awa-ᵏwurle	ka=rlelwa-na
El.Sib-first	SPEC-3a	3a=be.born-PAST	3aNAR-first	3a=be.born-PAST

ngayu	abi.
I	El.Sib

My only brother was born first, my big brother was born first.

When verbs (10.87a,b) and preverbs (10.87c) host *-ᵏwurle*, the suffix's clausal scope is clear:

(10.87a) Mana   aja   ngadoorriwurle.
          mana   aja   ngarr=nu-ᵏwurri-ᵏwurle
          3mDEF   sit   1pin=be-NUM-first
          Let's all sit down here first.

(b) Bengkaalkurle.
 ba=ya-ᵏwaal-ᵏwurle
 CFT=go-hither-first
 Come here first.

(c) Yorrwurle   ngarrwa
 yorr-ᵏwurle   ngarr=ᵇwa
 sit.together-first 1pin=fall
 Let's sit down together first.

Eleven: Complex predicates

11.1 Introduction

Complex predicates, also called verbal compounds, constitute the commonest means of verbal expression in Worora.[69] By text count such predicates are far more frequent than simplex verbal expressions. Complex predicates make use of a large and open word class that occurs in few other grammatical contexts: this is the lexical category that I will refer to as preverbal infinitives or *preverbs*. Worrorra preverbs are semantically verbal, while possessing syntactic properties of both nouns and adverbs. Complex predication, and the lexical category of preverbs it hosts, together constitute one of the defining features of Worrorra in typological terms, and is a characteristic areal feature of north-western Australia generally (see eg McGregor 2002, Amberber, Baker & Harvey (eds) 2010).

Complex predicates in Worrorra are typically composed of a preverb followed by an inflecting verb, here termed a *verb classifier* for reasons that will become apparent. Predicates of this type are not uncommon in Australia, where they have traditionally been referred to as compound verbs or verb-plus-auxiliary sequences (eg Capell 1976:615 ff). Other terminologies include 'root,' 'verb,' 'prefix,' 'infinitive,' 'particle,' 'uninflecting verb' and 'transparent event' for initial elements, and 'thematizing suffix,' 'root,' 'auxiliary,' 'classifier,' 'classifier complex,' 'light verb' and 'inflecting verb' for final elements (Dixon 1980:426, Nash 1982, Silverstein 1986, McGregor 1990, 2002 and references therein, and Amberber, Baker & Harvey (eds) 2010). The preverb carries the predicate's main semantic load, while the inflecting verb characterizes the event in terms of a small set of semantic features such as transitivity, telicity and control, as well as coding argument structure, tense and so on. I will use the term 'complex predicate' to refer to the combination of two such forms in some way within a single clause to compose a single although formally complex predication.

The approach to complex predication in Worrorra that I will prefer is based on Johnson's (1987, 2007) and Lakoff and Johnson's (1980) treatment of cognition, which engages with the embodiment of mental phenomena, and emphasizes the essential unity of bodily and mental experience. This perspective involves image schemata; that is, impressions that register in a non-specific and culturally defined fashion, the partitioning of the stream of experience into segments that manifest themselves as recurring kinetic, sensory enactments, configurations and performances. This approach is favoured as well by McGregor (2002) with respect to preverb and classifier combinations in north-western Australia generally, although what I am calling event schemata he refers to as *vectorial configurations*. Event schemata in Worrorra, as represented by preverbs, will be understood here as sets of specific and detailed gestures and configurations that are, in McGregor's terms, immanent; that is, operating without reference to external phenomena such as is coded, importantly, by argument structure. In

---

[69] Whether the combinations of preverb and inflecting verb described in this grammar are or are not compounded is probably a moot point. The majority of combinations described in this chapter are lexically appointed, and so meet lexical, if not phonological conditions for compound status.

Worrorra, argument structure is signalled entirely by the classifying verb with which preverbs are conjugated.

In the approach to generative theory taken by Jackendoff (1990) event denotation is decomposed into sets of semantic primes such as MOVE, CAUSE, BECOME, etc. Each element in such a decomposition is said to have its own argument structure which is projected upward to contribute to the argument structure of a complex predicate as a whole. This structural approach to the explication of complex predication is addressed by contributors to Amberber, Baker & Harvey (eds) (2010), and is elaborated in contributions by Baker & Harvey, Butt, Foley and Nordlinger, among others. The denotation of events is in this theory conceived of as having distinct tiers – importantly a thematic tier containing semantic information, and corresponding to event schemata as that term is used here; an action tier containing argument structure, an aspectual tier, and a temporal tier for coding sequential ordering. Event denotation by complex predication is said to be achieved by means of two grammatical processes – *event fusion* or *merger* unites semantic content, while *argument fusion* or *coindexation* rationalizes argument structure.

Complex predicates share with complement clause constructions in Worrorra properties that make them amenable to being treated as variations upon a single syntactic theme, or at least as showing syntactic features in common. Both constructions commonly, but not invariably, involve (i) the embedding of one predication within another, and (ii) the indexation of the embedded predicate on the matrix in undergoer position. While Lexical-Functional Theory allows complex predicates to evince two heads, and while Worrorra combinations also display two heads, there is an important difference: the preverb in Worrorra is the semantic head of the predication, while the classifying verb is its syntactic head. A large number of complex predicates in Worrorra are hypotactic: that is, the preverb appears as an object argument of its classifier. Lexical-Functional Theory admits of such hypotaxis: in that formulation, the process of argument fusion may involve a transparent event (≈preverb) being embedded as an argument of a light verb (≈classifier) (as outlined by Nordlinger 2010: 250 & fns 18, 19 & references therein).

Clearly this is a quite specific solution to the 'problem' of predicate linkage, and one characteristic of the language generally. To the extent that core arguments are indexed obligatorily on verbs as prefixes in S/U position, this coding device is available to signal grammatical relations of a certain kind. That predicate composition should make use of this ready-made morphological facility should not be surprising. It would appear that the language construes formal relations between predicates in much the same way as it construes morphosyntactic relations generally.

McGregor (2002:245 *et seq*) provides a comprehensive overview of the wide range of approaches taken to describing complex predication in Australian languages. His scenario for the origins of this phenomenon in Australia includes the use of ideophones with framing verbs (2002:345) (as in, eg, 'it went bang,' 'they're making whoopee,' and so on). In transitive constructions ideophones would have constituted object complements dependent upon matrix framing verbs. The transitive matrices involved would have comprised a smallish set of fairly generic verbs of the *do/say, get, put, make* variety, one or more of which would have taken on, or would have been selected because it already possessed, properties of *verba dicendi*.[70] The resulting hypotactic constructions would have reflected what we currently find in Worrorra.

While Worrorra verb classifiers bear many of the properties also associated with auxiliaries, the term 'auxiliary' is potentially confusing in cross-linguistic contexts in Australia. The label 'auxiliary' is probably better applied to the lexical category of that name occurring in Ngumpin languages such as Warlpiri, Walmatjarri and Djaru.

An example of a complex Worrorra predicate is provided in (11.1):

(11.1) We   ngawanerri.
       we   nga=ᵇwa-na-eerri
       lie   1=fall-TNS-PROG

---

[70] Just as English *go* and *be like* have recently turned into *verba dicendi*. Before this, *go* was a framing verb for ideophones in expressions like 'it went bang,' 'birds go tweet,' etc.

I'm lying down.

The preverbal infinitive (*we* 'lie down') is uninflected and carries the phrase's semantic load. The verb classifier *ngawanerri* is inflected for predicate argument structure, tense and aspect, with scope over the entire phrase. Although a fully-lexical verb meaning 'fall' in simplex constructions, in complex constructions =*ᵇwa* contributes no lexical information apart from a general sense of telic motion. Classifying verbs are schematic to the extent that for the most part they encode only general and abstract semantic properties, namely transitivity, control, telicity, motion and radial vector dynamics, more often than not by metaphorical extension.

Their schematic nature, and the way in which they combine with preverbs, should be borne in mind when reference is made to the auxiliary functions of verb classifiers in later sections. In attempting to provide a systematic account of complex predication in Worrorra, I will use the Role-and-Reference typology proposed by Foley & Van Valin (1984:238), consisting of a set of diagnostic criteria for classifying linked predicates and clauses. This is done on the basis of both formal, syntactic features and the semantic distinctions that motivate them. A quick outline of this theory and methodology is set out in Appendix 4. Where this analysis fails to best account for what we observe in Worrorra, I will refer to McGregor's (2002) exposition of this phenomenon in Australian languages more generally.

The Worrorra database contains 400 preverbs and 100 finite verbs, only 15 of which may serve as classifiers. By the end of the time I spent at Mowanjum I was encountering progressively fewer new finite verbs, but the rate at which I was encountering new preverbs was not diminishing. This suggests to me that a more complete lexicon might show a much higher ratio of preverbs to finite verbs.

11.2 Preverbs

In languages such as English, finite and infinitive predicators are distinguishable morphosyntactically. In Worrorra these two types are distinguished lexically, in that they belong to separate lexical categories. Preverbal infinitives in Worrorra constitute a category whose members may never take finite inflection. Members of this category denote events, actions and states, and may host aspectual derivational morphology (§11.3); this is to say that their denotations are entirely verbal. They also have inherent gender, they may take relational suffixes and they may occur as core arguments of finite verbs. Although exhibiting both verbal and nominal characteristics, preverbs are distinct from both finite verbs as defined in Chapter Five, and nouns as defined in Chapter Four.

As predicted by McGregor (2002:324-326), and reflecting their putative ideophonic origins, Worrorra preverbs have distinctive phonotactic features that set them apart from other word classes. A higher proportion of preverbs end in consonants than do members of other word classes, including words ending in /k/ (eg *ajak* 'sit down abruptly) and /y/ (eg *bariy* 'rise'), a situation not found at all in other classes. And a /rr+y/ cluster is found in the preverb *yorryorr* 'many people sit down together,' a reduplication of *yorr* 'sit down together.' Everywhere else in the language this cluster is hardened to /j/ by phonological rules 11 and 15 (but compare in this regard the preverbs *yurr* 'pull' and its reduplication *jujurr* 'haul along.' Here the central cluster has not only hardened, but has induced hardening on the initial consonant as well: **yurr-yurr* > **yujurr* > *jujurr*.) The diphthong /aai/ is also found word-finally uniquely in preverbs, and a relatively high proportion of preverbs are monosyllabic.

Finite verbs may never occur in uninflected form. Finite verbs and preverbs are therefore in formal complementary distribution: the former may never occur without inflection, while the latter may never occur *with* inflection. In functional terms as well, preverbs are in complementary distribution with their finite verb classifiers. Preverbs bear the semantic load of predication, with minimal grammatical encoding, while classifiers code syntactic relations and other grammatical properties with minimal semantic input. Nearly all the finite referential apparatus that predicates require in order to consummate linguistic semiotic function is borne by classifiers in the verb phrase. Both categories are required in order to constitute a formally complex predicate.

Preverbs are, then, semantic expansions or elaborations of the finite, reference-signalling, classifier heads of verb phrases. As such, preverbs typically denote *types* of event: only in combination with verb classifiers do they constitute predicates capable of referring to *instances* of such events. This distinction between type and instance of denotation (Langacker 1991:51) will be important in the description of other properties of Worrorra predicates. Most importantly, although preverbs are the semantic heads of their phrases, they are not the syntactic heads. The verb phrase in Worrorra is a projection of the verb classifier, not the preverb (see §5.1, §11.5.1). This means that in syntactic terms preverbs are underlyingly adverbial; that is to say that they are dependent forms in the predicates in which they occur.

11.2.1 Bare preverbs

One of the few situations in which preverbs may occur on their own, without the kind of referential setting otherwise provided by a classifier, is in imperative contexts, in which they function in a manner similar to that of English adverbial imperatives such as 'Quickly!' 'Careful!' 'This way!' or 'Over there!'

(11.2a) Yarribaa   wurriyaal!   Yarribaa!
        yarribaa   ᵏwuN-rra=yi-aal   yarribaa
        descend.PL   VCOMP-2p=do-hither   descend.PL
        Come down, you lot! Come down!

(b)   Wulaawirri   wulaa,   kuman-kuman   wurramra.
        wulaa-wirri   wulaa   kuman-kuman   ᵏwuN-rra=mra
        rest-quickly rest   close.eye-close.eye VCOMP-2p=gather
        Close your eyes at once and go straight to sleep.

(c)   Nyirri   marnuk!
        You.PL   lift
        You all lift! (Everyone lift!)

(11.3)
Ngani   waju   wali?   Kurdu   angarrwu!   Kurdu! Kurdu!
ngani   ᵏwuN-ngarr=yi   wali   kurdu   arr-ngarr=ᵇwu   kurdu   kurdu
what   VCOMP-1pin=do   PERF   follow 3p-1pin=hit   follow follow
What'll we do? Let's get after them! Chase them! Follow them!

Imperatives typically bear minimal inflexion cross-linguistically, often consisting of uninflected root morphemes. Worrorra preverbs are therefore suited to this function, although finite imperative forms are much more common here than preverbs (§8.5.3). In example (11.2b) the preverb *wulaa* 'rest' is not limited by any classifier, and the phrase *wulaawirri wulaa* constitutes an imperative expression distinct from the rest of the sentence. The following preverb *kuman* 'close (one's) eyes' is conjugated with the classifier =*ma* 'get' or its iterative form =*mra* 'gather.' *Wulaa* normally engages only with *kuN[ ]=yi* 'do' in complex predicates.

Preverbs may very occasionally substitute for an entire complex predicate, as in (11.4) below. Constructions of this sort are quite rare, are usually indicative of extra-linguistic interference (tiredness, distraction) and only occur when all the relevant referential indices are completely recoverable from a verb or verb classifier in the immediate environment. The opposite situation, in which a verb classifier substitutes for a complex predicate, is much more common (see §11.4.1). In (11.4) the bare preverbs are *minjarl* 'eat' in (11.4a) and *baawaa* 'ascend, appear, arrive' in (11.4b):

(11.4a) Arrka   karnmangku   wok   kawarrona,   ngeenya   minjarl.
        arrka   karnmangku   wok   ka-ᵇwarr-a=ᵇwu-na   ngeenya   minjarl
        3pNAR   yam   cook   3a-3p-EP=hit-PAST   honey   eat
        They cooked yams and ate honey.

(b)   Kaarringurru   dambeem   baawaa.
       kaarr=i-nga-ngurru   dambeem   bawaa
       3p=go-TNS-away   place   ascend.PL
       They went on and came to a camp.

11.2.2 Serial preverbs

Serial preverb constructions are reasonably common, as seen in (11.5) and (11.6) below, with the paired forms *we* 'lie down,' *kulunu* 'sleep' and *wulaa* 'rest:'

(11.5)
We   kulunu   ngawanerri.
we   kulunu   nga=ᵇwa-na-eerri
lie.down   sleep   1=fall-TNS-PROG
I'm going to sleep.

(11.6)
Jinalya   jadba   kawarraangurrurlu   kulunu   wulaa
jinalya   jad-ᵇwa   ka-ᵇwarr-a=ᵏwangurru-rla   kulunu   wulaa
spear   straight-PROG   3a-3p-EP-take-PAST   sleep   rest

kaajingeerri   maa.
ØN-ngka-ᵇwarr=yi-ng-eerri   maa
VCOMP-SJTV-3p=do-PAST-PROG   PROG
They threw spears at them while they were sleeping.

In serial constructions of this type one of the preverbs may appear postposed to the classifier. An example of this kind of arrangement may be seen in (5.17a) in §5.2.2. Such post-position may occur for pragmatic reasons, as in (11.7) (=8.36) where the preverb *kulunu* 'sleep' is a purposive complement comparable in this way to the postpositional forms seen in (11.8) (below):

(11.7)   Mana   we   ngarrwaarndu   kulunu.
         mana   we   ngarr=ᵇwa-aarndu   kulunu
         3mDEF   lie   1pin=fall-DU   sleep
         Let's lie down here and go to sleep.

11.2.3 Preverbs used substantively

Preverbs may also occur on their own when used substantively. Their use in a substantive syntax is signalled by a number of properties, among them their ability to take relational postpositions or suffixes:

(11.8a) Kumnyaangurrurlaal   bululuku   wurloowunya.
         kuN-Ø-mnya=ᵏwangurru-rla-aal   bululuku   wurloo-ᵏwunya
         3w-3-DD=carry-PAST-hither   foliage   purify.by.smoke-PURP
         She brought leaves and grass to perform the ceremony of purification by smoking.

(b) Nguru kanunaarndu yarrorlkunya.
nguru ka=nu-na-aarndu yarrorl-ᵏwunya
hear 3a=be-PAST-DU sound.of.voices-PURP
They listened for the sound of voices.

(c) Mangarri ding-ding kunjungunyarri minjarlkunya.
mangarri ding-ding kuN-Ø=yi-ng-a-nyarri minjarl-ᵏwunya
food ding-ding VCOMP-3=do-PAST-EP-1pxDAT eat-PURP
He rang the bell for us to have dinner.

None of the preverbs *wurloo* 'purify ritually by smoke' in (11.8a), *yarrorl* 'make a sound as of voices' in (b) or *minjarl* 'eat' in (c) are limited by any classifier, and all take a nominal purposive suffix *(-ᵏwunya)*. The reduplicated form of the construction in (11.8c) *(minjarl-minjarlkunya)* is translatable as 'edible,' as in (11.9):

(11.9)
Diwurl kanunangurraarndeerri karimbinjaa,
diwurl ka=nu-na-ngurru-aarndu-eerri karimba-inja-aa
kill.game 3a=be-PAST-away-DU-PROG bandicoot-3aDEF-and

rdungkulyinjaa, burnarri anja minjarl-minjarlkunya.
rdungkulya-inja-aa burnarri anja minjarl-minjarl-ᵏwunya
goanna.sp-3aDEF-and animals 3pDEF eat-eat-PURP
They (dual) killed bandicoots and goannas as they went along, and other animals that are good to eat.

In substantive use, preverbs may fall under the scope of a determiner, and so may display overt gender agreement. Most but not all preverbs are celestial (§4.1.3 (iii)), and may occur with a determiner of that gender:

(11.10) Wunu kuyoya wali nyijaningaayengaarndeerri.
wunu kuyoya wali nyirr-nya=ningaaye-ng-ᵏwarndu-eerri
3wDEF whisper PROG 2p-EP=do.MID-PRES-DU-PROG
You two are still whispering to each other.

In (11.11a & b) the respective preverbal object arguments *wala* 'cry' and *budurrwu* 'snore' accept a determiner *(wunu)* as an indicator of their grammatical function as predicate arguments. The syntax of this construction is treated below in §11.5.2.

(11.11a) Karle wala wunu durrba kumbunerri.
karle wala wunu durr-ᵇwa kuN-Ø=ᵇwu-na-eerri
then cry 3wDEF stop-PROG VCOMP-3=hit-PAST-PROG
Then he gradually stopped crying.

(b) Budurrwu maa wunu kumurrkarlanangkerri.
budurrwu maa wunu kuN-Ø=murrka-rla-nangka-eerri
snore PROG 3wDEF 3w-3=go.to-PAST-DAT-PROG
He_i went towards the sound of his_k snoring.

In (11.11b) the preverb *budurrwu* 'snore' is followed by the aspectual form *maa* 'PROG' and accepts a determiner of appropriate gender (celestial). As well as this, the preverb is indexed in undergoer position on the following verb, as *kuN*- '3w.' Note that this is not a simple collocational type of composition: linkages of this type are treated in §11.5.4 (iii).

The preverb *ngaja* in its more 'verbal' sense means something like 'be like (someone), emulate.' It has as well a nominal sense in which it translates as 'custom, tradition, precedent.' In its verbal sense its nominal properties are not evident (11.12a), but it may accept a determiner when its nominal sense meaning is in focus, even when combined directly with a verb classifier as in (11.12b).

(11.12a)
Awa	ngaja	kaanmanga.
awa	ngaja	kaarr-n-Ø=ma-nga
3aNAR	emulate	3p-INV-3=get-PAST

He's like them.

(b)
Nyangka	nyina	nyimrimaaingarrinya	wunu	ngaja	nyejamanga.
nyangka	nyina	nyimrimaaingarrinya	wunu	ngaja	nyaN-nyarr-nya=ma-nga
3fNAR	3fDEF	python.sp	3wDEF	emulate	3f-1px-EP=get-PAST

We follow the custom established by the black-headed python.

11.3 Derivational processes

While unable to inflect, preverbs may yet undergo derivational processes in order to signal aspect. Preverbs modified for aspect constitute lexical entries distinct from their base or uninflected forms. Members of other lexical categories may also be summoned to appear in preverbal function.

11.3.1 Plural actors

When a number of people perform some activity together, that activity appears to be conceived of in Worrorra as a multiplicity of separate, individual actions, constituting an essentially iterative event structure. Preverbs denoting events with multiple actors are given aspectual treatment, that is to say that such preverbs receive some kind of formal augmentation, by way of either reduplication or some

Table 11.1: plural-actor preverbs

		SINGULAR	PLURAL	
(a)		baa	baawaa, baawaard	*ascend, appear*
		baay	baawaa, baawaard	*climb*
		brrak	brrabrra	*wake up*
		jo	joyo	*drink*
		joli	joliyoli	*return*
		yorr	yorryorr	*sit together*
(b)		balya	balyaa	*go and visit someone*
		yala	yalabaa	*go hunting*
		yarriy	yarribaa	*descend*
(c)		rnala	rnalala, rnalowa	*make camp*
		wala	walaawirri	*cry*
		yola	yolow	*stand*
(d)		darak	darari	*enter*
		debarr	debadi	*die*
		yawak	yawarrarra	*sink underneath something*
		yawurlak	yawarrarra	*sink under water, drown*

other phonological extension, in a manner comparable to the way in which other types of aspect are marked (see §11.3.2). Plural-actor preverbs can be seen in sentence examples (11.2a) and (11.4b) above, and (11.13) below. The plural-actor forms typically signal three or more actors, and the singular forms signal one actor. Two actors may be signalled by either form.

Some plural-actor preverbs and their singular counterparts are displayed in Table 11.1 above. Group (a) in Table 11.1 displays stem-reduplication, also used for other kinds of aspectual meaning (often iteration). Group (b) appears to show an extended form of the morpheme -^{b}wa 'PROGRESSIVE', as does group (c), although in this group the continuous morpheme is more closely assimilated with preceding material. Group (d) displays other kinds of phonological augmentation.

Note that plural-actor forms may neutralize semantic distinctions encoded by singular-actor shapes: *baa* 'ascend' and *baay* 'climb' have the same plural-actor form, as do *yawak* 'sink' and *yawurlak* 'sink under water, drown' (cf the related and equally onomatopoeic *wurluk* 'swallow').

Preverbs do not bear coding features (such as number) for grammatical relations such as 'subject.' Plural-actor forms are underlyingly aspectual and denote certain kinds of event structures, not properties of arguments in subject grammatical function. As it happens, the kinds of event structures denoted by plural-actor forms take place typically when a number of instantiations of that event occur together in time and space. This semantic mismatch between coding for grammatical function and coding for predicate aspect is clearly revealed when the corresponding formal mismatch occurs. In (11.13) a plural-actor preverb accepts a singular subject argument:

(11.13)   Baawaard   maa   kanunaaleerri   inja   murlku.
          baawaard   maa   ka=nu-na-aal-eerri   inja   murlku
          ascend.PL   PROG   3a=be-PAST-hither-PROG   3aDEF   boil
          Boils kept on breaking out (all over him).

The subject *inja murlku* 'boil' is inanimate and so has no plural shape (§4.2.1). It also receives singular subject indexation on the verb classifier, as 3a *ka-*. Nevertheless, the fact that reference is being made to a multiplicity of entities is signalled by the form of the preverb. The preverb however does not itself refer directly to a multiplicity of entities; rather it codes the kind of event structure that is found when a number of instances of an event occur together in time and space. In (11.14) a *singular*-actor preverb (*yawak* 'sink down, disappear') accepts a *plural* subject argument:

(11.14)
Maa-maa   dalorr   wali maa,   yawak   barrwa   marru   ke.
maa-maa   dalorr   wali maa   yawak   ba-ngarr=^{b}wa   ma=rru   ke
3mREF-3mREF   sink.hole   PM   sink   CFT-1pin=fall   3m=LAT   3wREF
There's sink-holes over that way, and we might fall down one.

In this case the speaker is suggesting that only one person ('one of us') is likely to fall down a hole, ie, that it is unlikely that they would all fall down sink-holes simultaneously or even one-after-the-other. Again, the fact that reference is being made to a single event is signalled by the shape of the preverb.

11.3.2 Aspect

As well as the aspectual enclitics described in Chapter Ten, an aspectual morpheme -^{b}wa 'PROGRESSIVE' occurs as a suffix on preverbs. Its semantic range appears to be quite broad; Love (1934:108, 1939b:45) refers to its function as 'frequentative,' and in some of its occurrences it does seem to denote iterative aspect, as in *rdeyi* 'gash, smash open' and *rdeba* (< //rdeyi-^{b}wa//) 'smash repeatedly, smash a number of things open, go along smashing things open' as seen in (11.15b) below; but such instances seem usually to result from the semantics inherent in the base or underived form. The essentially progressive, rather than iterative denotation of -^{b}wa can be seen in (11.15a), a description of the setting sun, a continuous, uninterrupted event. In this example continuous aspect marking on both preverb and classifier is used to depict the gradual nature of the event.

(11.15a)
Yarriba   nyimnyawanangurreerri.
yarriy-ᵇwa   nyiN-mnya=ᵇwa-na-ngurru-eerri
descend-PROG   3f-DD=fall-TNS-away-PROG
It (the sun) was going down.

(b)
Wali maa	rdeyi-rdeyi	kumbunerri,	rdeba	maa
wali maa	rdeyi-redyi	kuN-Ø=ᵇwu-na-eerri	rdeyi-ᵇwa	maa
CONT	crack-crack	3w-3=hit-PAST-PROG	crack-PROG	PROG

nyengerri.
nya=ya-nga-eerri
3f=go-TNS-PROG
She was going along cracking them (celestial (oysters)) open as she went.

The word *maa* 'PROGRESSIVE' may signal progressive or extended aspect when it occurs after a preverb; examples of this use may be seen in (11.11b, 11.13) and (11.15b). *Maa* may also perform this function after finite verbs (example 11.6), after *kaarri* '3pNEG' (11.47b) and after some adverbs, such as *wali* 'yet, still' (examples 11.14, 11.15b) and after *jaa* 'PERFECTIVE.' The use in the same sentence of *maa* as a continuous aspect adverb after *wali* 'still,' and again after the preverb *rdeba* 'cracking, gashing' is shown in (11.15b).

The other kind of aspect-marking evidenced by preverbs is reduplication. Here there is stronger evidence that iteration is at least a part of the semantics of reduplicated forms. Reduplication is iconic of multiple instantiations of an event, that is to say that it is a form that lends itself naturally to iterative interpretation, as the following examples show:

(11.16a)
Manab-manab	bamarroyeerri	ajakarri	arrkanangkaya
manab-manab	ba-ma-rra–ᵇwu-yeerri	arr=yakarri	arr=ᵏwa-nangka-ya
steal-steal	CFT-VCOMP-2p=hit-PROG	3p=other	3p=NAR-DAT-3p

mangarri.
food
Don't go round stealing other people's food.

(b)
Mana-mana	kaard-kaard	kanunaarndeerri	mana	ngalarram,
mana-mana	kaard-kaard	ka=nu-na-aarndu-eerri	mana	ngalarram
3mDEF-REDUP	break.off-REDUP	3a=be-PAST-DU-PROG	3mDEF	long.grass

jinalya	warndi-warndi	kanunaarndeerri.
jinalya	warndi-warndi	ka=nu-na-aarndu-eerri
spear	make-make	3a=be-PAST-DU-PROG

Here's where they've been breaking off stalks of long grass and making toy spears.

(c)
Marno	ngarreyu	kuloorrkunya	jurujuru	ngarranoorri.
ma=rno	ngarr-a=ya	kuloorr-ᵏwunya	juruk-juruk	ngarr-a=nu-oorri
3m=DIST	1pin-OPT=go	water.lily-PURP	dive-dive	1pin-OPT=be-NUM

Let's all go and dive for water-lily roots.

Example (11.16c) demonstrates very nicely the underlying and essentially iterative nature of plural-actor aspect marking. Diving for water-lily roots (an esteemed food source) was an activity typically undertaken by women in groups, and invariably requiring a number of dives in order to bring up enough material to make the activity worthwhile. So here we can see an event being depicted as being performed by a number of actors who perform it iteratively, with the reduplicated form of the preverb serving to denote both plural-actor and iterative senses of this form of aspect marking.

However reduplication may also signal simply the extension of an event over a prolonged period of time (extended progressive aspect), as in English 'he ran and ran,' or 'she cried and cried.' Or it may simply signal continuous aspect, in which case there may be no semantic difference discernable between reduplicated forms and forms suffixed with -^{b}*wa* 'PROG.' For example the preverb *marnuk* 'lift' has a reduplicated form *marnu-marnu* and a suffixed form *marnowa*, both coding continuous aspect and both translatable as 'carry.' Moreover these forms appear to be interchangeable:

(11.17)
Wiyanu	marnu-marnu/marnowa	kunyajingeerringkurri
wiyanu	marnu-marnu/marnowa	kuN-nyarr=yi-ng-eerri-^{k}wurri
fire	carry/carry	VCOMP-1px=do-PAST-PROG-NUM

anja wangaya.
3pDEF women
We used to go and get firewood with the women.

In Worrorra, then, the reduplication of preverbs may signal (i) continuous aspect, (ii) extended progressive aspect, (iii) iteration or (iv) plural actors, depending upon context and more particularly upon the *Aktionsart* properties of the lexeme in question.

In observing the semantics of preverbal aspect it is useful to note the various forms of *kayal* 'hold hands.' The base form is combined with (conjugated with) the classifier =*ma* 'get' in a predicate meaning 'take (someone) by the hand, hold (someone's) hand.' Other shapes of *kayal*, bearing aspectual morphologies, combine with =^{k}*wangurru* 'carry,' which encodes the semantics of controlled or accompanying motion. So *kayalwa* =^{k}*wangurru* 'go along holding hands, hold hands while going along:'

(11.18)
Kengurraarndeerri	kayalwa	kaanbarrkangurrurlerri
ka=ya-nga-ngurru-aarndu-eerri	kayal-^{b}wa	kaarr-n-^{b}warr=^{k}wangurru-rla-eerri
3a=go-TNS-away-DU-PROG	hold.hands-PROG	3p-INV-3p=carry-PAST-PROG

anja wangalaalunguyu.
3pDEF children
They both went on, leading their children by their hands.

The base shape when reduplicated yields a form which may denote multiple instantiations of events in which people hold hands, such as occurs in the description of habitual or characteristic events:

(11.19)
Kenyini	malka	ajanaarndeerri,	karle	kayalkayal
ke-nyini	malka	arr-nya=nu-aarndu-eerri	karle	kayal-kayal
and-ENDPOINT	play	1px-EP=be-DU-PROG	then	hold.hand-hold.hand

ngankangurrurlu.
nga-n-Ø=^{k}wangurru-rla
1-INV-3-carry-PAST
Then she always used to play with me, and she would hold my hand wherever we went.

Alternatively the reduplicated shape may denote an event in which people keep on going along holding hands for an extended period:

(11.20)
'Kadaada binjiyeerri wali, dambeem mara
kadaada ba-kuN-nja=yi-eerri wali dambeem mara
tired CFT-VCOMP-2=do-PROG PERF place see

marrwaarndu,' kunjunganangka ngawanangka.
ma-ngarr=ᵇwu-aarndu kuN-Ø=yi-ng-a-nangka ngawa-nangka
3m-1pin=hit-DU VCOMP-3=do-PAST-EP-DAT el.sib-DAT

Kayalkayalwa kaangurrurlerri wali.
kayal-kayal-ᵇwa ka-Ø=ᵏwangurru-rla-eerri wali
hold.hand-hold.hand-PROG 3a-3=carry-PAST-PROG PERF
'Don't get tired, let's find our way home,' said his elder brother. He held his hand as they travelled along.

The precise reference of the kind of aspect denoted by reduplication is largely dependent upon the particular semantics of the lexeme involved. The reduplicated shape of *aja* 'sit, stay' is *ajaaja* 'dwell, inhabit, abide' not with reference to a single, extended, prolonged period of sitting, but to multiple, habitual instantiations of an act that is culturally constitutive of residence. The reduplicated form of *minjarl* 'eat' may refer to a number of instantiations of the event (ie a plural-actor interpretation) or to a temporally extended event, that is to the consumption of a meal rather than a snack. *Warnda* 'make camp' is typically a collective activity in Worrorra society, but the reduplicated forms (see below) refer to one or two people camping for an extended period of time. In reduplicated forms some degree of phonological alteration often occurs. The first phoneme of the (non-reduplicated) original may be altered under reduplication, as in (a), or the final phoneme of the original may be omitted from either or both reduplicated morphemes (b):

(a)	joli	*return*	joliyoli
	yurr	*pull*	jujurr
	aja	*sit*	ajaaja
	jo	*drink*	joyo
(b)	brrak	*wake up*	brrabrra
	juruk	*dive*	jurujuru
	baay	*climb*	baabaay
	daay	*pierce*	daadaay
	blaai	*pound*	blaablaai
	marnuk	*lift*	marnumarnu

A few preverbs exhibit alternative reduplicated shapes; one form showing a degree of phonological accommodation between the component morphemes, while the other does not:

jurro	*smoke (intr)*	jurrojurro,	jurroyurro
malka	*play*	malkamalka,	malkalka
wala	*cry*	walawala,	walaala
warnda	*camp*	warndawarnda,	warndaarnda

There is some evidence to suggest the possibility that the more blended shapes on the right might refer to multiple concurrent instantiations of an event while the unblended forms refer to multiple consecutive instantiations, however this is not certain. It is more likely that these are simply variant forms of reduplication, determined probably by speed of utterance. Example (11.21) seems to have caught the speaker in the process of selecting between synonymous alternatives:

(11.21)   Walawala   nyimnyanu,   walaala   nyimnyanu.
            wala-wala   nyiN-mnya=nu   wala-wala   nyiN-mnya=nu
            cry-cry   3f-DD=be   cry-cry   3f-DD=be
            She cried and cried.

Aspect is registered upon preverbs independently of its registration upon the classifiers with which they are conjugated. An event may be denoted as the punctual performance of a (punctual or progressive) act, or the progressive performance of such an act. These possibilities are illustrated below in the examples in (11.22) with the preverb *buluk* 'look for' and the classifier =*murrka* 'go (telic),' and the continuous preverbal shape *buluba* 'look for' and its classifiers =*ya* 'go' and =*nganyarro* 'look for.' In (11.22a) both preverb and classifier are unmarked for aspect, that is, they are both interpreted as punctual forms, and in (11.22b) an unmarked preverb is combined with a classifier marked for continuous aspect. In (11.22c) a preverb marked for progressive aspect is combined with a punctual-form classifier, and in (11.22d) both preverb and classifier are marked for progressive aspect.

(11.22a) (PUNCT - PUNCT)
Mee   ngunju   angujabirri   buluk   kanjamurrka   wunu?
mee   ngunju   angujabirri   buluk   ka-nja=murrka   wunu
I.don't.know   you   why   seek   3a-2=go.to   3wDEF
Why the hell did you have to go and look for him?

(b)   (PUNCT - CONT)
Wali   buluk   kaangamurrkerri!
wali   buluk   kaarr-nga=murrka-eerri
PERF   seek   3p-1=go.to-PROG
I'm still looking for them!

(c)   (CONT - PUNCT)
Kengerri   buluba   kenga   ajakekarri.
ka=ya-nga-eerri   buluk-ᵇwa   ka=ya-nga   arr=ya-ke-karri
3a=go-TNS-PROG   seek-PROG   3a=go-TNS   3p=↳-AUG-other
He set off to go and look for all the others.

(d)   (CONT - CONT)
Kaajengerri   buluba   kubarrkanyarronerri.
kaarr-nya=ya-nga-eeri   buluk-ᵇwa   kuN-ᵇwarr=nganyarro-na-eerri
3p-EP=go-TNS-PROG   seek-PROG   3w-3p=seek-PAST-PROG
They set out to go looking for it.

The reduplicated form of the preverb, *bulubuluba* 'look around for' denotes extended progressive aspect, and it, too, may be combined with classifiers either marked or unmarked for continuous aspect, as in (11.23).

(11.23a)   Bulubuluba   kaarringerri   mangarriwunya.
            buluk-buluk-ᵇwa   kaarr=i-nga-eerri   mangarri-ᵏwunya
            seek-seek-PROG   3p=go-TNS-PROG   food-PURP
            They were looking around for some food.

(b)   Ngeewunya wali bulubuluba arreyu.
        ngee-ᵏwunya wali buluk-buluk-ᵇwa arr-a=ya
        honey-PURP PERF seek-seek-PROG 1px-OPT=go
        We'll have a look around for some honey.

As mentioned, preverbs constitute the only lexical category whose members are able to end in /y/ (realized as [ç] word-finally, §2.5) or /k/, and they do so in significant numbers. There is a small amount of evidence that the phoneme /k/ at the end of a preverb may actively signal punctual aspect (as opposed to punctual being the default, ie, 'no aspect' category): the preverb *aja* 'sit' may also occur as *ajak* 'sit down abruptly.' This is however the only example of a productive or ideophonic use of /k/ in this setting that I have encountered.

11.3.3 Derived preverbs

As already discussed in §5.1, a number of different lexical categories may appear in preverbal position in complex predications. When material of this sort loses morphology that it would normally have, or when it accepts a typically preverbal morphology, we are justified in treating it as preverbal by derivation. Sometimes it is apparent from their syntax that words in preverbal position are functioning as derived preverbs, as is the noun *bijaku wunu* 'smoke' in (11.24), here conjugated with the transitive pro-verb =ᵇ*wu* 'hit:'

(11.24)   Bijaku kaanbuna.
             bijaku kaarr-n-Ø=ᵇwu-na
             smoke 3p-INV-3=hit-PAST
             She smoked them. (Ritual context)

The English verbs *work'm* and *lose'm* in (11.31a) and (11.31b) are preverbs derived syntactically, in just the same manner as the noun in (11.24). In (11.25) below, the terrestrial nouns *kulum mana* 'hot sand out of a fire, used to roast vegetables' and *marram mana* 'light' lose their gender marking suffix *(-m(a))* in preverbal position as derived preverbs. In (11.25b) *marruma* takes preverbal aspect-marking as well:

(11.25a)   Mana dambeem kulu ingkamangaarndu.
(=5.7)   mana dambeem kulu i-[Ø]-ngka=ma-nga-[aarndu]
             3mDEF place hot.sand 3a-[3]-SJTV=get-PAST-[DU_A]
             The place where they burned him with hot sand.

(b)   Marrawa nyenga.
        marra-ᵇwa nya=ya-nga
        light-PROG 3f=go-TNS
        She went about with a torch.

Predicate adjectives may also lose gender-marking affixes in preverbal position, as does the adjective *birdeen* in (11.26), which would otherwise take masculine gender marking (|birdeen-ya| [small-3a] > *birdeenja*) in agreement with the subject of the verb:

(11.26)   birdeen bangkaninya.
(=8.27c)   birdeen ba-ka=ni-nya
             small CFT-3a=be-PAST
             He should have been small.

Agreement-class indexation may also be lost from an adjective in predicate position when it functions as a preverb. Compare example (5.2) where the predicate adjective =*murlooku* 'well, healthy' takes an agreement-class prefix, with (11.27) where the adjective =*warr* 'wrong, bad' appears without any derivational affixation at all. In this syntax =*warr* is conjugated with =*ᵇwa* 'fall' to produce a predicate meaning 'look/appear wrong:'

(11.27)   Mana   warr   mawanerri   dambeem   mana.
          mana   warr   ma=ᵇwa-na-eerri   dambeem   mana
          3mDEF   wrong   3m=fall-TNS-PROG   place   3mDEF
          This place here doesn't look right.

Adverbs are the category most easily converted to use as preverbs. The word *wajulu* 'close' has in most of its occurrences a clearly adverbial syntax (see also ex. (5.4)):

(11.28)
Diyam   mamanga,   wajulu   maarndenga   awarnanya.
rdiyam   ma-Ø=ma-nga   wajulu   ma-Ø=ᵏwarnde-nga   awa-rnanya
fighting.club   3m-3=get-PAST   close   3m-3=place-PAST   3aNAR-LOC
He got his fighting-club and put it close by him.

But *wajulu* may also be used as a preverb, and in this role it is conjugated with =*ma* 'get' in transitive predicates:

(11.29)   Maaji-maaji   wajulba   angarrbaarndeerri.
          maaji-maaji   wajul-ᵇwa   arr-ngarr=ma-aarndu-eerri
          had.better-REDUP   close-PROG   3p-1pin=get-DU-PROG
          We'd better get up closer to them.

Even a directional marker such as -*ngurru* 'away', normally confined to verbal order class [10], may enter service as a preverb:

(11.30)
Kayal   kamangaarndu   ngurruba   kaankangurrurlu.
kayal   ka-Ø=ma-nga-aarndu   ngurru-ᵇwa   kaarr-n-Ø=ᵏwangurru-rla
hold.hand   3a-3=get-PAST-DU   away-PROG   3p-INV-3=take-PAST
She took them by the hand and led them away.

More commonly, the morpheme *ngurru* would be suffixed to the finite verb in this kind of sentence: *kaankangurrurlungurru* (//kaarr-n-Ø=ᵏwangurru-rla-ngurru// [3p-INV-3=take-PAST-away]). The alternation occurs presumably in response to requirements of a discourse-pragmatic nature, such as focus.

Preverbs exhibiting aspect-marking morphology often select different classifiers to combine with, than they do when in punctual or 'base' form. Table 11.2 below lists some frequently-occurring preverbs with the classifiers they most commonly combine with. This display shows the different classifier-selection requirements of a number of preverbs according to whether or not they bear aspectual morphology. This phenomenon raises the question of the nature of the process that results in complex predicates. It will be argued in the following section that predicates of the type listed below arise out of processes that are lexical rather than syntactic. Except in certain productive combinations discussed in §11.4.2, the set of classifiers with which a preverb is conjugated must be listed with that preverb as part of its entry in the lexicon. The varying selection requirements displayed by the preverbs in Table 11.2 give evidence that the aspectual and non-aspectual shapes of preverbs have different lexical specifications, that is to say that they have separate lexical entries. This in turn means that aspect marking on preverbs is a derivational rather than an inflexional process: aspectual morphology in this instance derives new lexical entries.

Table 11.2: aspect and conjugation

BASE-FORM PREVERB	DERIVED PREVERB
baa *'ascend,'* =ya *'go'*	baawaa(rd) kuN[ ]=yi *'do'*
baay *'climb,'* =nu *'be'* / =ya *'go'*	baawaa(rd) kuN[ ]=yi *'do'*
jiley *'carry on shoulder'* =ma *'get'*	jileba =ya *'go'* / =ᵏwangurru *'carry'*
jandu *'perform'* =ma *'get'*	jandu-jandu *'mock'* =rnaarna *'await'*
jarriy *'run'* kuN[ ]=ma *'get'*	jarriba =ya *'go'*
jo *'drink'* =ya *'go'*	joyo =nu *'be'* / kuN[ ]=yi *'do'*
joli *'return'* =nu *'be'*	joliyoli kuN[ ]=yi *'do'*
kayal *'hold hands'* =ma *'get'*	kayalwa =ᵏwangurru *'carry'*
marnuk *'lift'* =ma *'get'*	marnu-marnu *'carry'* kuN[ ]=yi *'do'*
minjarl *'eat'* kuN[ ]=yi *'do'*	minjarl-minjarl =nu *'be'*
rduwiy *'camp out'* =nu *'be'*	rduwiba =ya *'go'*
wala *'cry'* kuN[ ]=yi *'do'* / =nu *'be'*	walaawirri =nu *'be'*
yala *'hunt'* =nu *'be'*	yalaba/yalabaa kuN[ ]=yi *'do'*
yarriy *'descend'* =ᵇwa *'fall'*	yarriba/yarribaa kuN[ ]=yi *'do'*
yawak/yawurlak *'sink'* =ᵇwa *'fall'*	yawarrarra kuN[ ]=yi *'do'*
yorr *'sit togther'* =ᵇwa *'fall'*	yorryorr =nu *'be'*

A direct consequence of derivations of this nature is that most complex predicates containing the preverbs listed in Table 11.2 exhibit alternations in argument structure along active/agentive or 'split S' lines (Mithun 1991). The underived or base forms of *baa* 'appear,' *baay* 'climb,' *jo* 'drink,' *joli* 'return,' *yala* 'go hunting,' *yarriy* 'descend' and *yawak* 'sink' are all conjugated with intransitive verb classifiers, and so require subjects in S grammatical function. Their derived aspectual forms however are characteristically conjugated with transitive classifiers and so require agentive (A) subjects. For the preverbs *minjarl* 'eat,' *jiley* 'carry (something) slung over one's shoulder' and *jarriy*, 'run,' the opposite situation holds: the base forms are typically conjugated with transitive classifiers and take agentive subjects, while the aspectual forms are conjugated with intransitive classifiers and take S subjects. Again this should perhaps not be surprising: as lexically derived forms, the preverbs in the right-hand column of Table 11.2 strictly speaking do not exhibit aspectual properties at all, but rather *Aktionsart* (lexically aspectual) properties. And it is semantic alternations of just this sort that motivate active/agentive (split S) alignment systems in other languages that exhibit them (Mithun 1991:512-514).

11.4 Lexical status of complex predicates

Worrorra complex predicates may be described by reference to two grammatical parameters: their lexical status and their syntactic structure. In this section I will examine evidence for the lexical status of complex predicates, and in the following section (§11.5), that for their structural make-up.

11.4.1 Verb classifiers

At the beginning of this chapter it was noted that inflecting verbs in complex predicates serve to situate preverbs contextually within the semantic range of one of a set of generalizing lexemes. Inflecting verbs contribute a very abstract semantics to the predicates they take part in, and are essentially generalizing lexemes. In fact their semantics are so schematic that most inflecting verbs differentiate transitivity, motion, control and telicity, but not much more (see Table 11.3 below). It is this generalizing property in the majority of instances of their use that led Dixon (1976:13, 1982:225) to characterize these forms in northern Australia generally as classifying forms. Silverstein (1986) has applied this characterization to Worrorra inflecting verbs specifically:

the different [preverbs] select particular fixed and restricted sets of auxiliaries (from one to about three at most) as the range of possibilities for inflection. This means ... that in effect Worora ... [has] a system of verb classifiers. (1986:497)

In Worrorra, verb classifiers are the superordinate lexemes in a taxonomy of verbal reference (Silverstein *ibid*); in any particular instance of use they characterize their preverbs in terms of their sense meaning, as being one of this or that kind of event. So *wok* 'cook,' *kurdey* 'ask' and *kurleen* 'give birth' are all emically =^b*wu* 'hit [impact]' kinds of events; *marnuk* 'lift,' *yaarn* 'look for' and *mariny* 'gut' are all emically =*ma* 'get [centripetal]' kinds of events; *rok* 'bury,' *marneen* 'hang up' and *wamara* 'cover' are all =*ee* 'put [centrifugal]' kinds of events, and *krewa* 'walk awkwardly,' *darak* 'enter' and *wunurr* 'beg' are all =*ya* 'go [atelic motion]' kinds of events.

In Silverstein's view Worrorra verb classifiers are treated as the analogues of noun classifiers. In particular, an analogy is drawn between the mensural classification of nouns and the denotation of verbal aspect, as both code the kinds of intervals, 'lumps' or 'bits' in which a given (temporal or substantial) denotatum occurs. A further analogy is drawn between the sortal classification of nouns, and different types of predicate argument structure and predicate perspective (Silverstein 1986:511-512). While classifiers do register a general distinction between formally transitive and intransitive predicates, these formal coding features are only imperfectly matched up to verbal semantics. For example, some etically transitive preverbs such as *rdiwurl* 'kill (for food, as game)' are conjugated with intransitive classifiers (in this case with =*nu* 'be'), and some etically intransitive preverbs such as *braarr* 'be illuminated' may be conjugated with the formally transitive classifier *kuN[ ]=yi* 'do' (but see §11.5.2). Many classifiers fail to register argument structure altogether, for instance the predicate *minjarl kuN[ ]=yi* 'eat' may take an object (such as *mangarri* 'food'), but such an object is not indexed on the classifier. When third arguments are indexed on classifiers they appear as indirect objects in order class [11]. Worrorra verb classifiers and their component semantics are displayed in Table 11.3. The translations provided there are those of the verbs when used in simplex situations.

Table 11.3: verb classifiers

```
                    GENERAL
                    kuN[ ]=yi 'do'
           ┌────────────────────────────┐
           transitive           intransitive
           =ᵇwu 'hit'            =nu 'be' INCHOATIVE
      A    │                     │
           │                     MOTION
           CONTROL               =ᵇwa 'fall' (telic)
           =ma 'pick up' (centripetal)    =ya 'go' (atelic)

           =ee 'put down' (centrifugal)
           │
           MOTION
      B    =murrka 'go to' (telic)
           =yabu 'throw' (atelic)
           │
           CONTROLLED MOTION (accompanying motion)
           =ᵏwangurru 'carry'

      C    =rnaarna 'wait for'  =ᵏwana 'hold,'  =yora (1) 'seek,' (2) 'hate'

      D    =mra 'gather, collect,'  =yoolee 'go, travel'
```

It should be understood that preverbs co-occur with finite verbs in a variety of different syntactic arrangements, leaving it an open question as to which of these arrangements qualify as 'complex predicates' of the sort that might contain 'classifiers' as opposed to some other functional manifestation of the finite verb. In some of the syntactic arrangements in which preverbs and finite verbs are combined, it will be seen that inflecting verbs cannot be characterized as classifiers, even in broad terms (cf eg (11.11b)). Therefore the characterization of inflecting verbs in Worrorra as classifiers in any given construction will be contingent upon the particular syntactic environment in which the preverb and inflecting verb are linked. By and large, however (but see §11.4.2), the forms listed in Table 11.3 *do* function as classifiers. The reasons for the distinction between classifying and non-classifying predicates are discussed below, and predicate linkage in general is examined in §11.5.

The classifiers in Table 11.3 are divided into four groups, labelled A, B, C and D. These groups reflect the number of preverbs with which the verbs in them are found to combine in the Worrorra database. There can be no doubt that this database represents a far from complete picture of traditional language use; nevertheless the patterns evident in it are indicative of tendencies that in all probability and to a greater or lesser extent must reflect the traditional language-use situation. In this case the pattern is so stark that it may be assumed that the database really does contain a reflection of traditional usage, even if the pattern to emerge from a more complete corpus might be less well defined. The six classifiers in group A each combine with between 60 and 100 preverbs in the database, while the four in group B each combine with between 10 and 15. The ten classifiers in groups A and B constitute a classificatory system that characterizes complex predicates according to the semantics of transitivity, motion and control. Together the members of groups A and B define a semantic partitioning structure for verbal predication that accounts for the overwhelming majority of predicates, and constitutes the language's most important set of classifiers.

Both transitive and intransitive classifiers may denote motion, and motion is in turn categorized according to telicity. Transitive predicates also encode control in the form of prototypical verbs of manipulation; =*ma* 'get, take, pick (something) up,' or as Love (1934:91) puts it with characteristic perspicacity, 'a movement of the hands towards the body.' The complementary kind of manipulation is denoted by =*ee* 'place, set, lay (something) down.' These types of manipulation may be characterized as centripetal and centrifugal respectively. Because they most typically describe an actor's control over objects, they are employed in predicates involving control and causation generally. One transitive classifier, =^{k}*wangurru* 'carry, take' combines motion and control together in a form that denotes accompanying or controlled motion.[71]

The componential analysis of classifier semantics suggested in Table 11.3 is constrained by a high degree of metaphor and metonymy in classifier selection. The semantic relation between preverb and finite verb can be absolutely clear, as in the case of the synonymous relationships in (11.22d) and (11.31c) through to almost completely opaque, as for example is the case for the preverb *nguru* 'hear, listen, understand' when conjugated with =^{k}*wangurru* 'carry, [accompanying motion].' In this instance it may be that hearing is typically conceived of as listening to speech, in which case the speaker and hearer are mutually engaged ('structurally coupled' in Maturana & Varela's (1987) terms) in an act in which the speaker 'leads' the listener through a narrative, and the listener 'accompanies' the speaker through his or her depiction of a logically connected sequence of internal states or memories (as when in English the listener tells the speaker 'I'm with you' meaning 'I understand'). Be that as it may, the classifier in this instance encodes only the relatively skeletal semantics of accompanying motion.

The classifiers in group C do not participate in the same classificatory system as those in groups A and B. The classifier =*rnaarna* 'wait for' occurs with five preverbs in the database, and its semantic contribution is very opaque indeed. It occurs with *jandu-jandu* 'mock, make fun of, deride' (< *jandu* 'perform'), *jukurl-jukurl* 'be delighted with' (< *jukurl* '(be) happy') and *ngarlingka* 'torment, torture.' These preverbs seem to imply a meaning of something like 'feeling' or 'sensation,' but =*rnaarna* is also found with *kajurd* 'spear' and *low* 'splash.' The classifier =*yora* 'look for' combines with *murn* 'look, gaze' to produce 'scan, search visually,' and possibly in its second (homonymous) sense, meaning

---

[71] =^{k}*wangurru* 'carry' is transparently composed of the pan-Australian verb stem *ka-* 'carry' plus the Worrorra directional -*ngurru* 'away.'

'hate,' it combines with *kungurr* 'stab.' The classifier =^k*wana* 'hold, keep, look after' combines with *wurloo* 'purify ritually by smoke' and with *kurdurdumen* 'chase' (< *kurdu* 'chase').

The classifiers =*yoolee* 'go, travel' and =*mra* 'gather, collect' are quasi-aspectual variants of =*ya* 'go' and =*ma* 'get' respectively, and so have the potential to occur wherever the latter two are found. =*Yoolee* denotes movement in company over a reasonable distance ('walk around from place to place'), and =*mra* is essentially iterative. As variants, their distributional properties are essentially or potentially similar to their corresponding group A classifiers.

11.4.2 Predicate composition

Each preverb appears to be entered in the lexicon with a small set of classifiers that are part of its lexical specification (cf §11.3.3). The set of classifiers associated with a preverb contains from one to about three members, as noted by Silverstein in the quotation above. If a preverb lists more than one classifier in its lexical entry, then those classifiers define the range of sense meanings available to the preverb. For example the preverb *aja* 'sit' may be denoted as a =*nu* 'be [state]' kind of event (SUBJ exists in sitting position); as a =^b*wa* 'fall [telic motion]' kind of event (SUBJ moves into a sitting position); or as an =*ee* 'put [caused]' kind of event (SUBJ causes OBJ to exist in a sitting position). To take another example, the preverb *wala* 'cry' has the classifiers =*nu* 'be' and =*ma* 'get' in its lexical entry. The first, intransitive classifier refers to crying as a state of being, a state into which someone enters for a period of time. While the second, transitive classifier also refers to the state, it refers as well to the reason for that state: the person over whom you are crying is indexed on the classifier in undergoer position, in an inflexional applicative process. Preverbs select classifiers from their lexical entries in a way that appears to be quite analogous to the way in which free morphemes select bound morphemes in language generally; that is to say that morphological rules appear to play a significant part here as elsewhere in the language.

Two and possibly three of the classifiers listed in Table 11.3 do not appear to be part of the lexical entry of any preverb, and in these cases classifier selection is not mandated lexically. Rather, in some contexts preverbs are able to select a default classifier.

The superordinate pro-verb *kuN[ ]=yi* 'do,' although formally transitive, may be combined with any preverb, to compose both transitive and intransitive predicates. This is the general or default classifier, and as will be seen, its default status has a clear pragmatic function. At a lower level in Table 11.3, there is a split between transitive and intransitive classifiers, with =^b*wu* 'hit' the transitive pro-verb, and =*nu* 'be, INCHOATIVE' the intransitive pro-verb. The pro-verbal status of *kuN[ ]=yi* 'do' and =^b*wu* 'hit' is evident from their use with English lexemes:

(11.31a)
Garden	mana	*work'm*	wurri.
garden	mana	*work'm*	^kwuN-rra=yi
garden	3mDEF	work	VCOMP-2p=do

Work in the garden.

(b)
Kekaka	nyangka	nyinjorinya	nyangkem	kulanangka,	*lose'm*
kekaka	nyangka	nyinjorinya	nyangke-m	kula-nangka	*lose'm*
thus	3fNAR	widow	3fREF-?	husband-DAT	lose

ingkona.
i-Ø-ngka=^bwu-na
3a-3-SJTV=hit-PAST

That's the way it was for the widow when she lost her husband.

The subordinated predicate in (11.31b) was rephrased 'correctly' as (11.31c), with the metaphor of atelic motion traditionally employed in the denotation of bereavement:

(11.31c) waay ingkayabuna
waay i-Ø-ngka=yabu-na
throw 3a-3-SJTV=throw-PAST
when she lost him

It is likely that the classifiers *kuN[ ]=yi* 'do,' *=ᵇwu* 'hit' and possibly also *=nu* 'be' can combine with any preverb in context (for another example see (11.24) above), and so are not listed with each preverb individually. It is probably the case that these classifiers are listed elsewhere in the grammar as default selections (ie, as pro-classifiers) for all preverbs, with selection constrained in any instance by the semantics of the preverb. Although I have no clear evidence that *=nu* 'be' is a pro-classifier, this is likely to be the case, if only because of its symmetry with the other two default forms.

11.4.3 Compositional strategies: **buju** *'finish'*

For a more detailed study of how classifiers are associated with preverbs in the lexicon, we can look at the preverb *buju* 'finish,' and note the various ways, and the various argument structures, with which it is conjugated. The semantics of *buju* is quite close to that of its English translation, as 'something ceases to be, something goes out of existence.' Note its unconjugated use as an adverbial imperative:

(11.32) Buju *door!*
Shut the door!

In this case 'door' is understood to include the opening by means of which ingress and egress is effected through a wall, as well as the artefact used to block that opening. The expression in (11.32) is a command that the addressee cause that opening to cease to exist. The following classifiers are listed with *buju* in the lexicon:

=ᵇwu 'hit *(x, y)*'
kuN[ ]=ᵇwu 'hit *(x, V)*'
kuN[ ]=ᵇwu + DAT 'hit *(x, V (y))*'
=yabu 'throw'

Buju can also be conjugated with the general pro-verbal classifiers *kuN[ ]=yi* 'do' and *=nu* 'be,' but I will assume that these are not part of the lexical entry of *buju* because they seem to be able to combine with any preverb in the right context. If this is the case, then only two classifiers are specified for *buju*: *=ᵇwu* 'hit' with a number of argument structures, and *=yabu* 'throw.' Note that in this case *=ᵇwu* is not a default choice, rather it is in this particular instance listed with *buju* as that preverb's main classifier of choice.

The set of classifiers it may occur with defines the range of sense meanings able to be denoted by a preverb. When *kuN[ ]=yi* 'do' is combined with *buju*, the preverb's most general or least precise sense is denoted: 'SUBJ performs an act that results in the extinction of some entity; SUBJ ceases some activity,' as in (11.33):

(11.33)
School	buju	nyarrkunjungu	ke,	dambeenyinim
school	buju	ØN-nyarr-ngun=yi-ng	ke	dambee-nyini-m
school	finish	VCOMP-1px-SJTV=do-PAST	3wREF	place-ENDPOINT-3m

braarr	merrwuna.
braarr	ma-nyarr=ᵇwu-na
clean	3m-1px=hit-PAST

After we'd finished school we swept the grounds.

The classifier =*nu* 'be' brings an inchoative semantics to predicates with *buju*: 'SUBJ becomes nothing, SUBJ ceases to exist, goes out of existence' as in (11.34):

(11.34)
Nyirringkaal!	Minjarl-minjarl	nyirranu	mangarri,	karle
nyirr=i-^{k}waal	minjarl-minjarl	nyirr-a=nu	mangarri	karle
2p=go-hither	eat-eat	2p-OPT=be	food	CHANGE.OF.STATE

buju   kaadingeerri!
buju   kaarr=ni-ng-eerri
finish 3p=be-PRES-PROG
Come on! Come and get some food before it's all gone!

When conjugated with =^{b}*wu* 'hit,' *buju* has a causative sense meaning: 'SUBJ causes OBJ to cease to exist/die:'

(11.35)
Mawa	warrambam	baayje	manuna,	ke	buju
mawa	warrambam	baay-je	ma=nu-na	ke	buju
3mNAR	floodwater	climb-again	3m=be-PAST	and	finish

kaanbuna.
kaarr-n-Ø=^{b}wu-na
3p-INV-3=hit-PAST
The floodwaters rose higher still, and drowned them all.

When *buju* is conjugated with the object-demoting verb *kuN[ ]*=^{b}*wu* (§11.5.2), the sense meaning 'SUBJ ceases some activity' is created:

(11.36)
Kaarrbarrkaweenerri	kaarrweenerri,	ke	buju
kaarr=marrkawee-na-eerri	kaarr=^{b}wee-na-eerri	ke	buju
3p=fight.w.weapons-PAST-PROG	3p=hit.MID-PAST-PROG	and	finish

kubarrwuna.
kuN-^{b}warr=^{b}wu-na
VCOMP-3p=hit-PAST
They were fighting each other with spears and shields,[72] and then they stopped.

The complex predicate *buju kuN[ ]*=^{b}*wu* and predicates like it, with the preverb coded on the classifier in undergoer prefix position, is probably more accurately described as an agentive or S=A ambitransitive predicate (Dixon & Aikhenvald 2000). Nevertheless the alternation between transitive and intransitive uses of such labile predicates in Worrorra involves the demotion or deletion of an object. So here, any such alternation where an object in a transitive clause is deleted or lost in a corresponding (semantically) intransitive clause will be referred to as an 'object-demoting' construction. The object-demoting classifier *kuN[ ]*=^{b}*wu* can be 're-transitivized,' as it were, by the indexation of an indirect or non-subcategorized object (see Chapter 13) (glossed DAT) in suffix position at order class [11]. When this form is combined with *buju*, the resulting predicate appears to have the same meaning as the expression *buju* =^{b}*wu*, ie. 'SUBJ causes OBJ to cease to exist/die:'

---

[72] =*marrkawee* 'fight, skirmish with offensive weapons.'

(11.37) Buju   kubarrwunanangka   wara.
        buju   kuN-ᵇwarr=ᵇwu-na-nangka   wara
        finish   VCOMP-3p=hit-PAST-DAT   kangaroo
        They killed all[73] *the kangaroos.*

The DAT morpheme -*nangka* in this construction indexes the object *wara* 'kangaroo.' The reason for an alternation between the predicates *buju* =ᵇ*wu* and *buju kuN[ ]*=ᵇ*wu+DAT* is treated in §11.5.2 below, and is in all likelihood pragmatic, having to do with foregrounding an object *(buju kuN[ ]*=ᵇ*wu+DAT)* versus backgrounding an object *(buju* =ᵇ*wu)*.

Finally the classifier =*yabu* 'throw' in combination with *buju* creates an idiomatic expression meaning 'SUBJ eats all of [OBJ=food], SUBJ finishes off [OBJ=food],' as shown in (11.38):

(11.38) Bunjuma   waa   buju   bamayabeenya.
        bunjuma   waa   buju   ba-ma-Ø=yabu-yinya
        fig   not   finish   CFT-3m-3=throw-PAST
        He didn't finish off all the figs.

11.4.4 Productive composition

By way of contrast to the above, some complex predicates show preverbs and finite verbs combined in ways that seem to result from processes that are productive rather than lexical. In these cases preverbs appear to select their means of finite realization on semantic grounds. This difference points to an important distinction among complex predicates, between lexical and non-lexical types of composition.

Examples of non-lexical combinations are shown in (11.39) below:

(11.39a) Nyangka   aja   karnaarnarlaarndeerri.
         nyangka   aja   ka-Ø=rnaarna-rla-aarndu-eerri
         3fNAR   sit   3a-3=wait.for-PAST-DU-PROG
         She was sitting waiting for them both.

(b) Jarriba   kamarlaarndorna   inja   wara.
     jarriy-ᵇwa   ka-Ø=marlaarndo-rna   inja   wara
     run-PROG   3a-3=follow-PAST   3aDEF   kangaroo
     He ran after the kangaroo.

(c) Yarriy   kubarrkangurrurlaal   werrim   mana.
     yarriy   kuN-ᵇwarr=ᵏwangurru-rla-aal   werrim   mana
     descend   3w-3p=carry-PAST-hither   hill   3mDEF
     They brought it (celestial) down the hill.

(d) Bariy   imurrkangurru.
     bariy   i=murrka-ngurru
     rise   3a=go.to-away
     Get up and go over to him.

Another example of this type of composition already encountered is the combination of *buluba* 'seek PROG' with =*nganyarro* 'seek' in (11.22d). In these sentences the finite verbs do not have a generalizing

---

[73] *Buju* in this context refers to the extermination of a number of entities, or a mass of entities, hence the plural denotation of *wara* 'kangaroo' in this sentence. The killing of just one or two kangaroos could be referred to by preverbs such as *nguyul* 'strike, kill,' *barda* 'kill,' *kajurd* 'spear' or *rdiwurl* 'kill (as game).'

function, and so may not function as verb classifiers. Instead they are fully lexical – see especially (11.39a), where the verb =*rnaarna* 'wait for' has its full or simplex meaning, which never happens when it occurs in lexical compositions. Far from being lexically bleached, these arrangements are essentially serial constructions; they contain two fully lexical predicates sharing an actor in subject (A in these sentences) grammatical function (cf Nordlinger 2010). This kind of arrangement is discussed further in §11.5.4 (i) below.

This being the case, the inflecting verbs are not functioning here as classifiers: rather they bear finite coding features on behalf of the preverbs which are thereby dependent upon them. Classifiers, then, are found in lexical compositions, but not in non-lexical ones.

The potentially very productive nature of these non-lexical combinations suggests that in principle at least, just about any finite verb in the language could combine with just about any preverb if the appropriate semantic setting were presented. Nevertheless compositions of this sort are reasonably uncommon, most predicates consisting of preverb+classifier combinations that appear to have lexical status.

Worrorra also has a set of causative verbs that take complements in the form of preverbs. These are =*ᵏwanjoo* 'cause,' =*yanda* 'cause' and =*ᵏwarnda* 'set alight.' These verbs push their undergoer arguments onto their preverbal complements, which then appear as the subjects of those complements:

(11.40)   Yawarrarra   kaanjiyandarla.
          yawarrarra   kaarr-nja=yanda-rla
          sink.PL   3p-2=cause-PAST
          You caused them to drown.

In predicates of this sort the classifier's undergoer is interpreted as a preverbal subject. These compositions are discussed further in §11.5.4 (ii).

11.5 Syntactic status of complex predicates

Although complex predication might usually be thought to involve nuclear-level juncture, the linkage types under consideration here may involve juncture at either core or nuclear levels. From the discussion in §11.4 it can be seen that Worrorra preverbs and finite verbs may be combined in a number of different syntactic arrangements.

11.5.1 Headedness

The implications of the classifying status of finite verbs for the syntax of complex predicates are not insignificant. As mentioned previously (§4.1), and as other authors point out (eg Nichols 1986:57, Langacker 1991:165), classifiers are generally the syntactic heads of their phrases. Classifiers 'determine the possibility of occurrence of' a preverb in predicate function, and they determine the kind of arrangement in which a preverb appears.[74] Classifiers code predicate argument structure, tense, aspect, directionality, modality, voice, number and other categories (§5.2), and their encoding makes reference to the entire sentence in which they are found, not just to the finite verb or classifier. So although the preverb is the semantic head of the verb phrase, it is classifier that is the syntactic head, and the verb phrase is the projection of the classifier in syntax. Silverstein (1986:511-512) has remarked of Worrorra classifiers, that 'they are always present as the non-deletable component of the finite verb phrase, even where the lexical verb head of the projection does not occur.' Sentence example (11.41a) shows this phenomenon, where the preverb *kurruk* 'burst forth' is referred to anaphorically by the classifier *maajona*. The sentence that follows also shows a verb classifier used

---

[74] Verbal auxiliaries as well are generally the heads of constructions in which they occur with main verbs.

anaphorically. In (11.41b) the predicate involved is *warnda =nu* 'dwell, inhabit,' which occurs twice. In its second occurrence it is represented anaphorically by its classifier, inflected as *ngarrkunungeerrima*:

(11.41a)
Kurruk	mamnyona,	maajona	belangkarraya;
kurruk	ma-Ø-mnya=ᵇwu-na	ma-ᵇwarr-nya=ᵇwu-na	belangkarra-ya
burst	3m-3-DD=hit-PAST	3m-3p-EP=hit-PAST	everyone-3p

... karle	kurruk	mangkaarrwuna	dambeem.
karle	kurruk	ma-ngka-ᵇwarr=ᵇwu-na	dambeem
... then	burst	3m-SJTV-3p=hit-PAST	place

He burst up, they all did; ... they burst up out of the ground.

(b)
Mana	waa	warnda	baadinyeerri	mana	aalmarangarrim
mana	waa	warnda	ba-kaarr=ni-nya-eerri	mana	aalmara-ngarri-m
3mDEF	not	live	CFT-3p=be-PAST-PROG	3mDEF	European-REL-3m

kajirn	dambeem	ngarrkunungeerrima.
kajirn	dambeem	ngarr-ngun=nu-ng-eerri-ma
like	place	1pin-SJTV=be-PRES-PROG-3m

They didn't use to live in these European-style houses that we live in.

In (11.42a) the masculine undergoer is *manjawarra inja* 'berry sp.,' which does not appear in this particular sequence. The preverb *blaai* 'pound' is conjugated with =ᵇ*wu* 'hit' in its first two occurrences, and then with =*murrka* 'go (transitive, telic motion).' In this last occurrence, the classifier =*murrka* refers to the preverb *blaai* anaphorically:

(11.42a)
Blaai	kawarronerri,	blaai	kawarronerri,
blaai	ka-ᵇwarr-a=ᵇwu-na eerri	blaai	ka-ᵇwarr-a=ᵇwu-na-eerri
pound	3a-3p-EP=hit-PAST-PROG	pound	3a-3p-EP=hit-PAST-PROG

kawarramurrkarla	barlarlonmarnanya	mana	maniyama.
ka-ᵇwarr-a=murrka-rla	barlarlonma-rnanya	mana	ma=niya-m
3a-3p-EP=go.to-PAST	mortar-LOC	3mDEF	3m=good-3m

They pounded it and pounded it, they pounded it up on a good-sized grinding stone.

(b)
Wurrkunu	angujakunya	mara	kumbunaara	malyaama?
wurrkunu	angujakunya	mara	kuN-Ø=ᵇwu-na-aara	malyaama
trouble	what.for	see	3w-3=hit-PAST-1DAT	needlessly

Kubarrwunaara	ngayunyinoo.
kuN-ᵇwarr=ᵇwu-na-aara	ngayu-nyini-oo
3w-3p=hit-PAST-1DAT	I-ENDPOINT-EMPH

What did he have to go and make trouble for me for? They made trouble for me too.

In (11.42b) the predicate *mara =ᵇwu* 'see, find' has the sense 'find, come across,' and the adverb *malyaama* has a sense meaning 'unintentionally, accidentally.' The undergoer of the predicate, *wurrkunu wunu* 'trouble,' is indexed on the classifier as 3w *kuN-*. In the first sentence in (11.42b) the predicate is inflected as *mara kumbunaara* 'he found (trouble) for me.' In the second sentence the predicate occurs as *kubarrwunaara* 'They found (trouble) for me.' In this second sentence the preverb *mara* 'see' is deleted and the classifier substitutes for the predicate as a whole. Another example of this phenomenon may be seen in example (11.49). These examples show classifiers used anaphorically in the same way as the English pro-verb 'do' is used in the translation of (11.41a), and as an auxiliary such as *will* is used in sentences like *he told me not to tell you but I will*. The capacity to function anaphorically in this manner is a defining characteristic of phrasal head words. An important diagnostic of phrasal headedness has to do with the determination of argument structure. As the syntactic heads of their phrases, classifiers bear properties that encode predicate valency; that is to say that the classifier encodes the argument structure of the predicate in which it occurs.

Preverbs are typically conjugated or combined with one or another of a small set of classifiers which are listed with the preverb in the lexicon. In any particular instance of use, one member of the set will be selected, usually with close or not-so-close reference to the semantic features listed in Table 11.3 in §11.4.1 above. Classifier selection is governed by a number of grammatical considerations, not the least of which have to do with valency.

Worrorra preverbs select classifiers with different valencies to achieve a number of different construction types. Unlike what has been proposed for some other Arafuran languages (eg Reid 2000 for Ngan'gityemerri and Schultze-Berndt 2000 for Jaminjung), Worrorra preverbs do not bear valency. As denotative types they are entirely immanent, they depict events without reference to any actor-driven instantiation of those events. Rather, it is the classifier that imparts its valency to the predicate, or, as perhaps more accurately stated by McGregor (2002:266-281), it is the verb class (the 'indexed category'), of which the classifier is the lexicalization or representative, that bears valency. Either way, valency is largely, though not entirely as we shall see in Chapter 13, a property of, and encoded on, the classifier.

As an example of this, it may be interesting to observe the pragmatic motivation underlying the use of the transitive pro-verb =^{b}*wu* 'hit' as a valency-increasing morpheme. One of the commonest reasons for increasing the valency of a predicate is to bring an oblique or peripheral argument into its core. This type of construction is called applicative (cf eg Dixon & Aikhenvald 1997:78, 2000), except that in Worrorra the process is syntactic rather than derivational, as is apparently more often the case elsewhere. The motivations for this choice are essentially similar to those involved in noun–verb compounding or noun incorporation in other languages, which involve pragmatic strategies for foregrounding or backgrounding predicate arguments (Mithun 1984, 1986). For instance Leeding (1996) has described how noun incorporation in Anindilyakwa may denote culturally 'institutionalized' activities (cf in English *hunting for foxes* or *seeking attention*, where the object is chosen at random so to speak, and *fox-hunting* and *attention-seeking*, where the incorporation of the object is indexical of an institutionalized cultural activity).

In order to see how this is accomplished in Worrorra, we may return to a consideration of sentence example (11.16c) in §11.3.2. Note that the noun *kuloorr mana* 'water lily' in that example is a peripheral argument marked as such by the oblique suffix -^{k}*wunya* 'PURPOSIVE' (> *kuloorrkunya* 'for water-lily roots'). The predicate *juruk* =*nu* 'dive' is intransitive, and so its object arguments lie beyond the core and need to be marked by postposition or suffixation. In example (11.43) however, *kuloorr mana* 'water lily' is raised to undergoer status and brought into the core of the predicate *juruk* =^{b}*wu* 'dive.' To achieve this, the transitive pro-verbal classifier (=^{b}*wu* 'hit') is employed as a valency-augmenting device, in order to depict an institutionalized cultural activity:

(11.43)
Juruk	kaadunerri,	kuloorr	maa	juruk	maarrwunerri.
juruk	kaarr=nu-na-eerri	kuloorr	maa	juruk	ma-^{b}warr=^{b}wu-na-eerri
dive	3p=be-PAST-PROG	lily	3mREF	dive	3m-3p=hit-PAST-PROG

They were diving, they were diving for water-lily roots.

Evidence of the core status of *kuloorr* is to be found in its lack of inflexion and in its indexation on the classifier =^{b}*wu* in undergoer position as 3m *ma-*.

Valency augmentation is also available to clarify reference, by providing the facility for a core object argument to be indexed in undergoer position in those cases where its identification would otherwise be ambiguous. As an example of this process we could take note of the preverb *minjarl* 'eat,' conjugated with *kuN[ ]=yi* 'do' to produce an object-demoting predicate, or in derived form as *minjarl-minjarl*, conjugated with *=nu* 'be' to produce an intransitive predicate. The core objects of these predicates can only be identified compositionally, as in (11.44), where the object *kumbiyanu* 'yam *sp.*' occurs right next to the predicate:

(11.44)   Minjarl-minjarl   aduna   kumbiyanu.
          minjarl-minjarl   arr=nu-na   kumbiyanu
          eat-eat   1px=be-PAST   yam.sp
          We used to eat the yams called kumbiyanu.

In more involved constructions such as (11.45), where a full object NP is not available in the immediate vicinity, and where this kind of clarity is therefore not so easily achieved, the use of the transitive pro-verb allows a distant object to be coded as the predicate's undergoer argument:

(11.45)   Nyimnyeendarla   ke   minjarl   nyimnyona.
          nyiN-Ø-mnya=eenda-rla ke   minjarl   nyiN-Ø-mnya=^{b}wu-na
          3f-3-DD=cook-PAST   and   eat   3f-3-DD=hit-PAST
          He cooked her and ate her.

Use of the object-demoting expression *minjarl kunjungu* 'he ate' in this sentence would be as uneasy or as marked in Worrorra as would its counterpart in English: *he cooked her and then he ate*.

Another function of valency augmentation is topic maintenance. Topic chaining in Worrorra commonly takes the form of verb-initial absolutive (S/U) indices recurring in sequence. When this occurs the topic must be kept in S or U grammatical function if a topic shift (a pragmatically marked event) is to be avoided. Valency augmentation is one device available to hold a topic in U function. Take for example the preverb *rdiwurl* 'kill (as game).' This form is conjugated with the classifier *=nu* 'be' in the vast majority of its occurrences, as for example in (11.9) in §11.2.3, and its core objects are identifiable compositionally by being nearly always in immediately pre- or post-verbal position, as in (11.9). If however a speaker wishes to index the object of such a predicate in such a way that its co-referentiality with other indices in a chain is manifest, then the use of the transitive classifier will serve to raise the object to undergoer status, as in (11.46):

(11.46)
Nyangka   **nye**ngerri,   **nyi**mnyengerri,   ke   rdiwurl
nyangka   nya=ya-nga-eerri   nyiN-mnya=ya-nga-eerri   ke   rdiwurl
3fNAR   3f=go-TNS-PROG   3f-DD=go-TNS-PROG   and   kill

nyimbarrwunerri,   jeyi   **nyim**bajamanga   **nyi**na   jimbirrij.
nyiN-^{b}warr=^{b}wu-na-eerri   jey   nyiN-^{b}warr-nya=ma-nga   nyina   jimbirrij
3f-3p=hit-PAST-PROG   spear   3f-3p-EP=get-PAST   3FDEF   giant.groper
She went along, she kept going along, then they killed her, they speared the giant groper.

The speaker's ability to hold the feminine index *nyV(N)-* in verb-initial S/U position ensures that the foregrounded, topical status of the NP *nyina jimbirrij* 'the giant groper' is maintained.

Having reviewed some of the pragmatic motivations involved in the selection of classifiers, it will now be useful to look at the syntactic arrangements that produce the different types of predicate in question.

11.5.2 Nuclear-core subordination

Preverbs frequently function as undergoer (and less frequently subject) arguments of finite verbs. As pointed out in §11.2.3, preverbs, as a lexical category of non-finite denotative types, have something in common with nouns generally. One of their most striking nominal-like attributes is their propensity to function as predicate arguments, that is to be subordinated as arguments of a higher-level matrix predicate. In fact hypotaxis is generally the most characteristic syntax in which preverbs are found.

A preverb used substantively as the object argument of a complex predicate may be postposed to its predicate head, as in (11.47a), for discourse-pragmatic reasons:

(11.47a) Wala kanunerri,   durr kumbu   wala.
          wala ka=nu-na-eerri   durr kuN-Ø=*b*wu   wala
          cry   3a=be-PAST-PROG   stop VCOMP-3=hit   cry
          He was crying, then he stopped crying.

Here in the second clause the preverb *wala* 'cry' is postposed to its predicate head (inner preverb *durr* 'stop' plus classifier *kumbu*), and a stylistically elegant construction is achieved with *wala* at opposite ends of the sentence. In this construction *wala* is a core object argument of *durr kumbu* 'he stopped (it),' and so is not tightly bound to the inner predicate.

Reconsider the situation of the preverb *wala* 'cry' in example (11.11a) in §11.2.3. In that example *wala* 'cry' is again the core object argument of the complex predicate *durr =*b*wu* 'stop, cease (some activity).' And sentence example (11.47b) shows a different instantiation of the same construction:

(11.47b) Kaarri maa   waa   wala   durr   bungkonya.
          kaarri maa   waa   wala   durr   ba-kuN-Ø=*b*wu-nya
          in vain   not   cry   stop   CFT-VCOMP-3=hit-PAST
          He wouldn't stop crying.

This section will progressively outline evidence for an analysis in which this kind of construction involves a double embedding: (i) the preverb *durr* 'stop' is embedded in the classifier =*b*wu 'hit,' and (ii) the preverb *wala* 'cry' is embedded in turn in the complex predicate. This nested structure is shown in (11.47c):

(11.47c) (i)   [[durr] bungkonya]
          (ii) [[[wala] durr] bungkonya]

Bearing in mind the embedded syntactic status of the preverb *wala* 'cry' in the above example, it is now appropriate to turn our attention to the first type of embedding displayed in (11.47c), the embedding of a preverb inside a classifier.

One of the commonest and most revealing predicate syntaxes in Worrorra is an object-demoting construction produced by embedding a bare nucleus (a preverb) into the core of a classifier as the undergoer argument of that classifier. Preverbs have gender (§4.1.3 (iii)); most are celestial, and a few are terrestrial, eg *murn* 'gaze,' *beruk* 'finish a job of work,' *kurruk* 'burst up out of the ground,' *laariy* 'remove a scab from a sore,' *maarli-maarli* 'wave,' *rlaa* 'hold one's hand out to receive something,' and *manab* 'steal' (in (11.16a), indexed on the classifier =*b*wu 'hit' as VCOMP *ma-*). When a preverb is brought into a classifier's core, it is indexed on the classifier in undergoer position; a situation which can be observed in sentence examples (11.33), (11.36) and (11.37) above, where the celestial preverb *buju* is indexed as a 3w undergoer *(kuN-* or *ØN-)* and glossed VCOMP. This construction removes competing NPs from undergoer position and puts there instead a preverb, in this manner embedding the preverb within the classifier. The following examples illustrate exactly how preverbs compete with other nouns for indexation on their classifiers as undergoers. In these sentences the preverb illustrated is *juman* 'proceed along a line, follow a path' which is conjugated with =*ma* 'take, get.'

There is a common Worrorra metaphor of telling a story as procedure along a path. This metaphor is expressed by *juman* and also by *kurdu* 'follow, chase,' both of which have metaphorical as well as literal senses. The metaphor stems underlyingly from a very widespread religious narrative in which mythical (*Lalai* 'Dreaming') ancestors emerge out of the ground at specific places and travel along well-defined routes, creating the landscape as they go. They then either re-enter the earth or turn themselves into various features of the landscape. Religious ceremonies recount the deeds of these ancestors and culture heroes by following their progress in song from place to place along well-defined 'dreaming trails' across the countryside. The preverbs *juman* and *kurdu* therefore have metaphorical senses meaning 'narrate, retell, recount a story in temporal sequence.' In (11.48) the preverb *juman* is used in a literal sense meaning 'proceed along a line,' and in this instance the subject is actually creating the line as a Dreaming ancestor:

(11.48) [U = *mana dambeem* (3m)]
Nyina   dambeem   juman   mangkamanga   jimbirrij   nyangke.
nyina   dambeem   juman   ma-Ø-ngka=ma-nga   jimbirrij   nyangke
3fDEF   place   proceed   3m-3-SJTV=get-PAST groper   3fREF
It was the giant groper who made her way up through the land.

This sentence comes from a text describing the origin of the Prince Regent River. The Prince Regent River follows a long, straight fault line through the north-western Kimberley, and was made in the Worrorra account by an ancestral giant groper *(nyina jimbirrij)* ploughing her way up through the land and creating the channel for the river to run in. In (11.48) the predicate *juman =ma* refers to an act of not only following a line, but actually creating the line, although in the myth, as in most Worrorra myths, the event, and hence the geographical features that record the event, seem to have been in some sense pre-ordained, so that the giant groper really is following a (pre-ordained) line. The predicate's undergoer is *dambeem mana* 'the land,' indexed on the classifier as 3m *ma-*, and signalling the literal sense meaning of the predicate here. The following sentence examples employ the predicate in its metaphorical sense.

(11.49a) [U = *inja joonba* (3a)]
Arrkunumbalja   juman   kawarramanga   inja   joonba.
arr=ᵏwunumbal-ya   juman   ka-ᵇwarr-a=ma-nga inja   joonba
3p=wunumbal-3p   follow   3a-3p-EP=get-PAST 3aDEF   ceremony
Wunumbal people used to enact this ceremony.

(b)   [U = 'her' (3f)]
Arrka   joonbanyini   juman   nyimbarrbanga.
arrka   joonba-nyini   juman   nyiN-ᵇwarr=ma-nga
3pNAR   ceremony-ENDPOINT   follow   3f-3p=get-PAST
Then they performed this ceremony about her.

(c)   [U = *juman* (3w)]
Anja   ardungkuleya   burnarri   nganaya   ke   juman
anja   arr=rnungkule-ya   burnarri   ngana-ya   ke   juman
3pDEF   3p=ancient-3p   birds   PROB-PL   3wREF   follow

kubarrbanga.
kuN-ᵇwarr=ma-nga
VCOMP-3p=get-PAST
In the olden days I think it was the birds who used to tell this story.

In (11.49a) *inja joonba* 'ceremony' is present in the sentence and is the undergoer NP. In (11.49b) *inja joonba* is again a core argument, but it does not receive undergoer treatment. Instead the undergoer position is taken by another core argument, this time a human one (3f). From this we can see that the predicate *juman =ma*, in its metaphorical sense as 'narrate, perform, act out a narrative ceremony,' has three core arguments; an agent (the narrators or performers), a theme (the ceremony) and a topic-referent (who or what the ceremony is about). In (11.49b) we can see that the topic-referent, being typically a human, a deity or a personified animal, outranks the theme for access to undergoer position. In (11.49c) neither theme nor topic-referent arguments are present in the sentence, and the celestial preverb *juman* is indexed on the classifier =*ma* as undergoer. The nominal-like status of *juman* in this sentence is signalled by its co-occurrence with the deictic *ke* '3wREF.' The result is what I will refer to as an *object-demoting construction*, in that although both the core object arguments of *juman =ma* have been removed, this absence of objects is not signalled morphologically, as the classifier still indexes an undergoer. It is clear from this, that there is a hierarchy of accession to undergoer status with this three-place predicate, as follows: (1) animate topic-referent, (2) inanimate theme, (3) preverb. In the absence of (1) and (2), an object-demoting expression is created automatically, by virtue of the syntactic requirement that the transitive classifier *=ma* 'get' must index an undergoer argument.

It is probably the case that most if not all transitive predicates need to refer to a hierarchy of this sort. The terrestrial predicate *murn* 'look, gaze' has *=^{b}wu* 'hit' and *=yora* 'search' listed in its lexical entry for conjugation. The predicate *murn =^{b}wu* 'gaze, look about' may take an NP undergoer, as in (11.50):

(11.50) Nyangka   murn   kaanbuna.
         nyangka   murn   kaarr-n-Ø=^{b}wu-na
         3fNAR   gaze   3p-INV-3=hit-PAST
         She was looking out for them.

Usually, however, the terrestrial preverb *murn* is indexed on the classifier in undergoer position as terrestrial VCOMP *ma-*, and an object-demoting form results, as in (11.51). This construction is available whenever a speaker wishes to demote an object from focus or centre-stage position, and it is very frequently used.

(11.51) Mamangkunu   murn   maarrwuna.
         mamangkunu   murn   ma-^{b}warr=^{b}wu-na
         morning   gaze   VCOMP-3p=hit-PAST
         In the morning they looked all around.

The preverb *kurdu* 'chase, follow' is normally conjugated with *=^{b}wu* 'hit' as in (11.52a), but note how *kuN[ ]=yi* 'do' may be used as a ready-made object-demoting classifier in (11.52b):

(11.52a)
Maniyam   maan   ngana   mana   kurdu   kungoyeerri
ma=niya-m   maan   ngana   mana   kurnu   kuN-nga=^{b}wu-yeerri
3m=good-3m   SPEC   probably   3mDEF   chase   VCOMP-1=hit-PROG

kunjungu.
kuN-Ø=yi-ng
VCOMP-3=do-PAST
He thought this would be a good place to go chasing after it.

(b)
Wunu-wunu   angujakunya   anguja   inja   kurdu   kunjeenga
wunu-wunu   angujakunya   anguja   inja   kurdu   kuN-nja=yi-ng
3wDEF-3wDEF   what.for   something   3aDEF   chase   VCOMP-2-do-PAST

wunu?   Darr   banjamnyeenba   wara   inja!
wunu   darr   ba-ka-nja-mnya=ee-n-ba   wara   inja
3wDEF   stand   CFT-3a-2-DD=place-NON.P-EP   kangaroo   3aDEF
What'd you have to go chasing after that thing for? You should have let the kangaroo go!

In (11.52a & b) the speakers are interested in the actors and their trajectories, and are not at all interested in the objects. Example (11.52a) contains a main clause (*kunjungu* 'he thought') and a complement clause (the rest of the sentence: the third person subject of the complement clause receives formal first person singular marking). Note that the complement clause does not contain an object: the object recoverable from the environment is *inja wara* 'kangaroo.' A more accurate but stilted translation of the complement clause would be, 'a good place in which to perform an act of chasing.' In (11.52b) the object (also a kangaroo) is referred to in the first sentence as *anguja inja* 'that something' as an indicator of its unimportance in the speaker's estimation. It is not indexed in undergoer position, as it is the inconvenience of the addressee's actions, not the fate of the kangaroo that concerns the speaker.

Sentence example (11.53) shows an object-demoting variant of the predicate seen in (11.29); here again the object is deleted as old or given information, against which the gestures and trajectories of the actors are promoted as being more important in this section of discourse:

(11.53)   Wajulu   kumangaalkarndeerri.
           wajulu   kuN-Ø=ma-nga-ᵏwaal-aarndu-eerri
           close   VCOMP-3=get-PAST-hither-DU-PROG
           They (dual) were coming closer.

So far we have seen how object-demotion can be used for pragmatic purposes, that is to alter focus: to shift an object NP out of the foreground of discourse, as in sentence example (11.52b), or to remove object NPs offstage altogether, as in examples (11.51), (11.52a) and (11.53). However object-demotion can have a syntactic discourse function as well, in those situations where there is a clear coding advantage in suppressing an undergoer. Sentence (11.54) may be taken as an example here, showing the relativization of an instrumental argument:

(11.54)
Karrku	wunu	ruluk	kubarrbanga	burr	kaajungu.
karrku	wunu	ruluk	kuN-ᵇwarr=ma-nga	burr	ØN-ngka-ᵇwarr=yi-ng
rock	3wDEF	move	3w-3p=get-PAST	enclose	VCOMP-SJTV-3p=do-PAST

They moved away the rock they'd shut them in with /
They moved away the rock with which they'd shut them in.

In this complex sentence the main clause is *karrku wunu ruluk kubarrbanga* 'they moved (away) the rock.' The undergoer here is *karrku wunu* 'the rock,' indexed on the classifier =*ma* 'get' as 3w *kuN*-. There is also a subjunctive-mood subordinate relative clause, *burr kaajungu* 'they enclosed.' The relative clause is an object-demoting construction which indexes the preverb *burr* 'be enclosed' on the classifier *kuN[ ]=yi* 'do' in undergoer position as ØN- 'VCOMP.' Now the 'problem' for constructions of this sort is how to code the undergoer of the main clause, *karrku wunu* 'the rock,' as the head of the relative clause with an instrumental role interpretation; or put another way, how to give the subordinate clause a relative interpretation, with the matrix undergoer as its head.

The preverb *burr* 'be enclosed' is a state predicate with the same semantic frame as *aja* 'sit,' and although, like *aja*, it can be causativized in conjugation with the classifier =*ee* 'put, place' (§11.5.4 (ii)) (SUBJ cause OBJ to become enclosed), the undergoer of such a construction could only be interpreted as the patient, not as an instrumental NP. The use of such a construction (*burr angkaanbarreerla* 'when they had shut them in') would yield an adverbial subordinate reading of the sentence: 'they moved away the rock after they had shut them in' (see §15.6.1). The only way to relativize a subordinate clause of the type shown in (11.54) and endow it with an instrumental head, is to use an object-demoting construction which leaves the interpretation of headedness open to pragmatic rather than morphological cues. Syntactically, then, the only NPs in the main clause that could be candidates for head-of-relative-clause status are the subject (3p -ᵇwarr- 'they') and the undergoer *karrku wunu* 'the rock.' An interpretation with the main clause subject as relative clause head ('having shut them in, they moved the rock away') does not make sense: the act of shutting them in has already occurred some time previously in the narrative, with a number of events and a good deal of text intervening. The only candidate left is the main clause undergoer, which receives instrumental interpretation by virtue of the real-world, physical properties of its denotatum. Another example of this kind of use of pragmatic implicature for argument coding may be seen in (15.41) in §15.6.3.

Finally, observe the two variants in (11.55), demonstrating the predicate *bloy =ma* 'drop/slip,' with an active, transitive syntax in (11.55a), and the corresponding object-demoting construction in (11.55b):

(11.55a)　　Bloyba　　maa　　kerrbangerri.
　　　　　　bloy-ᵇwa　maa　　ka-nyarr=ma-nga-eerri
　　　　　　drop-PROG　PROG　3a-1px=get-PAST-PROG
　　　　　　We couldn't hold on to him / He kept slipping out of our grasp / We dropped him.

(b)　　　　Bloy　　kumanga.
　　　　　　bloy　　kuN-Ø=ma-nga
　　　　　　slip　　VCOMP-3=get-PAST
　　　　　　S/he slipped.

In dispensing with an object, the construction in (11.55b) acquires a reflexive interpretation, which is completely congruent with the semantics of middle-voicing processes (including antipassivization) generally.[75]

11.5.3 Collocation

This section deals with the commonest, least marked type of predicate syntax in Worrorra, one which McGregor (2002) refers to as collocation. Collocation is the juxtaposition in separate packages of the lexical and grammatical components of a single predicate (*idem:* 266-281). In being collocated with a preverb, a classifier bestows a distinct sense meaning to it. Put another way, classifiers invoke and apply the kinds of valency and vectorial configuration schemata by means of which events are instantiated.

In terms of the role-and-reference typology employed in other sections, collocation represents an instance of nuclear-nuclear subordination; that is, an arrangement where a (preverb) nucleus is embedded as an adverbial modifier of another (classifying) nucleus, so that the two form a compounded nucleus sharing all core and peripheral arguments. Consider the sentences in (11.56):

(11.56a)　　Aja　　nganingeerri.
　　　　　　aja　　nga=nu-ng-eerri
　　　　　　sit　　1=be-PRES-PROG
　　　　　　I'm sitting down.

(b)　　　　Aja　　ngawana.
　　　　　　aja　　nga=ᵇwa-na
　　　　　　sit　　1=fall-TNS
　　　　　　I sat down.

(c)　　　　Kanangkurri　　mara　　kangona.
　　　　　　kanangkurri　　mara　　ka-nga=ᵇwu-na
　　　　　　dog　　　　　　see　　　3a-1=hit-PAST
　　　　　　I saw a dog.

In these examples the preverbs *aja* 'sit' and *mara* 'see' modify the phrasal heads *=nu* 'be,' *=ᵇwa* 'fall' and *=ᵇwu* 'hit.' That this is so, and not the other way around, is evident when we consider the syntactic status of the two elements. As phrasal heads (§11.5.1), the classifiers have their own lexical meaning in simplex constructions: under linkage, this lexical meaning is drastically modified. In contrast, the

---

[75] Also called 'patientive ambitransitive' and 'unaccusative' processes by different writers.

lexical meaning of the preverbs is in no way modified; their status as types of predicate is unaltered, classification affecting only the way in which they are instantiated, eg as atelic states (11.56a) or telic events (11.56b).

In this section however, role-and-reference typology will be suspended in favour of an analysis that highlights the classifying function of finite verbs in Worrorra. The reason for this is that this kind of predicate exhibits formal but only schematic semantic linkage; that is, their formal status as linked predicates is not reflected in their semantics. Rather than being semantically complex, their denotation is of single, simplex events, not even chained in the way that verbs in languages like Kalam are (Pawley 1993). Yet formally they are complex; classifiers may function as simplex verbs in their own right, and most perverbs may combine with more than one classifier. Semantically, then, and in terms of grammatical outcomes, collocation is not really a form of predicate linkage at all: it results in semantically simplex predicates.

In Silverstein's (1986) exposition classifiers are lexicalizations of the intensions of their categories, and as such are overt ('privileged') prototypes for systems of classification generally. By contrast nominal gender systems, for example, are covert; their intensions are not lexicalized and are only discoverable, if at all, by observing the derivational functions of their tokens. If Worrorra complex predicates really do constitute a system of verbal classification, then by Silverstein's account their classifiers should be lexicalizations of the intensional properties of the categories of which they are the superordinate lexemes (see Table 11.4 below). And if this is the case, then at least some of their lexical meanings are likely to be retained under composition. And this is indeed more or less what we find in Worrorra (see Table 11.3 in §11.4.1 above). McGregor (2002:266-281) denies that classifiers have a predicative function, or that complex predicates are semantically complex. Rather, classifiers each invoke a particular kind or class of event, one with a specific valency and image schema ('vectorial configuration' in his exposition). It follows, then, that such languages should have a finite set of verb classes or categories, each headed by a particular classifier. Again, Table 11.3 in effect constitutes a list of verb classes in Worrorra, defined by the valencies and vectorial configurations they exhibit, and headed by a classifier in each case.

This arrangement may be clarified by looking at some examples. Table 11.4 presents nine of the Worrorra verb classes, excluding the universal pro-classifier *kuN[ ]=yi* 'do/say' and the members of sets C and D in Table 11.3. Next to each class is listed a small selection of the preverb members of that class.

Table 11.4: examples of verb classes

VERB CLASS	EXAMPLE MEMBERS
=ᵇwu *'hit'* <BIVALENT>	duk *'hit something and knock it over'*
	durr *'cut'*
	gee *'be represented totemically by OBJ'*
	balya *'visit someone'*
	mara *'see, find'*
=nu *'be'* <MONOVALENT> <INCHOATIVE>	nguru *'hear, listen'*
	keekeey *'peer, peep'*
	imbard *'lie prostrate'*
	bakurl *'miss, pine for someone'*
	burr *'enclose'*
=ᵇwa *'fall'* <MONOVALENT> <TELIC MOTION>	ngurak *'cross over'*
	yala *'hunt'*
	balaj *'(tide) ebb'*
	balyarr *'slip'*
	juward *'jump'*
	darr *'stand'*

VERB CLASS	EXAMPLE MEMBERS
=ya 'go' <MONOVALENT> <ATELIC MOTION>	rdorl 'explode, pop, crack' juward 'jump' marduk 'walk' ruluk 'move' wanga 'be senseless, lost'
=ma 'get' <BIVALENT> <CONTROL> <CENTRIPETAL>	duk 'hit something and knock it over' warrey 'summon' wayarl 'remove' aarl 'cook food in an earth oven' irri 'not want, not like'
=ee 'put, place' <BIVALENT> <CONTROL> <CENTRIFUGAL>	durloo 'set down, lay out, present' marneen 'hang up' darr 'stand' burr 'enclose' duru 'light a fire'
=murrka 'go to OBJ' <BIVALENT> <TELIC MOTION>	balala 'run to meet someone' baraan 'shave head for OBJ in mourning context' bardi 'come home to OBJ' joli 'return to OBJ'
=yabu 'throw' <BIVALENT> <ATELIC MOTION>	burrkay 'enquire' leewurr 'turn aside' warlaai 'turn around' wurluk 'swallow'
=ᵏwangurru 'carry' <BIVALENT> <CONTROL> <MOTION>	nguru 'hear, listen' durloo 'set down, lay out, present' doori 'live with as wife' iyaaw 'tell off' joli 'return'

The right-hand column headed 'example members' represents *categories* or *classes:* a group of preverbs here are all members of a particular class. In the left-hand column the features in angle brackets represent a category's *intension*, some of the things the members all have in common, so to speak. The classifying verb in the left-hand column is the *lexicalization* of this intension, and as such it is also the *superordinate lexeme* for its category. The features listed with each class by no means exhaust the intensional meanings of classes; rather, each set represents a skeletal outline of an intension, constrained by the limits of our experience of the language. Prolonged exposure would inevitably enable us to elaborate on the intensional meanings of Worrorra verb classes.

The most important thing to note about the above list is that class membership is determined emically; there is no point in trying to devise etic explanations for membership. Some allocations may seem fairly clear; experiences such as listening and pining for someone, states such as being enclosed, and stances such as lying prostrate may be recognized as inherently monovalent and inchoative. Likewise hunting, crossing over and the ebbing of the tide are sensibly monovalent telic movements. Yet these characterizations are by no means inevitable; we may imagine why lighting a fire involves a centrifugal schema, but it could perhaps just as easily involve a centripetal one. And it is not at all etically obvious why cooking food in an earth oven involves a centripetal schema.

The second point of note is that preverbs are fairly promiscuous, most being amenable to instantiation in more than one valency and vectorial configuration.

It is instructive to consider collocation along with the second most common type of complex predicate in the language, namely nuclear-core subordination, involving object-demoting constructions (§11.5.2). Pairs of this sort, of the type shown in (11.55), are common, and it is worth considering what kind of process is involved in this alternation. From formal juxtaposition with a classifier (collocation), it would seem that a preverb may enter into a hypotactic relationship with the classifier, appearing in its core as an undergoer argument. Alternations of this sort are common and are pragmatically motivated.

We are now in a position to compare in more detail three common and related types of complex predicate: (i) collocated predicates, (ii) object-demoting (nuclear-core subordinate) predicates and (iii) 're-transitivized' object-demoting constructions, as seen previously in example (11.37). By way of example we may observe the preverb *nguru* 'hear, listen, understand,' first in collocated predicates:

Collocation
(11.57a)   Nguru   banu!
           nguru   ba=nu
           hear   CFT=be
           Listen!

(b)   Nguru   kerrkangurreerri.
           nguru   ka-nyarr=ᵏwangurru-eerri
           hear   3a-1px=carry-PROG
           We're listening to him.

Nuclear-core subordinate (object-demoting)
(c)   Nguru   minyaangurru!
           nguru   minya=ᵏwangurru
           hear   2>3w=carry
           Listen!

Re-transitivized object-demoting construction
(d)   Nguru   kunyajaangudakerri
           nguru   kuN-nyarr-nya=ᵏwangurr(u)-nangka-eerri
           hear   VCOMP-1px-EP=carry-DAT-PROG
           We're listening to him.

Note that the object-demoting construction in (11.57c) is semantically equivalent to the intransitive form in (11.57a). Note also the correlation between the collocated form in (11.57b) and the re-transitivized object-demoting form in (11.57d). In (11.57b) a human participant is indexed on the classifier in undergoer position as 3a *ka-*. In the re-transitivized object-demoting construction, the preverb has usurped the undergoer position on the classifier, and the human argument has been pushed outward into indirect object (DAT) position. As the preverb moves into the classifier's core it dislodges the human object, which is then propelled outward from undergoer position to indirect-object position, in a chain-reaction process.

11.5.4 Serialization

Some complex predicate compositions involve serializations, that is, a pair of connected events rather than a single (complex) event. In predications of this sort the preverb is dependent upon an associated finite verb for operators such as tense, directionality, illocutionary force and modality. Of course the preverb cannot be independently specified for mood; rather the whole composition must be so specified, with the result that the preverb and the finite verb share the same core operators. They also share a core argument, and all peripheral constituents and operators, and so are combined at the core level of juncture. These productive, non-lexical compositions have been touched on in §11.4.4 above.

Serial compositions may be differentiated by reference to the way in which their finite verbs frame the event denoted by the associated preverb. One of the finite verb's arguments will be interpreted as the preverb's subject. This newly-appointed preverbal subject may be co-referential with the finite verb's actor, its undergoer, or with some other object not provided for in the finite verb's lexical entry. This last kind of argument, a non-subcategorized object, is discussed in §13.2.

Preverbs in serialized predicates will be referred to, then, as having subjects that are the same as, or different from that of their associated finite verbs. Different-subject compositions are commonly found in causative constructions.

11.5.4 (i) same-subject serialization

The status of core-level juncture in Worrorra as the syntactic framework most suited to serial constructions is best seen when the finite verb is intransitive; then the finite verb has only one argument, which it shares with its preverb:

(11.58)   Ajakekarri   wulaawa   kaarringa   wiyarnanya.
          arr=ya-ke-karri   wulaa-ᵇwa   kaarr=i-nga   wiyanu-rnanya
          3p-↳-AUG-other   rest-PROG   3p=go-TNS   fire-LOC
          All the others went and lay down by the fire.

When the finite verb is transitive, it shares its actor argument with the preverb. We have already seen some predicates of this type in (11.39) in §11.5.4, and two more are shown below. In (11.59a) the predicate *baay kawarraangurrurlu* is the serial composition:

(11.59a)
Kawarraarndenga   nanjanma.   Baay   kawarraangurrurlu.
ka-warr-a=ᵏwarnde-nga   nanjan-ma   baay   ka-warr-a=ᵏwangurru-rla
3a-3p-EP=place-PAST   fork-EP   climb   3a-3p-EP=carry-PAST
They placed him up in the branches of a tree.⁷⁶ They climbed up there with him.

(b)
Manjumanjungarrim   maa   bariy   kaanmurrkarla   rlarlangkarram.
manju-manju-ngarri-m   maa   bariy   kaarr-n-Ø=murrka-rla rlarlangkarram
wind-wind-REL-3m   3mREF   rise   3p-INV-3=go.to-PAST   sea
The wind blew up and the sea rose up around them.

The composition in (11.59b) is the same as that seen in (11.39d) (*bariy* 'rise'+=*murrka* 'go (tr)'). In these sentences the subject of the preverb (*rlarlangkarram* 'the sea') is co-referential with that of the finite verb.

11.5.4 (ii) different-subject serialization

The subject of a preverb may be co-referential with the undergoer of its associated finite verb, as seen in the examples shown below:

(11.60a)   Awanja   baa   kaangurrurlaal.
           awanja   baa   ka-Ø=ᵏwangurru-rla-aal
           boy   ascend   3a-3=carry-PAST-hither
           He brought (=carried) the boy up.

It could be argued in (11.60a) that the subject of *baa* 'ascend' is ambiguous, since both the boy and the person who carried him ascended. This observation shows up the *ad hoc* nature of the analytical

---

⁷⁶ *Nanjan mana*: 'forked branch of a tree; ladder, step, ledge.'

convenience of ascribing arguments to preverbs: here a carrying-and-ascending event is depicted as involving two actors; pragmatic implicature does the rest.

(11.60b) Kanangkuja   baa   nyirnaarnarlerri.
          kanangkuja   baa   nyiN-Ø=rnaarna-rla-eerri
          bitch   appear   3f-3=wait.for-PAST-PROG
          He was waiting for his dog (feminine) to show up.

This particular syntactic framework is tailor-made, as it were, for causative constructions. We have already seen an example of this in (11.40) in §11.5.4. Some others are shown below in (11.61):

(11.61a) Wangarr   nyinjandarla.
          wangarr   nyiN-Ø=yanda-rla
          forget   3f-3=cause-PAST
          He made her forget.

(b)   Inja   imarumarulya,   yorryorr   ingkaajandarla.
          inja   imaru-marulya   yorr-yorr   i-ngka-ᵇwarr=yanda-rla
          3aDEF   REDUP-round   sit.together-REDUP   3a-SJTV-3p=cause-PAST
          Their round cakes, which they had stacked up all together.

(c)   Jawalaa   kaankanjoona.
          jawalaa   kaarr-n-Ø=ᵏwanjoo-na
          scatter   3p-INV-3=cause-PAST
          He made them scatter.

The control classifiers =*ma* 'get' and =*ee* 'put' occur frequently in serial causative constructions. The transitive pro-classifier =ᵇ*wu* 'hit' may also occur with a causative function in these predicates, as has already been seen with the preverb *buju* 'finish' in (11.35 =11.62):

(11.62)   Buju   kaanbuna.
          buju   kaarr-n-Ø=ᵇwu-na
          finish   3p-INV-3=hit-PAST
          S/he killed them.

The classifier in (11.62) has a causative sense: 'SUBJ cause OBJ to finish/cease to exist,' and so the classifier's undergoer (3p *kaarr-*) is co-referential with the subject of the preverb *buju*.

Other constructions of this sort with the classifier =*ee* 'place, put down' also have causative meaning, as shown in (11.63) below. The preverbs *burr* 'be enclosed,' *aja* 'sit' and *we* 'lie down' are all intransitive state predicates when combined with intransitive classifiers: *aja* and *burr* are conjugated with =*nu* 'be,' and *we* is conjugated with =ᵇ*wa* 'fall' in collocated compositions. In (11.63) they occur with =*ee*:

(11.63a) We   kawarreerla.
          we   ka-ᵇwarr=ee-rla
          lie.down   3a-3p=put-PAST
          They knocked him down. (ie they killed or seriously wounded him)

(b)   Aja   nyeerla.
          aja   nya-Ø=ee-rla
          sit   3f-3=put-PAST
          He sat her down.

(c)   Burr   anbajeerla.
        burr   arr-n-ᵇwarr-nya=ee-rla
        enclose   1px-INV-3p-EP=put-PAST
        They locked us up inside.

The control classifier =*ma* 'get' may also be used causatively, again with preverbs that are otherwise found in intransitive collocated arrangements. The preverbs shown below are *ruluk* 'move,' *barlkarr* 'be offended' and *yangarnay* 'abscond.' *Ruluk* 'move' is conjugated with =*ya* 'go' in collocation, or with *kuN[ ]=yi* 'do' in nuclear-core subordinate predicates:

(11.64a)   Ruluk   bayaara.
            ruluk   ba=ya-aara
            move   CFT=go-1DAT
            Make room for me (move over for me).

(b)   Ruluk   jaal.
        ruluk   ØN=yi-aal
        move   VCOMP=do-hither
        Move over this way.

However it can be causativized (transitivized) by conjugation with =*ma* 'get,' as has already been seen in (11.54 =11.65):

(11.65)   Karrku   wunu   ruluk   kubarrbanga.
            karrku   wunu   ruluk   kuN-ᵇwarr=ma-nga
            rock   3wDEF   move   3w-3p=get-PAST
            They moved away the rock.

The preverb *barlkarr* 'be offended' is conjugated with *kuN[ ]=yi* 'do' in nuclear-core subordination (11.66a), but with =*ma* 'get' in causative constructions (11.66b):

(11.66a)   Barlkarr   kungenga.
            barlkarr   kuN-nga=yi-ng
            offended   VCOMP-1=do-PAST
            I was offended.

(b)   Barlkarr   nganmanga.
        barlkarr   nga-n-Ø=ma-nga
        offended   1-INV-3=get-PAST
        He offended me.

When the preverb *yangarnay*, which means something like 'disappear' or 'abscond,' is collocated with =ᵇ*wa* 'fall,' it forms a complex predicate meaning 'escape' (11.67a). When causativized with =*ma* 'get' in serial constructions, it forms a predicate meaning 'steal,' as in (11.67b):

(11.67a)   Ininjaarndeerri   yangarnay   bangkawaardu.
            i=ninja-aarndu-eerri   yangarnay   ba-ka=ᵇwa-aarndu
            3a=watch-DU-PROG   abscond   CFT-3a=fall-DU
            Watch them so they don't escape.

(b)   Koorlangi   aaya   yangarnay   kamangaarndu.
        koorlangi   aaya   yangarnay   ka-[Ø]=ma-nga-[aarndu]
        berry.sp   3aREF   abscond   3a-[3]=get-PAST-[DU$_A$]

They have stolen the koorlangi *berries.*

11.5.4 (iii) demoted-object serialization

Non-subcategorized objects are indexed upon verbs in order class [11], and are here glossed by the mnemonic DAT. They are essentially object arguments outranked for undergoer status by some other argument, or the undergoer arguments of formally intransitive verbs, where there is no site for their indexation in undergoer position (see §13.2).

The subjects of preverbs in serial constructions may be co-referential with NPs indexed on the finite verb in order class [11] as non-subcategorized object arguments. This occurs for pragmatic and coding reasons, when a preverb dislodges a nominal object from undergoer slot on a finite verb. The erstwhile undergoer is consequently propelled or demoted into indirect object position as a DAT form.

These constructions are typically quite opaque to translation. We have already seen one in (11.11b), repeated here as (11.68a):

(11.68a) Budurrwu   maa   wunu   kumurrkarlanangkerri.
          budurrwu   maa   wunu   kuN-Ø=murrka-rla-nangka-eerri
          snore   PROG   3wDEF   3w-3=go.to-PAST-DAT-PROG
          He$_k$ went towards the sound of his$_l$ snoring.

Elsewhere in the grammar, DAT morphemes may signal possession (a function reflected in the English translation of (11.68a)), but in this and in the following sentence example they are used to encode grammatical relations in predicate argument structure. In (11.68a) the subject of the preverb *budurrwu* 'snore' is indexed on the verb *=murrka* 'go (tr)' as a non-subcategorized object (DAT *-nangka*). The preverb itself is the undergoer argument of *=murrka*, marked by the appropriate gender index, celestial *kuN-*. Example (11.68a) has the logical structure shown in (11.68b):

(11.68b)   *=murrka*   (-Ø-,   [*budurrwu*   (-*nangka*)])
           go.to   (he$_k$, [snore   (he$_l$)])

Consider as well the sentence in example (11.69a):

(11.69a)   Anguja   jurro   kunjandanangkerri?
           angujua   jurro   kuN-Ø=yanda-nangka-eerri
           what   smoking   3w-3=cause-DAT-PROG
           What's he got that's making all that smoke?

In this sentence the preverb *(jurro* 'smoking') is again the classifier's undergoer argument, marked by celestial *kuN-*. The unspecified object (DAT *-nangka*) is co-referential with the interrogative anaphor *anguja* 'what?' and refers to the subject of *jurro* 'smoking.' Example (11.69a) has the logical structure shown in (11.69b), which is exactly the same as that shown in (11.68b):

(11.69b)   *=yanda*   (-Ø-,   [*jurro*   (*anguja*)])
           CAUSE   (he,   [smoke   (what)])

This example is particularly interesting because it shows that an NP nested as an argument of another argument can be questioned, that is, extracted and preposed in an interrogative construction. English is unable to do this, which is why the translation of (11.69a) is unrevealing of its structure. A structurally more faithful but unnatural translation would be 'what is he causing the smoking of?/what is he causing to smoke?' or possibly the emphatic but pragmatically misleading 'he's causing *what* to smoke?'

An intransitive counterpart of this object-demoting composition, one in which a subject is demoted to DAT position, may be seen in example (12.6) in §12.2.

Twelve: experiencer constructions

Experiencer constructions in Worrorra are, in general terms and for the time being, complex constructions involving one of a set of preverbs that will be referred to as *sensation preverbs*. These denote usually experiences or states felt by someone, or affecting someone. A stricter, more specific formulation of experiencer constructions will be offered in §12.3. Sensation preverbs do not always occur in experiencer constructions, nor need experiencer constructions necessarily contain sensation preverbs, although they almost always do. There are round about 24 sensation preverbs in the database, or about 5% of all the preverbs recorded there:[77]

PHYSICAL SENSATIONS		MENTAL STATES	
rdurlurr	*full (of food), swollen*	rley	*aware, realize*
bayaa	*hungry*	laai	*like, be pleased*
bungkuru	*thirsty*	larr	*like, be pleased*
imaya	*cold*	=yula inja	*anger*
yali	*cold*	kulunu	*sleep*
jajarrwa	*shivering, trembling*	ngambal	*satisfied*
jarrarra	*cramp*	yaji	*delighted*
kadaada	*tired*	bakurl	*miss, be lonely for someone*
ko	*tired*	irri	*not like*
IRREVERSIBLE CHANGES		NON-VOLITIONAL ACTS	
burnu	*die (euphemistic), perish*	dinjirr	*sneeze*
ingak	*die*	ngoy	*breathe*
awarl	*be cooked*		
		AFFLICTION	
		kurnkarriya	*cold, influenza*

12.1 Experiencers with subject coding

Constructions involving sensation preverbs with experiencers in S grammatical function depend on the classifiers =*nu* 'be' or =*bwa* 'fall.' Some examples have already been seen in (5.17a) and (11.1b), and more are shown in (17.44) and (12.1):

---

[77] Because of the limitations of the database it is not always possible to know if a given preverb can be used in experiencer constructions.

(12.1a) Imaya nganungu.
 imaya nga=nu-ng
 cold 1=be-PRES
 I'm cold.

(b) Ngambal ngunngulum maa ngunbananangka.
 ngambal ngun=ngulum maa ngun=ᵇwa-na-nangka
 pleased 2=stomach 3mREF 2=fall-TNS-DAT
 You will feel/are feeling pleased with/happy about it.

(c) Yaji nyimbananangka.
 yaji nyiN=ᵇwa-na-nangka
 delighted 3f=fall-TNS-DAT
 She was delighted with him.

(d) Kaarriyaka waa ngambal bangawanjeerri.
 kaarri-y₂aka waa ngambal ba-nga=ᵇwa-n-yeerri
 3pNEG-EMPH not satisfied CFT-1=fall-NON.P-PROG
 No way, I'm not at all happy about that.

In (12.1b) the inalienable noun =*ngulum mana* 'stomach,' the seat of feelings, is used either in apposition to the subject (*ngun-* '2' indexed on the verb =*ᵇwa* 'fall'), or as an adverbial adjunct ('pleased in your stomach/heart'). The non-subcategorized (DAT) object refers to a clause in the complex sentence from which this example is taken (for the entire sentence and discussions see (13.23) in §13.2.1 (iii)) and (15.40a) in §15.6.3).

Experiencers may also be encoded as transitive subjects of the object-demoting classifier *kuN[ ]=yi* 'do.' In these cases, the sensation preverb may be understood as the classifier's formal undergoer, indexed on it as 3w *kuN-* in a nuclear-core subordinate syntax. Nevertheless, the use of an object-demoting classifier signals that these constructions are semantically objectless, that is that they are essentially intransitive. Examples are shown in (12.2):

(12.2a) Durlurr kungayeerri.
 rdurlurr kuN-nga=yi-eerri
 full VCOMP-1=do-PROG
 I'm full.

(b) Yali kungayeerri.
 yali kuN-nga=yi-eerri
 cold VCOMP-1=do-PROG
 I'm cold.

(c) Aakuwunya bungkuru kunyajeerri.
 aaku-ᵏwunya bungkuru kuN-nyarr=yi-eerri
 water-PURP thirsty VCOMP-1px=do-PROG
 We're getting thirsty for water.

(d) Kadaada kunjungu nyilardu wunu.
 kadaada kuN-Ø=yi-ng nyiN=lardu wunu
 tired/aching VCOMP-3=do-PAST 3f=back 3wDEF
 Her back was aching.

Unfortunately I did not elicit a paradigm for the construction in (12.2d), so I cannot tell whether the possessor-experiencer (she/her) or the body-part noun (back) is indexed in A position on the verb *kuN[ ]=yi*. Options for meanings such as 'my back was aching' could be *?kadaada kunjungu ngalardu wunu* with the body-part noun indexed on the verb *kuN[ ]=yi* in A position as 3sg; or a possessor-ascension construction such as *?kadaada kungenga ngalardu wunu,* with the possessor-experiencer (in this case 1sg) raised to subject relation and indexed as such on the verb, as well as on the body-part noun. A possessor-ascension syntax in an inalienable part-whole construction may be seen in (6.27b) in §6.3. I suspect that both the above putative constructions could be valid, either option being selected pragmatically.

Another object-demoting classifier found in the database is *kuN[ ]=ma* 'get,' with the sensation preverb *ingak* 'die.' Again, the preverb may be interpreted as its classifier's formal undergoer in this semantically objectless construction:

(12.3)   Mamaamangkunu   wunu   ingak   kumnyama.
         ma-maa-mangkunu   wunu   ingak   kuN-Ø-mnya=ma
         ↳-AUG-morning   3wDEF   die   VCOMP-3-DD=get
         In the early morning he died.

The inalienable noun =*yula inja* 'anger' may appear in experiencer constructions, functioning as if it were a sensation preverb. The noun =*yula inja* occurs as the undergoer of the verb =*ma* 'get,' indexed on it as '3a,' and with the experiencer encoded as the verb's subject. This construction has been discussed already in §6.3, and is shown in example (6.30). The arrangement creates an expression of the form 'AGENT/EXPERIENCER grabs/gets his/her anger,' again meaning 'SUBJECT gets angry.' Its paradigm is shown in Table 12.1:

Table 12.1: =*yula inja* =*ma* 'get angry'

ngayula	kangamerri	*I'm getting angry*
nga=yula	ka-nga=ma-eerri	
1=anger	3a-1=get-PROG	
ngunjula kanjamerri		*you're getting angry*
iyula kamerri		*he's getting angry*
nyinjula kamerri		*she's getting angry*
wunjula kumerri		*it's getting angry (celestial)*
mayula mamerri		*it's getting angry (terrestrial)*
ngajula karrberri		*we're getting angry*
ajula kerrberri		*we're getting angry*
nyijula karramerri		*you're getting angry*
ajula kawarramerri		*they're getting angry*

Comparing this paradigm with that in Table 5.3 in §5.3.2, it can be seen that the inflecting verb's U prefix is coded as 3a *ka-*, and the only noun available for interpretation in this slot is =*yula inja* 'anger.' The non-human macrogender behaves differently here, but we will come to that below in §12.3.1.

This syntax is exemplified again in (12.4), where the NP in the semantic role of THEME ('with him') is encoded as a non-subcategorized object (DAT):

(12.4)   Arri   ajula   kerrbanganangkerri.
         arri   arr=yula   ka-nyarr=ma-nga-nangka-eerri
         we(exc)   px=anger   3a-1px=get-PAST-DAT-PROG
         We were getting angry with him.

By reference to Table 12.1, it is clear that the verb's 3a undergoer *ka-* is in agreement here with *ajula,* and is not indexing the theme argument.

12.2 Preverbs with subject coding

At this point we should note an idiomatic use of =*yula inja* 'anger.' In intransitive constructions it occurs as the subject of the complex predicate *bariy =nu* 'rise,' to create an idiomatic expression of the form 'SUBJECT's anger rises,' meaning 'SUBJECT gets angry,' as in (12.5):

(12.5) Iyula   inja   bariy   kanunerri.
       i=yula   inja   bariy   ka=nu-na-eerri
       3a=anger   3aDEF   rise   3a=be-PAST-PROG
       He was getting angry.

In these expressions the inalienable noun =*yula inja* is coded as the verb's subject, and the experiencer is encoded by the dependent NP index on the inalienable noun (*i*- '3a - he, his' in 12.5).

Sentence example (12.6a) contains a demoted-subject serialization, an intransitive analogue of the demoted-object serialization process described in §11.5.4 (iii). This composition links the preverbs *jajarrwa* 'shiver, tremble' and *wala* 'cry' to depict the trembling cry of a distressed baby:

(12.6a) Wala   jajarrwa   kununanangka.
        wala   jajarrwa   kuN=nu-na-nangka
        cry   tremble   3w=be-PAST-DAT
        He was crying and trembling.

This sentence example is unusual in the database, in having a preverb (the celestial preverb *wala* 'cry') in subject grammatical relation. *Wala* is indexed in S position on the verb =*nu* 'be' as 3w *kuN*- (cf 11.11a). A literal translation of (12.6a) is: 'his cry was trembling,' with the preverb *wala* promoted to subject relation under metaphorical licence. The logical structure of this sentence is captured in (12.6b):

(12.6b)   *jajarrwa*   *(wala*   *(-nangka))*
          tremble   (cry   (he))

The human experiencer, the demoted subject of *wala* 'cry,' appears as the non-subcategorized object of the finite verb *kununanangka*, indexed as DAT -*nangka*. Further constructions involving experiencers with object (undergoer, non-subcategorized object) verbal agreement are discussed below.

12.3 Experiencers with object coding

In a stricter formulation, experiencer constructions in Worrorra may be re-defined as those in which an experiencer appears as the syntactic subject of a verb, but receives formally objective agreement marking, as either an undergoer (U) or a non-subcategorized object (DAT).[78] Cross-linguistically, it is not all that unusual to find syntactic subjects being given formal marking as objects to encode the typically patientive semantic role of experiencers, and this is the case in Worrorra as well. Although displaying in these situations formal agreement as objects, they are nevertheless the syntactic subjects of their constructions. Arrangements of this sort will be treated here as experiencer constructions in a strict sense, as they exhibit a type of verbal agreement that is idiosyncratic and distinctive.

Subject arguments effected by sensations, afflictions and states of all sorts not uncommonly receive object agreement cross-linguistically. Split intransitivity case-marking systems[79] regularly treat experiencer subjects in this manner (see Merlan 1985, Mithun 1991, Dixon & Aikenvald (eds) 2000).

---

[78] Experiencers in Worrorra may also take objective case-marking *without* being syntactic subjects: this situation is discussed below in §13.2.2 (vi). Although these are also experiencer constructions in a broad sense, they lie outside of the concerns of this chapter and are more appropriately treated in Chapter 13.
[79] Also called 'active-stative,' 'active-agentive,' 'Split S' or 'Fluid S' systems among others.

For example Lakhota (Mithun 1991:514-515) has a first person singular morpheme *ma* used to mark patient undergoers in transitive expressions such as *maktékte* 'he'll kill me.' This shape is also used to refer to experiencer subjects in expressions such as *machúwita* 'I'm cold,' *imaphí* 'I'm full' and *wamátikha* 'I'm tired.' Old English did, and Icelandic still does encode experiencer subjects by means of dative case marking (Allen 1995). Early Modern English retained vestiges of dative case-marking of subjects in expressions such as *methinks* 'I think,' and Modern German has expressions such as *mir ist kalt* 'I am cold' with the first person singular dative-case pronoun *mir*, or *mich friert/mich friert es* 'I'm freezing,' with the first person singular accusative-case pronoun *mich*.[80] Note that in both the Early Modern English and Modern German examples, verb agreement is for a third person singular subject *(thinks, ist, friert)*. Allen (1995:137 footnote) accounts for this phenomenon by claiming that third person singular verb forms are unmarked forms, and as such are selected by default when no predicate argument is in a position to control verbal agreement. This is likely to be the case in Worrorra as well, where ergative third person singular subjects receive zero marking formally (§5.3.2).

The semantics of object agreement for experiencer subjects should be fairly clear from the Lakhota examples. Experiencers are underlying patients, who are effected by sensations, states and afflictions: they do not exhibit the characteristics of initiation, volition, performance or control typically associated with semantic subjects. This being the case, it is perhaps unsurprising to find grammars finding ways to avoid granting agentive (nominative, ergative) formal agreement to such patientive arguments. Allen (1995:321) discusses this phenomenon in Old English in terms of 'the grammatical compromise of making the topical experiencer a subject, but marking it with dative case to express [its] non-volitionality.'

12.3.1 Experiencers with non-subcategorized object coding

Experiencers in Worrorra may be encoded by way of non-subcategorized object (DAT) verbal agreement marking. The following example demonstrates DAT marking of experiencers in Worrorra:

(12.7a)　　Durlurr　　kunjungaara.
　　　　　rdulurr　　kuN-Ø-yi-ng-aara
　　　　　full　　　　VCOMP-3=do-PAST-1DAT
　　　　　I'm full.

The verb classifier in (12.7a) presents three grammatical function-slots, for A, U and D. By comparison with (12.2a) we can see that the sensation preverb *rdurlurr* 'full' is indexed as the classifier's undergoer, as VCOMP *kuN-*. The experiencer receives D coding as 1DAT *-ᵏwara*. The A function-slot is empty: there is just no argument available that could fill it. Nevertheless the A slot may not remain formally empty, and so accepts a morpheme of the unmarked, default third person singular category, which is in this case Ø. The paradigm of expressions of which (12.7a) is a part includes the following, with suffixed morphemes *-nu* '2DAT,' *-nangka* 'DAT' and *-nangkorri* '3pDAT' respectively:

(12.7b)　　Durlurr　　kunjunganu.
　　　　　rdurlurr　　kuN-Ø-yi-ng-a-nu
　　　　　full　　　　VCOMP-3=do-PAST-EP-2DAT
　　　　　You're full.

(c)　　　Durlurr　　kunjunganangka.
　　　　rdurlurr　　kuN-Ø-yi-ng-a-nangka
　　　　full　　　　VCOMP-3=do-PAST-EP-DAT
　　　　S/he's full.

---

[80] Of course in the second variant *es* 'it' is here the formal dummy subject, but note how *mich* 'me' takes the subject's clause-initial position, in contrast to other impersonal constructions such as *es tut mir leid* 'I am sorry/pained,' where dummy subject *es* assumes the subject's initial position.

(d)   Durlurr   kunjunganangkorri.
            rdurlurr   kuN-Ø-yi-ng-a-nangkorri
            full   VCOMP-3=do-PAST-EP-3pDAT
            They're full.

This paradigm clearly shows how DAT-marked experiencer arguments take on the subject grammatical relation, where the ergative A form-order class codes for third person singular. Another example of a construction with *rdurlurr* may be seen in (15.24).

In (12.8) below the same considerations apply: here the sensation preverb *ngoyba* 'pant, breathe heavily' receives U marking, and the subject gets D marking:

(12.8)   Ngoyba   kumnyenganangka.
          ngoy-^{b}wa   kuN-Ø-mnya=yi-ng-a-nangka
          breath-PROG   VCOMP-3-DD=do-PAST-EP-DAT
          S/he was panting / his/her breathing was laboured.

These predicates, 'be full' and 'pant,' are unequivocally monovalent, cross-linguistically. Even in a grammar that embeds a semantic predicate in its classifier as an undergoer, there is no possibility of a third argument that could be interpreted in A function.

The formally intransitive predicates *laai* =^{b}*wa* 'like' and *larr* =^{b}*wa* 'like' also obligatorily index experiencers as DAT arguments. The result is that the sensation preverbs *laai* 'like' and *larr* 'like' are found only in impersonal constructions, as seen in (12.9):

(12.9a)   Laai   kumbanaara.
           laai   kuN=^{b}wa-na-aara
           like   3w=fall-TNS-1DAT
           I like it.

(b)   Larr   kumbananu.
            larr   kuN=^{b}wa-na nu
            like   3w=fall-TNS-2DAT
            You liked it.

These preverbs are used when the CAUSE of the experience is an event, indexed in S position as 3w *kuN*-. So even here, in these apparently impersonal constructions, the reference of the 3w S index is recoverable as some event in the immediate linguistic or extra-linguistic environment. Although the formal subject in these expressions is clearly 3w 'EVENT,' the syntactic subject is equally clearly the experiencer.

12.3.2 Experiencers with undergoer coding

The final kind of experiencer construction I will review here is one in which the experiencer is indexed on a transitive verb classifier as an undergoer. There is no DAT argument in these constructions and the A function-slot is marked for third person singular *(Ø)*. This kind of construction for uncontrolled events is apparently quite common in Papuan languages (Foley 1986:121-127). In Worrorra, these constructions are found in complex predicates conjugated with =^{b}*wu* 'hit' and =*ma* 'get,' as shown in (12.10) and (12.11) respectively:

(12.10a)   Imaya   banganbeerri.
            imaya   ba-nga-n-Ø=^{b}wu-eerri
            cold   CFT-1-INV-3=hit-PROG

I might get cold.

(b) Kulunu   nganbu.
     kulunu   nga-n-Ø=ᵇwu
     sleep   1-INV-3=hit
     I'm tired.

(c) Bungkuru   ngunbeerri?
     bungkuru   ngun-Ø=ᵇwu-eerri
     thirsty   2-3=hit-PROG
     Are you thirsty?

(d) Dinjirr   koyeerri.
     dinjirr   ka-Ø=ᵇwu-yeerri
     sneeze   3a-3=hit-PROG
     He's sneezing.

(12.11a) Jajarrwa   nganmanga.
         jajarrwa   nga-n-Ø=ma-nga
         shiver   1-INV-Ø=get-PAST
         I was shivering.

(b) Jarrarra   nganmerri.
     jarrarra   nga-n-Ø=ma-eerri
     cramp   1-INV-3=get-PROG
     I've got a cramp.

(c) Kurnkarriya   kaanmerri.
     kurnkarriya   kaarr-n-Ø=ma-eerri
     cold   3p-INV-3=get-PROG
     They've all got colds.

(d) Ke   yali   nyimanga   karle   wajeng.
     ke   yali   nyiN-Ø=ma-nga karle   kuN-ngarr-nya=yi-ng
     and   cold   3f-3=get-PAST then   VCOMP-1pin-EP=do-PAST
     We used to say, then she was getting cool.

(e) Wali maa   awarl   kamnyamenya   wara.
     wali maa   awarl   ka-Ø-mnya=ma-yinya   wara
     CONT   cook   3a-3-DD=get-HORT   kangaroo
     Let the kangaroo keep on cooking.

The syntax of these sentences can be construed in at least two interesting ways. In the first scenario, the sensation preverb itself may be understood as the syntactic subject: this is the explanation preferred by Foley (*ibid*) for similar phenomena in Papua New Guinea (and cf §12.2 above). In this explanation, sensation preverbs have nominal status as NPs in A function, in constructions of the form, 'SENSATION hits/grabs EXPERIENCER.' Constructions of this sort are not uncommon for highly patientive experiencers; in English, sensations are nominalized and granted agency status in this way, in expressions like 'panic siezed him,' 'fear overcame him,' 'relief overwhelmed me' and so on. In French, sensations may be nominalized and function as undergoers of the verb *avoir* 'have,' in constructions like *J'ai faim* 'I'm hungry' and *J'ai soif* 'I'm thirsty.' And in Worrorra, anger is nominalized as an inalienable noun, =*yula inja*, and may appear with absolutive verbal agreement as either an undergoer, as in (12.4), or an intransitive subject, as in (12.5).

Note however that in those instances in Worrorra where preverbs or sensations do unequivocally take on predicate argument functions, as seen in (12.4, 12.5) and (12.6), they appear with absolutive indexation, that is with S or U marking, not with A marking. The most clearly nominal sensation, =*yula inja* 'anger' never occurs in A function as it might be expected to. This suggests another explanation for constructions of the type seen in (12.10) and (12.11), and one more in line with the observations noted about the DAT-marked subjects seen in (12.7, 12.8) and (12.9). And that is simply that arguments marked for absolutive agreement in undergoer position in experiencer constructions are functioning as the syntactic subjects of the sentences in which they appear. In morphological terms, this explanation implies a kind of passivization or valency reduction, in which formally transitive verbs become intransitive, and their absolutive-marked indices switch from coding U grammatical function to coding S function. This is congruent with the erstwhile marking of A function on these verbs, which is zero: in this scenario there really is no A morpheme present, as the verbs have become intransitive.

This phenomenon has been observed as well in Yawuru, where Hosokawa (1996) refers to a quasi-passive construction operating with body-part nouns. In Yawuru a verbal prefix that 'ought' to index an ergative subject, instead indexes an absolutive-case object:

> Like the transitive, the core constituents are an ergative NP and an absolutive NP. Unlike the transitive, however, the verbal prefix does not agree with the ergative NP, but agrees with the undergoer. (Hosokawa 1996:165)

Recall here the phenomenon reviewed in §6.3, in which inalienable nouns appear to change gender in agreement with a dependent NP of the non-human macrogender, as seen in Table 12.1 and in sentences such as (6.31), repeated here as (12.12):

(12.12a)   Wunu   marirri   wunjula   kumerri.
(=6.31a)   wunu   marirri   ᵏwuN=yula   kuN-(Ø)=ma-eerri
           3wDEF   parrot.sp   3w=anger   3w-(3)=get-PROG
           The red-winged parrot is getting angry.

(b)   Mana   darraanma   mayula   mamerri.
           mana   darraanma   ma=yula   ma-(Ø)=ma-eerri
           3mDEF   cockatoo.sp 3m=anger   3m-(3)=get-PROG
           The red-tailed black cockatoo is getting angry.

A more parsimonious explanation might see the verb =*ma* 'get' in these constructions as having reduced valency, such that the prefixed indices are now effectively in S function, showing agreement with their syntactic subjects, here *wunu marirri* and *mana darraanma*.[81] If this really is the case, then of course the subjects are in S, not U function, so their undergoer status is merely erstwhile in this context.

If it should turn out that this kind of process is indeed responsible for constructions in which experiencer subjects are found in undergoer position, then it might be expected that it could be productive, and could extend into other types of predication that involve highly patientive experiencers. And to a certain extent this is found in the database, as seen in example (12.13). This example involves the formally transitive predicate *burnu* =ᵇ*wu* 'die, perish,' with an experiencer in absolutive verbal agreement, and another transitive predicate, *yawurlak* =*yabu*, productively assembled to produce an experiencer construction meaning 'drown:'

(12.13)
¹Bloy   kumanga   ²ke   rlarlangkarranyinim   burnu   ko,
bloy   kuN-Ø=ma-nga   ke   rlarlangkarra-nyini-m   burnu   ka-Ø=ᵇwu
slip   VCOMP-3=get-PAST   and   sea-ENDPOINT-3m   3wPRO   3a-3=hit

---

[81] Ungarinyin has an intransitive verb of this form *(=ma* 'do') (Rumsey 1982:81, 157).

³yawurlak	kayabuna.	⁴Yawurlak	maa	kawanangurreerri
yawurlak	ka-Ø=yabu-na	yawurlak	maa	ka=ᵇwa-na-ngurru-eerri
sink	3a-3=throw-PAST	sink	PROG	3a=fall-TNS-away-PROG

rlarlangkarram.
sea

He slipped over and perished in the sea, he drowned. He sank down under the sea.

This sequence involves four clauses, numbered with superscripts for clarity. The first clause is described in relation to (11.55b) in §11.5.2.

In the fourth clause the predicate *yawurlak kawanangurreerri* 'he sank down' is formally as well as functionally intransitive, and the terrestrial noun *rlarlangkarram* 'the sea' appears in a clearly locative role without suffixation, as is usual for terrestrial nouns denoting places.

And in the second clause as well, despite its lack of locative suffixation, the noun *rlarlangkarram* appears in the semantic role of LOCATION, and does not appear to be functioning as an agent.[82] The complex predicate *burnu ko* 'he perished' contains the celestial pro-form *burnu*, here denoting disaster euphemistically as a sensation preverb, and the transitive classifier =ᵇwu, with the boy indexed on it as *ka-* '3a' in U position but in S grammatical function.

The complex predicate in the third clause, *yawurlak kayabuna* 'he drowned,' is also revealing. The preverb *yawurlak* 'sink' does not normally function as a sensation preverb. Nor does it denote, in its usual meaning, a sensation that could be said metaphorically to impact upon an experiencer. Rather than a sensation, it denotes a state, one of descent. The transitive classifier =*yabu* 'throw' also conveys only the semantics of atelic motion. The motivation for projecting a state of motion into an experiencer construction is to foreground the actor's patientive status, and to dramatize the experienced nature of the event. It is therefore quite unlikely that the preverb *yawurlak* 'sink' occurs in A function in this predicate. Here it would appear that there is an absolutive-agreement subject in undergoer position (3a *ka-*), again involving a labile passivization process that deletes underlying Ø-marked arguments in A function, and promotes an erstwhile U index to S grammatical function.

It is not unknown cross-linguistically for arguments to be removed from labile predicates without morphological signalling. English object-demoting expressions such as *he's eating* are without morphological marking, and sentences such as *they're fighting* can have antipassive or reflexive interpretation, again without morphological cueing.

This interpretation of the experiencer data brings the syntactic evidence into line with the semantic and pragmatic facts: experiencers in these constructions are animate and sentient, and so are clearly topical. Pragmatically, they are equally clearly terms, about which predications are being made. Both semantic and pragmatic considerations of this sort may be expected to motivate syntactic subjecthood. Objective agreement-marking of subjects in these constructions can be demonstrated with respect to DAT-marked arguments, and it is therefore conceivable that erstwhile undergoers showing absolutive verbal agreement might also be found in subject grammatical function.

---

[82] In (11.59b) the sea is not a location, but an actor.

Thirteen: objects and possession

In this chapter we will look at a set of person and number suffixes occurring on pronouns, verbs and kinship nouns. On pronouns and kinship nouns they serve to mark possession, and on verbs in form-order class [11] they mark various kinds of objects (see Table 5.1 in §5.2). The homophony of possessive and dative (indirect object) case markers is not uncommon in Australia,[83] and this morphology will be glossed DAT for convenience. I will argue in §13.2 that these forms code overt syntactic dependency in both complex NPs and complex predicates. Their shapes, with glosses, are set out in Table 13.1:

Table 13.1: possessive/non-subcategorized object (DAT) suffixes

FUNCTION		FORM	MORPHOLOGY	GLOSS
singular:	*first*	-ᵏwara		1DAT
	second	-nu		2DAT
	third	-nangka		DAT
plural:	*first inc*	-ngarri		1pinDAT
	first exc	-nyarri		1pxDAT
	second	-noorri	nu-ᵏwurri	2pDAT
	third	-nangkorri	nangka-ᵏwurri	3pDAT
dual:	*first inc*	-ngarrerndu	ngarri-ᵏwarndu	1pinDAT-DU
	first exc	-nyarrerndu	nyarri-ᵏwarndu	1pxDAT-DU
	second	-nurrerndu	[nu-ᵏwurri]-ᵏwarndu	2pDAT-DU
	third	-nangkaarndu	nangka-ᵏwarndu	DAT-DU

Note the following features of these forms:
- The singular and first person plural forms are unsegmentable.
- In second and third persons, plurality is marked by the collective morpheme -ᵏwurri attached to the singular shape.
- In first and second persons the dual morpheme is attached to the plural shape.
- In third persons the dual morpheme is attached to the singular shape.

Love (1934:14-15) lists a paucal ('trial') number series for these suffixes as well, with participant shapes 1 inc *-ngarringkurri*, 1 exc *-nyarringkurri*, and 2 *-nurringkurri*. His third person paucal shape is homophonous with the plural form. Although it is important to note that these forms are found in his grammar, as discussed in §9.6 they are not found in the database.

---

[83] Nor in other languages for that matter; cf this homophony in, eg, the Latin 1st & 5th (singular) nominal declensions.

Of pronouns, only personal pronouns may host DAT morphemes, and only the third person shapes in Table 13.1 are hosted. Possessive pronouns are described in §7.7 in Chapter Seven, and their formation will not be dealt with here.

13.1 Possessive constructions

Three morphosyntactic categories may be marshalled beneath a rubric of 'possession' in Worrorra. We have already looked at the class of inalienable nouns in §6.3, a head-marking morphology with syntactically dependent possessors indexed by prefixation. Another head-marked morphology, this time with dependents indexed as suffixes, will be addressed below in §13.1.1. These two head-marking morphologies are reserved quite specifically for what are typically body-part nouns and kinship nouns respectively (two kinds of arguably 'inalienable' possession). Alienable possession is dependent-marked; here possessive morphology attaches to the possessor, not to the thing possessed, as discussed in §13.1.2. These three types of possession are summarized in Table 13.2 below:

Table 13.2: possession types

	MORPHOLOGICAL TYPE	MARKEDNESS TYPE
BODY PARTS	derivational	head
KINSHIP	inflectional	head
ELSEWHERE	inflectional	dependent

13.1.1 Kinship nouns

The suffixes in Table 13.1 may be attached to kinship nouns, to index the propositus or 'owner' of the person denoted by the relationship term. An inventory of Worrorra kinship terms is provided in Chapter 18.

In the tables that follow, the first person singular propositus ('my') shapes are the citation forms. In this chapter primary stress will be marked on kinship nouns with an acute accent, and secondary stress is taken up by unaccented long vowels, if present. This convention is aimed at making the sometimes lengthy and compositional nature of such nouns easier to read.

Table 13.3: 'mother' stem *karra-*

PROPOSITUS	'MOTHER'	MORPHOLOGY	GLOSS
my	karráanya	karra-aa-nya	Mo-1DAT-3f
your	karránya	karra-Ø-nya	Mo-Ø-3f
his/her	karranangkánya	karra-nangka-nya	Mo-DAT-3f
our (inc)	karraangarrínya ~	karra-aa-ngarri-nya	Mo-1DAT-1pinDAT-3f
our (inc)	karráanyangarri	karra-aa-nya-ngarri	Mo-1DAT-3f-1pinDAT
our (exc)	karraanyarrínya ~	karra-aa-nyarri-nya	Mo-1DAT-1pxDAT-3f
our (exc)	karráa(nya)nyarri	karra-aa-nya-nyarri	Mo-1DAT-3f-1pxDAT
your (pl)	karranóorrinya	karra-[nu-ᵏwurri]-nya	Mo-[2pDAT]-3f
their	karranangkórrinya	karra-[nangka-ᵏwurri]-nya	Mo-[3pDAT]-3f

- All forms with a first person propositus contain a segment *-aa-*, which I take to be a reduced version of the 1DAT morpheme *-ᵏwara/-aara* in Table 13.1. This appears redundantly on first person plural forms.
- Singular kinship nouns show alternative placements of the possessive (propositus, DAT) morpheme in their first person plural shapes; one with the possessive morpheme inside, and one with it outside the gender marker. There appears to be no preference for one of these forms over the other.
- Elsewhere however the propositus marker appears inside the word-final gender marker.

- Forms with a second person singular propositus are somewhat variable: in *karraanya* and feminine nouns like it, it appears that the first person marker *-aa-* is simply dropped out of the citation shape, leaving a bare stem *karra-* to mark a second person propositus. Nouns that pattern like this are, among others, *mangkanya* 'your wife, your father's mother,' *kawurlanya* 'your (woman's) brother's daughter' and *ngawanya* 'your elder sister, your father's father's sister.' Other feminine nouns show their penultimate vowel modified to /i/: *bamarinya* 'your (man's) daughter, your father's sister,' and *jaminya* 'your mother's brother's daughter, your mother's father's sister' (cf first person propositus forms *bamaraanya* and *jamaanya*).
- Bi-morphemic second and third person plural propositus markers are enclosed within square brackets.

Table 13.4: 'father' stem *irra-*

PROPOSITUS	'FATHER'	MORPHOLOGY	GLOSS
my	irráaya	irra-aa-ya	Fa-1DAT-3a
your	irrólija	irra-wulija	Fa-2KIN.POSS
his/her	írranangka	irra-nangka	Fa-DAT
our (inc)	irráangarri ~	irra-aa-ngarri	Fa-1DAT-1pinDAT
our (inc)	irráayangarri	irra-aa-ya-ngarri	Fa-1DAT-3a-1pinDAT
our (exc)	irráanyarri ~	irra-aa-nyarri	Fa-1DAT-1pxDAT
our (exc)	irráayanyarri	irra-aa-ya-nyarri	Fa-1DAT-3a-1pxDAT
your (pl)	irranóorri	irra-[nu-ᵏwurri]	Fa-[2pDAT]
their	irranangkórri	irra-[nangka-ᵏwurri]	Fa-[3pDAT]

In masculine singular nouns the second person singular propositus marker is reconstructable as *-wulija*. This morpheme does not appear to be related to any other in the language. Other nouns in the database with this suffix are *kakólija* 'your mother's brother,' *kulélija* 'your husband,' *jamólija* 'your mother's father, your mother's brother's son,' *ngawarlólija* 'your elder brother, your father's father,' and *ibólija* 'your (woman's) son, your husband's father.'[84]

The nouns *káwurla* and *káwurlànya* 'woman's brother's son/daughter,' already commented on in §7.7, attract propositus suffixes more transparently, as seen in Table 13.5. Here the unreduced first person singular propositus marker is apparent, with the conventional second person singular marker in the masculine noun, as seen in Table 13.1. The second singular propositus in the feminine noun is Ø-marked. The rest of the paradigm is quite transparent, with suffixes from Table 13.1 attached directly to the stem *kawurla-*, and the feminine suffix *-nya* coming word-finally.

Table 13.5: *kawurla* 'woman's patrilineal son,' *kawurlanya* 'woman's patrilineal daughter'

PROPOSITUS	'SON'	MORPHOLOGY	'DAUGHTER'	MORPHOLOGY
my	kawurláara	kawurla-ᵏwara	kawurlanyáaranya	kawurla-nya-ᵏwara-nya
your	kawurlánu	kawurla-nu	káwurlanya	kawurla-Ø-nya

Many if not most nouns denoting humans and dogs, including all kinship nouns, form plurals by stem augmentation and suffixation (see §4.2.1). The 3p suffix *-ya* is added to an augmented stem. The stem is augmented in Type 3 manner, targeting the first consonant of the noun's second syllable (see §6.2.6 (ii)). This consonant is copied, preposed and followed by /aa/, as shown:

$$\emptyset \longrightarrow C_iaa / \#[\$_1 ... \$_1] \_\_\_ C_i ...$$

This process produces infixes that are inserted into the stem in front of the erstwhile second syllable, as exemplified in Table 13.6:

---

[84] Corresponding to first person singular propositus forms *kakaaya*, *kulaaya*, *jamaaya*, *ngawaaya* and *ibaaya*, respectively.

Table 13.6: stem augmentation by Type-3 infixation

SG NOUN	TRANS	STEM	INFIX	PL NOUN
kawurla	(W)BrSo	ka_wurla-	-waa-	ka**waa**wurlaya
awanja	boy	a_wa-	-waa-	a**waa**wanja
ngawaaya	ElBr, FaFa	nga_wa-	-waa-	nga**waa**waya
irraaya	Father	i_rra-	-rraa-	i**rraa**rreya
kurruma	WiMoBr	ku_rruma-	-rraa-	ku**rraa**rramaya
karraanya	Mother	ka_rra	-rraa-	ka**rraa**rreya
kajaaya	MoMoBr	ka_ja-	-jaa-	ka**jaa**jeya
mrnangkanya	teenage girl	m_rnangka-	-rnaa-	m**rnaa**rnangkaya
kanangkurri	dog	ka_nangkurr-	-naa-	ka**naa**nangkurri
bamaraanya	(M)Da, FaSi	ba_mara-	-maa-	ba**maa**mareya
kakaaya	MoBr	ka_ka-	-kaa-	ka**kaa**kaya
nyangkanya	girl	nya_ngka-	-ngkaa-	nya**ngkaa**ngkaya

As indicated in §2.2, and as seen here in the word *nyangkaangkaya* 'girls,' this morphology treats the prenasalized stop /ngk/ as a unit phoneme for the purposes of stem augmentation: the stem appears to be syllabified as indicated in Table 13.6. This phenomenon is seen again in the plural stem *mangkaangka-* (|ma-ngkaa-ngka-|) 'wives' in example (13.1) below.

Although phrases like 'my mothers' or 'my fathers' may seem odd in English, Worrorra kinship nouns denote sets of classificatory relations (such as 'mothers'), as well as a single socially and emotionally important individual. Therefore all kinship nouns in Worrorra have frequently-used plural forms. Propositus markers are suffixed to the augmented stems of plural kinship nouns before the plural suffix *-ya* is attached, as seen in Table 13.7:

Table 13.7: 'mothers' and 'fathers'

PROPOSITUS	'MOTHERS'	'FATHERS'	MORPHOLOGY (i-rra-)
my	karraarréya	irraarréya	i-rraa-rra-aa-ya
your	karraarraníya	irraarraníya	i-rraa-rra-nu-ya
his/her	karraarranangkáya	irraarranangkáya	i-rraa-rra-nangka-ya
our (inc)	karráarrangarri	irráarrangarri	i-rraa-rra-ngarri
our (exc)	karráarranyarri	irráarranyarri	i-rraa-rra-nyarri
your (pl)	karraarranóorri	irraarranóorri	i-rraa-rra-[nu-ᵏwurri]
their	karraarranangkórri	irraarranangkórri	i-rraa-rra-[nangka-ᵏwurri]

- The plural marker *-ya* and the word-final segment *-rri* are in complementary distribution in these forms.
- The underlying first person singular propositus marker *-aa-* (from *-aara* from *-ᵏwara*) is fronted to *-é-* before /y/.
- Likewise the second person singular propositus marker *-nu* appears as *-ni* before /y/.
- The first person singular propositus marker *-aa-* is omitted from first person plural forms.

Duality is an important social concept in Worrorra, and two people may frequently be referred to as the propositi of a kinship relation.

Table 13.8: 'two people's mother'

PROPOSITUS	'MOTHER'	MORPHOLOGY
our (dual inc)	karraangarrérndinya	karra-[aa-ngarri-ᵏwarndu]-nya
our (dual exc)	karraanyarrérndinya	karra-[aa-nyarri-ᵏwarndu]-nya
your (dual)	karranurrérndinya	karra-[[nu-ᵏwurri]-ᵏwarndu]-nya
their (dual)	karranangkáarndinya	karra-[nangka-ᵏwarndu]-nya

Therefore dual propositus markers may be attached to kinship nouns as shown in Table 13.8 above, where the dual-marked propositus material is enclosed within square brackets.

And of course it follows that two people may be the propositi of a kinship relation occupied by a set of people in that relationship. In this case dual propositus markers are attached to the plural shapes of kinship nouns:

Table 13.9: 'two people's mothers'

PROPOSITUS	'MOTHERS'	MORPHOLOGY
our (dual inc)	karraarrangarrérndiya	ka-rraa-rra-[ngarri-^kwarndu]-ya
our (dual exc)	karraarranyarrérndiya	ka-rraa-rra-[nyarri-^kwarndu]-ya
your (dual)	karraarranurrérndiya	ka-rraa-rra-[[nu-^kwurri]-^kwarndu]-ya
their (dual)	karraarranangkáarndiya	ka-rraa-rra-[nangka-^kwarndu]-ya

An example of the use of a plural kinship noun with a dual propositus is shown in (13.1). This reference is specifically to two *men:* more than one wife is involved, but not necessarily just two:

(13.1)
Warnda	kanunaarndeerri	mangkàangkanangkáarndiya	kurde.
warnda	ka=nu-na-^kwarndu-eerri	ma-ngkaa-ngka-[nangka-^kwarndu]-ya	kurde
dwell	3a=be-PAST-DU-PROG	↪-AUG-wife-[DAT-DU]-3p	ASSOC

They (dual) lived (there) with their (dual) wives.

A variant on plural kinship noun morphology was used by Patsy Lulpunda, who alternated forms like *irraarranangkaya* with *irraadakaya* 'his/her fathers,' and *irraarranangkorri* with *irraadakorri* 'their fathers.' These shapes come about by eliding the final vowel of the stem, leaving the DAT morpheme abutting the consonant /rr/, which induces Distance-Hardening Rule 13. The morphology of these words is exemplified in (13.2):

(13.2)
	irraadakaya	karraadakorri
	i-rraa-rr(a)-nangka-ya	ka-rraa-rr(a)-[nangka-^kwurri]
	↪AUG father-DAT-3p	↪AUG-mother-[DAT-NUM]
	his/her fathers	*their mothers*

A noun *karrèrnbarrínya* 'mother-of-many' denotes a woman as being a mother of more than one person. It has a plural shape *karràarrernbárriya*, and its use is exemplified in (13.3):

(13.3)
Arrerndu	ninjarrungunya	karrernbarrinya
arri-^kwarndu	nyiN=yarrungu-nya	karrernbarrinya
we(exc)-DU	3f=QUANT-3f	mother.of.many

karraanyarrerndinya,	ninjarrungunya.
karra-[aa-nyarri-^kwarndu]-nya	nyiN=yarrungu-nya
mother-[1DAT-1pxDAT-DU]-3f	3f=QUANT-3f

S/he and I had the same mother/the one woman was the mother of us both.

There is some evidence that kinship nouns may be able to delegate propositus marking to dependents in their phrase; in particular the quantifier =*yarrungu* in kinship contexts is used to refer to the sole member of a particular kinship category, as in (13.3) above. Further examples are offered below in (13.4), where in (13.4a) the 1px propositus marker appears on the quantifier, while the head noun reverts to default first person singular marking. In kinship contexts =*yarrungu* may take suffixial head marking as if it were a kinship noun.

(13.4a) iyarrungunyarrerndu   irraaya
         i=yarrungu-[nyarri-ᵏwarndu] irra-aa-ya
         3a=QUANT-[1pxDAT-DU]   father-1DAT-3a
         the one man who was the father of him/her and me
         s/he and I had the same father

(b)   iyarrungaara   inja
         i=yarrungu-ᵏwara   inja
         3a=QUANT-1DAT   3aDEF
         my only (son)

A nominal propositus is placed invariably in front of its kinship noun head, either with or without a possessive pronoun determiner (see §13.1.2 below), as seen in (13.5):

(13.5a) Kurnak   ngawanangka.
         Kurnak   ngawa-nangka
         NAME   ElSib-DAT
         Kurnak's elder brother.

(b)   Amy   nyangkanangka   ngawanangkanya.
         Amy   nyangka-nangka   ngawa-nangka-nya
         NAME   3fNAR-DAT   ElSib-DAT=3f
         Amy's elder sister.

13.1.2 Dependent-marked possession

Dependent-marked possessive phrases may be used to denote kinship relations, in conjunction with the head-marking arrangements described above. Other kinds of possession are shown exclusively by dependent-marking, and in the database this syntax is used to depict people's relationships with the following kinds of things: (i) people, including kin, children, dogs, and teachers; (ii) places, including country, houses, caves, cliffs, rivers, etc; (iii) utensils and artefacts, money; (iv) food; (v) totems, and (vi) language. Dependent-marked possessive phrases in Worrorra are compound and frequently complex, and in this section we will seek to unpack and display them using generative X-bar notation. As possessive phrases may consist of several layers of embedding, this approach is quite well suited to exposing the geometry of their structure.

The simplest kind of possessive phrase in Worrorra consists of a head noun modified by a possessive pronoun (see §7.7), as shown in (13.6a). The constituents of this phrase are labelled in (13.6b) and their relationships are displayed in (13.6c). Constituent order in these phrases may be varied, and the reverse of (13.6a) is shown in (13.6c). In these trees NP is the complement of D´.[85]

(13.6a) aanangka   karraki
         awa-nangka   karraki
         3aNAR-DAT   bag
         his bag

---

[85] In this exposition D = determiner, N = noun, P = phrase, and ['] represents an intermediate or bar-level projection. DP (Determiner Phrase) is an extended or functional projection of the phrase's lexical head, which is N *(karraki* 'bag' and *mayaram* 'house' in the following few examples). For a succinct exposition of the DP hypothesis, see Bernstein (2001). For arguments critical of functional projections generally, see Matthews (2007). The formalism as employed here is modified to avoid phonologically empty terminal nodes.

(b)   POSSESSIVE DETERMINER   HEAD
       aanangka   karraki

(c)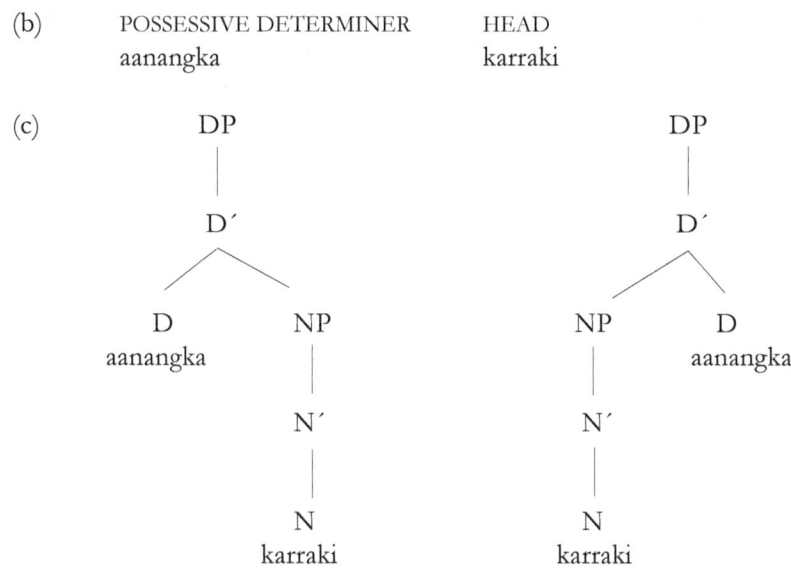

Other possessive phrases in Worrorra, as in English, consist typically of a sequence of <possessor NP, possessive determiner, head noun>, as in (13.7). This arrangement is the citation form for possessive phrases generally. Note that the Worrorra determiner must agree with *both* the possessor *and* the head of the phrase:

(13.7)   eeja   aanangkama   mayaram
            eeja   awa-nangka-ma mayaram
            man   3aNAR-DAT-3m   house
            (the) man's house

In English the possessive determiner is enclitic *'s*, while in Worrorra it is a possessive pronoun. This isomorphy is shown in (13.8a), and the structure of the phrase in (13.7), in two configurations, is shown in (13.8b):

(13.8a)   POSSESSOR   POSSESSIVE DETERMINER   HEAD
           eeja   aanangkama   mayaram
           man   *'s*   *house*

(b)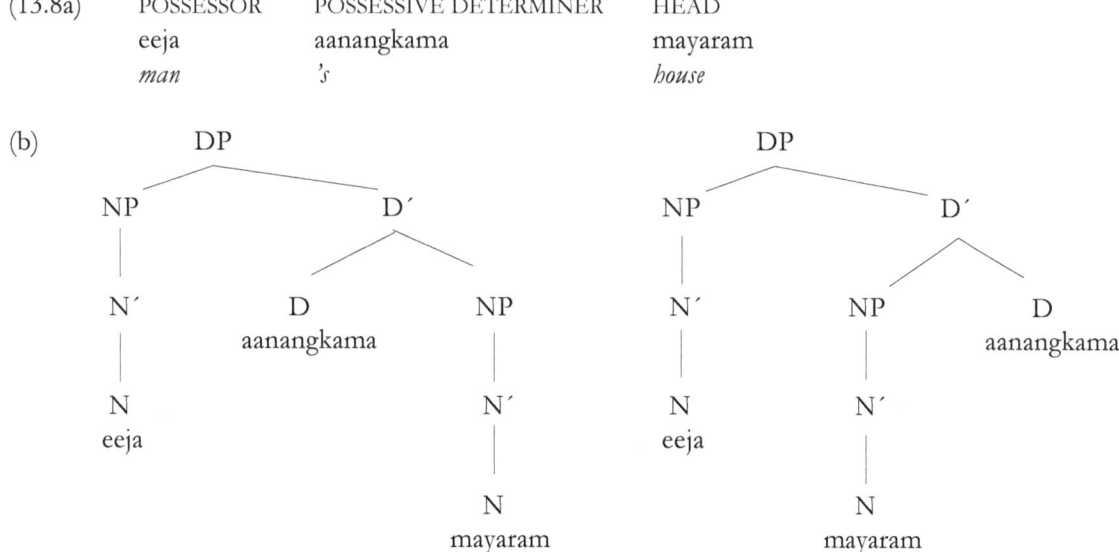

Here *eeja* is the specifier of DP, and *mayaram* is the complement of D´. Another phrase of this kind is *ajakarri arrkanangka mangarri* 'other people's food,' as seen in (11.16a).

That possessive pronouns in these phrases are functioning as determiners, is indicated by the fact that free pronouns and possessive pronouns are frequently found together, ostensibly pleonastically, as seen in (13.15a) and (13.9) below. In these situations free pronouns function as possessor noun specifiers of DP, just as *eeja* does in (13.7) and (13.8); the possessive pronouns here function as determiners:

(13.9a)   bunjuma   ngayu   ngayanangkama
            bunjuma   ngayu   ngaya-nangka-ma
            fig   I   I-DAT-3m
            my figs

(b)   nyangkaangkamaanja   arrkanangka   arri
         nya-ngkaa-ngka-maan-ya   arr=^{k}wa-nangka   arri
         ↳AUG-girl-SPEC-3p   px=NAR-DAT   we(exc)
         belonging only to us girls

(c)   Jimbirrij   [kajaanya   anja   arrkanangka].
         jimbirrij   kajaanya   anja   arr=^{k}wa-nangka
         rock-cod   MoMo   3pDEF   px=NAR-DAT
         The giant rock-cod is these (people)'s (totemic) mother's mother.

(d)   Ngarri   wali   [ngarrkanaanangkaya   anja   wangalaalunguyu].
         ngarri   wali   ngarr=^{k}wa-naa-nangka-ya   anja   wangalaalanguya
         we(inc)   PM   1pin=NAR-AUG-DAT-3p   3pDEF   children
         They are our children.

In (13.9a) the first person singular free and possessive pronouns occur side by side. In this construction the phrasal head *(bunjuma* 'fig') is taken out of DP and fronted under a higher NP node:

(13.10) (=13.9a)

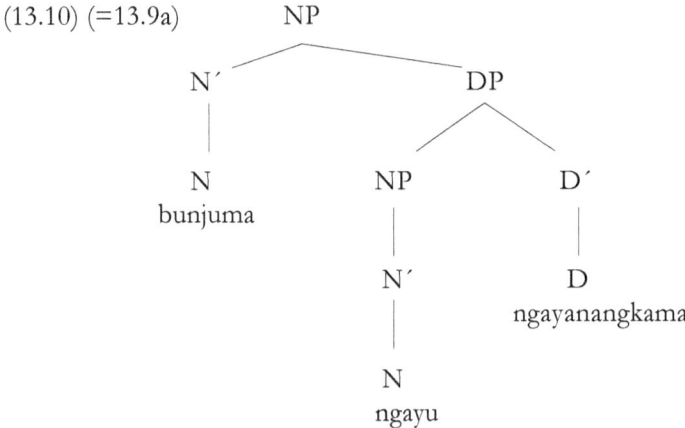

In (13.9b) it is the first person plural exclusive pronoun whose free and possessive shapes are juxtaposed. In this example the phrasal head is deleted, being recoverable from previous context. The free pronoun *arri* 'we (exc)' is in apposition to the noun *nyangkaangkamaanja* 'girls only.' This noun is also removed from DP and fronted under a higher NP node:

(13.11) (=13.9b)

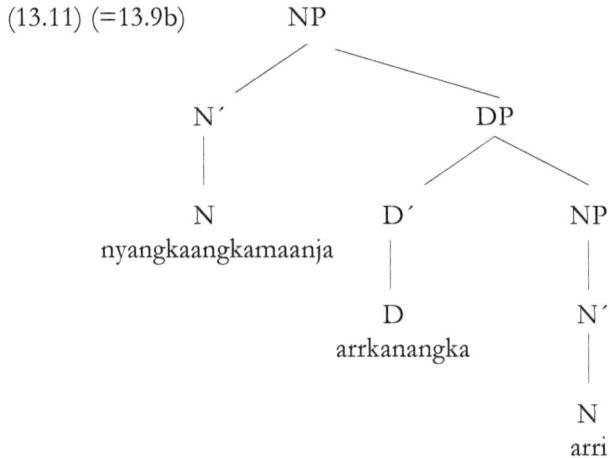

In (13.9c & d) the possessive phrases are bracketed. In (13.9c) the definite article *anja* is functioning as a third person plural pronoun, standing in for the possessor NP. Again, it occurs right next to the third person plural possessive determiner *arrkanangka*. The head of this phrase, *kajaanya* 'mother's mother,' is preposed in a structure similar to that seen in (13.10). The phrase contains an unusual kinship-noun construction, in that the noun *kajaanya* bears 'incorrect' coding, being marked for a first person singular propositus ('my mother's mother') when the associated article and possessive determiner clearly show that third person plural reference is involved.[86] The totemic status of this relationship is probably behind this phenomenon, as if this sentence could be paraphrased: *'the giant cod is (the one) they (call) 'grandmother'.'* In (13.9d) the two first person plural inclusive pronouns *ngarri* and *ngarrkanaanangkaya* occur in close proximity, but this time the free pronoun *ngarri* is just outside the possessive phrase. In this verbless sentence *ngarri* is the term, with the possessive phrase the predicate. The use of *wali* to mark predicates is discussed in §17.8. The structure of the possessive phrase in (13.9d) is shown in (13.13) below.

Possessive phrases may incorporate non-possessive determiners on a number of levels. The determiners most frequently found in possessive phrases are definite articles, as seen in (13.12). Note in this example a kinship noun not uncommonly exhibiting both head- and dependent marking syntaxes at once; with possessive marking suffixed to the head, and in the presence of a possessive determiner:

(13.12a) anja   kawaawurlanangkaya   nyangkanaanangkaya
          anja   ka-waa-wurla-nangka-ya   nyangka-naa-nangka-ya
          3pDEF   ↳-AUG-WBrCh-DAT-3p   3fNAR-AUG-DAT-3p
          her brothers' children

---

[86] Here *kajanangkorrinya* 'their MoMo' could be expected.

(b)

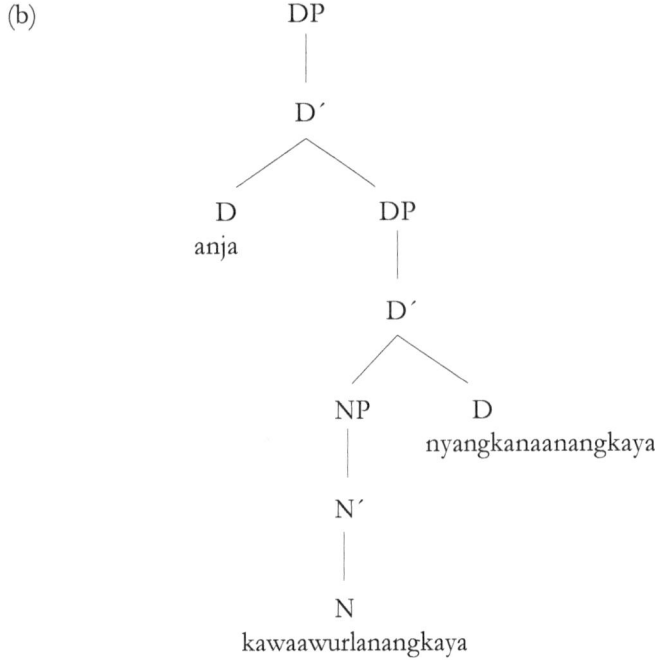

Non-possessive determiners may be imbedded within the possessive phrase, as in (13.13 (=13.9d)):

(13.13a) ngarrkanaanangkaya   anja   wangalaalunguyu
         ngarr=ᵏwa-naa-nangka-ya anja   wangalaalanguya
         1pin=NAR-AUG-DAT-3p   3pDEF   children
         (they are) our children

(b)

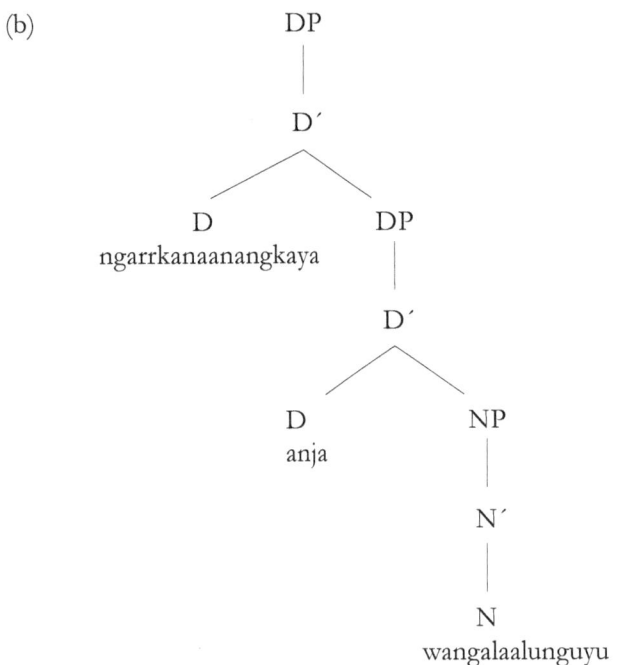

A more fully extended possessive phrase with definite articles at two levels, is seen in (13.14):

(13.14a)   anja   ngayu   ngayanaanangkaya   anja   nyangkaangkaya
             anja   ngayu   ngaya-naa-nangka-ya   anja   nya-ngkaa-ngka-ya
             3pDEF   I   I-AUG-DAT-3p   3pDEF   ↳-AUG-girl-3p
             these girls of mine

(b)

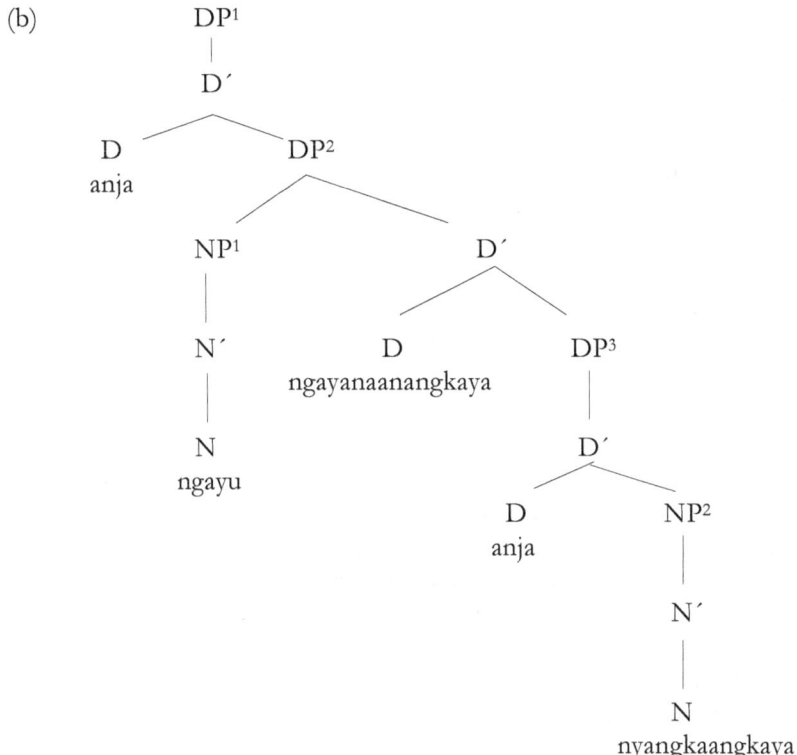

Here NP¹ is the specifier of DP², and DP², DP³, and NP² are successively more embedded complements under DP¹.

As mentioned, the typical possessive phrase is constructed as in (13.7); consisting, that is, of a possessor noun or free pronoun, a possessive determiner, and a head noun. As seen in (13.6), the possessor noun may be omitted, with coding for this constituent carried by the possessive determiner. Head nouns may also be omitted, their reference retrievable both from coding on the possessive determiner, and from context. Some examples may be seen in (13.9b) and (13.15):

(13.15a)
Durr	kunyajona	arrbri	kaarri.
durr	kuN-nyarr-nya=ᵇwu-na	arr=mri	kaarri
cut	VCOMP-1px-EP=hit-PAST	px=head	3pNEG

[Ngayu	ngayanangka]	durr	kungamnyona.
ngayu	ngayu-nangka	durr	kuN-nga-mnya=ᵇwu-na
I	I-DAT	cut	VCOMP-1-DD=hit-PAST

We used to gash our heads. I cut mine, too.

(b)
[Burrbu	nyangkanangkaya],	[Kurdu	nyangkanangkaya]	anja	wali
Burrbu	nyangka-nangka-ya	Kurdu	nyangka-nangka-ya	anja	wali
NAME	3fNAR-DAT-3p	NAME	3fNAR-DAT-3p	3pDEF	still

```
kaangarnaarnarla        bijakuwunya.
kaarr-nga=rnaarna-rla   bijaku-ᵏwunya
3p-1=wait.for-PAST      smoke-PURP
```
I still had to wait for Burrbu's (family), and Kurdu's (family) (to come) for the smoking (ceremony).

In (13.15a) the deleted head of the possessive phrase in the second sentence is retrievable from the first *(arrbri* 'our heads'). This body-part noun is referred to in the second sentence by a dependent-marked possessive construction, instead of by the expected head-marked morphology as *ngamri* or *ngayu ngamri* 'my head' (§6.3). In (13.15b) the deleted heads of the two possessive phrases are the same; something like 'family, kinsmen, children.' The plurality of the heads is marked on the possessive determiners, on the definite article, and on the verb in undergoer position. Example (10.60b) in Chapter Ten is interesting in this respect; here we see a possessive phrase predicated upon its head, which serves as the term in this verbless sentence. This example is repeated here as (13.16):

```
(13.16)     [TERM     ]    [PRED                              ]
(=10.60b)   Daraarlu       Bajawalakurdengarri   arrkanangka.
            rdaraarlu      Bajawala-kurde-ngarri arr=ᵏwa-nangka
            PLACE.NAME     NAME-ASSOC-REL        3p=NAR-DAT
```
Daraarlu is Bajawala's family's / Daraarlu belongs to Bajawala's family.

Although language, totems and stories are usually treated as alienably possessed, there is one occurrence in the database where a noun of this type is given inalienable treatment: in (13.17a) the DAT morpheme is suffixed to the head noun *(ngarlangarla* 'speech, story') as if it were a kinship noun. The person concerned is a dreamtime ancestor, and so she may be identified in terms of her story; that is, her story may be understood as being inalienably part of her.

```
(13.17a)    Ke      ngarlangarlanangka      wali wunu.
            ke      ngarlangarla-nangka     wali wunu
            3wREF   speech-DAT              PM
```
That is her story.

```
(b)         Aawali              school teacher-nyarri.
            aa(ya)-ᵇwali        school-teacher-nyarri
            3aREF-RESUM         school teacher-1pxDAT
```
He was our teacher.

Likewise in (13.17b) the social role 'teacher' is treated as a kinship noun for the purpose of coding a possessive-type relationship. This is entirely congruent; social roles in traditional Worrorra society are defined by kinship.

The coding of both possessor and head noun on the possessive determiner is isomorphic with other features of the language, most obviously the coding of both subjects and undergoers on transitive verbs. In this way an abstract syntactic phenomenon may be seen to have reflexes in more than one part of the grammar.

13.2 Non-subcategorized (lexically unspecified) objects

Worrorra verb roots obligatorily host either one (intransitive) or two (transitive) NP-indexing prefixes (§5.3). Where one is hosted, it codes a subject argument; where two are hosted, the subject and one object argument are coded. Most verbs require two argument prefixes, and so are formally transitive. A formally intransitive verb may never appear with two argument prefixes, and while formally transitive verbs may appear with only one argument prefix, they require a derivational valency-reducing marker to do so (see Chapter 16). We could thus contend that the number of argument prefixes a verb may host (one or two) is part of its specification in the lexicon; that is, is part of its lexical specification or subcategorization frame. There is scope, however, for all verbs optionally to code another argument – a second in the case of formally intransitive, and a third in the case of formally transitive verbs. These extra, lexically unspecified or non-subcategorized object markers take the form of the suffixes displayed in Table 13.1 above, occurring on the verb in order class [11].

It will be seen then that DAT morphology occurs in quite distinct environments: it marks possession in complex NPs, as well as being available to index the 'overflow' of clausal objects when for various reasons the prefixed verbal object slot is unavailable or already taken. With such widely diverse functions, we could expect DAT morphemes to be semantically underdetermined, their only obvious coding being for grammatical person and number features. This being the case we might look for a syntactic motivation for their occurrence, to account for their appearance in both nominal and clausal environments.

DAT morphemes appear to mark dependency status in both complex NPs and complex predicates; that is, they code forms that are syntactically dependent on some other form, which is the head. In possessive phrases DAT morphemes index the dependent possessor NP; in predicates the same morphology indexes objects dependent on the predicate's head, usually but not invariably a verb (see (13.33) in §13.2.2 (iii) below and discussion).

In §13.2.1 we will review a number of different lexical and syntactic classes of verbs, and the ways in which non-subcategorized objects are used within each class. Then in §13.2.2 we will look at the range of meanings that non-subcategorized objects may encode.[87] In the rest of this chapter and in the next, for convenience, the phrase 'non-subcategorized object' will be abbreviated to 'NSC object.'

13.2.1 Object-marking on a range of verbal subcategories

For the purposes of recording argument structure, we may discern formal distinctions among verbs in terms of (i) intransitive, (ii) object-demoting and (iii) fully transitive subtypes. Each subtype displays a somewhat different morphology with different syntactic consequences and different functional outcomes.

13.2.1 (i) objects on formally intransitive verbs
Complex predicates with intransitive classifiers may yet take objects, but of course such objects are not able to be registered as a verbal prefix (see example (11.44) in §11.5.1). Such occurrences are found when the classifier in a complex predicate is formally intransitive, but where the predicate itself is semantically transitive. Another example of this phenomenon is shown below, where the object *mangarri* 'vegetable food' is not indexed on the verb:

(13.18) Mangarri   minjarl-minjarl   kaaduna.
         mangarri   minjarl-minjarl   kaarr=nu-na
         veg.food   eat-eat   3p=be-PAST
         They used to eat vegetable food.

Pronoun objects, however, *are* able to be indexed on intransitive verbs as NSC objects in DAT position, as the following examples show:

(13.19a)
Aaja   yulul   kanunanangka.
aaja   yuluk   ka=nu-na-nangka
rain   approach   3a=be-PAST-DAT
Rain came towards him/her.

---

[87] The term 'indirect object' seems like an obvious choice to refer to this morphology, but it would nevertheless not always be accurate. As we will see, DAT morphemes often code semantic direct objects, and so the admittedly rather clumsy term 'non-subcategorized objects' will be preferred here.

(b)
Jaaljaal   kaadunaarerri,   marnumarnu
jaal-jaal   kaarr=nu-na-ᵏwara-eerri   marnuk-marnuk
carry.in.arms   3p=be-PAST-1DAT-PROG   carry.on.shoulder

kaadunaarerri   wangalangaanjanu.
kaarr=nu-na-ᵏwara-eerri   wangalang-aanjanu
3p=be-PAST-1DAT-PROG   child-ESS

They used to carry me in their arms, they used to carry me on their shoulders when I was a child.

(c)
Waa   laiburru   banganeenyanu.
waa   laiburru   ba-nga=nu-yinya-nu
not   know   CFT-1=be-PAST-2DAT

I didn't know you.

(d)
Angujakunya   irriwa   nyidunaarndaara?
anguja-ᵏwunya   irri-ᵇwa   [nyirr]=nu-na-[ᵏwarnda]-ᵏwara
what-PURP   hate-PROG   [2p]=be-PAST-[DU]-1DAT

Why do you two hate me?

(e)
Akurla   wanji   bangkaweenurrerndu.
akurlu   wanji   ba-ka=ᵇwee-[[nu-ᵏwurri]-ᵏwarndu]
devil   meet   CFT-3a=hit.MID-[[2pDAT]-DU]

A devil might find you both.

In each of these examples DAT morphology marks semantic direct objects; that is, patients who are directly effected by the verb's action; or themes. In (13.19e) the predicate *wanji =ᵇwee* 'find/meet up with someone, find/meet up with each other' employs an intransitive classifier derived from the transitive verb *=ᵇwu* 'hit.'

<u>13.2.1 (ii) object indexation in formally object-demoting constructions</u>
In object-demoting constructions the verb's undergoer slot is occupied by a celestial or terrestrial morpheme indexing a verbal complement or event, usually a speech event or the event denoted by a preverb if the verb is part of a complex predicate (§11.5.2). I have referred to predicates of this sort as object-demoting constructions. Here the predicate's preverb is indexed in undergoer position to the exclusion of any nominal object; no morphological process deletes nominal objects, rather object deletion comes out of the clause's information structure, specifically by way of the selection of a verbal complement rather than a noun as undergoer.

When a nominal object is to be indexed on a formally object-demoting verb classifier, it is accomplished by NSC object suffixes. In the following examples the object-demoting predicates shown are *maarlimaarli ma[ ]=ᵇwu* 'wave,' *jarriy kuN[ ]=ma* 'run,' *buju kuN[ ]=ᵇwu* 'finish, kill,' *rdurna kuN[ ]=yi* 'take hold,' *durr kuN[ ]=yi* 'stop,' *ngurr kuN[ ]=yi* 'strike,' and *nguru kuN[ ]=ᵏwangurru* 'listen,' and the nominal objects of these predicates are indexed in DAT position:

(13.20a)   Maarlimaarli   monanangka.
           maarlimaarli   ma-Ø=ᵇwu-na-nangka
           wave   VCOMP-3=hit-PAST-DAT
           He waved to him.

(b) Nyangka nyirno jarriy kumaaldaka Jimbirrij.
nyangka nyiN=rno jarriy kuN-Ø=ma-ᵏwaal-nangka jimbirrij
3fNAR 3f=DIST run VCOMP-3=get-hither-DAT rock.cod
The giant groper hurried back to her.

(c) Buju kubarrwunanangka wara.
(=11.37) buju kuN-ᵇwarr=ᵇwu-na-nangka wara
finish VCOMP-3p=hit-PAST-DAT kangaroo
They killed all the kangaroos.

(d) Inja rdurna wurrinangkaarndu.
inja rdurna ᵏwuN-[rra]=yi-nangka-[ᵏwarndu]
3aDEF take.hold VCOMP-[2p]=do-DAT-[DU]
You two grab hold of this.

(e) Durr kunjunangka nyineem mana.
durr kuN-Ø=yi-nangka nyiN=neem mana
stop VCOMP-3=do-DAT 3f=ear 3mDEF
He stopped her ears.

(f) Ngurr bungenangkeka.
ngurr ba-kuN-nga=yi-nangka-y₂aka
strike CFT-VCOMP-1=do-DAT-EMPH
I'll really belt her.

(g) Nguru kunyajaangudakerri.
(=11.57d) nguru kuN-nyarr-nya=ᵏwangurr(u)-nangka-eerri
hear VCOMP-1px-EP=carry-DAT-PROG
We're listening to him.

The sentence in example (13.20e) actually makes formal reference to three objects: the preverb *durr* 'stop, block' as a VCOMP object, the inalienable noun =*neem mana* 'ear' to the right of the predicate, and the 'owner' or 'whole' of which the ears are a part ('her') indexed on the classifier as -*nangka* 'DAT.' Sentence (13.20a) shows a terrestrial morpheme in VCOMP position; all the others have celestial VCOMPs.

<u>13.2.1 (iii) objects of *verba dicendi*</u>
If such a verb is not part of a complex predicate, then it may be a *verbum dicendi* or speech-framing verb, with the undergoer slot automatically filled by a celestial morpheme (glossed 'VCOMP') indexing the quoted or spoken material, either explicitly or implicitly (§4.1.3 (iii)). While classifiers need only index their preverbs in undergoer position when they enter into nuclear-core subordinate (object-demoting) constructions; Worrorra *verba dicendi* obligatorily index the celestial VCOMP morpheme in undergoer position. *Verba dicendi* register thought, speech or reported speech, or its denotation by means of a noun such as *ngarlangarla wunu* 'language, speech, discussion,' in undergoer position. I am aware of four *verba dicendi* in Worrorra:

kuN[ ]=yi *do; say, tell; think; want*
kuN[ ]=rloo *speak, talk*
kuN[ ]=miyangkana[88] *understand*
kuN[ ]=ᵇwaawaa *fail to understand*

---

[88] The verb =*miyangkana* has a second, possibly homophonous meaning 'recognize,' which is unconstrained in its selection of undergoer.

Verba dicendi are also able to code nominal objects by way of NSC object suffixes. 'Telling' and 'talking' are verbs of speech production, and these *verba dicenda* have addressee objects. The following examples show the verb *kuN[ ]=yi* used to frame direct (13.21a) and indirect (13.21b) speech. Note here how the direct speech example is in imperative mood, while its indirect counterpart is in hortative mood. Also shown in (13.21c) is the verb *kuN[ ]=rloo* used to denote a more extended or structured speech event. In all these examples addressee objects are indexed by DAT morphemes.

(13.21a)　'Bengkaalaaw,'　　　kubajenganangka.
　　　　　ba=ya-ᵏwaal-aaw　　kuN-ᵇwarr-nya=yi-ng-a-nangka
　　　　　CFT=go-hither-now　VCOMP-3p-EP=do-PAST-EP-DAT
　　　　　'Come here now,' they said to her.

(b)　　　Minyenangka　　　nyengkunyaal.
　　　　　minya=yi-nangka　nyiN=ya-ngku-nya-ᵏwaal
　　　　　2>3w=do-DAT　　 3f=go-EP-HORT-hither
　　　　　Tell her she can come over.

(c)　　　Kungarloonurreerri.
　　　　　kuN-nga=rloo-[nu-ᵏwurri]-eerri
　　　　　VCOMP-1=speak-[2pDAT]-PROG
　　　　　I'm talking to all of you.

Verbs of understanding or failing to understand have the opposite predicate perspective; they are verbs of speech perception. Accordingly their objects code the *speaker* in a speech event: the person whose speech is being, or failing to be, perceived. And the speaker in these clauses is coded by NSC object morphology on the verb:

(13.22a)　　Jaa maa　　minyamiyangkanaara.
(=10.11b)　 jaa maa　　minya=miyangkana-ᵏwara
　　　　　　 all.way　　 2>3w=understand-1DAT
　　　　　　 You must understand me properly.

(b)　　　Ngarlangarla　　kunjawaawaarlaara　　　　　　　　　　wunu.
　　　　　ngarlangarla　　kuN-nja=ᵇwaawaa-rla-ᵏwara　　　　　　wunu
　　　　　speech　　　　　VCOMP-2=not.understand-PAST-1DAT　3wDEF
　　　　　You didn't understand my argument.

Sentence (13.23) shows a complex sentence involving a form of *kuN[ ]=yi* 'say, tell; do' with *wunu ngarlangarla* 'speech, language, discussion' indexed in undergoer position as celestial ØN-:

(13.23) (=15.40a), (cf 12.1b)
Wardi　　ngana　ngambal　ngunngulum　　maa　　ngunbananangka
wardi　　 ngana　ngambal　ngun=ngulum　　maa　　ngun=ᵇwa-na-nangka
I.hope　　PROB　 pleased　　2=stomach　　　3mREF　2=fall-TNS-DAT

wunu　　ngarlangarla　　nganngunjunu　　　ke.
wunu　　ngarlangarla　　ØN-ngan-ngun=yi-nu　ke
3wDEF　 language　　　　VCOMP-1-SJTV=do-2DAT　3wREF
I think you might be pleased with the proposal I'm putting to you.

13.2.1 (iv) other uses of *kuN[ ]=yi*: naming and questioning

Although Worrorra has a simplex verb *=rima* 'name OBJ, call OBJ by name,' and a preverb *daleeba* 'recite, list (by name),' the verb *kuN[ ]=yi* is used for constructions of the 'SUBJ calls *x*, *y*' variety; where *x* is the person or thing named, and *y* is the name or status being bestowed upon *x*. In Worrorra *x*, the person or thing being named, is indexed on *kuN[ ]=yi* as an NSC object, with *y*, the name bestowed, marked compositionally by being close to the verb. The following sentences provide examples. In each case the DAT morpheme indexes the person or thing being named, even in (13.24b) where a tract of land is referred to. In (13.24c) the inalienable noun *=ngumbu wunu* 'name' is indexed in NSC object position on the verb, in a construction meaning 'called *x*=its name, *y*=Murray Springs.'

(13.24a)
Jijaaya   kurreenangka.
jijaaya   kuN-rra=yi-nangka
dad   VCOMP-2p=do-DAT
You can all call him 'dad.'

(b)
Kubajenganangka   dambeem   maa,   *Jujurr*
kuN-ᵇwarr-nya=yi-ng-a-nangka   dambeem   maa   jujurr
VCOMP-3p-EP=do-PAST-EP-DAT   place   3mREF   haul

Ingkaarrbanga   Dambeem.'
i-ngka-ᵇwarr=ma-nga   dambeem
3a-SJTV-3p=get-PAST   place
They called that country, 'The place where they carried him.'

(c)
Aalmara   kunjunganangka   wungumbu   *Murray Springs*
aalmara   kuN-Ø=yi-ng-a-nangka   ᵏwuN=ngumbu   murray springs
European   VCOMP-3=do-PAST-EP-DAT   3w=name   Murray Springs

kunjunganangka,   Wrewirri.
kuN-Ø=yi-ng-a-nangka   wrewirri
VCOMP-3=do-PAST-EP-DAT   PLACE.NAME
Europeans called Wrewirri *by the name 'Murray Springs.'*

The VCOMP undergoer of *kuN[ ]=yi* may index the interrogative sentential anaphor *ngani* 'what (event)?' (§10.5). When NSC object morphology is applied to *ngani kuN[ ]=yi* constructions, it codes objects effected, either positively or negatively, by the action questioned:

(13.25a)   Ngani   ngenangkorri   anja?
            ngani   ØN-nga=yi-[nangka-ᵏwurri]   anja
            what   VCOMP-1=do-[3Pdat]   3pDEF
            What can I do to/for them?

(b)   Ngani   kurringaarndaara?
            ngani   kuN-[rra]=yi-ng-[ᵏwarndu]-ᵏwara
            what   VCOMP-2p=do-PAST-DU-1DAT
            What have you two done to me?

13.2.1 (v) verbs of transfer

Transitive verbs may regularly be coded for two nominal objects; one in prefixed undergoer position, and the other in suffixed NSC object position. An inventory of uses for this kind of coding will be offered in §13.2.2, but for the moment, and to exemplify the kinds of syntactic arrangements and semantic constraints involved, we will look at the grammar of a typically trivalent situation, that of verbs of transfer; specifically those of giving and taking.

The Worrorra verb =*rno* 'give' has two objects, a recipient and a theme; here a theme will be understood as an entity not necessarily or immediately physically effected by the action of the verb, but one of interest or concern nonetheless, and in this case one whose location is at issue. Normally, however, only one of these objects, the recipient, being typically human, is indexed on the verb, in prefix position. The theme object is usually indicated compositionally, by occurring close to the verb. In (13.26) the theme *mangarri* 'food' is not indexed on the verb:

(13.26)   Mangarri   nganbardorna.
          mangarri   nga-n-^{b}warr=rno-rna
          veg.food   1-INV-3p=give-PAST
          They gave me some food.

The verb =*rno* may be used, as 'give' is in English, to denote the transfer of a person, usually a woman, between patrilines; that is, the act of giving someone away in marriage. In this situation both recipient and theme are human, and both must be indexed on the verb. However the rule that decides which object, the theme or the recipient, is coded in which object slot, is not straightforward; and in this case the grammar refers to the inverse hierarchy shown in Figure 5.4 in §5.3.4. The rule may be stated as follows:

1 A second-person object must be prefixed, regardless of whether it is recipient or theme.
2 In the absence of a second-person object, the recipient will be prefixed.

This rule automatically gives rise to formal coding ambiguity:

(13.27a)   Ngurnornaara.
           ngun-Ø=rno-rna-^{k}wara
           2-3=give-PAST-1DAT
           He gave me to you
           He gave you to me.

(b)   Ngurnornanangka.
           ngun-Ø=rno-rna-nangka
           2-1/3=give-PAST-DAT
           I/he gave you to him/her
           I/he gave him/her to you.

This ambiguity, however, is only formal: in any real-world exchange the identity, location and gender of speaker and addressee, and the context and occasion on which such utterances were made, would amply clarify reference.

In the absence of a second person actor, the recipient is coded in undergoer, and the theme in NSC object position:

(13.28a)   Kangarnornanangka.
           ka-nga=rno-rna-nangka
           3a-1=gave-PAST-DAT
           I gave her to him.

(b)   Kajirn   baangarnonangkorri   ngawaawanangkorri!
        kajirn   ba-kaarr-nga=rno-n-[nangka-ᵏwurri]   nga-waa-wa-[nangka-ᵏwurri]
        unable   CFT-3p-1=give-NON.P-[3pDAT]   ↳-AUG-El.Sib-[3pDAT]
        I can't give them to their own brothers!

Even though in (13.28b) both object slots on the verb are occupied by 3p morphemes, we know that it is the theme (the girls in this case, known from context) that receives DAT coding.

The matching verb with opposite predicate perspective is =*rnongku* 'take (something) away from (somebody),' with deprivee and theme objects. Again, it is the typically human deprivee who gets prefixed undergoer marking in most cases, while themes are adduced compositionally. In (13.29) the celestial theme is not indexed on the verb:

(13.29)   Wiyanu   wunu   angarnongku.
            wiyanu   wunu   arr-nga=rnongku
            fire   3wDEF   3p-1=take.away
            I'll take the fire away from them.

But again, a human theme must be indexed on the verb, by means of another hierarchical rule:

1 A first-person object must be prefixed, regardless of whether it is deprivee or theme.
2 In the absence of a first-person object, a second-person object must be prefixed, regardless of whether it is deprivee or theme
3 In the absence of first- and second-person objects, the deprivee will be prefixed.

Similar formal ambiguities result, again resolvable from information about speaker, addressee and context. Unambiguous coding only occurs in the absence of first or second person actors, as in (13.30b).

(13.30a)   Nganbardongkurlanangka   irraayaa   karraanya.
            nga-n-ᵇwarr=rnongku-rla-nangka   irra-aa-ya-aa   karra-aa-nya
            1-INV-3p=take.away-PAST-DAT   Fa-1DAT-3a-and   Mo-1DAT-3f
            They took me away from my mother and father
            They took my mother and father away from me.

(b)   Nyimbardongkurlanangka.
        nyiN-ᵇwarr=rnongku-rla-nangka
        3f-3p=take.away-PAST-DAT
        They took him/her away from her.

Having reviewed some of the patterns and constraints on the formal coding of NSC objects, we may now turn to a consideration of the variety of meanings they are able to be used for.

13.2.2 *Some uses for non-subcategorized objects*

In this section we will observe some of the functions that NSC objects in Worrorra may signal. Later this apparently straightforward list of etically-proposed semantic categories will break down and be seen to be rather less than straightforward; the categories prone to blurring and sliding into each other.

13.2.2 (i) beneficiaries

Cross-linguistically arguments in the semantic role of beneficiary are likely to appear as indirect or secondary objects, if a language has them or anything like them. And indeed this is the case in Worrorra: beneficiaries are coded as NSC objects. The following examples show a variety of situations in which beneficiaries occur.

(13.31a) Awa   wari   wirndiy   kanunanangkorri.
          awa   wari   wirndiy   ka=nu-na-[nangka-ʷwurri]
          3aNAR   kangaroos spear   3a=be-PAST-[3pDAT]
          He speared kangaroos for them.

(b)   Warndi   maajonanyarri.
          warndi   ma-ᵇwarr-nya=ᵇwu-na-nyarri
          make   3m-3p-EP=hit-PAST-1pxDAT
          They built it (a dormitory, mayaram mana) for us.

(c)   Mangarri   *ding-ding*   kunjungunyarri   minjarlkunya.
          mangarri   ding-ding   kuN-Ø=yi-ng-a-nyarri   minjarl-ʷwunya
          veg.food   ding-ding   VCOMP-3=do-PAST-EP-1pxDAT eat-PURP
          He used to ring the bell for us for dinner.[89]

(d)   Minyamaaldaka   *chair*   irrolija.
          minya=ma-ʷwaal-nangka   chair   irra-wulija
          2>3w=get-hither-DAT   chair   father-2KIN.POSS
          Get a chair for your father.

(e)   Ruluk   bayaara.
          ruluk   ba=ya-ʷwara
          move   CFT=go-1DAT
          Move over for me / make room for me.

(f)   Barra   nyimbarrkangurrurlaara   nyina   marangunya.
          barra   nyiN-ᵇwarr=ʷwangurru-rla-ʷwara   nyina   marangunya
          narrate   3f-3p=carry-PAST-1DAT   3fDEF   sun
          They told me the story about the sun.

In (13.31f) both a theme, *nyina marangunya* 'the sun,' and a beneficiary, 'me,' the listener, are indexed, with the theme in undergoer position.

13.2.2 (ii) affective dative[90]

The opposite situation occurs when an argument's referent is disadvantaged or adversely affected by an action; such arguments are also coded on verbs as NSC objects.

(13.32a) Anja   wangalaalunguyu   ngani   kurreenganangkorri?
          anja   wangalaalanguya   ngani   kuN-rra=yi-ng-a-[nangka-ʷwurri]
          3pDEF   children   what   VCOMP-2p=do-PAST-EP-[3pDAT]
          What have you done to these children?

---

[89] Literally, 'he did ding-ding for us to eat food.'
[90] Also called 'ethical dative.'

(b) Wurrkunu angujakunya mara kumbunaara?
wurrkunu angujaC-ᵏwunya mara kuN-Ø=ᵇwu-na-ᵏwara
trouble what-for see/find 3w-3=hit-PAST-1DAT
Why did he go and make ('find') trouble for me?

(c) Nanjan mana waay ngunngununanyarri.
nanjan mana waay ngun-ngun=nu-na-nyarri
ladder 3mDEF throw 2-SJTV=be-PAST-1pxDAT
When you threw away the ladder on us.

(d) Belangkarraya ngarru kaajengarrerndu?
belangkarraya ngarru kaarr-nya=ya-nga-[ngarri-ᵏwarndu]
many.people whither 3p-EP=go-PAST-[1pinDAT-DU]
Where's everyone gone?

(e) Arrke baawaard kaadunaara murlku.
(cf. 11.13) arrke baawaard kaarr=nu-na-ᵏwara murlku
3pREF rise:PL 3p=be-PAST-1DAT boil
Boils have broken out all over me.

In each example the referent of the DAT argument is adversely affected, even when this is not obvious from the English translation offered here. From the context in which (13.32a) is found it is clear that the children are suffering; likewise in (13.32c), the speakers are left stranded half-way up a cliff when the addressee throws away the ladder that got them up there. And in (13.32d) the first person inclusive dual (you and I) DAT object cannot be happily retained in translation while keeping the sentence a question. In this situation two children suddenly notice that their extended family has left them behind in the bush, with their own affectedness registered by DAT morphology.

13.2.2 (iii) external possession
Recalling its possessive use (§13.1), DAT morphology suffixed to a verb in NSC object position may be used to mark external possession. In this case the shape of the DAT morpheme codes the possessor, the dependent element in the construction, while the head, the possessed entity, will be some other argument in the clause. This construction constitutes a canonical instance of external possession, in which the possessor is coded as a grammatical relation of a verb, while the possessed item is expressed in a constituent separate from that which contains the possessor (cf Payne & Barshi 1999:3). The head of this construction in Worrorra may apparently be in any grammatical function except that of transitive subject.

Sentence (13.33) is a fuller version of the exchange shown in (1.1) in Chapter One:

(13.33)
'Wurlarnbirri nganiyaareya? Nganama kaanjaarndengaara?'
wurlarnbirri ngani-ᵏwara-ya ngani-ma kaarr-nja=ᵏwarnde-nga-ᵏwara
belongings where-1DAT-3p where-3m 3p-2=place-PAST-1DAT

'Karrangu kaangaarndenganu.'
karrangu kaarr-nga=ᵏwarnde-nga-nu
high 3p-1=place-PAST-2DAT
'Where's my things? Where did you put my (things)?'
'I put your (things) up there / I put them up there for you.'

The first question in (13.33) is verbless, predicate function being taken up by the inflected interrogative pronoun *nga-(ni)-* 'where?' (§7.4.1). Here the 1DAT morpheme codes the dependent possessor ('my'), while the head of the possessive construction is the noun *wurlarnbirri* 'possessions, things.' Similarly the other two sentences code possessors in DAT position, and possessed heads in verbal undergoer position, as 3p *kaarr-*. If *ngani* 'where?' in the first sentence may be understood as an intransitive predicate, a specifically interrogative form of *'be-at'*, then the head of the possessive construction (*wurlarnbirri*) is in S (intransitive subject) function. Another sentence with the head of an embedded possessive construction in S function is seen in (13.34) below:

(13.34)   Mayaranyinim   yorryorr   mawananangkorreerri.
          mayara-nyini-m   yorryorr   ma=ᵇwa-na-[nangka-ᵏwurri]-eerri
          house-ENDPOINT-3m   be.together   3m=fall-TNS-[3pDAT]-PROG
          Only their houses are left.

In this sentence the head of the possessive construction is *mayaram* 'house(s),' with the DAT morpheme *-nangkorri* indexing the dependent constituent.

Objects of formally intransitive complex predicates may also be heads of embedded possessive constructions, as seen in (13.35), with an object-demoting predicate in (a), and a formally intransitive one in (b):

(13.35a) Reey   kunjunganangkerri   iwajam.
          reey   kuN-Ø=yi-ng-a-nangka-eerri   i=ᵇwajam
          pluck   VCOMP-3=do-PAST-EP-DAT-PROG   3a=feather
          He_j pulled out all his_k feathers.

(b)   Kulnmerrba   rireey   nyinunangka   mana.
          kulnmerrba   reey-reey   nyiN=nu-na-nangka   mana
          tail   pluck-pluck   3f=be-PAST-DAT   3mDEF
          She stripped all the fur off his tail.

It is conceivable that DAT morphology could be coding the objects of these compositions, *iwajam* 'his feathers' and *kulnmerrba* '(his) tail,' respectively, instead of the owners of those objects. That this is not the case, but rather the DAT morphemes are coding possessor NPs dependent upon these objects, may be shown when the undergoer argument is coded on a formally transitive verb, as is (13.36):

(13.36a) Kulnmerrba   mamnyamanganangka.
          kulnmerrba   ma-Ø-mnya=ma-nga-nangka
          tail   3m-3=DD=get-PAST-DAT
          She grabbed his tail.

(b)   Kulnmerr   manjamangaara!
          kulnmerr   ma-nja=ma-nga-ᵏwara
          tail   3m-2=get-PAST-1DAT
          You grabbed my tail!

In both these sentences the terrestrial noun *kulnmerr* 'tail' receives undergoer coding *(ma-)* on the verb, while the owner of the tail gets DAT coding. Of the two arguments that could possibly be coded by DAT morphology in these constructions, it is clearly the dependent possessor that is so coded.

In (6.13a) (repeated below as (13.37)), there are three non-agent arguments, any one of which could potentially be receiving DAT coding: (i) *burnji* (plural/collective pro-form) 'magic,' (ii) =*neema* 'ears,' and (iii) *nyiN-* 'her:'

(13.37)   Burnji   anja   kaankarndenganangka   nyineemarnanya.
(=6.13a)   burnji   anja   kaarr-n-Ø=ᵏwarnde-nga-nangka   nyiN=neema-rnanya
           3pPRO   3pDEF   3p-INV-3=place-PAST-DAT   3f=ear=LOC
           He put a spell on her (lit: he put stuff (=magic) in her ears (=understanding, memory)).

Burnji 'magic' is here clearly indexed as 3p in undergoer position, while =*neema* 'ears,' as a locative adjunct, would not be expected to be encoded on the verb. So it is *nyiN-* 'her,' the owner of the adjunct, who receives DAT coding. Note that while, as an adjunct, the head of the possessive construction is not coded on the verb at all, its dependent *is* so coded, in DAT position.

13.2.2 (iv) themes

Objects (almost invariably people) of mental-state predicates meaning 'cry over/for (someone),' 'ask about (someone),' 'think (about someone),' 'be angry with (someone),' and 'be happy to see (someone),' and probably more, are all coded by NSC object morphology. These objects are goals towards which peoples' interests and emotions are directed, or with which they are preoccupied. They are also, more generally, the cause or source of the thought or emotion denoted in the instance under consideration. As formulated in §13.2.1 (v) above, they are objects of interest and/or concern to an agent, and are therefore themes. Note, however, that themes are not restricted to NSC object morphology; as mentioned in §11.4.2, undergoers of the transitive predicate *wala =ma* 'SUBJ cry for OBJ' are also themes. Constructions involving the preverb *wala* 'cry' with NSC object themes are shown in (13.38):

(13.38a) Wala kunjunganangkorri karranangkorrinya.
wala kuN-Ø=yi-ng-a-[nangka-ᵏwurri] karra-[nangka-ᵏwurri]-nya
cry VCOMP-3=do-EP-[3pDAT] Mother-[3pDAT]-3f
Their mother cried for them.

(b) Walaawirri kaadunanangka karranangkanyaa irranangka.
walaawirri kaarr=nu-na-nangka karra-nangka-nya-aa irra-nangka
cry.PL 3p=be-PAST-DAT mother-DAT-3f-and father-DAT
His mother and father cried for him.

Other NSC object constructions involving themes are illustrated below:

(13.39a) Nyina ngaard nyingamanganangka kawurlanangkanya.
nyina ngaard nyiN-nga=ma-nga-nangka kawurla-nangka-nya
3fDEF ask 3f-1=get-PAST-DAT daughter-DAT-3f
I asked his daughter about him.

(b) Arri ajula kerrbanganangkerri.
(=12.4) arri arr=yula ka-nyarr=ma-nga-nangka-eerri
We(exc) px=anger 3a-1px=get-PAST-DAT-PROG
We were getting angry with him.

(c) Waa jukurl-jukurl banganineerri.
waa jukurl-jukurl ba-nga=ni-n-nu-eerri
not happy-happy CFT-1=be-PRES-2DAT-PROG
I'm not happy to see you.

Sentence (13.39a) presents another example of the kind of inherent ambiguity discussed in §13.2.1 (v): the reported addressee, 'his daughter' is encoded by the definite article *nyina* and in undergoer postion *(nyiN-)*, as well as being stated in full as *kawurlanangkanya* 'his daughter.' The theme ('about him') is coded in NSC object position. From the narrative in which this statement was uttered, we know that this is the intended reading. Yet this sentence could also mean 'I asked her about her/(his) daughter,' again with reported addressee in undergoer position, but this time with the theme stated in full, as *kawurlanangkanya*, as well as being given DAT coding. And again, situation and context would clarify this kind of potential ambiguity.

The experiencer construction in (13.39b), discussed in §12.1, also involves a theme in DAT position. Sentence (13.39c) demonstrates the complex predicate *jukurl(-jukurl)* =*nu*+DAT with an apparently idiomatic meaning 'SUBJ be happy to see OBJ,' with the theme object given DAT coding.

<u>13.2.2 (v) emblematic representation</u>
This section addresses a particular kind of theme, involving relationships of emblematic or totemic representation between people, land and dreamtime ancestors. The preverb *gee* 'SUBJ be represented totemically by OBJ' is used in similar circumstances, but its grammar is relatively straightforward, and will not be discussed here.

Worrorra *joy* is a predicate adjective that only occurs with =*nu* 'be.' It is not found in the database in attributive function, nor compounded with any other finite verb. Daisy Utemorrah stated that this word means 'famous,' and translated it in some passages as 'represent.' Both people (13.40b), and ancestors (13.40a) may be said to be 'famous,' without specifying a relational context:

(13.40a) Ngarrunangkowa   joy   ngenu?
          ngarrunangkowa   joy   nga-nya=nu
          which.way   famous   1-OPT=be
          Where will I be famous? (ie, *where will I establish my totemic domain?*)

(b)   Ardirndeerri   anja   Dilangarri   joy   kaaduna.
          arr=rnirndeerr-i anja   dilangarri   joy   kaarr=nu-na
          3p=ancient-3p   3pDEF   CLAN.NAME   famous   3p=be-PAST
          The ancient Dog-people used to be famous.

In (13.40a) the speaker is a crocodile ancestor predestined to become a totemic emblem for a particular group of people in a particular place. In this usage *joy* seems to refer specifically to totemic status. On the other hand the extended family of humans referred to as being 'famous' in (13.40b) are *not* totems, rather they are represented by their totems, the giant dogs of their name (Clendon 2009). Places may also be 'famous:'

(13.41)
Maa maanma   joy   mamnyanunangka   mana   dambeem.
maa maan-ma   joy   ma-mnya=nu-na-nangka mana   dambeem
3mREF SPEC-3m   famous   3m-DD=be-PAST-DAT   3mDEF   place
That place became famous because of him.

Sentence (13.41) denotes a relationship between the 'famous' status of the land and a particular (quasi-historical) person. From these examples it is clear that ancestors, land and people can all be 'famous.' And as seen in (13.41) the source of the 'fame' of any one of these categories may be coded on these complex predicates in NSC object position *(-nangka* 'because of him' in this example). In the database at least, there is a symmetrical relationship between the 'famous' entity and the source or reason for its fame, as diagrammed in Figure 13.1:

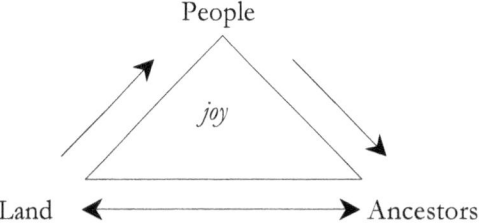

Figure 13.1: emblematic relationships denoted by *joy* 'famous'

Consider the further examples in (13.42):

(13.42a)

Ngayangkarnanya	wali wunu	kawa	wungumbu	ke,	joy
ngayaangkarnanya	wali wun	kawa	ᵏwuN=ngumba	ke	joy
Mt.Trafalgar	PM	3wNAR	3w=name	3wREF	famous

kumnyaninyanangkorri	Wurnbangkuwaaya	arrke.
kuN-mnya=ni-nya-[nangka-ᵏwurri]	Wurnbangku-waa-ya	arrke
3w-DD=be-HORT-[3pDAT]	PLACE.NAME-PERS-3p	3pREF

Ngayangkarnanya is its name, and it can represent the people of Wurnbangku.

(b)

Angujakunya	anja	yawarrarra	kaanjiyandarla,	anja
angugaC-ᵏwunya	anja	yawarrarra	kaarr-nja=yanda-rla	anja
what-PURP	3pDEF	drown.PL	3p-2=cause-PAST	3pDEF

belangkarraya	Dilangarri	anja?	Waawa	joy
belangkarra-ya	dilangarri	anja	waawa	joy
many.people-3p	CLAN.NAME	3pDEF	NEG.INTER	famous

baadinyaneerri?
ba-kaarr=ni-nya-nu-eerri
CFT-3p=be-PAST-2DAT-PROG

Why did you cause them to drown, all those Dilangarri people? Weren't they famous because of you?

(c)

Nyangka	Wurnbangkuwaamaanya	nyangke,	joy	mamnyanunangka
nyangka	Wurnbangku-waa-maan-nya	nyangke	joy	ma-mnya=nu-nangka
3fNAR	CLAN.COUNTRY-PERS-SPEC-3f	3fREF	famous	3m-DD=be-DAT

mana	dambeem.
3mDEF	place

She belongs only to the land of Wurnbangku, that place is [famous because of/ represents] her.

(d)

Mana	aja	bungkamnyaninya	wunu,	ke	ngarri
mana	aja	ba-kuN-mnya=ni-nya	wunu	ke	ngarri
3mDEF	sit	CFT-3w-DD=be-PAST	3wDEF	3wREF	we(inc)

joy	ngarrkuninyanangka.
joy	ngarr-ngun=ni-yinya-nangka
famous	1pin-SJTV=be-PAST-DAT

It should have been here, we wanted to represent it.

Example (13.42a), like (13.41), is an instance in which land is famous for, or emblematic of people: Mount Trafalgar is a large and spectacular mesa on the north shore of the St George's Basin, visible for miles around, and would certainly have been emblematic of the land in which it stood, just as its harbour bridge is emblematic of Sydney. In (13.42b) we see people famous because of their relationship with a dreamtime culture hero, in this case a giant talking dog. It is not clear whether those mythical people could be considered to be emblems of the culture hero in question. In (13.42c) a tract of land is famous for its association with a female dreamtime ancestor, and in (13.42d) a group of dreamtime ancestors are famous for, or emblematic of, Mount Trafalgar.

Translations of the adjective *joy* must therefore vary among 'represent,' 'be famous for,' and 'be emblematic of,' according to situation. We may nonetheless discern the set of partially reciprocal emblematic relations diagrammed in Figure 13.1, as they are represented in the database. In this figure the base of an arrow represents the famous entity, with the head of the arrow pointing to the cause or source of its fame. It is likely that recourse to a more complete corpus would enable all arrows to be double-headed. In every instance the source or cause of fame, or the entity for which a given denotatum stands as an emblem, is coded as a theme in DAT position on the verb =*nu* 'be.'

13.2.2 (vi) experiencers as syntactic objects

In §12.3.1 we observed how experiencers in some constructions may function as syntactic subjects while yet receiving objective case-marking. Some examples of experiencer subjects coded by NSC object morphology were offered in (12.7 – 12.9). There is another construction, however, not particularly well represented in the database, in which experiencers function as syntactic *objects* while receiving NSC object coding. Two examples are shown in (13.43):

(13.43a)   Mamangkunu   kununanangkaarndu.
           mamangkunu   kuN=nu-na-[nangka-^{k}warndu]
           morning   3w=be-PAST-[DAT-DU]
           It was morning.

(b)   Aalmara   kawi,   waa   bangkaninyanyarri.
         aalmara   kawi   waa   ba-ka=ni-nya-nyarri
         European   3aNEG   not   CFT-3a=be-PAST-1pxDAT
         There were no Europeans, they weren't around.

In neither of these sentences can the NSC objects be simply translated into English. This construction denotes an event, with what are effectively witnesses or bystanders to the event coded in DAT position; so: 'it was morning and they both experienced it,'[91] and 'we experienced a time when there were no Europeans.'

13.2.2 (vii) an approach less etic

In this section we have surveyed some of the functions in which NSC object morphology is called to serve. Of course this does not exhaust the possibilities, as it appears that DAT marking could potentially be available to index any object-like semantic role with a denotatum animate and salient enough to warrant it. For example, in (13.19a) and (13.20b) above, and in (13.45b) below, we can see the role of 'goal' indexed by NSC object morphology. Even the typically intransitive predicate *aja =nu* 'sit' appears in the database with a NSC object (13.44); the DAT morphology in this case apparently serving to host a dual morpheme with an outranked actor meaning (§9.2):

(13.44)   Jilinya   kurde   aja   nyinunangkaarndeerri.
          jilinya   kurde   aja   nyiN=nu-na-[nangka-^{k}warndu]-eerri
          demon   ASSOC   sit   3f=be-PAST-[DAT-DU]-PROG
          There was a female demon sitting with them both.

Non-subcategorized object morphology is employed as well to code argument structure in certain serial-predicate constructions (§11.5.4 (iii)), and to code direct objects in complement clauses, as will be seen in Chapter 14. This last grammar is formally a variety of indirect speech, the basics of which have been outlined in §13.2.1 (iii) above.

Finally, consider the pair of sentences in (13.45):

---

[91] A closer literal translation might be 'it dawned on them two,' but this has a completely different meaning in English.

(13.45a)   Aaku   kungkangurraalkarreerri.
           aku   kuN-Ø=ᵏwangurru-ᵏwaal-ngarri-eerri
           water   3w-3=carry-hither-1pinDAT-PROG
           He's bringing some water for us (inc).

(b)   Imnyaangurrunangka   karranangkanyawunya.
(=10.71a) i-mnya=ᵏwangurru-nangka   karra-nangka-nya-ᵏwunya
           3a-DD=carry-DAT   mother-DAT-3f-PURP
           Take him to his mother.

Both sentences involve DAT-marking on the verb =ᵏ*wangurru* 'take, carry.' In (13.45a) a beneficiary role is coded, while in (13.45b) the NSC object indexes a goal, marked by -ᵏ*wunya* 'PURP' on the following noun.⁹² Note, however, that -ᵏ*wunya*'s semantic scope is broad enough to include beneficiaries, as seen in (10.74a) in §10.6.3 (i); so its denotation of goalhood is not guaranteed. And anyway, in many cases it is just not clear whether goals or beneficiaries are being coded; that is, when used on verbs like =ᵏ*wangurru*, whether only the motion is being denoted, or its motivation as well. Consider the sentences in (13.46):

(13.46a)   Irranangka   kaankangurrunangkerri   mangarri.
           irra-nangka   kaarr-n-Ø=ᵏwangurru-nangka-eerri   mangarri
           father-DAT   3p-INV-3=carry-DAT-PROG   food
           S/he's taking food to his/her father.

(b)   Yarrkorli   irriyaara   ngurru.
           yarrkorli   i-rra=ee-y-ᵏwara   ngurru
           hang.down   3a-2p=place-EP-1DAT   here
           Hang it down here to/for me.

While in (13.46a) the father would appear to be a beneficiary, he could just as easily be a goal, or both. In (13.46b) a man at the bottom of a well is asking his friends to hang a rope *(mamurlanja inja)* down so he can climb out. The adverb *ngurru* 'here' clearly signals directional motion, but just as clearly the act is to be done for the speaker's benefit.

External possession (§13.2.2 (iii)) is another source of etic ambiguity. In the following examples the first person singular morpheme *(-ᵏwara)* could signal a variety of meanings: possessive, beneficiary, deprivee, affective, or combinations thereof:

(13.47a)   Kulaaya   karlewa   debarr   keng**aara**   inja.
           kula-aa-ya   karle-ᵇwa   debarr   ka=ya-nga-ᵏwara   inja
           husband-1DAT-3a now-PROG   die   3a=go-TNS-**1DAT** 3aDEF
           Now my husband has died.

(b)   Nyangkaangkaya   anja   angkuyu   kaanmr**aara**?
           nya-ngkaa-ngka-ya   anja   angkuyu   kaarr-n-Ø=mra-ᵏwara
           ↳-AUG-girl-3p   3pDEF   who   3p-INV-3=gather-**1DAT**
           Who will take these girls off me? / who will take my girls?

(c)   Wangalaalunguyu   arrke   akurla   kaanmrang**aara**.
           wangalaalanguya   arrke   akurla   kaarr-n-Ø=mra-nga-ᵏwara
           children   3pREF   demon   3p-INV-3=gather-PAST-**1DAT**

---

⁹² The 'him' on this occasion was a crying child, one whom the mother was at the time not keen to receive, and clearly did not consider herself to be a beneficiary of the transfer.

A demon took my children.

In (13.47a) first person singular morphology appears on both the kinship noun *kulaaya* 'my husband' and on the verb. If a possessive reading is involved in the verbal morpheme, then it is redundant, possession already being coded on the noun. It is more likely that the verbal morpheme signals an affective dative reading, or that both meanings are intended. Similarly in (13.47c), possessive and affective dative readings are both plausible for the 1DAT morpheme on the verb. In (13.47b) a man is wondering where he can find husbands for his grown-up daughters. In a possessive reading of the morpheme in question, he is asking 'who will take my girls?' In another reading he is a deprivee, and in yet another he is a beneficiary, as it is to his advantage to have them married off satisfactorily. It is not possible etically to decide which of these readings the speaker intended, or indeed, whether two or more of these readings were not intended simultaneously.

Fourteen: complement clauses

In Chapter 11 generally, and in §11.5.2 in particular, it was shown how preverbs may frequently enter into hypotactic relations with verb classifiers: in these cases the preverb is embedded in the classifier's core as a complement of the classifier, although the linkage is tighter than that usually envisaged when verbal complementation is considered. In this chapter another, looser, kind of complementation is brought into consideration, one that has been referred to intermittently throughout this grammar, in §4.1.3 (iii), §5.1, §5.3.1, §7.2, §8.2.1, §8.4.3, §9.6.2, §10.6.3 (i), §11.5.2, and §13.2.2 (vii). This construction involves the general-purpose pro-classifier *kuN[ ]=yi* 'do' in its non-classifier use as a simplex verb. A quick outline of this verb's basic usage, as a simplex verb, has been provided in §13.2.1 (iii), and the reader is referred to that section. The present chapter describes the use of *kuN[ ]=yi* as a matrix verb, and more particularly the kinds of clauses that may be subordinated to it, as a matrix. The sentences or speech events embedded under or subordinated to *kuN[ ]=yi* will be referred to as complement clauses$_1$.

A number of factors motivate the treatment of the framing verb–framed clause relationship in Worrorra as one of syntactic dependence. Such an analysis is isomorphic with the classifier–preverb relationship described in Chapter 11; in both cases the embedding of an eventive complement is signalled formally by celestial indexation on the verb *kuN[ ]=yi* in undergoer position. The status of *kuN[ ]=yi* as a superordinate framing verb for both preverbs and complement clauses$_1$ is guaranteed by its obligatory indexation of celestial morphology: *kuN[ ]=yi* can never appear without celestial indexation, and only this class is permitted in its undergoer slot. A comprehensive survey of the relationship between framing verbs and framed clauses is to be found in Rumsey (2010), who documents the widespread cross-linguistic treatment of framed clauses as grammatical undergoers.

Worrorra complement clauses$_1$ may represent any of three pragmatic functions, as illustrated in (14.1):

(14.1) [Wangarr ema] kubajungu.
 wangarr a-Ø-nya=ma kuN-^{b}warr=yi-ng
 forget 3a-3-OPT=get VCOMP-3p=do-PAST
 1. *They said, ['s/he'll forget him.']*
 2. *They said [s/he would forget him].*
 3. *They wanted [him/her to forget him].*

As shown, a single form may signal any or all of these pragmatic functions, represented here by their English translations numbered 1-3. The first function encodes direct speech, a way of reporting what is emically and ideally understood to be the more or less exact wording used in a speech event.[93] The

---

[93] It has long been recognized (eg Wierzbicka 1974) that 'direct speech' may not be used to report exact wording at all, but may serve as a device for dramatic effect and other discourse purposes. This is not material to the

second function codes indirect speech, a way of reporting the semantic content of a speech event, without claiming that exact wording is involved. The third function is that of the complement clause₂ more narrowly defined, the coding of some mental process (volition in the example above) that is not uttered, or at least whose utterance is immaterial to the context in which the clause₂ appears.[94] To clarify this terminology, the kinds of clauses under discussion are related as in the diagram in (14.2):

(14.2)

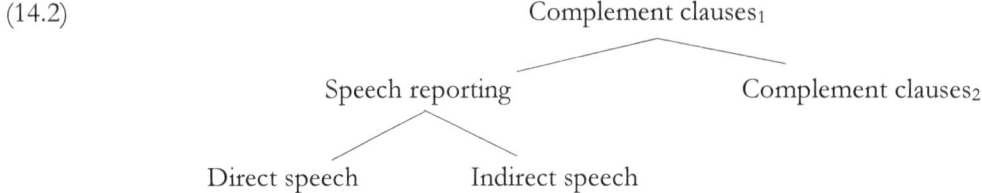

Here the expression 'complement clause₁' represents the entire range of types, while 'complement clause₂' represents a sub-type. The taxon 'Speech reporting' is discussed in §14.4. Sections §14.2 and §14.3 are concerned primarily with complement clauses₂.

As both *verbum dicendi* and pro-verb, *kuN[ ]=yi* is well suited to its role as general-purpose matrix predicate; and indeed its range of meanings, as discussed below, is wide: 'say, tell, think, suppose, know, want' in its role as a verb framing both speech and cognition, as well as 'do' more generally. As a *verbum dicendi* it may never appear without celestial indexation in undergoer position, so it obligatorily codes sentential material of some sort in object grammatical function. As a classifier, *kuN[ ]=yi* codes preverbs in undergoer position; as a matrix it codes sentences, thoughts and speech events generally.

14.1 *kuN[ ]=yi* as *verbum dicendi*

As noted in §13.2.1 (iii), after its pro-verbal function *kuN[ ]=yi* is at base a speech-framing verb. In this usage *kuN[ ]=yi* has three main semantic functions or 'meanings,' all denoting mental states and attitudes in either internal or external (spoken) manifestations. It is probably the case that at least all these mental stance meanings, 'say, think, know, want,' are related polysemously as sense meanings, in a manner comparable to that in which the *connaître* and *savoir* senses of the English verb *know* are related.

The material introduced or framed by this verb consists of a complement clause₁ representing an utterance or mental process which is indexed on the matrix in celestial undergoer position. In these constructions the complement clause₁ normally appears in front of the matrix verb, which is in turn usually at the end of the sentence it heads, as seen for example in (14.3a,b, 14.4) and (14.5) below. In these examples complement clauses₁ are circumscribed by square brackets.

(14.3a)   ['Angujakunya   wala   kunjiyeerri?']   kunjunganangka.
             anguja-ᵏwunya   wala   kuN-nja=yi-eerri   kuN-Ø=yi-ng-a-nangka
             what-PURP   cry   VCOMP-2=do-PROG   VCOMP-3=do-PAST-EP-DAT
             '*Why are you crying?*' *he asked him.*

(b)   ['Bengkaalaaw,']   kubajenganangka.
(=13.21a)   ba=ya-ᵏwaal-aaw   kuN-ᵇwarr-nya=yi-ng-a-nangka
             CFT=go-hither-now   VCOMP-3p-EP=do-PAST-EP-DAT
             '*Come here now,*' *they said to her.*

---

present discussion, which concerns a language-specific encoding of the direct–indirect distinction itself, rather than the motivations for each category.

[94] Rumsey (1990) has maintained for Ungarinyin that these three pragmatic functions are not emically distinguished, and that this situation is reflected in Ungarinyin sentence structure.

(c) Minyenangka [nyengkunyaal].
(=13.21b) minya=yi-nangka nyiN=ya-ngku-nya-^kwaal
  2>3w=do-DAT 3f=go-EP-HORT-hither
  Tell her she can come over.

The non-subcategorized (NSC)[95] object morphemes (DAT) on the matrix verbs here and in (14.4) index addressees (see §13.2.1 (iii)). We can note a difference in these sentences along the lines of the direct–indirect speech distinction observable in many languages. While the complement clause$_1$ verb in (14.3a) has a second-person subject; and while the complement$_1$ verb in (14.3b) is imperative, with an unmarked or understood second-person subject, that in (14.3c) is hortative, with a third-person subject. Sentence (14.3c) could conceivably have a direct-speech interpretation, as ?*tell him, 'she can come over'* with the referent of the complement-clause subject different from that of the matrix object. But this was not the case in the speech event in which this utterance was recorded: while it is possible or even likely that the Worrorra sentence *may* serve for the questioned translation, it was spoken with the meaning given. However, in other situations this kind of distinction may not be apparent at all:

(14.4)
Karle we nyirrwaarndu nganngunjungunurrerndu,
karle we nyirr=^bwa-^kwarndu ØN-ngan-ngun=yi-ng-u-[[nu-^kwurri]-^kwarndu]
now/then lie.down 2p=fall-DU VCOMP-1-SJTV=do-PAST-EP-[[2pDAT]-DU]

waa burnu birreenya.
waa burn-u ba-kuN-rra=yi-yinya
not PRO-3w CFT-VCOMP-2p=do-PAST
1. *When I told you both to lie down and go to sleep, you didn't do it.*
2. *When I told you both, 'lie down and go to sleep,' you didn't do it.*

The first part of this sentence contains a complement clause$_1$ ((*karle*) *we nyirrwaarndu*) in either imperative or hortative mood.[96] I am not sure whether the change-of-state conjunction *karle* should be included or excluded from the complement clause, as 'now lie down …' or 'then when I told you …' Whether it is or not, on the surface it seems that the direct–indirect distinction is irrelevant to sentences such as (14.4).

Thinking in Worrorra is represented as being analogous to speech, as internal conversation or monologue. The verb *kuN[ ]=yi* is able to frame thoughts as if they were speech:

(14.5a)
[Mangkaanya nyina ngarru nyengaara,]
mangka-aa-nya nyina ngarru nyaN=ya-nga-^kwara
wife$_i$-1DAT-3f 3fDEF whither 3f$_i$=go-PAST-1DAT

kungamnyenganu.
kuN-nga-mnya=yi-ng-a-nu
VCOMP-1-DD=do-PAST-EP-2DAT$_i$
I was thinking about you, wondering where that wife of mine had gone.

(b) (=11.52a)
[Maniyam maan ngana mana kurdu kungoyeerri]
ma=niya-m maan ngana mana kurdu kuN-nga=^bwu-yeerri
3m=good-3m SPEC PROB 3mDEF chase VCOMP-1=hit-PROG

---

[95] See Chapter 13.
[96] The hortative suffix *-(yi)nya* is absent from intransitive forms with plural participant subjects (§8.5.1).

kunjungu.
kuN-Ø=yi-ng
VCOMP-3=do-PAST
He thought/supposed he was chasing after it in a safe place.

(c) (=10.28b)
[Karle	kenga]	ngaali	kunyajunganu.
karle	ka=ya-nga	ngaali	kuN-nyarr=yi-ng-a-nu
now	3a$_i$=go-TNS	WRONG	VCOMP-1px=do-PAST-EP-2DAT$_i$

We thought/supposed you'd gone.

From these examples we can see that representations of speech and thought are formally indistinguishable. Although from context it is clear that a sense meaning 'thought' is intended in each case, the same *forms* could be used to represent utterances, but of course with different intonations and different meanings. For instance, the form of (14.5a) could be used to mean 'I asked you where my wife had gone/I asked you "where's my wife gone?"' with the complement subject not co-referential with the matrix object; the form of (14.5b) could be used to mean 'he said, I'm chasing it in what is probably a safe place;' and the form of (14.5c) could be used to mean 'we mistakenly told you he'd gone/we were wrong when we told you he'd gone.' Note however that in complement-clause$_2$ pragmatic function, the NSC object morphemes in (14.5a,c) do not index addressees; rather they have a thematic interpretation in these sentences (§13.2.2 (iv)).

The continuum from speaking to thinking to knowing is denoted by the verb *kuN[ ]=yi*. In (14.6) this verb in its matrix occurrence means 'know.' In example (14.6a) both clauses are discontinuous: this example has already been discussed in §5.1, and the reader is referred to that section, and to §14.3.4 below. In this sentence the matrix occurrence of *kuN[ ]=yi* denotes *knowing*, while its occurrence in the complement clause$_2$ denotes *doing*. Here, then, are two quite distinct sense meanings in compositionally adjacent forms (from now on actor identity will be co-indexed by subscripts):

(14.6a) (=5.8)
Waa	[kubajeerri]	bungkaajeenyanangkorri	[arrka
waa	kuN-^{b}warr=yi-eerri	ba-kuN-^{b}warr=yi-yinya-nangkorri	arrka
not	VCOMP-3p$_i$=do-PROG	CFT-VCOMP-3p=do-PAST-3pDAT$_i$	3pNAR$_i$

wangalaalunguyu.]
children$_i$
They didn't know [what their children were doing].

(b) (=10.52b)
[Ngani	kunjungu]	wardi	bungkaajaara.
ngani	kuN-Ø=yi-ng	wardi	ba-kuN-^{b}warr=yi-^{k}wara
what	VCOMP-3$_i$=do-PAST	hope	CFT-VCOMP-3p=do-1DAT$_i$

I hope they know [what happened to me].

We have found so far a semantic, but no formal distinction between *saying* and *thinking*. Here we still find no formal distinction, but another semantic one between *saying/thinking* on the one hand and *knowing* on the other. Example (14.6a) *cannot* mean **they didn't tell their children what to do/to do it*, and (14.6b) cannot mean **I hope they say to me, 'what happened?'* While the *saying* and *thinking* sense meanings may be more or less interchangeable in (14.5), those meanings are not interchangeable with *knowing* in (14.6).

14.2 *kuN[ ]=yi* as a tense-marking verb

In many of its occurrences as a matrix verb, *kuN[ ]=yi* appears to be semantically void, its only apparent function being to impart time reference to its complement clause$_2$, in circumstances where such complements are unable to code tense. In this section we will look at sentences where the subject of the complement clause$_2$ is the same as that of the matrix (that is, at 'same-subject' constructions). In this situation the matrix verb acquires whatever non-referential meaning it may exhibit, by raising it from its verbal complement. Observe tense and modality marking in (14.7):

(14.7a)   [Ngeyu]   kungayeerri.
          nga-nya=ya   kuN-nga=yi-eerri
          1-OPT=go   VCOMP-1=do-PROG
          I want to go.

(b)   [Ngeyu]   kungenga.
          nga-nya=ya   kuN-nga=yi-ng
          1-OPT=go   VCOMP-1=do-PAST
          I wanted to go.

Example (14.7a) is potentially synonymous with its complement clause$_2$: *ngeyu* can mean both 'I will go' and 'I want to go.' But whereas verbs in optative mood are usually ambiguous between future time reference and volition (§8.2.1), optative verbs in periphrastic complement-clause$_2$ constructions denote volition unambiguously (§8.2.2). Note also in these examples how time reference and modality are distributed: the optative-mood verb *ngeyu* is unable to mark tense (§8.2), its time-reference in this case being shown on the matrix verb, which marks tense as *present* in (14.7a) and *past* in (b). Likewise the semantics of volition resides solely in the complement clause$_2$ verb; it imparts a volitional sense upwards to its matrix. The matrix assumes control of time-reference for the entire sentence, leaving the complement clause$_2$ with access to only the modal, volitional sense of its optative mood. In constructions of this sort, then, tense flows down from the matrix to the complement, while modal semantics, in this case volition, moves up from the complement to the matrix, as diagrammed in (14.8):

(14.8)

MATRIX
tense   *modality*
COMPLEMENT

As Role-and-Reference theory predicts (Foley & Van Valin 1984:256), two predicates in a subordinate linkage of this nature cannot be independently specified for tense and modality, which is just what we find here.

The use of a matrix verb to code tense on a subordinate clause is transparently derived from a direct-speech situation: to paraphrase Rumsey (1990:349, ex 5), sentences like (14.7a) may be translated literally as *I am doing: 'I will go.'* Nevertheless there is evidence that something other than direct speech is being signalled in these constructions. While examples like (14.7) may not depict the kind of complement clauses found in English, we are yet able to distinguish in Worrorra direct speech and another kind of complement distinct from it.

The use of matrix *kuN[ ]=yi* to encode tense on complement clauses$_2$ is particularly evident in intransitive same-subject constructions. In (14.9) below, the complement clauses$_2$ are de-transitivized by means of a valency-reducing device, glossed MID (see Chapter 16):

(14.9a)   [Barda   ngewee]   kunjungu.
          barda   nga-nya=ᵇwee   kuN-Ø=yi-ng
          kill   1ᵢ-OPT=hit.MID   VCOMP-3ᵢ=do-PAST
          He wanted [to kill himself].

(b)   [Ngeninjiye]   binjee.
          nga-nya=ninja-ye   ba-kuN-nja=yi
          1-OPT=look.at-MID   CFT-VCOMP-2=do
          You might want [to look at yourself].

But this use holds as well for sentences with transitive complement clauses₂, as seen in (14.10):

(14.10a) [Awa   irranangka   mara   ingo]   kunjungu.
          awa   irra-nangka   mara   i-nga=ᵇwu   kuN-Ø=yi-ng
          3aNAR   fatherₖ-DATᵢ see   3aₖ-1ᵢ=hit   VCOMP-3ᵢ=do-PAST
          Heᵢ wanted [to see hisᵢ father].

(b)   Arri   [ngamuku   nyarrama]   kunyajeerri.
          arri   ngamuku   ØN-nyarr-a=ma   kuN-nyarr=yi-eerri
          we(exc)   milk   3w-1pxᵢ-OPT=get   VCOMP-1pxᵢ=do-PROG
          We want [to get some milk].

A present-tense version of example (14.10a) could be expressed in a simplex optative-mood construction: *awa irranangka mara ewu* 'he will/wants to see his father,' and a simplex version of (14.10b) would merely omit the matrix verb *kunyajeerri*. It would seem, then, that the functions of same-subject complement clause₂ constructions are restricted pretty much to (i) disambiguating optative sense meanings, and (ii) encoding tense on complement clauses₂.

A construction in which a matrix verb imparts its time-reference to a subordinate clause is potentially available to encode tense on any complement-clause₂ verb that cannot display it. The other formal class of verbs in Worrorra that cannot bear tense are potential forms, occurring when order-class [9] on a counterfactual verb is left empty (§8.3, Table 8.7), and used chiefly to denote hopes and fears as described in §8.4.4. But there are only a couple of examples of potential-mood complement clauses₂ in the database, and in both of them their subjects are different from those of their matrices. A potential-mood complement clause₂ is illustrated below in (14.27) in §14.3.4.

While tense-marking is a significant function of complement-clause₂ constructions, it is not their only one. Just as importantly, these constructions are used to track participants in constructions where the subject of the complement clause₂ is different from that of the matrix ('different-subject' constructions).

14.3 The syntax of complement clauses₂

The reader may have noticed that the subjects of complement clauses so far presented have on a number of occasions been coded as first person singular, in situations where such coding is not reflected in the English translation provided. This coding may be accounted for on the understanding that complement clauses₁ represent direct-speech quotations, as discussed in relation to Ungarinyin by Rumsey (1982:87-89, 95-96, 157-166; 1990:348-349), and as seen in (14.4). In this interpretation, the translations of the examples in question may be re-phrased as follows: (14.5b) *he thought, 'I'm probably chasing it in a safe place;'* (14.7) *I think/thought, 'I will go;'* (14.9a) *he thought, 'I will kill myself;'* and (14.9b) *you might think, 'I will look at myself.'*[97] However, and despite appearances, from further consideration it

---

[97] The grammar of (14.10a) will be considered below.

appears that the use of a first person singular morpheme indexes a non-quotational complement-clause₂ style.

14.3.1 Intransitive same-subject complements

For present purposes, we should note three types of intransitive complement clauses₂ in Worrorra: (i) clauses with simple intransitive verbs, as seen in (14.7), (ii) clauses with object-demoting predicates, as seen in (14.5b) and (14.12a) below, and (iii) derived intransitive clauses, as seen in (14.9). All these examples exhibit same-subject complement-clause₂ constructions.

Consider now the paradigm in (14.11), used for '(someone) wants to go.' Column (a) contains the complement clause₂, either *ngeyu* (|nga-nya=ya| [1-OPT=go]) 'I will/want to go,' *ngarreyu* (|ngarr-a=ya| [1pin-OPT=go]) 'we (inc) will/want to go,' or *arreyu* (|arr-a=yu| [1px-OPT=go]) 'we (exc) will/want to go.' Column (b) contains the matrix, forms of *kuN[ ]=yi* inflected for different classes of agent:

(14.11)

	(a)	(b)	
1	ngeyu	kungayeerri	*I want to go*
2	ngeyu	kunjiyeerri	*you want to go*
3	ngeyu	kunjeerri	*s/he wants to go*
1pin	ngarreyu	wajeerri	*we (inc) want to go*
1px	arreyu	kunyajeerri	*we (exc) want to go*
2p	ngeyu	kurriyeerri	*you all want to go*
3p	ngeyu	kubajeerri	*they want to go*

This paradigm is consistent with a direct-speech interpretation *(he thinks, 'I will go;' we think, 'we will go,'* etc) until the second and third person plural actor forms, where unexpectedly, the paradigm reverts to a first person singular index in the complement, as if each and every member of the indexed group (each individual of the 'you all' and 'they' sets) is depicted as thinking *I will go*. It is not clear why this depiction should not obtain as well for first person plural actors, or alternatively, why the second and third person plural complements should not use first person plural indices. This anomaly is even more apparent in spontaneous texts:

(14.12a)
Baay	kanunaarndu	werrim	mana,	[murn	mangayora]
baay	ka=nu-na-ᵏwarndu	werrim	mana	murn	ma-nga=yora
climb	3a=be-PAST-DU	hill	3mDEF	gaze	VCOMP-1=seek

kunjungaarndu.
kuN-[Ø]=yi-ng-[ᵏwarndu]
VCOMP-[3]=do-PAST-[DU]
They (dual) climbed a hill [in order to look around].

(b)
… [baay	ngenu]	kaajingeerri	[wunu
baay	nga-nya=nu	ØN-ngka-ᵇwarr=yi-ng-eerri	wunu
climb	1-OPT=be	VCOMP-SJTV-3p=do-PAST-PROG	3wDEF

karrku   rdaarreya.]
karrku   ØN=raarreya
hill   3w=big
… they were trying [to climb up into the high hills].

In these same-subject constructions, matrices with third person non-singular subjects dominate complement clauses with first person singular subject indices. In (14.12a) the matrix *kunjungaarndu* is marked for a third-person dual subject. The complement clause in this sentence is *murn mangayora,* literally 'I'll look around,' rather than either of the available 1pin shapes *murn marrayora* 'we'll look around,' or *murn marrayoraarndu* 'we'll both look around,' as would be expected if this construction really was one of direct speech. Instead, the direct speech version of this sentence would be, *baay kanunaarndu werrim mana: 'murn marrayora,' kaningaayenaarndu* – 'they climbed up a hill: 'let's have a look around,' they said to each other.' And indeed, not very far away in the same text we find a direct speech construction of just this sort, with the suppletive middle-voice allomorph of *kuN[ ]=yi* (see §16.1):

(14.13) 'Karle   ngarriyaarndu,'   kaningaayenaarndu.
         karle   ngarr-a=ya-ᵏwarndu   ka=ningaaye-na-ᵏwarndu
         now   1pin-OPT=go-DU   3a=do.MID-PAST-DU
         'Let's go' they said to each other.

Likewise in (14.12b), the complement clause₂ verb *ngenu* has a singular subject index rather than the plural index expected if this really were direct speech. The point is that first person singular indices always stand in for second and third person plural subjects in this kind of construction; the corresponding plural indices are just not found.

Further evidence for the grammaticization of first person singular in this role is seen in (14.14) below, where in order to denote iterative aspect the complement-clause verb is truncated and reduplicated in its entirety, as if it were a single (preverbal) morpheme (cf §11.3.3):

(14.14) [Ingam-ingam]   kaajingeerri.
         i-nga=ma–i-nga=ma   ØN-ngka-ᵇwarr=yi-ng-eerri
         3a-1=get–3a-1=get   VCOMP-SJTV-3p=do-PAST-PROG
         They were trying [to grab hold of him] / they almost [caught hold of him].

Notice as well in sentence example (10.49a) in §10.4.2 (ii), how the complement clause is discontinuous – the relevant part of that sentence is repeated here as (14.15):

(14.15)   ... [ngeyu]   jungunju   [dambeemangurru]
(=10.49a)   nga-nya=ya   ØN-nja-ngun=yi   dambeema-ngurru
             1-OPT=go   VCOMP-2-SJTV=do   place-ALL
           ... *when you want [to go home]*

Here the matrix verb *jungunju* 'when you want' splits the complement clause₂: this configuration can in no way be intended to represent actual utterance.

Despite that fact that constructions of the sort shown in (14.12) and (14.14) are clearly derived from or related to direct speech, with respect to synchronic grammar we are nonetheless able to entertain a *prima facie* case that in some contexts first person indices are found in constructions that do not involve direct speech. And indeed a good case can be made that first person singular subject marking is indexical of complement₂ constructions more generally. And when we observe as well constructions of the sort seen in (14.3a & b), it is equally clear that we need to distinguish direct speech from other kinds of construction in Worrorra.

Returning now to a reconsideration of the paradigm in (14.11), we can suggest a non-direct-speech interpretation of its grammar. In this interpretation first-person coding in same-subject complement clauses₂ constitutes dummy coding, with the subject's 'real' grammatical features projected onto the matrix, to appear as the matrix verb's subject index.

14.3.2 Transitive same-subject complements

The reader will also have noticed that sentence examples (14.5a, c) and those in (14.6) display matrix verbs suffixed with NSC object morphemes that do *not* denote addressees, and are not involved in direct-speech constructions. These examples all involve different-subject constructions; and indeed NSC objects are unable to appear on matrices involved in same-subject constructions with intransitive complement clauses$_2$. They may be found, however, in same-subject constructions with *transitive* complement clauses$_2$; we have already seen one such in (10.74b) in §10.6.3 (i), and another is shown below:

(14.16) [Burrkay ingayabu] kungeneerri.
         burrkay   i-nga=yabu kuN-nga=yi-nu-eerri
         ask   3a$_k$-1$_i$=throw VCOMP-1$_i$=do-2DAT$_k$-PROG
         I want to ask you something.

In this sentence the complement clause's$_2$ subject and object are both indexed twice. The complement object's real, second person, features appear in NSC object position on the matrix verb (2DAT), while it accepts dummy third person coding on the complement verb. Same-subject constructions, therefore, are produced according to the following specifications:

(14.17)
(1) A matrix subject is represented in the complement as a (dummy) first person,
(2) The complement object is relegated to third person,
(3) The real person features of a dummy third person index are projected onto the matrix.

As a corollary, when the complement object is an *actual* third person, no NSC object appears on the matrix. Observe in this context, the minimal pairs in (14.18) and (14.19), the latter taken from Appendix 1:

(14.18a) Ngarloonangka   kungayeerri.
          ØN nga⁻rloo-nangka   kuN-nga=yi-eerri
          VCOMP-1$_i$=speak-DAT   VCOMP-1$_i$=do-PROG
          I want to talk to him.

(b)   Ngarloonangka   kungeneerri.
          ØN-nga=rloo-nangka   kuN-nga=yi-nu-eerri
          VCOMP-1$_i$=speak-DAT$_k$ VCOMP-1$_i$=do-2DAT$_k$-PROG
          I want to talk to you.

(14.19a) Ingo   ngana   kubajungu   inja.
          i-nga=^{b}wu ngana kuN-^{b}warr=yi-ng   inja
          3a$_k$-1$_i$=hit PROB VCOMP-3p$_i$=do-PAST 3aDEF$_K$
          They must have wanted to kill him.

(b)   Ngayu ingo   ngana   kubajungaara.
          ngayu i-nga=^{b}wu   ngana   kuN-^{b}warr=yi-ng-^{k}wara
          I$_k$ 3a$_k$-1$_i$=hit PROB VCOMP-3p$_i$=do-PAST-1DAT$_k$
          They must have wanted to kill me.

Further examples of transitive same-subject constructions with third-person complement-clause$_2$ objects not marked on the matrix verb, may be seen in (14.10) and in Appendix 1.

For transitive same-subject constructions, then, there are three possibilities of expression: (i) in simplex form, (ii) in a hypotactic construction with a third person complement object, or (iii) in a hypotactic construction with a non-third person complement object, whose person features are coded on the matrix. These three possibilities are exemplified below:

(14.20a) Nyarloongarreerri.
ØN-Ø-nya=rloo-ngarri-eerri
VCOMP-3-OPT=speak-1pinDAT-PROG
He will/wants to talk to us.

(b) [Ngarloonangkorri]   kungayeerri.
ØN-nga=rloo-[nangka-^kwurri]   kuN-nga=yi-eerri
VCOMP-1$_i$=speak-[3pDAT]   VCOMP-1$_i$=do-PROG
I want to talk to them.

(c) [Ngarloonangkorri]   kunjungarreerri.
ØN-nga=rloo-[nangka-^kwurri]   kuN-Ø=yi-(ng)-ngarri-eerri
VCOMP-1$_i$=speak-[3pDAT$_k$]   VCOMP-3$_i$=do-(PAST)-1pinDAT$_k$-PROG
He wants/wanted to talk to us (inc).

Note that real number features are faithfully recorded for objects on complement clause$_2$ indices – they just happen to be attached to dummy person features. In (14.20c) the dummy third person object index on the complement clause$_2$ verb (3p *-nangkorri*) retains its plural number marking to agree with its 'real' manifestation (1pin *-ngarri*) as marked on the matrix verb.

14.3.3 *Indices of discourse status*

We have seen above in §14.3.1 how the dummy use of a first person singular morpheme in complement clauses$_2$ is an index of the indirect or non-direct status of a stretch of discourse. Deictic shifts mark indirect speech cross-linguistically; usually shifts from the 'original' or 'real' values in which deixis appears in corresponding direct-speech utterances (see, eg, Rumsey 1990 and references therein). It appears that person-marking in Worrorra complement clauses$_2$ is one such deictic, subject to shifting away from direct-speech contexts.

Two other phenomena in Worrorra may be noted in this regard. As mentioned, complement-clause$_2$ constructions in Worrorra may be indexed by the matrix verb's NSC object having a thematic rather than an addressee interpretation (§13.2.2 (iv)). The NSC object morphemes in (14.5a, c) above, for example, cannot be interpreted as addressees without radically altering their sentences' meanings. An interesting example of the contrast between thematic and addressee interpretations may be seen in (14.21), where the first sentence is indirect reportage, while the second repeats the information in direct speech style:

(14.21)
[Karle   *school*-kunya   *ready*   nyininyaal]   kubajengaara.
karle   *school*-^kwunya   ready   nyiN=ni-nya-^kwaal   kuN-^bwarr-nya=yi-ng-^kwara
now   school-PURP   ready   3f$_i$=be-HORT-hither   VCOMP-3p-EP=do-PAST-1DAT$_i$

'*School*-kunya   karle   ngunyangerri,'   kubajengaara
school-^kwunya   karle   ngun=ya-nga-eerri   kuN-^bwarr-nya=yi-ng-^kwara
school-PURP   now   2=go-PAST-PROG   VCOMP-3p-EP=do-PAST-1DAT

anja   aalmareya.
anja   aalmara-ya
3pDEF   European-3p
They said I should get ready for school. 'You're going to school, now,' the Europeans told me.

The first sentence here is an intransitive different-subject construction (§14.3.4) involving indirect reporting, while the second is direct quotation (see §14.4). As I will argue in §14.4, the hortative form of the complement-clause$_1$ verb in the first sentence constitutes a polite register used in reporting imperative speech acts: this phenomenon may be observed in (14.3c) as well. As will be seen below, the third person shape *nyininyaal* is indexical of a different-subject complement$_2$; it also means that the first person singular NSC object index on the matrix verb cannot, in the first sentence, have an addressee interpretation; rather it must be a theme. An addressee interpretation would require second-person or imperative coding in the complement clause$_1$. Another example is seen below, in which for the same reasons the NSC object cannot be an addressee, but must be a theme:

(14.22)
Kunyajunganangkerri awa barnarn kawana
kuN-nyarr=yi-ng-a-nangka-eerri awa barnarn ka=^{b}wa-na
VCOMP-1px=do-PAST-EP-DAT$_1$-PROG 3aNAR$_1$ married 3a=fall-TNS

karraanya.
karra-aa-nya
mother-1DAT-3f
We used to say that he'd married our mother / we used to say he's married our mother.

The NSC object on the matrix verb makes it improbable that this sentence is directly quoting what the speakers used to say, and its flat intonation contour confirms this interpretation (see discussion in §14.4).

Thirdly, possessive marking in complement clauses$_2$ shifts away from the deictic parameters that would apply in direct-speech situations. This phenomenon can be observed in (14.10a) above and in other examples:

(14.23) [Mangkanangkanya nyinganinja] kunjungu.
mangka-nangka-nya nyiN-nga=ninja kuN-Ø=yi-ng
wife$_k$-DAT$_i$-3f 3f$_k$-1$_i$=look.at VCOMP-3$_i$=do-PAST
He$_i$ wanted [to see his$_i$ wife].

In both (14.10a) and (14.23) there is a mismatch between possessive marking on the kinship nouns (third person singular) and formal marking of the possessor, the complement clause's$_2$ subject (as dummy first person singular). Possession *(-nangka* '3sg DAT') is marked on the complement-clause$_2$ object in formal agreement with the subject of the matrix verb, not with that of the complement verb, as we might expect if the complement clause really did represent a direct speech utterance.

14.3.4 Intransitive different-subject complements

Intransitive complement clauses$_2$ with subjects different from those of their matrix verbs may be seen in (14.3, 14.4) and in the second sentence of (14.21), but these examples all involve speech reporting, and will be discussed in §14.4. Sentence examples (14.5a, 14.5c), and the first sentence in (14.21) do not involve direct speech, and all have intransitive complement clauses$_2$ in different-subject constructions. Further examples are presented below:

(14.24a) [Nyeyu] kunjunganu.
nyaN-nya=ya kuN-Ø=yi-ng-a-nu
3f$_i$-OPT=go VCOMP-3=do-PAST-EP-2DAT$_i$
S/he wanted [you (fem) to go].

(b) [Eninjiye]   kunjungaara.
     a-nya=ninja-ye   kuN-Ø=yi-ng-ᵏwara
     3aᵢ-OPT-look.at-MID VCOMP-3=do-PAST-1DATᵢ
     S/he wanted [me (masc) to look at myself].

Each of these examples display (i) a dummy third person complement subject, with (ii) the complement subjects' real person features projected onto their matrix verb. This situation reverses one of the specifications for *same*-subject constructions noted in (14.17), which requires a dummy third-person complement *object*. We may now complete the specifications for constructing complement clauses₂, started in (14.17), as follows:

(14.25)
IN BOTH CONSTRUCTION TYPES:
ORDERED RULES:
   (1) A matrix subject is represented in the complement as a (dummy) first person,
   (2) A complement argument unaffected by (1) is relegated to third person, SUBJ > OBJ.
UNORDERED:
   (3) The real person features of a dummy third person index are projected onto the matrix.

IN DIFFERENT-SUBJECT CONSTRUCTIONS ONLY:
(4) A [{+I, +II}] complement subject is projected onto the matrix.

Although specifications (3) and (4) may seem to be equivalent, they are not, and both are required, as we will see. The ordering Rule (1) > Rule (2) accounts for the switching of obligatory third-person marking between the subject in different-subject, and the object in same-subject constructions. In same-subject complements Rule (1) applies first, effecting the complement subject. Only then can Rule (2) apply, and the only target left for it to effect is the complement object, which now becomes obligatorily third person. The rule only applies once, targeting first a subject, and if that has already been effected by Rule (1), it moves on to the object.

A further corollary is needed here, in addition to and along the lines of that provided for the specifications in (14.17): when a complement subject is [–I, –II], it *may* be projected onto the matrix verb, but is not *required* to be so. This optionality is illustrated in (14.26), where both sentences are legal:

(14.26a)   [Nyeyu]   kungayeerri.
           nyaN-nya=ya   kuN-nga=yi-eerri
           3f-OPT=go   VCOMP-1=do-PROG
           I want [her to go].

(b)   [Nyeyu]   kungenangkerri.
           nyaN-nya=ya   kuN-nga=yi-nangka-eerri
           3fᵢ-OPT=go   VCOMP-1=do-DATᵢ-PROG
           I want [her to go].

The only potential-mood complement clause₂ construction in the database is of this type (§14.2); the complement here is intransitive with a third-person subject which is not projected onto its matrix:

(14.27)   [Larlangkarram   maa   bangkawa]   kungayeerri.
           rlarlangkarram   maa   ba-ka=ᵇwa   kuN-nga=yi-eerri
           sea   3mREF   CFT-3a=fall VCOMP-1=do-PROG
           I am worried [that he might fall into the sea].

The sentences in (14.5a, 14.5c, 14.21, 14.24a) and (14.26) all show simple intransitive complement clauses₂ in different-subject constructions, and (14.24b) illustrates a derived intransitive complement in such a construction. The sentences in (14.6) contain complement clauses₂ with object-demoting predicates, and require further comment.

In (14.6b) the subject of the complement clause₂ (-Ø- '3') is co-referential with the first-person singular matrix NSC object. The interrogative anaphor *ngani* is the complement verb's object (see §10.5), and the real (first) person features of the complement subject have been projected onto the matrix verb. In Worrorra the question-frame *ngani kuN[ ]=yi?* 'what did [SUBJ] do?' corresponds in meaning to the English frame *what happened to OBJ?* (see also (6.14c)).

A third-person NSC object suffixed to a matrix verb is indexical of the different-subject status of a complement-clause₂ construction – this phenomenon is not found in same-subject constructions (see §14.3.2). And so: when different-subject status is referentially important, for, say, disambiguation or participant-tracking purposes, a third person complement subject will be projected onto its matrix verb as an NSC object, which is what we find in (14.6a/5.8), and which may be what the speaker had in mind when (14.26b) and (14.29b) were elicited. In (14.6a) the juxtaposed matrix and complement verbs share the same lexical root *(kuN[ ]=yi)*, and the same subject index (3p), which are, however, not co-referential. Projecting the complement subject onto the matrix as an NSC object ensures that this sentence will not be interpreted as a same-subject construction – the subjects of the two clauses can only refer to different actors.

14.3.5 Transitive different-subject complements

The first specification in (14.25) requires a matrix subject to be represented as a dummy first person if it appears in a complement clause₂. In transitive different-subject constructions, this occurs when the matrix subject is co-referential with the complement *object* (as opposed to the complement subject in same-subject constructions). The examples in (14.28) illustrate this kind of transitive construction:

(14.28a) [Nganyaninja]   kunjuneerri.
          nga-n-Ø-nya=ninja   kuN-Ø=yi-nu-eerri
          1$_i$-INV-3$_k$-OPT=look.at   VCOMP-3$_i$=do-2DAT$_k$-PROG
          He$_i$ wants [you to look at him$_i$].

(b)   [Nyarluwaara]   kungeneerri.
          ØN-Ø-nya=rloo-^{k}wara   kuN-nga=yi-nu-eerri
          VCOMP-3$_k$-OPT=speak-1DAT$_i$ VCOMP-1$_i$=do-2DAT$_k$-PROG
          I want [you to talk to me].

(c)   [Aai nganyo]   kubajunganangkerri.
          aai   nga-n-Ø-nya=^{b}wu   kuN-^{b}warr=yi-ng-a-nangka-eerri
          call 1$_i$-INV-3$_k$-OPT=hit VCOMP-3p$_i$=do-PAST-EP-DAT$_k$-PROG
          They$_i$ wanted [him to call out to them$_i$].

(d)   [Mara nganyo]   kungenganu.
          mara   nga-n-Ø-nya=^{b}wu kuN-nga=yi-ng-a-nu
          see   1$_i$-INV-3$_k$-OPT=hit VCOMP-1$_i$=do-PAST-EP-2DAT$_k$
          I wanted [you to see me].

In each of these sentences the matrix subject appears in the complement as dummy first-person singular, and the real person features of the third-person complement subject are projected onto the matrix verb. In (14.28c) the speaker has chosen to project a third-person complement subject onto the matrix, again, most likely to maximally distinguish the roles of the third-person actors in this sentence.

When the matrix subject does not appear as an argument of the complement clause₂, the complement object is not projected onto the matrix, and retains its real person coding:

(14.29a)
[Ngunyaninja]　　　　　kunjaareerri.
ngun-n-Ø-nya=ninja　　kuN-Ø=yi=ᵏwara-eerri
2-INV-3ᵢ-OPT=look.at　 VCOMP-3=do-1DATᵢ-PROG
He wants [me to look at you].

(b)
[Barrarloonu]　　　　　kungenangkorreerri.
ØN-ᵇwarr-a=rloo-nu　　 kuN-nga=yi-nangkorri-eerri
VCOMP-3pᵢ-OPT=speak-2DAT　VCOMP-1=do-3pDATᵢ-PROG
I want [them to talk to you].

(c)
Irno　　eeja　　[mangkanangkanya　　nyininja]　　　kunjaareerri.
i=rno　 eeja　　mangka-nangka-nya　 nyiN-Ø=ninja　kuN-Ø=yi=ᵏwara-eerri
3a-DIST manᵢ　 wife-DATᵢ-3F　　　　 3f-3ₖ=look.at　VCOMP-3ᵢ=do-1DATₖ-PROG
That manᵢ wants [me to look at hisᵢ wife].

Again, in these sentences the complement subject is third person, with its real person features projected onto the matrix. In (14.29b) a third-person complement subject is projected onto the matrix, so whether or not such forms are dummy, is moot.

The first-person coding of matrix subjects appearing as complement objects, in distinction to complement objects from other sources, has implications for participant tracking. The following minimal pair illustrates how coding the source of a complement object may support comprehension: in (14.30a) the complement object co-refers with the matrix subject, and in (14.30b) it does not.

(14.30a)　　[Nganyaninja]　　　kunjaarerri.
　　　　　　nga-n-Ø-nya=ninja　kuN-Ø=yi=ᵏwara-eerri
　　　　　　1ᵢ-INV-3ₖ-OPT=look.at　VCOMP-3ᵢ=do-1DATₖ-PROG
　　　　　　Heᵢ wants [me to look at himᵢ].

(b)　　　　 [Eninja]　　　　　kunjaarerri.
　　　　　　a-Ø-nya=ninja　　 kuN-Ø=yi=ᵏwara-eerri
　　　　　　3aₖ-3ₚ-OPT=look.at　VCOMP-3ᵢ=do-1DATₚ-PROG
　　　　　　Heᵢ wants [me to look at himₖ].

Different-subject constructions appear not to be required to project complement subjects onto their matrices in the following circumstances: (i) when all arguments in both clauses are third person, and (ii) when the matrix subject does not appear in the complement clause₂. Some examples follow, with intransitive complement clauses₂ seen in (14.31a, b), and a transitive complement in (14.31c)). Sentence example (14.1) is also of this type, with a transitive complement.

(14.31a)　　[Wangarr　nyewa]　　　kunjungu.
　　　　　　wangarr　 nyaN-nya=ᵇwa　kuN-Ø=yi-ng
　　　　　　forget　　 3fₖ-OPT=fall　 VCOMP-3ᵢ=do-PAST
　　　　　　He wanted [her to forget].

(b)　　　　 [Barda　arrawee]　　kunjungu.
　　　　　　barda　 arr-a=ᵇwee　 kuN-Ø=yi-ng
　　　　　　kill　　 3p-OPT=hit.MID　VCOMP-3=do-PAST

He wanted [them to kill themselves/each other].

(c)   [Wangarr nyewarrama]   kubajungu.
        wangarr   nyaN-nya-^{b}warr-a=ma   kuN-^{b}warr=yi-ng
        forget   3f-OPT-3p$_k$-OPT=get   VCOMP-3p$_i$=do-PAST
        They$_i$ wanted [them$_k$ to forget her].

This appears to be a strong tendency, but without more exemplification in the database it is difficult to rule out the possibility of projection altogether. Rather, in such circumstances the projection of the subject of a complement clause onto its matrix is likely to have been a device always available for disambiguation and to clarify participant tracking; but able to be omitted when not required.

14.3.6 Complement-clause$_2$ syntax: summary and extension

In the preceding sections we have observed a syntax transparently derived from a direct-speech scenario. This syntax consists of a set of formal dependencies and correspondences holding between the arguments of the matrix and complement clauses$_2$, that conspire to signal the identity of participants in discourse. And as seen in §14.2, these inter-clausal syntactic dependencies extend beyond argument structure to time-reference and tense-marking. Taken together, this set of syntactic and morphological forms collectively constitutes the grammaticization of complement clause$_2$ syntax in Worrorra.

It could be tempting to ignore the relationships described above in favour of a less formal approach, which would treat complement clauses$_2$ as direct mental quotations without reference to the set of dependency correspondences obtaining between them and their matrices. Despite their derivation, complement clauses$_2$ of the sort we have seen have structural properties that are not simply excrescences of a synchronic direct-speech style, and they are not able to be adequately described in those terms. Nevertheless it is possible to summarize the processes we have observed over the previous sections, and this has been attempted in the set of specifications set out in (14.25), and again, and perhaps more graphically, in (14.32):

(14.32)[98]   MATRIX SUBJ —> 1(sg) in COMP
                 COMP ARG —> 3
                 COMP ARG [+REAL] —> MATRIX OBJ

This summary employs the term ARG to represent either argument of a clause (subject or object, depending on clause type) that undergoes some syntactic process. The clause level, matrix or complement, is capitalized in front of the grammatical function under consideration. If (14.25) lists a set of specifications for each kind of clause, (14.32) summarizes (in a hopefully comprehensible fashion) the processes involved, without reference to clause type.

Having established specifications and processes, it remains to describe a revealing variation upon them. This occurs when an NP index contains a bundle of person features, namely [+I, +II] or [+I, [–I, –II]]. Complement-clause$_2$ constructions are able to decompose or separate out these features in the same way that outranked-actor number marking is able to distinguish grammatical classes indexed by a single form (§9.2). The sentences in (14.33) both contain intransitive complement clauses$_2$, a same-subject complement in (14.33a), and a different-subject one in (b). Both complements contain an index with a complex feature-bundle: 1px which is [+I, [–I, –II]].

---

[98] Abbreviations used in this formalism: MATRIX = matrix clause; COMP = complement clause; SUBJ = subject; OBJ = (non-subcategorized) object; ARG = either argument of a clause, one effected by a syntactic process; REAL = non-dummy person features; 1 = first person; 3 = third person.

(14.33a)   [Arriyoorri]   kungayeerri.
(cf. 9.39b)   arr-a=ya-oorri   kuN-nga=yi-eerri
              1px-OPT=go-U/AUG   VCOMP-1=do-PROG
              I want [to go with them].

(b)   [Arriyoorri]   kungenangkorreerri.
              arr-a=ya-oorri   kuN-nga=yi-nangkorri-eerri
              1px-OPT=go-U/AUG   VCOMP-1=do-3pDAT-PROG
              I want [them to come/go with me].

Sentence (14.33a) is the simplest type of construction (intransitive same-subject), and the only specification that applies to it is that the matrix subject should be represented in the complement as first person; which is what we find, although not in singular index form as could be expected. This example shows that the grammatical category affected by these syntactic processes are grammatical person *features*, rather than composite grammatical persons as such. In (14.33a) the matrix subject bears the feature [+I], and it is this feature, rather than a particular formal index, that must appear in the complement clause$_2$.

The matrix in sentence (14.33b) bears an NSC object morpheme, making it clear that its intransitive complement displays a different subject. Reviewing the specifications required for this kind of construction, again we see that the matrix subject finds representation in the complement by way of a [+I] grammatical feature. In this different-subject construction rule (2) (in (14.25)) is outranked by rule (1), so the complement subject is not required to appear in a third person index.

In accordance with specification (4), a complement subject is projected onto the matrix of (14.33b), but it bears neither of the features [+I] or [+II]. In effect, and as signalled by the outranked-actor morpheme appearing on the complement verb, this construction has split the feature-bundle of 1px. The feature [+I] remains behind in the complement clause$_2$, while only the third-person feature [–I, –II] is projected onto the matrix: and this turns out to be a precise coding device – in this sentence the semantic subject is invested only with the feature [–I, –II]. The outcome is that in this construction the complement-clause$_2$ verb *arriyoorri* has a third-person plural subject in line with its English translation: but only in the specific syntax in which it occurs in (14.33b) and sentences like it. Note how the semantic subjects of *arriyoorri* are switched in these two sentences: this switch can only be signalled by the syntax of the constructions in which they appear, a syntax which would not be apparent in an analysis which treated alike all manifestations of complement clauses.

Finally, observe a variation on this process in another intransitive different-subject construction, this time with a [+I, +II] feature-bundle in the complement:

(14.34)   [Ngarreyu]   kungenurreerri.
              ngarr-a=ya   kuN-nga=yi-noorri-eerri
              1pin-OPT=go   VCOMP-1=do-2pDAT-PROG
              I want [you all to come with me].

Here we find the matrix subject represented in the complement, again by the person feature [+I], and a [+II] complement subject feature projected onto its matrix. Again, the syntax has decomposed the feature bundle of the first person inclusive plural index, sending one feature up into the matrix while retaining the other in the complement.

The sentences in (14.33, 14.34) appear to have a syntactic foot in both same-subject and different-subject camps. This is because the matrix subjects in these sentences are, in feature terms, both the same as and different from the subjects of their complements. And the grammar uses this ambiguity as an opportunity to encode meaning in subtle and precise ways.

14.4 Reporting speech

In §14.2 and §14.3 we observed complementation$_2$ as the representation of mental processes by means of an array of syntactic dependencies between a matrix clause indexing an agent and a type of mental process (thinking, wanting, fearing etc), and its complement, denoting the propositional or semantic content of that process. In this section we will review a second kind of complementation, that used to record speech. We will need to distinguish further two kinds of speech reporting, that which purports to present actual wording, and that which conveys the propositional content of some speech event, without making claims about the actual wording used.

We may now return to a consideration of the examples of speech reporting shown above in (14.3, 14.4) and in the second sentence of (14.21). Example (14.13) also involves direct speech, and the morphology of the framing verb in this sentence will be discussed in Chapter 16. In formal terms the sentences in (14.3, 14.4) and (14.21) are all intransitive different-subject constructions in which the complement subject is an actual or implied second person. They violate complement clause$_2$ specifications in not having a third-person complement subject index, and complement-clause$_2$ semantics in having NSC objects that index addressees.

Reported speech may involve a complement clause$_1$ with a verb in optative mood, without requiring a volitional interpretation. The complement in (14.35) contains three verbs, the first two in hortative mood, the third in optative:

(14.35)
'Karle	nyardo,	wara	arrbanangka	nyarrarno,'
karle	nyaN-ngarr=rno	wara	a-ngarr=ma-nangka	nyaN-ngarr-a=rno
now	3f-1pin=give	kangaroo	3a-1pin=get-DAT	3f-1pin-OPT=give

kubajeng.
kuN-^{b}warr-nya=yi-ng
VCOMP-3p-EP=do-PAST
'Let's give it to her now, let's get a kangaroo and we'll give it to her,' they said.

Formally, the sequence *nyarrarno kubajeng* represents a transitive same-subject construction, and violates none of the specifications for complement clauses$_2$ of this kind. Yet this construction does not involve a complement of that sort. The optative-mood verb registers future time reference only, as supported by the hortative form of the two preceding verbs, and the sentence conveys a representation of direct speech in its complement.[99]

Direct speech is conveyed as well by altered intonation, pitch and volume. The material within quotation marks in (14.3a, b, 14.21) and (14.35) was spoken with pitch and intonation altered from that in adjacent text. Pitch is generally higher, volume may be increased, and intonation is more varied (more lively), depending on the content of quoted material. In a narration direct speech may be introduced by an interjection 'O,' repeated for each new speaker. The speech in (14.36) was quoted without a framing verb:

(14.36)
'O,	karle	nyardo,	marno	binyineerri	nyangke.'
O	karle	nyaN-ngarr=rno	marno	ba-nyiN=nu-eerri	nyangke
O	now	3f-1pin=give	3mDIST	CFT-3f=be-PROG	3fPRSNTIL

'Let's give it to her now, she might be (all alone) over there.'

---

[99] The speaker is here representing actual wording. Whether these exact words were uttered precisely as stated is irrelevant; in Worrorra as in other languages direct speech is a discourse style available for graphic and dramatic effect, as well as for accurate recording purposes. In (14.37) below Patsy Lulpunda recounts an event that had happened 80 years previously, and employs direct discourse style for effect. Of course speaker and hearers all understand the conventions associated with this style.

In fluent or dramatic renditions, as above, framing verbs may be dispensed with altogether. The speakers in (14.37) have just discovered the body of a recently-murdered dreamtime ancestor. This passage is reproduced here with the sentences separated out and numbered for convenience:

(14.37)
'Arri   angkuyu   nguyul   kumnyenganangka?
arri   angkuyu   nguyul   kuN-Ø-mnya=yi-ng-a-nangka
but   who   kill   VCOMP-3-DD=do-PAST-EP-DAT
1. 'But who killed him?

Angkuyu   nguyul   kunjunganangka?'
angkuyu   nguyul   kuN-Ø=yi-ng-a-nangka
who   kill   VCOMP-3=do-PAST-EP-DAT
2. Who killed him?'

'O,   Mee   angkuyu   ngana,   angkuyu   ngana.'
O   I.don't.know   who   PROB   who   PROB
3. 'I don't know who it could have been, who it might have been.'

Nyina   karranangkanya   nyengkunaal:
nyina   karra-nangka-nya   nya=ya-ngku-na-ᵏwaal
3fDEF   mother-DAT-3f   3f=go-EP-PAST-hither
4. His mother arrived:

'Karraa!   Karraa!   Karraa!   Karraa!'
mother!   mother!   mother!   mother!
5. 'O mother! O mother! O mother! O mother!'

Marnduma   mamnyawewuna.
marnduma   ma-Ø-mnya-ᵇwe=ᵇwu-na
stomach   3m-3-DD-AUG=hit-PAST
6. She pounded her stomach.

Karraa! is the vocative shape of *karraanya* 'mother,' and is employed as a cry of extreme grief. Here, as commented on in relation to (5.14b) in §5.2.2, the crocodile mother cries out in grief and pounds her stomach, possibly in reference to the place (her womb) where her son was conceived. No framing verbs appear in this passage, and each new speaker (in lines 1, 3 and 5) is introduced by alterations in pitch and intonation: the pitch in line 3 is higher than in lines 1 and 2, and the volume in line 5 is louder than in adjacent text. Sentence (14.38) also contains direct speech, part of which is whispered (shown by grey text and dotted underline):

(14.38)
'Ngarriyaarndu!   Bern   ngarranu   marno   werrim,'   kunjaara.
ngarr-a=ya-ᵏwarndu bern   ngarr-a=nu   marno   werrim   kuN-Ø=yi-ᵏwara
1pin-OPT=go-DU   climb   1pin-OPT=be   3mDIST   hill   VCOMP-3=do-1DAT
'Come with me! We'll climb that hill,' she told me.

Note how only part of the quoted material is whispered, the initial imperative is shouted, and the final framing verb is in neutral intonation. There is an intonation break between the quotation and the framing verb, as is also the case in (14.35) and in other sentence examples of this kind.

However there is no pause or intonation break between the complement clause and its matrix verb in (14.22) above, or in (14.39) below (taken from Appendix 1.1); in both these examples the entire sentence is contained in a single intonation contour:

(14.39)
[Wara	irno	imaal	drarr	iwu]	kubajunganangka.
wara	i=rno	i=ma-^{k}waal	drarr	i=^{b}wu	kuN-^{b}warr=yi-ng-a-nangka
k'roo	3a=DIST	3a=get-hither	gut	3a=hit	VCOMP-3p=do-PAST-EP-DAT

1. *They told him [to get that kangaroo and gut it].*
2. *'Get that kangaroo and gut it,' they said to him.*

Even though the complement contains two imperative verbs, intonation here is flat, in line with reading (1). On the strength of this, and of the contrast between this kind of intonation and the much more varied intonations seen in the direct-speech examples above, it may be claimed that Worrorra distinguishes both direct and indirect speech reporting styles. And it follows therefore that sentences (14.3a,b) are also examples of direct, and (14.1, 14.4) of indirect styles. But of course in (14.39) and in (14.4) there is no morphological or *textual* way of deciding between the two styles. The complement clauses in both sentence examples contain verbs in imperative form, just as would be used in direct speech. Note how (14.3b) and (14.40) also contain imperative verb forms in their complement clauses, but how the speech acts they record, questioning and commanding, are reproduced with realistic intonation, marking them as instances of direct speech reporting:

(14.40) (cf. 11.2a)
'Yarribaa	wurriyaal!	Yarribaa!	Anguja	karrolkunerri?'
yarribaa	^{k}wuN-rra=yi-aal	yarribaa	anguja	ka-rra=^{k}wulkuna-eerri
descend.PL	VCOMP-2p=do-hither	descend.PL	what	3a-2p=fear-PROG

kubajunganyarri	abaabiya.
kuN-^{b}warr=yi-ng-a-nyarri	a-baa-bi-ya
VCOMP-3p=do-PAST-EP-1pxDAT	↳-AUG-El.Sib-3p

'Come down! Come down! What are you frightened of?' our big brothers called to us.

So far then, we have identified a distinction between direct and indirect speech in Worrorra on the basis of suprasegmental features (stress and intonation). There is one context, however, in which morphology indexes the distinction. When imperatives are reported they may occur in the complement clause$_1$ as such, as seen in (14.39), or they may be shifted to hortative mood if the speaker is using a polite register. This has already been noted with respect to (14.3c) and the first sentence in (14.21), where hortative forms index the use of this register. The phenomenon may be seen again in the minimal pair in (14.41):

(14.41a) [Nyeyungurru] kungenga.
nyaN-nya=ya-ngurru kuN-nga=yi-nga
3f-OPT=go-away VCOMP-1=want-PAST
I wanted [her to go].

(b) [Nyengenyangurru] kungenga.
(cf. 8.33) nyaN=[ya-nga]-yinya-ngurru kuN-nga=yi-nga
3f=[go-TNS]-HORT-away VCOMP-1=want-PAST
I said [she could go] / I told [her to go].

Sentence (14.41a) contains an intransitive different-subject complement clause$_2$ expressing volition. Sentence (14.41b) contains a hortative-mood complement verb, marking this sentence as an instance of indirect reported speech – a polite-register imperative form, moreover.

We have, then, been able to identify three categories of complement clause₁ in Worrorra: direct speech, indirect speech, and complement clauses₂ more narrowly defined. We have also noted quite a lot of overlap between these categories; that is, they have fuzzy boundaries. Nevertheless core instances of each type are able to be identified, and the emic identification of any particular instance would have depended on each occasion upon factors having to do with pragmatic implicature and discourse context, as well as extra-linguistic circumstances.

The elicited sentence in (14.1) is a case in point: its form fits into any of the three categories, and its interpretation, and that of sentences like it, would have been subject to the particulars of the speech event in which it would have been produced, and the conventional implicatures involved. This categorial fuzziness does not, however, mean that discourse category distinctions, in their core manifestations at least, were unavailable to Worrorra speakers, or that Worrorra speakers did not reify mental processes and speech acts, as processes and acts. In (14.42) the 'thought' sense-meaning of *kuN[ ]=yi* is made explicit by adverbial qualification by means of a postpositional phrase based on the noun =*neema* 'ear,' the pan-Australian seat of cognition:

(14.42) (cf. 7.14e)
'Arrke   ngani   kubajeerri?'   kunjungu   ineemarnanya.
arrke   ngani   kuN-ᵇwarr=yi-eerri   kuN-Ø=yi-ng   i=neema-rnanya
3pREF   what   VCOMP-3p=do-PROG   VCOMP-3=do-PAST   3=ear-LOC
'What are they doing?' he wondered.

The expression =*neemarnanya kuN[ ]=yi*, literally 'do/say in (one's) ear' is an idiom denoting pondered or considered thought. By its intonation in the text in which it occurs, this complement clause₁ is clearly framed to depict direct speech. In (14.42) speech act discourse style is employed to portray a mental process. The ability to use one discourse style in the service of another is only available where speakers are able to distinguish and manipulate the relevant discourse categories.

Fifteen: subjunctive verbs

The subjunctive mood constitutes a class of verb forms along with the indicative, optative and counterfactual moods (see Chapters Five and Eight). Subjunctive status is signalled by a pair of allomorphs in form-order class [4], and by the use of the series-2 inflexional NP indices shown in Table 8.4 and discussion in §8.1.1. For convenience Table 8.1 from Chapter Eight is repeated here:

Table 15.1 (=8.1): mood-signalling

MOOD	NP INDEX TYPE	SLOT [1]	SLOT [4]	FUNCTION
Indicative	series-1	∅	∅	actualized events
Counterfactual	series-1	*ba*	∅	unactualized events
Optative	series-2	∅	*a, nya,* ∅	projected events
Subjunctive	series-2	∅	*ngun, ngka*	averted events

It will be seen that the optative and subjunctive moods share some formal features distinctive to themselves: both employ series-2 NP indices, and both insert material in form-order class [4]. And non-distinctively, both leave form-order class [1] empty.

J R B Love referred to these forms as 'subjunctive' because, like the Latin subjunctive, they may signal an irrealis meaning and are found in subordinate clauses. Of this form-class Love wrote: 'the subjunctive mood is used in hypothetical clauses, conditional clauses, and subsidiary clauses; i.e. in all dependent clauses that are not direct statement[s] of fact' (Love 1934:42). The Latin subjunctive encompasses both hypothetical and counterfactual events, meanings which are, however, formally distinguished in Worrorra. As Love observed, subjunctive verbs may convey irrealis meaning, but they are in many ways the opposite of the irrealis counterfactuals described in Chapter Eight: they are used to affirm or assert a proposition's validity on the basis of evidence. Nevertheless I will retain the label 'subjunctive' here: as Michaël Peyrot writes with regard to its use in Tocharian, 'it is an empty term … it is the name of a category, no more' (Peyrot 2013:4).

15.1 Overview

The most intriguing feature of Worrorra's subjunctive mood is the diversity of its functions, as follows:

<u>Modal</u>: averted action/event (Kuteva's (2004) 'avertive') and frustrative mood. These are events that could have happened, or nearly happen, but which do not.

<u>Evidential</u>: coding for the source of evidence for a statement's propositional content. In Worrorra two categories of evidence are coded, firsthand and non-firsthand.

Syntactic: coding for hypotaxis, that is, when a predicate is subordinated as a dependent upon some other constituent: in Worrorra this results in both adverbial and relative subordination.

The obvious question is how these three apparently quite disparate grammatical meanings can be related, as indeed they must be in some way related, as they are all expressions of a single class of forms. This question in turn devolves into two further issues: diachrony, that is, the putative evolution of two of these categorial meanings from another, supposedly prior or 'original' meaning; and synchrony, that is whether, in terms of speaker competence, these meanings were related homonymously, or as sense meanings, by way of participation in a system of conversational implicatures.

Because of its complementary distribution with the other form classes, the subjunctive mood's modal meaning should probably be seen as systematically prior, coding, like the other three, a reality-status modality. Note that while systematic priority may imply diachronic priority, it need not imply anything about synchronic priority, that is, speaker competence. Worrorra's avertive modality appears in two flavours: reality status, in which an event nearly happens but does not, and a root modal frustrative mood, in which someone wanted an event to happen which ultimately did not happen. Frustrative mood, as a kind of volition, is congruent with the formal parallels noted with the optative mood.

In Worrorra the four moods show varying degrees of event actualization or reality status, from indicative, in which events happen (realis), to counterfactual, in which events do not happen (irrealis). In between are two more irrealis moods; optative, in which an event does not happen but is expected to happen at some future time, and subjunctive, in which an event does not happen although it nearly happened. This set defines a scale of actualization, from indicative through optative and subjunctive to counterfactual. Using some *ad hoc* notation, the semantics may be simplified and the scale schematized as in Table 15.2:

Table 15.2: modal actualization scale

SCALE	MOOD	NOTATION
full actualization	indicative	$\exists e$
projected actualization	optative	$\neg \exists e_i \land (\exists e_i)_{FUT}$
averted/failed actualization	subjunctive	$\neg \exists e_i \land ((\exists e_i)_{FUT})_{PAST}$
no actualization	counterfactual	$\neg \exists e$

Where e stands for some event, the notation reads as follows:
- for indicative: some event exists
- for optative: it is not the case that some event exists, and in the future that event exists
- for subjunctive: it is not the case that some event exists, and in the past it was the case that in the future that event exists
- for counterfactual: it is not the case that some event exists

The notations for optative and subjunctive contain both of the terms $\exists e$ and $\neg \exists e$, and so are mid-way on the scale. Optative contains the least embedded or least qualified instantiation of $\exists e$, and so is higher on the scale than subjunctive, in which $\exists e$ is more embedded and more qualified. What this means for the grammar of Worrorra is that the semantics of avertive modality involve irrealis meanings well suited to framing inferential logic, including hypothesizing. Mid-way between non-actualization and projection, logical inference is grounded in the preconditions for event actualization.

Subjunctive morphology, along with the syntax of complement clauses, is probably the most complex part of Worrorra's verbal system, primarily because it has so many functions and because those functions are not related in transparent ways. The analysis offered here is not complete; I have not, for example, been able to establish clear criteria to predict where hypotaxis will and will not occur in clause linkage, nor in all circumstances to distinguish adverbial from relative subordination. Some discussion of these problems appears below at §15.6.4. The necessarily meta-linguistic analysis presented here is not intended as a model of speakers' competence: the outline presented in this chapter collapses synchronic and diachronic relations without distinction.

15.2 Subjunctive forms

The morpheme appearing in form-order class [4] (glossed SJTV), which together with the series-2 NP indices shown in Table 8.4 signal a verb's subjunctive status, is *-ngun-*, with an allomorph *-ngka-* used only when all NP indices appearing in the prefix cluster are third person. The following two tables show how the series-2 NP indices combine with SJTV allomorphs to produce the prefixes that signal the subjunctive form class.

Table 15.3: intransitive subjunctive prefix-clusters

	SINGULAR			PLURAL	
1	nganngun-	|ngan-ngun|	1pin	ngarrkun-	|ngarr-ngun|
2	ngunngun-	|ngun-ngun|	1px	arrkun-	|arr-ngun|
3a	ingka-	|i-ngka|	2p	nyirrkun-	|nyirr-ngun|
3f	nyangka-	|nyaN-ngka|	3p	angka-	|arr-ngka|
3w	ka-	|ØN-ngka|			
3m	mangka-	|ma-ngka|			

Table 15.4: transitive subjunctive prefix-clusters

1>2	ngunngun-	|ngun-(n)-Ø-ngun|
1>3a	inganngun-	|i-ngan-ngun|
1>3f	nyinganngun-	|nyiN-ngan-ngun|
1>3w	nganngun-	|ØN-ngan-ngun|
1>3m	manganngun-	|ma-ngan-ngun|
1>2p	nyinngun-	|nyirr-n-Ø-ngun|
1>3p	anganngun-	|arr-ngan-ngun|
2>1	janngun-	|jan-ngun|
2>3a	injangun-	|i-nja-ngun|
2>3f	nyinjangun-	|nyiN-nja-ngun|
2>3w	jungun-	|ØN-nja-ngun|
2>3m	manjangun-	|ma-nja-ngun|
2>1px	anjangun-	|arr-nja-ngun|
2>3p	anjangun-	|arr-nja-ngun|
3>1	nganngun-	|ngan-(n)-Ø-ngun|
3>2	ngunngun-	|ngun-(n)-Ø-ngun|
3>3a	ingka-	|i-Ø-ngka|
3>3f	nyingka-	|nyiN-Ø-ngka|
3>3w	ka-	|ØN-Ø-ngka|
3>3m	mangka-	|ma-Ø-ngka|
3>1pin	ngarrkun-	|ngarr-Ø-ngun|
3>1px	anngun-	|arr-n-Ø-ngun|
3>2p	nyinngun-	|nyirr-n-Ø-ngun|
3>3p	angka-	|arr-(n)-Ø-ngka|
1pin>3a	arrkun-	|a-ngarr-ngun|
1pin>3f	nyarrkun-	|nyaN-ngarr-ngun|
1pin>3w	warrkun-	|ᵏwuN-ngarr-ngun|
1pin>3m	marrkun-	|ma-ngarr-ngun|
1pin>3p	angarrkun-	|arr-ngarr-ngun|
1px>2	ngunngumbarr-	|ngun-(n)-ngun-ᵇwarr|

1px>3a	errkun-	|a-nyarr-ngun|
1px>3f	nyerrkun-	|nyaN-nyarr-ngun|
1px>3w	nyarrkun-	|ØN-nyarr-ngun|
1px>3m	merrkun-	|ma-nyarr-ngun|
1px>2p	nyinngumbarr-	|nyirr-n-ngun-ᵇwarr|
1px>3p	anyarrkun-	|arr-nyarr-ngun|
2p>1	jarrangun-	|jan-rra-ngun|
2p>3a	irrangun-	|i-rra-ngun|
2p>3f	nyirrangun-	|nyiN-rra-ngun|
2p>3w	wurrangun-	|ᵏwuN-rra-ngun|
2p>3m	marrangun-	|ma-rra-ngun|
2p>1px	arrangun-	|arr-rra-ngun|
2p>3p	arrangun-	|arr-rra-ngun|
3p>1	nganngumbarr-	|ngan-(n)-ngun-ᵇwarr|
3p>2	ngunngumbarr-	|ngun-(n)-ngun-ᵇwarr|
3p>3a	ingkaarr-	|i-ngka-ᵇwarr|
3p>3f	nyingkaarr-	|nyiN-ngka-ᵇwarr|
3p>3w	kaarr-	|ØN-ngka-ᵇwarr|
3p>3m	mangkaarr-	|ma-ngka-ᵇwarr|
3p>1pin	ngarrkubarr-	|ngarr-ngun-ᵇwarr|
3p>1px	anngumbarr-	|arr-n-ngun-ᵇwarr|
3p>2p	nyinngumbarr-	|nyirr-n-ngun-ᵇwarr|
3p>3p	angkaanbarr-	|arr-ngka-kaarr-n-ᵇwarr|

Some points to be noted in these paradigms are:
(i) Series-2 NP indices are used.
(ii) The first person singular index is *ngan-* rather than the expected *nga-*.
(iii) Initial CC reduction rule 28 applies to the 2>3w, 3>3w and 3p>3w clusters |ØN-nja-ngun|, |ØN-Ø-ngka| and |ØN-ngka-ᵇwarr| to produce the surface forms *jungun-*, *ka-* and *kaarr-* respectively.
(iv) Trill deletion rule 15 deletes /rr/ at the end of the plural indices *nyirr-* 'second person' and *arr-* 'exclusive' before a nasal consonant.
(v) General hardening rule 11 turns the initial nasal of the morpheme *-ngun-* into /k/ after /rr/, to produce the shape *-kun-*.
(vi) The subjunctive 3p>3p shape contains a redundancy, with the object index being repeated: |arr-ngka-kaarr-n-ᵇwarr| [3p_O-SJTV-3p_O-INV-3p_A]. Note that the object's second appearance is in its series-1 shape.
(vii) The subjunctive morpheme appears in the prefix cluster after the NP indices, except when the subject index is 3p *-ᵇwarr-* (or 1px in the 1px>2(p) clusters).

15.2.1 Tense-marking

Subjunctive verbs display three kinds of tense-marking:
(i) the first is the same as that appearing on indicative forms, as set out in §5.4 in Tables 5.4 and 5.5. This marking appears on subjunctive verbs in hypotactic and avertive functions.
(ii) The frustrative mood employs the past-tense morpheme *-(yi)nya* appearing in form-order class [9]. This morpheme in subjunctive verbs uniquely marks frustrative mood, and combines with the continuous aspect morpheme to produce *-nyeerri* (|nya-eerri|).

(ii) Subjunctive verbs coding evidential meaning display a distinct present-tense morpheme -*ny* in form-order class [9] (glossed MIR). This morpheme combines with the continuous aspect morpheme in slot [13] to produce the shape -*njeerri* (|ny-yeerri|).

15.3 Subjunctive functions

Subjunctive verbs occur in eight etically distinguishable functions; two modal-semantic, four evidential, and two syntactic. These functions are arrayed in Table 15.5:

Table 15.5: functions of subjunctive mood
(1) Modal   (i) averted reality
                   (ii) frustrative mood

(2) Evidential   (i) non-firsthand: (a) social general knowledge
                                         (b) inferred from stated antecedents
                   (ii) firsthand: (a) immediately apparent
                                         (b) mirative

(3) Syntactic   (i) adverbial subordination
                   (ii) relativization

A single sentence in Worrorra may contain instances of all three types of grammatical meaning; evidential, syntactic and modal-semantic, coded by subjunctive verbs. The following two sentence examples illustrate this range of functions.

Sentence example (15.1) below is from a story in which an old man has been slighted by a family living near him. In revenge, he invites them to climb up a ladder onto a cliff face where his fig trees[100] are growing, and eat the ripe figs there. Once they are there he takes the ladder away and leaves them stranded high on the cliff face. Figs ripen at the end of the hot season, and the sweet and sticky figs make people thirsty. After leaving them in the sun on the cliff face for an unspecified but presumably lengthy amount of time, during which the family have become frightened and distressed, he puts the ladder back up and lets them down. Once down, they say to him:

(15.1)
Nanjan	mana	waay	ngunngununanyarri	ke,	bungkurunyini
nanjan	mana	waay	ngun-ngun=nu-na-nyarri	ke	bungkuru-nyini
ladder	3mDEF	throw	2-SJTV=be-PAST-1pxDAT	3wREF	thirsty-ENDPOINT

anngumbuna	wunu:	wangalaalunguyu	anja	karle
arr-n-Ø=ngun=ᵇwu-na	wunu	wangalaalanguya	anja	karle
1px-INV-3-SJTV=hit-PAST	3wDEF	children	3pDEF	then

debadi	kaajingeerri.
debadi	ØN-ngka-ᵇwarr=yi-ng-eerri
die.PL	VCOMP- SJTV-3p=do-PAST-PROG

When you took the ladder away you knew we'd get thirsty, and these children nearly died.

All three clauses in this sentence are in subjunctive mood, and each codes a different grammatical meaning, as follows:

---

[100] The rock fig *Ficus platypoda*.

1. *Nanjan mana waay ngunngununanyarri ke,* 'when you took the ladder away,'
This is an adverbial subordinate clause: here the subjunctive shape codes the clause's syntactic dependence on the main clauses.
2. *bungkurunyini anngumbuna wunu:* 'you knew we'd get thirsty'
This verb codes subjunctive evidential meaning: the speaker is claiming that the old man could infer from evidence (hot weather, being stranded for a long time, eating figs) that they would get thirsty. This meaning is reinforced by the use of the definite article *wunu*, making this entire clause definite, the speaker asserting that its propositional content is already known to the old man (see §17.1.1). Evidentiality and definite marking here conspire towards an additional purpose: this clause constitutes an accusation that not only must the old man have known what would happen, but that he brought the situation about on purpose, maliciously. The morpheme *-nyini* 'ENDPOINT' also imparts a resultative meaning to the clause, as a logical and inferable outcome of the situation the old man had engineered.
3. *Wangalaalunguyu anja karle debadi kaajingeerri* 'the children nearly died.'
Subjunctive form here marks avertive reality status: an event that could have happened, or nearly happened, but did not. Note that this clause is in effect resultative, in that although containing neither of the resultative postpositions *-maade* or *-nyini*, it has an effective protasis in clause 2, constituting its logical antecedent.

(15.2)

Bulakangarri	arrke	wunu	ngarlangarla	barrabarra	kaajeerri,
bulaka-ngarri	arrke	wunu	ngarlangarla	barrabarra	ØN-ngka-ᵇwarr=yi-eerri
middle-REL	3pREF	3wDEF	story	narrate	VCOMP-SJTV-3p=do-PROG

wunu	bundurlb	mana	angkayoolinerri	wali	ke.
wunu	bundurlb	mana	arr-ngka=yoolee-na-eerri	wali	ke
3wDEF	bush	3mDEF	3p-SJTV=travel-PAST-PROG	PERF	3wREF

Long ago they used to tell this story when they were travelling around in the bush.

Both clauses in (15.2) are subjunctive, and again they code different meanings:
1. *Bulakangarri arrke wunu ngarlangarla barrabarra kaajeerri,* 'long ago they used to tell this story.' This clause bears non-firsthand cultural-knowledge evidential meaning. Daisy Utemorrah translated *bulakangarri* (/bulaka-ngarri/ [middle-REL]) as 'the people-in-the-middle,' meaning people who lived before living memory and beyond the range of genealogical reckoning, but subsequent to the mythical events of the dreamtime. This being the case, the speaker is unable to state from firsthand experience what such ancient people did: rather she defers to an emically reliable, non-firsthand authority as the source of evidence for her statement. The authority in this case is likely to have been cultural ideology or publically received understanding.
2. *wunu bundurlb mana angkayoolinerri* 'when they were travelling in the bush'
This adverbial subordinate clause provides the setting for the preceding main clause.

Another sentence with multiple subjunctive clauses may be seen in (15.41) in §15.6.3 below.

Well over 200 sentences in the database contain one or more subjunctive verbs, and the clear majority of these signal sentential hypotaxis in the form of either adverbial or relative subordinate clauses. However the marking of evidentiality and inference is likely to be one area in which the narrative style of most of the database imparts a bias to the sample.

15.4 Avertive

Avertive meaning quite specifically involves events which nearly happen; which some actor could have good reason to expect to happen, but which fail to happen (Kuteva 1998, 2004:78-112). Averted reality is found in the database in two clearly different senses, one involving reality-status modality, and one root-modal. The reality-status sense involves reasonable expectation; that is, some actor's expectation that an event will occur, but which fails to occur. The root-modal sense, here termed 'frustrative,' involves volition: some actor both expects and desires an event to happen, which does not happen.

Averted reality is patchy in the database at best. There are few examples of it, though verbal paradigms with the translation 'wanted to V' were readily elicited. Love (1934:57) also recorded this verbal category, which he called a 'past subjunctive.' There are some anomalies, and some forms have tantalizingly few instances. What follows is an attempt to make sense of the data that is evident, both in the database and in Love's thesis.

Verbs denoting averted reality are signalled both by subjunctive form and usually by the past-tense allomorph *-(yi)nya* (cf this allomorph on irrealis counterfactual forms as described in §8.3). Elicited forms translated by 'wanted to …' always involved this tense allomorph, some of which are presented as the frustrative mood paradigms in Appendices 2 and 3.

15.4.1 Averted reality

Events which are on the verge of happening, but which ultimately fail to occur, are denoted in Worrorra by subjunctive forms. Avertive reality is discussed by Kuteva (2004:78-112), as a grammatical meaning involving imminent aspectuality, past time-reference and counterfactual modality. Whether or not imminence in Worrorra is aspectual may be open to further investigation, but the link between avertive status and past time-reference seems sound, and it is clearly the case that averted events are coded as a kind of irrealis modality. Some unequivocal examples of avertive reality from the database are shown in (15.3):

(15.3a) (=14.12b)
Baay	ngenu	kaajingeerri	wunu	karrku
baay	nga-nya=nu	ØN-ngka-ᵇwarr=yi-ng-eerri	wunu	karrku
climb	1-OPT=be	VCOMP-SJTV-3p=do-PAST-PROG	3wDEF	hill

rdaarreya.
ØN=raarreya
3w=big
They were trying to climb up into the high hills.

(b) (cf 14.14)
Ingam-ingam	nyarrkunjingeerri	ke	kaarri maa.
i-nga=ma–i-nga=ma	ØN-nyarr-ngun=yi-ng-eerri	ke	kaarri maa
3a-1=get–3a-1=get	VCOMP-1px-SJTV-do-PAST-PROG	3wREF	in.vain

We tried to grab hold of him but we couldn't.

(c)
Arrka	wali	brrabrra	kaajingeerri	maa.
arrka	wali	brrabrra	ØN-ngka-ᵇwarr=yi-ng-eerri	maa
3pNAR	PERF	awake.PL	VCOMP-SJTV-3p=do-PAST-PROG	PROG

They were still just waking up / they still hadn't woken up yet.

In text subsequent to sentence (15.3a) the actors fail to get up out of reach of floodwaters, and perish. A more careful but cumbersome translation of this sentence might read 'they were trying, but ultimately failed to climb ...' The 'failed outcome' reading of (15.3b) is made explicit by the adverb *kaarri maa* 'in vain,' and in (15.3c) acts of waking up have begun but have failed to be achieved when surrounding and accompanying events overtake the sleepers.

These examples all use the verb *kuN[ ]=yi* as either a classifier (15.3c) or as a matrix verb in complement clause₂ constructions (see Chapter 14). Note that these textual examples all use this verb's indicative past-tense allomorph *-ng*. The following elicited examples, in contrast, all use the allomorph *-(yi)nya*:

(15.4a)
Bija	ngana	iwarnbarnngarri	aja	ngannguninyanangka.
bija	ngana	iwarnbarnngarri	aja	ngan-ngun=ni-yinya-nangka
FUT	PROB	brown.snake	sit	1-SJTV=be-PAST-DAT

I would have/nearly sat on a snake.

(b)
Bija	ngana	mara	inganngumbeenya.
bija	ngana	mara	i-ngan-ngun=ᵇwu-yinya
FUT	PROB	see	3a-1-SJTV=hit-PAST

I would have found him (if I'd gone a bit further).

(c)   Inganngurnonya.   (d)   Nganngunyenyanangka.
      i-ngan-ngun=rno-nya   ØN-ngan-ngun-nya=yi-yinya-nangka
      3a-1-SJTV=give-PAST   VCOMP-1-SJTV-EP=do-PAST-DAT
      I would have given it to him.   *I would have told him.*

Note how in the (a) and (b) examples here my instructors have underlined the irrealis import of these sentences by use of the dubitative adverb sequence *bija ngana* at the start of each. Although a volitional reading could be argued to be possible in (15.4b), this is out of the question in (15.4a), in which a completely involuntary situation is described.

15.4.2 Frustrative mood

Frustrative mood in Worrorra is an aspect or subset of avertive reality status, one incorporating the semantics of volition. A volitional interpretation ('wanted to ...,' 'would have ...') was volunteered for all the frustrative paradigms presented in the appendices. Consequently all the frustrative mood examples used here are unelicited.

There are a couple of sentences in the database denoting present-tense frustrative forms, one of which (15.5a) is both clear and spontaneous. Significantly, the present-tense frustrative morpheme used here is the irrealis counterfactual non-past marker *-n*, noted in §8.3. The use of epenthetic *-ba* word-finally after non-past *-n* may be seen again in sentence (8.26b). Other sentence examples involving past-tense forms are shown in (15.5b-d):

(15.5a)
Nganngunyenganba	kanangkuja	baanyini:	ngani
ngan-ngun-nya=[ya-nga]-n-ba	kanangkurr-nya	baa-nyini	ngani
1-SJTV-EP=[go-TNS]-NON.P-EP	dog-3f	appear-ENDPOINT	what

kunjeerri?
kuN-Ø=yi-eerri
VCOMP-3=do-PROG

I have to/want to go (but can't) until (my) dog shows up: what's she doing?

(b)
Marruminya	ngarrkunyengenya		dalorrba	maa,	dalorr	wali
marru-minya	ngarr-ngun-nya=[ya-nga]-yinya		dalorr-ba	maa	dalorr	wali
3mLAT- ?	1pin-SJTV-EP=[go-TNS]-PAST		well-EP	3mREF	well	PERF

manungu,	yawak	barrwa.
ma=nu-ng	yawak	ba-ngarr=ᵇwa
3m=be-PRES	sink	CFT-1pin=fall

We wanted to go/would have gone that way, but there's sink-holes there and we might fall down one.

(c)
Biju	nganngunyawenya	*motor-car,*	biju	nganngunyawenya.
biju	ngan-ngun-nya=ᵇwa-yinya	motor-car	biju	ngan-ngun-nya=ᵇwa-yinya
repeatedly	1-SJTV-EP=fall-PAST	motor-car	repeatedly	1-SJTV-EP=fall-PAST

Barda	ngewee	kungenga.
barda	nga-nya=ᵇwee	kuN-nga=yi-ng
kill	1-OPT=hit.MID	VCOMP-1=do-PAST

I wanted to fall out of the car, I kept trying to fall out. I wanted to kill myself.

(d)
Mana	aja	bungkamnyaninya	wunu,	ke	ngarri	joy
mana	aja	ba-kuN-mnya=ni-yinya	wunu	ke	ngarri	joy
3mDEF	sit	CFT-3w-DD=be-PAST	3wDEF	3wREF	we(inc)	famous

ngarrkuninyanangka.
ngarr-ngun=nu-yinya-nangka
1pin-SJTV=be-PAST-DAT

It (celestial) should have been here, we wanted to represent it.

Examples (15.5b & c) clearly involve unachieved volition: in the first sentence the reason why they didn't go that way is stated, and in the second sentence the speaker clearly did not throw herself out of a moving vehicle. Note the interesting and rather fine semantic distinction in (15.5c), between 'failed attempt,' encoded by the subjunctive frustrative verb form of the first two clauses, and the less marked kind of volition encoded by the complement₂ construction in the final clause. This last clause clearly distinguishes this sentence as involving frustrative mood, in which an actor wanted an event to happen, from one involving averted accomplishment as in (15.4a), in which an actor would certainly not have wanted something to happen. Daisy Utemorrah translated the second clause in (15.5d) as 'we wanted to represent it,' although a literal translation would be 'we wanted to be famous because of it.'[101]

15.5 Evidentiality

In another of its sense-meanings the subjunctive mood signals evidentiality. Worrorra displays one of the simplest kinds of evidential system in Aikhenvald's (2004) typology, formally marking statements for which evidence is invoked, against statements unmarked for evidence. In Aikhenvald's arrangement this appears to be a Type A2 system, however the extensions of this system are not simple.

---

[101] See §13.2.2 (v) for a discussion of constructions with *joy* 'famous.'

Etically, four kinds of evidentiality can be distinguished within the single formal device available in the language, and these kinds can be sorted into firsthand and non-firsthand categories:

(1) Cultural knowledge is non-firsthand evidence, and derives from the body of social understandings that every traditionally-educated Worrorra speaker would have possessed, and which could be appealed to, to validate a proposition.
(2) Inferential evidentiality is again non-firsthand, and invokes a set of circumstances as logical antecedents to a proposition, and which a speaker uses to validate the statement in which the proposition is contained.
(3) Immediately apparent evidentiality is firsthand, in which a speaker presents the addressee's observable environment as manifest evidence for a proposition.
(4) Mirativity is also firsthand, and presents information that is not only new, but unexpected as well.

Any evidential clause may involve one or more of these meanings at the same time: they are not mutually exclusive, in fact they often entail and support each other in the invocation of evidence. It is important to note the discourse function of evidential marking in Worrorra: evidentials are used to *support* propositions rather than to qualify them. This means that in most cases subjunctive forms constitute assertions, with a stronger epistemic force than if they constituted qualifications or caveats.

15.5.1 Non-firsthand evidence: cultural general knowledge

What I will refer to here as 'cultural knowledge' consists of background social and cultural understandings about religion, mythology, geography, kinship and the world generally, accessible to all traditionally-educated Aboriginal people in the north-west Kimberley. Merlan (1981:182) describes a comparable use of irrealis modality in Mangarayi, to encode a situation which the speaker knows about from hearsay or repute, but of which she herself has no firsthand knowledge. In Worrorra, evidentiality is not used to distance a speaker from the validity of a proposition, as appears to be the case in some other languages: rather it is used to achieve the opposite effect. In marking evidence as non-firsthand, a Worrorra speaker is appealing for validation to a higher authority than that of his or her own self. While non-firsthand evidentials in some languages convey, 'this is not my evidence, and so I cannot vouch for its reliability,' non-firsthands in Worrorra convey, 'this is not just *my* evidence, and so is more reliable than if it were.' The higher authority appealed to is likely to be religious doctrine, social custom and ideology, or received opinion, all of high importance in Australian Aboriginal society. In similar vein, an English speaker might say, at a crucial part of a narrative where he or she wishes to assert that the information is not merely his or her own opinion or interpretation, but rather is supported by other people's observations and evidence, something like: 'now apparently what happened then was this …' In utterances of this sort a speaker is indexing his or her evidence as non-firsthand, but as all the more reliable for being so. Non-firsthand evidentials, therefore, may represent assertions with a stronger epistemic warrant than indicative declarative utterances.

In talking about her life, Patsy Lulpunda started with just such an assertion, based on universal religious and cultural knowledge:

(15.6a)
Ngayu	gee	anganngumbu	mirimiringarrinya,	irlaangalya,	lalai.
ngayu	gee	arr-ngan-ngun=^{b}wu	mirimiringarrinya	irlaangalya	lalai
I	represent[102]	3p-1-SJTV=hit	echidna	possum.sp [103]	dreaming

My spirit-animals are the echidna and the scaly-tailed possum, from the dreaming.

However by no means all religious references require evidential marking; having established the authority for her assertion, Patsy repeats the statement a little later, without evidential marking:

---

[102] *gee* =^{b}*wu* 'represent': literally 'SUBJ has OBJ as his or her totemic representative.'
[103] The cuscus-like phalangerid *Wyulda squamicaudata*.

(15.6b)
Inja	gee	kango	ngayu	irlaangalya.
inja	gee	ka-nga=ᵇwu	ngayu	irlaangalya
3aDEF	represent	3a-1=hit	I	possum.sp

My spirit-animal is the scaly-tailed possum.

While traditional and mythical stories are by no means told exclusively in subjunctive form, at some stage, usually but not always at the start, a story-teller is likely to index the cultural mandate that constitutes the evidentiary source of the assertions she makes. The sentences in (15.7) all come from traditional stories, and show evidential marking used to signal the cultural source of the information being proffered:

(15.7a)
Nyina	dambeem	juman	mangkamanga	jimbirrij	nyangke.
nyina	dambeem	juman	ma-Ø-ngka=ma-nga	jimbirrij	nyangke
3fDEF	place	road	3m-3-SJTV=get-PAST	rock-cod	3fREF

The giant rod-cod made a road up through the land.

(b)
'Kunyila	inja	barraninjerri,'	kaajunganangkorri
kunyila	inja	ba-ka-rra=ninja-eerri	ØN-ngka-ᵇwarr=yi-ng-a-[nangka-ᵏwurri]
moon	3aDEF	CFT-3a-2p=look-PROG	VCOMP-SJTV-3p=do-PAST-EP-[3pDAT]

anja	wangalaalunguyu	wunu	wurnirndeerrngarri	wali	wunu.
anja	wangalaalanguya	wunu	ᵏwuN=rnirndeerr-ngarri	wali	wunu
3pDEF	children	3wDEF	3w=old-REL	PERF	3wDEF

'Don't look at the moon,' they used to tell their children long ago.

(c)
Wangalaalunguyu	anja	baawaard	kaajungu ...
wangalaalanguya	anja	baawaard	ØN-ngka-ᵇwarr=yi-ng
children	3pDEF	appear.PL	VCOMP-SJTV-3p=do-PAST

arrka	Dilangarri	dambeem	mana	brrak	kaajungu.
arrka	dilangarri	dambeem	mana	brrak	ØN-ngka-ᵇwarr=yi-ng
3pNAR	dog.people	place	3mDEF	awake	VCOMP-SJTV-3p=do-PAST

Children were born ... the Dog-clan's child-spirits were conceived in that land.

(d)
Jirrini	wunu-wunu,	jamaarri	ingkamnyaarnamaleena	lalai.
jirrini	wunu-wunu	jamaarri	i-ngka-mnya=ᵏwarnamalee-na	lalai
PLACE.NAME	3wDEF-3wDEF	mullet	3a-SJTV-DD=fight.MID-PAST	dreaming

Jirrini is here, where the mullet fought in the dreamtime.

(e)
Karle	kurruk	mangkaarrwuna	dambeem.
karle	kurruk	ma-ngka-ᵇwarr=ᵇwu-na	dambeem
then	burst.up	3m-SJTV-3p=hit-PAST	place

Then they (Wandjinas) burst up out of the ground.

All these sentences depict events about which the speaker has no first-hand knowledge, but which are nevertheless part of public cultural knowledge, and their validity is asserted by being marked as such.

The 'road' referred to in (15.7a) is the Prince Regent River, which flows along an ancient fault in a straight line SE to NW. Sentence (15.7b) bears the same import as the first clause in (15.2): the speaker has only cultural understanding as a basis for asserting what people actually did long ago. Sentence (15.7c) contains two metaphors; *baawaard kuN[ ]=yi* '(many people) appear/be born,' referring to succeeding generations of children, and *brrak kuN[ ]=yi* 'wake up,' referring to the appearance of child spirits out of the deep *wungkurr* pools where they dwell, and their metamorphosis into human form.

Sentence (15.8) is from the middle of a text, and represents the impression point of that story (see §17.3.1). Because this is the pivot around which the story turns, the speaker is re-asserting her evidentiary source for it, in reference to her character's motivation for behaving as she does at this particular point:

(15.8)
Ke	ko	kenga	wunu:	'maaji	aakuwunya
ke	ko	ØN-Ø-ngka=yi-ng	wunu	maaji	aaku-ᵏwunya
3wREF	tired	VCOMP-3-SJTV=do-PAST	3wDEF	had.better	water-PURP

ngeyu.'
nga-nya=ya
1-OPT=go

Then she must have/I think she got tired: 'I'd better go for some water.'

Another narrative impression point employing a subjunctive verb may be seen below in (15.24b).

Sentence (15.9) is not from a story, rather it describes a rock-shelter with Wandjina paintings. Where hands are stencilled on the wall, Patsy says, in reference to the Wandjina called Marrenbini:

(15.9) (=7.9a)
Injinja	inja	irnurnu	warndi	kona	lalai.
inja-inja	inja	i=rnurnu	warndi	ØN-Ø-ngka=ᵇwu-na	lalai
3aDEF-3aDEF	3a-DEF	3a=hand	make	3w-3-SJTV=hit-PAST	dreaming

This (Wandjina) painted his hands here in the dreamtime.

Not having seen Marrenbini do this, Patsy has no direct or firsthand evidence for her assertion; rather she is stating what is common knowledge. Subjunctive marking in contexts like this may have become more common since the advent of Christianity, a religion which is often seen to compete with traditional accounts of the way the world is.

15.5.2 *Immediately apparent firsthand evidence*

Immediately apparent evidence is typically manifest or ongoing at the time of speaking, and so is usually (but not always) coded by a verb with the evidential present-tense morpheme *-ny* (glossed 'MIR') in form-order class [9]. Immediately apparent evidentiality is presentational, in that a speaker typically holds an event up to a listener for his or her inspection, or presents a scene to an onlooker, in order to bring it to his or her attention. In the following sentences speakers are presenting situations to their listeners: notice how in (15.10a) a presentational pronoun is used (§7.3.2), to reinforce the presentational function of the utterance. The interesting sentence in (15.10d) is discussed in §6.2.6 (i); and (15.10e) contains three clauses, the last of which is of interest here: the speaker is pointing out that his body is freshly painted with white paint (pipe-clay):

(15.10a) (=7.38c)
Nyingaangurrurlaal	nyangkem	aja	nyangkaninjeerri.
nyiN-nga=ᵏwangurru-rla-kwaal	nyaN=ᵏwe-m	aja	nyaN-ngka=ni-ny-yeerri
3f-1=carry-PAST-hither	3f=PRSNTIL-?	sit	3f-SJTV=be-MIR-PROG

I brought her here, and there she is.

(b) (=7.9b)

Injinja	inja	we	ingkawanjeerri.
inja-inja	inja	we	i-ngka=^{b}wa-ny-yeerri
3aDEF-3aDEF	3aDEF	lie	3a-SJTV=fall-MIR-PROG

This is him lying down here.

(c)

Ngurru	aja	arrkunyawanjeerri	kaarrinyini.
ngurru	aja	arr-ngun-nya=^{b}wa-ny-yeerri	kaarri-nyini
here	sit	1px-SJTV-EP=fall-MIR-PROG	3pNEG-ENDPOINT

We're living here until the end.

(d) (=6.16)

Ngayu	nyinjorinya	nyinngalja,	yorr
ngayu	nyiN=yoru-nya	nyiN=n-ngal-nya	yorr
I	3f=widowed-3f	3f=DEF-several-3f	sit.together

nyangkawanjeerri	nyirno-nyirno.
nyaN-ngka=^{b}wa-ny-yeerri	nyiN=rno
3f-SJTV=fall-MIR-PROG	3f=DIST

I am one of these widows that (you can see) live all around here.

(e)

Wunu	marnowa	nganngunyaangurru,	jaa	wurlingkarr
wunu	marnu-^{b}wa	ØN-ngan-ngun-nya=^{k}wangurru	jaa	wurlingkarr
3wDEF	carry-PROG	3w-1-SJTV-EP=carry	PERFV	rub.off

bungkayaara:	wunu	rowa	ngannguninjeerri!
ba-kuN-Ø=yi-^{k}wara	wunu	rowa	ngan-ngun=ni-ny-yeerri
CFT-VCOMP-3=do-1DAT	3wDEF	white	1-SJTV=be-MIR-PROG

If I carry it (celestial) my (paint) might all rub off: look how white I am!

(f)

Wunngurrij	maa	barrabarra	warrkunyenjeerri.
^{k}wuN=n-ngurru-ji	maa	barrabarra	^{k}wuN-ngarr-ngun-nya=yi-ny-yeerri
3w=DEF-away-again	PROG	narrate	VCOMP-1pin-SJTV-EP=do-MIR-PROG

To this day we still tell (this story).

Congruent with the presentational function of immediate first-hand evidence, verbs of perception are frequent in this kind of sentence. Note *nguru =nu* 'hear' in (15.14b) below, and predicates of visual perception *(=ninja, kala =nu, murn ma[ ]=^{b}wu, mara =^{b}wu)* elsewhere (eg. 15.11, 15.16, 15.18, 15.19, 15.27b & g), and (15.41). Sentence (15.11) below illustrates this presentational function particularly clearly:

(15.11)

Maa	maa	kekaka	wurramnyaninja,	wurno	rdarlurn
maa	maa	kekaka	^{k}wuN-rra-mnya=ninja	wurno	rdarlurn
3mREF	3mREF	like.this	3w-2p-DD=look	3wDIST	looming

kamnyanunaaljeerri.
ØN-ngka-mnya=nu-na-ᵏwaal-yeerri
3w-SJTV-DD=be-PAST-hither-PROG
Look at it (celestial) there, looming up over there.

In this example immediate evidentiality is signalled after the directional morpheme, by the hardening of the first phoneme of the continuous aspect morpheme to produce the shape -*aaljeerri*, as if the morpheme -*ny*, covertly present, were yet effecting the shape of the following aspect morpheme. In other contexts (eg 8.46c, 9.27b, 11.13, and the indicative forms in Appendix 2.2) the morphemes -ᵏ*waal* 'hither' and -*(y)eerri* 'progressive' combine to produce the shape -*aaleerri*.[104]

Immediate marking is used to draw attention to new and evolving events: rather than presenting an existing situation, this involves pointing out new information. In (15.12) two children are lost. At one stage they hear their family in the distance, and say:

(15.12)
Arno   yarrorl   kaajinjeerri!
arr=rno   yarrorl   ØN-ngka-ᵇwarr=yi-ny-yeerri
3p=DIST   sound.of.voices VCOMP-SJTV-3p=do-MIR-PROG
There's their voices!

In (15.13) two people are desperately searching for assistance; seeing other people camped in the distance, the wife says:

(15.13) (=17.39d)
Arno-rno   jurroyurro   marrkunjandanjeerri
arr=rno-arr=rno   jurro-jurro   ma-ngarr-ngun=yanda-ny-yeerri
3p=dist-3p=dist   smoke.rising-REDUP 3m-1pin-SJTV=cause-MIR-PROG

maalkarram,   angarrburrkaarndu   arrke wali.
maalkarram   arr-[ngarr]=murrka-[ᵏwarndu] arrke wali
grass-fire   3p-[1pin]=go.to-[DU]   3pREF RESUM
Here, we'll light grass-fires to (send up) smoke (to signal) those (people) over there, (and then) let's go over to them.

The second clause in (15.13) is unequivocally hortative, while the first is an immediately-apparent evidential, indicating that the action is occurring while the actor is speaking; that is, in her anxiety she is setting fire to the grass without waiting for her addressee's consent. Neither of the expected optative or hortative forms are used here; it is as if the utterance's requirement to code evidentiality outranks other considerations. This first clause is presentational: by coding for evidentiality and a first person plural inclusive actor, the speaker is saying, 'look at what I'm doing, I invite you to do this too.' This expression is semantically hortative, but more immediate and urgent, because the denoted action is taking place at the same time as the exhortation is uttered. An English translation 'here, let's V' with the speaker initiating a performance of V while speaking, is probably as good as any.

In (15.14) the speakers are in hiding, and are reporting on what they are observing in (15.14a), and overhearing in (15.14b):

(15.14a)
Yaw,   ke   blaai   ingkaarrwunjeerri   rnokukajirn.
yaw   ke   blaai   i-ngka-ᵇwarr=ᵇwu-ny-yeerri   rnoku-kajirn
Yes   and   pound   3a-SJTV-3p=hit-MIR-PROG   mortar-like
Yes, and it looks like they're pounding it (masc) up in a mortar.

---

[104] The other exception is the counterfactual present paradigm of the irregular verb =*ya*-ᵏ*waal* 'come,' as discussed in §8.3.2.

(b)
Nguru	kanuna	inkarnd-inkarndu	aja	ingkaninykarndeerri.
nguru	ka=nu-na	i=n-ᵏwarndu-i=n-ᵏwarndu	aja	i-ngka=ni-ny-ᵏwarndu-eerri
hear	3a=be-PAST	3a=DEF-DU-3a-DEF-DU	sit	3a-SJTV=be-MIR-DU-PROG

He heard them both sitting there.

Notice how often the presentational dimension of evidential marking is supported by the reduplication of deictic determiners: *wunu-wunu, injinja, nyirno-nyirno* and *inkarnd-inkarndu* in (15.7d, 15.9, 15.10b, d) and (15.14b).

In (15.15) the speakers are identifying things in their immediate surroundings, one is pointing it out to an addressee in (15.15a), and the other to himself in (15.15b):

(15.15a)
Darak	bayungurru	rlaard	mangkenganjeerri.
darak	ba=ya-ngurru	rlaard	ma-ngka=[ya-nga]-ny-yeerri
enter	CFT=go-away	crevice	3m-SJTV=[go-TNS]-MIR-PROG

Go through there where there's a crevice.

(b)
Marneen	nyangee	mana	nanjarnanya	wurno	rlaard
marneen	nyaN-nga=ee	mana	nanjan-rnanya	ᵏwuN=rno	rlaard
hang.up	3f-1=place	3mDEF	ledge-LOC	3w-DIST	split

kenganjeerri.
ØN-ngka=[ya-nga]-ny-yeerri
VCOMP-SJTV=[go-TNS]-MIR-PROG
I'll put her on the ledge, up there where (the rock) is fissured.

These two sentences both use the word *rlaard* 'split, fissure, ledge, crack,' typically in sandstone cliffs or rocks, and often used as ossuary deposits, as in (15.15b). This word appears as a noun *rlaard mana* 'crevice' in (15.15a), and in (15.15b) as a preverb in the complex predicate *rlaard =ya* '(rock) be cracked, fissured.'

Immediately apparent evidentiality may consist of evidence of an event that happened in the past, in which case the present-tense morpheme *-ny* must be dispensed with. This situation is not common in the database, but one such occurrence is shown in (15.16), where an indicative past-tense morpheme is used. Here the speaker is showing two boys the body of a demon, and uses evidential form to present its past action:

(15.16)
Irramnyaninjaarndu	jadam;	aaya	wurluk
i-[rra]-mnya=ninja-[ᵏwarndu]	jadam	aaya	wurluk
3a-[2p]-DD=look.at-[DU]	closely	3aREF	swallow

nyinngunyiyabunaarndu.
[nyirr]-n-Ø-ngun-nya=yabu-na-[ᵏwarndu]
[2p]-INV-3-SJTV-EP=throw-PAST-[DU]
Take a good look at him, you two; he swallowed you both.

Evidential paradigms with *-ny* 'MIR' were readily elicited, as systematic alternatives to present indicative paradigms (see Table 15.6 below). Immediate/presentational meaning is therefore not confined to any particular set of agreement classes, it simply indexes an event that is occurring here-and-now as being evident to an addressee, where such indexation is pragmatically pertinent. These verb forms may be seen in spontaneous use in sentences (15.10a, e; 15.18a) and (15.27a, f). Other examples of the immediate/presentational use of subjunctive verbs can be seen in the final clause of (15.41) below, and at (10.60c) and (17.58), this latter set about with presentational/topicalizing/focusing determiners.

Table 15.6: present-tense evidential paradigm, *aja =nu* 'sit'

aja ngannguninjeerri	*I'm sitting down*
aja ngunnguninjeerri	*you're sitting down*
aja ingkaninjeerri	*he's sitting down*
aja nyangkaninjeerri	*she's sitting down*
aja kaninjeerri	*it (celestial) is sitting down*
aja mangkaninjeerri	*it (terrestrial) is sitting down*
aja ngarrkuninjeerri	*we (inc) are sitting down*
aja arrkuninjeerri	*we (exc) are sitting down*
aja nyirrkuninjeerri	*you're all sitting down*
aja angkaninjeerri	*they're sitting down*

15.5.3 Mirative

Mirativity is the semantics of 'unprepared mind,' as manifested in evidential meaning (DeLancey 1997, 2001; Aikhenvald 2004). Aikhenvald (2004:8) sums up mirativity as signalling 'unprepared mind, new information, speaker's surprise.' We have already seen that 'new information' is part of the meaning of immediately apparent evidentiality in Worrorra, but it is also possible to distinguish new information from the semantics of surprise or unprepared mind in comparable forms. In (15.17) a man has gone to sleep in a rock shelter. He is woken up by a noise, and looking up he sees:

(15.17)
Ey!	Wangayinyina	nyangkawalkeny!
ey	wangayinya-nyina	nyaN-ngka=^{b}walke-ny
ey	woman-3fDEF	3f-SJTV=stand-MIR

Hey! There's a woman standing there!

The following two examples distinguish a background event of unfocussed gazing or scanning, denoted by the complex predicate *murn ma[ ]=^{b}wu* 'gaze (typically out over landscape),' from what the viewer ends up seeing: in both cases what is seen causes surprise, and is set against the activity that preceded it:[105]

(15.18a)
Awanja	inja	kala	kanuna	nguwanu,	ke	murn
awanja	inja	kala	ka=nu-na	nguwanu	ke	murn
boy	3aDEF	look.up	3a=be-PAST	tree	3wREF	gaze

mona	dumbinyini	aja	ingkaninjeerri.
ma-Ø=^{b}wu-na	dumbi-nyini	aja	i-ngka=ni-ny-yeerri
3m-3=hit-PAST	barn.owl-ENDPOINT	sit	3a-SJTV=be-MIR-PROG

The boy looked up into a tree and saw an owl sitting up there.

(b)
Murn	mona:	'bijakunyini	jurro	kaniny,'
murn	ma-Ø=^{b}wu-na	bijaku-nyini	jurro	ØN-ngka=ni-ny

---

[105] *murn ma[ ]=^{b}wu* 'gaze' and =*nganyarro* 'search' may be understood as atelic and telic alternatives of what is essentially the same act.

gaze VCOMP-3=hit-PAST smoke-ENDPOINT smoking 3w-SJTV=be-MIR
kunjungu.
kuN-Ø=yi-ng
VCOMP-3=do-PAST
He looked around: 'there's smoke rising up,' he thought.

Notice how in both sentences the clauses containing the subjunctive verb also contain the morpheme *-nyini* 'ENDPOINT,' signalling that these clauses are conceptually separate from, and the outcomes of, the activity of gazing that leads up to them.

Sentence (15.19) shows unequivocal mirative meaning. Here two children are being warned against looking at the moon; not an easy injunction to obey when going to sleep in the open with a full moon overhead. Mirative marking on the verb =*ninja* 'look at' denotes accidental or inadvertent observation, of the sort that could easily happen in these circumstances. Here neither surprise nor new information are being signalled: this sentence codes 'unprepared mind' exclusively, as an act done inadvertently, without attention:

(15.19) (=8.42b)
Barraninjaarndeerri   kunyila   aaya;   irrangunyaninjanykarndu
ba-ka-[rra]=ninja-[ᵏwarndu]-eerri   kunyila   aaya   i-[rra]-ngun-nya=ninja-ny-[ᵏwarndu]
CFT-3a-[2p]=look.at-[DU]-PROG   moon   3aREF   3a-[2p]-SJTV-EP=look.at-MIR-[DU]

ke,   yarriy   bangkawaal.
ke   yarriy   ba-ka=ᵇwa=ᵏwaal
3wREF   descend   CFT-3a=fall-hither
Don't you two look at the moon; if you inadvertently look at it, it might come down.

15.5.4 Inferred evidence

Inferred or inferential evidence is non-firsthand and based on stated or otherwise known logical antecedents. The second clause in sentence example (15.1) above is a good example of this kind of marking: the stated antecedent occurs in the first clause, 'when you threw away the ladder.' The ANTECEDENT–RESULT structure of this kind of sentence is often made explicit by the use of either *-nyini* 'ENDPOINT' or *(-)maade* 'RESULT' in the apodosis, as in (15.20):

(15.20)
Maambulb   mana   kungurr   kunge   rlarlangkarram   mana,
ma=ᵏwambul-ma   mana   kungurr   kuN-nga=yi   rlarlangkarram   mana
3m=eye-3m   3mDEF   stab   VCOMP-1=do   sea   3mDEF

manmaadem   buju   angkamnyanuna.
ma=n-maade-m   buju   arr-ngka-mnya=nu-na
3m=DEF-RESULT-3m   finish   3p-SJTV-DD=be-PAST
I stabbed the Eye-of-the-sea, that's why they all died.

The 'Eye-of-the-sea' is the name of a particularly dangerous tidal whirlpool off the north-west Kimberley coast.

Even when result status is not specifically marked, the evidential nature of such sentences is usually clear. In (15.21) a man is searching for evidence of what has happened to two missing children:

(15.21)
Akurla	kamangaarndu;	mana	braarr	kamnyeng
akurla	[ka]-Ø=ma-nga-[ᵏwarndu]	mana	braarr	ØN-Ø-ngka-mnya=yi-ng
demon	[3a]-3=get-PAST-[DU]	3mDEF	clear	3a-3-SJTV-DD=do-PAST

mana	ngalarram,	rdiwa-rdiwa	mangkamurrkarlaal.
mana	ngalarram	rdiwa-rdiwa	ma-Ø-ngka=murrka-rla-ᵏwaal
3mDEF	long.grass	break-break	3m-3-SJTV=go.to-PAST-hither

A devil took them; here's where he must've flattened the long grass and trampled it down.

In (15.22) two women have just recounted the horrific details of their adventures or sojourn in their husband's country. They end their account by declaring that on the basis of what has happened to them:

(15.22) (=7.37a)
Wunngarri	maa	bardi	arrkunyaninykarndeerri
ᵏwuN=n-ngarri	maa	bardi	arr-ngun-nya=ni-ny-ᵏwarndu-eerri
3w=DEF-REL	PROG	be.at.home	1px-SJTV-EP=be-MIR-DU-PROG

mana	dambeem.
3mDEF	place

From now on we're staying at home.

Subjunctive inferential marking in this case indexes the antecedent narrative that leads up to this declaration. In (15.23) evidential marking appears again on the outcome or result ('we ran away') of the situation indexed by inferential morphology ('we were afraid of him'):

(15.23)
Arri	arrkunjooleenangurru	wangalaalunguyu	kerrkulkunarla.
arri	arr-ngun=yoolee-na-ngurru	wangalaalanguya	ka-nyarr=ᵏwulkuna-rla
we(exc)	1px-SJTV=go-PAST-away	children	3a-1px=fear-PAST

The reason us children ran away is that we were afraid of him.

Example (15.24) is from Daisy Utemorrah's account of her childhood at the Kunmunya Mission. Here she is describing the ways in which as girls she and her friends helped older women. The first part of the extract is not glossed, and describes the kind of work girls did after school. The second part, which is glossed, is an assertion based on evidence, that girls at that time actively helped their parents and relations:

(15.24a)
School buju nyarrkunjungu ke dambeenyinim braarr merrwuna. Wiyanu marnowa kunyajingeerringkurri anja wangaya. Ke aaku kurley kunyajingeerringkurri mangarringarrim.dambeem mana.
When we finished school we used to clean up around our camps. We carried firewood with the women, and with them we watered [splashed water on] the gardens.

(b)
Wunu	anyarrkurnawajangerri;	marno-marnowa
wunu	arr-nyarr-ngun=rnawaja-nga-eerri	marno-marno-ᵇwa
3wDEF	3p-1px-SJTV=help-PAST-PROG	carry-carry-PROG

nyarrkunjingeerri	wiyanu,	wunu
ØN-nyarr-ngun=yi-ng-eerri	wiyanu	wunu
VCOMP-1px-SJTV=do-PAST-PROG	fire	3wDEF

anyarrkurnawajangerri	anja	wangaya.
arr-nyarr-ngun=rnawaja-nga-eerri	anja	wangaya
3p-1px-SJTV=help-PAST-PROG	3pDEF	women

That's how we helped them; we used to carry firewood, we helped the women that way.

From the same story as example (15.1), sentence (15.25) also shows subjunctive inferential marking on a result clause. In Worrorra culture a full stomach is invariably accompanied by thirst, and thirst happens to be a crucial consequence in this story. The speaker is here stating how it came about that they became full, and so became thirsty:

(15.25)
Wangalaalunguyu	anja	minjarl	kaajanunerri	ardernayurriya,
wangalaalanguya	anja	minjarl	kaarr-nya=nu-na-eerri	arr-rne=rnayurr-iya
children	3pDEF	eat	3p-EP=be-PAST-PROG	3p-AUG=adult-3p

ke	rdurlurr	kenganangkorri.
ke	rdurlurr	ØN-Ø-ngka=yi-ng-a-[nangka-ᵏwurri]
3wREF	full.of.food	VCOMP-3-SJTV=do-PAST-EP-[3pDAT]

The children and adults all ate (figs), and [that's how they got/ they must have been] full.

This construction involves a kind of causation; the speaker is not specifically saying that their eating was the cause of their being full: they were eating figs (which swell inside the stomach), and so in this case we may logically infer that they were full. This is an example of a conversational implicature coming out of what Levinson (1983:146) calls a principle of informativeness, allowing a listener to 'read into an utterance more information than it actually contains.'

15.5.5 Aetiological formulæ

Third-person narratives make up a significant proportion of the database, and a significant proportion of these are traditional stories. And a significant proportion of these, in turn, are ætiologies. This being the case, it is appropriate to note an evidential formula, or set of formulæ, that almost invariably end ætiologies. In these contexts the etic distinction drawn here between immediate and inferential evidentiality is collapsed. Observe this phenomenon in (15.26), which comes at the end of a story in which Mount Trafalgar was stolen and then returned to its rightful place on the north shore of the St. George's Basin:

(15.26)
Aja	kamnyaninjeerrimaade	wurno	Malandumarnanya.
aja	ØN-ngka-mnya=ni-ny-yeerri-maade	ᵏwuN=rno	Malanduma-rnanya
sit	3w-SJTV-DD=be-MIR-PROG-RESULT	3w=DIST	Prince.Regent.Riv-LOC

So there it (celestial) stands, out there on the Prince Regent River.

As an ætiology, the story ends by representing the outcomes of a traditional story as being observable today. Note however that it is impossible to tease out immediate from inferential status: the outcome of the story is immediately apparent, as anyone can observe Mount Trafalgar. But the outcome of the story is also evidenced by the narrated events that caused the phenomenon under consideration to come into being; and these events constitute antecedents for the final outcome or result that comprises ætiological status. In other stories it is the thorns on an echidna, the black head and reduced wings of an emu, the lack of hair on the scaly-tailed possum's tail, and the red splashes on the wings of the red-winged parrot that are readily observable, and that are also the outcomes of events narrated in each case.

In the following examples certain natural phenomena are held up as the manifest results of the events that have just been recounted. Note in these examples the frequent appearance of the postposition *maade* 'RESULT' or *-nyini* 'ENDPOINT' used to make explicit the logical connection between the narrative and the currently-observable phenomena which have been its outcome. Such sentences have been seen in (7.36c), (10.17a) and (10.40b); others are presented below:

(15.27a)
Ke	wunu	jarlewamaade	nyangkaninjeerri	wunu.
ke	wunu	jarlewa-maade	nyaN-ngka=ni-ny-yeerri	wunu
3wREF	3wDEF	red-RESULT	3f-SJTV=be-MIR-PROG	3wDEF

That's why she's red now.

(b)
Weni	arrkuninjanjeerri:	kunyilarnanya	maa	aja
weni	a-ngarr-ngun=ninja-ny-yeerri	kunyila-rnanya	maa	aja
now	3a-1pin-SJTV=look.at-MIR-PROG	moon-LOC	3mREF	sit

kaningeerri.
ka=ni-ng-eerri
3a=be-PRES-PROG

We can see him now: he's up there in the moon.

(c)
Ke	wunu	warnanjakurde	nyangkamnyaninjeerrimaade.
ke	wunu	warnanja-kurde	nyaN-ngka-mnya=ni-ny-yeerri-maade
3wREF	3wDEF	thorn-ASSOC	3f-SJTV-DD=be-MIR-PROG-RESULT

And so that's how she is now, covered in thorns.

(d)
Kanbanerri	awa	burnu	kenga,	bulmarrwaaya	maa
kanbanerri	awa	burnu	ØN-Ø-ngka=yi-ng	bulmarrwaaya	maa
crab	3aNAR	3wPRO	VCOMP-3-SJTV=do-PAST	squashed	PROG

ingkenganjeerrimaade.
i-ngka=[ya-nga]-ny-yeerri-maade
3a-SJTV=[go-TNS]-MIR-PROG-RESULT

The crab was injured, and he still goes around all squashed.

(e)
Ke	birdeennyinim	yarrkay	mangkamnyaninjeerri.
ke	birdeen-nyini-m	yarrkay	ma-ngka-mnya=ni-ny-yeerri
3wREF	small-ENDPOINT-3m	hang.down	3m-SJTV-DD=be-MIR-PROG

And so now there's just little (wings) hanging down there.

(f)
Wunu	nyirrbriaarndu	wakumaada	maade	kaninjeerri
wunu	nyirr=mri-ᵏwarndu	wakumaada	maade	ØN-ngka=ni-ny-yeerri
3wDEF	2p=head-DU	black	RESULT	3w-SJTV=be-MIR-PROG

wunu,	manjawarra	wali	aaya	durloo	irrangunyeerlaarndu.
wunu	manjawarra	wali	aaya	durloo	i-[rra]-ngun-nya=ee-rla-[ᵏwarndu]
3wDEF	berry.sp	PERF	3aREF	place	3a-[2p]-SJTV-EP=place-PAST-[DU]

So now you see that both your heads are black from where you carried the **manjawarra** *berries.*

(g)

Wunmaamaade	wunu	nyarrkunyaninjanjeeerri
ᵏwuN=n-maa-maade	wunu	nyaN-ngarr-ngun-nya=ninja-ny-yeerri
3w=DEF-SPEC-RESULT	3wDEF	3f-1pin-SJTV-EP=look.at-MIR-PROG

rdiwurl	angkamnyaningeerri.
rdiwurl	arr-ngka-mnya=ni-ng-eerri
kill	3p-SJTV-DD=be-PRES-PROG

And so this is how we see them (fem), now when they kill (them).

Sentences (15.27f & g) both show a pair of subjunctive clauses; in each case the first clause is evidential while the second is adverbial-subordinate. Example (15.27g) clearly shows both kinds of subjunctive present-tense marking: the evidential present-tense marker *-ny* is seen in the first verb, while non-evidential indicative-type present tense marking *(-ng)* occurs on the second. Sentence (15.27d) also shows two subjunctive clauses, this time both are evidential. The first clause here indexes cultural knowledge as an evidentiary source, while the second is ætiological.

The second clause in (15.27f) is clearly adverbial-subordinate: it denotes the background or prior condition for the information in the first clause, as well as containing the perfect aspect marker *wali*, indexing past events as being still pertinent to the present. The second clause refers to the preceding narrative: two emus stole cakes of black berries and ran off with them on their heads; this is expected of the backgrounding function of this kind of clause. But in serving this function the second clause assumes a *de facto* causative role: again, implicature from the principle of informativeness is probably involved here. In stating antecedent conditions, this clause thereby and in this instance states the cause of the situation in the first, evidential clause.

15.6 Clause subordination

In Worrorra texts it is not uncommon to find ambiguity between evidentiality and backgrounding: sentence example (15.25) has already been discussed in this regard. Another example may be seen in (15.28) below. This example comes from a text in which a divine injunction is broken and a Wandjina floods the land, drowning everyone except for two children who survive. The story ends as in (15.28); for transparency, intonation breaks are here marked by diagonal slashes, and intonation units are numbered in superscripts.

(15.28)

[1] kaangurrurlaarndu	mayakarrinyinim	dambeem	/[2] arrka
[ka]-Ø=ᵏwangurru-rla-[ᵏwarndu]	ma=yakarri-nyini-m	dambeem	arrka
[3a]-3=carry-PAST-[DU]	3m=other-ENDPOINT-3m	place	3pNAR

karle	buju	angkona	inja	Wanjurna
karle	buju	arr-(n)-Ø-ngka=ᵇwu-na	inja	wanjurna
change.of.state	finish	3p-(INV)-3-SJTV=hit-PAST	3aDEF	DEITY

/[3] yawarrarra	kubajeng	/[4] dambeenyinim	karamalo.
yawarrarra	kuN-ᵇwarr-nya=yi-ng	dambee-nyini-m	karamalo
sink.PL	VCOMP-3p-EP=do-PAST	place-ENDPOINT-3m	empty

[1]*It took them_j both to another country* /[2] *now the Wandjina had destroyed them_k* /[3] *they_k drowned* /[4] *the land was*

empty.

It is likely that intonation unit 3, recapitulating as it does the preceding narrative, constitutes the antecedent material for the evidential/inferential clause in unit 2. Unit 4 constitutes a second, verbless, result clause with unit 3 as its precedent. Nevertheless the information in unit 2 could also be understood as background or prior condition for the information in unit 1; perhaps more realistically, this sequence may be decoded in both ways: as indexing an antecedent source of knowledge (3) about propositional content (2), while at the same time indexing that propositional content as a sufficient condition for the situation in (1). It is likely that conversational implicature licences the extension of formal evidential marking into other linguistic categories.

15.6.1 *Adverbial subordinate clauses*

Worrorra clauses may frequently be juxtaposed, especially when events occur concurrently. Verbs may be serialized to depict sequences of related events, as in (16.10) in §16.2.3. In (15.29) clauses which would normally be subordinated in English are linked paratactically to each other. Example (15.29a) uses a parallel format in which each clause is introduced by *karle* 'CHANGE-OF-STATE:'

(15.29a)
Karle	wali	ajeendaarndu	wunu,	[karle	budurrwu
karle	wali	a-[ngarr]-nya=eenda-[ʷwarndu$_A$]	wunu	karle	budurrwu
Then	PERF	3a-[1pin]-EP=cook-[DU$_A$]	3wDEF	then	snore

kengerri].
ka=ya-nga-eerri
3a=go-TNS-PROG
Then we both burned him, [while he was snoring].

(b)
Ke maa	kubajingeerri	[wori	kaarrweenerri].
ke maa	kuN-ᵇwarr=yi-ng-eerri	wori	kaarr=ᵇwee-na-eerri
thus	VCOMP-3p=do-PAST-PROG	go.around	3p=hit.MID-PAST-PROG

They did these things [while they were travelling around].

(c) (=10.84b)
Mangarriwurle	minjarl	ju,	[bija	joli	ngenaal].
mangarri-ᵏwurle	minjarl	ØN=yi	bija	joli	nga-nya=nu-(ᵏw)aal
food-first	eat	VCOMP=do	FUT	return	1-OPT=be-hither

I'll come back [after you've had lunch]. (Lit: '*eat lunch first, I'll come back here.*')

Clauses may also be subordinated by means of the relativizing suffix *-ngarri* (see §10.6.2 (i)). For negative subordinate clauses, this may be the only means available:

(15.30) (=10.62b)
[Wali waa	nyaa	bangawenyangarri,]	karraanya
wali waa	nyaa	ba-nga=ᵇwa-yinya-ngarri	karra-aa-nya
not.yet	born	CFT-1=fall-PAST-REL	mother-1DAT-3f

ngankangurrurlerri	marndumarnanya.
nga-n-Ø=ᵏwangurru-rla-eerri	marnduma-rnanya
1-INV-3=carry-PAST-PROG	stomach-LOC

[Before I was born,] my mother carried me in her womb (stomach).

However by far the most frequent means of clausal subordination is by the use of subjunctive morphology; indeed, this is the most frequent function of subjunctive forms in the database, which is strongly biased towards a narrative third-person, referring-and-predicating discourse style. This kind of subordinating morphology may be used to set up temporal backgrounds:

(15.31a) (=10.58b)
Wrrorra	maa	kunyarloorlerri	[wangalang	arrkununa].
wrrorra	maa	kuN-nyarr=rloo-rla-eerri	wangalang	arr-ngun=nu-na
Worrorra	only	VCOMP-1px=speak-PAST-PROG	child	1px-SJTV=be-PAST

We only spoke Worrorra [when we were children].

(b) (=8.28c)
Ngurr	bungenangkeka,	[wunu	joli	nyangkanungaal].
ngurr	ba-kuN-nga=yi-nangka-y₂aka	wunu	joli	nyaN-ngka=nu-ng-ᵏwaal
strike	CFT-VCOMP-1=do-DAT-EMPH	3wDEF	return	3f-SJTV=be-PRES-hither

I'll really belt her [when she gets back].

(c)
[Wunu	marangunyina	maramara	nyangkaningeerri,]
wunu	marangunya-nyina	maramara	nyaN-ngka=ni-ng-eerri
3wDEF	sun-3fDEF	hot	3f-SJTV=be-PRES-PROG

nyinaarringeenya	wajunangka.
nyinaarringeenya	kuN-ngarr=yi-nangka
midday	VCOMP-1pin=say-DAT

[When the sun is hottest], we say it's midday.

(d) (=10.48a)
Minyiyaara	[ngamba	ngeyu	jungunju	dambeemangurru].
minya=yi-ᵏwara	ngamba	nga-nya=ya	ØN-nja-ngun=yi	dambeema-ngurru
2>3w=do-1DAT	when	1-OPT=go	VCOMP-2-SJTV=do	place-ALL

Tell me [when you want to go home].

(e)
Karle	waay-waay	kanunangurru	wurno;
karle	waay-waay	ØN-ngka=nu-na-ngurru	wurno
CHANGE.OF.STATE	throw-throw	3w-SJTV=be-PAST-away	3wDIST

iyakarra	iwaraaleya	baay	ingkenga ...
i=yakarra	iwaraaleya	baay	i-ngka=ya-nga
3a=other	month	rise/appear	3a-SJTV=go-TNS

Then when after a while she had recovered (from the worst of her grief); when another month had gone by ...

(f)
[Mara	errkumbu]	kajirn	berrwundaka.
mara	a-nyarr-ngun=ᵇwu	kajirn	ba-ka-nyarr=ᵇwu-n-y₂aka
see	3a-1px-SJTV=hit	NEG	CFT-3a-1px=hit-NON.P-EMPH

[If/when we see/find him], we certainly won't hurt him.

(g)
Nguru   kerrkangurreerri   [karloorlanyarreerri].
nguru   ka-nyarr=ᵏwangurru-eerri   ØN-Ø-ngka=rloo-rla-nyarri-eerri
hear   3a-1px=take-PROG   VCOMP-3-SJTV=speak-PAST-1pxDAT-PROG
We used to listen to him [when he talked to us].

(h) (=4.3a)
Waawa   nguru   banyankangurrun   [wunu   nganngunjineerri]?
waawa   nguru   ba-jan=ᵏwangurru-n   wunu   ØN-ngan-ngun=yi-nu-eerri
NEG.INTER   hear   CFT-2>1=carry-NON.P   3wDEF   VCOMP-1-SJTV=do-2DAT-PROG
How come you don't listen to me [when I'm talking to you]?

(i)
Bardi   nyinyamurrkaarndu   ngayu,   [wunu   yala
bardi   [nyirr]-n-Ø-nya=murrka-[ᵏwarndu]   ngayu   wunu   yala
at.home   [2p]-INV-3-OPT=go.to-[DU]   I   3wDEF   hunting

nganngumbana   wariwunya].
ngan-ngun=ᵇwa-na   wari-ᵏwunya
1-SJTV=fall-TNS   kangaroos-PURP
I'll come back home to you [after I've gone hunting for kangaroos].

(j)
Jinalya   jadba   kawarraangurrurlu   [kulunu   wulaa
jinalya   jada-ᵇwa   ka-ᵇwarr-a=ᵏwangurru-rla   kulunu   wulaa
spear   straight-PROG   3a-3p-EP=take-PAST   sleep   rest

kaajingeerri].
ØN-ngka-ᵇwarr=yi-ng-eerri
VCOMP-SJTV-3p=do-PAST-PROG
They_k threw their_k spears at him [while they_l were sleeping].

(k)
Ngarramnyeyu   dambeem   [ingkamnyaninjawa,   karle
ngarr-a-mnya=ya   dambeem   i-ngka-mnya=ninjawa   karle
1pin-OPT-DD=go   place   3a-SJTV-DD=be.burned   CHANGE.OF.STATE

iwujarra   ingkamnyanungu].
i=ᵏwujarra   i-ngka-mnya=nu-ng
3a=ripe/cooked   3a-SJTV-DD=be-PRES
We'll go home [when it's cooked, when it's ready to eat].

Other examples can be seen at (14.4) in §14.1, and in the first clause in (15.41) below. The subjunctive verbs in (15.31b,c) and (k) show indicative-type present-tense marking *(-ng)*, reinforcing the analysis that they are not evidential forms. These examples involve the depiction of a background or context in time, against which the events in the main clause are to be understood. The definite status of the backgrounding or contextualizing subordinate clauses in examples (15.31b,c,h & i) is signalled by the celestial definite article *wunu*.

Other sentences use subordinate clauses to depict something about the circumstances or the manner in which main clause events occur; that is, about the circumstances accompanying and effecting those events. In Worrorra these *manner-adverbial* subordinate clauses also employ subjunctive morphology; some examples may be seen below:

(15.32a)
Juwalyanyini	warndi	kawarrona	[yarludoo	angkengerri
juwalya-nyini	warndi	ka-ᵇwarr-a=ᵇwu-na	yarludoo	arr-ngka=ya-nga-eerri
path-ENDPOINT	make	3a-3p-EP=hit-PAST	break	3p-SJTV=go-PAST-PROG

jindimaa	yanarri	injaa	nguwanu	wunaa].
jindima-aa	yanarri	inja-aa	nguwanu	wunu-aa
mangrove-and	undergrowth	3aDEF-and	tree	3wDEF-and

They made a road [by breaking down all the mangroves, bushes and trees].

(b)
Ke	juman	nyimbajamanga	[wunu	barnbarreyi
ke	juman	nyiN-ᵇwarr-nya=ma-nga	wunu	barnbarreyi
3wREF	enactment	3f-3p-EP=get-PAST	3wDEF	thrash.about

kamnyenga,	rdeyi-rdeyi	nyangkamnyaweena
ØN-Ø-ngka-mnya=yi-ng	rdeyi-rdeyi	nyaN-ngka-mnya=ᵇwee-na
VCOMP-3-SJTV-DD=do-PAST	gash-gash	3f-SJTV-DD=hit.MID-PAST

karrkunyine].
karrku-nyine
rock-INST

They enact this story about her, [in which she thrashes about (in grief) and gashes herself with a rock].

(c)
Kunyajenganangkerri	weninyine,	[mangkaardimarla
kuN-nyarr-nya=yi-ng-a-nangka-eerri	weni-nyine	ma-ngka-ᵇwarr=rima-rla
VCOMP-1px-EP=do-PAST-EP-DAT-PROG	now-INST	3m-SJTV-3p=name-PAST

mangumbam	mana	dambeem].
ma=ngumba-m	mana	dambeem
3m=name-3m	3mDEF	place

We still tell (the story) today, [how they gave that place its name].

(d)
Juloorr-juloorr-juloorr	kumnyengaalkarndeerri	[wunu
juloorr-juloorr-juloorr	kuN-[Ø]-mnya=yi-ng-ᵏwaal-[ᵏwarndu]-eerri	wunu
carry.along.over.shoulder	VCOMP-[3]-DD=do-PAST-hither-[DU]-PROG	3wDEF

imrirnanya	aja	ingkeerlaarndu	inja	manjawarra].
i=mri-rnanya	aja	i-[Ø]-ngka=ee-rla-[ᵏwarndu]	inja	manjawarra
3a=head-LOC	sit	3a-[3]-SJTV=place-PAST-[DU]	3aDEF	berry.sp

They were coming along with their bags over their shoulders and [with the manjawarra cakes placed up on their heads].

It follows that manner-adverbial subordinate clauses may quite naturally serve as protases for result clauses that are themselves marked for inferential evidentiality. In arrangements of this kind an evidential clause indexes or points to the circumstances that constitute a source of knowledge about some propositional content, as seen in (15.33) below, in which a subjunctive manner-adverbial clause precedes an evidential clause:

(15.33)
[karrku	ke	marnuk	kamanga],	ke	iwarndu
karrku	ke	marnuk	ØN-Ø-ngka=ma-nga	ke	i=ᵇwarndu
rock	3wREF	lift	3w-3-SJTV=get=PAST	3wREF	3a=arm

wunu	burnumaade	kenga.
wunu	burnu-maade	ØN-Ø-ngka=yi-ng
3wDEF	3wPRO-RESULT	VCOMP-3-SJTV=do-PAST

[It was when he lifted up that rock], that's how he broke his arm.

In an etic analysis such as this, manner-adverbial subordinate clauses blend fairly seamlessly into those that constitute causes: that is, clauses whose propositional content is understood to be a sufficient condition for the events in the main clause. And such causal clauses are also, naturally enough, marked by subjunctive morphology; some analytical indeterminacy along these lines has already been noted with respect to (15.28). And as noted, example (15.27f) above is a clear instance of causation: the first clause is an immediately-apparent evidential; the second is a manner-adverbial subordinate clause involving causation, and so becomes a *de facto* causal clause. Example (15.34a) below is from the same story, and here the causal function of the subordinate clause is even clearer. Other subordinate clauses with causal functions are shown in (15.34b–d):

(15.34a)
Imriyaarndu	wakumaada	kumnyanungaarndu	wunu,	[aja
i=mri-ᵏwarndu	wakumaada	kuN-mnya=nu-ng-ᵏwarndu	wunu	aja
3a=head-DU	black	3w-DD=be-PRES-DU	3wDEF	sit

ingkeerlaarndu	inja	manjawarra].
i-[Ø]-ngka=ee-rla-[ᵏwarndu]	inja	manjawarra
3a-[3]-SJTV=place-PAST-[DU]	3aDEF	berry.sp

*Both their heads are black [from where they put the **manjawarra** berries].*

(b)
Ardernayurriya	marndum	maangurru	[wunu	minjarl
arr-rne=rnayurr-iya	marndum	maa-ngurru	wunu	minjarl
px-AUG=adult-3p	stomach	3mREF-away	3wDEF	eat

angkanunerri	bunjuma	mana].
arr-ngka=nu-na-eerri	bunjuma	mana
3p-SJTV=be-PAST-PROG	fig	3mDEF

The adults with their stomachs extended/swollen [from all the figs they'd eaten/from their eating of the figs].

(c)
Marnduma	rnima	mamangerri	[wunu	wurluk
marnduma	rnima	ma-Ø=ma-nga-eerri	wunu	wurluk
stomach	heavy	3m-3=get-PAST-PROG	3wDEF	swallow

ingkayabunaarndu].
[i-Ø-ngka=yabu-na-[ᵏwarndu]
[3a]-3-SJTV=throw-PAST-[DU]

His stomach was heavy [from having swallowed them both].

(d)
Dress	anbardorna	[*school*-kunya	arrkunyenga].
dress	arr-n-ᵇwarr=rno-rna	school-ᵏwunya	arr-ngun-nya=ya-nga
dress	1px-INV-3p=give-PAST	school-PURP	1px-SJTV-EP=go-TNS

They gave us dresses [for when we went to school].

15.6.2 Hypothesizing

Hypothesizing necessarily involves inference; hypothesis is explanation on the basis of (incomplete) evidence. Hypothetical constructions involve pairs of irrealis clauses, an antecedent prior condition and an outcome. Hypothetical constructions differ from other ordered matrix–subordinate syntaxes in that the apodosis is irrealis, not realis. In Worrorra the hypothetical protasis is in subjunctive form, and the apodosis is in either counterfactual-potential or optative mood. Hypothetical constructions from the database may be seen in §8.4.3 in the examples in (8.30). One of these is presented above in (15.10e) (the first two clauses of that example), another may be seen in (15.19), and another is repeated in (15.35a) below. More examples may be seen in (15.35b & c), both from an ætiology about the origin of marriage rules and patrimoieties:

(15.35a) (=8.30b)
Arri	ingujulum	ingannguunyamaalima,	ke	bangamaalimaarndu.
arri	i=ngujulum	i-ngan-ngun-nya=maalima	ke	ba-[ka]-nga=maalima-[ᵏwarndu]
but	3a=ribcage	3a-1-SJTV-EP=spear	3wREF	CFT-[3a]-1=spear-[DU]

But if I were to spear him in the ribs, I might get those two (boys).

(b)
Ngunju	nyangkaangkayanyale	angkaanbarrburrkaal	anja ngayu
ngunju	nya-ngkaa-ngka-ya-nyale	arr-ngka-kaarr-n-ᵇwarr=murrka-ᵏwaal	anja ngayu
you	↳-AUG-girl-3p-then	3p-SJTV-3p-INV-3p=go.to-hither	3pDEF I

ngayanaanangkaya	iwaawurleya,	ke	wardi	wurlarl	bungkanunu.
ngaya-naa-nangka-ya	iwaawurleya	ke	wardi	wurlarl	ba-kuN=nu-nu
I-AUG-DAT-3p	teenage.boys	3wREF	HOPE	suitable	CFT-3w=be-2DAT

Then if your girls could come over to be with my big boys, I hope that might be suitable to you.

(c)
Wunu	ngunjanangkaya	nyangkaangkaya	anja	angkengkaal
wunu	ngunja-nangka-ya	nya-ngkaa-ngka-ya	anja	arr-ngka=ya-ᵏwaal
3wDEF	I-DAT-3p	↳-AUG-girl-3p	3pDEF	3p-SJTV=go-hither

ngayurnanya,	ke	wurlarl	baade	nyanu.
ngayu-rnanya	ke	wurlarl	maade	ØN-nya=nu
I-LOC	3wREF	suitable	RESULT	3w-OPT=be

If your girls come over to my place, then that will be appropriate.

15.6.3 Relative clauses

The distinction in Worrorra between adverbial, adjoined, and relative subordinate clauses might be an entirely etic one, were it not for a phenomenon involving the terrestrial and plural agreement classes: some subjunctive verbs exhibit class-marking suffixes, which, when taken together with their series-2 NP prefixes, give them the formal appearance of adjectives (see §6.1). Terrestrial suffixation on subjunctive verbs marks such forms as being relativized or nominalized,[106] and structurally dependent upon actual or implied head nouns in locative semantic roles, as seen in (15.36). In the following examples the external heads of relative clauses are marked by a subscripted H:

(15.36a)
[Ngayu   mana   aja   nyinngunyeerlaarndum]
ngayu   mana   aja   [nyirr]-n-Ø-ngun-nya=ee-rla-[ᵏwarndu]-m
I   3mDEF   sit   [2p]-INV-3/1-SJTV-EP=place-PAST-[DU]-**3m**

dambeemarnanya_H   waa   aja   binyidinyaarndeerri.
dambeem-rnanya   waa   aja   ba-nyirr=ni-nya-ᵏwarndu-eerri
place-LOC   not   sit   CFT-2p=be-PAST-DU-PROG
You two didn't stay at the place where I left you.

(b)
Bunjuma   minjarl-minjarl   nyirranu   werrim   maa,   werrim_H
bunjuma   minjarl-minjarl   nyirr-a=nu   werrim   maa   werrim
fig   eat-eat   2p-OPT=be   hill   3mREF   hill

[manganngunyaarndenga**ma**].
ma-ngan-ngun-nya=ᵏwarnde-nga-**ma**
3m-1-SJTV-EP=place-PAST-**3m**
You can eat your fill of the figs on the hill, the hill where I've planted them.

The presence of the locative morpheme -*rnanya* in such sentences seems to be stylistic; overt locative marking may be on the relative-clause head as in (15.36a), on a dependent constituent such as a determiner as in (15.37a) below, on the relativized or nominalized verb itself as in (15.37b), or absent altogether, as in (15.36b & 15.37c):

(15.37a)
Maangurrunyini   ngayanangkamarnanya   ngunyaangurru,
maa-ngurru-nyini   ngaya-nangka-ma-rnanya   ngun-Ø-nya=ᵏwangurru
3mREF-away-ENDPOINT   I-DAT-3m-LOC   2-3/1-OPT=take

[arri   brrak   nyarrkunju**ma**   maa].
arri   brrak   ØN-nyarr-ngun=yi-**ma**   maa
we(exc)   awake   VCOMP-1px-SJTV=do-**3m**   3mREF
So now I'll take you away to my own (country_H), where our child-spirits are found.

(b)
Dambeem_H   joli   mangamurrka   ngayanangkama_(H),   [brrak
dambeem   joli   ma-nga=murrka   ngaya-nangka-ma   brrak
place   return   3m-1=go.to   I-DAT-3m   awake

nyarrkunju**ma**rnanya].
ØN-nyarr-ngun=yi-**ma**-rnanya
VCOMP-1px-SJTV=do-**3m**-LOC
I'll go back to my own country, where our child-spirits are found.

---

[106] Perhaps more accurately 'adjectivalized.'

(c) (=6.9)

Aja	ajanuna	mana	barnjama_H	[ingkaangkarrenga**ma**],
aja	arr-nya=nu-na	mana	barnjama	i-ngka=ᵏwangkarre-ng-a-**ma**
sit	1px-EP=be-PAST	3mDEF	cave	3a-SJTV=image.exist-PRES-EP-**3m**

[irnurnu	warndi	kona**ma**].
i=rnurnu	warndi	ØN-Ø-ngka=ᵇwu-na-**ma**
3a=hand	create	3w-3-SJTV=hit-PAST-**3m**

We stayed in the cave where his picture is, where he painted his hands.

The gerund-like root =ᵏ*wangkarre* 'SUBJECT'S image exists' is discussed in relation to example (6.9) in §6.2.4. Terrestrial class-marking on subjunctive verbs in locational constituents may be observed as well in sentence examples (1.2) in §1.7, and (11.41b) in §11.5.1, along with accompanying discussions.

In the database there are two instances of subjunctive verbs with plural suffixation, shown in (15.38) below. The relativized verb in (15.38a) modifies a head in S grammatical function, while that in (15.38b) modifies one in U function:

(15.38a)

Arrka_H	[iwaawurleya	angkanune**ya**]	maa	maanma	buju
arrka	iwaawurleya	arr-ngka=nu-na-**ya**	maa	maan-ma	buju
3pNAR	teenage.boys	3p-SJTV=be-PAST-**3p**	3mREF	SPEC-3m	finish

kaaduna.
kaarr=nu-na
3p=be-PAST

They who were young men died there (=they died there when they were young men).

(b)

Anja	kawaawurlanangkaya_H	nyangkanaanangkaya_H	[kurleen
anja	ka-waa-wurla-nangka-ya	nyangka-naa-nangka-ya	kurleen
3pDEF	↳-AUG-woman's.son-DAT-3p	girl-AUG-DAT-3p	bear

angkonaa**ya**]	bijaku	kaanyiyaalkarla.
arr-n-Ø-ngka=ᵇwu-na-**ya**	bijaku	kaarr-n-Ø-nya=yaalka-rla
3p-INV-3-SJTV=hit-PAST-**3p**	smoke	3p-INV-3-EP=stand.TR-PAST

She stood the sons and daughters she'd given birth to in the smoke.[107]

Subjunctive verbs with agreement-class suffixes bear formal testimony to their status as constituents dependent upon nominal heads, and so themselves qualify as heads of relative clauses. Yet the majority of verbs in the database with proposed relative status show no such suffixation, and a relativization analysis is dependent upon an interpretation based on pragmatic and semantic, as well as structural considerations.

The examples below may be understood as subordinate relative constructions, using semantic and pragmatic considerations alone. The most pertinent structural consideration appears to be the appearance of a relative clause immediately adjacent to its main-clause head, as these examples show.

(15.39a)

Angujakane	inja:	kaakaajinjaa	['ka-ka-ka'
angujakane	inja	kaakaaja_H-inja-aa	ka-ka-ka
all.kinds.of.things	3aDEF	spirit-bird[108]-3aDEF-and	ka-ka-ka

---

[107] Although redundant in English, this qualification distinguishes classificatory from biological kin.

kenga   ke].
ØN-3-ingka=yi-ng   ke
VCOMP-3-SJTV=do-PAST   3wREF
(There were) all kinds of things: (there was) the kaakaaja *bird, that goes 'ka-ka-ka.'*

(b)
Ngarru   inja   kanangkurri_H   [wali   burnu   angkona],
ngarru   inja   kanangkurri   wali   burnu   arr-n-Ø-ngka=^bwu-na
whither   3aDEF   dog   PERF   3wPRO   3p-INV-3-SJTV=hit-PAST

[yawarrarra   angkayandarla]?
yawarrarra   arr-n-Ø-ngka=yanda-rla
sink.PL   3p-INV-3-SJTV=cause-PAST
Where's the dog who destroyed them, who made them disappear?

(c)
Ke   wiyanbali   [ke   wurluk   kayabuna   wunu
ke   wiyanu_H-wunbali   ke   wurluk   ØN-Ø-ngka=yabu-na   wunu
3wREF   fire-3wRESUM   3wREF   swallow   3w-3-SJTV=throw-PAST 3wDEF

ngarrkunjaangarri].
ngarrkunjaa-ngarri
long.ago-REL
That's the fire that he swallowed long ago.

(d)
[Ngayu   baba-baba   nganngunju]   karle   kanunangurru   maa.
ngayu   baba-baba   ØN-ngan-ngun=yi   karle   ka=nu-na-ngurru   maa
I   MoFa-MoFa   VCOMP-1-SJTV=do   then   3a=be-PAST-away   3mREF
(The man_H) whom I called grandfather passed away there.

(e)
Anjanyale   [yorr   angkawanerringkurri]   kaarringanyale.
anja_H-nyale   yorr   arr-ngka=^bwa-na-eerri-^kwurri kaarr=i-nga-nyale
3pDEF-then   sit.together   3p-SJTV=fall-TNS-PROG-NUM   3p=go-TNS-then
Then they who were sitting with them went away too.

(f)
Wayurrkarri   anja_(H)   [kabalbarnanya   dalulu   angkanuna]   anja
wayurr-ngarri   anja   kabalba-rnanya   dalulu   arr-ngka=nu-na   anja
under-REL   3pDEF   ground-LOC   shed   3p-SJTV=be-PAST   3pDEF

marrukuya_H   arrke   minjarlminjarl   nyinunerri.
marruku-ya   arrke   minjarl-minjarl   nyiN=nu-na-eerri
flower-PL   3pREF   eat-eat   3f=be-PAST-PROG.
She ate the flowers underneath that had fallen on the ground.

---

[108] Two onomatopoeically-named spirit-birds haunt the night forests of the north-west Kimberley: *kaakaaja inja* and *meemeenya nyina*.

(g)
Nalala	kunjungu	anja	wurlarnbirri_H	[jaalba
rnalala	kuN-Ø=yi-ng	anja	wurlarnbirri	jaal-^bwa
set.down	VCOMP-3=do-PAST	3pDEF	belongings	carry.in.arms-PROG

nyangkengerri].
nyaN-ngka=ya-nga-eerri
3f-SJTV=go-PAST-PROG

She set down all the things that she had been carrying.

(h)
Arrka	wijingarra_H	[bardbard	kenga]	gee
arrka	wijingarra	bardbard	ØN-3-ingka=yi-ng	gee
3pNAR	quoll	shake.out.water	VCOMP-3-SJTV=do-PAST	represent

kawarramnyo.
ka-^bwarr-a-mnya=^bwu
3a-3p-EP-DD=hit

Their spirit-animal is the quoll that shook the water out of its fur.[109]

(i)
Eeja_H	anja	[yala	angkawana	wariwunya]	yawarrarra
eeja	anja	yala	arr-ngka=^bwa-na	wari-^kwunya	yawarrarra
man	3pDEF	hunt	3p-SJTV=fall-TNS	kangaroos-PURP	sink.PL

kubajeng.
kuN-^bwarr=yi-ng
VCOMP-3p=do-PAST

The men who had gone hunting for kangaroos all disappeared.

There is a strong preference for relative clauses to appear to the right of their heads, the only exception in these examples being (15.39f) above and (15.40b) below. And in (15.39f), the first appearance of the determiner *anja* '3pDEF' could be taken as a head: indeed, in the terms of the DP hypothesis (Bernstein 2001) determiners *are* the heads of their phrases.

Sentences (15.39a–c) have verbless main clauses in which their relative clause NP heads cannot be assigned a grammatical function. In sentences (15.39d–e) main clause NPs in S grammatical function head up relative clauses, and sentences (15.39f–h) have NPs in U function heading relative clauses. There is no convincing, unelicited example in the database of an NP in A function heading up a relative clause, but this may be a result of the statistically less likely occurrence of this type of clause in natural discourse, rather than an indication of its impossibility.[110] The main clause of sentence (15.39i) is an object-demoting construction, with a semantically intransitive subject given formal agentive marking as 3p *-^bwarr-*. Here at least we see a relative-clause head indexed by a formally agentive morpheme.

NPs in other grammatical functions can also head relative clauses: in (15.40) below we see (a) a non-subcategorized object NP, and (b) a possessor NP dependent upon a set of heads in U function, both heading up relative clauses:

---

[109] Literally: 'they *gee* the quoll that shook water out of its fur.'
[110] An elicited example of an agent NP heading up a relative clause is: *inja eeja_H [warndi nyangkonerri yarnkalja], kanangkurrinyini nguyul kunjunganangka* 'the man [who was making a spear-thrower] hit the dog;' but this may not be an unequivocally relative construction, even though the subjunctive predicate immediately follows its head. The morpheme *-nyini* 'ENDPOINT' suggests a sequence of events, rather than the embedding of an event inside an NP.

(15.40a) (=13.23), (cf 12.1b)
Wardi	ngana	ngambal	ngunngulum	maa	ngunbananangka	wunu
wardi	ngana	ngambal	ngun=ngulum	maa	ngun=ᵇwa-na-nangkaᵢ	wunu
HOPE	PROB	satisfied	2=feelings[111]	3mREF	2=fall-TNS-DAT	3wDEF

ngarlangarlaᵢ₍ₕ₎	[nganngunjunu	ke].
ngarlangarla	ØN-ngan-ngun=yi-nu	ke
speech	VCOMP-1-SJTV=do-2DAT	3wREF

I think you might be pleased with the proposal I'm about to put to you.

(b)
[Debarr	ingkenga]	aaya₍ₕ₎	kulanangka	kakaakanangkaya,
debarr	i-ngka=ya-nga	aaya	kulaₕ-nangka	ka-kaa-ka-nangka-ya
die	3a-SJTV=go-TNS	3aREF	Hu-DAT	↳-AUG-MoBr-DAT-3p

kajaajeyanangkaya,	bamaamaranangkaya	wurloo	kaanyona.
ka-jaa-ja-ya-nangka-ya	ba-maa-mara-nangka-ya	wurloo	kaarr-Ø-nya=ᵇwu-na
↳-AUG-MoMoBr-3p-DAT-3p	↳-AUG-FaSi-DAT-3p	smoke	3p=3-EP=hit-PAST

She performed the smoking ceremony for the men of the mother's patriline, for the people of the mother's mothers' patriline, for the women of the father's patriline of her husband who had died.

In (15.40a) the head of the relative clause, *wunu ngarlangarla* 'utterance, word, idea' is indexed on the main clause verb, *ngunbananangka*, as a DAT object in this experiencer construction (see §12.1). In (15.40b) an NP is relativized *(kulanangka* 'her husband') which is structurally dependent upon an undergoer NP, or in this case a set of undergoers (coded by 3p *kaarr-* on the main-clause verb). This sentence follows on directly from (17.29f) in §17.4, which shows the same phenomenon.

Relativized NPs may take on instrumental roles in their relative clauses. Although there is no instrumental marking in (15.41), the main-clause undergoer *wunu karrku* 'rock, stone' gets an instrumental-role interpretation in its relative clause by virtue of its context. Again, and for clarity, the component clauses of this sentence are numbered by superscripts:

(15.41)
¹Weni	ngamba	burramiwa	angkenga	ajakekarri
weni	ngamba	burramiwa	arr-ngka=ya-nga	arr=ya-ke-karri
now	when	travel.around	3p-SJTV=go-TNS	3p=↳-AUG-other

anja,	²mara	kubajonya		wunu	karrkuₕ
anja	mara	kuN-ᵇwarr-nya=ᵇwu-nya		wunu	karrku
3pDEF	see	3w-3p-EP=hit-HORT		3wDEF	stone

³[ingkaarrkarnaarnamalunerri	ke,]	⁴jok
i-ngka-ᵇwarr-ᵏwarn-ᵏwarnamalu-na-eerri	ke	jok
3a-SJTV-3p-AUG= hit.with.missile -PAST-PROG	3wREF	heap.up

kamnyaninjeerri.
ØN-Ø-ngka-mnya=ni-ny-yeerri
3w-3-SJTV-DD=be-MIR-PROG

¹Now when other people go past ²theyⱼ can see the rocks ³that theyₖ threw at him, ⁴all piled up in a heap.

The first clause is adverbial-subordinate, denoting those times or occasions when the action of the main clause occurs. The second clause is the main clause, in hortative mood. The third clause is

---
[111] =*ngulum mana* 'stomach, feelings'

relative, with *wunu karrku* 'the rocks' as its head in the main clause; and the verb in the fourth clause has evidential present-tense marking *(-ny)*, and is an immediately-apparent evidential form. This example should be compared with sentence (11.54) in §11.5.2 and the discussion there: in both cases a matrix undergoer *(karrku* 'rock, stone') appears in an instrumental role in a relative clause. (In (15.41) the relative-clause undergoer is 3a 'him,' not 'rock' as in the English translation.)

15.6.4 Adjoined relative clauses

It is far from being inevitably clear which subordinate clauses may be adverbial, and which relative: there are many instances where it is just not possible to decide. Rather, some subjunctive clauses are clearly relative, and some are clearly adverbial; and there is a fuzzy zone between these two categories. Rather than being syntactically embedded, many such clauses in Worrorra appear to be adjoined to the main clause in some way, along the lines described by Hale (1976) for Warlpiri and other Australian languages. An adjoined relative interpretation is consistent with sentences whose syntax, and therefore whose meanings, would otherwise be ambiguous. In Worrorra adjoined subordinate clauses may have NP-relative, time-relative or place-relative interpretations. Two examples are shown below, the first from an oral history:

(15.42a)
Mana	arrkunyenga	merrkunjanduwerla	ajengerri
mana	arr-ngun-nya=ya-nga	ma-nyarr-ngun=yanduwe-rla	arr-nya=ya-nga-eerri
3mDEF	1px-SJTV-EP=go-PAST	3m-1px-SJTV=leave-PAST	1px-EP=go-PAST-PROG

juwalya	inja	kerrbarlaarndornerri.
juwalya	inja	ka-nyarr=marlaarndo-rna-eerri
path	3aDEF	3a-1px=follow-PAST-PROG

1. *We came away and left that (place) and went further on along the road.*[112]
2. *When we came away and left that (place) we went further on along the road*

(b) (=10.48c)
Ngamba	wurnarnngarri	ingkenga	wunu,	kolkol
ngamba	wurnarn-ngarri	i-ngka=ya-nga	wunu	kol-kol
when	EXCHANGE-REL	3a-SJTV=go-TNS	3wDEF	share/trade

ngarrkunungaayenga
ngarr-ngun=ningaaye-ng
1pin-SJTV=do.MID-PRES
We'll share it out when it goes into the wurnarn *exchange cycle.*

Example (15.42a) involves a serial pair of subjunctive verbs that could be cultural-knowledge evidentials, or hypotactic: there is nothing in the surrounding discourse to indicate which, if either, is intended. The first clause in (15.42b) is adverbial-subordinate, while the second contains the suppletive middle-voice allomorph *=ningaaye* of *kuN[ ]=yi* 'do' (see Chapter 16). As in (15.13), optative or hortative morphology could be expected here, but a subjunctive form is used instead. This clause is not a result clause, nor an outcome, nor evidential; rather it is volitional, it codes the speakers' intentions for the future. It is likely that the meanings of constructions like these were distinguished pragmatically by the operation of conversational implicatures (Grice 1975, Levinson 1983).

Sometimes lexical or structural cues are available, as in the set in (15.43) below, showing an externally-headed NP-relative clause in the (a) example, and adjoined subordinate clauses in the (b) and (c) examples. In these and in the following sentences, the first of the translations offered is NP-relative, the second time-relative:

---

[112] The Gibb River Road is referred to here.

(15.43a)
Nyangka	maa	ngoy	kumnyengaa	anja	eeja_H
nyangka	maa	ngoy	kuN-Ø-mnya=yi-ng-aa	anja	eeja
3fNAR	PROG	breath	VCOMP-3-DD=do-PAST-and	3pDEF	men

[karrangurnanya	nyangkarnanya	angkanunerri].
karrangu-rnanya	nyangka-rnanya	arr-ngka=nu-na-eerri
high-LOC	3fNAR-LOC	3p-SJTV=be-PAST-PROG

She was still alive, as well as the men who were with her high up (on the hill).

(b)
Warrabarl	kaanyarrwuna	mangarri	[ke	Andrew	anngunjaariwuna].
warrabarl	kaarr-nyarr=^bwu-na	mangarri	ke	Andrew	arr-n-Ø-ngun=yaariwu-na
throw.out	3p-1px=hit-PAST	food	3wREF	Andrew	1px-INV-3-SJTV=give-PAST

1. We threw away the food that Andrew gave us
2. We threw away the food when Andrew gave it to us.

(c)
Barra	nyimbarrkangurrurlaara	nyina	marangunya	[ke
barra	nyiN-^bwarr=^kwangurru-rla-^kwara	nyina	marangunya	ke
narrate	3f-3p=take-PAST-1DAT	3fDEF	sun	3wREF

iwarnbarnngarri	nyangkaningkarla	mana	karrangu].
iwarnbarnngarri	nyaN-Ø-ngka=ningka-rla	mana	karrangu
brown.snake	3f-3-SJTV=bite-PAST	3mDEF	high

1. They told me about the sun which the snake bit up in the sky.
2. They told me about the sun and how the snake bit her up in the sky.

Sentence (15.43a) contains the NP–NP conjunction *aa* 'and,' linking *nyangka* 'she' and *eeja* 'men,' making a relative interpretation feasible and likely. Sentences (15.43b–c) on the other hand contain the VP–VP conjunction *ke* '3wREF/and' joining two clauses. Instead of *ke* in (15.43b) we would expect a 3p determiner such as *arrke* '3pREF' to agree with the collective noun *mangarri*, if this subordinate clause were to have an embedded NP-relative interpretation. Similarly, *ke* in (15.43c) links two clauses; it does not join the two nouns. In this example the subjunctive clause could be either a cultural-knowledge evidential, a manner-adverbial subordinate clause, or an adjoined relative clause.

In the sentences that follow we are not able to be sure whether relative or adverbial coding could be intended; they are all examples where an adjoined-relative analysis would appear to be the most parsimonious:

(15.44a)
Arrkeka	nyejarnawajanga	[arri	ajoyoriya	arrkunu].
arrka-y_2aka	nyaN-nyarr-nya=rnawaja-nga	arri	arr-yo=yoru-ya	arr-ngun=nu
px-EMPH	3f-1px-EP=copy-PAST	we(exc)	px-AUG=widow-3p	1px-SJTV=be

1. We who are widows do what she did.
2. We do what she did when we are widows.

(b)
Arrka	jukurl-jukurl	kawarrarnaarnarla	inja	imarumarulya
arrka	jukurl-jukurl	ka-^bwarr-a=rnaarna-rla	inja	imaru-marulya
3pNAR	happy-REDUP	3a-3p-EP=await-PAST	3aDEF	REDUP-cake

[yorryorr   ingkaajandarla].
yorr-yorr   i-ngka-ᵇwarr=yanda-rla
sit.together-REDUP   3a-SJTV-3p=cause-PAST

1. *They were very pleased with all the cakes that they'd piled up together.*
2. *They were very pleased with all the cakes when they'd piled them up together.*

(c)
Wardi   banganbarrbiyangkana   wunu,   [ngamri   maai   nganngunyenga].
wardi   ba-nga-n-ᵇwarr=miyangkana   wunu   nga=mri   maai   ngan-ngun-nya=ya-nga
HOPE   CFT-1-INV-3p=recognize   3wDEF   1=head   blacken   1-SJTV-EP=go-TNS

1. *I hope they recognize me who have shaved and blackened my head.*
2. *I hope they recognize me now that I've shaved and blackened my head.*

(d)
Arrbri   maai   kaanyajamurrka   anja   kulaayanyarri   [debarr
arr=mri   maai   kaarr-nyarr-nya=murrka anja   kula-aa-ya-nyarri   debarr
px=head   blacken   3p-1px-EP=go.to   3pDEF   Hu-1DAT-3a-1pxDAT   die

angkenga].
arr-ngka=ya-nga
3p-SJTV=go-TNS

1. *We shave and blacken our heads for our husbands who have died.*
2. *We shave and blacken our heads for our husbands when they die.*

If right-hand adjacency to a potential main-clause head were taken as a *post hoc* criterion for relative status, then the subjunctive verbs in (15.44b & d) would be relative (with heads *imarumarulya* 'cakes' and *kulaayanyarri* 'our husbands'), and those in (15.44a & c) would be adverbial. But it is not clear that adjacency on its own can be taken as criterial.

15.6.5 Place- and time-relative clauses

Sentence examples (15.36) and (15.37) above show place-relative clauses with verbs bearing terrestrial suffixation. Locative suffixes may be attached directly to subjunctive verbs in such contexts, without terrestrial marking, as in (15.45) and (15.48a), or alternatively neither terrestrial nor locative suffixation may be present, as in (15.46):

(15.45a)
Nyengkunaal   [mana   kroomarnanya   mangkawalkenyarnanya].
nya=ya-ngku-na-ᵏwaal   mana   krooma-rnanya   ma-ngka=ᵇwalke-nya-rnanya
3f=go-EP-PAST-hither   3mDEF   cypress-LOC   3m-SJTV=stand-PAST-LOC

She came to where_H the cypress pine[113] was standing.

(b)
Awa   bariy   kanunaal   [debarr   ingkengarnanya].
awa   bariy   ka=nu-na-ᵏwaal   debarr   i-ngka=ya-nga-rnanya
3aNAR   rise   3a=be-PAST-hither   die   3a-SJTV=go-TNS-LOC

He got up from where_H he had died.

---

[113] *Callitris sp.*

(15.46a)
kawarramurrkarlerri	mana	dambeem_H	[kulu	ingkamangaarndu].
ka-ᵇwarr-a=murrka-rla-eerri	mana	dambeem	kulu	i-[Ø]-ngka=ma-nga-[ᵏwarndu]
3a-3p-EP=go.to-PAST-PROG	3mDEF	place	burn	3a-[3]-SJTV=get-PAST-[DU]

They_j went to him at the place where they (dual)_k had burned him with hot coals.

(b)
Maa	dalorr_H	manungunyale	[rlaburd	ingkamanga].
maa	dalorr	ma=nu-ng-nyale	rlaburd	i-Ø-ngka=ma-nga
3mREF	sink.hole	3m=be-PRES-then	seize	3a-3-SJTV=get-PAST

There's a sink-hole there where he seized it.

Subjunctive verbs may constitute time-relative clauses, dependent upon covert or stated temporal adverbs or determiners. In the following examples the celestial determiners *ke*, *kawa* and *wunu*, the celestial adjective *wurnirndeerr* 'old,' the aspectual adverbs *wali* and *karle*, and the temporal noun *lalai* 'dreamtime' all refer to times that are further specified by subsequent relative clauses. Note how in (15.47c) the adverb *karle* introduces each relative clause in turn:

(15.47a)
Wurnirndeerr	wali	ke	lalai,	[waay	nyangkayabuna	wunu].
ᵏwuN=rnirndeerr	wali	ke	lalai	waay	nyaN-Ø-ngka=yabu-na	wunu
3w=old	PERF	3wREF	dreaming	throw	3f-3-SJTV=throw-PAST	3wDEF

It was long ago in the dreamtime, when he threw her.

(b)
Awanyale	kulnmerrbarnanya	iwajam	irnora,	[wunu	nyangka
awa-nyale	kulnmerrba-rnanya	i=ᵇwajam	i=rnora	wunu	nyangka
3aNAR-then	tail-LOC	3a=fur	3a-not.have	3wDEF	3fNAR

yurrwa	ingkaangurrurlaal].
yurr-ᵇwa	i-Ø-ngka=ᵏwangurru-rla-ᵏwaal
pull-PROG	3a-3-SJTV=carry-PAST-hither

And so he's got no fur on his tail, from when she pulled it.

(c) (=17.32)
Kawa	wunu	karle	[arrkumnyenga	aalmara]	karle
kawa	wunu	karle	arr-ngun-mnya=ya-nga	aalmara	karle
3wNAR	3wDEF	then	1px-SJTV-DD=go-TNS	European	then

[marno	Karnmanya	yorr	arrkunyawana].
ma=rno	Karnmanya	yorr	arr-ngun-nya=ᵇwa-na
3m=DIST	Kunmunya	sit.together	1px-SJTV-EP=fall-TNS

That was the time then, that we went with the white people and we all moved to Kunmunya.

15.6.6 Nominalizations

As a consequence of their adjoined syntax and especially of their adjectival function, that is their ability to head up constituents that are in turn dependent upon external NP heads, subjunctive verbs may function as absolute nominal phrases in their own right.[114] In such usage they constitute

---

[114] As do, for example, substantive adjectives in languages such as Latin.

exocentric lexicalizations that I will refer to here for convenience as nominalizations. Consider the phrases used to express 'waterfall,' 'witness' and 'world war' in the following sentence examples:

(15.48a)
Ajengorri	[warrambam	wo	mangkawana]rnanya	marno.
arr-nya=ya-nga-^kwurri	warrambam	wo	ma-ngka=^bwa-na-rnanya	marno
1px-EP=go-TNS-NUM	flood	roar	3a-SJTV=fall-TNS-LOC	3mDIST

We all went out to the waterfall / (to where the floodwaters roar).

(b)
Arrinyini	ajenga	*courthouse*	Broome	[mara
arri-nyini	arr-nya=ya-nga	courthouse	Broome	mara
we(exc)-ENDPOINT	1px-EP=go-TNS	courthouse	Broome	see

nyarrkumbuna]	bamaraanya	ngayu.
ØN-nyarr-ngun=^bwu-na	bamaraanya	ngayu
3w-1px-SJTV=hit-PAST	Fa.Si	I

So my aunt and I went to court in Broome as witnesses.

(c)
[Wunu	angkaweenerri	anja	aalmareya]	marru	kenga.
wunu	arr-ngka=^bwee-na-eerri	anja	aalmareya	marru	ka=ya-nga
3wDEF	3p-SJTV=hit.MID-PAST-PROG	3pDEF	Europeans	3mLAT	3a=go-TNS

He went away to the World War (=when the Europeans were fighting)

The bracketed phrases in these sentences were unhesitatingly translated as 'waterfall,' 'witnesses' and '(First) World War' respectively, and upon enquiry it transpired that *warrambam wo mangkawana* was the usual (lexicalized) term for this seasonal phenomenon. From (15.48b) it likewise transpired that a complex predicate of the form *mara ØN-[ ]-SJTV=^bwu* serves the function of the English noun 'witness,' with built-in variable reference of agreement-class for the phrase's exocentric head. The expression used for 'fighting ground' seen in (1.2) in §1.7 is a further example.

Place-names may be place-relative clauses with exocentric heads: two such recorded in the database are:

(15.49a) Imalala   jujurr   ingkaarrbanga
          i=malala   yurr-yurr   i-ngka-^bwarr=ma-nga
          3a=attractive   pull-pull   3a-SJTV-3p=get-PAST
          Where they carried the handsome man

(b)   Jilinya   jaarr   nyangkawana
          jilinya   jaarr   nyaN-ngka=^bwa-na
          spirit-woman[115] upstream   3f-SJTV=fall-TNS
          Where the spirit-woman travelled upstream

Daisy Utemorrah gave many of her traditional stories titles with subjunctive verbs. Two explanations are available: they could be either cultural-knowledge evidentials, or *ad hoc* nominalizations, as that term is used here; that is, relative clauses with omitted heads. Some examples are provided, with Daisy's translations:

---

[115] *Jilinya*, translated as 'spirit-woman,' is essentially a female version of *akurla* 'demon.'

(15.50a)   Kunyila   ingkaninjangaarndeerri
           kunyila   i-[Ø]-ngka=ninja-nga-[ᵏwarndu]-eerri
           moon   3a-[3]-SJTV=look.at-PAST-[DU]-PROG
           They looked at the moon / when they looked at the moon

(b)   Iwarnbarnngarri   nyangkaningkarla   marangunya
           iwarnbarnngarri   nyaN-Ø-ngka=ningka-rla marangunya
           brown.snake   3f-3-SJTV=bite-PAST   sun
           The snake that bit the sun / when the snake bit the sun

(c)   Jujurr   kaarrbanga   Ngayangkarnanya
           yurr-yurr   ØN-ngka-ᵇwarr=ma-nga   Ngayangkarnanya
           pull-pull   3w-SJTV-3p=get-PAST   Mt.Trafalgar
           How they carried Mount Trafalgar

(d)   Jilinya   wurda   angkamanga
           jilinya   wurda   arr-n-Ø-ngka=ma-nga
           spirit.woman   go.looking[116]   3p-INV-3-SJTV-get-PAST
           The spirit-woman who fell in love / how the spirit-woman fell in love

In these instances it may not be necessary to have to decide between competing etic explanations; it may be that the various relevant senses of subjunctive morphology combine in a gestalt manner to produce an outcome that is more than the sum of its components.

---

[116] This preverb was translated as 'go looking for (something),' but appears to have a wide range of metaphorical extensions.

Sixteen: middle voice

The term 'middle' in this chapter will serve as a rubric for what is essentially predicate valency-reduction fulfilling a variety of ends, all of which are marked on the verb by the morpheme *-ye* in form-order class [8], immediately to the right of the verb root.[117] Paradoxically however, not all the uses to which middle morphology is put result in a reduced number of arguments for any given predicate.

As its adjacency to the root morpheme suggests, the morpheme *-ye* is derivational, creating formally intransitive from transitive verb roots. This morpheme performs reflexive, reciprocal, passive and antipassive operations; it is a 'patientless antipassive' and an 'agentless passive' morpheme in Dixon's (2002:535-536) typology, and a 'backgrounding antipassive' in Foley & Van Valin's (1984:338) exposition.

Starting with Austin (1981:151-157) this function with variations has been recognized in a number of Australian languages. Dixon (2002:206-207, 530-536) has proposed an 'original' pan-Australian valency-reducing morpheme *-dharri-*, although he is not specific about the sense in which this form could have been original, as either a proto-form in phylogeny or in some other sense. From the first syllable he derives subsequent shapes -*dha-*, -*dhi-*, -*ji-*, and -*yi-*. These forms are very widespread: they are found, for example, in the Gulf of Carpentaria, on Cape York and in the Lake Eyre Basin. Languages in south-east Arnhem Land (Wubuy, Ngandi, Warndarrang, Ngalagkan; Dixon *op. cit:* 535) show the morphemes -*i-*, -*yi-*, or -*ji-* in this function, as do languages elsewhere in Arnhem Land: Gurrgoni and Njebbana, as well as Wardaman (Merlan 1993:189-191).

In the Kimberley region the non-Worrorran language Gooniyandi employs two verb classifiers, =*arni₂* and =*marni*, in a reflexive/reciprocal role (McGregor 1990:195, 557 *et seq*), while the Worrorran language Wunambal accommodates this function without any dedicated marker (Carr 2000:183). However Ungarinyin has a morpheme -*yi-* occurring immediately after the verbal root morpheme (Rumsey 1982:102-105). The Worrorra valency-reducing morpheme -*ye* is formally, functionally and compositionally similar to the Ungarinyin morpheme, and more widely comparable with morphemes used in this role in other Arafuran languages across northern Australia.

The treatment of valency reduction in this chapter (and elsewhere, see §11.5.1 and §13.2.1 (ii)) is based on Givón's (1994) broad functional characterization, and on Dixon & Aikhenvald's (2000) typological discussion. On statistical grounds Givón treats canonically active structures as basic, and passive and antipassive structures as derived. So passivization (in the broad sense he employs) involves the removal (or demotion) of an active subject, as seen in lexical sense-alternating pairs such as *he opened the door* and *the door opened*, in which the subject of the first, active, member of the pair has

---

[117] Dixon & Aikhenvald (2000:11) rightly point out that 'the term 'middle' is used with a frightening variety of meanings.' Nevertheless in the work of a number of authors, such as Kemmer (1993), that variety has begun to converge on 'valency reduction' in all or most of its manifestations, and it is in this spirit that the term is employed here.

been removed to form the second member.[118] Likewise, antipassivization may involve the removal of an active object, as seen in a labile sense-alternating pair such as *he's eating beans* and *he's eating*, in which the object of the active sentence has been 'removed' to form the antipassive one. In this broad functional treatment morphological cueing is not critical: note how a verb such as *eat* can have both active and antipassive senses, just as a labile verb such as *fight* can have a number of uncued pragmatic senses, as in *they're fighting the enemy* (active), *they're fighting* (reciprocal), and *they're away fighting* (antipassive).

16.1 Middle forms

Valency reduction is signalled by the morpheme *-ye* in form-order class [8], in combination with one of the intransitive NP-indexing prefixes listed in Table 5.2 in §5.3.2. If originally transitive, the verb so marked now becomes formally intransitive, and accepts only the tense morphemes *-ng* 'PRESENT' and *-na* 'PAST,' as noted in §5.4.1. Morphemes to the left of *-ye* are affected by regressive vowel harmony (see §2.6.1): the short vowels /a/ and /u/ are frequently but not invariably changed to /i/ (see sentences (16.1, 3, 4, 5 ,7, 10) below and elsewhere for examples).

A few verbs do not accept *-ye*, but rather display lexically-specific middle-voice allomorphs ending in /ee/ or /e/, and those known to me are listed below:

Table 16.1: verbs with middle-voice allomorphs

	ACTIVE SHAPE		MIDDLE SHAPE	
(a)	=ᵇwu	'hit; transitive pro-verb'	=ᵇwee	'middle pro-verb'
	=rno	'give'	=rnawee	'exchange'
	=ᵏwarnamalu	'hit with missile'	=ᵏwarnamalee	'fight with missiles'
	=ᵏwanjoo	'cause'	=ᵏwanjee	'become'
(b)	=rnawaja/e	'imitate; help'	=rnawaje	'idem'
	=ᵏwulkuna	'fear'	=ᵏwulkune	'be afraid'
	=ngarnda	'rain fall on OBJ'	=ngarnde	'rain'
(c)	kuN[ ]=yi	'do, say'	=ningaaye	'middle pro-verb'

The items in set (a) show the [+round] final vowel of an active root becoming /ee/ in middle form, while in set (b) are verbs with a final /a/ which becomes /e/. These alternations are likely to have resulted from an historical application of V-expansion rule 18 (/u-yi/ > /ee/, /a-yi/ > /e/). While the sole member of set (c) ends with the middle-voice morpheme *-ye*, it exhibits a suppletive alternation with its active counterpart.

Rumsey (1982:103-104) describes the Ungarinyin verb root *=ininga* as the suppletive shape used to replace the active intransitive verb *=ma* 'do, say,' in reflexive-reciprocal contexts. The root *=ininga* is suffixed with the Ungarinyin reflexive-reciprocal morpheme *-yi* when it appears in this function, to produce a shape *=iningayi*. Ungarinyin *=ma* is the functional equivalent of Worrorra *kuN[ ]=yi* 'do, say,' and in other, active, contexts Ungarinyin *=ininga* means 'put.' The Worrorra root *=ningaaye* is never found without its middle-voice segment, nor in any function other than that of suppletive counterpart of *kuN[ ]=yi*. It is transparently composed of a shape /ningaa/ suffixed by the middle morpheme, and is formally and functionally directly comparable to Ungarinyin *=ininga* in reflexive-reciprocal usage. Both languages have suppletive middle-voice forms of a verb meaning 'do, say,' and both languages use essentially the same shape for that function. What is intriguing is the difference in the active forms in each language; an historical scenario that may account for this has been suggested in Clendon (2006:55-56).

---

[118] The second sentence manifests other operations specific to English, such as the raising of the active object to subject in the medio-passive or anticausative version. This is not particularly germane to a discussion of Worrorra.

16.2 Middle functions

The use of the term 'middle' as a rubric is justifiable by our inability in many cases to distinguish among the various functions of valency-reduced forms in Worrorra. Not only is it frequently impossible to differentiate etically-determined sense meanings for Worrorra middle-voice verbs, it is frequently doubtful whether such an imposition could be warranted. The following sentence examples show forms that could be interpreted in any or all of passive, antipassive, reflexive or reciprocal functions:

(16.1) (=17.61)
Kowa ke maanbali	wurnirndeerrngarri	angkarnongkiyena
kowa ke maanbali	ᵏwuN=rnirndeerr-ngarri	arr-ngka=rnongku-ye-na
that's.what.happened	3w=old-REL	3p-SJTV=take.away-MID-PAST

inja	manjawarra.
3aDEF	berry.sp

That's what happened long ago when they had the manjawarra berries taken off them/when they stole the manjawarra berries.

The grammar of the trivalent transitive verb =*rnongku* 'take away' is described in §13.2.1 (v). A third person deprivee must be indexed in undergoer position on this verb: the indicative active form of the verb in (16.1) is *kaanbardongkurla* (|kaarr-n-ᵇwarr=rnongku-rla| [3p-INV-3p=take.away-PAST]) 'they took (something) away from them.' It is impossible, then, to tell in (16.1) whether the 3p prefix on the middle verb is indexing the erstwhile active agent or the active undergoer, and it is therefore not possible to tell whether this is a passive or antipassive, or even a reciprocal, verb form (although this latter is highly unlikely, given the preceding context).

(16.2)
Nyingumbu	Kankanarlonya	wali nyina,	ke	yankarndamanyinyim
nyiN=ngumbu	kankanarlonya	wali nyina	ke	yankarnda-ma-nyini-m
3f=name	NAME	PM	3wREF	star-3m-ENDPOINT-3m

warndi	nyimnyaweena	inja	Baalamara.
warndi	nyiN-mnya=ᵇwee-na	inja	baalamara
make	3f-DD=hit.MID-PAST	3aDEF	Venus

Her name was Kankanarlonya, and she turned into a star, the evening star.

In this sentence the valency-reduced predicate *warndi nyimnyaweena* could be interpreted as passive ('she was made into a star,' with implied external agency), as medio-passive (anticausative)[119] ('she turned into a star,' with no agency implied) or as reflexive ('she made herself into a star'). Certainly the text from which it is taken offers no clues, and it is anyway doubtful whether distinctions of this sort are able to be coded in Worrorra by morphology alone.

(16.3) (=9.20c)
Nyina	ngawanangkorrinya	laburru	kamnyamiyengoorri,
nyina	ngawa-[nangkorri]-nya	laburru	ka-mnya=ma-ye-ng-oorri
3fDEF	El.Sib-[3pDAT]-3f	follow	3a-DD=get-MID-PRES-U/AUG

---

[119] This term is from Dixon & Aikhenvald's (2000) typology. Different treatments of valency alternation employ slightly different terminologies; for instance Keenan & Dryer (2007) provide another useful typological discussion.

ajarrungaarndiya.
arr=yarrungu-ᵏwarndu-ya
px=QUANT-DU-3p
They both followed after their elder sister.

A larger context for this example, including specifics of number-marking morphology, may be seen in (9.20c) in §9.4.2, and in subsequent discussion. In the historical context from which this sentence is taken, the woman died first and her two younger brothers died shortly after her. The definite-marked term *nyina ngawanangkorrinya* 'their elder sister' appears at the start of this sentence, a position in which subjects are frequently found. The middle-voice verb could, then, be passive ('she was followed by them two'), although a reciprocal interpretation might be just as feasible ('they all followed each other'). The topic of the larger text, however, including the immediately preceding section, is the two brothers, and if they are the subject (that is, the term upon which the utterance is predicated), then the middle verb must be antipassive ('the elder sister (died and) they followed').

The bivalent predicate *laburru [OBJ] [SUBJ]=ma* 'follow' in this sentence occurs with tokens of both its arguments, *nyina ngawanangkorrinya,* as mentioned, and *ajarrungaarndiya* 'the two of them,' with reference to the brothers. Clearly then, the middle form of the verb is not used here in order to reduce its valency: something else must be involved, and there are at least two compatible possibilities. This sentence constitutes a metaphor for that semantically most highly-marked topic, death. Middle-voice verbs in Worrorra are highly marked, they occur with significantly less frequency in the database than do other kinds of verbs. It is likely that the use of middle morphology in this instance signals the metaphorical nature of the 'following' denoted; and not metaphor only, but the actual reference of the metaphor used in this instance. Dying is an intransitive state, and the metaphor is detransitivized to index that reference iconically. This sentence involves an instance of what I will refer to below as 'mutual action,' in which a number of actors take part in the same event, performing essentially the same or complementary acts together (see below §16.2.3). It may be that a metaphor of death has in this instance motivated the schema of mutual motion.

An approach likely to arrive at a realistic account of this kind of coding is one that does not force etic distinctions, but is aware of a range of often compatible semantic and discourse-pragmatic motivations for detransitivization in Worrorra.

16.2.1 *Reflexive actions*

Such considerations notwithstanding, reflexivity is one meaning able to be clearly distinguished in middle morphology. Reflexive meaning involves agentive acts performed with the actor as patient. In (16.4) we see just such a series of violent, prototypically agentive acts, coded by middle morphology in the denotation of intense grief:

(16.4)

Nyangka	rdeyi	nyimbeenerri,	nguyulwa	nyangkangurriyena,
nyangka	rdeyi	nyiN=ᵇwee-na-eerri	nguyul-ᵇwa	nyaN=ᵏwangurru-ye-na
3fNAR	gash	3f=hit.MID-PAST-PROG	strike-PROG	3f=carry-MID-PAST

bardawaai	nyimbeena,	karrku	kumanga	rdeyi-rdeyi
bardawaai	nyiN=ᵇwee-na	karrku	kuN-Ø=ma-nga	rdeyi-rdeyi
roll	3f=hit.MID-PAST	stone	3w-3=get-PAST	gash-gash

nyimbeenerri,	bimbinalb	mamanga	rok	nyimiyena.
nyiN=ᵇwee-na-eerri	bimbinalb	ma-Ø=ma-nga	rok	nyiN=ma-ye-na
3f=hit.MID-PAST-PROG	ash	3m-3=get-PAST	bury	3f=get-MID-PAST

She gashed herself, she struck herself, she writhed on the ground, she grabbed a rock and slashed herself, she threw ashes over herself.

Here we see the middle-voice predicates *rdeyi* =*ᵇwee* 'gash oneself,' *nguyulwa* =*ᵏwangurriye* 'strike oneself' and *rok* =*miye* 'bury oneself' (ie, throw dirt or ash over oneself). Some preverbs in the database combine with the middle-voice pro-verb =*ᵇwee* to denote forceful, agentive movements that involve and effect only the actor(s); one of these is *bardawaai* 'roll, thrash about,' seen here; others are *manja* 'come face-to-face with someone,' *wanji* 'idem,' *rdurdu* 'move, walk around,' *barnbarrey* 'throw oneself down,' *nambarr* 'gather together' and *wori* 'move, travel around.' Other sentences with typically reflexive meanings are presented below in (16.5):

(16.5a)   Barda   ngewee   kungenga.
          barda   nga-nya=ᵇwee   kuN-nga=yi-ng
          kill   1-OPT=hit.MID   VCOMP-1=do-PAST
          I wanted to kill myself.

(b)   Kuraa   nganingaayena.
        kuraa   nga=ningaaye-na
        chop.with.axe   1=do.mid-past
        I cut myself with an axe.

(c)   Anmolba   dinda   ngamiyena.
        anmolba   dinda   nga=ma-ye-na
        white.clay   paint   1=get-MID-PAST
        I've painted myself with pipe-clay.

(d)   Mara   nyimbeena,   nyungumanja   aaya   mara   kona.
        mara   nyiN=ᵇwee-na   nyungumanja   aaya   mara   ka-Ø=ᵇwu-na
        see   3f-hit.MID-PAST   reflection   3aREF   see   3a-3=hit-PAST
        She saw herself, she saw her reflection.

(e)   We   kamnyawana   ke   ngarli   kurneen   kamiyena.
        we   ka-mnya=ᵇwa-na   ke   ngarli   kurneen   ka=ma-ye-na
        lie   3a-DD=fall-TNS   3wREF   paperbark   cover   3a=get-MID-PAST
        He lay down and covered himself over with paperbark.

(f)   'Yaw,'   kaningaayena   iyarrungumaanja   inja.
        yaw   ka=ningaaye-na   i=yarrungu-maan-ya   inja
        yes   3a=do.MID-PAST   3a=QUANT-SPEC-3a   3aDEF
        'Yes,' he said to himself, all on his own.

16.2.2 Reciprocal and antipassive meanings

Reciprocal actions involve a number of agents acting on each other, and as seen in the English example used above, fighting and arguing are prototypically reciprocal events. The Worrorra verb =*ᵇwee* 'hit.MID' is frequently employed in this function; note two nominalizations in which this form is found:

(16.6a)   wunu   angkaweenerri   anja   aalmareya
(=15.48c)   wunu   arr-ngka=ᵇwee-na-eerri   anja   aalmareya
               3wDEF   3p-SJTV=hit.MID-PAST-PROG   3pDEF   Europeans
               When the Europeans were fighting (=the world war)

(b) marno angkaweenerrima
(=1.2) ma=rno arr-ngka=ᵇwee-na-eerri-ma
  3m=DIST 3p-SJTV=hit.MID-PAST-PROG-3m
  The fighting-ground

An example containing the middle shape =*ᵏwarnamalee* 'fight with missiles' may be seen at (15.7d), and a passivized form of =*maalima* 'spear' is shown in (16.7). Other sentences with reciprocal meanings are shown in (16.8):

(16.7)
Kaarrbaalimiyena ngana, angkuyu ngana kawarrona?
kaarr=maalima-ye-na ngana angkuyu ngana ka-ᵇwarr-a=ᵇwu-na
3p-spear-MID-PAST PROB who PROB 3a-3p-EP=hit-PAST
They must be fighting with spears; I wonder if they've killed anyone?

(16.8a)
Mungurr kaningaayenaarndu marruku ke.
mungurr ka=ningaaye-na-ᵏwarndu marruku ke
argue 3a=do.MID-PAST-DU flower 3wREF
They argued over flowers.

(b) (=17.54b)
Ke maa kaningaayenaarndeerri ke maa.
ke maa ka=ningaaye-na-ᵏwarndu-eerri ke maa
thus 3a=do.MID-PAST-DU-PROG thus
They (dual) did this to each other time and again.

(c)
Kangamurrkarla ke arrburrkayena.
ka-nga=murrkarla ke arr=murrka-ye-na
3a-1=go.to-PAST 3wREF 1px=go.to-MID-PAST
I went to him and we met one another.

(d)
'Mana we ngarrwaarndu kulunu,' kunjunganangka
mana we ngarr=ᵇwa-ᵏwarndu kulunu kuN-Ø=yi-ng-a-nangka
3mDEF lie 1pin=fall-DU sleep VCOMP-3=do-PAST-EP-DAT

kaningaayenaarndu.
ka=ningaaye-na-ᵏwarndu
3a=do.MID-PAST-DU
'Let's lie down here and go to sleep,' he said to him, they said to each other.

(e)
Karnaweenaarndu Jrr'nkurn aa Wadoy wangalaalunguyu.
ka=rnawee-na-ᵏwarndu jrr'nkurn aa wadoy wangalaalanguya
3a=give.MID-PAST-DU owlet.nightjar and spotted.nightjar children
Jinkun and Wadoy exchanged their children.

Note here the functional equivalence of *kuN[ ]=yi* and =*ningaaye* as seen in (16.8d): the former signalling active, the latter middle voice.

In the absence of any token specific to the effected actor (ie, of some kind of reciprocal anaphor) these constructions are patientless antipassives, in that the objects from their active equivalents are unstated but understood. Unlike the object-demoting constructions described in §11.5.2 and §13.2.1 (ii), these are morphological antipassives, as the presence of their dedicated middle-voice morpheme indicates. Here predicate actors are not distinguished, agent from undergoer; so in the first clause of (16.7) the opposing participants in the fight are all indexed by the same prefix (3p *kaarr-*), and in (16.8e) each culture hero is both source and recipient of the theme object *wangalaalunguyu* 'children.'

The examples in (16.7) and (16.8) involve typically reciprocal events: each participant does to the other what the other does to him or her, be it arguing, fighting, meeting, telling or exchanging. The events in (16.9) could also be argued to be reciprocal, although perhaps less typically so:

(16.9a) Kol   kaadingaayenerri,   minjarl   kaadunerri.
         kol   kaarr=ningaaye-na-eerri   minjarl   kaarr=nu-na-eerri
         distribute 3p=do.MID-PAST-PROG   eat   3p=be-PAST-PROG
         They shared it all out and ate it.

(b)   Wunu   kuyoya   wali   nyijaningaayengaarndeerri.
(=11.10) wunu   kuyoya   wali   nyirr-nya=ningaaye-ng-ᵏwarndu-eerri
         3wDEF   whisper   PROG   2p-EP=do.MID-PRES-DU-PROG
         You two are still whispering together.

The functional equivalence of *kuN[ ]=yi* and *=ningaaye* may again be noted with respect to (16.9b): note the various conjugational possibilities of the preverb *kuyoya* 'whisper' in the database. These include the intransitive predicate *kuyoya =nu* 'whisper (immanent),' the transitive *kuyoya kuN[ ]=yi+DAT* 'whisper (something) to someone (uni-directional),' and the middle-voice predicate seen here, *kuyoya =ningaaye* 'whisper to each other (bi-directional).'

16.2.3 Mutual action

The most frequent use of middle morphology in the database is to encode an image schema that I will refer to as 'mutual action' as indicated above with respect to (16.3); that is, more or less the same action performed by a number of people together, more or less in the same place, and for more or less the same ends. Indeed, the reciprocal/antipassive meanings described above in §16.2.2 should probably be subsumed under a rubric of mutual action: they are kept separate here only for the sake of exposition. And again, a schema of mutual action could be argued to be central to the psychology and anthropology of a small-scale society living in closely-knit family groups, for whom close cooperation in social, economic and religious ventures was indispensible.

In example (16.10) we can see how mutual action and reciprocal/antipassive meanings merge. This example describes a procedure for dispute resolution involving ritualized or at least formalized armed conflict. It contains three middle-voice verbs and four clauses, the latter numbered for clarity with superscripts. The third clause consists of a string of three verbs, two of which are in middle voice:

(16.10)
¹Anja   ardaarrawaaya   belangkarraya   jaruk   kaarrbiyena   ²ke
anja   arr=raarrawa-ya   belangkarra-ya   jaruk   kaarr=ma-ye-na   ke
3pDEF   3p=many-3p   group-3p   gather   3p=get-MID-PAST   3wREF

kaarringa   malanim   we   maarreerla.   ³Kaarringerri
kaarr=i-nga malanim   we   ma-ᵇwarr=ee-rla   kaarr=i-nga-eerri
3p=go-TNS   battle   lie   3m-3p=place-PAST   3p=go-TNS-PROG

kaarrbarrkaweenerri	kaarrweenerri,	⁴ke	buju
kaarr=marrkawee-na-eerri	kaarr=ᵇwee-na-eerri	ke	buju
3p=fight.w.weapons-PAST-PROG	3p=hit.MID-PAST-PROG	3wREF	finish

kubarrwuna.
kuN-ᵇwarr=ᵇwu-na
VCOMP-3p=hit-PAST

¹A big crowd of people had gathered together, ²they went out and made preparations for a fight. ³They went and fought with their weapons, they fought ⁴and then brought the fight to an end.

The first clause here contains the middle predicate *jaruk =miye* 'gather together,' a good example of the mutual action schema; the action is undertaken by a group but is not reciprocal, rather it is collective and cooperative. In the third clause two more middle-voice verbs occur, the deponent *=marrkawee* 'fight with weapons' and *=ᵇwee* 'hit.MID, fight.' These are clearly reciprocal/antipassive forms, but in this context it is equally clear that they are part of the mutual action described in this passage.

The transitive, telic motion verb *=murrka,* in middle form, is quite common in the denotation of mutual action, where it seems to refer specifically to mutual centripetal motion:

(16.11a)
Inside dormitory	-nyini	ajamurrkayena	burr	anyeerla.
inside dormitory	nyini	arr-nya=murrka-ye-na	burr	arr-Ø-nya=ee-rla
inside dormitory	ENDPNT	1px-EP=go.to-MID-PAST	enclose	1px-3-EP=place-PAST

We all went into the dormitory together and he shut us up in there.

(b)
Kaarrburrkayenerri	bundurlb	mana.
kaarr=murrka-ye-na-eerri	bundurlb	mana
3p=go.to-MID-PAST-PROG	bushland	3mDEF

They were travelling around through the bush.

(c)
Warnda	kaarrburrkayenerri	mana	dambeem.
warnda	kaarr=murrka-ye-na-eerri	mana	dambeem
camp	3p=go.to-MID-PAST-PROG	3mDEF	place

They were camping in their own country.

(d)
Blaai	kawarramnyonerri,	blaai	kaarrburrkayena
blaai	ka-ᵇwarr-a-mnya=ᵇwu-na-eerri	blaai	kaarr=murrka-ye-na
pound	3a-3p-EP-DD=hit-PAST-PROG	pound	3p=go.to-MID-PAST

ardaarrawaamaanja	anja	burnarri.
arr=raarrawa-waa-maan-ya	anja	burnarri
3p=many-PERS-SPEC-3a	3pDEF	birds

They were pounding them up, all the birds were pounding them up together.

The centripetal schema involved in these sentences may not be immediately clear: in (16.11a) teenage girls from different camps around Kunmunya are brought into a central dormitory building. The predicates in (16.11b & c) denote a traditional domestic and economic pattern in which people radiated out from a central camp in the morning, and returned thither, or to another predetermined location, at nightfall. In (16.11c) dreamtime birds are pounding up vegetable matter with pestles on a big mortar. Here middle voice signals not only mutual action, but the centripetal motion of a number of pestles surrounding and striking a single grindstone.

Further examples of the use of middle voicing to invoke the mutual action schema may be seen in (16.12):

(16.12a)
Ke maa   kubajingeerri   wori   kaarrweenerri.
ke maa   kuN-^bwarr=yi-ng-eerri   wori   kaarr=^bwee-na-eerri
thus   VCOMP-3p=do-PAST-PROG   move.around   3p=hit.MID-PAST-PROG
They did these things while they were travelling around together.

(b)
Ajooleena   baawaard   ajaangurriyena   werrim   marno   karrangu.
arr=yoolee-na   baawaard   arr-nya=^kwangurru-ye-na   werrim   marno   karrangu
1px=travel-TNS   ascend.PL   1px-EP=carry-MID-PAST   hill   3mDIST   high
We took ourselves off and climbed to the top of a hill.

(c)
Murndaaleya   mana   baawaard   kaadingaayena,   yarribaa
murndaaleya   mana   baawaard   kaarr=ningaaye-na   yarribaa
plateau   3mDEF   ascend.PL   3p=do.MID-PAST   descend.PL

kaajaangurriyena.
kaarr-nya=^kwangurru-ye-na
3p-EP=carry-MID-PAST
They climbed up onto the plateau together, they all came down together.

(d)
Dambeewunyinim   ruluk   kaajimiyena.
dambee-^kwunya-nyini-m   ruluk   kaarr-nya=ma-ye-na
place-PURP-ENDPOINT-3m   move   3p-EP=get-MID-PAST
They all went back home together.

(e)
Karle   laiburru   ajanungurroorri,   kayalkayal   ajaangurriyena.
karle   laiburru   arr-nya=nu-ngurru-^kwurri   kayal-kayal   arr-nya=^kwangurru-ye-na
then   know   1px-EP=be-away-NUM   hold.hands-RDP   1px-EP=carry-MID-PAST
By then we had got to know each other, and we held hands with them.

(f)
Nanjan   maarndenganangkorri,   baawaard   kaadingaayenerri,
nanjan   ma-Ø=^kwarnde-nga-[nangka-^kwurri]   baawaard   kaarr=ningaaye-na-eerri
ladder   3m-3=place-PAST-[3pDAT]   rise.PL   3p=do.MID-PAST-PROG

baawaard   kubajingeerri   karrangunyini   warnangkali   wunu.
baawaard   kuN-^bwarr=yi-ng-eerri   karrangu-nyini   warnangkali   wunu
rise.PL   VCOMP-3p=do-PAST-PROG   high-ENDPOINT   cliff   3wDEF
He put a ladder up for them and they all climbed up, they climbed up to the top of the cliff.

These sentences illustrate a range of undertakings done together in company, and signalled as such by middle-voice morphology: travelling together, climbing hills, coming down hills, holding hands; these and similar events reflect the importance of companionship and concerted action in Worrorra society. Note again the functional equivalence of *kuN[ ]=yi* and *=ningaaye* in (16.12f), denoting active and middle discourse perspectives respectively.

Middle voice is a marked category, and so is relatively rare in the database. This being the case, much of what can be said about such verbs must remain tentative, simply because there are not enough examples from which to draw firm conclusions. With this caution, I will attempt to make sense of a couple of forms that occur infrequently.

In at least part of their meanings, the two verbs =*yoolee* 'travel' and =*ladee* 'be' appear to be middle-voice, mutual-action equivalents of the active verbs =*ya* 'go' and =*nu* 'be' respectively. For one of these verbs at least, =*yoolee*, this supposition is borne out by its morphology, which is largely isomorphic with that found on =*ya* 'go' and =*ya-ᵏwaal* 'come' (see §5.4.1). The centripetal directional morpheme used with =*yoolee* appears as -*ngkaal* in spoken form (16.13), and a redundant tense allomorph -*nga* is bonded to the root in hortative forms (see (17.63d) in §17.8). This is the same morphology as that found on =*ya* 'go,' in counterfactual ((8.18) in §8.3.2) and hortative ((8.33) in §8.5) moods. The long high front vowel at the end of these verbs is reminiscent of the middle-voice signalling function of this vowel in the section (a) verbs in Table 16.1. These vowels may be shortened to accommodate global stress patterns, so the variants =*yooli* and =*ladi* are found. =*Ladee* takes the two intransitive tense morphemes -*ng* and -*na*, signalling present and past tense respectively, while =*yoolee* appears to have only one tense morpheme, -*na*, marking non-future tense, just as -*nga* 'TNS' does for =*ya* 'go.' Of 32 occurrences in the database, =*yoolee* is found only once with a singular subject, and both occurrences of =*ladee* are with plural subjects. The more common verbs of movement are intransitive =*ya* 'go' denoting atelic movement generally, and transitive =*murrka* 'go to OBJ,' requiring a goal to consummate its meaning. =*Yoolee*, then, appears typically to have denoted travel undertaken in company over a distance; examples of this verb may be seen in (8.13, 10.7, 10.42, 15.4, 15.23) and (16.12b). In typical usage it is likely to have described the movement of a group of people around their home country; hunting, finding food, visiting religious sites and visiting relations. Its semantics would have contained two important parts: travel over distance, and travel in company. However it appears that either, but not both, of these meanings could be dispensed with:

(16.13) Nyijooleengkaal *school*-kunya!
nyirr=yoolee-ᵏwaal school-ᵏwunya
2p=travel-hither school-PURP
You lot all come to school!

In this sentence the children's homes at Kunmunya were presumably not a great distance from the school, so the denotation is of travel undertaken together, as a group, with the distance meaning in abeyance.

The verb =*ladee* appears to denote stative existence, again in a group. In both sentences in (16.14) reference is being made to groups of people and houses located together. Note that the singular terrestrial NP index in (16.14b) refers to a number of houses (see §6.2.6 (i)).

(16.14a) Anja aarra kaajaladinerri.
anja aarra kaarr-nya=ladee-na-eerri
3pDEF sick 3p-EP=be-PAST-PROG
They were all getting sick.

(b) Ngani kubaje nyini mana mayaram?
ngani kuN-ᵇwarr-nya-yi nyini mana mayaram
what VCOMP-3p-EP=do ENDPOINT 3mDEF house

Mawe maa maladinyeerri.
ma=ᵏwe maa ma=ladee-nya-eerri
3m=PRSNTIL PROG 3m=be-HORT-PROG
Then what are they going to do with the houses? Let them stay the way they are.

In a mutual-action schema middle-voice constructions may be re-transitivized or reactivated, just as object-demoting verb forms may be, as described in §11.4.3 and §11.5.3. We have already seen in

(16.3) a formally intransitive mutual-action predicate with both subject and object NPs present. Two more reactivated middle-voice constructions may be seen in (16.15) below:

(16.15a) (=10.15a)
Birriyaarndeerrije,	akurlanyini	wanji
ba-kuN-rra=yi-ᵏwarndu-eerri-je	akurla-nyini	wanji
CFT-VCOMP-2p=do-DU-PROG-again	devil-ENDPOINT	find

bangkaweenurrerndu	wuneerda.
ba-ka=ᵇwee-[[nu-ᵏwurri]-ᵏwarndu]	wunu-yirda
CFT-3a=hit.MID-[[2pDAT]-DU]	3wDEF-try

Don't do it again; another time a demon might find you both.

(b)
Ke maa	kubajingeerri,		kaardawajenanangka.
ke maa	kuN-ᵇwarr=yi-ng-eerri		kaarr=rnawaje-na-nangka
thus	VCOMP-3p=do-PAST-PROG		3p=imitate.MID-PAST-DAT

That's how they did it, by working together/helping each other.

The first sentence example involves the middle-voice form of the predicate *wanji* =ᵇ*wu* 'find,' reactivated by means of non-subcategorized object morphology (see §13.2.1 (ii)). The second clause in this sentence therefore has a subject *(akurla* 'demon') and an object *(-nurrerndu* 'you two'). The predicate is both semantically and morphologically transitive, despite its de-transitivizing middle-voice morphology. The denotation is probably that of mutual action, in which the speaker envisages both the demon and the two boys walking through the bush, and the boys being opportunistically found by (meeting up with) the demon. Sentence (16.15b) employs the transitive verb =*rnawaja* '[SUBJ] does what [OBJ] does,'[120] seen here with a single intransitive NP index in middle-voice form. The meaning of this verb is not straightforward: it can be used of someone who 'got there before' someone else ('she's doing what I was going to do'); it can refer to following a custom laid down by a dreamtime ancestor, and, as in this sentence, to helping, or working together to achieve a common goal. The function of middle voicing in this sentence probably has to do with the depiction of collective, concerted group action.

16.2.4 Passivization

Passive constructions occur when an active subject is removed in the formation of a middle-voice predicate, leaving only an active object, now in derived subject grammatical function. In Worrorra the question arises as to whether the single prefixed NP index of a middle form represents the subject or object of the underlying active version (see (16.1) above). In this section I will argue that passive derivations are found in a number of Worrorra constructions. The sentences in (16.16) show two examples from the database. Sentence (16.16a) describes the traditional consequence of violating the prohibition against sexual relations within one's own patrimoiety:

(16.16a)
Wurrkunu	kununa	karle maa	ke,	kaarrbaalimiyena,
wurrkunu	kuN=nu-na	karle maa	ke	kaarr=maalima-ye-na
trouble	3w=be-PAST	REM.P	3wREF	3p=spear-MID-PAST

---

[120] This verb's active shape may apparently end in either /a/ or /e/ (see Table 16.1). =*rnawaja* has an apparent synonym, =*rnaajo*.

nyangka	barda	nyimbarrwuna,	awa	barda	kawarrona.
nyangka	barda	nyiN-ᵇwarr=ᵇwu-na	awa	barda	ka-ᵇwarr-a=ᵇwu-na
her	kill	3f-3p=hit-PAST	him	kill	3a-3p-EP=hit-PAST

There used to be trouble in the old days, they were speared, they killed both the woman and the man involved.

(b)
Aambulkarndu	jilibeerd	kumiyenangkaarndu.
a=ᵏwambul(u)-ᵏwarndu	jilibeerd	kuN=ma-ye-(na)-[nangka-ᵏwarndu]
3a=eye-DU	close	3w=get-MID-(PAST)-[DAT-DU]

Their eyes were stuck together.

If the 3p index *kaarr-* on the verb in the second clause in (16.16a) referred to the agents of the act of spearing, we would expect the verb to maintain its active form, as *kaanbarrbaalimarla* (|kaarr-n-ᵇwarr=maalima-rla| [3p-INV-3p=spear-PAST]) 'they speared them;' there would be no obvious motivation for patient removal. Indeed, in the next two clauses it is the patients *nyangka* 'her/the girl/woman' and *awa* 'him/the boy/man' who are preposed in topic position, and we would expect their topic status to be reflected in the previous clause, by the removal of competing agent morphology from the middle-voice verb. In (16.16b) the subject of the middle-voice predicate is =ᵏ*wambulu wunu* 'eye,' with tokens of the dependent possessors (two boys) affixed to the body-part noun and suffixed to the classifying verb. Here the verbal predicate is *jilibeerd =ma* '[SUBJ] close, enclose [OBJ] by manual manipulation; [SUBJ] fold up [OBJ].' Sentence (16.16b) is without agent indexation, there is only a celestial token of the enclosed patients, the boys' eyes, stuck together by what is probably bacterial conjunctivitis, prefixed to the now intransitive verb in subject position.

The following examples are taken from the same story as the last; the first involves the predicate *nyambalak =ma* '[SUBJ] stick/glue [OBJ] together,' in which a typically human AGENT uses some medium or INSTRUMENT, typically spinifex gum, to stick two objects together, coded as undergoer PATIENT(S). This predicate's active use is illustrated in (16.17), with two human patients as undergoers, and the moon as subject/agent:

(16.17)
Nyambalak	binyinmaarndu	nyirrkumbulaarndu.
nyambalak	ba-[nyirr]-n-Ø=ma-[ᵏwarndu]	nyirr=ᵏwumbulu-ᵏwarndu
stick/glue	CFT-[2p]-INV-3=get-[DU]	2p=eye-DU

It might glue your (dual) eyes together.

The middle-voice versions of this predicate seen in (16.18) redirect the active patients of (16.17) to subject status, with the erstwhile agent, along with the instrument, uncoded by verbal NP indices:

(16.18a)
Nyambalak	kamiyenyaarndu.
nyambalak	ka=ma-ye-nya-ᵏwarndu
stick.together	3a=get-MID-HORT-DU

Let them (dual) be stuck together/they (dual) will just have to be stuck together.

(b)
Wurlingkarr	kunjingeerri	burnma	kuma,	wunu
wurlingkarr	kuN-Ø=yi-ng-eerri	burnma	kuma	wunu
rub.off	VCOMP-3=do-PAST-PROG	3mPRO	glue	3wDEF

nyambalak	angkamiyena.
nyambalak	arr-ngka=ma-ye-na
stick.together	3p-SJTV=get-MID-PAST

He rubbed away at that stuff, the gum with which they were stuck together.

The second clause in (16.18b) is a subordinate relative clause of the sort seen in §15.6.3, headed by *kuma* 'glue, gum' in the main clause. In this instance the determiner *wunu* appears to refer to *kuma* anaphorically: for the gender ambiguity involved here, see (6.13c (=16.20 below)) and discussion in §6.2.5.

From the same story, the preverb *wayarl* is used to denote cleaning or removing some (sticky or dirty) substance off an object, such that an AGENT cleans some material THEME off some PATIENT. It is found in the database in two compositions, intransitive *wayarl =ya* '[THEME] be removed,' and transitive *wayarl =ma* '[AGENT] remove [THEME]; [AGENT] get [THEME] off ([PATIENT]).' Its use in an active intransitive construction is shown in (16.19a), and in a transitive one in (16.19b):

(16.19a)
Karle	wayarl	menga	mana	kuma.
karle	wayarl	ma=ya-nga	mana	kuma
PERF	remove	3m=go-TNS	3mDEF	glue

The glue has gone.

(b)
Ngarrunangkowa	wayarl	karrba	inja	kunyila?
ngarrunangkowa	wayarl	ka-ngarr=ma	inja	kunyila
which way/how	remove	3a-1pin=get	3aDEF	moon

Kajirnba	wayarl	bangamandaka.
kajirnba	wayarl	ba-ka-nga=ma-n-y₂aka
can't	remove	CFT-3a-1=get-NON.P-EMPH

How can we remove this moon (stuff)? I can't get it off.

Here we see the offending substance (the semantic THEME in both sentences) in S function (as 3m) in the intransitive, and O function (as 3a) in the transitive sentence. In the passive sentence in (16.20), however, the semantic PATIENT(S), the boys' eyes, are indexed in subject position, to the exclusion of both agent and theme:

(16.20) (=6.13c)
Aambulkarndu	wunu	karle	wayarl	kumiyena
a=ᵏwambul-ᵏwarndu	wunu	karle	wayarl	kuN=ma-ye-na
3a=eye-DU	3wDEF	then	remove/clean	3w=get-MID-PAST

wunu	burnma,	kuma	mana.
3wDEF	3mPRO	gum	3mDEF

Their eyes were cleansed of that stuff, that gum.

The above examples illustrate agent deletion and the concomitant foregrounding of both non-agent arguments: of the theme in (16.19a), and of the patient in (16.20). Note however that in all the examples in this section passivization in Worrorra targets semantic *patients*: competing semantic roles, such as instruments and themes in the above examples, are not targeted; other strategies are employed to foreground non-core (non-agent and non-patient) semantic roles.

Being marked, middle voicing is relatively rare in the database. Its mutual-action function is by far the most frequent, and its passivization function possibly the least frequent. Nevertheless there is good evidence from the few examples we have that a fully passive, patient-targeting operation was an integral part of the syntax of the Worrorra middle voice.

16.3 Deponent verbs

Deponent verbs are those that have passive or middle form, but active meaning. For the time being, middle form will be seen in intransitive verbs ending in the segments /ye/, /e/ or /ee/, or intransitive verbs with uniquely middle tense-marking morphology. Of concern is the fact that some middle verbs are so rarely attested, or unattested outside of elicitation contexts, that there is a real possibility of their having active forms that have simply not been recorded. These forms will be noted, but in the meantime a core of genuinely deponent forms can be identified.

The transitive verb =*ᵏwulkuna* '[SUBJ] fear [OBJ]' takes the past-tense allomorph *-rla*, and has a middle-voice form =*ᵏwulkune* '[SUBJ] be afraid' (see Table 16.1). The middle form takes the tense morphemes *-ng* 'present' and *-nya* 'past.' In Worrorra *inja aaja* 'rain' is grammaticized in a number of ways, including *aaja yulul* =*nu(+DAT)* 'rain approaches (someone),' *aaja* =*ᵇwa* 'rain falls' and *aaja [OBJ]-[3]*=*murrka* 'rain approaches some object.' There are as well at least two weather verbs, shown in Table 16.1: transitive =*ngarnda* '[SUBJ=rain] falls on [OBJ], and its middle-voice equivalent *[3a]*=*ngarnde* 'rain falls.' The middle form =*ngarnde* takes the past tense allomorph *-nya*, although I have no record of its present tense allomorph. It is likely however, that this verb patterns like =*ᵏwulkune* 'fear,' with active and middle forms, and *-ng/-nya* middle-voice tense allomorphy.

This morphology is distinctive: although a past-tense morpheme *-(yi)nya* is found with counterfactual verbs (§8.3.2), and the same shape may signal both hortative (§8.5.1) and frustrative (§15.4.2) moods, this allomorph is not found on indicative verbs except in a few specific instances. The other instances along with =*ᵏwulkune* and =*ngarnde* are the intransitive verbs =*ᵇwalke* 'stand' and =*ᵇwarnke* 'grow' (see §5.4.1), which also, and uniquely, take *-ng* and *-nya* as indicative present- and past-tense allomorphs respectively. The verb =*ᵇwalke* has a causative shape =*ᵇwalkenju* '[SUBJ] erect [OBJ],' but this is transparently a secondary form incorporating the north-western Australian causative morpheme *ju-*, widely found in this function. By analogy with =*ᵏwulkune* and =*ngarnde*, then, I will claim that =*ᵇwalke* and =*ᵇwarnke* exhibit middle morphology (final segment /e/ and distinctive tense allomorphy) without corresponding active forms, and so are deponent.

Love (1934:108) identified a class of deponent verbs in Worrorra, citing =*ᵇwalke* and =*ᵇwarnke* as its members.[121] It also seems likely that the verbs =*yoolee* and =*ladee* discussed in §16.2.3 above are deponent, in having an essentially middle form and function, without corresponding active shapes.

A list of deponent and potentially deponent verbs, arranged by semantic category, is presented below in Table 16.2:

Table16.2: deponent verbs by semantic type

Existential state:	=ladee	*exist*
	=ᵇwalke	*stand*
	=ᵇwarnke	*grow*
	=ᵏwangkarre	*exist as image*
Mutual motion:	=yoolee	*travel*
	=marrkawee	*fight with weapons*
	=ᵇwaje	*separate, part company*
Emotion:	=rnaarriye	*love*
	=rnangajaaye	*regret, apologize*

All these verbs have final segments /e/, /ee/ or /ye/, and where they have been recorded, all have a present-tense allomorph *-ng*, and a past-tense allomorph *-na*, except for =*ᵇwalke* and =*ᵇwarnke* as discussed above.

The verb =*marrkawee* 'fight with weapons, engage in armed conflict' denotes a typically mutual-action schema, and this, coupled with its transparent incorporation of the middle shape =*ᵇwee* of the

---

[121] Unfortunately the 2000 Lincom Europa reprint of his thesis reproduced this section under the sub-heading 'dependent verbs.'

impact verb =*ᵇwu* 'hit' (see Table 16.1) guarantees its middle-voice status. The two emotion verbs likewise transparently incorporate the middle morpheme *-ye* as their final segment, making it also likely that these are middle-voice forms. The verb =*rnaarriye* 'love' may be based on the body-part noun =*rnaarri inja* 'bone(s),' in a metaphor of powerful affection: indeed its one instantiation in the database is as the form *nyirnaarriyenanangka* (|nyiN=rnaarri-ye-na-nangka| [3f=love/bone-MID-PAST-DAT]) 'she loved him dearly.'

The status of the verbs =*ᵏwangkarre* 'exist as image' (see (6.9) in §6.2.4 and discussion) and =*ᵇwaje* 'part company' is less certain; they are poorly attested in the database. All that can be said is that their semantics, their tense allomorphy and their final segments make them likely candidates for deponency status.

Of the 89 simplex verbs in the Worrorra dictionary (excluding allomorphic shapes as in Table 16.1), only 15 are intransitive, so there is a restricted set to consider. Of those 15, nine are found in Table 16.2, while another three are classifiers, shown in Table 11.3 in §11.4.1. The remaining three are =*yawa* 'rub oneself,' =*ninjawa* 'be burned' and =*rlelwa* 'be born.'

Seventeen: discourse cohesion

Pronouns, especially the demonstratives reviewed in Chapter Seven, combine in a variety of ways with each other and with adverbs to produce an extensive pragmatic system with referential, deictic and indexical functions. We have already seen some of these pragmatic devices in the existential interrogatives in §7.4.3, the contrastive forms in §7.5.2 and §7.5.5, and the presentational forms in §7.5.4. In this chapter we will briefly observe an array of configurations that encode a number of important pragmatic categories, and which are in turn important in discourse cohesion.

As discussed in §5.3.1, subject and object grammatical relations are indexed on verbs as prefixes, by way of a set of tokens of the agreement-class of the nouns entering into those relations. This is quite a different state of affairs from signalling grammatical relations on the nouns themselves. Verb morphology merely codes the *class* of the noun in such-and-such a grammatical relation, and *any* instance of that class in the linguistic or extra-linguistic environment is a potential candidate for interpretation in that relation. The problem for this kind of grammar is that individuals rather than classes are usually required to be encoded in core grammatical relations. For instance *eeja inja* 'man' and *warrala inja* 'boy' are both members of the masculine singular agreement class, but the coding of that agreement class in a particular grammatical function fails to distinguish between the two nouns themselves. And of course in transitive subject function, the zero-marked third person singular ergative form does not even distinguish between genders. Verbal agreement alone will not identify arguments exhaustively; the identification of denotata in particular grammatical relations needs to be achieved by other means.

Within the context of the section of discourse in which it occurs, the pragmatic status of a noun phrase, as being, say, more important, better known or more topical than some other noun, may distinguish it from other members of its class. In doing so, its pragmatic status may also qualify such an NP to be a candidate for interpretation in some particular grammatical function to which its class membership entitles it. What results is a system of grammatical-function signalling that relies on both morphological and syntactic cueing, in which individual nouns are primed pragmatically to serve in the grammatical relations signalled by verbal morphology.

In broadly characterizing pragmatic reference, the metaphor of the theatre employed by Foley (1993:133), is a useful one. If nouns are characters and verbs are the script, then pragmatic devices amount to *staging effects*: the particular effects we will be concerned with here are *prominence* (at the front of the stage or at the back, that is, foregrounding and backgrounding) and *lighting* (in the spotlight or out of it). In this analogy, prominence and lighting together constitute an indexical system, the purpose of which is to encode grammatical function by offering up selected arguments for service in particular syntactic roles.

17.1 Definiteness

The definite article =*n* 'DEF,' realized as *inja* 'masc,' *nyina* 'fem,' *wunu* 'celestial,' *mana* 'terrestrial' and *anja* 'plural;' and discussed in §7.3.1 and seen in Table 7.4, encodes definiteness as a major part of its functional load. By definiteness is meant the linguistic marking of a speaker's belief that the identity of a particular denotatum is already known to the listener when a phonetic token of its type is produced (Lyons 1999). What any speaker imagines a listener to know is, of course, culture-specific. There exists in any society a large set of cultural givens which all its adult members are expected to know as part of their membership endowment. An understanding of what constitutes definiteness in a language, therefore, is not a purely linguistic enterprise: it involves as well considerable cultural sophistication. As a simple example of this in Worrorra, observe the marking of definiteness in (17.1) below.

Being a pragmatic phenomenon, definiteness makes reference to whole stretches of discourse, and its causes and effects are rarely observable in single sentences. Because of this, detailed glossing will be suspended from time to time in this chapter, in favour of a more schematic system. This will be done in order to make larger stretches of discourse available to the reader, than can be conveniently displayed in a closely-glossed format. When this is done, the relevant morphemes will be in bold.

(17.1)
Jaarra	maarrwunerri	**mana**	Malandum,
upstream	they.were.doing	the	Prince.Regent.River

ke	murn	maajorarlerri	dambeem	**mana**.
and	gaze	they.were.doing	place	the

'Warnangkali	**wunu**	ngarru	kumnyenga?'
mountain	the	whither	it.went

They were travelling up the Prince Regent River, and looking all around at the countryside. 'Where's the mountain gone?'

This passage occurs right at the start of a narrative text, yet three nouns in it are definite: *mana Malanduma* 'the Prince Regent River,' *mana dambeem* 'the place/countryside, and *warnangkali wunu* 'the cliff, mountain.' These occurrences are instances of what Lyons (1999:233, 278 *et seq*) refers to as resulting from people's encyclopaedic knowledge of the world; they are in his terms situational or general knowledge definites. The name of the river is definite because as a name, its reference is unique. The mountain/cliff/mesa *(warnangkali wunu)* is also definite because in Worrorra culture one mountain above all others is associated with the Prince Regent River: *Ngayangkarnanya* 'Mount Trafalgar,' the large and spectacular mesa that guards the entrance to the river. Any traditionally-educated Worrorra person would know the referent of *warnangkali wunu* in this context.

Typically, however, the first occurrence of a noun in a text is not definite. For example common household utensils such as *angkam mana* 'wooden bowl,' *namarrkama mana* 'large wooden bowl,' *kambananya nyina* 'shovel, poker,' *karraki inja* 'bag' and *ngarli wunu* 'paperbark' are usually introduced without definite marking, only becoming definite on subsequent appearances. In some contexts, however, definite marking of such items is granted on first appearance, as in (17.2):

(17.2)
Manjawarrawunya	buluba	kaarringa,	kawarramrangerri	angkam	**mana**.
for.m.berries	searching	they.went	they.were.gathering.them	bowl	the

They were going out looking for manjawarra *berries, they were gathering them in bowls.*

In this sentence *angkam mana* 'bowl' is definite, because such items are co-located contextually with the particular food-gathering activity denoted; that is to say that they are presupposed to occur within the context of such activity. Similarly in English, such contextually backgrounded items may be introduced with definite marking, as in, eg, *I've spilt some on the carpet*, where neither the name of the item nor the item itself have figured in previous conversation.

17.1.1 Definite clauses

In Worrorra, clauses as well as nouns may be marked as definite. Definite clauses contain a propositional content that a speaker believes is already known to his or her listener, and they are marked by the determiner *wunu*. When clauses are marked for definiteness, there is a strong tendency for the article to occur clause-finally. Observing the occurrence of this phenomenon in other languages, Lyons (1999:60) supports this interpretation: 'a definite article can sometimes serve to introduce an entire finite clause, thus functioning somewhat as a complementizer. [...] This phenomenon may be particularly characteristic of polysynthetic languages.'

Identifying such clauses in Worrorra is not all that straightforward, however, as in a language which is only loosely configurational, and in passages where intonation contours are unclear, ascertaining which function of *wunu* is intended can be problematic. Nevertheless there appear to be a number of pragmatic reasons for marking a clause as definite.

(i) The first of these, and by far the most common, is in the marking of subordinate time-relative clauses (see §15.6.5). Such clauses are subjunctive, and definiteness-marking frequently occurs as part of the syntactic apparatus that produces subordinate forms. The function of these subordinate clauses is specifically to refer to an event as representing backgrounded or known information, in the light of which the information presented in the main clause is to be understood. Two examples of this kind of construction are shown in (17.3), where the subordinate clauses are enclosed in square brackets.

(17.3a)
Kaanyardawaje	[**wunu**	ajora	arrkununa]
kaarr-nyarr=rnawaje	wunu	arr=yora	arr-ngun=nu-na
3p-1px=copy	3wDEF	px=widow	1px-SJTV=be-PAST

We do the same as they did [when we are widows]

(b)
Bardi	nyinyamurrkaarndu	ngayu,	[**wunu**	yala
bardi	nyirr-n-Ø-nya=murrka-ᵏwarndu	ngayu	wunu	yala
come.home	2p-INV-3/1-OPT=go.to-DU	I	3wDEF	hunting

nganngumbana]
ngan-ngun=ᵇwa-na
1-SJTV=fall-TNS

I will come back home to you both, [after I've gone hunting]

Sometimes the determiner *wunu* may mark the backgrounded or conditional status of a clause in the absence of a subjunctive verb, as in (17.4), or even in the absence of any verb at all, as in (17.5):

(17.4)
[Larlangkarram	mana	kaarri maa	keekeey	kanunerri	**wunu**
rlarlangkarram	mana	kaarri maa	keekeey	ka=nu-na-eerri	wunu
sea	3mDEF	in.vain	peer	3a=be-PAST-PROG	3wDEF

kalam	mana],	ke	bloy	kumanga		ke	rlarlangkarranyinim
kalam	mana	ke	bloy	kuN-Ø=ma-nga		ke	rlarlangkarra-nyini-ma
raft	3mDEF	and	slip	VCOMP-3=get-PAST		and	sea-ENDPOINT-3m

burnu	ko.				
burnu	ka-Ø=ᵇwu				
3wPRO	3a-3=hit				

[As he was peering into the sea from the raft], he slipped over and perished in the sea.

(17.5)
Marduk	kengkunaaleerri		aaya,	[kaarri	maa
marduk	ka=ya-ngku-na-aal-eerri		aaya	kaarri	maa
walk	3a=go -EP-PAST-hither-PROG		3aREF	3pNEG	3mREF

dambeenyinim	**wunu**],	ke	mana	aja	kanunerri.
dambee-nyini-m	wunu	ke	mana	aja	ka=nu-na-eerri
place-ENDPOINT-3m	3wDEF	and	3mDEF	sit	3a=be-PAST-PROG

He came walking along, and [there being nobody at home], he sat down there.

(ii) The second function of *wunu* is to substitute for a definite clause; that is, to serve as a sentential anaphor of an expression of known propositional content, just as 'it' is a sentential anaphor in English (cf *I didn't see it*, where 'it' substitutes for an instantiation of 'Fred kicked a goal'). Some examples are seen in (17.6):

(17.6a)
	Wunu	ngenangka	kungenu.
	wunu	ØN-nga=yi-nangka	kuN-nga=yi-nu
	3wDEF	VCOMP-1=do-DAT	VCOMP-1=do-2DAT

I want to tell you about it.

(b)
	Kaarriyaka	wunu.
	kaarri-y₂aka	wunu
	3pNEG-EMPH	3wDEF

That won't/ doesn't/ didn't happen at all.

(c)
	Wunu	nge,	marram	angarno	dambeem.
	wunu	ØN-nga=yi	marram	arr-nga=rno	dambeem
	3wDEF	VCOMP-1=do	light	3p-1=give	place

I want to do it, I want to give light to them on the earth.

Sentence (17.6a) is a complement-clause construction with *kungenu* 'I want (with respect to yourself)' the matrix, and *wunu ngenangka* 'I will tell (you) about it' the complement; and sentence (17.6b) is a verbless construction. In these examples *wunu* functions in a manner equivalent to its English translation, as 'it' or 'that' with reference to events.

(iii) A third important function of sentential definiteness-marking is to signal questions, most commonly rhetorical questions. In this function *wunu* appears at the end of questions. In making questions definite, a speaker is declaring his or her belief that either the answer, that is, the information content of the question, or the reason for asking, is known to the listener. Note that only the information content of questions is marked as being definite: the question-word itself lies beyond the scope of the determiner, as is suggested both by semantics and by observation of intonation contours, as shown in (17.7):

(17.7)
	[Ngarru]	[nyina	nyim **n y e** nga	wunu?]
	ngarru	nyina	nyiN-mnya=ya-nga	wunu
	whither	3fDEF	3f-DD=go-TNS	3wDEF

Where did she get to?

Other examples of definite-marked questions are shown in (17.14) & (17.8):

(17.8a) Yaada ngarlangarla kunjawaawaarlaara wunu?
yaada ngarlangarla kuN-nja=ᵇwaawaa-rla-ᵏwara wunu
ENQ speech VCOMP-2=misunderstand-PAST-1DAT 3wDEF
Can it be that you didn't understand what I said?

(b) Angkuyu baangamnyarnonangkorri wunu?
angkuyu ba-kaarr-nga-mnya=rno-nangkorri wunu
who CFT-3p-1-DD=give-3pDAT 3wDEF
Who can I give them to?

(c) Arri wunu baraankarndu wunu?
arri wunu baraan-ᵏwarndu wunu
but 3wDEF shaved-DU 3wDEF
So how come your (dual) heads are shaved?

Sentence (17.8c) is highly elliptical, in omitting both a question word, a verb and the phrasal head. However its sense is completely recoverable from the context in which it occurs, and the repetition of the article emphasizes the speaker's belief that not only is the answer known to the listeners, but they also know his reason for asking, and are deliberately withholding information from him.

(iv) A speaker may acknowledge his or her belief that information is already known to a listener when he or she is repeating that information, or when the depiction of some event is repeated. Sentences containing repeated information are usually definite in Worrorra. The following discourse sections show this phenomenon:

(17.9)
Waay kawarrayabuna karrangu. Yarriy kawanaal ke
throw they.threw.him high descend he.fell.here and

waayje kawarrayabunangurru karrangu, ke yarriyje kawanaal.
throw.again they.threw.him.away high and descend.again he.fell.here

Ke **wunu** waayje kawarrayabuna.
and the throw.again they.threw.him
They threw him up in the air. He fell down and again they threw him up, and again he fell down. Then they threw him up again.

Key words in this text are *waay* 'throw,' *waayje* 'throw again,' *yarriy* 'descend,' *yarriyje* 'descend again' and *karrangu* 'high.' The sentence containing the second repetition of *waay* 'throw' receives definiteness marking.

(17.10)
Barnbarrey kumnyengeerri nyangka nyina karranangkanya.
throw.self.down she.did.it she the his.mother

Deyi-rdeyi nyimbeenerri karrkunyine, ke barnbarrey kunjingeerri.
gash-gash she.hit.self with.rock and throw.self.down she.did.it

Bardawaai	nyimbeenerri	wangalanguwunya	**wunu**.
thrash/writhe	she.hit.self	for.child	the

His mother threw herself down on the ground and thrashed about. She gashed herself with a sharp rock, and rolled about. She thrashed about [in her grief] for her child.

The key terms here are the preverbs *barnbarrey* and *bardawaai*, both of which refer to a response specific to newly bereaved women, of throwing themselves down on the ground and writhing and thrashing about in an agony of grief. These two terms appear to be synonyms, and although they possibly may not be, they are closely collocated at any rate. On the third occurrence of this denotation, the sentence in which it occurs receives marking for definiteness, as it essentially repeats information already contained in the previous two sentences.

(17.11)

Wunu-wunu	karle	wali	kunyajunganoorri	**wunu**,
this	now	still	we.told.you	the

[dumbi	mara	irrangunbu,	malka	barroyeerri],	kunyajunganoorri.
owl	see	when.you.do.him	play	you.do.not.him	we.told.you

We told you and told you: [if you find an owl, don't play with it;] we told you.

The key word here is *kunyajunganoorri* (|kuN-nyarr=yi-ng-a-noorri| [VCOMP-1px=do-PAST-EP-2pDAT]) 'we (exc) told you (pl),' and the reported speech is indicated in square brackets. In this sentence definiteness marking refers to both the *verbum dicendi* ('we told you'), in that the speakers are claiming rhetorically that the listeners knew that they had been told, as well as to the reported content, which the listeners are also being told that they already knew.

(17.12)

[Yawurlak	kawana]	rlarlangkarrama,	[kawana],
sink	he.fell	sea	he.fell

balangkarranya	bariy	anmurrkarlaal	ke	keekeey	kanunerri,
storm.wave	rise	it.came.to.us	and	peering	he.was

[yawurlak	kamnyawanangurru	**wunu**].
sink	he.fell.away	the

[He sank down under] the sea, [he drowned], storm waves rose up all around us and he was peering over the side, [he drowned under] the sea.

In (17.12) the key words are *yawurlak* 'sink, drown' *rlarlangkarrama* 'sea,' *balangkarranya* 'storm wave,' *bariy* 'rise' and *keekeey* 'peep.' The complex predicate *yawurlak* =^{b}*wa* 'sink down, drown' appears three times here; its tokens enclosed in square brackets. The second time it appears, the classifier *kawana* is used anaphorically to substitute for the entire predicate (see §11.5.1). The third time the predicate appears, it is marked as definite, that is, as repeated information by this time known to the listener.

(v) In presenting information, a speaker may wish to declare that the information is, or should be, already known to his or her listener, and to emphasize that the listener ought to be aware of it. In these situations, too, definiteness marking is used rhetorically to point out to a listener that what is being said is nothing new. In (17.13a) a man has for some time been asking a certain woman to let her son go out turtle-fishing with him and his friends. At one stage of this process he says to her:

(17.13a)
Wali	erraangurru	wunu	kunyajeerri	warliwunya	ke.
wali	a-nyarr-a=ᵏwangurru	wunu	kuN-nyarr=yi-eerri	warli-ᵏwunya	ke
PERF	3a-1px-OPT=carry	3wDEF	VCOMP-1px=do-PROG	turtle-PURP	3wREF

We still want to take him out hunting for turtles /
We want, as I say, to take him out hunting for turtles.

(b) (=11.10)
Wunu	kuyoya	wali	nyijaningaayengaarndeerri.
wunu	kuyoya	wali	nyirr-nya=ningaaye-ng-ᵏwarndu-eerri
3wDEF	whisper	PROG	2p-EP=do.MID-PRES-DU-PROG

You two are still whispering together.

Sentence (17.13a) contains a matrix *verbum dicendi*, *kunyajeerri* 'we want' and a complement-clause verb *erraangurru* 'we want to take him.' Because the speaker wishes to make it clear to the boy's mother that he knows that the information in the complement clause is already known to her, and that it should therefore come as no surprise to her, he marks it as definite. In (17.13b) a mother is scolding her children; they clearly know what they have been doing, and the predicate is marked as definite.

Example (17.14) consists of a definite-marked question (cf. 17.8), followed by a definite statement, with both sentences marked by *wunu* in final position:

(17.14)
Arri	ngani	kunjinganangkorreerri	wunu?
arri	ngani	kuN-nja=yi-ng-a-nangkorri-eerri	wunu
but	what	VCOMP-2=do-PAST-EP-3pDAT-PROG	3wDEF

Baanjamurlomurlonyeerri	wunu!
ba-kaarr-nja=murlomurlo-nya-eerri	wunu
CFT-3p-2=look.after-PAST-PROG	3wDEF

But what have you been doing to them? You should have been looking after them!

Here in the second sentence the speaker is declaring not only what the listener's obligation was, but also that the listener was, or should have been, well aware of it. The repetition of sentence-final definiteness-marking in sequences such as this is very effective in producing an eloquent rhetorical pattern of accusation and condemnation.

Another exchange is reproduced in (17.15), a good deal of which consists of two people telling each other what they already know (a not uncommon discourse phenomenon in any society). This exchange is from a mythical text in which a dead man comes back to life and goes to see his wife. She, however, has already instituted funerary rites for him, and does not want to see him. Here the definite clauses are enclosed in square brackets. When he appears before her, she says:

(17.15)
'Waa	jukurljukurl	banganineerri;	[**wunu**	ngunyengkunaal,]	[karle wali
not	happy	I.am.not.to.you	the	you.came	CHANGE

waay	ngunjabuneka	**wunu**]	karle	ngamri	ke	maai
throw	I.threw.you.really	the	now	my.head	it	shave-blacken

ngunmurrkarla.	Angujabirri	bariy	ngununaal?'	kunjunganangka.
I.did.for.you	why	rise	you.were.here	she.said.to.him

'[Mee	bariy	ngamnyanunaal	ke	buluba	ngunyanganyarrona	**wunu**].'
just	rise	I.was.here	and	searching	I.looked.for.you	the

'I'm not happy to see you; [although you've come back] [already by now I have really lost you] and I've shaved and blackened my head in mourning for you. Why did you have to come back?' she asked him.
'[I just got up and went out looking for you (as you can see)].'

The first listener, the husband, obviously knows that he has come back, so *ngunyengkunaal* 'you have come back' receives definite-marking. The wife then declares that she has already lost him (*waay ngunjabuneka* 'I have really lost you') and that this too he must know, or at least ought to know, in the normal course of things. She then declares the means by which she has instituted funeral rites, by shaving and blackening her head. As a new social institution, the significance of this process cannot be known to her husband, indeed the point of the narrative so far is that it is not known to him, and so her declaration of it is not marked as definite. In reply, the husband states what must be obvious to his wife, that he has come back to life and come looking for her, and so this sentence too receives definite marking.

In this part of its grammar we see how Worrorra logically extends the reference of definiteness from nominal denotata that the speaker believes the listener can identify, to information in general, that is, to events and whole stretches of discourse that the speaker believes are known to the listener. The determiner used to signal this assumption is the celestial one, the determiner from the category of events, denotata occurring in time (§4.1.3 (iii)).

17.2 Topicality

In this section the notion of 'topic' will be understood rather informally, as the entity or activity that is what a sentence is primarily about. Topics are often, but not necessarily, old or given information from which, or against the background of which, new information is introduced. It seems that in at least some languages explicit topic-marking serves to confer an artificially 'given' status to constituents, that is to confer 'given' status on them despite their failure to qualify for such status on discourse-internal grounds. Using such a facility, language is able to introduce new references and treat them as if they are old. Given information attracts staging privileges resulting from considerations of relevance, importance, salience and other pragmatic properties. The purpose of conferring 'givenness,' then, is to expose such constituents under highlighting on centre stage. In English *this* may be used to mark its referents as topics, that is as the constituents that provide the setting for a discourse, and from which the narrative departs (cf Levinson 1983:85). In its other senses, *this* denotes an entity that is spatially proximate to the location of the speech act; that is typically visible or known to the listener, as old or given information. In Worrorra, deictic principles are employed to serve such ends.

17.2.1 Contextual deixis

The uses of the pronoun =^{k}*waya* 'CONTEXTUAL' (glossed REF, see Table 7.8) as a contextual deictic and distal demonstrative have been discussed in §7.3.3. Contextual deictics serve quite naturally as topic markers in Worrorra because what is salient in a referential context is, of course, also salient at a pragmatic level. By way of example of this collapse, observe contextual deictic marking in (17.16). This utterance was made during a dispute over the allocation of wives. As the object of an ongoing dispute between the members of two clans, the woman concerned is contextually salient on an ongoing basis. At the same time she is also the topic of this particular exchange, in the sense that she is what the exchange is all about. She is referred to by CONTEXTUAL marking *(nyingke)* on both counts, but observe how readily the one meaning fades into the other:

(17.16)
Nyingke	nyimnyiyabaal!	Angujakunya	nyinjaangurreerri?
nyiN=^{k}waya	nyiN-mnya=yabu-aal	anguja-^{k}wunya	nyiN-nja=^{k}wangurru-eerri
3f=REF	3f-DD=throw-hither	why	3f-2=carry-PROG

Send her over here! What are you holding onto her for?

The first occurrence of a reference in a Worrorra text is typically marked by a contextual deictic if the entity concerned is topical. Subsequent references are usually definite (marked by =*n* 'DEFINITE'). In this situation =*ᵏwaya* 'REF' cannot mark entities as being somehow known from context: rather the pronoun serves to introduce a referent, by announcing it as a new and topical entity. In (17.17a-d) the topical nouns occur in translation with the English articles 'a' or 'some,' indicating their indefinite or 'new' status. In each of the sentences in (17.17) the speaker is introducing the noun marked by a contextual deictic to his or her listener or audience as a new and important reference:

(17.17a)
Jilinya	nyingke	mara	nyingona.
jilinya	nyingke	mara	nyiN-nga=ᵇwu-na
spirit-woman	3fREF	see	3f-1=hit-PAST

I have found a spirit-woman.

(b)
Kanbanerri	birdeenja	aaya	rlerlewa	kamurrkarlerri.
kanbanerri	birdeen-ya	aaya	rlerlewa	ka-Ø=murrka-rla-eerri
crab	small-3a	3aREF	crawl	3a-3=go.to-PAST-PROG

A little crab went crawling up to him.

(c)
Dumbi	aaya	mara	irrangunbu,	ngarlingka	barrarnaarnerri.
dumbi	aaya	mara	i-rra-ngun=ᵇwu	ngarlingka	ba-ka-rra=rnaarna-eerri
owl	3aREF	see	3a-2p-SJTV=hit	torment	CFT-3a-2p=await-PROG

If you find an owl, don't hurt it.

(d)
Wangalaalunguyu	arrke	wumbirli	nganbarrbangerri.
wangalaalanguya	arrke	wumbirli	nga-n-ᵇwarr=ma-nga-eerri
children	3pREF	mock	1-INV-3p=get-PAST-PROG

Some children were making fun of me.

(e)
Mara	nyimbeena,	nyungumanja	aaya	mara	kona.
mara	nyiN=ᵇwee-na	nyungumanja	aaya	mara	ka-Ø=ᵇwu-na
see	3f=hit.MID-PAST	reflection	3aREF	see	see3a-3=hit-PAST

She saw herself, she saw her own reflection.

(f)
Wangalaalunguyu	arrke	akurla	kaanmrangaara.
wangalaalanguya	arrke	akurla	kaarr-n-Ø=mra-nga-ᵏwara
children	3pREF	devil	3p-INV-3=gather-PAST-1DAT

A devil has taken my children.

(g)
Arrkeka	yakurnu	burrkay	angarramurrkerda	anja	darraanma.
arrke-y₂aka	yakurnu	burrkay	arr-ngarr-a=murrka-yirda	anja	darraanma
3pREF-EMPH	try	enquire	3p-1pin-OPT=go.to-try	3pDEF	cockatoo

Here, let's try and find out from those black cockatoos.

Topic marking is not of course reserved for first occurrences. Any noun that a speaker wants to hold under a spotlight on centre stage may receive such marking, as shown in the examples in (17.18):

(17.18a)
Karle	waay	kangayabuna	aaya	kulaaya	ngayanangka.
karle	waay	ka-nga=yabu-na	aaya	kulaaya	ngaya-nangka
now	throw	3a-1=throw-PAST	3aREF	husband	I-DAT

I've lost my husband (=he has passed away).

(b)
Mangkanangkanya	marno	nyimnyenga	mayakarrimarnanya
mangka-nangka-nya	ma=rno	nyiN-mnya=ya-nga	ma=yakarri-ma-rnanya
wife-DAT-3f	3m=DIST	3f-DD=go-TNS	3m=other-3m-LOC

nyinjorinya	nyangke.
nyiN=yoru-nya	nyangke
3f=widow-3f	3fREF

His wife, the widow, would go over to another place.

(c)
Nyangke	ngeenya	waa	wali	binyangarreendandaka	nyangke.
nyangke	ngeenya	waa	wali	ba-nyaN-ngarr=eenda-n-y₂aka	nyangke
3fREF	honey	not	PERF	CFT-3f-1pin=cook-NON.P-EMPH	3fREF

That honey; we don't cook it at all.

(d)
Kewunya	mungurr	kaningaayenaarndu,	marruku.
ke-ᵏwunya	mungurr	ka=ningaaye-na-aarndu	marruku
3wREF-PURP	argue	3a=do.MID-PAST-DU	flower

That's what they were arguing about, flowers.

(e)
Arrigrarlya	arrke	gee	kaanbarrwu	anja	burnarri.
arr=igrarl-ya	arrke	gee	kaarr-n-ᵇwarr=ᵇwu	anja	burnarri
3p=CLAN.COUNTRY-3p	3pREF	represent	3p-INV-3p=hit	3pDEF	animals

Those Arrigrarlya clan people have these animals as their totemic emblems.

17.2.2 Definite topics

The three pronouns =*n* 'DEFINITE,' =ᵏ*wa* 'ANAPHORIC' (glossed NAR) and =ᵏ*waya* 'CONTEXTUAL' may all appear inside the same NP, where their co-occurrence and configuration signal a number of pragmatic functions (§7.3.3). The most straightforward of such orderings is simply the juxtaposition of =*n* and =ᵏ*waya* within the same NP. This construction signals that a topical NP is also definite (recall from §17.2.1 that topics in Worrorra need not be definite). Examples are shown in (17.19); the determiner *wunu* in (17.19a) marks the subordinated verb phrase headed by *ingkaarrwu* 'when they kill it (masc)' as definite, that is, as background information to a preceding main clause:

(17.19a)
… inja	koyoya	aaya	ingkaarrwu	minjarlkunya	wunu.
inja	koyoya	aaya	i-ngka-ᵇwarr=ᵇwu	minjarl-ᵏwunya	wunu
… 3aDEF	crocodile	3aREF	3a-SJTV-3p=hit	eat-PURP	3wDEF

… when they kill the crocodile for food.

(b)
Yawarrarra	angkayandarla	kanangkurri	inja	iraarreya	aaya.
yawarrara	arr-Ø-ngka=yanda-rla	kanangkurri	inja	i=raarreya	aaya
sink.PL	3p-3-SJTV=cause-PAST	dog	3aDEF	3a=big	3aREF

The dog, that big one that caused them to disappear.

(c)
Iyarrungu	aaya	inja	kurleen	kangona
i=yarrungu	aaya	inja	kurleen	ka-nga=^{b}wu-na
3a=QUANT	3aREF	3aDEF	bear	3a-1=hit-PAST

The one and only (child) born to me

(d)
Karle	arrke	ankurle	wali,	anja	Mawanjamangarriwurle.
karle	arrke	arr=n-^{k}wurle	wali	anja	Mawanjama-ngarri-^{k}wurle
then	3pREF	3p=DEF-first	PERF	3pDEF	Mowanjum-REL-first

Then (I did) those ones first, these Mowanjum people first.

Another syntactically important way of ordering pronouns is described in §17.4.

17.2.3 Topical adverbs

Adverbial phrases as well as clauses may be topicalized by 3wREF *ke*. We have already seen one such phrase in (17.13) in §17.1.1: *warliwunya ke* 'for (the purpose of getting) turtles.' This suffixial phrase, like suffixial and postpositional phrases generally, functions adverbially, as seen again in (17.20a & b). The examples in (17.20) show the adverbial suffixial phrase *wangalangaanjanu* 'as children, when (we were) children,' and the adverbs *ngamba* 'soon, TIME RELATIVE' and *ngarrkunjaangarri* 'long before our time:'

(17.20a)
Weni-weni	korru	anmarlaarndonya	[warliwunya	**ke**].
weni-weni	korru	arr-n-Ø=marlaarndo-nya	warli-^{k}wunya	ke
now-now	alright	1px-INV-3=follow-HORT	turtle-PURP	3wREF

Now you can let him go with us after turtles.

(b)
'Yarrorl birriyeerri,'	kubajunganyarri
yarrorl ba-kuN-rra=yi-eerri	kuN-^{b}warr=yi-ng-a-nyarri
voices CFT-VCOMP-2p=do-PROG	VCOMP-3p=do-PAST-EP-1pxDAT

[wanglangaanjanu	**ke**].
wangalang-aanjanu	ke
child-ESS	3wREF

'Don't make too much noise,' they used to tell us when we were children.

(c) (=5.43b, 7.42b)
Kawarro	wali	aaya	[ngamba	**ke**].
ka-^{b}warr-a=^{b}wu	wali	aaya	ngamba	ke
3a-3p-EP=hit	PERF	3aREF	now	3wREF

They're going to kill him soon.

(d)

Wiyanbali	ke	wurluk	kayabuna	[wunu
wiyanu-ᵏwuN-nbali	ke	wurluk	ØN-Ø-ngka=yabu-na	wunu
fire-3w-RESUM	3wREF	swallow	3w-3-SJTV=throw-PAST	3wDEF

ngarrkunjaangarri	ke].
before.our.time	3wREF

That's that same fire that he swallowed way back in the dreamtime.

Note how the term *ngarrkunjaangarri* 'before our time/before we were born' receives definite marking as well (*wunu* '3wDEF'), in a narrative in which the mythical or dreaming context of the events described is in focus.

17.2.4 Clause conjunction

Probably related historically to its contextual deictic function, *ke* has a further and very frequent use in clause-clause conjunction, where it means 'and.' Typical examples of clause conjunction by *ke* 'and' are seen in (17.21):

(17.21a)

Wangawa	kengaarndu	**ke**	baay	kanunaarndu	werrim	mana.
wanga-ᵇwa	ka=ya-nga-aarndu	ke	baay	ka=nu-na-aarndu	werrim	mana
lost-PROG	3a=go-TNS-DU	and	climb	3a=be-PAST-DU	hill	3mDEF

They got lost and climbed up the hill.

(b)

Dambeem	braarrbraarr	monaarndu	**ke**	we	kawanaarndu.
dambeem	braar-braarr	ma-Ø=ᵇwu-na-aarndu	ke	we	ka=ᵇwa-na-aarndu
place	clean-clean	3m-3=hit-PAST-DU	and	lie	3a=fall-TNS-DU

They cleared away an area of ground and lay down.

(c)

Braarru	kuninjangaarndu	**ke**	bariy	kanunaarndu.
braarru	kuN-Ø=ninja-nga-aarndu	ke	bariy	ka=nu-na-aarndu
dawn	3w-3=look-PAST-DU	and	rise	3a=be-PAST-DU

They saw the first light of dawn appear, and they got up.

17.3 Climactic clauses

Whole clauses may be highlighted and placed at centre stage by the use of a couple of syntactic devices in Worrorra. Clauses are so foregrounded in order to mark the importance of their propositional content, in processes that may be subsumed under a heading 'climactic,' as this adjective sums up the general motivation for these processes. Foley (2010:99) recognizes a similar (climactic, punchline) function for chain-final serial verb constructions in the Papuan language Watam.

17.3.1 Impression points

The determiner *wunu* may again be used rhetorically, to mark predicates that are pivotal to the narrative in which they occur. These are the intense and dramatic events upon which a narrative turns, that is, the impression points which the speaker considers to be of key importance in his or her account of something.¹²² Such sentences are in effect super-predicates, that is, the pragmatic goals of entire stretches of discourse, not of single sentences only, and may occur in mundane gossipy accounts of daily activities as well as in narrative texts. The predicates marked by *wunu* as being impression points usually contain a verb in aorist mood (§5.4.5 (i),(iv)), with the vivid or imminent sense meanings of this mood foregrounded. Examples of sentences that constitute impression points, and which are marked as such by the article *wunu* are:

(17.22a)
Jarrangurlak	kamaarndu	**wunu**.
jarrangurlak	[ka]-Ø=ma-[ᵏwarndu_U]	wunu
lift.up	[3a]-3=get-[DU_U]	3wDEF

He lifted them both up.

(b)
Jarra	kowaarndu	**wunu**.
jarra	[ka]-Ø=ᵇwu-[ᵏwarndu_U]	wunu
charge	[3a]-3=hit-[DU_U]	3wDEF

He charged at them.

(c)
[Karle wali	ajeendaarndu	**wunu**],	karle	budurrwu
karle wali	a-[ngarr]-nya=eenda-[ᵏwarndu_A]	wunu	karle	budurrwu
CHANGE	3a-[1pin]-EP=cook-[DU_A]	3wDEF	then	snore

kengerri.
ka=ya-nga-eerri
3a=go-TNS-PROG

[Then we both burned him], while he was snoring.

(d)
Kanbanerri	birdeenja	aaya	rlerlewa	kamurrkarlerri,
kanbanerri	birdeen-ya	aaya	rlerlewa	ka-Ø=murrka-rla-eerri
crab	little-3a	3aREF	crawl	3a-3=go.to-PAST-PROG

[kaningka	**wunu**]	ke	yarrmun	kumnyeng.
ka-Ø=ningka	wunu	ke	yarrmun	kuN-Ø-mnya=yi-ng
3a-3=bite	3wDEF	and	fright	VCOMP-3-DD=do-PAST

A little crab crawled up to him [and bit him], and he got a fright.

Aorist mood is usual in this function, but not inevitable, as the sentences in (17.23) show:

(17.23a)
	Marrirri	wunu	aja	kumnyanunerri	**wunu**.
	marrirri	wunu	aja	kuN-mnya=nu-na-eerri	wunu
	parrot	3wDEF	sit	3w-DD=be-PAST-PROG	3wDEF

The red-winged parrot came and sat down.

(b)
	Kamarlamarlaarndorna	**wunu**.
	ka-Ø-marla=marlaarndo-rna	wunu
	3a-3-REDUP=follow-PAST	3wDEF

She followed along after him.

---

¹²² The idea of narrative impression points (German *Eindruckspunkt*) employed here is adapted from the work of Frank Kermode (1979), whose understanding is in turn based on that of the philosopher Wilhelm Dilthey.

In (17.23a) the arrival of the red-winged parrot is pivotal to the myth in which this event occurs, in that this bird is totemically associated with fire, and is able now to show the other birds how to obtain it. In (17.23b) the special (pivotal) status of the predicate is reinforced not by aorist mood, but by the reduplication of the root morpheme (§5.2.2).

Related to the rhetorical function of *wunu* discussed in §17.1.1, is its occurrence with the modal adverbs *wardi* 'hopefully' (§8.4.3) and *mee/mee maa* 'just, only' (§6.4.2 (iii)). In this position *wunu* takes on an adverbial emphatic function, as seen in (17.24):

(17.24a) Wunu   mee   ngenu ...
          wunu   mee   ØN-nga=yi-nu
          3wDEF   just   VCOMP-1=do-2DAT
          I really just want to tell you ...

(b)   Wunu   mee maa   minjarl   binjeen.
          wunu   mee maa   minjarl   ba-kuN-nja=yi-n
          3wDEF   just   eat   CFT-VCOMP-2=do-NON.P
          You should really just eat it.

(c)   Wardi   bangkayungurru   wunu.
          wardi   ba-ka=ya-ngurru   wunu
          I.hope   CFT-3a=go-away   3wDEF
          With any luck he might just go away.

(d)   Mee   wardi   wunu,   wardi   murlard   barroyeerringkurri.
          mee   wardi   wunu   wardi   murlard   ba-ka-rra=ᵇwu-yeerri-ᵏwurri
          just   I.hope   3wDEF   I.hope   look.after   CFT-3a-2p=hit-PROG-NUM
          I really just hope you'll be looking after him.

17.3.2 Topical clauses

In Worrorra it appears to be the case that whole propositions, not just nouns, may be invested with topicality. As a discourse-level property, it would not be unfeasible if topicality were to apply to sentences. Although the database does not provide conclusive evidence on this point, it would appear that the form of the contextual deictic used to topicalize sentences is the celestial shape, *ke*. And just as is the case with the topicalized nouns shown in (17.18), it is the clauses and sentences marked by *ke* in (17.25) that the speakers seem to want to place in the spotlight on centre stage. Here the proposed topicalized clauses are enclosed in square brackets:

(17.25a)
Marrungurru   bungunyeyeerri,   maa-maa   dalorr   wali maa,
ma=rru-ngurru   ba-ngun=ya-yeerri   maa-maa   dalorr   wali maa
3m=LAT-ALL   CFT-2=go-PROG   3mREF-3mREF   sink-hole   PM

[yawak   barrwa   marru   ke].
yawak   ba-ngarr=ᵇwa   ma=rru   ke
sink   CFT-1pin=fall   3m=LAT   3wREF
Don't go over there, there are sink-holes over there, and [we might fall down one].

(b)
Ngayu	mana	aja	nyinngunyeerlaarnduma		
ngayu	mana	aja	[nyirr]-n-Ø-ngun-nya=ee-rla-[aarndu]-ma		
I	3mDEF	sit	[2p]-INV-3/1-SJTV-EP=put-PAST-[DU$_O$]-3m		

dambeemarnanya,	waa	aja	binyidinyaarndeerri:	[arri
dambeema-rnanya	waa	aja	ba-nyirr=ni-nya-aarndu-eerri	arri
place-LOC	not	sit	CFT-2p=be-PAST-DU-PROG	but

ngalarram	maa	marramurrkarlaarndu	**ke**].
ngalarram	maa	ma-[rra]=murrka-rla-[aarndu]	ke
long.grass	3mREF	3m-[2p]=go.to-PAST-[DU$_A$]	3wREF

You didn't stay at home where I left you: [instead you went over into the long grass].

(c)
[Ngarrunangkowa	ngunyangerri	**ke**?]
ngarrunangkowa	ngun=ya-nga-eerri	ke
IN.WHICH.DIRECTION	2=go-TNS-PROG	3wREF

[So where are you off to?]

In (17.25a) the topicalized clause conveys a sense of urgency, consisting as it does of a warning about an imminent danger. In (17.25b) topic marking is used to bring out the contrast between what the two boys were told to do, and what they actually did. In (17.25c) the question is topicalized, probably for purposes of focus, as is suggested by the use of 'so' in the translation.

Topical clauses and sentences typically constitute background information, against which the information contained in surrounding clauses is to be understood (cf eg Haiman 1978). In Worrorra topic-marked sentences are indeed frequently subordinate, as indicated by the subjunctive shapes of their verbs, examples of which are shown in (17.26). Again, the subjunctive, topicalized sentences are shown in square brackets:

(17.26a)
[Kawa	karrku	maa	marnuk	kamanga	**ke**],	blaai
kawa	karrku	maa	marnuk	ØN-Ø-ngka=ma-nga	ke	blaai
3wNAR	rock	3mREF	lift	3w-3-SJTV=get-PAST	3wREF	pound

kona.
ka-Ø=^{b}wu-na
3a-3=hit-PAST

[When he lifted up the rock there], it crushed him.

(b)
Wunu	angkaweenerri	anja	aalmareya	marru
wunu	arr-ngka=^{b}wee-na-eerri	anja	aalmareya	ma=rru
3wDEF	3p-SJTV=hit.MID-PAST-PROG	3pDEF	Europeans	3m=LAT

kenga	wali,	[wali	weerla	ingkanuna	**ke**].
ka=ya-nga	wali	wali	weerla	i-ngka=nu-na	ke
3a=go-TNS	PERF	PERF	young.man	3a-SJTV=be-PAST	3wREF

He had gone away to the great war [when he was still a young man].[123]

---

[123] The great war: *wunu angkaweenerri anja aalmareya* 'when the Europeans were fighting each other.'

(c)
Nguru	kerrkangurreerri	[karloorlerri	**ke**].
nguru	ka-nyarr=ᵏwangurru-eerri	ØN-Ø-ngka=rloo-rla-eerri	ke
hear	3a-1px=carry-PROG	VCOMP-3-SJTV=speak-PAST-PROG	3wREF

We used to listen to him [when he spoke].

The NP in example (17.27) below is another example of one containing a topicalized subordinate relative clause. The proximity of *ke* to the subjunctive verb suggests that in this situation topic marking is primarily a feature of the relative clause (shown here in square brackets), and only applies secondarily to the entire NP. The exocentric head of the relative clause is *ngarlangarla* 'story, speech, word,' here translated as 'thing:'

(17.27)
Wunmaanbali	ngarlangarla	jarrungu	[nganngunjunu	**ke**].
ᵏwuN=n-maanbali	ngarlangarla	ØN=yarrungu	ØN-ngan-ngun=yi-nu	ke
3w=DEF-FOCUS	story	3w=QUANT	VCOMP-1-SJTV=do-2DAT	3wREF

The very same thing [that I want to talk to you about].

It is by no means the case, however, that all topical sentences need to be in subjunctive form. One reason for conferring given status to a clause (topicalizing it) is in order to mark it as a prior condition of an event depicted in some other clause, that is, to constitute it as in some sense the cause of some other event expressed in another clause (Clendon 1988:199-200). Causal constructions of this sort need not be subjunctive, as may be seen in the sentences in (17.28):

(17.28a)
[Wurrkunu	kununa	karle maa	**ke**],	kaarrbaalimiyena.
wurrkunu	kuN=nu-na	karle maa	ke	kaarr=maalima-ye-na
trouble	3w=be-PAST	REM.PAST	3wREF	3p=pierce-MID-PAST

[For that sort of trouble in the old days], they used to get speared.

(b)
[Wumbirli	nganmangaarndeerri	**ke**],	nguyul
wumbirli	nga-n-[Ø]=ma-nga-[aarndu]-eerri	ke	nguyul
deride	1-INV-[3]=get-PAST-[DU_A]-PROG	3wREF	strike/kill

kungenganangkaarndu.
kuN-nga=yi-ng-a-[nangka-ᵏwarndu]
VCOMP-1=do-PAST-EP-[DAT-DU]

[They were sneering at me], so I killed them.

(c)
[Wangalaalunguyu	dumbi	ngana	kawarronerri	**ke**],
wangalaalanguya	dumbi	ngana	ka-ᵇwarr-a=ᵇwu-na-eerri	ke
children	owl.sp	PROB	3a-3p-EP=hit-PAST-PROG	3wREF

Wanjurna	waay	kayabuna	inja	aaja.
wanjurna	waay	ka-Ø=yabu-na	inja	aaja
Wandjina	throw	3a-3=throw-PAST	3aDEF	rain

[The children must have killed the owl], that's why the Wandjina has sent the rain.

17.4 Periphrastic subject-marking

The pronouns =^{k}*wa* 'ANAPHORIC' (Table 7.2 in §7.2) and =*n* 'DEFINITE' (Table 7.4 in §7.3.1) appearing together and most often in that order within an NP, provide a periphrastic marking of topicality that serves, in the overwhelming majority of its occurrences, as a *de facto* signal of subjecthood. The two pronouns need not be closely juxtaposed, the important constraint is that in nearly all cases they must be configured in the right order (example 17.30a below is one of the very few exceptions in the database). Examples may be seen in (17.44) in §17.6, and in (17.29):

(17.29a) (=4.5)
Awa	inja	angujakana	baa	kamurrkarla.
a=^{k}wa	i=n-ya	angujakana	baa	ka-Ø=murrka-rla
3a=NAR	3a=DEF-3a	something	rise/appear	3a-3=go.to-PAST

Something came up towards him.

(b)
Nyangka	nyina	'Ngarreyu!	Ngarreyu!'	kunjaara	Aalkaalja.
nyangka	nyina	ngarr-a=ya	ngarr-a=ya	kuN-Ø=yi-^{k}wara	Aalkaalja
3fNAR	3fDEF	1pin-OPT=go	1pin-OPT=go	VCOMP-3=do-1DAT	NAME

'Let's go! Let's go!' Aalkaalja said to me.

(c)
Arrka	anja	kawarrarnaarnarlerri	eeja.
arrka	anja	ka-^{b}warr-a-rnaarna-rla-eerri	eeja
3pNAR	3pDEF	3a-3p-EP=await-PAST-PROG	man

Certain people were waiting for the man.

(d)
Arrka	anja	eeja	belangkarraya	Arnngarrngoyu	kaarringurru.
arrka	anja	eeja	belangkarraya	Arnngarrngoyu	kaarr=i-nga-ngurru
3pNAR	3pDEF	men	large.group	patriclan.name	3p=go-TNS-away

All the men of the Arnngarrngoyu clan departed in a group.

(e)
Awaarndu	inkarndu	wumbirli	kamangaarndeerri
awaarndu	inkarndu	wumbirli	ka-[Ø]=ma-nga-[^{k}warndu$_A$]-eerri
3aNAR.DU	3aDEF.DU	deride	3a-[3]=get-PAST-[DU$_A$]-PROG

irranangkorri	inja.
irra-nangkorri	inja
father-3pDAT	3aDEF

They were both making fun of their father.

(f)
Wurloo	kaanyonerri	kakaakanangkaya,	inja
wurloo	kaarr-n-Ø-nya=^{b}wu-na-eerri	ka-kaa-ka-nangka-ya	inja
smoke[124]	3p-INV-3-EP=hit-PAST-PROG	↳-AUG-MoBr-DAT-3p	3aDEF

---

[124] *Wurloo* 'smoking, purify ritually by smoking:' a ceremony performed at a specified time after a death to remove mortuary prohibitions from relatives of the deceased.

```
kulanangka         kakaakanangkorri,    kakaakanangkaya        awa
kula-nangka        ka-kaa-ka-nangkorri  ka-kaa-ka-nangka-ya    awa
Hu-DAT             ↳-AUG-MoBr-3pDAT     ↳-AUG-MoBr-DAT-3p      3aNAR

inja       debarr    ingkenga.
inja       debarr    i-ngka=ya-nga
3aDEF      die       3a-SJTV=go-TNS
```
She would perform the smoking ceremony for his mothers' brothers, for her husband's (and his siblings') mothers' brothers, for the mothers' brothers of he who had died.

Because the kinship-possessive morpheme (-*nangka* 'DAT') does not code for gender, sentences such as (17.29f) are potentially ambiguous as to whose (his, the husband's, or her, the wife's) uncles are being referred to. The use of the topicalizing =*ᵏwa* =*n* word order makes it clear that it is the husband's relations that are being referred to here. In (17.29e) dual pronouns are used.

Verbless equational sentences are not usually said to have subjects as such, but in predicate logic we may distinguish terms and predicates within such sentences (Searle 1969:113). A logical term is functionally equivalent to a grammatical subject; in fact most subjects are terms by virtue of the pragmatic motivations underlying grammatical relations. In this situation the =*ᵏwa* =*n* configuration marks terms, and so supports the contention that this word order is intrinsically involved in marking subjects. The examples in (17.30) show equational sentences with terms marked periphrastically:

(17.30a)
```
[TERM                       ]    [PRED                        ]
Mana     dambeem    mawa         Dilangarri   manbali    mana.
3mDEF    place      3mNAR        'Dog'        3mRESUM    3mDEF
```
That place is Dog-clan country as well.

(b)
```
[TERM                       ]    [PRED                        ]
Nyangka    karranangkanya        nyirnayuja         nyangke,    ke
nyangka    karra-nangka-nya      nyiN=rnayurr-nya   nyangke     ke
3fNAR      mother-DAT-3f         3f=adult-3f        3fREF       and

[TERM                         ]    [PRED    ]
nyangka    nyina    marangunya      birdeenya.
nyangka    nyina    marangunya      birdeen-nya
3fNAR      3fDEF    sun             small-3f
```
Her mother is the big one, and the sun is the little one.

(c)
```
[TERM         ]    [PRED              ]
Kawa    wunu       Wunumbal   wali wunu
3wNAR   3wDEF      Wunumbal   PM
```
That one is a Wunumbal (story)

In (17.30a) the term is *mana dambeem mawa* 'this/that country,' topicalized by the two pronouns, and with its definite status highlighted by the initial position of the determiner *mana*. Example (17.30b) contains two contrasting verbless clauses. In the first one the term is *nyangka karranangkanya* 'her mother,' and in the second the term is *nyangka nyina marangunya* 'the sun.' In the first clause the predicate (*nyirnayuja* 'adult (fem)') is topicalized morphologically by the contextual deictic *nyangke*, while in the second clause it is the term that is topicalized, this time configurationally by the pronouns *nyangka nyina*. This construction produces a highly contrastive sentence, with terms and predicates contrasted on a number of levels. In (17.30c) the topicalizing pronouns themselves (*kawa wunu* 'that (celestial) one') constitute a term, with *Wunambal* 'group/language name' the predicate. The phrase *wali wunu* is a predicate marker (glossed PM), described in §17.8.

While pronominal ordering is *available* to mark subjects, as an essentially topicalizing construction it is, of course, not *required* for this purpose. Rather it functions pragmatically to produce emphasis, foregrounding, disambiguation etc, in a manner comparable to movement rules in English. As a topicalizing device it may, of course, occur with non-subject NPs, although this is surprisingly rare in the database. The examples in (17.31) show a process comparable to the movement called object fronting in English, first with an undergoer object (17.31a), and then with a non-subcategorized object (17.31b):

(17.31a)
Nyangka	nyina	nyimrimaaingarrinya	wunu	ngaja	nyejamanga
nyangka	nyina	nyimrimaaingarrinya	wunu	ngaja	nyaN-nyarr-nya=ma-nga
3fNAR	3fDEF	python.sp	3wDEF	custom	3f-1px-EP=get-PAST

It is the black-headed python whose precedent we followed

(b)
Nyangka	nyina,	'Juward	bawa'	kunjunganangka,
nyangka	nyina	juward	ba=ᵇwa	kuN-Ø=yi-ng-a-nangka
3fNAR	3fDEF	jump	CFT=fall	VCOMP-3=do-PAST-EP-DAT

'mana	wiyanu'
3mDEF	fire

Her he ordered to jump into the fire

Note in (17.31b) that *wiyanu wunu* 'fire' controls terrestrial agreement on the determiner to denote a fire as a location. Example (17.31b) also contains a good example of a not uncommon stylistic device, in which a *verbum dicendi (kunjunganangka)* is encliticized to the first constituent (in this case the complex predicate) in a direct speech quotation (cf also 17.29b). The non-subcategorized object is referred to by the pronouns *nyangka nyina* 'her,' and indexed on the *verbum dicendi* by the morpheme *-nangka* 'DAT.'

Subjecthood defines a pragmatically-motivated phenomenon, and the =ᵏwa =n configuration marks subject status in the vast majority of instances of its use, in situations that call for the marking of topicality as well as subjecthood.

In summary we can say that there are two main topicalizing devices in the language, the first being the set of contextualizing deictics *(=ᵏwaya)*, and the second being the ordered =ᵏwa =n configuration. While the former is used generally, the latter appears to be dedicated (largely but not exclusively) to marking subject status.

As well as non-subject NPs, pronominal ordering may also be used to topicalize adverbial phrases, as in (17.32). In this example the sequence *kawa wunu* has temporal reference, forming with *karle* 'CHANGE-OF-STATE' a topicalized time-adverbial phrase:

(17.32) (=15.47c)
Kawa	wunu	karle,	arrkumnyenga	aalmara	karle
kawa	wunu	karle	arr-ngun-mnya=ya-nga	aalmara	karle
3wNAR	3wDEF	then	1px-SJTV-DD=go-TNS	European	then

marno	Karnmanya	yorr	arrkunyawana.
ma=rno	Karnmanya	yorr	arr-ngun-nya=ᵇwa-na
3m=DIST	Kunmunya	sit.together	1px-SJTV-EP=fall-TNS

That was the time then, that we went with the white people and we all moved to Kunmunya.

The remaining logical combination of pronouns involves =ᵏwa 'ANAPHORIC' and =ᵏwaya 'CONTEXTUAL,' however these two do not appear to be combined in any systematic way. The few examples in the database where they do co-occur within an NP appear to involve non-systematic instances of topicalized anaphors or of predicate marking (§17.8). Examples of equational term-predicate constructions involving =^kwa and =^kwaya are seen in (17.33). In (17.33a), *nyangka* is the term and the rest of the utterance the predicate:

(17.33a)
[TERM	[PRED	]
Nyangka	Wurnbangkuwaamaanya	nyangke.
nyangka	Wurnbangku-waa-maan-nya	nyangke
3fNAR	clan.country-PERS-SPEC-3f	3fREF

She's the one who belongs only to the land of the Wurnbangku clan.

(b)
[PRED	]	[TERM		]
Ngayangkarnanya	wali wunu	kawa	wungumbu	ke.
Ngayangkarnanya	wali wunu	kawa	ᵏwuN=ngumbu	ke
Mt.Trafalgar	PM	3wNAR	3w=name	3wREF

Ngayangkarnanya is its name.

(c) (=7.16c)
Awanyale	inja	koyoya	aaya ...
awa-nyale	inja	koyoya	aaya
3aNAR-too	3aDEF	crocodile	3aREF

There was this crocodile ...

Sentence examples (17.33b & c) appear to involve highly presentational constructions, the (c) example introducing as subject a pivotal character in a myth (a crocodile), and the (b) example recording a performative act by which a mountain was named, with corresponding emphasis on the noun =*ngumbu wunu* 'name.' Note in (17.33b) that just as in the sentences in (17.30), the term in this equational sentence is marked configurationally (here by *kawa ... ke*), although the linear order of term and predicate is reversed.

17.5 Identity maintenance

Identity maintenance in Worrorra is another form of definite reference, as in other languages. The bound morpheme -^bwali (in this context glossed 'RESUM') in Worrorra has an essentially similar meaning to that of the free adverb of the same form (§10.1.1 (i)), namely 'perfect aspect; ongoing, continuing state.' The function of -^bwali is to maintain a referent's identity within an unfolding speech event, that is, to maintain the referent's known (definite) status as the event unfolds. The bound form is suffixed to the pronouns =*n* 'DEF,' =*rno* 'Distal' and =^kwaya 'Contextual.' Although the language has a suffixial adjective *jawe-* '(the) same,' it is rare in the database, and identity maintenance of the type covered by the English adjective 'same' is usually achieved by the use of DEF-^bwali. The definite form =*nbali* is used for unmarked reference, and the distal =*rnowali* form for reference to distant things. There is also an identity-maintaining topic form =^kwaya-wali, as shown in Table 17.1. Note that the 3w and 3p forms with this meaning consist of two words rather than one:

Table 17.1: identity-maintenance pronouns

	THE SAME	THE SAME DISTAL	THE SAME TOPIC
3a	inbali	irnowali	aawali
3f	nyinbalinya	nyirnowalinya	nyingkewalinya
3w	wunbali	wurnowali	ke wali
3m	manbalima	marnowalima	maawalima
3p	anbali	arnowali	arrke wali

Identity maintenance in Worrorra is found when reference is resumed after an interval of time. Such an interval may be of real (extra-linguistic) time, or of narrative time, as when reference to an NP in a narrative is resumed after discussion of other things.

In (17.34) some children have been warned not to hurt owls. Later on that day they find an owl in a tree, and call out:

(17.34)
Inbali!	Inbali!	Dumbi	inbali!	Arrowurri!
inbali	inbali	dumbi	inbali	a-ngarr-a=^{b}wu-^{k}wurri
3a.RESUM	3a.RESUM	owl	3a.RESUM	3a-1pin-OPT=hit-NUM

Here it is! Here it is! There's that owl! Let's all kill it!

In (17.34) a highly definite reference is resumed after an interval of time, and the fact of the resumption is registered by the use of an appropriate form of the identity-maintaining pronoun. Two other resumptions in real time are shown in (17.35). In (17.35a) a husband arrives at a camp some time after his wife has arrived there previously, and in (17.35b) the speaker realizes the identity of a culprit some time after a crime has been committed:

(17.35a)
Mangkanya	nyinbalinya	marno,	jawarnda	maa	rnala	kunjungu.
mangkanya	nyinbalinya	marno	jawarnda	maa	rnala	kuN-Ø=yi-ng
your.wife	3f.RESUM	3mDIST	apart	PROG	camp	VCOMP-3=do-PAST

That wife of yours is over there, she's made her camp away from everyone else.

(b)
Nyinbalinya	ngunju,	ngunju	maambulba	kungurr	manjona.
nyinbalinya	ngunju	ngunju	ma=^{k}wambul-ma	kungurr	ma-nja=^{b}wu-na
3f.RESUM	you(sg)	you(sg)	3m=eye-3m	stab	3m-2=hit-PAST

So it was you (fem), you stabbed its eyes.

In both these examples reference is resumed after an interval of time during which the people in question have not been referred to.

Participant persons may receive identity-maintenance marking, in which case they may either attract gender-marking appropriate to their sex, as shown in (17.35b) above (*nyinbalinya ngunju* 'so it's you (fem)/you (fem) are the one'), or else be marked by a celestial form, as in (7.2c, 17.36) and (7.2d =17.63a). In the following example someone standing outside a house has called out to someone inside to find out if anyone is at home, in which case the person inside may reply:

(17.36)
	Ngayu	wunbali!
	I	3w.RESUM

I'm (still) here!

A resumption in narrative time is shown in (17.37): here the narrator returns to her central theme after consideration of other things:

(17.37)
Nyinbalinya	jilinya	jandu	nyimbajamanga	joonbanyiniya.
nyinbalinya	jilinya	jandu	nyiN-^{b}warr-nya=ma-nga	joonba-nyini-ya
3f.RESUM	spirit.woman	perform	3f-3p-EP=get-PAST	ceremony-ENDPOINT-3p

They used to perform ceremonies about that spirit-woman.

In many instances of its occurrence, DEF-*bwali* and REF-*bwali* cover much the same semantic ground as the English adjective phrase 'the same:'

(17.38a)
Hey!	Nguru	banu!	'Du-rdu-rdu'	ke wali!
hey	nguru	ba=nu	rdu-rdu-rdu	ke wali
hey	hear	CFT=be	rdu-rdu-rdu	3wREF RESUM

Hey! Listen! It's that 'du-du-du' noise again!

(b)
Ke wali	kurdu	kungoyeerri?	
ke wali	kurdu	kuN-nga=^{b}wu-yeerri	
3wREF RESUM	follow	VCOMP-1=hit-PROG	

Should I be talking about that same thing?

(c)
Anbali	anja,	ngayanangka	ibaaya	aaya	kawana	rlarlangkarrama.
anbali	anja	ngayanangka	ibaaya	aaya	ka=^{b}wa-na	rlarlangkarrama
3p.RESUM	3pDEF	my		son	3aREF	3a=fall-TNS	sea

They're the very ones (that caused) my son to fall into the sea.

(d)
Wunbali	wunu	joli	nganungaal.
wunbali	wunu	joli	nga=nu-ng-aal
3w.RESUM	3wDEF	return	1=be-PRES-hither

I'll come straight back.

In (17.38d) the 3w pronoun phrase makes reference to time, namely the same general time-period as that in which the utterance is made.

In other occurrences, DEF-*bwali* and REF-*bwali* are used anaphorically when the referent of a phrase is re-stated, usually to clarify or reinforce that referent's identification by maintaining and emphasizing its definite status:

(17.39a)
Kunyilarnanya	maa	aja	kaningeerri	inja	kanangkurri,
kunyila-rnanya	maa	aja	ka=ni-ng-eerri	inja	kanangkurri
moon-LOC	PROG	sit	3a=be-PRES-PROG	3aDEF	dog

inbali	irraarreya	inja.
inbali	i=raarreya	inja
3a.RESUM	3a=big	3aDEF

The dog$_i$ is still up there in the moon; that big one$_i$.

(b)
Mr Love	aaya	irnayurri,	aawali	minister.
Mr Love	aaya	i=rnayurr-i	aa(ya)-^{b}wali	minister
Mr Love	3aREF	3a=adult-3a	3aREF-RESUM	minister

Mr. Love was an elder, he was the minister.

(c)
Ingumbu	Dawarra;	ingumbu	ke wali	Dawarraweyi.
i=ngumbu	Dawarra	i=ngumbu	ke wali	Dawarraweyi
3a=name	NAME	3a=name	3wREF RESUM	NAME

His name was Dawarra, or rather Dawarraweyi.

(d) (=15.13)

Arno-rno	jurroyurro	marrkunjandanjeerri
arr=rno-arr=rno	jurro-jurro	ma-ngarr-ngun=yanda-ny-yeerri
3p=dist-3p=dist	smoking.rising-REDUP	3m-1pin-SJTV=cause-MIR-PROG

maalkarram,	angarrburrkaarndu	arrke wali.
maalkarram	arr-[ngarr]=murrka-[ᵏwarndu]	arrke wali
grass-fire	3p-[1pin]=go.to-[DU]	3pREF RESUM

Here, we'll light grass-fires to (send up) smoke (to signal) those (people) over there, (and then) let's go over to them.

In none of the examples in (17.39) is the use of identity-maintaining pronouns essential to consummate referential meaning; rather they are employed as stylistic and/or pragmatic devices to reinforce a referent's identity.

17.6 Discourse deixis

A morpheme *-mnya-*, glossed DD 'discourse deictic,' occurs in verbs in form-order class [5], just before the verb root, or before root augmentation in form-order class [6]. This morpheme appears to function rhetorically; it is used more by some speakers than by others, and is found in particular kinds of discourses and in particular places in discourse. It appears to be a stylistic device with a discourse-deictic role. Its occurrence appears to mark a speaker's assessment that the predicate in which it occurs has a particular logical or emotional connection to an earlier section of discourse. It indicates a speaker's wish to highlight a link between the predication in which it occurs, and the propositional content of some previous utterance or situation, not too far back in some spoken or even unspoken discourse. In elicitation the morpheme is produced typically in responses to questions, as seen in sentences such as (7.26b), repeated here as (17.40), in which a speaker wishes to be seen to be cooperating with the questioner:

(17.40)
Ngarrunangkowa	nyenga?	Marrunangkowa	nyimnyenga.
ngarrunangkowa	nya=ya-nga	marrunangkowa	nyiN-**mnya**=ya-nga
which.way	3f=go-TNS	that way	3f-DD=go-TNS

Which way did she go? She went that way.

The phonetics of *-mnya-* are discussed in §2.3.1. The morpheme has no indispensible coding function, which means it's optional; it cannot appear after *-nya-* in epenthetic function *(nya-*epenthesis rule 26), but may occur after this morpheme when it is found in optative function:

(17.41)
Ruluk	bamnyayu,	wook	ngunyamnyongurru.
ruluk	ba-**mnya**=ya	wook	ngun-∅-nya-**mnya**=ᵇwu-ngurru
move	CFT-DD=go	pass	2-1/3-OPT-DD=hit-away

Move aside, I want to get past you.

The morpheme does not occur naturally after (plural) subject NP indices ending in /rr/, as this would require initial /m/ to harden to /b/ to produce a shape *-bnya-*. That this is a phonological rather than a morphosyntactic restriction is shown by the fact that it is found in plural-subject index clusters *not* ending in /rr/: *kawarramnyo* (|ka-ᵇwarr-a-mnya=ᵇwu| [3a-3p-EP-DD=hit]) 'they hit him.' Hardened forms occur in an elicited paradigm, but they are absent from every other part of the database; an example is *warrbnye* (|ˌwɒtpɨ̍ˈɲeː|) (|kuN-ngarr-mnya=yi| [VCOMP-1pin-DD=do]) 'we do it/we'll do it.'

This morpheme is readily comparable to the Ungarinyin definite subject morpheme (Rumsey 1982:105-106). The Ungarinyin morpheme, *-iwa-* or *-irra-*, occurs in form-order class [8] in the Ungarinyin verb (*idem*: 75), to the left of, and immediately adjacent to the root morpheme. Of this morpheme Rumsey states that 'the subject of the verb so marked is an NP which is coreferential to one which has occurred in previous discourse.' In the Worrorra database the morpheme appears to have a wider reference than to subjects only: part participant-tracking mechanism, part rhetorical device, it appears to have referential scope over either an entire previous predication or just specific parts of it, selected and decoded by conversational implicature.

In texts the morpheme may occur in clusters, in parts of a narration the speaker judges to be of particular emotional or connective significance. Textual example (17.42) comes after a conversational exchange, without framing *verba dicendi*, between a dying man and a person caring for him. Discourse deixis is absent from this exchange, and then the narrator says:

(17.42)
'Karle	ngawarru,	ku**mny**enga,	karle	ngoyba	ku**mny**enganangka.
now	I.sick	he.said	now	breath	he.did.it

Iman	ka**mny**anu,	debarr	ka**mny**enga.	Kawarra**mny**aarndenga,	debarr	ka**mny**enga,
he.dead	he.is	die	he.went	they.placed.him	die	he.went

walaawirri	kaajanu.	Mangkanangkanya	maangurru	nyi**mny**enga,	nyinjorinya	nyimri
wailing	they.are	his.wife	away	she.went	widow	her.head

durr	kumbuna.	Nyi**mny**enga,	marno	kawarra**mny**aarndenga	karndirrim	maa.
cut	she.did.it	she.went	there	they.placed.him	platform	that

'I'm sick,' he said, then he stopped breathing. He was dead, he had died. They put him up, he had died, they <u>grieved</u>. His wife went away, the widow <u>gashed</u> her head. She went away, they put him up on a burial platform.

Here the discourse deictic morpheme is in bold. In a passage with 11 verbs, discourse-deictic marking is found in 9 of them; the two without such marking are underlined in the translation. The section involves three participants: the deceased man, his wife, and a group of others ('they'); all are at one time or another the subjects of verbs marked for discourse deixis. This passage includes the first reference to *mangkanangkanya* 'his wife' in the text, but the predicate in which she occurs, as a subject, also receives discourse deictic marking.

This kind of clustering is reasonably common in the database, in dramatic or important sections of discourse, or sections involving climaxes or impression points. It is found in descriptions of Patsy's own widowhood, the activities of Wandjina ancestors, a demon cannibal feast, the commission and discovery of crimes, and conclusions, climaxes, retributions, realizations, tense and exciting episodes, and warranted or deserved outcomes generally.

The use of discourse deixis in (17.42) is rhetorical, as befits its tragic content. But its rhetoric comes out of its structural context: all the events depicted ensue from the text that precedes it; it represents an outcome or consequence of the preceding passage. A little later in the same text, after a description of women's grieving practices, the following sentence occurs, with reference to the widespread traditional belief that deaths not resulting from old age are brought about by (supernatural) human agency:

(17.43)
Jakarri,	'ngani	kumnyenga	wunu?	Yaada	ngani
ØN=yakarri	ngani	kuN-Ø-**mnya**=yi-ng	wunu	yaada	ngani
3w=other	what	VCOMP-3-DD=do-PAST	3wDEF	ENQ	what

```
kumnyenga                wunu?'
kuN-Ø-mnya=yi-ng         wunu
VCOMP-3-DD=do-PAST       3wDEF
```
One day/the next day [they asked], 'what happened to him? What had he done?'

Discourse deictic marking occurs here because the question necessarily follows on from, and refers back to, the preceding event, the man's death.

Sentence example (17.44) comes near the end of a story about the origin of patrimoieties. The culture hero Jrr'nkurn (Jinkun), the owlet nightjar, has resisted attempts to make him give his daughters away to men of the opposite patrimoiety, preferring to keep them for their own brothers. Finally he becomes aware of the enormity of what he has been wanting:

(17.44)
```
Ineem     karle    rley    kunjungu          awa       Jrr'nkurn    inja,
i=neem    karle    rley    kuN-Ø=yi-ng       awa       jrr'nkurn    inja
3a=ear    now      open    VCOMP-3=do-PAST   3aNAR     Jinkun       3aDEF

ke       'Yaw,    korru     angamnyarnerno,'         kumnyeng.
ke        yaw     korru     arr-nga-mnya-rne=rno     kuN-Ø-mnya=yi-ng
3wREF     yes     alright   3p-1-DD-AUG=give         VCOMP-3-DD=do-PAST
```
Then Jinkurn realized,[125] and he said, 'yes, it's right that I should give them away completely.'

This is an outcome or consequence of the story so far, and its climax. The crucial verb *angamnyarnerno* is augmented ('give them away completely, with no thought of their return') and marked for discourse deixis.

Consider as well the clustering seen in (17.45), again with discourse-deictic marking in bold:

(17.45)
```
Maa-maa        kerreendarla.   Dande       maa      kerreendarla    marno     aakurnanya
there-there    we.cooked.it    out.bush    there    we.cooked.it    there     by.water

yorr            ajawana.
sit.together    we.did

'Yaw,    karlewa    ngajengerri.'
yes      now        we.may.be.going

'Wali maa    awarl    kamnyamenya    wara,       ke     ngarramnyeyu    dambeem
keep.on      cook     let.it.do      kangaroo    and    we.will.go      place/home

ingkamnyaninjawa,    karle    iwujarra     ingkamnyanungu.    Ngarramnyeyu
when.it.is.cooked    then     it.cooked    when.it.is         we.will.go

joli      ngarramnyanu    dambeemangurru    dormitory-rnanya.'
return    we.will.be      to.home           in.dormitory
```
We cooked it right there. We sat down together by a pool of water and cooked it out in the bush.
'Alright, let's go now,' (he said).
'Let the kangaroo cook first, and then we'll go home when it's done, when it's cooked properly. Then we'll go back home to the dormitory.'

---

[125] Literally: 'now Jinkun's ears (=understandng) opened.'

Here a group of girls' European teacher is trying to hurry the cooking process, which must have been taking an inordinate amount of time by his standards. In the girls' reply every verb contains discourse-deictic marking, as a response to and rebuttal of what their teacher has just said.

The previous context indexed by deictic marking may not be an utterance at all: it may be an extra-linguistic situation manifest to discourse participants. In (17.46) a woman finds her husband sleeping-in one morning. The first thing she says to him is:

(17.46) Bariy   bamnyanu,   karle   mamangkunu.
         bariy   ba-**mnya**=nu karle   mamangkunu
         rise   CFT-DD=be   now   morning
         Get up now, it's morning.

No preceding *discourse* context can be involved here; deictic marking refers to *situational* context, in this case the rising sun. Sentence (17.41) above is another example arising out of an extra-linguistic context in which a man finds his wife asleep on a narrow path, and (17.56b) and (17.57b) below are two more.

In other situations discourse deixis in Worrorra may be a feature of rhetorical anaphora, as a group of words repeated across a series of sentences, as seen in (17.47), in which Patsy talks about her early childhood development:

(17.47)
Wali	maa	karleng	ngawana,	karleng	ngamnyawana	karle
wali	maa	karleng	nga=ᵇwa-na	karleng	nga-**mnya**=ᵇwa-na	karle
PERF	PROG	turn	1=fall-TNS	turn	1-DD=fall-TNS	then

ngarnayurr	nganunangurru,	karle	ngarnayurr	ngamnyanungurru,
nga=rnayurr	nga=nu-na-ngurru	karle	nga=rnayurr	nga-**mnya**=nu-ngurru
1=grown	1=be-PAST-away	then	1=grown	1-DD=be-away

rlerlewa	ngamnyenga,	rlerlewa	ngamnyengangurru,	karle
rlerlewa	nga-**mnya**=ya-nga	rlerlewa	nga-**mnya**=ya-nga ngurru	karle
crawl	1-DD=go-TNS	crawl	1-DD=go-TNS-away	then

bariy	ngamnyanu	mardow-mardowa	ngamnyenga
bariy	nga-**mnya**=nu	mardow-mardowa	nga-**mnya**=ya-nga
rise	1-DD=be	walk-walk	1-DD=go-TNS

I could turn over, then I grew bigger and started to crawl, and then I could stand up and I started to walk.

Three verbal expressions are repeated here:[126] *karleng* =ᵇ*wa* '(an infant) turn over,' =*rnayurr* =*nu-ngurru* 'develop physically,' and *rlerlewa* =*ya* 'crawl.' Discourse-deictic marking is seen on the second occurrence of each of the first two predicates, and on all subsequent predicates. The last two predicates ('I rose,' 'I walked') are marked as arising out of, and as being logically connected to the preceding discourse. Marking for subject-tracking alone would be redundant in this passage, and may anyway occur without specific deictic marking.

The marking of rhetorical anaphora is not unusual in Worrorra; a poem by Daisy Utemorrah about the characteristic movements of the northern quoll, reproduced here as (17.48), employs it in each occurrence of the verb:

---

[126] This repetition is not reflected in the translation.

(17.48: Daisy Utemorrah)
    Wijingarra ka**mny**eng
    Wijingarra ka**mny**eng
    Wijingarra dankewa dankewa ka**mny**eng
    Wijingarra krewa krewa ka**mny**eng
    Wijingarra rdurdurduwa darak ka**mny**eng

    The quoll goes along
    The quoll is going along
    The quoll goes along swaying from side to side
    The quoll goes along with its hindquarters raised
    The quoll scuttles off into its burrow

Discourse-deictic marking is ubiquitous in Worrorra, especially in Patsy Lulpunda's texts. It may be seen in many sentence examples in this chapter, and in most other chapters. Its occurrence is sometimes puzzling, as may be expected of a rhetorical-stylistic device. As an expression of a speaker's mood or intention, the motivation for its appearance may remain unclear if in any instance that intention is not overtly or explicitly evident.

17.7 Specific reference

By 'specific reference' is meant here our ability to identify a single instance of some type of thing; a 'uniquely determined instance' of something (Langacker 1991:103, see also Bickerton 1981:146-154). Uniqueness is central to the meaning of specificity: specific reference is reference made to a particular thing and to no other thing of its kind. Specificity is encoded anaphorically in language by way of grammatical forms that enable us to make such identifications.

17.7.1 Specificity

Specificity is marked in Worrorra by the adverbial suffix or postposition *-maan-* 'Specific' (glossed SPEC), with agreement forms as shown in Table 17.2:

    Table 17.2: *-maan-* 'SPECIFIC'

3a, 3p	maanja
3f	maanya
3w	maa (~maan)
3m	maanma (~maanba)

The 3w shape *-maan-* appears to be confined to the pronoun *=n* 'DEF' in *wunmaan* (see Table 17.3), the form *maa* appearing elsewhere.[127] The 3m shape *maanba* has an epenthetic suffix *-ba*, and occurs as a separate phonological word. These forms are attached as suffixes or postpositions, with no consistent pattern to the way in which the strength of the boundary is decided. Compare, for example, the suffixial form *Wurnbangkuwaamaanya* 'she of the Wurnbangku clan country/the Wurnbangku clan country is her own' in (17.33a) above, with the postpositional form *karraanya maanya* 'my own mother' in (17.49a) below.

    Specificity in Worrorra highlights a referent's uniqueness, by picking one item out from a background of similar items. So in (17.49a) the speaker refers to an action performed by one particular person, identified by being set apart from all the other people to whom the kinship term *karraanya* 'mother, mother's sister, classificatory mother' could apply. Likewise in (17.49b) the

---

[127] The homophony of *maa* '3mREF' and *maa* '3wSPECIFIC' appears to be fortuitous.

reference of the kinship noun *abiya* 'elder brother, father's father, son's son; clansman, etc' is narrowed down to just one particular person:

(17.49a)
Karraanya	maanya	karlaa	konerri	rambarrba
karraanya	maanya	karlaa	ka-Ø=ᵇwu-na-eerri	rambarrba
my.mother	3fSPEC	cover	3a-3=hit-PAST-PROG	avoidance.kin

nyangkanangkama,	ke	waa	bawarronya.
nyangka-nangka-ma	ke	waa	ba-ka-ᵇwarr-a=ᵇwu-nya
3fNAR-DAT-3m	and	not	CFT-3a-3p-EP=hit-PAST

It was my own mother who covered her avoidance-category kinsman (with her body), so they didn't kill him.

(b)
Abiyorle	maanja	karlelwana;	aworle	karlelwana
abiya-ᵏwurle	maanja	ka=rlelwa-na	awa-ᵏwurle	ka=rlelwa-na
El.Br-first	3aSPEC	3a=be.born-PAST	3aNAR-first	3a=be.born-PAST

ngayu	abi,	ngayanangka	maanja.
ngayu	abi	ngaya-nangka	maanja
I	El.Br	I-DAT	3aSPEC

My own elder brother was born first; he was born first, my elder brother, my own one.

(c)
Wundu-wundukum	maanma	bariy	kanunaarndu.
wundu-wundukum	maanma	bariy	ka=nu-na-aarndu
REDUP-dark	3mSPEC	rise	3a=be-PAST-DU

They got up very early one morning.

(d)
Mayarrungum	maanma	ajaaja	nganuna.
ma=yarrungu-ma	maan-ma	aja-aja	nga=nu-na
3m=QUANT-3m	SPEC-3m	sit-sit	1=be-PAST

I just stayed at the one place.

(e)
Marnu-marnu	kunyajengaal,	arri	arrkanangka
marnu-marnu	kuN-nyarr-nya=yi-ng-aal	arri	arr=ᵏwa-nangka
carry.on.shoulders	VCOMP-1px-EP=do-PAST-hither	we(exc)	px-NAR-DAT

maa,	nyangkaangkamaanja	arrkanangka	arri.
maa	nyangkaangka-maan-ya	arrkanangka	arri
3wSPEC	girls-SPEC-3p	our	we(exc)

We carried it back on our shoulders, it was only for us, just for us girls.

In (17.49c) one particular morning is singled out for attention, and in (17.49e) a quantity of food is referred to as belonging to one particular group of girls only, and to no-one else. Participant persons marked as SPECIFIC appear to attract adverbial celestial agreement forms (cf §17.5), as seen in *arri arrkangangka maa* 'belonging just to us (exc)' in (17.49e).

In keeping with its denotation of a single instance of some type of thing, *-maan-* often occurs with a sense meaning 'only,' as in (17.49e). In this function, specificity serves to *exclude* other members of a class from consideration. Some more examples of this sense of *-maan-* are seen in (17.50):

(17.50a)
Ricky-   maanja   kengenya.
Ricky   maan-ya   ka=[ya-nga]-yinya
NAME   SPEC-3a   3a=[go-TNS]-HORT
Only Ricky can go.

(b)
Wakumaada   maa.
black   3wSPEC
(I) only (have) black (tea)/only black (tea for me).

(c)
Eejamaanja   barnmarnja.
eeja-maan-ya   barnmarn-ya
man-SPEC-3a   sorcerer-3p
Only men are sorcerers.

(d)
Wrrorra   maa   kunyarloorlerri   wangalang   arrkununa.
wrrorra   maa   kuN-nyarr=rloo-rla-eerri   wangalang   arr-ngun=nu-na
Worrorra   SPEC   VCOMP-1px=speak-PAST-PROG child   1px-SJTV=be-PAST
We only spoke Worrorra when we were children.

(e)
Darrkawala   maanya   kubajunganangka   mana   Karnmanya.
Darrkawala   maan-nya   kuN-bwarr=yi-ng-a-nangka   mana   karnmanya
NAME   SPEC-3f   VCOMP-3p=do-PAST-EP-DAT   3mDEF   Kunmunya
Only Darrkawala got her name at Karnmanya.

(f)
Waa   barndaya   binyengenyeerri   kaarri.   Wondum   maanma
waa   barndaya   ba-nya=[ya-nga]-yinya-eerri kaarri   wondum   maanma
not   mainland   CFT-3f=[go-TNS]-PAST-PROG   3pNEG   sea   3mSPEC

rlerlewa   nyengerri,   jaa maa   rlerlewa   nyengerri
rlerlewa   nya=ya-nga-eerri   jaa maa   rlerlewa   nya=ya-nga-eerri
crawl   3f=go-TNS-PROG   all.the.way   crawl   3f=go-TNS-PROG

mangubam   maanma.
mud   3mSPEC
She didn't go up onto the land at all; she only crawled along through the sea, she crawled all the way through the mud.

Love (1934:31) describes a comparative degree formation in adjectives using *man'daga*, almost certainly *-maandaka* (|-maan-y₂aka| [SPEC-EMPH]).[128] Unelicited comparative expressions using *-maan-* 'SPEC' are rare in the database, those examples shown in (17.51) being exceptions:

---

[128] In elicitation my instructors agreed to forms modelled on Love's examples, such as those shown in (17.66):

(17.66a)
Awa   darranku   maandakeya   eeja   ardaarrawaya.
awa   darranku   maan-y₂aka-ya   eeja   arr=raarrawa-ya
3aNAR   strong   SPEC-EMPH-3p   man   3p=many-3p
He is stronger than the other men.

(17.51a)
Awa	imalalamaanja	inja.
awa	i=malala-maan-ya	inja
3aNAR	3a=handsome-SPEC-3a	3aDEF

He is particularly handsome/he is very handsome.

(b)
Ardaarramaanja	anja	dobiji	kawarronerri
arr=raarra-maan-ya	anja	do-biji	ka-^{b}warr-a=^{b}wu-na-eerri
3p=many-SPEC-3p	3pDEF	stone-REPEAT	3a-3p-EP=hit-PAST-PROG

karrku	wunu.
stone	3wDEF

A very large crowd of people stoned him.

While the sequence |-maan-y₂aka| [SPEC-EMPH] does occur in the database, the semantics of this construction is not comparative. In (17.52) a group of people are looking for a pair of dogs, a dog (*kanangkurri*) and a bitch (*kanangkuja*). When they spot them in the distance they say:

(17.52)
Nyina	ninjarrungumaandakuwalinya,	iyarrungumaandakuwali,
nyina	nyiN=yarrungu-maan-y₂aka-^{b}wali-nya	i=yarrungu-maan-y₂aka-^{b}wali
3fDEF	3f=QUANT-SPEC-EMPH-RESUM-3f	3a=QUANT-SPEC-EMPH-RESUM

kanangkurri	inja.
dog	3aDEF

There she is, (I mean) there he is, it's the dog.

Here the narrator has mistakenly used a feminine form and corrected herself to produce the masculine form of the adjective. As this is the only construction of this sort in the database, it is difficult to say very much about it except that (i) it is clearly a highly presentational form, (ii) it is also highly definite by virtue of the incorporated identity-maintenance morpheme, and (iii) the morphemes =*yarrungu* 'Quantifier' (here meaning 'one') and -*maan*- SPEC ('unique, only') co-occur, which is expected and quite typical, there being nine instances altogether in the database of these two morphemes co-occurring (cf 17.49d, 17.53c 17.57c & 17.60a).

The shape -*maan*- occurs systematically with the pronouns =*n* 'DEF' and =^{k}*wa(ya)* 'Contextual,' but the forms it occurs with appear to be very limited. Why this should be so is not clear: the most obvious answer is that neither Love nor I collected paradigms of these forms, but even so, there is a

---

(b)
Mana	darraanma	marnayurr	baandakama	mawa.
mana	darraanma	ma=rnayurr	maan-y₂aka-ma	mawa
3mDET	cockatoo	3m=adult	SPEC-EMPH-3m	3mNAR

This black cockatoo is bigger than that one.

In (17.66b) is seen an instance of nasal hardening across a word boundary, probably haplologically motivated from underlying *marnayurrba maandakama*, with the 3m allomorph -*ba* suffixed to the adjective. These examples are, however, possibly unconvincing as instances of traditional, pre-contact language use. The adjective =*rnayurr* 'adult, grown' Love appears to have interpreted as 'big' (1934:31), an interpretation followed apparently by Capell & Coate (1984), who wrongly use it to qualify *rdiyama* 'fighting club.' In (17.66b) my instructors probably used it to signify 'more fully grown, more fully fledged, elder.' Opposed to this, however, the consistent agreement of the adverb with the following object (3p and 3m respectively) suggests that these really may have been grammaticized constructions.

reasonably large number of =*n-maan* forms in the database inflected for agreement with the non-human macrogender, but none agreeing with the human macrogender. In contrast, forms in =*n-maanbali* are common in all non-participant agreement classes, and it is possible that the two sets are in partial complementary distribution (§17.7.2). Specific pronoun forms attested in the database are as shown in Table 17.3:

Table 17.3: specific pronouns

	=*n-maan*	=^{k}*waya-maan*
3a		aamaanja
3w	wunmaan	ke maa
3m	manmaan	maa maanma
	manmaanma	maamaan

It is impossible to say now whether the gaps in this paradigm are real or simply an artefact of fieldwork. Note the proliferation of terrestrial shapes compared to the paucity of human macrogender forms: the terrestrial expressions are used almost exclusively with reference to places. The 3m shapes listed are alternatives: the 3m specific-topic shape occurs as two words *maa maanma* when the 3m suffix appears, or as one word *maamaan* if it does not. Examples of their use in sentences are shown in (17.53):

(17.53a)
Irranangka	debarr	kenga,	ke	aamaanja
irra-nangka	debarr	ka=ya-nga	ke	a=^{k}wa(ya)-maan-ya
father-DAT	die	3a=go-PAST	and	3a=REF-SPEC-3a

kaangurrurlerri.
ka-Ø=^{k}wangurru-rla-eerri
3a-3=carry-PAST-PROG
His$_i$ father had died, and he$_i$ was all she had.

(b)
Wunmaan	joli	ngamnyanungaal.
^{k}wuN=n-maan	joli	nga-mnya=nu-ng-aal
3w=DEF-SPEC	return	1-DD=be-PRES-hither

I'll come straight back.

(c)
Maa	mayarrungum	maanma	kaaduna.
maa	ma=yarrungu-ma	maan-ma	kaarr=nu-na
3mREF	3m=QUANT-3m	SPEC-3m	3p=be-PAST

They all lived in the one place.

(d)
Manmaanma	dalorrba	kamnyanungu.
ma=n-maan-ma	dalorrba	ka-mnya=nu-ng
3m=DEF-SPEC-3m	sink.hole	3a-DD=be-PRES

He's still there in that sink hole.

The celestial reference of *wunmaan* in (17.53b) is to time (cf. 17.38d). Note in (17.53c) how the two words of the specific-topic shape (*maa ... maanma*) surround the adjective *mayarrunguma* 'one (terrestrial).'

The celestial specific-topic form *ke maa* has a widespread and semi-idiomatic identity-maintenance meaning: 'that same thing (= event, action)/again' (see also §10.2.2 (iv)). Related to this core meaning is a recapitulatory meaning: 'that's what/that's how ... (EVENT happened).' Its identity-maintenance use is shown in (17.54), and its more strictly recapitulatory use is exemplified in (17.55).

(17.54a)
Ke maa	kubajunganyarri		mamangkunu	rdaarrawa	wunu.
ke maa	kuN-ᵇwarr=yi-ng-a-nyarri		mamangkunu	ØN=raarrawa	wunu
thus	VCOMP-3p=do-PAST-EP-1pxDAT		morning	3w=many	3wDEF

They used to tell us the same thing every morning/ that's what they used to tell us every morning.

(b)
Ke maa	kaningaayenaarndeerri	ke maa.
ke maa	ka=ningaaye-na-ᵏwarndu-eerri	ke maa
thus	3a=do.MID-PAST-DU-PROG	thus

They did the same thing to each other all over again.

(c)
Ke maa	kunjinyaarndeerri.
ke maa	kuN-[Ø]=yi-nya-[ᵏwarndu]-eerri
thus	VCOMP-[3]=do-HORT-[DU]-PROG

They'll have to keep doing the same thing/ that's what they'll have to keep doing.

(d)
Ke maa	kunjingeerri	awa	irranangkorri	inja.
ke maa	kuN-Ø=yi-ng-eerri	awa	irra-nangkorri	inja
thus	VCOMP-3=do-PAST-PROG	3aNAR	father-3pDAT	3aDEF

Their father was doing the same thing again.

(17.55a)
Ke maa	kumnyengaara.
ke maa	kuN-Ø-mnya=yi-ng-ᵏwara
thus	VCOMP-3-DD=do-PAST-1DAT

That's what she said to me.

(b)
Ke maa	wali maa	warnda	kaaduna.
ke maa	wali maa	warnda	kaarr=nu-na
thus	PROG	dwell	3p=be-PAST

That's how they used to live.

(c)
Ke maa	daadaay	kunyarrbrangerri,	warlbirri	maa,
ke maa	daay-daay	kuN-nyarr=mra-nga-eerri	warlbirri	maa
thus	wear-REDUP	VCOMP-1px=gather-PAST-PROG	apron	3wSPEC

yawurna.
apron

That's what we used to wear, ((just) the pubic aprons called) warlbirri and yawurna.

The SPECIFIC morpheme *-maan-* occurs in some situations in the absence of any substantive to which it could refer. In these situations it appears to have an adverbial meaning, as 'only' or 'really.' In this function it may appear in suffixial form as *-maan* (17.56c), or in either of the 3m shapes *maanma* (17.56a) or *maanba* (17.56b & d):

(17.56a)
Malka	kanungaarndeerri	maanma.
malka	ka=nu-ng-a-ᵏwarndu-eerri	maanma
play	3a=be-PRES-EP -DU-PROG	only

They're only playing.

(b)
Bariy	bamnyanu	ngunju,	mee	maanba	ˈkaanjamnyaninjerri!
bariy	ba-mnya=nu	ngunju	mee	maanba	kaarr-nja-mnya=ninja-eerri
rise	CFT-DD=be	you	just	only	3p-2-DD=look-PROG

Get up, you! You're only just watching them!

(c)
Wali maa,	wali	yorr	kaajawanerri	ngurru,
wali maa	wali	yorr	kaarr-nya=ᵇwa-na-eerri	ngurru
PROG	PERF	sit.together	3p-EP=fall-TNS-PROG	here

malyaamaan	wali	yorr	kaajawanerri.
malyaa-maan	wali	yorr	kaarr-nya=ᵇwa-na-eerri
NO.REASON-just	PERF	sit.together	3p-EP=fall-TNS-PROG

They still go on living together here, just all hanging out around here.

(d)
Baanbaan	nyirdeen	kurri	maanba	wunu.
baanbaan	nyirr=reen	kuN-rra=yi	maanba	wunu
ignore	2p=real	VCOMP-2p=do	really	3wDEF

You really did ignore it/you just completely ignored it (= everything we'd told you).

Example (17.56d) is quite idiomatic, with the adjective =*reen* 'real' used in an adverbial sense fortuitously matching its English translation.

Far more frequently, however, the SPECIFIC morpheme occurs in its 3w shape, *maa*, in adverbial constructions of this kind. We have already seen it in this function in (17.49e) and (17.55c) above, as *ke maa* 'SPECIFIC TOPIC' above, as *maa* 'CONTINUOUS' when used with preverbs (§11.3.2), and as a frozen component of the adverbial expressions *wali maa* 'EXTENDED PROGRESSIVE' (§10.1.1 (ii)), *jaa maa* 'all the way, always' (§10.1.1 (v)), *mee maa* 'just, only' (§10.2.2 (i)), *kaarri maa* 'in vain' (§10.2.2 (ii)), and *karle maa* 'REMOTE PAST' (§10.4.1 (ii)). In this light observe that the expression *mee maanba* in (17.56b) is simply a terrestrial variant of the more usual celestial form *mee maa*. The use of terrestrial shapes in the sentences in (17.56) and in others like them probably has to do with the greater markedness value of the terrestrial class over the celestial: the SPECIFIC morphemes used in (17.56) convey the asymmetric semantics of markedness in the expressions in which they occur.

17.7.2 Definite and specific

The morphemes -*maan*- 'SPECIFIC' and -ᵇ*wali* 'RESUMPTIVE' are commonly combined to produce a form -*maanbali* (glossed FOCUS), used to refer to things that are both unique and highly definite within the context of discourse. These two shapes have already been seen together in (17.52), in words the literal translation of which must be something like 'that's the very one/that's just the one (we've been looking for).' The morpheme -*maanbali* is used to put an NP in front and centre stage under highlighting; it demands that a listener uniquely identify something highly pertinent and intensely topical. The word *maanbali* on its own may be used as an adverb modifying other adverbs (17.57a & b), adjectives (17.57c) or personal pronouns (17.57d & e), in which case it has a focusing function, usually translatable by 'just,' 'really' or something similar:

(17.57a)
Niji   maanbali   wunu   ajarrungoorri   maa   aja   kaadingeerri.
niji   maanbali   wunu   arr=yarrungu-oorri   maa   aja   kaarr=ni-ng-eerri
truly   FOCUS   3wDEF   3p=QUANT-TRI   3mREF   sit   3p=be-PRES-PROG
There really are only three of them out there.

(b)
Wenmaanbali   ngamnyengkunaal.
weni-maanbali   nga-mnya=ya-ngku-na-aal
now-FOCUS   1-DD=go-EP-PAST-hither
I've only just got here.

(c)
Juwalya   iyarrungu   maanbali   inja   kamarlaarndornaarndeerri.
juwalya   i=yarrungu   maanbali   inja   ka-[Ø]=marlaarndo-rna-[^{k}warndu$_A$]-eerri
path   3a=QUANT   FOCUS   3aDEF   3a-[3]=follow-PAST-[DU$_A$]-PROG
They had both come along on just this one path.

(d)
Awa   maanbali   akurla   inja.
3aNAR   FOCUS   demon   3aDEF
He really is a demon.

(e)
Angujabirri   ngunju   maanbali   ngurnaarnarlerri?
angujabirri   ngunju   maanbali   ngun-n-Ø=rnaarna-rla-eerri
why   you   FOCUS   2-INV-3/1=await-PAST-PROG
What the hell did I have to keep waiting for you for?

The shape *-maanbali* is also found combined systematically with the pronouns =*n* 'DEFINITE' and =^{k}*waya* 'CONTEXTUAL.' In this morphology these pronouns may be translated by something like 'this/that particular one.' Their forms are shown in Table 17.4:

Table 17.4: focal pronouns

	=*n-maanbali*	=^{k}*waya-maanbali*
3a	inmaanbali	aamaanbali
3f	nyinmaanbalinya	nyingke maanbali
3w	wunmaanbali	ke maanbali
3m	manmaanbalima	maamaanbalima
3p	anmaanbali	arrke maanbali

Unlike the specific pronoun shapes in Table 17.3, the focal pronouns in Table 17.4 show a full set of agreement-classes, through both human and non-human macrogenders. In fact it is likely that the focal forms serve both purposes in the human macrogender; that is, that the distinction between specific and focal pronoun reference is collapsed in the human macrogender. The exception of course is the 3a specific topic form *aamaanja*, which contrasts with the focal topic shape *aamaanbali*.

Although specific and focal pronouns do appear to have distributions and hence meanings that coincide closely, in some situations they can be seen to contrast. Observe the sentence in (17.58): here the words *wunmaanbali* and *wunmaanjirda* refer to *wunu ngaja* 'custom, precedent,' implied from context. In talking about Worrorra marriage arrangements the speaker corrects herself to take into account modern practices that deviate from the traditional ideal. In uttering this sentence the speaker realizes that modern practices are indeed not the same as those established in the dreamtime, and so replaces the identity-maintenance morpheme of the focal shape *wunmaanbali* with the suffix *-yirda* 'try' on the specific pronoun *wunmaan*:[129]

(17.58)
Wunmaanbali,	wunmaanjirda	kurdu
ᵏwuN-n-maan-ᵇwali	ᵏwuN-n-maan-yirda	kurdu
3w-DEF-SPEC-RESUM	3w-DEF-SPEC-try	follow

warrkunyonjeerri.		Nyarrkunyonjeerri
ᵏwuN-ngarr-ngun-nya=ᵇwu-ny-yeerri		ØN-nyarr-ngun-nya=ᵇwu-ny-yeerri
VCOMP-1pin-SJTV-EP=hit-MIR-PROG		VCOMP-1px-SJTV-EP=hit-MIR-PROG

aayaarndu	maanbali	ngaja	kaanyarrbanga,	Wadoy
a=ᵏwaya-ᵏwarndu	maanbali	ngaja	kaarr-nyarr=ma-nga	wadoy
3a=REF-DU	FOCUS	custom	3p-1px=get-PAST	spotted.nightjar

aa	Jrr'nkurn.
and	owlet.nightjar

This is the same [custom], this is the very [custom] that we (inc) still follow, are still trying to follow. We (exc) follow and keep the custom those two [established], Wadoy and Jinkurn.

Note also in this interesting sentence the occurrence of a dual focal-topic construction *(aayaarndu maanbali)*, and the anaphoric use of the verb classifier *nyarrkunyonjeerri* (§11.5.1). In the second sentence the speaker has altered the subject's person reference from 'we (inc)' to 'we (exc),' to take into account a non-Worrorra audience, and has used the inflected classifier of the predicate *kurdu kuN[ ]=ᵇwu* 'follow, adhere to a practice or custom' anaphorically to substitute for the whole predicate. Specificity *(-maan-)* and identity-maintenance *(-ᵇwali)* are both denoted in focal pronouns, and the semantics of either or both may be brought to the fore in any utterance. In (17.58) *wunmaanbali* carries an identity-maintaining sense, while *aayaarndu maanbali* has both specific and identity-maintenance sense meanings. More examples of focal forms with specific sense meanings are shown in (17.59). Other examples of focal pronouns used with an identity-maintenance sense are shown in (17.60). There (17.27) is repeated as (17.60a).

(17.59a)
Inmaanbali!	Inmaanbali!	Burnja	aaya	dindiwalya.
i=n-maanbali	i=n-maanbali	burn-ya	aaya	dindiwalya
3a=DEF-FOCUS	3a=DEF-FOCUS	PRO-3a	3aREF	falcon

That's the one! He's the very one! — that what's-his-name, the peregrine falcon.

(b)
Awa	anmaanbali	Jrr'nkurn	aanaanangkaya
awa	arr=n-maanbali	jrr'nkurn	awa-naa-nangka-ya
3aNAR	3p=DEF-FOCUS	spotted.nightjar	3aNAR-AUG-DAT-3p

wangalaalunguyu.
children
They're the ones, those children of Jinkurn's.

---

[129] See §10.2.1 (v).

(17.60a) (=17.27)

Wunmaanbali	ngarlangarla	jarrungu	nganngunjunu	ke.
ᵏwuN=n-maanbali	ngarlangarla	ØN=yarrungu	ØN-ngan-ngun=yi-nu	ke
3w=DEF-FOCUS	story	3w=QUANT	VCOMP-1-SJTV=do-2DAT	3wREF

The very same thing that I want to talk to you about.

(b)

Arrke	maanbali	burnarri	anja	ngaja	kaanyarrbanga.
arrke	maanbali	burnarri	anja	ngaja	kaarr-nyarr=ma-nga
3pREF	FOCUS	animals	3Pdef	custom	3p-1px=get-PAST

Those very same animals are the ones whose precedent we follow.

Just as the 3w SPECIFIC expression *ke maa* is used most often with a recapitulatory meaning (§17.7.1), so the 3w focal form *ke maanbali* occurs most often in the database in a quasi-idiomatic recapitulatory formula at the end of narrative texts: *kowa ke maanbali* 'that's the way it is (was)/that's how it came to be so.' The word *kowa* is a variant of *kawa* '3wNAR' confined to this expression. A typical example of this formula is seen in (17.61):

(17.61) (=16.1)

Kowa ke maanbali	wurnirndeerrngarri	angkarnongkiyena
kowa ke maanbali	ᵏwuN=rnirndeerr-ngarri	arr-ngka=rnongku-ye-na
that's.how.it.was	3w=old-REL	3p-SJTV=take.away-MID-PAST

inja	manjawarra.
3aDEF	berry.sp

That's what happened long ago when the manjawarra *berries were stolen.*

17.8 Predicate Marking

In §17.4 ideas from predicate logic were employed to characterize equational sentences, namely concepts of *terms* and *predicates*, and the equivalence of terms with subjects. Subjects, defined pragmatically, are what you are talking about; the things about which you have something to say. Predicates on the other hand are the pragmatic goals of a speech act: they are what motivate you to say something in the first place, the reason for undertaking a referring-and-predicating kind of act. In this section we will take note of a construction that signals predication in Worrorra; a syntax that will be referred to as predicate marking (PM).

Predicate marking in Worrorra is accomplished by the word *wali* followed by a form of either =*n* 'DEF' or =ᵏ*waya* 'CONTEXTUAL': that is, by either of the constructions *wali* =*n* or *wali* =ᵏ*waya*. The pronoun in these markers agrees in gender and number with the term in most cases (examples 17.62e & 17.63a are exceptions), that is to say that the predicate marker refers anaphorically to the term. This is not uncommon in languages; for example in Roper River Kriol in an expression such as *san im odwan* 'the sun is hot,' the predicate marker *im* refers anaphorically to the term, *san* 'sun.'

Predicate marking of this sort occurs only in verbless predicates, and serves to mark one of the expressions in a sentence as a predicate. We have already seen the predicate markers *wali maa* (7.14a, 11.14, 17.25a), *wali wunu* (9.25, 17.30c, 17.33b), *wali aaya* (7.13e) and *wali ke* (7.14a). The selection of either the =*n* or =ᵏ*waya* forms of a predicate marker has to do with whether or not the speaker considers the predicate to be topical in discourse context. Examples of predicate marking have already been seen in §17.4; some more examples are shown in (17.62):

(17.62a)
[TERM   ]   [PRED   ]
Inbali   irnayurri   wali inja.
i=n-ᵇwali   i=rnayurr-i   wali inja
3a=DEF-RESUM   3a=adult-3a   PM
He is the leader.

(b)
[PRED   ]   [TERM   ]
Kajaaya   wali aaya,   irlarlangkarra.
MoMoBr   PM   crocodile
He is my mother's mother's brother, the crocodile.

(c)
      [TERM   ]   [PRED   ]
Ke   awa   wijingarra,   inja   eeja   wali inja.
and   3aNAR quoll   3aDEF   man   PM
Now the quoll, he was the man.

(d)
[TERM   ]   [PRED   ]
Jrr'nkurn   inja   imalarri   wali inja.
jrr'nkurn   inja   i=malarr-i   wali inja
owlet.nightjar 3aDEF   3a=patrimoiety-3a PM
The owlet nightjar belongs to the Arrbalarriya moiety.

(e) (=6.26)
[TERM   ]   [PRED   ]
Nyingumbu   Kankanarlonya   wali nyina.
nyiN=ngumbu   kankanarlonya   wali nyina
3f=name   NAME   PM
Her name is Kankanarlonya.

(f) (=9.25)
[TERM   ]   [PRED   ]
Nyingumbu   wunu   jarrungaarndu   wali wunu.
nyiN=ngumbu   wunu   ØN=yarrungu-ᵏwarndu   wali wunu
3f=name   3wDEF   3w=quant-DU   PM
She has two names.

(g)
[TERM]   [PRED   ]
Awa   imalaleka   wali inja.
awa   i=malala-y₂aka wali inja
3aNAR   3a=handsome-EMPH PM
He's very handsome.

Note that in (17.62f) the predicate marker agrees in gender with the term (=*ngumbu wunu* 'name'), but that in (17.62e) the marker agrees with an NP dependent upon the same term (the referent of the 3f prefix *nyiN-*). In this example it appears that the gender of the predicate noun (*Kankanarlonya* - feminine) overrides that of the term. Again note in (17.63a) below that the participant pronoun *ngayu* 'I' takes celestial agreement markers (cf 17.36 above).

Some expressions of this sort lack terms (that is, are 'subjectless'); we have already seen examples in (7.14a): *Darraanma wali maa!* 'that's a black cockatoo!' *Marrirri wali ke!* 'that's a red-winged parrot!' These expressions consist of pure predication; that is to say that their 'terms' are extralinguistic, being the already-observed presence of the birds themselves. In other situations as well, narrative or extralinguistic contexts throw up unuttered terms upon which predications are made: non-narrative, non-'predicating-and-referring' speech is full of such expressions, which are pure predication, probably accounting for the majority of speech acts in everyday life. Example (17.63a) is an observed example, and (17.63b & c) are examples in which previous discussion provides instantiation of the term.

(17.63a) (= 7.2d)
'Angkuyu?' 'Ngayu   wali wunu!'
  who   I   PM
'Who is it?' 'It's me!'

(b) (=7.13e)
Irnayurri   wali aaya.
i=rnayurr-i   wali aaya
3a-ult-3a   PM
That one's an elder.

(c)
Nyangka   wali nyangke.
3fNAR   PM
That's her.

(d)
Arrwaawarnkarraya   wali anja,   karle   kaajooleengenya.
arr-waa=warnkarra-ya   wali anja   karle   kaarr=[yoolee-nga]-yinya
3p-AUG=grown-3p   PM   change-of-state   3p=[travel-TNS]-HORT
Now that they're grown up, let them go/They're grown up now, so let them go.

The term in (17.63d) is missing, presumably *arrka* '3pNAR' or similar. This appears to be a stylistic option not prohibited even from narrative contexts.

In some sentences the terms are subjunctive evidential clauses, which appear to be functioning as terms in these situations. Some examples of verbless matrices with subjunctive clauses acting as terms are shown in (17.64):

(17.64a)
[PRED   ]   [TERM   ]
Wurnirndeerr   wali ke   lalai,   waay   nyangkayabuna   wunu.
ʷwuN=rnirndeerr   wali ke   lalai   waay   nyaN-Ø-ngka=yabu-na   wunu
3w=old   PM   dreaming   throw   3f-3-SJTV=throw-PAST 3wDEF
It was way back in the dreamtime that he threw her up.

(b)
[TERM
'Kunyila   inja   barraninjerri,'   kaajunganangkorri
kunyila   inja   ba-rra=ninja-eerri   ØN-ngka-ᵇwarr-yi-ng-a-nangkorri
moon   3aDEF   sjtv-2p=look-cont   VCOMP-nom-3p=do-past-ep-3pdat

```
                                  ]          [PRED                                          ]
anja        wangalaalunguyu              wunu        wurnirndeerrngarri          wali wunu.
anja        wangalaalanguya              wunu        ᵏwuN=rnirndeerr-ngarri       wali wunu
3pDEF       children                     3wDEF       3w=old-REL                   PM
```
It was back in the old days, that they used to tell their children not to look at the moon.

(c)
```
[TERM
Wunu        nyirrbriaarndu         wakumaada       maade           kaninjeerri
wunu        nyirr=mri-ᵏwarndu      wakumaada       maade           ØN-ngka=ni-ny-yeerri
3wDEF       2p=head-DU             black           RESULT          3w-SJTV=be-MIR-PROG

          ]          [PRED                                                              ]
wunu,       manjawarra     wali aaya      durloo      irrangunyeerlaarndu.
wunu        manjawarra     wali aaya      durloo      i-[rra]-ngun-nya=ee-rla-[ᵏwarndu_A]
3wDEF       berry.sp       PM             present     3a-[2p]-SJTV-EP=place-PAST-[DU_A]
```
So now both your heads are black from where you put the manjawarra *berries.*

The sentences in (17.64) may be paraphrased in order to make their structures explicit, with the English copular verb 'be' substituting for the Worrorra predicate marker, as follows:

(17.64a)   [TERM his throwing her up TERM] [PRED *WAS* back in the dreamtime PRED]

(b)   [TERM their telling their children not to look at the moon TERM]
            [PRED *WAS* back in the old days PRED]

Example (17.64c) is more complex, as the predicate as well as the term contains a subjunctive clause, this time a relative clause dependent upon the noun *manjawarra* 'berry *sp.*' In this context the predicate still lacks a verb as its head constituent; the subjunctive predicate *durloo irrangunyeerlaarndu* 'where/when you (dual) placed it (masc)' functioning only to modify the predicate noun *manjawarra*:

(17.64c)   [TERM the cause of your heads being black TERM]
            [PRED *IS* those berries, and your placement of them PRED]

These are fairly complex constructions, and it is probably not coincidental that they all come from the final, recapitulatory sections of stories told by an articulate and accomplished narrator.

The sequences *wali =n* and *wali =ᵏwaya* do *not* function as predicate markers in predicates with head verbs. Of course these sequences are not uncommon in the language, and care must be taken to distinguish their use as predicate markers in verbless predicates from their functions in other situations. The Examples in (17.65) show these sequences in predicates with head verbs:

(17.65a)
```
Ngani       kurringaarndeerri                  wali        wunu?
ngani       kuN-rra=yi-ng-a-ᵏwarndu-eerri      wali        wunu
what        VCOMP-2p=do-PAST-EP-DU-PROG        PERF        3wDEF
```
What have you two been doing?

(b)
```
Yawarrarra      bungaju                 wali        ke.
yawarrara       ba-kuN-ngarr=yi         wali        ke
sink.PL         CFT-VCOMP-1pin=do       PERF        3wREF
```
We might all get drowned.

(c)
Eeja	maa	wali	yawak	kawana.
eeja	maa	wali	yawak	ka=ʷwa-na
man	3mREF	PERF	sink	3a=fall-PAST

A man had fallen down there.

In each of these sentences the word *wali* codes perfect aspect, that is, an indication that events in some non-present time are important for the way we react and behave in the present. In (17.65a) the determiner *wunu* marks the utterance as a definite-marked question (§17.1.1), and in (17.65b) the pronoun *ke* marks the projected event as highly salient (§17.3.2). In (17.65c) the pronoun *maa* substitutes anaphorically for the noun *dalorrba mana* 'sinkhole,' occurring in the preceding stretch of discourse.

Just as in Chapters Five and Seven we saw how pragmatic categories such as subject and topic are signalled morphologically by agreement marking, in this chapter we have seen how those categories are signalled morphologically as well as periphrastically. In Worrorra both agreement and word-order contribute to the coding of grammatical relations. The subject grammatical relation is coded at both levels: morphology reveals the class of the denotatum to receive subject coding, and word-order identifies which real-world member of that class is intended.

Eighteen: kinship terms

Worrorra kinship nouns are nominal expressions which include reference to the propositus (the 'owner,' a structurally dependant NP) as well as to the structural head, the person designated as being in such-and-such a relation to the propositus. Although the grammar of Worrorra kinship nominals has been discussed in §13.1, it is relevant here to provide an inventory of Worrorra kinship terms with their equivalents in the usual anthropological metalanguage. As well as being of interest in its own right, such an inventory can be useful in comparative exercises such as that undertaken by McConvell (1997).

Elkin (1954:49-79, see also Berndt & Berndt 1964:76) identifies the north Kimberley or Ungarinyin kinship system as one of five major types of kinship system found in Australia. It is based on the extended patrilineal family or clan as the basic-level category for the purpose of reckoning relatedness. In this system all members of an extended family are to a certain extent equivalent for kinship-reckoning purposes, and terminology reflects this situation. It is what Elkin calls a 'vertical' system, in the sense that entire extended families or clans are egocentrically labelled, with either all generations referred to by a single term, or with different terms used for alternating generations. This situation is evident in Lucich's (1968) exposition, and made explicit in Silverstein (nd 1).

Following Silverstein's arrangement, then, the inventory offered here will be considered in terms of patrilines, on the understanding that each Worrorra person is (among other things) a social expression of the intersection of four patrilines. In Worrorra society these patrilines are practically and functionally, if not theoretically, equivalent to patriclans. All patrilines/clans are shared out among the two sociocentrically-named, exogamous patrimoieties, *Arrbalarriya* (phonetic *Adbalarriya*) and *Arrwunarriya*. Unless otherwise stated, the kinship terms presented here are the default forms, indexed for a first person singular propositus ('my x').

As in most Australian societies, kinship dynamics are generated by patrilineage exogamy, and constrained by (i) equivalence of same-sex siblings, and (ii) equivalence of alternate generations. Marriages are arranged as exchanges of daughters between patrilines, a state of affairs the origin of which is described explicitly in the story *Jrr'nkurn aa Wadoy* 'The owlet nightjar and the spotted nightjar' (Lalbanda & Utemorrah 2000:43-50).

The system exhibits a degree of Omaha-type skewing (Lucich 1968) in which adjacent generations are collapsed in some contexts, and which makes it difficult clearly to distinguish generational moieties. So for example, sons and fathers call each other by the same term *(irraaya)*, and fathers' sisters and brothers' daughters call each other by the same term *(bamaraanya)*. More covertly, husbands and wives occupy harmonic generations in most contexts having to do with kinship reckoning, although it is clear from the prescribed marriage rule that husbands and wives may regularly come from adjacent or disharmonic generation levels (see Figure 18.2).[130] One of the outcomes of this situation is anomalous generational reckoning for categories such as *walbaya*

---

[130] North-eastern Arnhem Land or 'Murngin'-type marriage rules also display an alternation in the generation levels from which wives or husbands may be selected (Berndt & Berndt 1964:103).

'(woman's) DaHu,' which is a harmonic term when applied to a HuSiHu, but disharmonic when applied to a DaHu (see below). Nevertheless the cyclic alternation of kinship terms within patrilines and between generations is the most significant feature of Worrorra kinship terminology, and the clearest expression of the underlying meanings of these terms.

Most kinship nouns occur in male-female pairs, with the feminine form being based on the masculine shape with the addition of the feminine suffix *-nya*. Pairs of this sort are always related consanguineally, as brother and sister, never affinally. Three important brother-sister pairs however do *not* have the same phonological stem shapes: *irraaya* 'father, mans son' and his sister *bamaraanya*; *karraanya* 'mother, man's son's wife' and her brother *kakaaya*, and *mangkaanya* 'father's mother, wife' and her brother *waaya*. All others share stem shapes with siblings, eg *kulaaya* 'husband' and *kulaanya* 'husband's sister.'

Instead of using the usual first person Latin shifter *ego* to stand for a datum point in kinship reckoning, I will for the sake of clarity use the English second person shifters 'you' and 'your.' Also note that the system as described here is without doubt an idealized model of what should happen, and not necessarily what actually does happen to real people in real families. This is to say that the Worrorra kinship system is depicted here at the level of ideology, and that practice probably reflects this ideology to a greater or lesser extent.

18.1 Your own patrimoiety

18.1.1 Father's father's family

This is your 'own' clan, reckoned in terms of the dominant patrilineal ideology, and referred to by the inalienable noun *=rambim mana* 'patriclan,' so: *ngarambim mana* 'my family/clan.' This is the patriline of which you are identifiably a member, and to which you owe social allegiance.

Irraaya: male-male pairs in adjacent generations are *irraaya* to each other, hence 'father,' '(man's) son.' Also '(woman's) brother's son.' *Jijaaya* 'dad' is the baby-talk form. Plural: *irráarrèya*, vocative: *irra*.

-SJTV=^{k}wurlu: this term is formally a nominalized verb, unable to bear tense or aspect marking (§6.2.4). It refers to G^{-1} males in your own patriline, hence '(man's) son,' '(woman's) brother's son.' This term appears to be cognate with, and equivalent to the simplex nouns *kawurla* and *kawurlanya* 'patrilineal son, daughter' (see §7.7, §13.1.1).

Bamaraanya: male-female pairs in adjacent generations are *irraaya* and *bamaraanya* to each other. Hence 'FaSi,' '(man's) Da,' '(woman's) BrDa.' *Jijeenya* is the baby-talk form. Plural: *bamàamaréya*.

Ngawaaya (baby-talk *abiya*): ascending harmonic generation kinsman in your own patriline, hence 'ElBr,' 'FaFa.' Note that a *ngawaaya*'s wife (your FaMo) is referred to by the same term as your own wife, *mangkaanya*. By extension, *ngawaaya* is also used in other contexts to refer to all men in your own (your FaFa's) clan. Plural: *ngawaawaaya* and *abaabiya*, usually used to refer to all your clansmen as a group. Vocative: *abi*.

Ngawaanya (baby-talk *abeenya*): ascending harmonic generation kinswoman in your own patriline, hence 'ElSi,' 'FaFaSi.' Also 'clanswoman' by extension. Plural: *abàabiyéya*. Alternate generations of both men and women are *abi-abi* to each other.

=^{b}w(a)male: descending harmonic generation kinsperson in your own patriline. This nominal form takes derivational affixes as shown:

Ngawmaleya: 'my YrBr,' 'my (man's/woman's brother's) SoSo.' Also *iwamaleya/iwamaleyanangka* 'his little brother,' *nyimbamaleya/nyimbamaleyanangka* 'her little brother,' *ngarrwmaleya* 'our (inc) little brother' etc. Plural: *ngawmaamaleya* etc.

Ngawmalenya: 'my YrSi,' 'my (man's/woman's brother's) SoDa.' Also *iwamaleyinya/iwamaleyanangkanya* 'his little sister,' *nyimbamaleyinya/nyimbamaleyanangkanya* 'her little sister,' *ngarrwmalenya* 'our (inc) little sister' etc. Plural: *ngawmaamalenya* and *ngawmaamaleya* etc.

18.1.2 Mother's mother's family

This patriline contains a man's (or a woman's brother's) wife's mother, and full or partial avoidance constraints apply to people in this clan.

Kajaanya: 'MoMo,' 'MoBrWi.' All women of this patriline are *kajaanya* to you.

Kajaaya: 'MoMoBr,' 'MoMoFa.' All men of this patriline are *kajaaya* to you.

Kajaajeya (plural): all members of this clan.

Kaja: vocative form for any member of this clan, applied to all generation levels.

Kurrumaanya: 'WiFaWi (=WiMo),' 'WiBrWi' (ie 'FaMoBrWi,' 'FaMoBrSoWi').

Kurruma: 'WiMoBr.' *Kurruma* and *kurrumaanya* are in a full avoidance relationship to yourself, and are in the strong avoidance category called *rambarr mana:* (Ungarinyin 'barrier' - Alan Rumsey, pers comm).

18.2 Opposite patrimoiety

18.2.1 Mother's father's family

This clan represents your matriline, and contains your most important matrilineal kin. It is the patriline into which disharmonic kinsmen in your own clan (ie *irraaya*, both 'Fa' and '(man's) So') marry, hence it contains 'FaWi (=Mo)' and 'SoWi.'

Karraanya: disharmonic generation kinswoman in this patriline, hence 'Mo,' '(man's/woman's brother's) SoWi.' Plural: *karraarreya*. By extension, *karraarreya* is also used to refer to all the women in this clan. Baby-talk: *amakunya*,[131] plural *amaamakuyu*. Vocative: *karraa*.

Kakaaya: disharmonic generation kinsman in this patriline, hence 'MoBr,' 'MoBrSoSo,' 'SoWiBr.' Plural *kakaakaya*, also refers to all men of this clan.

Jamaaya: harmonic generation kinsman in this patriline, ie your matrilateral cross cousins and your mother's father, hence 'MoFa,' 'MoBrSo,' 'MoBrSoSoSo.' Baby talk: *babaaya*.

Jamaanya: harmonic generation kinswoman in this patriline, ie your female matrilateral cross cousins, hence 'MoFaSi,' 'MoBrDa.' Baby talk: *babaanya*. Vocative for both *jamaaya* and *jamaanya*: *jama*.

Maangkarreya: (plural) all members of this clan.

18.2.2 Father's mother's family

This is the clan that gives away its sisters and daughters to men in your own clan, in generations harmonic to yours, as wives.

Makamaka: all members of this clan

Maka: vocative form for any member of this clan, applied to all generation levels.

Mangkaanya: woman of opposite patrimoiety and in generation level harmonic to yours, hence 'FaMo.' Also a man's prescribed wife, 'FaMoBrDa' or 'FaMoBrSoDa,' hence 'Wi' and 'WiSi.' All women of this patriline are *mangkaanya* to you.

Makamangkaanya: all the women of this clan.

Waaya: 'FaMoBr (=WiFa),' 'FaMoBrSo (=WiBr).' All men of this patriline are *waaya* to you.

Waawaaya: (plural) all the men of this clan.

There is a further set of relations best understood as 'woman's in-laws,' that is, as the family of a woman's husband, and/or of a man's sister's husband. Although these people too may be members of one or more of the patrilines referred to above, their structural definitions come about by virtue of their affinal relationship to your own patriline. So, for instance, although *walbaya* '(woman's/man's sister's) DaHu,' *walbayinya* '(woman's/man's sister's) DaHuSi, *burda* '(woman's/man's sister's) DaSo' and *burdinya* '(woman's/man's sister's) DaDa' are all defined in terms of their membership of the

---

[131] *Amakunya* 'mum' is probably derived from *ngamuku-nya* 'breast-fem.'

patriline into which a woman's daughter marries, these same people are also members of your own MoMo patriline, and in some contexts you may refer to them as such, ie as *kajaanya* '(structural) MoMo' and *kajaaya* '(structural) MoMoBr.' We may therefore examine as well a woman's (or man's sister's) husband's family:

18.3 Woman's (man's sister's) husband's family

18.3.1 Husband's father's father's family

The clan into which a woman marries has four terms associated with it, which effectively partition the patriline by gender and generation. Terms in this patriline need to be understood from two points of view, from egocentric and sociocentric perspectives (Silvserstein n.d.1:12-13). In egocentric perspective the terms *kulaaya/kulaanya* and *ibaaya/ibaanya* refer to harmonic and disharmonic generation levels respectively, while in sociocentric perspective those terms refer less abstractly to 'woman's husband/husband's sister' and 'woman's child' respectively. The point to be noted is that the egocentric perspective maintains an alternation of generation levels, while in sociocentric perspective those levels are collapsed.

Kulaaya: (i) Viewed egocentrically, as a woman married into this line: male in harmonic generation to yourself, hence 'Hu,' 'HuFaFa,' '(woman's) SoSo.' (ii) Viewed sociocentrically, from the point of view of your own clan: husband of any woman in your patriline, hence 'FaFaSiHu,' FaSiHu,' 'SiHu,' '(man's) DaHu.' Note that 'FaSi' and '(man's) Da' are both *bamaraanya*, and that 'ElSi' and 'FaFaSi' are both *ngawaanya* or *abeenya*, so *kulaaya* may in this reckoning be resolved as 'husband of some sister or daughter,' or more broadly as 'man of the patriline to whom our sisters and daughters are given.'

Kulaanya: sister of *kulaaya*, hence 'HuSi' and '(woman's) SoDa' among others.

Ibaaya: Viewed egocentrically: male in disharmonic generation to yourself, hence 'HuFa,' '(woman's) So.' Viewed sociocentrically: son of any woman in your patriline, ie son of some *bamaraanya* or *ngawaanya*, hence 'SiSo,' '(man's) DaSo,' 'FaSiSo.'

Ibaanya: sister of *ibaaya*, hence 'HuFaSi,' '(woman's) Da,' 'SiDa' '(man's) DaDa,' 'FaSiDa.' Vocative for both *ibaaya* and *ibaanya: iba*.

Waraku and his sister *warakunya*: These kin are structurally equivalent to *ibaaya* and *ibaanya*, and may be considered as a specialized subset of those relations. (i) 'FaSiCh,' ie patrilateral cross-cousin, and (ii) 'HuFa' and 'HuFaSi.' Just as his *waaya* provides a man with a wife, so her *waraku* provides a woman with a husband. To understand how these two functions are congruent with each other and are equivalent to *ibaaya* 'woman's son,' the structure of Worrorra prescribed or ideal marriage relations must be noted.

Ideal marriage arrangements from a man's point of view are with a (classificatory) FaMoBrDa or FaMoBrSoDa (Silverstein nd 1:11). This arrangement is shown in Figure 18.1: note here that all the women in the patriline into which a man marries are *mangkaanya* to him, and all the men are *waaya*:

Figure 18.1: Man's prescribed marriage to a FaMoBrDa or a FaMoBrSoDa

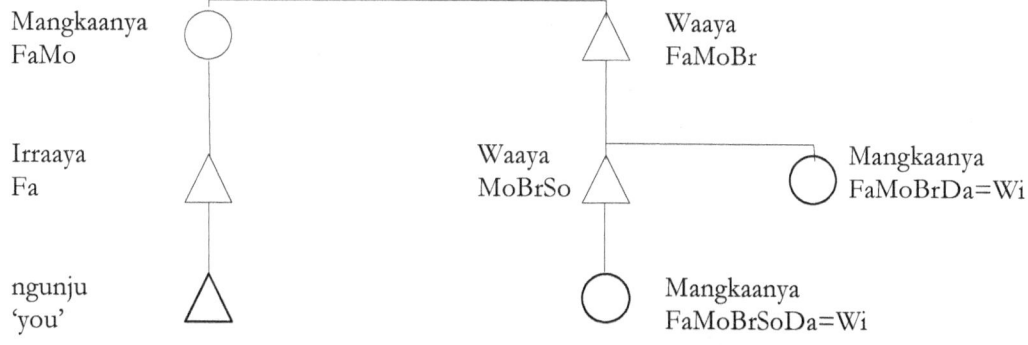

The key point here is that there are two possible locations in which a wife may be found. Now consider the same arrangement from a woman's point of view, with the first possibility shown in Figure 18.2, and the second in Figure 18.3.

Figure 18.2: Woman's prescribed marriage to a FaSiSoSo

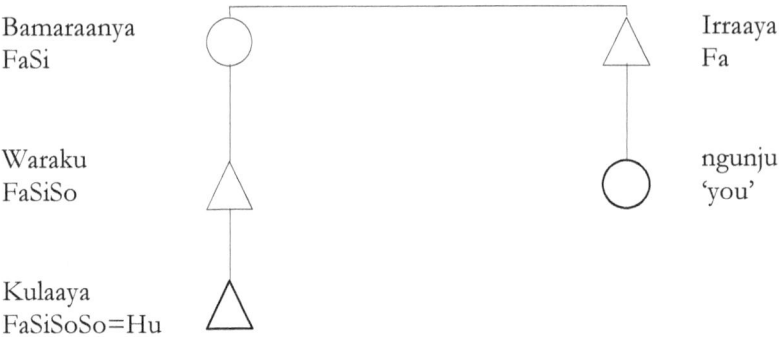

Figure 18.3: Woman's prescribed marriage to a FaFaSiSoSo

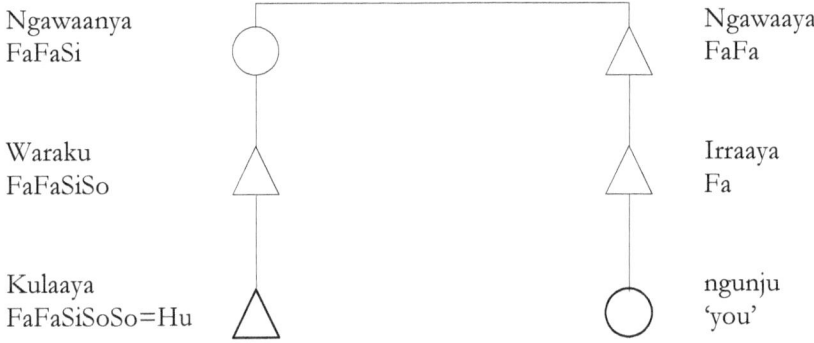

Note in Figure 18.2 that *waraku* appears in its 'correct' relation as patrilateral cross-cousin, ie as 'FaSiSo.' A *bamaraanya*'s husband is *kulaaya*, so the men in the patriline into which a woman marries alternate *kulaaya-waraku-kulaaya*, with *waraku* occupying in this instance the structural position otherwise occupied by *ibaaya* in this patriline. A woman's father-in-law or 'husband-giver' really is in this case a structural patrilateral cross-cousin.

Now note Figure 18.3: here *waraku* is not *bamaraanya*'s son at all, but the son of a *ngawaanya* 'FaFaSi,' a structural 'ElSi:' because of the rule of alternate generation equivalence, this *ngawaanya* is equivalent to an elder sister. And because of the rule of same-sex sibling equivalence, *ngawaanya*'s children are equivalent to your own children. Therefore *waraku* is indeed a structural (woman's) son, and again is equivalent to *ibaaya* 'woman's son.' In both positions, note, *waraku* consistently maintains its apparently most important denotation as 'husband's father/husband-giver.' Once this point is understood, its other interpretations, as 'son' and 'patrilateral cross-cousin' cease to be anomalous. And it becomes apparent that kinship nouns such as *waraku* cannot be understood in terms of focal relations only, but must be seen as indices or tokens ultimately of more abstract functional relationships within a particular structure.

18.3.2 Husband's mother's father's family

This clan is your husband's matriline, partitioned only by terms that encode gender.

Ngalinjaanya: any woman whom your husband refers to as *karraanya* 'mother/(man's) SoWi,' hence 'HuMo,' '(woman's) SoWi.' Also your husband's female (structural) matrilateral cross cousins (ie his *jamaanya*), 'HuMoBrDa' and 'HuMoFaSi.'

Ngalinjaaya: any man whom your husband refers to as *kakaaya* 'MoBr' or *jamaaya* 'matrilateral cross cousin.' Hence 'HuMoBr,' 'HuMoBrSo' and 'HuMoFa,' as well as '(woman's) SoWiBr.'

HuMo-SoWi pairs are *ngalinjaanya* to each other, and are also *rambarr* to each other. All people in this patriline, ie all your husband's *maangkarreya*, are referred to as either *ngalinjaanya* or *ngalinjaaya*, and all are *rambarr* with respect to yourself.

18.4 Woman's (man's sister's) husband's sister's husband's family

This is the family of your husband's sister's in-laws, ie the patriline that your husband and his sister in their turn refer to as *kulaaya/kulaanya* and *ibaaya/ibaanya*. By the logic of kinship geometry this patriline is equivalent to your own MoMo patriline, and accordingly you may refer to its members as *kajaaya* and *kajaanya*. People in this clan are structurally complementary to the people in your HuMoFa patriline, *ngalinjaanya* and *ngalinjaaya*. Note that as with the HuFaFa patriline (§18.3.1), the terms used to name people in this patriline employ a sociocentric view of it.

Walbaya and his sister *walbayinya*: most importantly, this category includes a woman's DaHu and his sister. DaHu-WiMo pairs are *walbaya* and *kurrumaanya* to each other respectively, and constitute the strongest form of the *rambarr* relationship category. More broadly, *walbaya* and *walbayinya* refer to all the relations that your husband calls *kulaaya* and *kulaanya*, hence: 'HuFaFaSiHu,' 'HuFaSiHu,' 'HuSiHu,' DaHu' and 'HuSiSoSo' and their sisters. Note that just as the terms *kajaaya* and *kajaanya* ignore generation levels, so the relationships listed here for *walbaya* and *walbayinya* range over G^{+2}, G^{+1}, G^{0}, G^{-1} and G^{-2}. That is, *walbaya* and *walbayinya* name the husband and husband's sister of any woman in your husband's patriline.

Burda and his sister *burdinya*: most importantly, this category includes a woman's DaSo and DaDa. More broadly, *burda* and *burdinya* refer to all the relations that your husband calls *ibaaya* and *ibaanya*, hence: 'HuFaSiSo,' 'HuFaSiDa,' 'HuSiSo,' 'HuSiDa,' 'DaSo' and 'DaDa,' as well as '(man's) SiDaSo' and '(man's) SiDaDa.' That is, *burda* and *burdinya* name the child of any woman in your husband's patriline.

An important skewing effect is evident here: although a husband's use of *kulaaya* and his wife's use of *walbaya* name the same person, *kulaaya* is a harmonic generation term, while *walbaya* is a disharmonic one. The same holds true for the generational references of *ibaaya* and *burda*. This asymmetry results from the generational mis-match inherent in a woman's prescribed marriage to a FaSiSoSo as shown in Figure 18.2, such that while *ibaanya* 'Da' is G^{-1}, *walbaya* 'DaHu' is G^{-2}, ie *walbaya* really is a harmonic generation relative after all. Nevertheless a *walbaya*'s children, *burda* and *burdinya*, follow their mother's generational position and are G^{-2} as well, thus pushing *walbaya* up into a structural G^{-1} position. This state of affairs gives evidence that male marriage to a FaMoBrDa is more underlyingly prescriptive than the alternative (to a FaMoBrSoDa).

A couple of cyclic patterns are evident in this account.[132] One pattern manifests an alternation of terms along harmonic/disharmonic generation lines within patrilines. These are the patrilines defined by reference to a parent's or husband's *father*:

---

[132] For a more detailed account of these cycles see Lucich (1968).

FaFa patriline	harmonic:	ngawaaya/ngawaanya (G^O, G^{+2}), ngawmaleya/ngawmalenya (G^O, G^{-2})
	disharmonic:	irraaya/bamaraanya ($G^{\pm 1}$)
MoFa patriline	harmonic:	jamaaya/jamaanya
	disharmonic:	karraanya/kakaaya
HuFaFa patriline	harmonic:	kulaaya/kulaanya
	disharmonic:	ibaaya/ibaanya
HuSiHuFaFa patriline	harmonic:	burda/burdinya
	disharmonic:	walbaya/walbayinya

Another pattern manifests no such alternation; these are the patrilines defined by reference to a parent's or husband's *mother*:

MoMo patriline:	kajaanya/kajaaya
FaMo patriline:	mangkaanya/waaya
HuMoFa patriline:	ngalinjaanya/ngalinjaaya.

Ultimately, Worrorra kinship terminology cannot be understood as referring to prototypical, focal members of some kinship category as proposed by Lounsbury (1965). Rather, kinship terms denote abstract relations that refer underlyingly to categories. As an example, take the noun *mangkaanya*, usually translated as 'wife.' This translation runs into difficulty with one of *mangkaanya*'s other translations, 'father's mother.' For a young child in a virilocal society a doting FaMo could indeed be the 'focal' denotation of *mangkaanya*, but as the child grows, so then the woman with whom he would come to live on intimate terms, and who bears his children would be likely to take over from his FaMo as the focal denotation of *mangkaanya*. The point is that a term like *mangkaanya* has no unique focal denotation; rather the term refers underlyingly to an entire set of women in a particular relationship to yourself within social structure. To capture the proper meaning of *mangkaanya*, a formula such as 'woman of opposite patrimoiety to propositus, and in harmonic generation level' is required, even though *mangkaanya*, as 'man's wife,' may only be a harmonic relation when adjusted out of the disharmonic position that results from generational skewing. Such a formula refers at base to a particular abstract relationship or social function, rather than to a unique focal relation. This is not to deny that the underlying denotation of *mangkaanya* may have to do with a function translatable by the English word 'wife;' what it does mean, however, is that wifehood in Worrorra and English involve quite different concepts. Rather the claim made here is that while reference is to one of a set of people in a particular social function, no one member of that set is prototypically representative of it, ie that no instance of the set stands for the set as a whole. An even clearer example is seen in the noun *irraaya* 'Fa,' '(man's) So:' fathers and sons refer to each other as *irraaya*, a term which clearly indexes both males as members of the same patriline. The part of the meaning that might be said to capture a so-called 'biological' basis, by which is or ought to be meant intimate interpersonal relations within a nuclear family, is of course the generational one, by the denotation of both persons as members of adjacent generations within their patriline.

Appendices

Appendix 1: texts

Appendix 1.1: Amy Peters, extract from Dawarraweyi

Ke   ingo   kubajeng,
ke   i-nga=ᵇwu   kuN-ᵇwarr-nya=yi-ng
3wREF   3a-1=hit   VCOMP-3p-EP=do-PAST
1. *Now they wanted to kill him,*

ke   nyina   kunjungaara,
ke   nyina   kuN-Ø=yi-ng-ᵏwara
3wREF   3fDEF   VCOMP-3=do-PAST-1DAT
2. *and she said to me,*

'kawarro   wali   aaya   ngamba   ke.
ka-ᵇwarr-a=ᵇwu   wali   aaya   ngamba   ke
3a-3p-EP=hit   PERF   3aREF   now   3wREF
3. *'they're going to kill him now.*

Wara   drarr   iwu   kaajunangka
wara   drarr   i=ᵇwu   ØN-ngka-ᵇwarr=yi-nangka
kangaroo   gut   3a=hit   VCOMP-SJTV-3p=do-DAT
4. *When they tell him to gut the kangaroo*

bariy   imurrkangurru,'   kunjungaara.
bariy   i=murrka-ngurru   kuN-Ø=yi-ng-ᵏwara
rise   3a=go.to-away   VCOMP-3=do-PAST-1DAT
5. *get up and go over to him,' she told me.*

Ke   Kengkunaaleerri,
ke   ka=ya-ngku-na-ᵏwaal-eerri
3wREF   3a=go-EP-PAST-hither-PROG
6. *And then he arrived,*

wara	irno	imaal	drarr	iwu	kubajunganangka.
wara	i=rno	i=ma-ᵏwaal	drarr	i=ᵇwu	kuN-ᵇwarr=yi-ng-a-nangka
k'roo	3a=DIST	3a=get-hither	gut	3a=hit	VCOMP-3p=do-PAST-EP-DAT

7. *and they told him to get that kangaroo and gut it.*

Ke	kamangaal	drarr	kamnyona,
ke	ka-Ø=ma-nga-ᵏwaal	drarr	ka-Ø-mnya=ᵇwu-na
3wREF	3a-3=get-PAST-hither	gut	3a-3-DD=get-PAST

8. *So he brought it over and set about gutting it,*

ke	nyangka	kunjungaara,	'bariy	imurrkangurru;
ke	nyangka	kuN-Ø=yi-ng-ᵏwara	bariy	i=murrka-ngurru
3wREF	3fNAR	VCOMP-3=do-PAST-1DAT	rise	3a=go.to-away

9. *and she said to me, 'get up and go over to him;*

ingo	kubajeerri	wali	aaya,'	kunjungaara.
i-nga=ᵇwu	kuN-ᵇwarr=yi-eerri	wali	aaya	kuN-Ø=yi-ng-ᵏwara
3a-1=hit	VCOMP-3p=do-PROG	PERF	3aREF	VCOMP-3=do-PAST-1DAT

10. *they want to kill him,' she said.*

Bariy	kangamurrkarlangurru	ngawurriy	kunyajungaarndu;
bariy	ka-nga=murrka-rla-ngurru	ngawurriy	kuN-nyarr=yi-ng-ᵏwarndu
rise	3a-1=go.to-PAST-away	drink.gravy	VCOMP-1px=do-PAST-DU

11. *I got up and went over to him, and drank the gravy in the body-cavity with him;*

ke	awa	laiburru	kanuna:
ke	awa	laiburru	ka=nu-na
3wREF	3aNAR	know	3a=be-PAST

12. *and so then he knew:*

ingo	ngana	kubajungu	inja.
i-nga=ᵇwu	ngana	kuN-ᵇwarr=yi-ng	inja
3a-1=hit	PROB	VCOMP-3p=do-PAST	3aDEF

13. *they must have wanted to kill him.*

'Ngayu	ingo	ngana	kubajungaara,
ngayu	i-nga=ᵇwu	ngana	kuN-ᵇwarr=yi-ng-ᵏwara
I	3a-1=hit	PROB	VCOMP-3p=do-PAST-1DAT

14. *'They must want to kill me,*

nyina	nganmurrkarlaal.'
nyina	ngan-n-Ø=murrka-rla-ᵏwaal
3fDEF	1-INV-3=go.to-PAST-hither

15. *she has come over to me.'*

Waa	ngawurriy	bungajin
waa	ngawurriy	ba-kuN-ngarr=yi-n
not	drink.gravy	CFT-VCOMP-1pin=do-NON.P

16. *We don't drink the cooked blood in the body-cavity of the kangaroo*

wunu	mrnangkanya	ngarrkunungu,
wunu	mrnangkanya	ngarr-ngun=nu-ng
3wDEF	teenage.girl	1pin-SJTV=be-PRES

17. when we are young teenage girls,

ke	arrka	maa	ngarrbardo.
ke	arrka	maa	ngarr-ᵇwarr=rno
3wREF	3pNAR	3wSPEC	1pin-3p=give

18. unless they give it to us.

Appendix 1.2: Amy Peters, Kanunerri Warruwarlu

Kanunerri	Warruwarlu.	Awa	iyarrungu	maa,	ke
ka=nu-na-eerri	Warruwarlu	awa	i=yarrungu	maa	ke
3a=be-PAST-PROG	PLACE	3aNAR	3a=QUANT	3mREF	and

1. *He used to live at Warruwarlu. He was on his own there, and*

buju	kenga	jubakuyaa	*flour,*	*sugar,*	kengkunaal
buju	ØN-Ø-ngka=yi-ng	jubakuya-aa	flour	sugar	ka=ya-ngku-na-ᵏwaal
finish	VCOMP-3-SJTV=do-PAST	tobacco-and	flour	sugar	3a=go-EP-PAST-hither

2. *when he had finished his tobacco, flour and sugar, he came*

Warruwarlaalb	barrawarranyine	Ngokonyini.	Arrka	anja
warruwarlu-aalb	barrawarra-nyine	ngoko-nyini	arrka	anja
PLACE-from	canoe-INST	PLACE-ENDPOINT	3pNAR	3pDEF

3. *from Warruwarlu in a canoe to Ngoko. Those*

kawarrarnaarnarlerri	eeja.	Ke	kawarrona,	we	kawarreerla.
ka-ᵇwarr-a=rnaarna-rla-eerri	eeja	ke	ka-ᵇwarr-a=ᵇwu-na	we	ka-ᵇwarr=ee-rla
3a-3p-EP=await-PAST-PROG	men	and	3a-3p-EP=hit-PAST	lie	3a-3p=place-PAST

4. *men were waiting for him. They bashed him and left him lying there.*

ke	we	kawanerri	ke	bariy	kanuna.	Karle	karlumarlum	wali.
ke	we	ka=ᵇwa-na-eerri	ke	bariy	ka=nu-na	karle	karlumarlum	wali
and	lie	3a=fall-PAST-PROG	and	rise	3a=be-PAST	now/then	evening	PERF

5. *He lay there, then [later] he got up. By then it was evening.*

Jaaya	karle	irnurru.	Ardurru	kaaduna	jaaya.	Kengkunaal
jaaya	karle	i=rnurru	arr=rnurru	kaarr=nu-na	jaaya	ka=ya-ngku-na-ᵏwaal
fish	now	3a=stinking	3p=stinking	3p=be-PAST	fish	3a=go-EP-PAST-hither

6. *His fish were by that time stinking. The fish were stinking. He came*

dambeenyinim.	'Angujaaw	ngunyangkunaal,	waraku?'	kungenganangka.
dambee-nyini-m	anguja-aaw	ngun=ya-ngku-na-ᵏwaal	waraku	kuN-nga=yi-ng-a-nangka
place-ENDPOINT-3m	what-time	2=go-EP-PAST-hither	FaSiSo	VCOMP-1=do-PAST-EP-DAT

7. *to the camp. 'When did you get here, cousin?' I asked him.*

'Wenmaanbali	ngamnyengkunaal,'	kunjungu.	'Anja	jaaya
weni-maanbali	nga-mnya=ya-ngku-na-ᵏwaal	kuN-Ø=yi-ng	anja	jaaya
now-FOCUS	1-DD=go-EP-PAST-hither	VCOMP-3=do-PAST	3pDEF	fish

8. *'I came in just now,' he said. 'The fish*

ardurrunyini,	weya?'	'Wenmaanbali	ngamnyengkunaal,'
arr=rnurru-nyini	weya	weni-maanbali	nga-mnya=ya-ngku-na-ᵏwaal
3p=stinking-ENDPOINT	hey	now-FOCUS	1-DD=go-EP-PAST-hither

9. *are stinking, hey?' 'I came in just now,'*

kunjungaara.	Walambarr	kunyajungu	anja	jaaya.
kuN-Ø=yi-ng-ᵏwara	walambarr	kuN-nyarr=yi-ng	anja	jaaya
VCOMP-3=do-PAST-1DAT	throw.out	VCOMP-1px=do-PAST	3pDEF	fish

10. *he told me. We threw out all the fish.*

Ardurrunyiniya	karle,	jaaya	walambarr	kunyajeng.
arr=rnurru-nyini-ya	karle	jaaya	walambarr	kuN-nyarr-nya=yi-ng
3p=stinking-ENDPOINT-3p	now	fish	throw.out	VCOMP-1px-EP=do-PAST

11. *By now they were all stinking, we threw out all the fish.*

Ke	anja	iyaaw	kawarraangurrurlu	irraaya,	ngayu irraaya
ke	anja	iyaaw	ka-ᵇwarr-a=ᵏwangurru-rla	irra-aa-ya	ngayu irra-aa-ya
and	3pDEF	abuse	3a-3p-EP=carry-PAST	father-1DAT-3a	I father-1DAT-3a

12. *Then they*[133] *abused my father, my own father,*

ngayu-ᵏwunya.	'Nyingke	nyimnyiyabaal!	Nyingke	nyimnyiyabaal!
ngayu-ᵏwunya	nyiN=ᵏwaya	nyiN-mnya=yabu-ᵏwaal	nyiN=ᵏwaya	nyiN-mnya=yabu-ᵏwaal
I-PURP	3f=REF	3f-DD=throw-hither	3f=REF	3f-DD=throw-hither

13. *because of me. 'Send her over here! Send her over here!*

Angujakunya	nyinjaangurreerri?	Ngurru	nyimnyengkunyaal	arrirnanya!'
anguja-ᵏwunya	nyiN-nja=ᵏwangurru-eerri	ngurru	nyiN-mnya=ya-ngku-nya-ᵏwaal	arri-rnanya
what-PURP	3f-2=carry-PROG	hither	3f-DD=go-EP-HORT-hither	we(exc)-LOC

14. *What are you hanging on to her for? Let her come over here to us!'*

kubajunganangka		ngayu	irraaya.	Ke awa
kuN-ᵇwarr=yi-ng-a-nangka		ngayu	irra-aa-ya	ke awa
VCOMP-3p=do-PAST-EP-DAT		I	father-1DAT-3a	and 3aNAR

15. *they said to my father. Then he*[134]

kunjunganangkorri,	'Angkuyu	iyaaw	kaangurreerri	
kuN-Ø=yi-ng-a-[nangka-ᵏwurri]	angkuyu	iyaaw	ka-Ø=ᵏwangurru-eerri	
VCOMP-3=do-PAST-EP-3pDAT	who	abuse	3a-3=carry-PROG	

16. *said to them, 'who is calling out abuse*

kakaaya	ngayanangka?	Nyirringkaal	ngurru	nyinyamanjoo!'
kaka-aa-ya	ngayu-nangka	nyirr=i-ᵏwaal	ngurru	nyirr-n-Ø-nya=manjoo
MoBr-1DAT-3a	I-DAT	2p=go-hither	hither	2p-inv-1/3-opt=kill

17. *to my uncle? Come here and I'll kill you!'*

kunjunganangkorri.	Ke	wali	kengkunaalkarndu
kuN-Ø=yi-ng-a-[nangka-ᵏwurri]	ke	wali	ka=ya-ngku-na-ᵏwaal-ᵏwarndu
VCOMP-3=do-PAST-EP-3pDAT	and	PERF	3a=go-EP-PAST-hither-DU

18. *he said to them. Then straight away two of them came*

jarriy	kumangaalkarndu	ke	kaajaweena,	ke
jarriy	kuN-Ø=ma-nga-ᵏwaal-ᵏwarndu	ke	kaarr-nya=ᵇwee-na	ke
run	VCOMP-3=get-PAST-hither-DU	and	3p-ep=hit.MID-PAST	and

19. *running over here and they fought, and*

jadbengurru	maa	wangarr	kawarrona.	Ke kawarraangurrurlu
jadbengurru	maa	wangarr	ka-ᵇwarr-a=ᵇwu-na	ke ka-ᵇwarr=ᵏwangurru-rla
for.good	3mREF	strike/kill	3a-3p-EP=hit-PAST	and 3a-3p=carry-PAST

20. *they knocked him down and killed him. They carried him*

---

[133] The men who had attacked Amy's cousin.
[134] Amy's cousin, the man from Warruwarlu.

hospital-kurru,   we   kawarreerla.   Nyina   ngaard nyingamanganangka
hospital-ngurru   we   ka-ᵇwarr=ee-rla   nyina   ngaard nyiN-nga=ma-nga-nangka
hospital-ALL   lie   3a-3p=place-PAST   3fDEF   ask   3f-1=get=PAST-DAT
21. *to the hospital and laid him down there. I asked*

kawurlanangkanya,   'Ngani kumnyeng,   irrolija?'   'Karle kaarri'
kawurla-nangka-nya   ngani   kuN-Ø-mnya=yi-ng   irra-wulija   karle   kaarri
BrCh-DAT-3f   what   VCOMP-3-DD=do-PAST   father-2KIN.POSS now   3pNEG
22. *his daughter about him, 'how is your father?' 'He is gone,'*

kunjungaara.   Ke   wundu-wundukum   maanma
kuN-Ø=yi-ng-ᵏwara   ke   wundu-wundukum   maanma
VCOMP-3=do-PAST-1DAT   and   REDUP-night   3mSPEC
23. *she told me. And that same night, before dawn,*

wali   wulaa   kaajingeerri   maa,   arrka   anja   eeja   belangkarraya
wali   wulaa   ØN-ngka-ᵇwarr=yi-ng-eerri   maa   arrka   anja   eeja   belangkarra-ya
PERF   sleep   VCOMP- SJTV-3p=do-PAST-PROG   PROG   3pNAR   3pDEF   men   many.people-3p
24. *while they were still sleeping, all the men*

Arnngarrngoyu   kaarringurru.   Jinalya   jadba   kawarraangurrurlu
Arnngarrngoya   kaarr=i-nga-ngurru   jinalya   jad-ᵇwa   ka-ᵇwarr-a=ᵏwangurru-rla
CLAN.NAME   3p=go-PAST-away   spear   straight-PROG   3a-3p-EP-take-PAST
25. *of the Arnngarrngoyu clan set out. They threw their spears at them*[135]

kulunu wulaa   kaajingeerri   maa.   Ke   kaanbajaangurrurlu
kulunu wulaa   ØN-ngka-ᵇwarr=yi-ng-eerri   maa   ke   kaarr-n-ᵇwarr-nya=ᵏwangurru-rla
sleep   rest   VCOMP-SJTV-3p=do-PAST-PROG   PROG   and   3p-INV-3p-EP-carry-PAST
26. *while they were still sleeping, until others dragged them*

marnonyinim.   Aworle   kawarrona   we   kawarreerla
ma=rno-nyini-m   awa-ᵏwurle   ka-ᵇwarr-a=ᵇwu-na   we   ka-ᵇwarr=ee-rla
3m=DIST-ENDPOINT-3m   3aNAR-first   3a-3p-EP=hit-PAST   lie   3a-3p=place-PAST
27. *away. They attacked the [younger] one first, and laid him out*

dambeemarnanya,   Arrigrarlya   dambeem   we   kawarreerla.
dambeema-rnanya   arr=grarlya   dambeem   we   ka-ᵇwarr=ee-rla
place-loc   3p=CLAN.NAME   place   lie   3a-3p=place-PAST
28. *in the camp, they laid him out in the camp of the Arrigralya clan.*

Arri   inja   iwarnkarra   kengangurru   marno   angkaweenerrima.
arri   inja   i=warnkarra   ka=ya-nga-ngurru   ma=rno   arr-ngka=ᵇwee-na-eerri-ma
CONJ   3aDEF   3a=elder   3a=go-TNS-away   3m=DIST   3p-SJTV=hit.MID-PAST-PROG-3m
29. *But the elder [brother] went over to the fighting-ground.*

Karraanya   maanya   karlaa   konerri.
karra-aa-nya   maanya   karlaa   ka-Ø=ᵇwu-na-eerri
mother-1DAT-3f   3fSPEC   cover   3a-3=hit-PAST-PROG
30. *My own mother covered him.*[136]

---

[135] at the men who had killed Amy's cousin.
[136] with her body.

Awa	maa	we	kawarreerla	aalkunya.	Karraanya	maanya
awa	maa	we	ka-ᵇwarr=ee-rla	aalkunya	karraanya	maanya
3aNAR	3mREF	lie	3a-3p=place-PAST	young.man	my.mother	3fSPEC

31. *They laid the young man out there. My own mother*

karlaa	konerri	rambarrba	nyangkanangkama,	ke
karlaa	ka-Ø=ᵇwu-na-eerri	rambarrba	nyangka-nangka-ma	ke
cover	3a-3=hit-PAST-PROG	avoidance.kin	3fNAR-DAT-3m	and

32. *protected her (classificatory) son-in-law and*

waa	bawarronya.	Karle.
waa	ba-ka-ᵇwarr-a=ᵇwu-nya	karle
not	CFT-3a-3p-EP=hit-PAST	that's.all

33. *they didn't kill him. That's all.*

Policeman-nyini	kaanyamurrkarlaal,	kaanyaangurrurlu	barndaya.
policeman-nyini	kaarr-n-Ø-nya=murrka-rla-ᵏwaal	kaarr-n-Ø-nya=ᵏwangurru-rla	barndaya
police-ENDPOINT	3p-INV-3-EP=go.to-PAST-hither	3p-INV-3-EP=carry-PAST	mainland

34. *Then a policeman came for them, and took them away overland.*

Karle.	kaarri.	Arrinyini	ajenga	*courthouse*	Broome,
karle	kaarri	arri-nyini	arr-nya=ya-nga	courthouse	Broome
now	3pNEG	we(exc)-ENDPOINT	1px-EP=go-TNS	court	PLACE.NAME

35. *That's all. We went to court in Broome,*

mara	nyarrkumbuna,	bamaraanya	ngayu.	Ngayu	mangkanangkanya
mara	ØN-nyarr-ngun=ᵇwu-na	bamara-aa-nya	ngayu	ngayu	mangka-nangka-nya
see	3w-1px-SJTV=hit-PAST	FaSi-1DAT-3f	I	I	wife-DAT-3f

36. *as witnesses, my aunt and I. His wife and I*

ajengaarndu	*courthouse*	Broome.	Karle.
arr-nya=ya-nga-ᵏwarndu	courthouse	Broome	karle
1px-EP=go-TNS-DU	court	PLACE.NAME	that's.all

37. *went to court in Broome. That's all.*

Appendix 2: irregular verb paradigms

Appendix 2.1: =ya 'go'

	NON-FUT PROG *I am/was going*	PAST *I went*	OPTATIVE *I will go*
1	ngengerri	ngenga	ngeyu
2	ngunyangerri	ngunyenga	ngunyayu
3a	kengerri	kenga	eyu
3f	nyengerri	nyenga	nyeyu
3w	kunyengerri	kunyenga	nyayu
3m	mengerri	menga	meyu
1pin	ngarringerri	ngarringa	ngarreyu
1px	arringerri	arringa	arreyu
2p	nyirringerri	nyirringa	nyirreyu
3p	kaarringerri	kaarringa	arreyu

	SUBJUNCTIVE *when I go/have gone*	HORTATIVE *let me go*	FUTURE PROG *we will be going*
1	nganngunyenga	ngengenya	ngeyeerri
2	ngunngunyenga	ngunyangenya	—[137]
3a	ingkenga	kengenya	—
3f	nyangkenga	nyengenya	—
3w	kenga	kunyangenya	—
3m	mangkenga	mengenya	—
1pin	ngarrkunyenga	ngarreyu	ngarriyeerri
1px	arrkunyenga	arreyu	arriyeerri
2p	nyirrkunyenga	nyirreyu	nyirriyeerri
3p	angkenga	kaarringenya	—

	CNTRFCT NON-PAST *I should go*	CNTRFCT PRES PROG *I should be going*	CNTRFCT PAST *I should have gone*
1	bangengan	bangenganjeerri	bangengenya
2	bungunyangan	bungunyanganjeerri	bungunyangenya
3a	bangkengan	bangkenganjeerri	bangkengenya
3f	binyengan	binyenganjeerri	binyengenya
3w	bungkengan	bungkenganjeerri	bungkengenya
3m	bamengan	bamenganjeerri	bamengenya
1pin	barringan	barringanjeerri	bangarringenya
1px	berringan	berringanjeerri	berringenya
2p	binyirringan	binyirringanjeerri	binyirringenya
3p	baarringan	baarringanjeerri	baarringenya

	CNTRFCT PAST PROG *I should have been going*	POTENTIAL *I might go*	AVERSIVE *I don't want to go*
1	bangengenyeerri	bangayu	bangayeerri
2	bungunyangenyeerri	bungunyeyu	bungunyeyeerri
3a	bangkengenyeerri	bangkayu	bangkayeerri
3f	binyengenyeerri	binyiyu	binyiyeerri
3w	bungkengenyeerri	bungkayu	bungkayeerri

---

[137] Unattested forms.

3m	bamengenyeerri		bamayu		bamayeerri
1pin	bangarringenyeerri		bangarriya		bangarriyeerri
1px	berringenyeerri		berriya		berriyeerri
2p	binyirringenyeerri		binyirriya		binyirriyeerri
3p	baarringenyeerri		baarriya		baarriyeerri

FRUSTRATIVE MOOD *I wanted to go/I nearly went*

1	nganngunyengenya	3m	mangkengenya
2	ngunngunyengenya	1pin	ngarrkunyengenya
3a	ingkengenya	1px	arrkunyengenya
3f	nyangkengenya	2p	nyirrkunyengenya
3w	kengenya	3p	angkengenya

IMPERATIVE *Go!*

Imp singular	bayu	*go!*
Imp sg continuous	bayeerri	*keep going!*
Imp plural	nyirriya	*you all go!*
Imp pl cont	nyirriyeerri	*you all keep going!*
Negative imp sg	bungunyeyeerri	*don't go!*
Neg imp pl	binyirriyeerri	*don't go, you lot!*

Appendix 2.2: =ya-ᵏwaal *'come'*

	AORIST	PRESENT PROG	PAST
	I come	*I'm coming*	*I came*
1	ngengkaal	ngengkaaleerri	ngengkunaal
2	ngunyangkaal	ngunyangkaaleerri	ngunyangkunaal
3a	kengkaal	kengkaaleerri	kengkunaal
3f	nyengkaal	nyengkaaleerri	nyengkunaal
3w	kunyangkaal	kunyangkaaleerri	kunyangkunaal
3m	mengkaal	mengkaaleerri	mengkunaal
1pin	ngarringkaal	ngarringkaaleerri	ngarringkunaal
1px	arringkaal	arringkaaleerri	arringkunaal
2p	nyirringkaal	nyirringkaaleerri	nyirringkunaal
3p	kaarringkaal	kaarringkaaleerri	kaarringkunaal

	PAST PROG	OPTATIVE	SUBJUNCTIVE PRES
	I was coming	*I will come*	*when I come*
1	ngengkunaaleerri	ngeyengkaal	nganngunyengkaal
2	ngunyangkunaaleerri	ngunyengkaal	ngunngunyengkaal
3a	kengkunaaleerri	eyengkaal	ingkengkaal
3f	nyengkunaaleerri	nyeyengkaal	nyingkengkaal
3w	kunyangkunaaleerri	nyayengkaal	kengkaal
3m	mengkunaaleerri	meyengkaal	mangkengkaal
1pin	ngarringkunaaleerri	ngarriyengkaal	ngarrkunyengkaal
1px	arringkunaaleerri	arriyengkaal	arrkunyengkaal
2p	nyirringkunaaleerri	nyirriyengkaal	nyirrkunyengkaal
3p	kaarringkunaaleerri	arriyengkaal	angkengkaal

	SUBJUNCTIVE PAST	SUBJUNCTIVE PAST PROG
	when I came	*when I was coming*
1	nganngunyengkunaal	nganngunyengkunaaleerri
2	ngunngunyengkunaal	ngunngunyengkunaaleerri
3a	ingkengkunaal	ingkengkunaaleerri
3f	nyingkengkunaal	nyingkengkunaaleerri
3w	kengkunaal	kengkunaaleerri
3m	mangkengkunaal	mangkengkunaaleerri
1pin	ngarrkunyengkunaal	ngarrkunyengkunaaleerri
1px	arrkunyengkunaal	arrkunyengkunaaleerri
2p	nyirrkunyengkunaal	nyirrkunyengkunaaleerri
3p	angkengkunaal	angkengkunaaleerri

	HORTATIVE	CNTRFCT NON-PAST	CNTRFCT PRES PROG
	let me come	*I should come*	*I should be coming*
1	ngengkunyaal	bangengkunaal	bangengkunaaljeerri
2	ngunyangkunyaal	bungunyangkunaal	bungunyangkunaaljeerri
3a	kengkunyaal	bangkengkunaal	bangkengkunaaljeerri
3f	nyengkunyaal	binyengkunaal	binyengkunaaljeerri
3w	kunyangkunyaal	bungkengkunaal	bungkengkunaaljeerri
3m	mengkunyaal	bamengkunaal	bamengkunaaljeerri
1pin	ngarringkunyaal	bangarringkunaal	bangarringkunaaljeerri
1px	arringkunyaal	berringkunaal	berringkunaaljeerri
2p	nyirringkunyaal	binyirringkunaal	binyirringkunaaljeerri
3p	kaarringkunyaal	baarringkunaal	baarringkunaaljeerri

	CNTRFCT PAST	POTENTIAL	AVERSIVE
	I should have come	*I might come*	*I don't want to come*
1	bangengkunyaal	bangengkaal	bangengkaaleerri
2	bungunyangkunyaal	bungunyengkaal	bungunyengkaaleerri
3a	bangkengkunyaal	bangkengkaal	bangkengkaaleerri
3f	binyengkunyaal	binyengkaal	binyengkaaleerri
3w	bungkengkunyaal	bungkengkaal	bungkengkaaleerri
3m	bamengkunyaal	bamengkaal	bamengkaaleerri
1pin	bangarringkunyaal	bangarringkaal	bangarringkaaleerri
1px	berringkunyaal	berringkaal	berringkaaleerri
2p	binyirringkunyaal	binyirringkaal	binyirringkaaleerri
3p	baarringkunyaal	baarringkaal	baarringkaaleerri

FRUSTRATIVE MOOD   *I wanted to come / I nearly came*

1	nganngunyengkunyaal	3m	mangkengkunyaal
2	ngunngunyengkunyaal	1pin	ngarrkunyengkunyaal
3a	ingkengkunyaal	1px	arrkunyengkunyaal
3f	nyingkengkunyaal	2p	nyirrkunyengkunyaal
3w	kengkunyaal	3p	angkengkunyaal

IMPERATIVE *Come!*

Imperative singular	bengkaal	*come!*
Imp sg continuous	bengkaaleerri	*keep coming!*
Imp plural	nyirringkaal	*you all come!*
Imp pl cont	nyirringkaaleerri	*you all keep coming!*
Negative imp sg	bungunyengkaaleerri	*don't come!*

| Neg imp pl | binyirringkaaleerri | *don't come, you lot!* |

The 1pin counterfactual series prefix *bangarr-* is in free alternation with *barr-*.

Appendix 2.3: kuN[ ]=yi *'do'*

	AORIST	PRES PROG	OPTATIVE
	I do it	*I'm doing it*	*I will do it*
1	kunge	kungayeerri	nge
2	kunjee	kunjiyeerri	je
3	kunju	kunjeerri	nye
1pin	waju	wajiyeerri	warre
1px	kunyaju	kunyajeerri	nyarre
2p	kurree	kurriyeerri	wurre
3p	kubaju	kubajeerri	barre

	PAST	PAST PROG
	I did it	*I was doing it*
1	kungenga	kungengeerri
2	kunjeenga	kunjeengeerri
3	kunjungu	kunjingeerri
1pin	wajungu	wajingeerri
1px	kunyajungu	kunyajingeerri
2p	kurreenga	kurringeerri
3p	kubajungu	kubajingeerri

	SUBJUNCTIVE PRES	SUBJUNCTIVE PAST
	when I do it	*when I did it*
1	nganngunju	nganngunjungu
2	jungunju	junngunjungu
3	ke	kenga
1pin	warrkunju	warrkunjungu
1px	nyerrkunju	nyarrkunjungu
2p	wurrangunju	wurrangunjungu
3p	kaaju	kaajungu

	CNTRFCT PRES	CNTRFCT PAST	POTENTIAL
	I should do it	*I should have done it*	*I might do it*
1	bungen	bungenya	bunge
2	binjeen	binjeenya	binjee
3	bungken	bungkenya	bungke
1pin	bungajin	bungajeenya	bungaju
1px	binyajin	binyajeenya	binyaju
2p	birreen	birreenya	birree
3p	bungkaajin	bungkaajeenya	bungkaaju

	AVERSIVE	HORTATIVE	FRUSTRATIVE MOOD
	I don't want to do it	*Let me do it*	*I wanted to do it / I nearly did it*
1	bungayeerri	kungenya	nganngunyenya
2	binjiyeerri	ju	jungunyenya
3	bungkayeerri	kunjinya	kenya

1pin	bungajeerri	waju	warrkunyenya
1px	binyajeerri	kunyaju	nyarrkunyenya
2p	birriyeerri	wurri	wurrangunyenya
3p	bungkaajeerri	kubajeenya	kaajenya

IMPERATIVE *Do it!*

Imp singular	ju ~ minye	*do it!*
Imp sg continuous	jiyeerri ~ minyiyeerri	*keep doing it!*
Imp plural	wurri	*you all do it!*
Imp pl cont	wurriyeerri	*you all keep doing it!*
Negative imp sg	binjiyeerri	*don't do it!*
Neg imp pl	birriyeerri	*don't do it, you lot!*

Appendix 3: transitive verb paradigm: =ᵇwu 'hit'

	PRES PROG *I'm hitting you*	PAST *I hit you*	OPTATIVE *I will hit you*
1>2	ngunbeerri	ngunbuna	ngunyo
1>3a	kangoyeerri	kangona	ingo
1>3f	nyingoyeerri	nyingona	nyingo
1>3w	kungoyeerri	kungona	ngo
1>3m	mangoyeerri	mangona	mango
1>2p	nyinbeerri	nyinbuna	nyinyo
1>3p	kaangoyeerri	kaangona	ango
2>1	janbeerri	janbuna	janyo
2>3a	kanjoyeerri	kanjona	injo
2>3f	nyinjoyeerri	nyinjona	nyinjo
2>3w	kunjoyeerri	kunjona	jo
2>3m	manjoyeerri	manjona	manjo
2>1px	kaanjoyeerri	kaanjona	anjo
2>3p	kaanjoyeerri	kaanjona	anjo
3>1	nganbeerri	nganbuna	nganyo
3>2	ngunbeerri	ngunbuna	ngunyo
3>3a	koyeerri	kona	ewu
3>3f	nyimbeerri	nyimbuna	nyewu
3>3w	kumbeerri	kumbuna	nyo
3>3m	moyeerri	mona	mewu
3>1pin	ngarrweerri	ngarrwuna	ngajo
3>1px	anbeerri	anbuna	anyo
3>2p	nyinbeerri	nyinbuna	nyinyo
3>3p	kaanbeerri	kaanbuna	anyo
1pin>3a	karrweerri	karrwuna	arro
1pin>3f	nyarrweerri	nyarrwuna	nyarro
1pin>3w	warrweerri	warrwuna	warro
1pin>3m	marrweerri	marrwuna	marro
1pin>3p	kaangarrweerri	kaangarrwuna	angarro
1px>2	ngunbarrweerri	ngunbarrwuna	ngunbarro
1px>3a	kerrweerri	kerrwuna	erro
1px>3f	nyerrweerri	nyerrwuna	nyerro
1px>3w	kunyarrweerri	kunyarrwuna	nyarro
1px>3m	merrweerri	merrwuna	merro
1px>2p	nyinbarrweerri	nyinbarrwuna	nyinbarro
1px>3p	kaanyarrweerri	kaanyarrwuna	anyarro
2p>1	jarroyeerri	jarrona	jarrewu
2p>3a	karroyeerri	karrona	irrewu
2p>3f	nyirroyeerri	nyirrona	nyirrewu
2p>3w	kurroyeerri	kurrona	wurrewu
2p>3m	marroyeerri	marrona	marrewu
2p>1px	kaarroyeerri	kaarrona	arrewu
2p>3p	kaarroyeerri	kaarrona	arrewu

3p>1	nganbarrweerri	nganbarrwuna	nganbarro
3p>2	ngunbarrweerri	ngunbarrwuna	ngunbarro
3p>3a	kawarroyeerri	kawarrona	ewarro
3p>3f	nyimbarrweerri	nyimbarrwuna	nyewarro
3p>3w	kubarrweerri	kubarrwuna	barro
3p>3m	maarrweerri	maarrwuna	mewarro
3p>1pin	ngarrbarrweerri	ngarrbarrwuna	ngarrbarro
3p>1px	anbarrweerri	anbarrwuna	anbarro
3p>2p	nyinbarrweerri	nyinbarrwuna	nyinbarro
3p>3p	kaanbarrweerri	kaanbarrwuna	anbarro

		SUBJUNCTIVE PRES	HORTATIVE
		when I hit you	*let me hit you*
1>2		ngunngumbu	ngunbeenya
1>3a		inganngumbu	kangonya
1>3f		nyanganngumbu	nyangonya
1>3w		nganngumbu	kungonya
1>3m		manganngumbu	mangonya
1>2p		nyinngumbu	nyinbeenya
1>3p		anganngumbu	kaangonya
2>1		janngumbu	janbeenya
2>3a		injangunbu	kanjonya
2>3f		nyinjangunbu	nyinjonya
2>3w		jungunbu	kunjonya
2>3m		manjangunbu	manjonya
2>1px		anjangunbu	kaanjonya
2>3p		anjangunbu	kaanjonya
3>1		nganngumbu	nganbeenya
3>2		ngunngumbu	ngunbeenya
3>3a		ingko	konya
3>3f		nyangko	nyimbeenya
3>3w		ko	kumbeenya
3>3m		mangko	monya
3>1pin		ngarrkumbu	ngarrweenya
3>1px		anngumbu	anbeenya
3>2p		nyinngumbu	nyinbeenya
3>3p		angko	kaanbeenya
1pin>3a		arrkumbu	arrwu
1pin>3f		nyarrkumbu	nyarrwu
1pin>3w		warrkumbu	warrwu
1pin>3m		marrkumbu	marrwu
1pin>3p		angarrkumbu	angarrwu
1px>2		ngunngumbarrwu	ngunbarrweenya
1px>3a		errkumbu	erro
1px>3f		nyerrkumbu	nyerrwu
1px>3w		nyarrkumbu	nyarro
1px>3m		merrkumbu	merrwu

1px>2p	nyinngumbarrwu		nyinbarrweenya
1px>3p	anyarrkumbu		anyarro
2p>1	jarrangunbu		jarronya
2p>3a	irrangunbu		karronya
2p>3f	nyirrangunbu		nyirronya
2p>3w	wurrangunbu		kurronya
2p>3m	marrangunbu		marronya
2p>1px	arrangunbu		kaarronya
2p>3p	arrangunbu		kaarronya
3p>1	nganngumbarrwu		nganbarrweenya
3p>2	ngunngumbarrwu		ngunbarrweenya
3p>3a	ingkaarrwu		kawarronya
3p>3f	nyangkaarrwu		nyimbarrweenya
3p>3w	kaarrwu		kubarrweenya
3p>3m	mangkaarrwu		maarrweenya
3p>1pin	ngarrkubarrwu		ngarrbarrweenya ~ ngarrbarronya
3p>1px	anngumbarrwu		anbarrweenya ~ anbarronya
3p>2p	nyinngumbarrwu		nyinbarrweenya
3p>3p	angkaanbarrwu		kaanbarrweenya

		CNTRFCT PRES	CNTRFCT PAST
		I should hit you	*I should have hit you*
1>2		bungunbun	bungunbeenya
1>3a		bangon	bangonya
1>3f		binyingon	binyangonya
1>3w		bungon	bungonya
1>3m		bamangon	bamangonya
1>2p		binyinbun	binyinbeenya
1>3p		baangon	baangonya
2>1		banyanbun	banyanbeenya
2>3a		banjon	banjonya
2>3f		binjon	binjonya
2>3w		binjon	binjonya
2>3m		bamanjon	bamanjonya
2>1px		baanjon	baanjonya
2>3p		baanjon	baanjonya
3>1		banganbun	banganbeenya
3>2		bungunbun	bungunbeenya
3>3a		bangkon	bangkonya
3>3f		binyimbeen	binyimbeenya
3>3w		bungkon	bungkonya
3>3m		bamon	bamonya
3>1pin		bangarrwun	bangarrweenya
3>1px		benbun	benbeenya
3>2p		binyinbun	binyinbeenya
3>3p		baanbun	baanbeenya
1pin>3a		barrwun	barrweenya

1pin>3f	binyangarrwun ~ binyarrwun	binyangarrweenya ~ binyarrweenya	
1pin>3w	bungarrwun	bungarrweenya	
1pin>3m	bamangarrwun	bamangarrweenya	
1pin>3p	baangarrwun	baangarrweenya	
1px>2	bungunbarrwun	bungunbarrweenya	
1px>3a	berrwun	berrweenya	
1px>3f	binyerrwun	binyerrweenya	
1px>3w	binyarrwun	binyarrweenya	
1px>3m	bamerrwun	bamerrweenya	
1px>2p	binyinbarrwun	binyinbarrweenya	
1px>3p	baanyarrwun	baanyarrweenya	
2p>1	banyarron	banyarronya	
2p>3a	barron	barronya	
2p>3f	binyarron	binyarronya	
2p>3w	burron	burronya	
2p>3m	bamarron	bamarronya	
2p>1px	baarron	baarronya	
2p>3p	baarron	baarronya	
3p>1	banganbarrwun	banganbarrweenya	
3p>2	bungunbarrwun	bungunbarrweenya	
3p>3a	bawarron	bawarronya	
3p>3f	binyimbarrwun	binyimbarrweenya	
3p>3w	bungkaarrwun	bungkaarrweenya	
3p>3m	bamaarrwun	bamaarrweenya	
3p>1pin	bangarrbarrwun	bangarrbarrweenya	
3p>1px	benbarrwun	benbarrweenya	
3p>2p	binyinbarrwun	binyinbarrweenya	
3p>3p	baanbarrwun	baanbarrweenya	

	POTENTIAL	AVERSIVE	FRUSTRATIVE MOOD
	I might hit you	*I don't want to hit you*	*I wanted to/nearly hit you*
1>2	bungunbu	bungunbeerri	ngunngumbeenya
1>3a	bango	bangoyeerri	inganngumbeenya
1>3f	binyango	binyangoyeerri	nyanganngumbeenya
1>3w	bungo	bungoyeerri	nganngumbeenya
1>3m	bamango	bamangoyeerri	manganngumbeenya
1>2p	binyinbu	binyinbeerri	nyinngumbeenya
1>3p	baango	baangoyeerri	anganngumbeenya
2>1	banyanbu	banyanbeerri	janngumbeenya
2>3a	banjo	banjoyeerri	injangunbeenya
2>3f	binjo	binjoyeerri	nyinjangunbeenya
2>3w	binjo	binjoyeerri	jungunbeenya
2>3m	bamanjo	bamanjoyeerri	manjangunbeenya
2>1px	baanjo	baanjoyeerri	anjangunbeenya
2>3p	baanjo	baanjoyeerri	anjangunbeenya
3>1	banganbu	banganbeerri	nganngumbeenya
3>2	bungunbu	bungunbeerri	ngunngumbeenya

3>3a	bangko	bangkoyeerri	ingkonya
3>3f	binyimbu	binyimbeerri	nyangkonya
3>3w	bungko	bungkoyeerri	konya
3>3m	bamo	bamoyeerri	mangkonya
3>1pin	barrwu	barrweerri	ngarrkumbeenya
3>1px	benbu	benbeerri	anngumbeenya
3>2p	binyinbu	binyinbeerri	nyinngumbeenya
3>3p	baanbu	baanbeerri	angkonya
1pin>3a	barrwu	barrweerri	arrkumbeenya
1pin>3f	binyangarrwu ~ binyarrwu	binyangarrweerri ~ binyarrweerri	nyarrkumbeenya
1pin>3w	bungarrwu	bungarrweerri	warrkumbeenya
1pin>3m	bamangarrwu	bamangarrweerri	marrkumbeenya
1pin>3p	baangarrwu	baangarrweerri	angarrkumbeenya
1px>2	bungunbarrwu	bungunbarrweerri	ngunngumbarrweenya
1px>3a	berrwu	berrweerri	errkumbeenya
1px>3f	binyerrwu	binyerrweerri	nyerrkumbeenya
1px>3w	binyarrwu	binyarrweerri	nyarrkumbeenya
1px>3m	bamerrwu	bamerrweerri	merrkumbeenya
1px>2p	binyinbarrwu	binyinbarrweerri	nyinngumbarrweenya
1px>3p	baanyarrwu	baanyarrweerri	anyarrkumbeenya
2p>1	banyarro	banyarroyeerri	jarrangunbeenya
2p>3a	barro	barroyeerri	irrangunbeenya
2p>3f	binyarro	binyirroyeerri	nyirrangunbeenya
2p>3w	burro	burroyeerri	wurrangunbeenya
2p>3m	bamarro	bamarroyeerri	marrangunbeenya
2p>1px	baarro	baarroyeerri	arrangunbeenya
2p>3p	baarro	baarroyeerri	arrangunbeenya
3p>1	banganbarrwu	banganbarrweerri	nganngumbarrweenya
3p>2	bungunbarrwu	bungunbarrweerri	ngunngumbarrweenya
3p>3a	bawarro	bawarroyeerri	ingkaarrweenya
3p>3f	binyimbarrwu	binyimbarrweerri	nyangkaarrweenya
3p>3w	bungkaarrwu	bungkaarrweerri	kaarrweenya
3p>3m	bamaarrwu	bamaarrweerri	mangkaarrweenya
3p>1pin	bangarrbarrwu	bangarrbarrweerri	ngarrkubarrweenya
3p>1px	benbarrwu	benbarrweerri	anngumbarrweenya
3p>2p	binyinbarrwu	binyinbarrweerri	nyinngumbarrweenya
3p>3p	baanbarrwu	baanbarrweerri	angkaanbarrweenya

IMPERATIVE *Hit me!*

	SG	PROG SG	PL	PROG PL
1	janbu	janbeerri	jarro	jarroyeerri
3a	iwu	iweerri	irro	irroyeerri
3f	nyimbu	nyimbeerri	nyirro	nyirroyeerri
3w	minyo	minyoyeerri	wurro	wurroyeerri
3m	mo	moyeerri	marro	marroyeerri
1px	anbu	anbeerri	arro	arroyeerri
3p	anbu	anbeerri	arro	arroyeerri

	NEGATIVE IMPERATIVE	*Don't hit me!*
	SG	PL
1	banyanbeerri	banyarroyeerri
3a	banjoyeerri	barroyeerri
3f	binjoyeerri	binyirroyeerri
3w	binjoyeerri	burroyeerri
3m	bamanjoyeerri	bamarroyeerri
1px	baanjoyeerri	baarroyeerri
3p	baanjoyeerri	baarroyeerri

Appendix 4: the Role-and-Reference account of predicate linkage

A predicate is the pragmatic goal of a speech act; that is to say, a predicate is the reason why someone embarks on an act of predicating-and-referring in the first place. For the purpose of investigating linkage phenomena, clauses may be considered as expanded predicates, and grammatically equivalent to them. In Role-and-Reference grammar the clause is understood to be a layered structure, with an inner level called a nucleus, an intermediate level called a core and an outer layer called a periphery. The nucleus contains the non-finite manifestation of a lexical predicate — a denotative *type* in Langacker's (1991:51) terms. The core contains the nucleus and its 'core arguments,' which are nowhere well defined, but which are considered generally to be the subject and in transitive predicates one or two of its objects, selected on morphosyntactic grounds by access to a privileged position within the clause, and on semantic grounds by reference to a hierarchy of semantic roles (Foley & Van Valin 1984:59). The periphery contains everything outside the core. Also distinguished (*ibid*: 208) are two relevant categories in the clause, a substantive category called 'constituents' and a non-substantive one called 'operators.' The operators over a predicate are aspect, directionality, modality, reality status, tense, evidentiality and illocutionary force. These operators are said to have scope over (be an integral part of, make specific reference to) different layers of the clause. Aspect and directionality have scope over the nucleus, with aspect the innermost operator. Modality has scope over the core, and reality status, tense, evidentiality and illocutionary force have scope over the periphery, proceeding outwards from reality status as the innermost peripheral operator to illocutionary force as the outermost one (*ibid*: 224).

Turning to a consideration of linkage patterns between predicates, the authors propose a theory of juncture (*ibid*:188), in which it is claimed that when predicates are joined, the juncture occurs at one and (usually) only one particular structural level; either nuclear, core or peripheral. So that when predicates are joined at the nuclear level (nuclear juncture), the combined nuclei form a complex nucleus and share all core and peripheral arguments. When predicates are joined at the core level, two cores usually share at least one core argument and all peripheral arguments. Peripheral junctures are the loosest sort of union and allow for a variety of different syntactic arrangements. Predicates, then, may be joined at any one of the three structural levels, and the level of juncture will have grammatical consequences in each instance.

While the theory of juncture refers to the clausal level at which linkage occurs, a second parameter, called nexus, refers to the syntactic nature of that linkage (*ibid*: 238). The two diagnostics of nexus type are embeddedness and dependency. Embeddedness refers to a part-whole relationship between predicates, as when one predicate is a part of another. In this situation the embedded constituent is typically a core argument or an adverbial component of another predicate, which is in turn superordinate. Dependency refers to whether or not two linked, non-embedded predicates may be independently specified for the operators that have scope over the level at which the juncture occurs. If the predicates may be independently specified (for, say, modality at a core-level juncture), then the nexus is said to be *independent*. If independent specification is not possible, the nexus is said to be *dependent*. When a nexus is both non-embedded and independent, it is said to be an instance of *coordinate* nexus. When a nexus is non-embedded but dependent, it is said to be an instance of *cosubordinate* nexus. And when a nexus is embedded, it is also dependent, and is said to be an instance of *subordinate* nexus (*ibid*: 241). For descriptive purposes, this amounts to a diagnostic flow-chart: at the first decision-node, linkages are distinguished embedded from non-embedded, and embedded linkages are labelled subordinate. At the second decision-node, non-embedded linkages are distinguished dependent from independent: dependent, non-embedded linkages are labelled cosubordinate, while independent, non-embedded ones are labelled coordinate.

Each type of nexus may be represented at all three levels of juncture and vice-versa: each level of juncture may exhibit all three types of nexus, making a total of nine types of linkage, defined jointly by nexus type and juncture level. The typology created by this methodology is therefore discovered from the interaction of three independent diagnostic parameters: embeddedness, dependency and level of juncture. As mentioned, the theory of juncture claims that generally, juncture occurs between predicates (or 'juncts' – member units of a juncture – *ibid*: 188) at the same structural level of each conjoined clause; that is to say, nuclear with nuclear, core with core and peripheral with peripheral levels. However there is one nexus type in which we might expect this not to be necessarily the case. Subordinate nexus involves the possibility of not only a core-level predicate becoming embedded in the core of a superordinate junct, but also an entire periphery becoming embedded as a core argument of some other predicate. As Foley & Van Valin (*ibid*: 256) point out, direct or indirect speech quotation is probably the most common occasion on which an entire periphery is embedded in the core layer of a *verbum dicendi* as a core argument (a sentential object). Bare nuclei may also be embedded as core arguments of superordinate predicates, as is seen in §11.5.2. Peripheral- and nuclear-core subordinations are marked nexus types (*ibid*: 251), being exceptions to the general principle that predicate linkage occurs between juncts at the same structural level.

It is claimed that the type of predicate linkage available in any context has grammatical consequences that may be discerned both inside and outside the clause. Certainly, the methodology described here is able to make distinctions among complex predicates in Worrorra, and these distinctions have significance for our understanding of the grammar as a whole. In Chapter 11 various types of predicate linkage in Worrorra are described in terms of the theory of nexus and juncture outlined above, on the understanding that a systematic syntactic account of these phenomena will permit an appreciation of their semantics.

Appendix 5: bibliographical note

This appendix briefly outlines just a few of the more interesting and accessible publications on Worrorra culture and society, and some on related and neighbouring languages.

Although by now a little out of date, the best bibliography of manuscripts and publications directly relating to Worrorra may be found in William McGregor (1988) *Handbook of Kimberley Languages v 1*, as well as references to materials on related and neighbouring languages. McGregor's *Languages of the Kimberley, Western Australia* (2004) likewise contains extensive information on Worrorra and its neighbouring languages. The Australian Institute of Aboriginal and Torres Strait Islander Studies' on-line Mura catalogue (<http://www.aiatsis.gov.au/collections/muraread.html>) has an even longer list of references (over 250), found by searching under both 'Worora' and 'Worrorra.'

The predecessors to this description of Worrorra grammar are *A Grammar of Worrorra* (Clendon 2000) and a Worrorra Dictionary, both available from the Kimberley Language Centre. The dictionary has been published by the language centre as *A Provisional Worrorra Dictionary* (Clendon et al 2000). Both these works are intended for use as resources in any future language revival programme that Worrorra people may decide to undertake.

Major accessible published accounts of Worrorra society and culture include pre-eminently J R B Love's *Stone-Age Bushmen of To-day* (1936, reissued 2009), and the film *Lalai Dreamtime*. The eminent scholar of Kimberley rock art, David Welch, has re-issued Love's book under the title *Kimberley people: Stone-Age Bushmen of To-day*. Welch has added a wealth of additional photographs taken from a variety of early twentieth-century sources, additional text, and a brief biography of J R B Love. This book is beautifully produced and is a valuable compilation of original sources and photographs of Worrorra society at and near the time of European contact, and well worth close attention.

An historical account dealing with missionaries and their activities in and around Worrorra country is provided by Maisie McKenzie in *The Road to Mowanjum* (1969). Of McKenzie's history and others like it Noel Pearson has written (1986:161): 'The works of the Church authors are a product of a mission tradition of paternalism and they are inadequate, misleading and offensive.'

Other important descriptions of Worrorra society published in journals are Love 1917 and 1935, and Blundell 1980 and Blundell & Layton 1978. Love's master's dissertation, *The Grammatical Structure of the Worora Language of north-western Australia* (1934) is widely referred to in this book, and was published by Lincom Europa in 2000.

Also of considerable cultural interest is Andreas Lommel (1952) *Die Unambal: Ein Stamm in Nordwest Australien*, recently translated into English by Ian Campbell (1997) as *The Unambal: a tribe in northwest Australia*. This is an account of the Frobenius expedition to the north Kimberley in 1938, and while mainly concerned with Wunambal-speaking people to the north of Worrorra country, is yet a fascinating and very important early study of the north Kimberley culture complex. In similar vein, Valda Blundell and Donny Woolagoodja (2005) have produced a worthwhile emic account of religion and land in the north-west Kimberley.

Peter Lucich worked at Mowanjum in the 1960s, and produced a monograph on kinship (Lucich 1968), relating to Worrorra, Ngarinyin and Wunambal people there. However as the author's concern is to investigate a particular problem in typology this book is not intended to provide a comprehensive description of the kinship system. It contains some omissions, and is somewhat confusing in the way it is set out. Lucich 1969 is a set of transcriptions and translations of Worrorra stories told by Heather Umbagai's mother, the late Elkin Umbagai. The transcriptions are not phonemic and appear to omit some discourse-cohesive material; nonetheless they overlap with the stories recorded by Daisy Utemorrah and provide a very important perspective on those stories.

Capell and Coate's (1984) comparative-typological monograph *Comparative Studies in Northern Kimberley Languages* surveys aspects of the grammars of Wunambal, Worrorra, Ungarinyin and an unnamed speech variety which they refer to as the Forrest River Language. Their study makes reference to other north Kimberley speech varieties as well. Many of their Worrorra sentence examples are taken from Love's (1934) thesis, and many of those that are not, are wrong. The volume includes nonetheless some interesting observations.

Eric Vasse (Eric Vászolyi) worked extensively on Wunambal in the 1970s (see eg Vászolyi 1976, Vasse 1991), and more recently Thérèse Carr (2000) has described this language. An important unpublished resource on Wunambal is Vászolyi 1972.

Alan Rumsey's 1982 *Intra-Sentence Grammar of Ungarinyin* remains the definitive description of Ungarinyin, and Rumsey has more recently described the Kimberley language Bunuba (2000).

William McGregor has written extensively on Kimberley languages, not only on Gooniyandi (1990), Warrwa (1994) and Nyulnyulan (eg 1996b & 1999), but also on the northern Wororan language called Gunin or Kwini (1993). William McGregor and Alan Rumsey (2009) is a detailed argument in support of an hypothesis that the north-west Kimberley (Wororan) languages are related phylogenetically; this monograph contains many insightful observations and comparisons among the languages of this region.

Three important recent publications are Utemorrah (2000), Lalbanda & Utemorrah (2000) and Lalbanda, Peters & Utemorrah (2000). These bilingual collections of traditional stories and oral histories provide a definitive perspective on Worrorra culture and folklore, and contain a good deal of the written material upon which this account is based.

References

Aikhenvald, Alexandra, 2004, *Evidentiality*. Oxford: Oxford University Press.
Aikhenvald, Alexandra & R M W Dixon (eds), 2003, *Studies in evidentiality*. Amsterdam: John Benjamins.
Akerman, Kim, 1975, 'The double raft or *kalwa* of the west Kimberley.' *Mankind* 10 (1): 20-23.
Allen, Cynthia, 1995, *Case marking and reanalysis: grammatical relations from Old to Early Modern English*. Oxford: Oxford University Press.
Amberber, M, B Baker & M Harvey (eds), 2010, *Complex predicates: cross-linguistic perspectives on event structure*. Cambridge: Cambridge University Press.
Andrews, Avery, 1985, 'The major functions of the noun phrase.' In Tim Shopen (ed), *Language typology and syntactic description*. Cambridge: Cambridge University Press (62-154).
Austin, J L, 1955, *How to do things with words*. Oxford: Oxford University Press (1976 edition).
Austin, Peter, 1981, *A grammar of Diyari, South Australia*. Cambridge: Cambridge University Press.
Austin, Peter, & Joan Bresnan, 1996, 'Non-configurationality in Australian Aboriginal languages.' *Natural Language and Linguistic Theory*, 14: 215-268.
Baker, Brett & Mark Harvey, 2003, 'Word structure in Australian languages.' *Australian Journal of Linguistics*, 23 (1): 3-33.
Berndt, R M & C H Berndt, 1964 [1977], *The world of the first Australians*. 2nd edition, Sydney: Ure Smith.
Bernstein, Judy, 2001, 'The DP hypothesis: identifying clausal properties in the nominal domain.' In M Baltin & C Collins (eds), *Handbook of contemporary syntactic theory*. Malden, MA: Blackwell (536-561).
Bickerton, Derek, 1981, *The roots of language*. Ann Arbor MI: Karoma.
Bloomfield, Leonard, 1933, *Language*. London: George Allen & Unwin.
Blundell, Valda, 1975, *Aboriginal adaptation in northwest Australia*. Doctoral dissertation, Madison: University of Wisconsin.
Blundell, Valda, 1976, *A dictionary of Worrorra terms for material culture, environmental features and related items, with Ngarinjin equivalents*. Typescript, 69 pp, Ottawa.
Blundell, Valda, 1980, 'Hunter-gatherer territoriality: ideology and behaviour in northwest Australia.' *Ethnohistory*, 27 (2): 103-117.
Blundell, Valda & Robert Layton, 1978, 'Marriage, myth and models of exchange in the west Kimberleys.' *Mankind*, 11 (3): 231-245.
Blundell, Valda, & Donny Woolagoodja, 2005, *Keeping the Wanjinas fresh*. Fremantle: Fremantle Arts Centre Press.
Brisard, Frank, 1997, 'The English tense system as an epistemic category: the case of futurity.' In M Verspoor, K Lee & E Sweetser (eds), *Lexical and syntactical constructions and the construction of meaning*. Series: Current Issues in Linguistic Theory, vol 150. Amsterdam: John Benjamins (271-285).
Brock, Peggy, 1993, *Outback ghettos: Aborigines, institutionalization and survival*. Cambridge: Cambridge University Press.

Capell, Arthur, 1976, 'Rapporteur's introduction and summary.' In R M W Dixon (ed) (615-625).
Capell, Arthur, & Howard H J Coate, 1984, *Comparative studies in northern Kimberley languages*. Canberra: Pacific Linguistics, Series C, no 69.
Carr, Thérèse, 2000, *Wunambal: a language of the north-west Kimberley region, Western Australia*. Masters dissertation, University of New England, Armidale.
Chappell, Hilary, & W B McGregor, 1996, 'Prolegomena to a theory of inalienability.' In Chappell & McGregor (eds) (3-30).
Chappell, Hilary, & W B McGregor (eds), 1996, *The grammar of inalienability: a typological perspective on body-part terms and the part-whole relation*. Berlin: Mouton de Gruyter.
Clendon, M, 1988, 'Some features of Manjiljarra nominalized relative clauses.' In Peter Austin (ed), *Complex sentence constructions in Australian languages*. Amsterdam: John Benjamins (193-204).
Clendon, M, 1999, 'Worora gender metaphors and Australian prehistory.' *Anthropological Linguistics*, 41 (3): 308-355.
Clendon, M, 2000, *A grammar Of Worrorra*. Halls Creek: Kimberley Language Resource Centre.
Clendon, M, 2006, 'Re-assessing Australia's linguistic prehistory.' *Current Anthropology*, 47 (1): 39-62.
Clendon, M, 2009, 'Dog-people: the meaning of a north Kimberley story.' In H Koch & L Hercus (eds), *Aboriginal placenames: naming and re-naming the Australian landscape*. (Aboriginal History Monograph 19) Canberra: Aboriginal History Inc and ANU E Press.
Clendon, M, Patsy Lalbanda, Amy Peters & Daisy Utemorrah, 2000, *A provisional Worrorra dictionary*. Halls Creek: Kimberley Language Resource Centre.
Corbett, Greville, 1991, *Gender*. Cambridge: Cambridge University Press.
Cusack, Susan, & Michael Cusack, 1989, 'Our year in the wilderness.' *Australian Geographic*, 15: 72-91.
DeLancey, Scott, 1997, 'Mirativity: the grammatical marking of unexpected information.' *Linguistic Typology*, 1: 33-52.
DeLancey, Scott, 2001, 'The mirative and evidentiality.' *Journal of Pragmatics*, 33: 369-382.
Dixon, R M W (ed), 1976, *Grammatical categories in Australian languages*. Canberra: Australian Institute of Aboriginal Studies.
Dixon, R M W, 1979, 'Ergativity.' *Language*, 55: 59-138.
Dixon, R M W, 1980, *The languages of Australia*. Cambridge: Cambridge University Press.
Dixon, R M W, 1982, *Where have all the adjectives gone?* Amsterdam: Mouton.
Dixon, R M W, 2002, *Australian languages: their nature and development*. Cambridge: Cambridge University Press.
Dixon, R M W, 2010, 2012, *Basic linguistic theory, volumes 1-3*. Oxford: Oxford University Press.
Dixon, R M W, & Alexandra Aikhenvald, 1997, 'A typology of argument-determined constructions.' In J Bybee, J Haiman & S Thompson (eds), *Essays on language function and language type, dedicated to T Givón*. Amsterdam: John Benjamins (71-113).
Dixon, R M W, & Alexandra Aikhenvald, 2000, 'Introduction.' In R M W Dixon & A Aikhenvald (eds), *Changing valency: case studies in transitivity*. Cambridge: Cambridge University Press (1-29).
Elkin, A P, 1954, *The Australian Aborigines: how to understand them*. Sydney: Angus & Robertson.
Evans, Nicholas, 2003, *Bininj Gun-Wok: A pan-dialectal grammar of Mayali, Kunwinjku and Kune*. Canberra: Pacific Linguistics.
Fillmore, Charles, 1968, 'The case for case.' In E Bach & R Harms (eds), *Universals of linguistic theory*. New York: Holt, Rinehart & Winston (1-90).
Foley, William, 1986, *The Papuan languages of New Guinea*. Cambridge: Cambridge University Press.
Foley, William, 1991, *The Yimas language of Papua New Guinea*. Stanford, CA: Stanford University Press.
Foley, William, 1993, 'The conceptual basis of grammatical relations.' In W Foley (ed), *The role of theory in language description*. Berlin: Mouton de Gruyter (131-174).
Foley, William, 2010, 'Events and serial verb constructions.' In Amberber, Baker & Harvey (eds) (79-109).
Foley, William, & Robert Van Valin, 1984, *Functional syntax and universal grammar*. Cambridge: Cambridge University Press.
Givón, Talmy, 1994, 'The pragmatics of de-transitive voice: functional and typological perspectives of inversion.' In T Givón (ed), *Voice and inversion*. Amsterdam: John Benjamins.

Greenberg, J H, 1988, 'The first person inclusive dual as an ambiguous category.' *Studies in Language,* 12 (1): 1-18.

Grice, H Paul, 1975, 'Logic and conversation.' In Peter Cole & Jerry Morgan (eds), *Syntax and semantics 3: speech acts.* New York: Academic Press (41-58).

Grossman, Lt Col Dave, 1995, *On killing.* Boston: Little, Brown & Co.

Haiman, John, 1978, 'Conditionals are topics.' *Language,* 54: 564-588.

Hale, Kenneth, 1976, 'The adjoined relative clause in Australia.' In R M W Dixon (ed), *Grammatical categories in Australian languages.* Canberra: Australian Institute of Aboriginal Studies (78-105).

Harvey, Mark, 1992, *The Gaagudju people and their language.* Doctoral dissertation, University of Sydney.

Heath, Jeffrey, 1975, 'Some functional relationships in grammar.' *Language,* 51: 89-104.

Heath, Jeffrey, 1976, 'Substantival hierarchies: addendum to Silverstein.' In R M W Dixon (ed) (172-190).

Heath, Jeffrey, 1978, *Ngandi grammar, texts and dictionary.* Canberra: Australian Institute of Aboriginal Studies.

Heath, Jeffrey, 1984, *Functional grammar of Nunggubuyu.* Canberra: Australian Institute of Aboriginal Studies.

Hosokawa, Komei, 1996, "'My face *am* burning!': quasi-passive, body parts, and related issues in Yawuru grammar and cultural concepts.' In Chappell & McGregor (eds) (155-192).

Hyman, Larry, 1975, *Phonology: theory and analysis.* New York: Holt, Rinehart & Winston.

Johnson, Mark, 1987, *The body in the mind: the bodily basis of meaning, imagination and reason.* Chicago: University of Chicago Press.

Johnson, Mark, 2007, *The meaning of the body: aesthetics of human understanding.* Chicago: University of Chicago Press.

Keen, Ian, 1997, 'A continent of foragers: Aboriginal Australia as a 'regional system."' In P McConvell & N Evans (eds), *Archaeology and linguistics.* Melbourne: Oxford University Press.

Keenan, Edward & Matthew Dryer, 2007, 'Passive in the world's languages.' In Tim Shopen (ed), *Language typology and syntactic description, vol. 1: clause structure.* Cambridge University Press (325-361).

Kemmer, Suzanne, 1993, *The middle voice.* Amsterdam: Benjamins.

Kermode, Frank, 1979, *The genesis of secrecy.* Cambridge MA: Harvard University Press.

Kuteva, Tania, 1998, 'On identifying an evasive gram: action narrowly averted.' *Studies in Language,* 22: 113-60.

Kuteva, Tania, 2004, *Auxiliation: an enquiry into the nature of grammaticalization.* Oxford: Oxford University Press.

Lakoff, George, 1987, *Women, fire and dangerous things.* Chicago: University of Chicago Press.

Lakoff, George & Mark Johnson, 1980, *Metaphors we live by.* Chicago: University of Chicago Press.

Lalbanda, Patsy, Amy Peters & Daisy Utemorrah, 2000, *Ngarlelwana Karnmanya: I was born at Kunmunya, and other Worrorra stories.* Halls Creek: Kimberley Language Resource Centre.

Lalbanda, Patsy & Daisy Utemorrah, 2000, *Wanjurna: the Wandjina and other stories from Worrorra folklore.* Halls Creek: Kimberley Language Resource Centre.

Langacker, Ronald, 1991, *Foundations of cognitive grammar, vol. 2: descriptive application.* Stanford, CA: Stanford University Press.

Leeding, Velma, 1996, 'Body parts and possession in Anindilyakwa.' In H Chappell & W B McGregor (eds), *The grammar of inalienability.* Berlin: Mouton de Gruyter (193-249).

Levinson, Stephen, 1983, *Pragmatics.* Cambridge: Cambridge University Press.

Lommel, Andreas, 1997 [1952], *The Unambal: a tribe in northwest Australia.* Carnarnvon Gorge, Queensland: Takarakka Nowan Kas Publications. Translation by Ian Campbell of *Die Unambal: Ein Stamm in nordwest-Australien.* Monographien zur Völkerkunde herausgegeben vom Hamburgischen Museum für Völkerkunde, Nr 11: *Ergebnisse der Frobenius-Expedition von 1938-39 nach Nordwest-Australien.*

Lounsbury, Floyd, 1965, 'Another view of the Trobriand kinship categories.' In E Hammel (ed), *Formal semantic analysis.* Washington: American Anthropological Assn (142-185).

Love, J R B, 1917 [1915], 'Notes on the Worora tribe of north-western Australia.' *Transactions of the Royal Society of South Australia,* vol 41, pp 20-38.

Love, J R B, 1934, *The grammatical structure of the Worora language of north-western Australia*. Masters dissertation, Adelaide: University of Adelaide.
Love, J R B, 1935, 'Mythology, totemism and religion of the Worora tribe of north-west Australia.' *Report of 22nd meeting of ANZAAS*, pp 222-232.
Love, J R B, 1936, *Stone-age bushmen of to-day*. London: Blackie & Son.
Love, J R B, 1939a, 'The double raft of north-western Australia.' *Man*, 39: 158-160.
Love, J R B, 1939b, *English-Worrorra vocabulary*. 136 page typescript, Canberra: Australian Institute of Aboriginal & Torres Strait Islander Studies, Ms no 17b.
Love, J R B, 1941a, *Worrorra-English vocabulary*. 121 page handwritten ms, Canberra: Australian Institute of Aboriginal & Torres Strait Islander Studies, Ms no 17a.
Love, J R B, 1941b, 'Worrorra kinship gestures.' *Transactions of the Royal Society of South Australia*, vol 65 pt 1 (108-109).
Love, J R B, 1950 [1939], 'Worrorra kinships.' *Transactions of the Royal Society of South Australia*, vol 73 pt 2 no 2 (280-281).
Love, J R B, 2000, *The grammatical structure of the Worrorra language of north-western Australia*. München: Lincom Europa (Edited by R M W Dixon).
Lucich, Peter, 1968, *The development of Omaha kinship terminologies in three Australian Aboriginal tribes in the Kimberley Division, Western Australia*. Canberra: Australian Institute of Aboriginal Studies, Social Anthropology Series no 2.
Lucich, Peter, 1969, *Children's stories from the Worrorra*. Canberra: Australian Institute of Aboriginal Studies, Australian Aboriginal Studies no 18, Social Anthropology Series no 3.
Lyons, Christopher, 1999, *Definiteness*. Cambridge: Cambridge University Press.
Lyons, John, 1977, *Semantics*. Cambridge: Cambridge University Press.
MacKnight, Campbell, 1986, 'Macassans and the Aboriginal past.' *Archaeology in Oceania*, 21 (1): 69-75.
Matthews, P H, 2007, *Syntactic relations: a critical survey*. Cambridge: Cambridge University Press.
Maturana, Humberto & Francisco Varela, 1987, *The tree of knowledge: the biological roots of human understanding*. Boston: New Science Library.
McConvell, Patrick, 1997, 'Long lost relations: Pama-Nyungan and northern kinship.' In P McConvell & N Evans (eds), *Archaeology and linguistics*. Melbourne: Oxford University Press.
McGregor, William B, 1986, 'The Love papers.' *Australian Aboriginal Studies*, 2: 76-79.
McGregor, William B, 1988, *Handbook of Kimberley languages, vol 1*. Canberra: Pacific Linguistics, Series C, no 105.
McGregor, William B, 1989, 'Greenberg on the first person inclusive dual: evidence from some Australian languages.' *Studies in Language*, 13 (2): 437-451.
McGregor, William B, 1990, *A functional grammar of Gooniyandi*. Amsterdam: John Benjamins.
McGregor, William B, 1993, *Gunin/Kwini*. München: Lincom Europa.
McGregor, William B, 1994, *Warrwa*. München: Lincom Europa.
McGregor, William B, 1996, 'Introduction.' In W B McGregor (ed), *Studies in Kimberley languages in honour of Howard Coate*. München: Lincom Europa.
McGregor, William B, 1996b, 'The grammar of nominal prefixing in Nyulnyul.' In Chappell & McGregor (eds) (251-292).
McGregor, William B, 1999, 'External possession constructions in Nyulnyulan languages.' In Payne & Barshi (eds) (429-448).
McGregor, William B, 2002, *Verb classification in Australian languages*. Berlin: Mouton de Gruyter.
McGregor, William B, 2004, *The languages of the Kimberley, Western Australia*. London: Routledge Curzon.
McGregor, William B, & Alan Rumsey, 2009, *Worrorran revisited*. Canberra: Pacific Linguistics.
McKay, Graham, 1978, 'Pronominal person and number categories in Rembarrnga and Djeebbana.' *Oceanic Linguistics*, 17 (1): 27-37.
McKenzie, Maisie, 1969, *The road to Mowanjum*. Melbourne: Angus & Robertson.
Merlan, Francesca, 1981, 'Some functional relations among subordination, mood, aspect and focus in Australian languages.' *Australian Journal of Linguistics*, 1: 175-210.

Merlan, Francesca, 1983, *Ngalakan grammar, texts and vocabulary*. Pacific Linguistics, series B, No 89. Canberra: Australian National University, Research School of Pacific Studies, Department of Linguistics.

Merlan, Francesca, 1985, 'Split intransitivity: functional oppositions in intransitive inflection.' In J Nichols & A C Woodbury (eds), *Grammar inside and outside the clause: some approaches to theory from the field*. Cambridge: Cambridge University Press (324-362).

Merlan, Francesca, 1993, *A grammar of Wardaman*. Berlin: Mouton de Gruyter.

Mithun, Marianne, 1984, 'The evolution of noun incorporation.' *Language*, 60: 847-893.

Mithun, Marianne, 1986, 'On the nature of noun incorporation.' *Language*, 62: 32-37.

Mithun, Marianne, 1991, 'Active/agentive case marking and its motivations.' *Language*, 67 (3): 510-543.

Nash, David, 1982, 'Warlpiri verb roots and preverbs.' In Steve Swartz (ed), *Papers in Warlpiri grammar in memory of Lothar Jagst*. Work Papers of SIL-AAB, A-6 (165-216).

Nichols, Johanna, 1986, 'Head-marking and dependant-marking grammar.' *Language*, 62 (1): 56-119.

Nordlinger, Rachel, 2010, 'Complex predicates in Wambaya: detaching predicate composition from syntactic structure.' In Amberber, Baker & Harvey (eds) (237-258).

Nordlinger, Rachel, 2011, 'Transitivity in Murrinh-Patha.' *Studies in Language*, 35 (3): 702-734.

Nordlinger, Rachel, to appear, 'Constituency and grammatical relations.' In H Koch & R Nordlinger (eds), *The languages and linguistics of Australia: a comprehensive guide*. Berlin: De Gruyter.

Pawley, Andrew, 1993, 'On meeting a language that defies description by ordinary means.' In W Foley (ed), *The role of theory in language description*. Berlin: Mouton de Gruyter.

Payne, Doris, & Immanuel Barshi, 1999, 'External possession: what, where, how and why.' In Payne & Barshi (eds) (3-29).

Payne, Doris, & Immanuel Barshi (eds), 1999, *External possession*. Philadelphia, PA: Benjamins.

Pearson, Noel, 1986 [1998], *Hope Vale Lutheran Mission (1900-1950)*. Reprinted in J Kociumbas (ed) (1998), *Maps, dreams, history: race and representation in Australia*. Sydney: University of Sydney (131-236).

Peyrot, Michaël, 2013, *The Tocharian subjunctive: a study in syntax and verbal stem formation*. Leiden: Brill.

Pinker, Steven, 1999, *Words and rules*. London: Weidenfeld & Nicolson.

Reid, Nicholas, 1991, *Ngan'gityemerri*. Doctoral dissertation, Canberra: Australian National University.

Reid, Nicholas, 2000, 'Complex verb collocations in Ngan'gityemerri: a non-derivational strategy for encoding valency alternations.' In R M W Dixon & A Aikhenvald (eds), *Changing valency: case studies in transitivity*. Cambridge: Cambridge University Press (333-359).

Rosch, Eleanor, 1977, 'Human Categorization.' In N Warren (ed), *Advances in cross-cultural psychology, vol 1*. London: Academic Press (1-49).

Rosch, Eleanor, 1978, 'Principles of Categorization.' In E Rosch & B Lloyd (eds), *Cognition and categorization*. Hillsdale, N J: Erlbaum (27-48).

Rose, Deborah Bird, 1991, *Hidden histories: black stories from Victoria River Downs, Humbert River and Wave Hill Stations*. Canberra: Aboriginal Studies Press.

Rumsey, Alan, 1982, *An intra-sentence grammar of Ungarinyin*. Canberra: Pacific Linguistics Series B, no 86.

Rumsey, Alan, 1990, 'Wording, meaning, and linguistic ideology.' *American Anthropologist*, 92 (2): 346-361.

Rumsey, Alan, 2000, 'Bunuba.' In R M W Dixon & B J Blake (eds), *The handbook of Australian languages vol 5: grammatical sketches of Bunuba, Ndjebbana and Kugu Nganhcara*. Melbourne: Oxford University Press (35-152).

Rumsey, Alan, 2010, ''Optional' ergativity and the framing of reported speech.' *Lingua* 120 (7): 1652-1676.

Sansom, Basil, 1980, *The camp at Wallaby Cross: Aboriginal fringe dwellers in Darwin*. Canberra: Australian Institute of Aboriginal Studies.

Schultze-Berndt, Eva, 2000, *Simple and complex verbs in Jaminjung: a study of event categorization in an Australian language*. Doctoral dissertation, Katholieke Universiteit Nijmegen.

Searle, John, 1969, *Speech Acts*. Cambridge: Cambridge University Press.

Silverstein, Michael, 1976a, 'Hierarchy of features and ergativity.' In R M W Dixon (ed) (112-171).

Silverstein, Michael, 1976b, 'Shifters, linguistic categories and cultural description.' In K Basso & H Selby (eds), *Meaning in anthropology*. Albuquerque: University of New Mexico Press (11-55).

Silverstein, Michael, 1981, 'The limits of awareness.' *Working Papers in Sociolinguistics, 84*. Austin, TX: Southwestern Educational Laboratory.

Silverstein, Michael, 1986, 'Classifiers, verb classifiers and verbal categories.' *Proceedings of the 12th annual meeting of the Berkeley Linguistics Society,* 12: 497-514.

Silverstein, Michael, nd 1, *Naming sets among the Worora (northern Kimberley, Australia)*. Typescript.

Silverstein, Michael, nd 2, *Worora spelling*. 10 pp typescript held at Kimberley Language Resource Centre, Halls Creek.

Sweetser, Eve, 1990, *From etymology to pragmatics*. Cambridge: Cambridge University Press.

Utemorrah, Daisy, 2000, *Worrorra lalai: Worrorra dreamtime stories*. Halls Creek: Kimberley Language Resource Centre.

Vasse, Eric, 1991, 'Nouns and nominals in Wunambal.' In I Macolm (ed), *Linguistics in the service of society: essays in honour of Susan Kaldor*. Perth: Institute of Applied Language Studies, Edith Cowan University (25-34).

Vászolyi, Eric, 1972, *Wunambal language data*. Unpublished ms held in the AIATSIS library, Canberra.

Vászolyi, Eric, 1976, 'Wunambal.' In R M W Dixon (ed), *Grammatical categories in Australian languages* (629–646).

Welch, David (compiler), 2009, *Kimberley people: stone-age bushmen of to-day*. Re-edition of Love (1936) with additional photographs and text. Australian Aboriginal Culture Series no 6. Virginia, NT: David Welch.

Wierzbicka, Anna, 1974, 'The semantics of direct and indirect discourse.' *Papers in Linguistics*, 7: 267-307.

This book is available as a free fully-searchable PDF from
www.adelaide.edu.au/press

www.ingramcontent.com/pod-product-compliance
Lightning Source LLC
Chambersburg PA
CBHW050713090526
44587CB00019B/3361